Prevention from the Inside-Out

By

Jack Pransky

ISBN: 1-4107-0374-6 (e-book)
ISBN: 1-4107-0375-4 (Paperback)

This book is printed on acid free paper.

For information address Jack Pransky, NorthEast Health Realization Institute, 234 Pransky Rd, Cabot, VT 05647.

Editing By Pam Parrish.

1stBooks - rev. 4/18/03

With the aid of the scientific method, we have gained an encompassing view of the physical world far beyond the dreams of earlier generations. The great adventure is now beginning to turn inward, toward ourselves.

— Edward O. Wilson, *Consilience*, 1998

ACKNOWLEDGEMENTS

This book is dedicated to the memory of my father, Kermit Pransky, 1918-1999, the kindest man who ever lived and the embodiment of everything I try to teach.

I also want to thank my wife, Judy, without whose unfailing encouragement I would not have made the decision to enter a doctoral program where I became exposed to many new ideas that subsequently became an integral part of this book.

I want to very much thank sociologist Marvin Sussman, Ph.D., my core faculty member; community psychologist Donald Klein, Ph.D., my second core reader; and the rest of my doctoral Learning Committee: Keith Blevens, Ph.D., George Brown, M.D., Annika Hurwitt Schahn, Ph.D., and Patricia Deer, Ph.D., and my learning consultants Peter Perkins, M.A. and Elena Mustakova-Possardt, Ph.D.

Very much thanks goes to my primary editor, Pam Parrish, to Dr. Barbara Disley and Dr. Donald Klein who all contributed many helpful editorial suggestions, and to Georgina Mavor and Wendy Baker-Thompson for reviewing the final draft. Thanks also to Janet Westervelt for transcribing tapes of the interviews. I am very grateful to Jeanne Rosenberg Chin, my wonderful cousin, for producing many of the diagrams in this book.

Last but not least, from the bottom of my heart, I thank Sydney Banks, whose incredible insights pointed not only me but the world in this inside-out direction; Dr. Roger Mills, who took the initial risks to show how this direction could be applied as an effective approach to prevention; and Dr. George Pransky, my primary teacher, from whom I learned so very much.

TABLE OF CONTENTS

PREFACE

You could have knocked me over with a feather.

In 1991 when I first became exposed to this new inside-out approach to the prevention of problem behaviors, what I heard went against everything I believed. All my life I had fought against oppression in the form of violence against others, in the form of poverty, in the form of a system keeping wealth and power consolidated in the hands of a few at the expense of the many, in the form of drug pushers (including the corporate kind) and environmental profiteers who put profit over people's health. Even more, I worked to improve conditions in the more immediate environments of family and school to build healthy self-perceptions in young people to reduce problem behaviors. Now I was being told the answer lay within? No way! I was a trained community organizer. I had written a book, *Prevention: The Critical Need* (Pransky, 1991), espousing that the answer to prevention lay primarily in changing external conditions. This direction seemed crystal clear. How could I accept that instead of changing external conditions that put people at risk and building resiliency through creating healthy environments, my focus should be the internal, within people's minds? I could not fathom it.

Still, I couldn't turn away. Why? Because it worked better than anything I had seen in all my years in prevention. I had always been about what works. Besides, this new approach sounded intriguing. I had begun traveling my own spiritual path, and this understanding seemed aligned. It had a ring of truth. As my initial book was about to go to press I managed to squeeze in a little something about it, but at the time I saw it merely as a new, innovative approach. I didn't realize it was a completely new paradigm (a term I do not use lightly), a completely new direction, a completely new way of conducting prevention business, or any business for that matter. I had been looking at problems and solutions from the outside-in; this approach required looking from the inside-out. It played tug-of war with my mind, because no way could my thinking about prevention change—or so I thought.

Yet that is precisely the point: My thinking changed! The fact of *thought*— that no matter what terrific things we do in the name of prevention, even if precisely researched-based, **if people's *thinking* does not change, their feelings and behavior *will not* change**—is one of the two critical elements I realized I had missed entirely. And I was not alone. Nearly the entire field had left out *the key variable* that determines people's behavior. The significance of this cannot be understated.

I realized, too, that I missed another critical factor. I realized that subtly, inadvertently, certainly not intentionally, I saw the people with whom we work as incomplete, not whole— *unless* we did something with them or to them or for them. This shocked me, because I had always insisted on seeing people's strengths, not their deficits. But a closer look revealed that I believed *if* we only changed unhealthy conditions or created healthy conditions then people would do fine. *If* we provided them supports or skills with the right information then they would do fine. *If* we built resiliency or healthy self-perceptions then they would do fine. In other words, people weren't fine or whole *unless we* did something. This was humbling. Again, I was in good company. Nearly the entire field appeared to miss that within everyone's spiritual essence, so to speak, they are already perfectly whole and complete, that **when people are connected with their "Health" or internal well-being or "spiritual essence" they do not commit the acts we are trying to prevent**. Now I see that everyone has within them all the wisdom and common sense they will ever need to overcome any problem behavior or difficulty they encounter. Instead of doing all these things from the outside in hopes it will strengthen them on the inside, we could help them realize the inside directly—help them see they already have all the resources within that they will ever need to make it out of their plight. We could help them *see* their innate essence that provides automatic strength and hope, and what separates them from it, so on their own they would be guided toward Health and well-being and away from problems.

I consider these two points so crucial that I repeat them in a slightly different way in Chapter II.[1] But remember, none of this is the real reason I changed. The reason I turned away from a focus on external conditions and inward toward the human mind and human spirit is because it works better. People change to a far greater extent. Their lives truly become healthier on a grand scale. Their relationships improve. And these people, now changed from within and seeing themselves and their lives from a new, healthier perspective, then work to create healthier conditions and change the oppressive conditions in which they find themselves. This is the paradox. By focusing within, the external ends up changing to an even greater extent than if we focused directly on it. The more I explored this inside-out direction, the more I had no choice but to completely change my approach to prevention.

Does this mean I am suggesting that the outside-in focus practiced by most of the field and extolled in *Prevention: The Critical Need* is the wrong direction or a waste of time? Not at all! Outside-in prevention is helpful to people; it does reduce problems—to a certain extent. All I am saying is, from what I have observed first-hand—and I now speak from personal experience as well as the experience of hundreds of others around the country and world who practice it—prevention from the inside-out has far more life-changing impact. **Therefore, if we are truly interested in reducing problem behaviors and enhancing well-being, it is critically important for the field to thoroughly examine this inside-out approach and become trained in it.** Then prevention and health promotion practitioners can make their own informed decisions.

All I want is equal time and resources. I would settle for 50% of prevention time and resources to be devoted to the inside-out approach. Right now it is probably more like .01% (that's a wild guess). The scale needs to be tipped.

Because I have seen its results firsthand, both in myself and others, I gave up trying to convince others of the worth of this inside-out approach. "Convincing" is not this book's intent. Its intent is "exposure." The message will either strike you or it won't, and if it doesn't it won't matter because you will continue to do what you are doing. But if out of it

---

[1] In fact, throughout this book I repeat many points in different ways because some people will relate to them better when stated differently, or they will hear them differently later after they have absorbed more. Therefore, what may sound redundant in some places is for a purpose.

you become as intrigued as I was, or have an insight that opens your eyes to something new, then on your own you will want to pursue it further, as I did. And if the field of prevention begins to change a little as a result, so much the better.

This book is for anyone who works with others, or anyone who wants to understand themselves better, or anyone interested in their own or others' well-being. It is geared for those who work with others preventively, but it has implications and relevance for all of health and human services, as well as for those who work in treatment, corrections, education, and human resources.

So I invite you to settle back and enjoy something within the prevention field that I hope is refreshingly different. I invite you to be open to the new. I invite you to see the potential and power of inside-out prevention. It is not necessarily easy to grasp at first—at least it wasn't for me (but it takes me a while). It may take a few readings or further exploration. But if you are touched by its power and its hopefulness, perhaps you too will not be able to turn away from this direction, as I couldn't.

Jack Pransky
Cabot, VT
August, 2001

FOREWORD

Donald C. Klein, Ph.D.
Union Institute and University

Every now and then a single book precipitates a revolution in human understanding and practice. Examples that come to mind are Sir Francis Bacon's *Novum Organum*, which opened the door to an empirical science grounded in inductive reasoning; Thomas Paine's *Common Sense*, which fanned the spirit of the American revolution; and Thomas Kuhn's *The Structure of Scientific Revolutions*, which illuminated the paradigmatic nature of fundamental change in our understanding of the world around us. Whether Jack Pransky's latest book on prevention – *Prevention from the Inside Out* – turns out to have an equally revolutionary effect on the mental health field remains to be seen. I have no doubt, however, that it should. At the very least, it deserves the thoughtful attention of mental health practitioners and those who set priorities and shape the field's future.

Both scholarly and impassioned, it is grounded in thoroughgoing familiarity with theory and practice having to do with prevention and health promotion in mental health. It is based on Pransky's personal wisdom drawn from his own and others' intimate life-transforming experiences. And it is informed by a lucid synthesis of the writings of sages, scholars, and scientists who in recent years have been delving into the mysteries of energy fields and mind-body relationships. It conveys knowledge of a simple, yet transcendent, insight that is capable of transforming one's life.

In my view, Pransky's work is compatible with the familiar tri-partite public health model of host, agent, and environment. It singles out the host as the focus for the "inside-out approach." However, Pransky faults the concentration of traditional host-oriented approaches that seek to shore up individuals' deficiencies or to impart knowledge, skills, and understandings that will overcome their inabilities to cope successfully with life challenges. His contribution is oriented to the *strength* of the host. It is based on the simple, yet profound recognition that every human being is born with the capacity to function successfully and, despite virtually whatever adversities life has to offer, continues to possess that capacity throughout life. What he terms the "inside-out approach" adds a major new and exciting possibility to the armamentarium of prevention and promotion in mental health.

I am one of those who, from my own personal experience, knows whereof Pransky speaks. Much of my professional lifetime was spent on exploring approaches to primary prevention in the mental health field. From 1953-63 I directed an experimental preventively-oriented community mental health program in Wellesley, Massachusetts associated with the Harvard School of Public Health (Klein, 1968). The next ten years saw a dramatic upsurge in the development of community-based programs in the field. In 1976 I was one of the prime movers of the Pilot Conference on Primary Prevention sponsored by the National Institute of Mental Health. In the mid-1970s, however, I became aware of a promising new development. A friend and colleague (Dr. Roger Mills, then Director of the Lane County, Oregon mental health program) alerted me to the impressive effect a wise teacher, Sydney Banks, had been having on the emotional and physical well-being of hundreds of people in British Columbia simply by talking with them about the wisdom he had gained from his own sudden and unexpected personal enlightenment. At Roger's urging, my wife Lola and I paid two visits to British Columbia to see for ourselves. We talked with couples whose lives had been dramatically transformed by, to use a slang expression common to that area of Canada at the time, "twigging" to what Sydney had to say. Even more impressive was the second visit, during which we spent three days at a resort with individuals and their families who had been affected by Sydney's teachings. Among them were about twenty children of varying ages, who spent much of their time playing with one another in and out of the pool. We were amazed to notice that during the entire three days we did not hear one child cry. Neither did we notice any instance of a child teasing or getting angry at another. Nor did we observe any parents scolding or disciplining their children. Clearly something extraordinary was going on here. These were healthy, active, apparently normal children. Absent were the usual flare-ups of negative emotions or indicators of sibling rivalry that one would ordinarily expect to observe not once but many times in a group such as this over a three-day period.

When we talked with Sydney, his only response was, "All you need to do is set your mind aside." When I replied that I was an intellectual whose mind was a tool of his trade, he responded, "Don't worry about it." Towards the end of our second visit, we spent a memorable winter's evening with Sydney, his wife, and mother-in-law in their home by the edge of a ship channel on SaltSpring Island, British Columbia. We walked through a tunnel of over-arching, snow covered trees to the house and sat quietly talking with Sydney about the wisdom he had discovered, as through a picture window we saw an occasional ghostly freighter glide by. We came away from that evening with at least a glimmer of understanding of what Sydney was talking about. From that time on, our lives, too, were transformed as we discovered what I have in recent years come to speak and write about as one's inherent "power of appreciation" (Klein, 1988, 2001.)

I use the term "appreciation" to refer to the capacity we are born with to feel at one with the universe and to experience the awe and wonderment of life. Everybody I've talked with has experienced such appreciation more than once in their lives but, with rare exceptions, only under special circumstances. After leaving SaltSpring Island that evening in the 1970s we realized that we felt such awe and wonderment when we watched beautiful sunsets. What happens, we asked ourselves, when the sun goes down and that wondrous feeling disappears? Where does that feeling go? And where is it now? The answer was obvious. The feeling does not go down with the sun. It remains within each of us. Somehow we had bought into the idea that we needed special occasions, such as sunsets, to make it okay to experience that good feeling. Then we remembered something Sydney had said, which neither of us understood at the time, to the effect that the way to gain knowledge and understanding was to "allow" oneself to have "good" feelings. Until that moment we had interpreted his remarks as the equivalent of the kind of advice Pollyana might offer, such as: "See the good in everything" or "In every cloud there's a silver lining." Now, however, the light dawned. We became aware that it was the good feeling that mattered, not having to justify those feelings. We now knew that we had such feelings within ourselves and we were in control of them. That is, we could, if we chose, experience those feelings no matter what was happening in our lives!

From that time on, with occasional lapses into anger and other negative ways of responding, we viewed life and one another through the remarkable lens of appreciation. It was as if our windows to the world had been scrubbed clean of all manner of intellectual and emotional dirt. We experienced deep joy, more available energy, creative possibilities, and a far clearer sense of how to deal with whatever challenges presented themselves.

To help others understand what gets in the way of experiencing our capacity to bring appreciative knowing to bear on our lives, I developed the metaphor of the transparent curtain that theater people refer to as the "scrim." On that transparent curtain they paint background scenes. When the footlights and spotlights on the audience side of the stage shine on the scrim, all the audience sees is the scenery painted on the otherwise transparent curtain. When, however, the scrim is back lighted, the scenery grows dim or disappears altogether, and an entirely new reality is revealed to the audience, the reality of life "behind the scrim."

The scrim metaphor suggests that from birth on we humans paint bits and pieces of scenery on our internal, mental scrims. Years ago, Erich Berne, founder of Transactional Analysis, created the wonderful image of a "little professor" inside each of us, whose lifework is to help us make sense out of our experiences (Berne, 1972.) By the time we're adults, our conscientious, inventive, and remarkably creative little professors have made sure that our inner curtains contain literally millions of thoughts, i.e., values, ideas, beliefs, and convictions, about ourselves, other people, and the world. Viewed through everyday consciousness, all we can see are those thought-scenes we've painted on what is, and will always remain, a potentially transparent curtain. Appreciation, that is the feelings of awe and wonderment, the "good feeling" of which Sydney Banks spoke, turns out to be the way to back light the scrim, to allow all those images to fade away, and thus enable ourselves to see new possibilities and to know what needs to be done.

Thus, from two decades of immersion in community-based preventive programs in mental health plus my own transformative personal discoveries, I welcome Jack Pransky's important contribution. Drawing from my own professional and personal discoveries, I believe that, provided the field is ready for a paradigm shift, *Prevention from the Inside Out* offers the basis for a profound revolution in the nature and focus of mental health work.

INTRODUCTION

How effective have we been in preventing problem behaviors and promoting health and well-being? I know of two ways to answer this question. Both are important.

We can look to the results we've achieved. The prevention and health promotion fields have accomplished wonderful things. Any life changed for the better as a result of our efforts is beautiful—and we have seen changed lives. We have turned people away from a life of alcohol and other drug abuse. We have turned people away from violence and child abuse and delinquency and crime and teenage pregnancy and suicide and more. We have helped create healthier communities. No words can describe the meaning this has; no price can be put on it. Any lessened misery or pain perpetrated upon others is a relief to citizens and society. The prevention and health promotion fields should be commended for their incredible efforts, against many odds, toward these ends.

We can look to the lives we have not yet been able to reach. What if we could achieve even more of the above? What if we could be even more effective than we are now? What if we could massively increase our efficacy? After all, can we really say with certainty we're as effective as we can possibly be? Can we really say we know all there is about how to effect change in others' lives and in communities? Can we afford to be complacent, thinking we already know what works best? If we are not successful in helping *every* person turn away from problem behaviors to a life of well-being, it may mean we still need to know things we now don't.

This book asserts that we *can* be even more effective than we are now—far more effective. I have seen it with my own eyes. I have seen the results in others. I have seen the results in myself. I have seen the results in those with whom I've worked. All since I turned to prevention from the inside-out. But that's what it takes: looking in a completely different direction than most of us are used to.

* * *

In November, 1987, an event of enormous magnitude occurred in the field of prevention—only no one knew it. Dr. Roger Mills began a new experiment. He attempted for the first time to effect community change from an entirely different direction—from the inside-out. Results from this event would not appear until 1990 [see Chapter X]. Results showed that two low-income housing projects replete with violence, drug gangs, shootings, crack addicts and alcoholics, child abuse and spouse abuse, were completely turned around. In 2½ years they became healthy communities. Many residents' lives were completely altered. Unfortunately, the quality of research left something to be desired, went unpublished, and very few took notice.

Yet, Mills had proven something. He demonstrated that in fact it was *possible* to achieve community change, reduce problems and improve well-being by taking a completely different approach. Not only was it possible, it looked quite promising. This was not a new program; this was an entirely new way of conducting prevention. Mills took an enormous risk. People called him crazy, stating that trying to point people inside themselves when they are surrounded by external problems not only would never work, it was insulting. But Mills proved them wrong. And, he had attempted this in some of the most difficult and problem-laden environments. If it could happen there, it could happen anywhere.

I am grateful for Mills paving the way. Since then, similar results from this inside-out prevention approach have rippled across the country, changing thousands of lives and improving scores of communities and organizations.

* * *

As I write this, yet another horrible school shooting left two students dead and many others wounded. Children shooting children. Children shooting teachers, the people there to help them! What have we come to as a society when this kind of thing can happen?

I watch as Dan Rather says, "The important question is, what could be done to prevent incidents like this from happening in the first place?"

It is the right question. The world has changed. In 1990 no famous news anchorman would have asked such a question. Prevention was not in the national consciousness. Now it is.

As terrific as the question was, to answer it Rather called in "experts." One spoke of beefing up school security. Another talked about ensuring less access to guns. Another about helping kids feel more accepted. None are the right answer. Good sentiments, but not the right answer. Why? They do not get to the heart of the matter.

To find the heart of the matter we must ask what created these students' actions? Our tendency has been to look to the outside world for answers. I submit that the real answers are found inside. These students' horrendous actions could only have occurred because they had thoughts of hatred or revenge! They perceived those who wronged them as people to hate and revenge. But we must look deeper.

Where did those perceptions or thoughts come from? It is tempting to look for the answers in the outside world or in the past. It is tempting to look to how they were treated by others. Yet many others who are treated badly or picked on do not commit such terrible acts. Different people act differently in similar circumstances. External events don't dictate how everyone will act. Nor does the past hold present answers. It is over, gone, too late. No one can change the past. We are talking *prevention* here!

We can look instead to people's own creative power of *Thought,* to their power to think anything and to experience whatever they created with their own thinking.

I know this sounds strange. It sounded very odd to me at first—almost unfathomable. But unless these kids' thinking changed, they were going to follow it no matter what! Unless we could have done something up front to preclude their destructive thinking, they would have tried anything to carry it out, or they would have had to continually fight against those compelling thoughts and feelings.

Beefing up school security is long after the fact of such thinking. Ensuring less access to guns is after the fact—so they would do it with knives or Molotov cocktails instead (they may cause less harm but they would still cause harm). Helping kids feel more accepted is closer but still after the fact. Why? Because despite our best efforts those kids still may have felt wronged and vengeful. Why? Because whether or not they ended up feeling "accepted" is solely determined by their own thinking. *We will never get to the heart of the matter unless we are able to affect people's thinking.*

Interestingly, I am not talking about cognitive psychology here. I am not talking about helping people to change their thoughts. I am talking about getting closer to heart of the matter. We can look to very the power of Thought that allows people to create thoughts in the first place.[2] For example, before this shooting took place, suppose this boy had come to understand how whatever he sees in life comes from his own thinking, not from the outside world. In other words, suppose he had been helped to realize that it only looks on the surface as if other people can make him feel anger or hatred and revenge; his own thinking really does that. Suppose he had been helped to realize that he has an awesome gift within him, the power to create anything with his own thinking, and how whatever he creates with this power looks "real" but is not "truth." Suppose he had been helped to see that sometimes his mind—and all of our minds—create faulty messages we do not have to believe. Suppose he had learned beforehand that he could always tell which thoughts to follow because he always has access to inner wisdom and common sense, when his mind is quiet enough to hear it. Suppose he had been helped to see that in a calmer state, the world and those people look very different than when his thinking is riled up, so he would not have to take the "reality" he is seeing at the time so seriously, so he would not have to act on it. Suppose he had come to realize that other people's thinking is what made them pick on him in the first place, and their thinking was way off-base at those times, so he didn't have to take it to heart or take it personally. Suppose he had come to understand that despite what people say about him and despite how they treat him, he has something so much more beautiful and wise and important and special and precious inside him that can bring him harmony and peace. Suppose he had come to see that if all those who treated him badly, including family and peers, understood the same things, it would have spared him a lot of pain and heartache— but because they didn't see this themselves, they had no choice but to act out of their self-created thinking, just as he does. If he had truly realized all this, he may not have felt so compelled to follow his thinking down a destructive path, and so much death and misery may have been prevented.

Prevention is the most important thing we can do to preclude such tragedies, but the approach we take is equally important. I think it is safe to say most of the field has not been looking in this direction. Perhaps it is a reason we have not prevented more such incidents.

* * *

A review of my book, *Prevention: The Critical Need* (Pransky, 1991) called it "a prevention classic that will guide the field into the 21st century…[and]…inspire its readers to push beyond current accepted theories and practices in the human services arena" (Miller,

---

[2] If this is a reader's first time being exposed to this inside-out approach, I don't expect what follows to make much sense right now. It will be dealt with thoroughly in the rest of this book. Here I just want the reader to get a sense of it.

1991, p.28). As the 21st century is beginning to unfold, again I now see prevention with new eyes. Again it may be time for the prevention field to push beyond currently accepted theories and practices and take a fresh look at itself.

Inside-out prevention, to borrow an old phrase from Klein & Goldston (1977), is "an idea whose time has come." It is a bold statement, some might say presumptuous. Why do I say this?

Prevention is now a common idea, and if not exactly common practice it is now at least fairly well accepted. It was not always that way. In 1977 the fields of mental health and human services were at a crossroads. These fields could have continued their then-present direction and ignored the logic and mounting evidence of the need for prevention. It may have taken nearly twenty more years for prevention to become accepted by the mainstream (some would say it still isn't), but in 1977 Klein and Goldston's book served as a clarion call for action. At the time the mainstream thought prevention an impractical, wasteful, almost foolish notion. As late as the mid-1980s, perhaps early 1990s, prevention was dismissed by many as incomprehensible, by others as worthless, by others as too radical. Why? Perhaps they did not understand what it really meant or how to accomplish it, and not enough scientific research existed to convince the powers-that-be of its worth.

Today I see the prevention field at a similar crossroads with regard to inside-out prevention. We could continue our present direction. We could continue to look toward the outside world as the reason people do what they do, and continue to see solutions there, or we could look within. We could continue to look toward ever-increasing social-ecological complexity and break the "causes" down into smaller and smaller, distinct components—or we could look to simplicity and find the common denominator for all. We could continue to narrow our prevention focus to so-called "research-proven" programs that have had large research grants behind them—or we could be open to new, innovative directions. Some in the current prevention mainstream may dismiss inside-out prevention as an impractical, wasteful, incomprehensible, worthless, too radical, almost foolish notion. Why? Perhaps only because they do not yet understand what it really means or how to accomplish it, and not enough "scientific" research exists to be wholly convincing. We are at a very similar crossroads.

Which path will we take? This book attempts to clarify the path of inside-out prevention, so practitioners in the field can decide for themselves.

* * *

I had become complacent. I thought I knew the answers. I didn't realize at the time that I had closed myself off to new possibilities.

The first inkling that I might be missing something with my and the field's approach to prevention came in November 1991 when basketball icon Magic Johnson announced to the world that he was HIV positive. Like magic, he accomplished in moments what the AIDS prevention field had been trying to achieve for years without much success. Suddenly in a three-month period use of condoms tripled, HIV testing quadrupled, and media reports about AIDS/HIV quintupled. Why did this happen? Other celebrities and athletes had come forward, but without the same results. The more I reflected on it, the more I couldn't escape the conclusion that, for whatever reason—his personality, his unbelievable skills, his enthusiasm, his winning ways, his public image, his smile, or all in combination—Magic

Johnson touched people in the heart. And those he touched were somehow moved to change their behavior.

At the time I remember thinking, "Does this mean that if people aren't touched they don't change?" I recalled that the most powerful prevention efforts I, personally, had seen over the years were those where participants were touched in the heart, such as the Council for Unity in New York City or the early days of the Green Mountain Teenage Institute (GMTI) in Vermont (in Pransky, 2001). But did it mean lasting change? I admitted I didn't know, but in the case of GMTI anyway, I doubted it. Even in Magic's case, its effect faded over time. Besides, it made no sense to rely on celebrities like him to move others. Something still seemed to be missing.

I then realized—and this came as a real shock—that, as a field, *we did not know what made people change!* Here we were, in the business of change, and we did not know the first thing about what moves people to change. It began to shake my certainty that I knew what I was doing.

Then, serendipitously, I was invited to a child abuse prevention conference where Roger Mills spoke about the incredible results achieved in the Modello and Homestead Gardens Housing Projects in Dade County, Florida. At the time I didn't really know what it meant, but the lives of two residents who Mills brought with him from the projects—Cynthia Stennis and Elaine Burns—had obviously changed to an almost unbelievable extent. I didn't realize then that this inside-out approach (which later came to be known as "Health Realization") provided a real answer about how and why people change, and therefore was a piece of the puzzle we were missing in prevention. So I began to look into it.

In 1993 I spent a few weeks around Modello and Homestead Gardens interviewing people to write the story of how that project unfolded from beginning to end, which culminated in the book, *Modello: A Story of Hope for the Inner-City And Beyond* (Pransky, 1998). During those interviews I realized I could no longer see prevention as I had. This inside-out approach had produced changes in people's lives that stood head and shoulders above any prevention results I had seen in all my years in this field. I could not turn away from it.

I decided to fully immerse myself in trying to understand it. I attended as many trainings as I could. Most surprising to me, my own life began to change for the better, even though I wasn't looking for it.

The final blow to my old view of prevention came with my own attempts to teach this new understanding to others. To my amazement I saw others' lives change as a result. In fact, I began to have a greater effect on people than in all my previous work combined. That did it for me. There was no turning back. Since then it has been only a matter of deepening my understanding, because no one ever can fully get to the bottom of the inside world. Fortunately, my own effectiveness in helping others to gain this understanding has continued to improve.

* * *

What you will see on these pages sometimes looks too simple, and sometimes baffles like a mystery that can't possibly be unraveled. This is not surprising since looking from the inside-out is an attempt to boil down all human behavior to its simplest elements, to its essence—yet this essence cannot be truly understood by the intellect. This is one of many paradoxes in inside-out prevention. It is too simple to be comprehended. One can never get to the bottom of it, for the depth of understanding is limitless—far beyond what I understand now. If I had to guess, I would say that my own understanding of inside-out prevention is beginning to approach the bottom of the tip of the iceberg—the bottom of the tip! And even this has taken me ten years. Still, my limited understanding has been enough to change lives. That is hopeful!

With inside-out prevention I see endless possibilities, for the limitless cannot possibly grow stale. It continues to yield increasingly deep insights and understandings, new insights on how to effectively reach others so their lives improve. What could be better than that?

This book attempts to present the simplicity of the inside-out approach. However, to write about simplicity presents an automatic dilemma. Simplicity implies "essence," and essence implies spiritual, and no words can adequately describe the spiritual. A description of simplicity is only an approximation of the essence; therefore, in attempting to explain it, it sometimes seems necessary to get more complex than I would like. Therefore, the reader is encouraged to ignore the words as much as possible and simply pick up the feeling or the essence of them.

* * *

My intent in writing *Prevention from the Inside-Out* is to convey the understanding that everyone—the community members with whom we work, all young people, all families, our clients, our co-workers, government workers, the powers-that-be, even the oppressors—can look inside and find the innate wisdom to overcome oppression and to stop oppressing, to cease abuse and to refuse to be abused, to truly live lives of well-being and not be consumed by worry or bother or anger or fear or hate or any of the things that keep ourselves less at peace, less calm and content or hurtful toward others. This book is more a vision of who we can be as human beings.

I want to make one thing very clear. This vision has nothing to do with me. I did not make it up. It is within everyone, waiting to be unveiled. Prevention from the inside-out is simply *knowing* that everyone has *inside* them everything they need to live healthy and humane lives. This book is a celebration of this innate, limitless capacity. When found, it unfurls and comes *out* into the world and makes it a slightly better place for us all. And all those "slightly betters" begin to add up and keep adding up and then multiply and ripple out to affect others. Then before we know it we have prevented many, many problems and made our communities and the world a better place because people are living healthier, wiser lives. This vision is of who we all really are deep inside. The purpose of this book is to provide as comprehensive a look as I can muster at the many aspects of prevention from the inside-out. Like *Prevention: The Critical Need* (which could be renamed "Prevention from the Outside-In"), I expect many readers will read only those chapters they find interesting.

For instance, Chapters I, IV, VII, IX, XI, XX and XXII offer extensive, compelling interviews with people whose lives have been touched and changed from the inside-out and who are now using this approach as their own work. Some readers will choose to read only these inspiring stories.

Chapter II examines what "inside-out prevention" means, what it is and is not, and why it is a completely new paradigm. Chapter III reexamines the field of prevention from an inside-out perspective. Chapter V explores research that makes a case for why inside-out prevention is an essential approach for prevention and health promotion. Chapter VI presents the Principles behind inside-out prevention (one of the book's two central chapters). Chapter VIII offers a bit of history: where this understanding and approach arose from. Chapter X presents research demonstrating the effectiveness of this inside-out prevention approach. Chapter XII offers a summary of my own qualitative research study, with wonderful quotes from participants. Chapter XIII is about how this approach is *applied* in communities and organizations (the other central chapter). Chapter XIV shows the application in action, through interviews with people in the trenches. Chapters XVI and XVII offer a new look at alcohol and other drug abuse and violence prevention, respectively, from an inside-out perspective. Chapter XVIII provides a glimpse into what counseling from an inside-out perspective looks like. Finally, Chapter XIX explores other spiritual approaches to prevention, and XXI examines some scientific evidence that makes a case for how the formless becomes manifest in form within human beings.

This explains this book's length. All these aspects seem important for a comprehensive view. In this book I also attempt to strike a balance between head and heart.

Interestingly, while inside-out prevention can be applied as a stand-alone program structure and process, as an understanding it can be superimposed over most existing outside-in prevention structures. In other words, it is something that can be applied within most already existing programs. This will become clearer later.

One final note: In this book I attempt to distinguish between what the field generally thinks of as "principles" and what I mean by "Principles," and between what people generally think of as "health" and what I mean by "Health." To help make the distinction, throughout the book I capitalize these words when using them as I mean them (for the most part). The same holds true for "Mind," "Consciousness" and "Thought." These definitions are found herein.

I. HELEN

Interview with Helen Neal-Pore. *Helen is a miracle. Abused, depressed and suicidal one day, overnight she became happy and peaceful—a completely new person. Changes of this nature are rare; they are not the norm. What this does show is the possibility. It raises the question, "How could this happen?" Some shift of enormous magnitude must have occurred. Here is Helen's story. I interviewed her at her home in Tampa, Florida in November, 2001.*

JP: What were you like before you got involved with this understanding?

HNP: I was very nervous and very insecure. I had very low self-esteem—felt real bad about myself. Back from my beginning I thought there was something about me that wasn't right.

JP: What made you think that?

HNP: Well, I was born into a home where there was a lot of violence. My parents were very hard workers, so I always was kind of comfortable that way, but no hugging, no time, no loving. My father was a weekend alcoholic. Friday was payday and my dad would come home drinking. Now he's going to be gone for a whole weekend, so then my mom would start, "You go every weekend, you've got to stay home," and here it go. My mom was very verbal, and she would just tell him off, so the only way he knew to shut her up was to start punching her. And that would give him an excuse: "See what you made me do? Now I've got to leave!" And then, maybe Sunday we'd see him again, and then he'd be sobering up for work, and when he sobered down everything would be real quiet. Even as a little kid I took responsibility for them and for their happiness. So on Sunday I would grab my dad's uniform, boots and hat—he was a heavy construction equipment operator—and put it on, and I would come in the living room where they weren't even speaking to each other, and I'd just sit there. And all of a sudden they'd bust out laughing, and I would break that cycle of quietness and silence in the house. Then things would be normal until Thursday. Then my mom decided to go to work early so she would not be abused over the weekend. So then I was dropped here and there and went to feeling like I wasn't wanted at a early, early age.

And then, when I was real small, probably between five and seven, my older cousin molested me. And he made me feel like it was my fault, something that I did, and that I couldn't tell anybody because I'd get in trouble. So I kind of held that in for a lot of years, thinking that there was something wrong with me.

Then the very first boy I liked when I was about fourteen and dated for four years, ended up rejecting me right prior to our marriage at eighteen. He just kind of disappeared—

JP: You mean he left you at the altar?

HNP: A month before—and I had no idea why, other than there had to be something wrong with me. I thought maybe it was because I was heavy, so I just had these very insecure thoughts.

Then I kind of flipped the switch and I said, "Okay, I'm going to make people like me." I thought, maybe if I just do whatever people ask me to do, just run myself raggedy, then people would like me. So I was trying to buy my friendship, with girlfriends too. If they needed a ride I'd take them; if they needed money I'd give it. It wasn't working [laughs].

JP: When you say, "It wasn't working," what do you mean?

HNP: It didn't make me happy. I started feeling, "Now they just using me. The only reason they like me is because I have a little money or I have a car, I can take them places." So nothing I was doing was working. But being Black, we never think of psychologists or going to get help. This was normal. My cousins were the same way, because the same thing was going in their home. You know what it was, Jack? I was always there for everybody else, even the adults in my life, so I wondered, where was my person?

JP: So what happened after being left a month before the altar—

HNP: I was so angry because I wanted to get back at him. I was the admission clerk at a hospital and this cook in the hospital was my friend, and we started hanging out together. She was just doing things that I would never be bold enough to do, like going with other men and partying, and it wasn't good stuff [laughs]. It was not the typical Helen.

So I met a guy one night and we danced, and the next day he called me and I had to go to work, and he said, "Can I borrow your car?" And I was naïve and not smart at all, and said, "Sure." So he picked me up that evening, and I said, "Where do I need to take you, because I'm really tired, and I want to go home and go to bed." He said, "Oh you're my bitch now. You belong to me!" And I'm going, "Excuse me!?" So then he smacks me. That was my first experience with domestic violence. And he goes, "Yeah, I've just moved into your house!" And he moved his stuff into my apartment. And when we got to the apartment he was like, "Well, come on in!" And I was, like, "No no no," because I didn't want him to rape me. I didn't know what was going to happen—I was scared. So I said, "I need to go somewhere. Just give me my car keys." And I took off driving. And I was wanting to go to my parents but they're going to want to kill me because I let this guy have access to my whole apartment, everything.

And I drove around and went by this filling station where me and my friend would stop and get gas. And this guy was there, and we'd seen him but I didn't know him, and I told him what had happened. And he said, "Don't worry, I'll get him out of there. I'll help you out. I'll pretend I'm your big brother." And when he got off work he went and he beat this guy up and threw his stuff out of my house. And I was so grateful! Somebody cared about me. So now I'm in *love* with this guy, I thought, not knowing him.

We dated for about a year, and then he asked me to marry him. He was from a different kind of life-style. His family lived in, like, really the predominantly ghetto-kind of area where there was always drug-dealers on the street, always stuff happening, the police was always there, and he wanted to move on that side of town. So he found a duplex, but it was in an area that wasn't safe and it wasn't anything that I was used to. But he knew the lady and her little kids next door. And I said, "Well, okay, they're always home. They'll watch the house."

So two weeks after we got married, one day I was at home, and he spent a lot of time with that woman and her three kids. I was thinking this was a friend, no big deal. And his phone rang, and it was his mother, so I went over to tell him that and knocked on the door. The little kids were sitting there and I said, "Is my husband over here?" And this little kid said, "Oh yeah, he's in the bedroom with mom." So now I'm like, "Oh God, he's moving next door to his woman!" So I busted in the bedroom, and to my surprise she was shooting him up with heroin. I'd married a heroin addict.

That day I got beat so bad I didn't recognize my own face. Now that I knew his secret, every time he'd think about me busting into that room he'd just beat me for no reason. And then right after the fight, or when he'd go to sleep and wake up he'd say, "What happened to you?" He didn't even remember abusing me. About two months of him was about all I could take.

After that I moved away for a little while, then came back and met my next husband. He was a honky—handsome, tall, big and really cute. He'd asked me, "Will you go to church with me?" And I was, like, *"Wow!"* Nobody had ever asked me to go to church. So we'd party on Saturday and go to church on Sunday. [laughs] But when I got pregnant I didn't want to go out any more. Then I started listening in church, and I'm finding out about Jesus, and it took me to a level that there was a peace, and I didn't want to go out partying anymore. My husband and I had been together four years and we had a wonderful relationship, or so I thought—because one day he came home one day with a woman in the car and pulled into our driveway and said, "I don't love you anymore, because you love God and that baby more than you love me. I'm leaving you." I'm going, "What?!" I mean, we never had a problem before! So now I'm rejected again, and it was devastating. I got real depressed. I lost a lot of weight, wouldn't eat, and just took care of my baby—he was probably the only reason I wanted to live. I even thought suicide and had a handgun. Then one day my baby picked up that handgun, and that was the last day I ever had a gun in my house, period.

So I let a year or two go by and I'm really praying that God's going to bring him back. I was doing all this praying and feeling real low in myself. I was a real good Sunday school teacher—I was so good, Jack, for everybody but me. I could get in that church and I could teach, and I would get this energy from somewhere that was just so great. But then I'd get home and I would just cry. I had a good 38-year pity-party [laughs] before I got into this understanding. (But now that I look back and know what I know now, I was in my innate wisdom when I'd do other things for other people—but I never pulled on that for me.)

Then I met this guy who was not attractive, glasses taped together in the middle, wore really old clothes, stuff like that. So I thought, "I don't want him, so maybe nobody else is going to want him either." [laughs][But we got to talking. It was more like a friendship, and it went on for about four years. I had told him that I was still waiting for my husband to come back (of course, my husband is probably on woman number six by now and he wasn't heading back my way no way.) [laughs]

Then this guy decided that he wanted to be intimate. I wasn't attracted to him, but we start a sexual relationship. And the first time I got pregnant. So the right thing for a Sunday school teacher to do is to get married. So I married someone I wasn't in love with, just so other people wouldn't think I was this person who did something that she shouldn't have did. [laughs] So in this relationship I wasn't as intimate as a wife should be to her husband, and I just wasn't doing what he wanted. And he just got really ugly, verbal abusive, and started calling me names, and I had my own business at that time, I had my own company, and I started losing everything.

JP: What was the business?

HNP: I had a boarding home where I took care of elderly people. I had a four-bedroom house with a couple of apartments in back. And I was able to be home with my son. This guy had helped me for four years with this business, but when we got married he said, "These people got to go." And I'm saying, "This is my income! I make good money." I mean, I was going on cruises, living a good life. I said, "I don't think we can live off of your paycheck. I don't think you make enough to take care of me or this household." But he thought he could. So I quit my job, and that's when the verbal abuse really started, because then it became a financial strain on him. So now he wants me to work. So I had to go off to work. Then he'd say, "You don't spend enough time with the boys!" So then I'd quit that job and stay home and then he'd say, "There's not enough money to take care of you. Go to work!" And I was trying to be what I thought at that time in my religious beliefs that I had to be a perfect wife and submissive to my husband. So being submissive to my husband caused me a couple of nervous breakdowns [laughs].

JP: You're talking nervous breakdown, literally?

HNP: Literally. Mental hospital. I had had these episodes where I would cry and couldn't stop, and then I'd feel like something was crawling all over me. It felt like bugs were in the top of my head and then crawling all over me. Then my children would play and it would just sound like a freight train coming through the living room. And I would be, "Just shut up!" I couldn't stand to even hear them laugh. And they would then cry because they didn't know what was happening. As soon as they'd get quiet I would kind of calm down.

Then it got so bad this one particular time that I woke up and just stared crying and I couldn't stop. So my mom took me to my doctor, and he sent me to a psychologist. And I'm going, "Oh my God, I'm crazy!" Now this was really validating everything I had thought in the past that something was wrong with me. So I go telling him how I was feeling but I never related what was going on in my relationship: My husband would play mind games with me. He'd say things real nasty, like scream at me, "Iron my shirt!" And I'd say, "Well you don't have to talk to me like that." And then he'd go, [real sweet voice] "Well, all I said was would you please iron my shirt. You make such a big deal out of little stuff. "And I'd go, "Okay?" And the next thing you know I'm ironing his shirt, and I'm going, "That ain't what I heard." Then he'd go, "You just crazy!" He'd say that all the time. It never dawned on me that I'm getting mentally and emotionally abused.

The doctor put me in Memorial Hospital, and when this man took a key and unlocked that door, it hit me, "I have a mental problem, and I'm going into a *psych ward*!" And when he closed that door behind me I really cried then. I mean, I broke down and I *cried*.

And then all of a sudden I looked up from my tears and feeling sorry for myself and I saw all these people, and they were looking so out of it. They were just zonked out, and the women's hair was just a mess like it hadn't been combed and nobody had took care of them. And my nurse instinct just jumped in there immediately and I wanted to take care of these women. And I started doing their hair. And in two weeks my doctor said, "You are doing so much better I think I'm going to let you go home." Now I was feeling good about myself, I was away from my husband and all that chaos, and taking my Zanax and Tolfinal as prescribed. Then I went right back into that relationship. And then everything just started all over again. Then I had a second breakdown.

JP: What do you remember about that?

HNP: My third husband has a stepdaughter. One night we were home watching a movie, and we were laughing and just having a wonderful time, and he came in and started screaming at both of us. And it felt like those things were just crawling all over me again. I mean, it came to a point where I was just like [sucks in breath] speechless. I couldn't talk. I have never had anything that severe happen to me. It was such a panic. Then I started having panic attacks. I'd get real scared—it was just like jumping. And it got to the point after that night I just would jump at the least little thing, like if somebody would walk up on me.

JP: How long were you in the hospital this time?

HNP: Probably four weeks. But I had a horrible dream one night that I shot him. It was so real. I shot him for every man that had ever hurt me in my life. Then I knew I couldn't be in that relationship. I knew that when he did get violent that I was capable of doing something like that, and I had to be out of it. I couldn't be in an abusive relationship.

JP: How long from the time you got out of the hospital until you left him?

HNP: A few months. What happened was, my younger son wanted to go to a birthday party that my older son was going to, and he went to screaming. And my husband went to grab him and was shaking him: "You ain't going, so just shut up!" And he had never went off on the kids before. So when I grabbed my son to take him, he grabbed him and threw him on his bed, then he went to choking me. So my older son runs to a neighbor's house and calls my parents. And the police came and I told them, "Make him give me my car keys. I'm trying to leave." We had two cars and his car was there, plus he had a truck. And the police officer said, "Is his name on the title?" And I said, "Yuh." And he said, "Well, then we can't." And I said, "He just abused me, he choked me." And they go, "We don't see any bruises." So they told me that I could leave, but they couldn't make him give me my car keys. So I left there walking with one child on one hip and dragging the other one behind me. And my parents pulled up and we got in the car with them.

I had heard about The Spring, which was a shelter for battered women, and I called them. I said, "I have to feed my kids and I only have $35 left and I have nowhere else to go to." I felt really bad because for so many years I had helped so many people, and everybody that I called, Jack, turned me down because they didn't want to get involved in our business—all these friends that I had housed and given money to and took places. Family members too. So the Shelter told me they had a bed for us, and me and my sons went to the shelter. And they got me clothes. I was able to go to work as a Kindergarten teacher at my Church school. I was there twenty-one days.

And I met my [future] daughter there—she and her mom were my roommates—she was three years old at that time, and we kind of became friends. Then after me getting out of the shelter, we still kept in touch and the little girl became my Goddaughter. The next year her mother got back into her bad relationship and ended up shooting at the baby's father. The police knocked on my door at 3:00 in the morning with her, because the baby told them, at almost three, she goes, "Don't arrest me. I didn't do nothing. Take me to my Godmom's." This little baby showed them where I lived, and she's been with me ever since. I've adopted her since. She's thirteen now.

So now it's me and my three kids now, and we're living in low-income housing on welfare in the projects in Tampa, and I'm feeling really low. In 1993 I decided to go back to the shelter to say thank you for what they did for me and my kids. They said to me, "Helen, we need you to go and speak, we need a survivor, someone who's gotten out of a bad relationship and has made it for herself and her kids. I didn't think I had made it; I'm still on welfare and feeling sorry for myself, but they thought I had made it just because I'd gotten out of the abusive relationship. And I said, "No, I can't do that. I'm not a speaker. You got the wrong person." So then they sicked Mable Bexley on me. I admired her highly because she was the woman that started this shelter. Then I felt obligated because I owe Miss Mable.

One day I was on a panel in 1996, and Jeannie Williamson—who at the time was deputy director at Bay Area Legal Services—she saw me speak. Somewhere in my talk I had talked about my "stinkin' thinkin'," and how I was making these bad choices, and that I have a choice to make better ones but I didn't choose to do it at that time in those relationships. And she came up to me afterwards and she said, "Oh my God, you were awesome!" And I said, "Really?" I didn't think so. I was getting ready to get to my car and get back to my Zanax so I could calm down [laughs]. So she says, "There's going to be a Health Realization training. Elsie Spittle is doing a training, and I would love for you to come." And I said, "How much is it?" "And she said $250 for four days, and I said, "Oh ma'am, I'm sorry, I'm on welfare and I don't have any money." And she said, "No, we'll take care of it. Bay Area Legal will pay for you to go." And I said [under breath], "Oh shoot, now, she's going to pay for me to go, like I need something else." I'm already seeing my psychiatrist, I'm taking Zanax, I'm seeing a counselor, I'm taking my Tolfinal, what do I need with a Health Realization

5

class?" I was not happy about this. But I'm a people-pleaser, so the first thing that comes out of my mouth is, "Okay." [laughs]

The day before the class started I had to go see my psychologist, so I thought the best way to get out of this class is to go ahead and have another good breakdown. So I go in there remembering all the things that happened to me from my birth, and examining my life and these marriages and how awful they was, and I was really in a bad, bad space.

JP: This was when you were talking to the psychologist?

HNP: The day before. I was doing a reminiscing. I was going down memory lane [laughs]. So by the time I went to see her, I am a nervous wreck. I'm crying, snotting and everything. I was just out of it. So she thinks I'm having another breakdown and starts calling around trying to find a bed. Couldn't find one! And this was my seventh psychologist, by the way. Seven years of therapy with seven different people. And they didn't find a bed, so I might as well go to this stupid Health Realization class. So I go in there the next day, and I was the only Black in the audience. And I felt, "I'm in the wrong place. There's nobody my color here." There were two Black ladies but they were presenters: Theresa Roberson, from Tampa, and Cynthia Stennis [from the Modello project (Pransky, 1998)]. And Elsie talks with this soft voice.

The other thing about them was, I had never seen so many happy people at one place—all of the presenters: Jeannie (the lawyer that introduced me), Elsie, Theresa, Cynthia and Reese [Coppage]— they had this peace about them that I had never experienced and never seen. And Elsie went to talking about how that we all had this innate wisdom, and that we were all connected to a greater source, greater than us—which immediately, because of my religious background, I thought of the Holy Spirit and God—yeah, okay I can buy that; I'm okay with that part. That's cool. And then she started talking about Thought. How our thoughts create our reality. And I was lost there. I didn't understand that. And then she drew the thought cycle, where she says a thought gives you a feeling, and then you get a behavior, and then you get a result. And I'm like, no, it's what I'm feeling that make me think about stuff—I thought it was the other way around: because I'm feeling bad, I think bad. But when she went through it, the way she did it, it was so powerful that I knew that it was something to it. But it was too easy. When she was saying that we could let go of that stuff, and everything that had happened to us in the past was past, it was just memory, it was just thought, it was no longer alive, and it was only when we start validating it and accepting it that it becomes alive. And it was weird to me, very weird. It was too simple. She couldn't tell me that I could just start thinking better or I can start looking at things a different way and then feel different. It was just too easy.

So the first day I was just doing a whole lot of head-thinking, not saying anything, but one thing I wanted to do was make this little lady out a liar. That was on my agenda. Because I had a thirteen-year-old son, and we have not gotten along, and he wouldn't even move unless I'm screaming and hollering at him. Nothing's working. So after the end of the class this day, I just had to prove that this couldn't work. I was going to go home and try this out, and then I was going to come in the next day and tell her how this didn't work.

So I thought about my boy coming home from school when I'm not home, and he drop his book-bags in the middle of the floor, the remotes would be everywhere, he would make a mess with the food, whatever. So I would have to go in and scream at him. So I said, "No, I learned this new stuff, I'm not going to scream today. I'm going to do like Miss Lady said. I'm going to be nice and quiet and calm, and I'm going to see what happens." So I go in and sure enough everything was a mess. So I go, "You know, Shevon, this is your house. I went to this class today, and I learned that this is my baby's house, and I would love a nice living room for people to come walk into, but you live here too, and it is your responsibility to keep your living room clean too. But if you don't want to, that's okay. When people come in I'm going to tell them that this is my baby's living room too, and if he wants a messy living room then it's all right by me." So I went in my room and started putting on some more casual clothes to do dinner, and all of a sudden I heard his door slam. So I came back out and I went in the kitchen, I looked in the living room and the remote controls were all back in the thing, and his books and stuff was up. Now, before I would have had to yell, "*Pick up your stuff!*" and he would have picked up one item and *slowly* took it out, then I'd have to scream again for the second item. So I said, "Wait a minute, this stuff works! This lady's not lying." You know? He didn't change. He didn't go to that class. *I* went. *I* did something different. I handled it a different way. She's right, we get what we give. If I give out love and kindness, it's going to be different.

Then I knew if I passed this next test, this stuff was good. My ex-husband calls my son every day. He has always been a good father. But usually when he calls, I'd throw the phone: "*Your daddy want to talk to you!*" I just didn't even want to hear his voice, I had so much hatred for him because I felt like I had lost everything—I had lost my business, I lost my home, I'm on welfare—and it all was because of him! So he called, and I answered and I said [cheerfully], "Hi!" And he's, like, real quiet on the other end of the phone. I had never in 5 years said hi, not in that tone of voice [laughs]. So he was like, "Hello? Is C.J. there?" And I said, "Yes. I went to this class today, and it was really nice, and I realized that we will never be husband and wife, but because of C.J. we need to be the best parents he could have. We need to be the best for him. So I think we should just get along, for him, what do you think?" And there's silence on the other end of the phone. This man is just, like, speechless. And he says, [meekly] "Okay." So I say, "Well, hold on, let me get C.J." And it was the first time that it felt like these weights just lifted off my shoulders, with this person.

Then I remembered her talking about this innate wisdom that we all had, and that night I started thinking about that even more in my bed. I went to looking back over my life and I realized, my dad was only doing the best he could with what he knew. He saw his dad come home drunk and abuse his mom. My mom wasn't rejecting me, she was just trying to be safe. My cousin molested me: He took advantage of me. That was not my fault. The boyfriend that left me, I had no idea why, but he had came back into my life by then—

JP: The first guy who left you?

HNP: Yes. A year before getting into this understanding, I was living back at my parent's house because they had bought another house. And he had came knocking on the door looking for me when his mother passed away. And he said, "Are you married?" That's the first thing came out of his mouth. And I'm going, "What do you mean I'm married?" And he says, "I came back to marry you." And I'm going, "I think you're about twenty-some years late on this marriage thing. [laughs] Why did you ever leave me?" And he said, "Do you remember when I used to come visit you, and on Fridays your dad would wave the gun at me because he'd be drunk and he'd be cussing and going and fighting your mom?" And I said, "Well, yuh." And he said, "Well, I got scared and I thought if I married you, your dad would shoot me one day." And I said, "Well there was no bullets in the gun!" He goes, "What do you mean? " I said, "Because on Thursday night we'd take the bullets out of the gun, because we know he's going to come home Friday and swing the gun. And on Sunday before he comes home we put them back in there because we know he's going to clean his gun on Monday." So this guy left me and I'm thinking "rejected," and getting into all these relationships trying to get back at him. And it was all because he thought that my dad was going to hurt him.

JP: Well, he could have told you.

HNP: Yuh. I agree. I would have at least known what was up. But he didn't. He said, "I didn't want to hurt you." "But you hurt me worse by not telling me, because then I had to leave it to my own imagination to know why!"

JP: So back to that night—

HNP: I'm going back and reevaluating my whole life. Then I realized that, wait a minute, he was just doing the best he could at the time. He was scared. I jumped the gun and went to thinking something else. Then I went to thinking about giving that guy my car keys—I allowed him to take advantage of me because I turned over my car keys. And then this other boy, I saw that there was abuse in his family, and I still married someone that I saw abuse in. And I took for granted that those things on his arm were whatever lie he told me—I bought into it. And the other relationship with the husband that ran off with this woman: Well, when his mom got saved, his mom and dad separated, his dad ran around a few years, then he came back home. He thought he was going to run around for ten years like his dad did and then come back home. Then I was thinking, he was husband number two, and I was looking for husband number three [as in "strike three"]. And with husband number three I married somebody that I wasn't really in love with. And it finally dawned on me when I went to this Health Realization class that day, because Elsie said something like, "Even if you got into a relationship with someone that did something to you or hurt you in some way, there was something about that person—everybody has some good inside of them—and there was something good about that person that attracted you to that person in the first place, even before the dislike or the disagreement happened." So I went to thinking about this last husband, and he was a good father, and what I didn't have was a relationship that him and his daughter had. Then I realized why I couldn't be intimate with him. I wanted him to treat me like he treated his children. He was looking for a wife, and I was looking for a father. And it was just so eye-opening for me that, wait a minute, the reason this relationship didn't work was because we were looking for two different things. You don't be intimate with your father! So I didn't want to be intimate with him. That was just so relieving—I was just having one insight after another—

JP: While you were lying in bed.

HNP: Lying in bed! I mean, I was just like, "*Wow!*" [laughs] I just had one insight after another and I just kept cleaning up my life. And then the nervous breakdowns and the abuse and all this other stuff, by me thinking that this was my last chance at marriage, I was the one that stayed in that abusive relationship, and not really knowing that emotional and mental abuse is abuse. I didn't learn that until I went to the battered women's shelter when it got physical. So I realized all that stuff is just *thought* because it's not real anymore.

And that night [pause]—now I get teary-eyed because this is the turning point in my life—that night I made a promise to myself [emotional pause] that nothing, no matter what episode happened in my life [pause], would ever have as much control over me as the last thirty-eight years of my life had. And I vowed that I would take one day at a time. And when things happened to me and when people did things to me, I knew that they had this innate wisdom, this innate health that Elsie was talking about. And I would always, no matter who I was dealing with, no matter how poor they were, no matter who they were, no matter what problems they had, I would always speak to their innate wisdom. I would never look at the person and judge another human being in my life. And it was *powerful*! I mean, it was a wake-up call for me. And I now knew that I had the person to make me happy [pause], and that was *myself* and my connection to the spiritual whatever-she's-talking-about. [laughs] I didn't know what it was [laughs]. But I knew that if I could tap into that for everybody else, now I'm going to start tapping into it for myself. And that was my flip. I was always there for other people, I've always had that gift, but I never had that gift for me—to love me. It wasn't important anymore to think of what anyone else thought about me—how fat I was or how ugly I was or however unwanted I was, *I love me*! Right where I was. And I knew from that day forward, laying in my bed that night, that this was something that I was going to do for the rest of my life. Because I knew there were a lot of Helen's out there that were feeling like I was, and no one was telling them that they were *one thought away* from being healthy—mentally healthy.

By the time I got ready for that class the next day, I was just so sold on this stuff. I'm lit up like a Christmas tree. And Jeannie noticed right away that there was something different about me. But it's like that one night I shedded thirty-eight years of Hell. And I just let it all go.

JP: Incredible.

HNP: Mm hmm, and took it for what it was—it was just *Thought*. But no one had ever told me that. Elsie used that circle, and I *saw* it. I saw how I was thinking. And I saw that things are going to happen to me, people aren't going to like me and it's just what I think about it that matters. And when I catch myself I can just recognize that, "Wait a minute, it's just that my thinking is off, and I don't have to deal with that right now. It's going to be okay." Ain't that *powerful*?

JP: I'll say!

HNP: So the second day of class I came and I shared the experience and how it felt like a ton of bricks had just lifted away from me. By the third day I was just glowing, and by the fourth day, Elsie hired me as a trainer.

JP: [laughs]

HNP: And I started working with her company, which at that time was Life Core Consulting, or something like that. And they were doing a program in a housing project with some residents, working with the children and the older ladies, but no one was touching the teen moms. And I said, "Why don't I start teaching this to the teen moms?" And Elsie said, "I don't have any money to pay you." And I said, "Oh, I don't need to get paid, I just need to do this." So I would get my food stamps and I'd buy a bottle of coke and chips, and I started meeting with the teen moms. And soon that group grew tremendously, and six months went by, and I told Elsie, "OK, I'm ready to start my company now. I want to do what you're doing." And she first said, "Helen, it took me twenty years to really get to this point." And I'm saying, "That was you."

JP: [laughs]

HNP: "I'm ready!" I think at first she was thinking I was kidding. Then the opportunity came where she was moving to California. And I said, "I want you to do this for me and help me through this before you leave." And she helped me get Life Changing Consultants started. And that's the name of my consulting business.

And my life changed. The first thing that happened was that a week after that first training I had gone to, I went up to my psychiatrist and I said, "I'm through with taking this medication." And she said, "What do you mean?" And I said, "I don't need it any more. I'm free." And I've been off it to this day. Never even thought about needing it again.

JP: Wow!

HNP: Then I wanted to do something different. My first real job was at Alpha House, which is a home for pregnant teen moms. These ladies were at the same training, and the lady that ran the housing part of this saw how I changed immediately, and when they told her that I had started a company, they were my first paid job. In March I learned my understanding, and in September I

9

started my company, and by November I was working for Alpha House doing groups with the teen moms, teaching Health Realization.

JP: Amazing.

HNP: It was! The next year was kind of slow. I gave back to The Spring, the battered women's shelter. Then by word of mouth people went there watching me. Then some of the same clients I was working with went to drug rehab' and went to telling that Miss Helen was doing great things and would come and do groups. So I started doing three different sessions for the drug rehab, the moms and infants group, and then I stared doing their men, and then the residential. And it just has flourished from there.

JP: Did you start seeing changes in the people you were working with?

HNP: Oh yes! Especially after I started Life-changing Support Groups [with help from Reese Coppage]. Then in there, I saw miracles happen.

JP: Give me one example.

HNP: One day we were having a group, and one of the guys who was driving the residential treatment van—he had been going to commit suicide when he first came into the group, and he's now in the Health Realization and living a good life, just got married, just bought a house, doing wonderful—so he was driving the van, and there was a homeless lady sitting on the bench outside the church, crying. He sees her and he goes over to her and he says, "You need to come inside and see Miss Helen." And she says, "No, I'm gonna kill myself." And he says, "Yeah, I know the look, I was going to do that last year, but now I'm doing good. But you need to come in because I was feeling this way almost a year ago." And she said, "I don't want to see Miss Helen or nobody. I don't want anything." So I went out, and she was a bag lady—dirty, smelly, the whole nine yards. And something just said, "Hug her. She just needs you to hug her." So I thought, "Oooo, I'm going to hug her," and then all of a sudden the odor went away. It was like somebody just took their fingers and plugged up my nose, and I just laid her into me and she just cried on my shoulder, and I just hugged her. I said, "I love you. I don't know why, but I just need to tell you. I don't know who you are, but I love you, and I want you to just come inside and get you some food and get you cleaned up, and we here to help you. This is a support group." So she came in, and we went to talking about Thought, and she went to sharing about how she had been molested as a child, and how her mom didn't like her, and she had been a school teacher, and after her husband had died she got into a relationship with someone on drugs, and it just kind of pulled her down. And she had been on the streets for the past seven years, had lost her children, and she had just given up hope. And she started coming to the group and started dressing better and the next thing you know, she had a job back in the school system. And she rented this apartment that we're in right now, and stayed here for a while. And she went back and forth and back and forth, but I was always there for her with unconditional love. Now she just bought a condominium and she's working for the State. Now she's totally drug free. She's not doing any crack or anything now. She's been totally clean for the past year and a half. Isn't that great? I mean, I've seen miracle after miracle. She walks in the door now and people don't recognize her. She's become so pretty—a beautiful African woman, and she's my best friend. And she's just one of the many, many stories.

JP: Thank you! Well, this was great.

HNP: Good [laughs]. This life is so great. I'm just so grateful for Jeannie—I'll be forever indebted to her for the rest of my life. And now I'll share it with anybody who will listen. Anybody that wants a new life, I have the key to open that door [laughs].

Jack Pransky

II. DISCOVERING THE MEANING OF INSIDE-OUT PREVENTION

Whether we operate from the outside-in or from the inside-out, in prevention and health promotion we are after the same thing: behavior change. We want either reduced problem behaviors or improved health and well-being resulting in increased healthy behaviors, or both. The only question is, which route might best get us there?

Usually if we want to get somewhere and have a choice, we take the most direct route. To get south, we wouldn't first go north then west then south (unless we were sightseeing); we would go directly south. In prevention, we could go more directly to the heart of the matter. This book suggests that the most direct route to behavior change is within, for that is where behavior originates.

Helen [Chapter I] is an example. She changed from the inside-out. She had a massive insight that changed her forever. I am suggesting that the true source of behavior change is *insight*. If we looked closely we would see the *only* way anyone can really change is if they have an insight that alters their perspective.

On the surface it looks otherwise. If we have a gun to someone's head and are forcing him to do something, it certainly looks as if the gun is making him do it. A closer look reveals otherwise. Even at gunpoint, at some point that person must have a thought that says (something like), "Okay, I give up. Whatever you say!" or "I'd rather die!" Ultimately, the internal thought determines the behavior. Thought causes behavior. The person holding the gun also had a thought or set of thoughts that caused his behavior.

I suggest community or organizational or institutional change can only occur when a critical mass of individuals think differently than they have, and those thoughts lead to action.

Prevention from the inside-out is, first, a recognition that true change can only come from within—*through a shift in perspective that leads to a change in consciousness.*

If true that all change comes from within, it raises an interesting question: If people change internally, why do we attempt to foster change by first traveling in an external direction? As examples, to change the course of destructive or troubling behavior among young people, some might try to scare them straight, some might send them to treatment or lock them up, some might tell them to "just say no"—all with the hope they will change. Some of us might give them information. We might teach skills. We might provide supports or mentors. We might try to reduce their stress. We might try to change destructive conditions in the environment that put people at risk for developing behavior problems. We might try to build healthy conditions—in the family, school, peer group, and the rest of the community—that foster resiliency. We might try to provide assets. We might try to put "research-proven" programs in place. We might try to build healthy relationships. Whichever we select (certainly, some have been found to work better than others), we are hoping that by doing these external things people's perspective will change, which will lead to behavior change.

What if we could go directly to a change in perspective? What if we could go directly to that point of internal change?

Despite all our wonderful work in prevention and health promotion, I am suggesting we may be missing the essential ingredient in creating change.

I do not make this statement lightly. It is a humbling thought for those of us who, like myself, have worked for so many years to prevent the behavior problems that plague this society. Everything we have tried in the name of prevention has been with the best of intent. Many of our efforts have been effective. But how effective? What has been the extent of our success?

I am suggesting that if we move directly to the point where true change occurs, we can be even far more effective than we are now.

What We Have Missed

What we have missed, in my view, is this: We have forgotten, or ignored, or not realized where behavior comes from. All behavior arises from *Thought*. No matter what wonderful things we do in the name of prevention or health promotion, **unless people's thinking changes, their behavior will not change.** Our behavior always follows our thinking. This is an irrefutable fact one only has to reflect on to see its truth.

If I walk into a bar to have a drink, I must have had the thought that I want to, and the thought to do it. If I have those thoughts but also have another thought such as, "I'd better not; it's not good for me," the initial thoughts would be overridden, unless still another thought said, "Forget that. I've got to"—or something like that. If I never have the thought (which for me, personally, is more likely), I'm never even tempted to walk into a bar.

In fact, the thoughts of prevention practitioners determine which prevention strategies they choose. When it comes to behavior of any kind, *Thought* is fundamental. Our behavior always follows our thinking.

In traditional prevention, whether we realize it or not, we are doing something from the outside in hopes people's thinking will change on the inside and lead to behavior change.[3] No matter what our approach, our program or effort will *not* be successful for any individual *if* that person's thinking *does not* change as a result. No matter what our approach, our efforts in a community will not be successful unless enough people's collective thinking changes. Since most of our efforts do not attempt to affect *Thought* directly, we are, in effect, leaving it to chance.

I believe this has been the fundamental flaw in our approach [see Chapter V]. It's nobody's fault. Believe me, I was there! I spent 23 years working from the outside-in perspective and even wrote a book about it (Pransky, 2001/1991).

Beyond this, something else appears to lie within. **When people are connected to or aligned with what might be called their "spiritual essence" or their "innate Health" or**

---

[3] I know a few, rare prevention efforts are exceptions to this generalization, and I will address this later.

wisdom (or any number of other terms people may use), **they do not engage in problem behaviors.**

Unfortunately, this second point cannot be proven. It can never be proven. Unlike the connection between thought and behavior, this connection cannot be considered irrefutable, but it sure looks true to me and to many others. Yet, our "outside-in" approaches have not, for the most part, attempted directly and purposefully to connect people to this internal dimension. I realize that some do, and where this happens it can make a real difference.

Thus, the most critical factor in behavior change—*Thought*—and perhaps another essential factor—our spirit or *innate Health*—have been left out of the equation in most all our prevention efforts.

This book attempts to make a compelling argument for why turning the opposite way, to look within, is critically important, if for no other reason than to reach the people we have not yet been able to reach. If we operate from the inside-out, evidence suggests we may be able to get even better results than we do now [Chapter X].

Defining "Inside-Out"

The term, "inside-out" has already become overused in a number of fields. Many different meanings have been ascribed to it. Because of this I considered not using the term at all. Unfortunately I could find no other term that works as well. Here is what "inside-out" means, as I use it throughout this book:

The word before the hyphen (in "inside-out" or "outside-in") refers to *the point where the intervention begins.* It is the initial focus of our efforts. The word following the hyphen refers to *our intention: what we hope will transpire as a result of the intervention.* This will become clearer as we go along.

The best way to see inside-out prevention is in contrast with traditional, outside-in prevention. In "outside-in" prevention our beginning point is with external conditions that are either harmful and need to be changed or are constructive and need to be built or fostered or supported or nurtured. The end point, "in," refers to our intention that these external changes will manifest within and yield healthier people. For example, we might attempt to reduce high-risk conditions in hopes it will make people healthier and reduce problem behaviors. We might attempt to build resiliency or internal assets, or build strengths to make people healthier. We might provide supports or teach skills or information, implying that if people only had these, problems would be prevented. Any time we think we must do something to people or for people or with people for them to be fully healthy and whole and free of problems, we are in the realm of outside-in prevention. If we believe our external program or anything we can do externally will make people healthier, we are operating outside-in.

In contrast, in inside-out prevention, the first part of the equation, "inside" means beginning with *knowing* that everyone is already completely whole and healthy within—with all the wisdom they will ever need to guide them, and this is the only place where answers arise—and people can be helped to understand and experience this "innate Health," and realize when they are not in touch with it, so their lives can be guided by it. Or, it means beginning with looking to the spiritual world within—the world of formless energy and creative potential that can be brought forth to manifest in healthy form. Or it is a combination of these. These are merely different explanations for the same force or source, but it is our beginning, our focal point, for "inside-out" prevention. "Inside," then, refers not so much to something we do as to something we *see* in people. What we do then naturally follows from what we see.

The "out" part of the "inside-out" equation—the end point—refers to the intention for this Health to manifest *out* in the world to ultimately affect one's relationships, the community and its institutions . With the realization of what lies within, one's own life first becomes more aligned with well-being. One's relationships then begin to improve. Then, when a critical mass of people in a community or organization become affected in a similar way, they work to change the unhealthy conditions in their communities and organizations and systems. Thus, what is naturally *inside* is brought *out* into the world.

To say this in a slightly different way, with inside-out prevention the starting point is seeing that every person is a fully whole, healthy human being who needs absolutely nothing from us because everything is already within. In a sense this is seeing people's "spiritual essence," which lacks absolutely nothing. With that as "given" we come to understand that, as prevention practitioners, we can do nothing to make people healthy and whole—because they already *are* perfectly whole and healthy. All we can do is help them see who they already really are and help them see what keeps them from realizing it. Once seen, people's internal perspective changes; then it ripples out from there. In inside-out prevention we *know* people have the wisdom within to overcome any problem or situation they may encounter—if they know how to access it! We know they have the wisdom within to overcome poverty and other oppressive conditions. We know they have the wisdom within to overcome anger or fear or depression or violence or victimization or anything else. All they need is to *see* this.

This implies, in inside-out prevention, our job is to do whatever we can to help others see that innate part of themselves. This begins within ourselves, for *unless we are able to see our own Health, and what keeps us from experiencing it, we would not be able to help anyone else know what to look for.* Unless we have seen our own lives improve as a result of looking within to our own Health, we will not have much to communicate to others; anything we say or do will have a hollow ring. Thus, inside-out prevention begins with us— inside us. We must walk our talk. Only then can we be of assistance to others in helping them see their Health.

Because, unfortunately (or thankfully), we cannot dive directly into people's minds initially we often have no choice but to do something from the outside—even talk with them—to help people see what is within that they don't now see. We are inhibited in that respect, but with inside-out prevention we understand that nothing we can ever do can possibly make them see their Health. If they see it, it is only because they had an insight; if they do not see it, it is because they did not have such an insight. If they have an insight, it has nothing to do with us. We can point them in the direction of the inside world, but whether they see it or not is entirely their own realization.

Does this make our work with others superfluous? Not at all. On the contrary, it makes it extremely interesting and exhilarating. There is no limit to the depth of the inside world. We can never get to the bottom of it. When we work with others, the only thing keeping us from seeing what another person might see that could trigger an insight is the temporary limitations of our own little minds.

Inside-out prevention means getting to the essence of what is inside human beings that makes them behave and function as they do. It means getting to the heart of human behavior.

Stress Management as an Example of the Difference Between Outside-In and Inside-Out Prevention

Dealing with stress is one place where the difference between outside-in and inside-out prevention may be most clear. The Vermont State Employee Wellness Program, for example, issued a fairly typical flyer about "Handling Stress." The first thing it says is, "You need stress in your life!…Without stress, life would be dull and uninteresting."

From the inside-out perspective, nothing could be further from the truth. Do we need stress to appreciate a beautiful sunset? If we love the feeling of lying on a beach in the sun, does that mean we would need stress to be motivated to do it again, or do anything else? If we are having fun at our work and are so totally involved we don't even realize how much time has passed, are we stressed? The fact is, when we are connected to the moment and do not have a lot of extraneous thoughts on our minds, we feel internally motivated to do whatever feels right. We don't need stress to make work interesting; we don't need stress to make life interesting.

The flyer then gives some suggestions for ways to handle stress: "Try physical activity. Share your stress (by talking it out with others). Take care of yourself (by getting enough rest and eating well). Make time for fun. Check off your tasks (after making a list of what needs to be done). Be a participant. When other people upset you, use cooperation instead of confrontation. Avoid self medication. It's okay to cry. Create a quiet scene (in your mind)."

All are outside-in strategies. The last two only seem on the surface to be inside-out. All assume stress is a given. All are strategies for dealing with stress *after* we already experience it. All assume stress is caused by things in the outside world to which we must react. In inside-out prevention stress is never considered a given, no matter what happens in the outside world. Inside-out prevention asserts that stress is caused by the way we see the outside world—from within.

It sure looks as if stress comes from the outside world, but not if we look deeper. We think having to do too much work in too little time causes us stress. But some people seem to handle this better than others. In fact, sometimes we're more stressed about it than at other times—given the same amount of work! Our stress *must* come from the way we think about it. Sometimes it looks as if stress is caused by our having to produce and keep producing to make enough money. Yet, if we look closely we see this too looks different to us at different times. Or, we think stress is caused by poverty. But some poor people aren't stressed, and some rich people are! Sometimes it looks as if our boss is causing us stress. But a few of our coworkers think our boss is funny when he blows up, and they laugh about it. Inside-out prevention asserts that stress can only be caused by the way we see the outside circumstances—with our own thinking.

Thus, the inside-out approach to "dealing with" stress is to help the person see the source of stress; that it comes from within ourselves, not from anything "out there": to realize the amount of stress we have is completely determined by our own stressful thinking; to see that our stress level shifts when our thinking shifts; to realize we don't have to take our stressful thinking so seriously.

We need to look inside to affect whether stress is experienced in the first place.

Looking Deeper into the Inside World?

If inside-out prevention looks in the direction of the inside world for answers to social problems, we need to take a deeper look into the world within. When I say "the world within" I am talking about beginning as far "in" as we can go.

When we look outside, we see behaviors. What happens when we look within? At first glance we might see our feelings. But that is not the inside I am talking about. Our feelings have already been produced; we already feel them. In that sense they are already "out" in the world—at least in our own world. Whether we have expressed those feelings or not, whether we are aware of them or not, they are already "out" affecting us. I am referring to something deeper.

I am talking about what *creates* the feelings we have. We could say our feelings are produced, as scientist Candace Pert (1997) says, by the movement of molecules in our bodies, the "molecules of emotion." While proven true by science, this is not the inside I am talking about. Often the molecules in our bodies move via some internal force.[4] The "inside" I am talking about is the *creative force* that makes the molecules move in the first place.

If we look deeper within, we would see that our feelings come from our thoughts. Often we are not aware of those thoughts, but they are acting on us. Yet, thoughts too have already been thought—in that sense they are "out" in the world. Whether we have expressed them or not, and whether we are aware of them or not, they are already "out" affecting us. The deep inside I am talking about is what *creates* our thoughts in the first place, what creates all thoughts. I don't deny that many of our thoughts come from our memories. But of the trillions of thoughts stored in our memories, what makes us think of certain ones at certain times and not others? It is a mystery. Even more mysterious, where do thoughts come from that we have never thought before? Does our brain manufacture them from nothing? Even if it does, how would the brain know what to manufacture—and where does it get its power? These are deep questions. Some other mysterious, creative force seems to be at work.

To truly look within is to look at creation. Anything already produced by this creative force within is already after the fact, a product of creation, "out" there. If we are talking about the most primary prevention—prevention at the earliest possible moment—we must look directly at the creative force itself. This is our beginning point in prevention from the inside-out.

Before we get there, our exploration might lead us to consciousness. What makes us conscious of life? Mystics and philosophers have pondered this question for centuries without being able to reach a definitive answer. Even more mysterious, where does our consciousness come from? What gives us the power to have Consciousness? Some would say the brain manufactures consciousness (Dennett, 1991), but even if true (which I sincerely doubt), what would give the brain its power to do so? Some kind of life force must give the brain the power to do its work; otherwise it is just a lump of tissue.

Here we come to something so indefinable and so unfathomable that it is beyond intellectual understanding. The power of Thought and the power of Consciousness are already

---

[4] I do not dispute that some outside physical forces can also make those molecules move, but this will be dealt with later in Chapter XXI.

Distinguishing Between Outside-In and Inside-Out Prevention Approaches

Where do current prevention strategies fall within this definition? It might be helpful to examine the prevention strategies implied by Albee's landmark prevention formula (1980), as adapted by Pransky in *Prevention: The Critical Need* (2001).

$$\text{rate of problem behavior} = \frac{\text{cultural expectations} + \text{stress} + \text{organic problems} + \text{lack of opportunity}}{\text{healthy perceptions} + \text{life skills} + \text{supports} + \text{awareness}}$$

Were we to examine the factors in the numerator of Albee's equation, it is easy to see in most cases how we would be operating outside-in. For example, with regard to cultural expectations or stress from the social environment, the formula suggests that those external factors affect an individual, and we can create preventive strategies to minimize those harmful external effects.

For organic problems this is less clear. Are not organic problems internal? By this book's definition, if organic factors such as traumatic head injury or fetal alcohol syndrome are outside the person's control, if we look to prevent their "causes," we still are operating from the outside-in.

What about "lack of opportunity?" Here, people feel subjected to outside forces over which they have little or no control, and if our approach is to minimize those external forces we again would be operating outside-in. If, on the other hand, lack of opportunity is seen as an internal perception we are attempting to change, we then could be operating inside-out, but it depends on the approach we take. If we do something with people externally, such as providing meaningful work in hopes that their perception will change, we are operating outside-in. If we are attempting to change attitudes about work, we may be operating inside-out (but again it depends how we achieve it).

The items in the denominator can appear even more muddy, but only on the surface. If the intent is to build self-esteem or healthy self-perceptions by helping people learn or do certain things or by creating healthy conditions so they can gain self-esteem, our approach would be from the outside-in. If the intent is to help people realize their own innate self-esteem and have their own realizations affect their relationships and the community, our approach would be from the inside-out. If the teaching of skills implies that people are lacking something they have to get from outside, individual or group skill-building would be an outside-in approach. If people do not have external supports and the intent is to help people gain those, it is outside-in. If the intent is to provide information, build awareness or *teach* new attitudes, by this definition it is an outside-in approach.

Moving beyond Albee's formula, if the intent is to use counseling as a preventive approach but there is no intent to help people use their new understanding to affect outside conditions, it would not qualify as inside-*out*, for it remains internal. An argument could be made that Gandhi employed an inside-out approach to social change, because it began with getting himself right first, and having his highly moral stance affect others and an entire nation (Gardner, 1993).

Spiritual approaches to prevention may be considered inside-out approaches (Pransky, 2001), but a subtle distinction can be observed in implementation. A reliance on techniques such as meditation or yoga may assume something external must be practiced for the inside to be affected. If the focus is on the practice or technique instead of on the internal state of calm or peace, then it may not be an inside-out approach. Perhaps, too, if one's "higher power" is viewed as outside oneself, that may suggest an outside-in approach; if one's higher power is seen within, it suggests an inside-out approach.

What about resiliency and asset building? Research shows that both external and internal factors affect one's resilience. Affecting external factors is obviously operating outside-in. What about internal factors? Here another subtle but important distinction can be made. Though many of us talk strengths and health when we talk resiliency and prevention, whenever we see an incomplete human being who needs something from outside oneself to change, such as information, skills, supports, a mentor, or even a healthy environment, we are in the realm of outside-in prevention.

This is not meant to imply that outside-in prevention is not a valid direction. Both inside-out and outside-in directions are important and useful in prevention. For the field to be wholly effective neither should be neglected. Yet, currently, by this definition, nearly all funding for prevention programming is directed to outside-in efforts.

beyond intellectual understanding, but these powers themselves must come from somewhere. From where? Here we "find" the formless—formless energy that appears to have an Intelligence attached. Only we can't find it, because it is formless. We can't even conceive of it, really. Perhaps this is The Ultimate Power, the Ultimate Source. People give it various names: Spirit, Mind, God, Allah, The Creator, and lots more. But it doesn't matter what it is called. For purposes of this book I choose to call it "Mind" or "Spirit"—or I may make reference to "formless energy" or "the life force" or I may use some other terms—but it really doesn't matter. Whatever It is, It is the Source of all creation.

I submit that the "inside"—the true inside—consists of the power of Thought and the power of Consciousness, all powered up and created by and from and of the power of Mind. These powers are the very process of creation within ourselves and everyone with whom we work and ultimately of all things. This process of creation becomes our starting point in the world of inside-out prevention.

In traditional outside-in prevention and human services, human resources, and most psychotherapy, we look to the already created and try to do something constructive with it or change it. In inside-out prevention we look to the creative process or creative force itself. It is an entirely different world in which to operate. This is not to say we shouldn't care about building healthy environments—we absolutely should. It is to say we might consider directing efforts at where the true source of change occurs.

I now realize this is where answers lie to the most impactful prevention, because this creative process when used differently to yield healthier creations from within, then radiates "out" to affect people's thoughts, then feelings, then behavior, then relationships, then communities, then societies and the world.

As philosopher Sydney Banks says, "The inside creates the outside."

The key to prevention is for people to experience a "change in consciousness," which as we shall see later is really a change in Thought, and to see how this is all brought about by Mind. For most of us, Thought has been our greatest enemy, when it could be our greatest and most powerful ally.

So this is where our inquiry begins.

Before we get there, however, let's examine why operating solely from the outside world can only take us so far.

III. A NEW PERSPECTIVE ON PREVENTION PRACTICE

What is our end point in prevention? What we are really trying to achieve? Using Lofquist's (1986) definition, if prevention is "an active process of changing conditions…that promote the well-being of people," is our "end" to achieve "well-being," or is it "changed conditions," or is it to reduce the incidence of various social problems?

To answer this question it is worthwhile to ask what kind of change are we satisfied with in the name of prevention?

Levels of Change

Are we satisfied, for example, to change the magnitude of drug education in a school and involve students in program development, thereby changing a condition in the school system? On the surface it seems so, but suppose even with such drug education we find young people abusing alcohol and drugs as much as ever. Would we be satisfied? Compare this with the kind of change that could occur within young people's very consciousness so it would not even occur to them to want to abuse drugs.

When we help people move through a community development process we can change detrimental conditions. This is terrific, but will community members' overall well-being improve? If so, by how much? How much change is enough change? If we remove a grain of sand from a beach, that beach is forever changed, but is this level of change satisfactory? What if we were able to help improve people's well-being first, without changing conditions? Would that be considered "good" prevention practice? These are compelling questions.

In our attempts to create change through prevention program development we might consider the example of an effort to reduce the incidence of AIDS:

Because AIDS is a manifestation of HIV, logic tells us we must reduce the incidence of people contracting HIV. Since HIV is carried only through blood and semen, logic dictates that we should attempt to prevent HIV from being passed from an infected to an uninfected person. Therefore, if we could just get people to stop having sex, and get heroin and other needle-using addicts to stop sharing needles, and ensure HIV-free blood supplies, we might stop 99% of HIV transmission. One strategy, then, is to test all blood supplies. What about trying to get people to stop having sex? Not likely—as unlikely as trying to get addicts to have the presence of mind in the moment to not share needles (although some would argue these are the only ways).

Since we can't stop sex ("just say no" or just say "abstinence" just don't seem to have the impact on young people most adults would like), if we could get people to have safe sex through using condoms, and ensure that addicts would use clean needles, we could substantially prevent the spread of HIV/AIDS. But since most people having sex don't always have condoms at their fingertips at the needed moment, and most addicts don't have access to clean needles, logic dictates that we must get enough condoms and clean needles into people's hands. This becomes another prevention strategy. [Some people, of course, despise this idea—in fact, a lot of these ideas—but that's another story.] Some prevention practitioners stop there.

Even if condoms and clean needles are in people's hands, does that mean they will use them? How can we get people to use them? Some people do not realize the danger, so we must educate them by whatever means necessary—through the media, school curricula, community pamphlets and posters—and that becomes another prevention strategy. Some prevention practitioners stop there.

Even if people understand the need to use condoms, some don't know how to use them properly to ensure complete safety, so we need to teach them these skills—and that becomes another strategy. Some prevention workers stop there.

Even if people have the information and skills, there may be too much pressure from their peers or from their subculture to act as "society" might desire. In some areas, it may not be considered manly or macho to use condoms. In other places they might say, "No way! It doesn't feel good enough to use a condom," or "People who use condoms are wusses"—and many people, even if they disagree, do not have the inner strength to go it alone. So another strategy might be to try to turn around peer pressure and provide the supports needed for people to feel enough strength in numbers—even if it is one other buddy or mentor—so they can carry out what they have the education to do. This becomes another strategy. Some practitioners stop there.

Or we say, if people only had high self-esteem or inner strength they could resist the temptation, despite peer pressure. So we try to build self-esteem through a school curriculum or through educational support groups in the community. Some stop there.

Others say, wait, let's go to the research and find out what really works to ensure self-esteem, and they discover that healthy self-perceptions appear largely the result of how people are treated in their families and in school. Thus, if we can change unhealthy environments into environments that build resilience—through parenting education and school climate improvement—then people might be strong enough to resist the pressure. Some stop there.

Still others say, suppose we could alter an entire community norm in support of healthy behaviors and to discourage the unhealthy. We could organize people through a solid community development process to create the changes we need. Further, because there appears to be much overlap in many of our HIV/AIDS prevention strategies with other fields—such as substance abuse prevention, teenage pregnancy prevention, sexual abuse prevention, public health promotion, mental health promotion and others—we could collaborate to create one concerted effort, while directly involving young people in developing strategies. We could even decide to build a community that fosters resilience and develop a host of programs found by research to work. Most remaining prevention practitioners stop there.

Through all this logic and creative prevention one problem remains. No matter what strategies we employ, if people still think, "I don't need to use condoms (or clean needles)," or, "It won't happen to me," or, "I don't give a damn what happens," or, "It's not worth thinking about," or, if they're caught up in the passion of the moment—"Forget this!"—or they don't think of using a condom at all, all our wonderful attempts at prevention have not been successful. No matter how creative our strategies, no matter how comprehensive our approach, if people still *think* in ways that lead to these risk-taking behaviors, we have not reached them. Only when people's thinking actually changes will their behaviors follow.

As asserted in Chapter II, people truly change when their perspective shifts. If you reflect upon a time in your life when you changed a really important behavior, and then ask yourself what caused the change, if you questioned yourself hard enough, you would likely find that you changed from within. Some outside event or something someone said may have triggered it, but that same event or those same words could have happened or been said to thousands of other people, and they would not have changed the way you did, or you may not have changed all the other times you heard those comments. True change happens from within! This is how everyone changes. Not many of our prevention efforts focus on consciously affecting internal change. As I have said, this has been the missing link in prevention.

"Change" within prevention has often meant changing community or institutional conditions, and we never want to stop doing that. But now we realize an additional ingredient is needed that changes people at the most fundamental level, within their very consciousness, just as happened within us in the example above. *We do not want to be doing only half the job in prevention, for we will be only half as successful as we could be.* We can help people change all the detrimental conditions around them, but if they still think the same way about their lives, their well-being will not be affected. They may still think in ways that cause problems for themselves or others.

THE TWELVE DEPTHS OF PREVENTION

The field of prevention has achieved some very worthwhile results. Whether we have had the kind of wide impact on a grand scale that we and most others desire is debatable. As of this writing, the (modern) field of prevention has been at work for at least four decades. Has it achieved wide impact? If not, why not? I do not pretend to know the answer. I know many factors are at play, including limited funding for prevention. But we need to ask ourselves whether we have been as successful as we would like, even within adequately funded programs. One answer may be found in a somewhat different-than-usual perspective on prevention: an examination of prevention's vertical dimension.

Despite training prevention practitoners since 1971 and being a student of prevention research since 1977, it was not until the mid-late 1990s that the following observations occurred to me about prevention practice:

1. People who talk about and work in prevention operate at different depths.
2. The depth at which people operate is determined by what they see; that is, by what they believe to be true or "the way to go."
3. The deeper the prevention depth, the more impact it appears to have in changing people's lives toward well-being and away from problems.
4. The deeper the depth, the fewer people are currently engaged in its practice.

What follows is not science. It is simply one person's view based on observation. But it does hold a certain logic. The fact is, most practitioners and preventionists in the field have looked at prevention horizontally; in other words, we have looked to a series of things that need to be done over time to produce change. This is fine, but I now realize there is a vertical dimension to prevention as well. The vertical dimension consists of a series of levels or depths. Others may have varying ideas about what each of the depths should be named, or whether some should be added or subtracted. The point is there are different levels of prevention depth at which people operate, no matter what the various levels are called, and the deeper the depth the more potential power to create preventive change. [Note: In this section I will touch upon a number of themes that will be presented later in more detail.]

Finding the Essence of Prevention

The definition of prevention I like best is based on the root of the word, the Latin *praevenire*, meaning, "to come before." (Pransky, 2001). When combined with a principle of physics that two objects cannot occupy the same space at the same time, this means if healthy, constructive conditions that *come before* a problem are built up-front, the problem or destructive conditions cannot materialize. If prevention means "to come before," the question might be asked, "What is the earliest *before*?" In other worlds, if we keep boiling down the contributing factors to arrive at the very essence, to find what lies at the crux of what creates problem or healthy behaviors, we may get closer to what might have the most impact. Where would we end up? The idea is to move closer to the essence.

The metaphor of rugs on a floor may be useful. We walk upon a rug's surface, but if we want to know what the floor is made of, we have to lift up the rug and look under it. We would never know the essence of the floor by simply standing on the rug's surface and operating there. So we lift up the rug and take a look. Suppose we find another rug. We are closer to the essence than before, but to truly find that essence, we have to look under this next rug. Suppose we uncovered another rug. We would have to look still deeper. Suppose we lifted the next and found another, then another, then another, and so forth. We have to continue to look deeper until we reach the essence of the floor itself. Only then would we know what materials we need to fix it, or to build a stronger floor. The rugs tell us only about the surface and obscure the true essence.

If we pictured these rugs as prevention layers, anyone stepping onto the top rug would recognize that many people appear to have problems that adversely affect others or themselves, and something needs to be done. Everyone standing on this rug makes a choice—often inadvertently—about how deeply to look to determine what needs to be done. The depth they reach is the depth they see or have learned to see, and *what people see is the realm in which they naturally operate* [Figure 1].

My view of the twelve depths of prevention follows. The seasoned preventionist will note that the first few depths—in fact, more than the first half—are levels most of us are all too familiar with and use different terms to describe.

Depth # 1 — *See problems, do nothing*
People who step onto the rug's surface know there are problems. They see those problems, they complain about them. They know something has to be done, but they choose to do nothing. It is important to understand that this level is already a leap from not getting

on the rug at all—from not even recognizing problems exist that we could impact. It is better than being oblivious. It is also a leap from those who choose to ignore the problems. It is an enormous leap from those who actually cause the problems. But it is not very effective for solving those problems. To do something constructive, we must look beyond this surface.

Depth # 2 — *Fix problems after the fact*

People who lift up the first rug and step onto the second layer know that if we can see a problem, something can be done to fix it. These people see that the problem behaviors are serious. Once they see those problems occur they are so concerned that, depending on the specific nature of the problem, they may lock people up, or offer treatment, or services. At this level these people want to do something constructive about a problem after it has already materialized and become serious. It is important and necessary to operate at this level, yet some people see this level as the only prevention, and it does nothing to reduce the incidence (new cases) of those problems.

Depth # 3 — *See problems emerge, then intervene*

These people see a little more deeply. They see that serious problems had to evolve; they didn't simply start that way. If problems can be fixed, they can be caught earlier. These people see the early signs of problems, and they want to stop them in their tracks before they become serious. When they see problems emerge they want to intervene at the earliest possible time, or to stop or manage crises. To catch problems earlier is often more effective and less costly than waiting for them to become serious, but still it will not reduce incidence.

Depth # 4 — *See primary prevention, before the fact of problems*

These people see that behind nearly every emerging problem is something that could have been prevented in the first place. People operating at this level want to do more than just cut off problems at the pass; they do not want the problems to materialize at all. Simply seeing this possibility of primary prevention is a huge leap, because it asks the question, "What can be done up front to reduce the incidence of problems?" In other words, instead of fishing people out of the river after they have already fallen in, it recognizes that we can go upstream and build a fence so people won't fall in the first place or, better, help people see how wise it is (and therefore how much healthier it is) to not get too close to the river bank.

Depth # 5 — *Pick a prevention strategy that sounds good*

These people not only recognize the possibility of primary prevention, they actually try to do it. They may hear of a program or approach that sounds good, sounds like it could logically work, and they leap on the chance to do something. While noble, at this depth people do not ask whether the approach will actually work. For example, if kids are getting into trouble and the community says, "It's because they have nowhere to go and nothing constructive to do," they may conclude, "Let's get the kids a youth center!" These people have the best of intentions, and youth centers are very nice things for kids, but youth centers may not prevent anything. "Just Say No" is another example. Some would say the original DARE program is another example. Because implementation of a community "asset-building" approach (Benson et al, 1995) has not yet been proven effective (as of this writing), that may or may not be another. It is not that such efforts are inadvisable; it is that research has not shown, to date, that they prevent the problems they claim to.

Depth # 6 — *See risk factors that lie behind problems, and reduce them*

These people look deeper and take the leap into research. They see that research shows correlations, that certain external and internal factors contribute to the problems, or that certain factors appear to lie behind the development of problems. They see research shows that people who come from certain "high risk" conditions have a greater tendency to become involved in problems (Hawkins et al., 1992). They either single out "high risk" people for special treatment (thus retreating to depth # 3), or better, they identify existing risk factors and work to reduce those risks.

Depth # 7 — *See root "causes" behind the risks, and change conditions*

While closely related to the above, at this level people look even deeper to see that behind the long lists of risk factors identified by research in various fields there appear to be a few key "root causes," or more accurately, "root contributing factors" (because cause and effect cannot be shown). In other words, no matter what lists of risk factors we examine, some risks seem to be repeated over and over and therefore appear to have the most influence. [For research on what these root factors are, specifically, see section titled, *The Conceptual Framework of Prevention, Revisited,* later in this chapter.] The social-ecological model (Kelley, 1968; Belsky, 1980) helps us see the connections between and the effects upon all parts of this system, including many depths above and below this. However, George Albee (1996) reminds us that within this depth lie two opposing forces, one geared to finding the "root cause" of social problems in organically/genetically-based origins with its resulting implications for solutions, and the other seeing the root cause as fundamental economic injustice and corruption of power, causing the ever-widening gap between rich and poor, with its resulting stressors and problems. The latter implies the solution lies in fundamental social change. People operating at this depth can work to change these conditions, and certainly some important changes here can and should be accomplished. Unfortunately, to truly make a dent at this important level may require a "movement" of great magnitude often beyond the scope of the few who work in the prevention field.

Depth # 8 — *See that not everyone succumbs to risks; focus on resiliency and strengths*

These people see that research shows even when people grow up in high risk/"root cause" situations, not all become involved with problems; not everyone succumbs to the risks (Werner, 1992; Rutter, 1979; Garmezy, 1991). This indicates that some other mediating factors stand between the risks and emergent behaviors. Some research calls these "protective factors" (Hawkins et al., 1992) or factors that make people "resilient" in spite of the risks. Thus, the focus becomes identifying the key factors that make people resilient. (Benard, 1991; Wilson et al., 1995; Henderson & Milstein, 1997) [See Chapter V]. The idea is to ensure that every environment that significantly touches young people's lives builds these. The focus is on building strengths or assets, as opposed to reducing risks. As Benard (1996a) eloquently states, "Prevention program planners and evaluators must move beyond seeing prevention as specific programs...and specific content...to the understanding that prevention is a developmental process of making connections to healthy people, places, ideas, and interests that give one's life meaning and hope." Researchers speak of the need to build both external and internal assets (Benson et al., 1994) and resiliency (Benard, 1996b), but observation suggests that action in the field has largely focused on building the external. [See Chapter V for a more in-depth look at this.]

Depth # 9 — *See what resiliency hopes to build: healthy self-perceptions*

These people see beyond the lists of assets or protective or resiliency factors to what we hope will occur as a result of building resiliency; in other words, to what we hope our resiliency efforts will achieve. In short, it is hoped people will emerge with healthy self-perceptions, which research suggests makes the primary difference in how people behave. Despite different terminology used by different researchers in different fields this essentially means people who perceive that they are 1) *capable*, that is, they have self-worth and competence; 2) *important* to something greater than themselves; and 3) have the *power to affect what happens* to them in life; plus, they have the skills of self-discipline, communication, responsibility, and judgment (Glenn & Nelsen, 1988; Pransky, 2001). To focus at this level is to ensure—within whatever resiliency approach or asset-building approach is applied within families, schools, the peer group and community—that people are developing these healthy perceptions. This is the depth H. Steven Glenn has been talking about since the mid-1970s. [Note: Depths 7, 8 and 9 were the primary focus of *Prevention: The Critical Need*].

Depth # 10 — *See what lies behind perceptions: thoughts*

These people see that even when resiliency factors are built, not everyone emerges with healthy self-perceptions and free from problems; something lies behind "self-perceptions." This means there is a further mediating influence. What makes the difference? What lie behind people's perceptions of themselves are *thoughts*. For example, people with thoughts of violence will follow their thinking unless and until they have other thoughts. Relapse Prevention in the substance abuse field (Marlatt & Gordon, 1985) and the sexual abuse field Bays & Freeman-Longo, 1989) recognizes this, and when they help people restructure their cognitive distortions so they will not go down a destructive path, they have a much higher success rate (Pithers, 1989). But why wait until people are coming out of treatment? Such cognitive approaches could be applied as primary prevention, for example through school curricula, to have far wider impact. A few creative cognitive approaches have begun to crop up in primary prevention over the past few years; for example, within *Positive Paths* of Information & Referral Services/EMPACT-SPC in Tucson/Phoenix, Arizona (Parrish & Shaw et al.,1997) and *In My House* (Responsible Decisions, Inc., 2000). One of the most successful primary prevention programs employs "interpersonal cognitive problem solving" as its key ingredient in an early childhood education curriculum (Shure & Spivak, 1988).

Depth # 11 — *See what lies behind thoughts: Thought + Consciousness*

These people see that something lies even behind the content of people's thoughts. Where do thoughts come from? Behind thought content lies the power of people to think, the power to formulate thoughts. Close examination suggests that *Thought* is the source of anything we can possibly create. Plus, we must have a way to experience life. This is where *Consciousness* comes in. Consciousness allows us to experience our creations. Close examination suggests *we are capable of experiencing only what our thinking creates*. [See Chapter VI] At this depth, then, people are helped to realize that with their own thinking they are in a continual process of creating whatever they experience of life. When people see how they create not what happens to them but *how they experience whatever happens to them, and how they feel as a result*, they experience what some would call a shift or a change in consciousness. With this shift, they gain new understanding of what they experience in life. Healthier thinking, feelings, and actions naturally follow. Further, when people see they have within them an innate, healthy thought process, and how to access it and trust it, they are able to pull themselves out of problems and live in well-being. This is a recognition that people have *natural, internal resiliency, and people can realize it and draw it forth*. They can also lose sight of it, but see how to get back on track (Pransky, Mills, Sedgeman & Blevens, 1997; Pransky, 1998). This depth recognizes that *unless people experience a change in consciousness they will not fundamentally change.*

Depth # 12 — *See what lies behind Thought + Consciousness: Mind or Spirit*

Some people see even deeper to the very source of Thought and Consciousness. Where does the power to have Thought and to have Consciousness come from? If it were possible to connect with the Source of creation itself, problems might vanish as the illusions they may well be (Banks, 1998). Some call this a connection with the intelligence or formless energy behind life, or *Mind*; others call it a connection with Spirit or God or The Creator or many other things. Some refer to this depth as the link between spirituality and prevention. This is the ultimate depth because there is no getting to the bottom of this Source. Many of us know of people whose lives have completely turned around as a result of some spiritual epiphany of great magnitude (Foreman & Engel, 1995; Maslow, 1968). The difficulty here is that no one knows how to make an epiphany happen. To truly reach this depth is to transcend what we commonly see and how we commonly feel and behave; it is to see *the essence of humanity in relation to the spiritual world.* When we talk about what *comes before* problems, this depth is the earliest possible *before*, because it is the Source itself. This depth, of course, can never be "proven," and some deny its very existence. It is difficult to dispute, however, that some people's lives have changed markedly after they have what they describe as a spiritual experience.

Again, the deeper the level or depth, the more powerful the potential for affecting people and for turning around lives, for each deeper level is closer to the essence or source. Yet at the deeper depths fewer people are engaged in current prevention practice. In my view, most of our work in prevention does not yet go deep enough.

Again, the *twelve depths of prevention* is not a scientific taxonomy. The point is there are different levels of prevention at which people operate, no matter what the levels are called, and the deeper the level the more potential power we have to create preventive change.

It may appear that certain key approaches to prevention are not built into these "depths" For example: Where is community development (Lofquist, 1986)? Where is a focus on outcomes? Where is research about "What Works?" Where is the focus on what constitutes effective prevention practice? These I see as sub-depths within each of the depths, because they could be employed at most of the different depths to make them more effective. For example, for most of the different levels, the more effective community development practices are employed, the more people focus on results, the more people focus on what has been found by research to work, and the more people focus on the specific qualities of effective prevention programs, the more effective the effort will be at those depths. But wherever they operate, they are still operating at that particular depth, and it is always possible to go deeper—if people see those levels.

Again, I want to be exceptionally clear, I am not suggesting we abandon attempts to change outside conditions such as inequitable institutions and socio-economic conditions that breed poverty and hopelessness and that put people at high risk for developing problems. I am not suggesting we stop trying to build environments and relationships that foster resilience. Of course we should continue these! I am saying, once again, that to be most effective we need to give at least equal time and effort to what goes on *within* human beings that shapes their behavior.

Prevention Paradigm Shifts

The evolution of the prevention field may be viewed as a consolidation of these depths into three or four major paradigm shifts that have occurred and are still in process. "Paradigm shift" has become an overused phrase; it really means "a pervasive world view for a given domain that establishes the kinds of questions that can be asked and determines which types of answers are acceptable within this perspective" (Kuhn, in Bloom, 1996, p. 88).

Perhaps the first major paradigm shift within the fields of mental health, criminology, health care and human services was the shift to primary prevention. The idea that problems could be prevented up front, before they manifest, proved to be a completely different view of solving social behavior and health problems. This coincided with the shift of focus from the individual (called by some, "blaming the victim") to one of changing societal, community or environmental conditions.

Another huge leap for the prevention field, although not meeting the criteria of a "paradigm shift," occurred with the recognition that research into risks or causal/contributing factors could define and guide prevention efforts and make them far more effective.

The next major paradigm shift occurred in changing the focus from the negative (risks) to the positive (resiliency, assets, or strengths). Some would say this shift in the field is still in its early stages.

A new major shift may now be in the embryonic stage, a shift from an outside-in focus to an inside-out focus. By this I do not mean what John McKnight (1997) portrays as an "inside-out" approach. McKnight advocates a preventive or community development approach that begins with connecting people to their own, internal personal resources (skills) and community resources to effect community change. While certainly an innovative and worthwhile approach, McKnight appears to operate at depth 7 and perhaps 8 above, while the "inside-out" approach advocated here refers to a far deeper intervention—at depths 11 and 12—beginning with what takes place internally, within the human mind.

This still relatively new field of prevention is in a continual process of evolution. Prevention has been a field of "fads"—whatever catches preventionists' attention is "in," for a while. The twelve depths of prevention offer a perspective on where new "fads" or new directions fit into the big picture. It is also noted that nearly every time a new paradigm is introduced, proponents of the earlier paradigm have shown resistance (Klein, 1981; Pert, 1997). This is understandable when a completely new way of thinking emerges. For example,

Figure 1
TWELVE DEPTHS OF PREVENTION

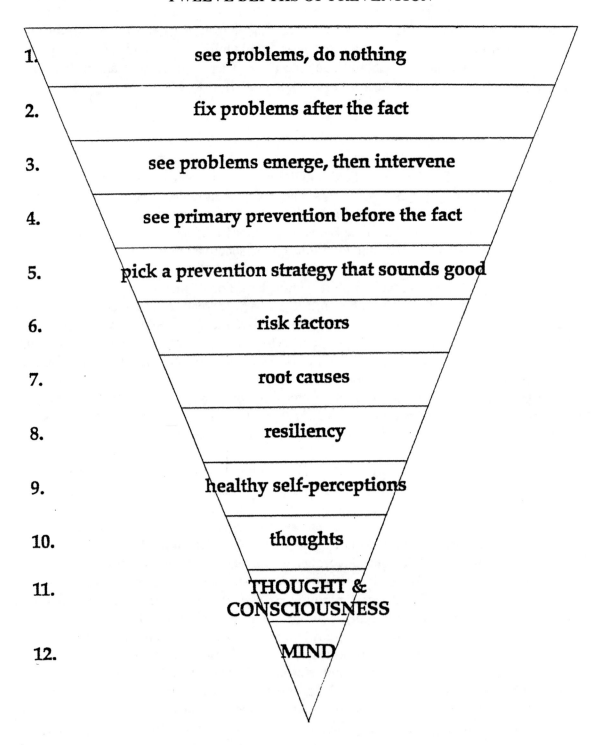

1. see problems, do nothing
2. fix problems after the fact
3. see problems emerge, then intervene
4. see primary prevention before the fact
5. pick a prevention strategy that sounds good
6. risk factors
7. root causes
8. resiliency
9. healthy self-perceptions
10. thoughts
11. THOUGHT & CONSCIOUSNESS
12. MIND

Figure 2
PREVENTION PARADIGM SHIFTS

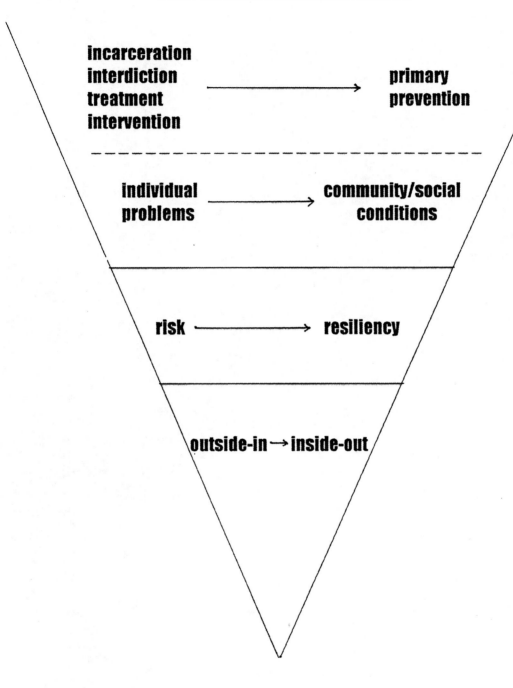

the seminal resiliency studies of Garmezy (1974), Rutter (1979) and Werner (1982) were conducted in the 1970s but only since the 1990s has the resiliency/asset paradigm become generally accepted by the field and desired as an approach. Some would say it is still not wholly accepted. The last of these major shifts—to an inside-out focus—may be no exception.

THE CONCEPTUAL FRAMEWORK OF PREVENTION, REVISITED *from an Inside-Out Perspective* [5]

When I was struck by the unrelenting logic of the inside-out direction in prevention, I was suddenly confronted with having to reexamine my entire conceptual framework for prevention that had formed the basis for my book, *Prevention: The Critical Need* (Pransky, 1991/2001). This proved a major wrench, for it had been the lens through which my entire philosophy and practice of prevention had been based.

My book showed research clearly identified the conditions or variables that contribute to problem behaviors and help people resist those problems. The prevention field has developed programmatic responses that have become generally accepted by practitioners.

According to research, the conditions or variables that most contribute to or put people at risk of developing problem behaviors are-

- cultural messages that model inappropriate behavior
- stress from the social environment
- organic problems
- lack of opportunity
- family "dysfunction"

The conditions or variables that most help people resist those problems are healthy or resilience-fostering environments within families, schools, peers, and community that build -

- healthy self-perceptions
- life skills
- supports

The reader will recognize these from Albee's adapted prevention formula in Chapter II. Let's consider these one at a time. Each contains at least a grain of truth. Each also could be viewed from an inside-out perspective, and I offer an example from the book *Modello* (Pransky, 1998) of how it has been applied.

1. Cultural Messages

Research shows the more people are subjected to messages communicated via the media that model problem behaviors, subjected to subcultural values that create difficulties for the larger society, and the more they are severed from their cultural roots, the more they will act in ways that cause problems for society or themselves.

The grain of truth: What is modeled appears to be what we get. For example, the more violence seen on TV, the more violence in society. The more alcohol is shown to be the prime way to celebrate any occasion, the more we find drinking and alcoholism. The more we are told to self-medicate our problems away, the more we find drug use and abuse. If a subcultural group, like a gang, espouses violence, the more violence will occur around them. Of course, there is more to culture than this. Culture offers a way of being in the world, a guidance system for families and individuals passed down through the generations, a link to spiritual development, and severed from their cultural roots, many Native peoples are cast adrift and without that balance many problems occur.

Therefore, s*ome generally accepted community-based prevention solutions* are: 1) to counter destructive media messages with constructive messages, 2) to desensitize consumers to the influence of the media messages; 3) to attempt to change subcultural norms perceived as problems; 4) to rebuild traditional culture in cultural groups; 5) to embrace and celebrate diversity.

An inside-out perspective might suggest*:* It is great to use such strategies, and celebrating unique cultural traditions is a wonderful thing, but a key element is missing. Beyond messages, beyond culture, beyond diversity, all human beings function via the same "mechanism." At the very essence of all human beings lies innate Health and wisdom that is equally accessible by all [See Chapter VI]. Without this connection to a greater, common source we only see differences. Thus, we lose connection to humanity, and to how in the most basic way, "you are just like me."

For example, in the Modello Housing Project (Pransky, 1998), instead of encouraging the African American community to celebrate its unique and special cultural heritage, Dr. Roger Mills helped residents see that, no matter what their culture, all human beings have equal access to innate Health and well-being, and we all tend to use our thinking in ways that get in our own way and keep us from seeing it. We're all in

---

[5] Much of this section's content originally appeared as the paper, "The Renaissance of Prevention Prevention's Missing Link: Health Realization" (Pransky, J., with Pransky, G., 1997)

that same boat. Once the residents saw this common sense and began to feel better about themselves as human beings, on their own they went out of their way to create opportunities to celebrate their cultural heritage.

2. Stress from the Social Environment

Research shows the more people experience stress as a result of living in poverty, in run-down or overcrowded housing conditions, in social isolation, of being traumatized, of being in difficult situations, and of compromising their physical needs through poor nutrition or lack of sleep, the more they will act in troubling or troubled ways.

The grain of truth: "High risk" situations tend to affect people's thinking in negative ways, which lead to stress and resulting problems and diminish their experience of well-being.

Some generally accepted community-based prevention solutions are: 1) to identify community conditions that put people at risk and through a community development process work to change those conditions; 2) to identify communities or neighborhoods with an overabundance of high risk conditions and work with everyone within those areas; 3) to identify individuals most "at risk" and involve them in personal development activities such as support groups, mentoring, conflict resolution, skill development, etc.; 4) to promote radical social change to eliminate poverty and resulting conditions through community, state and national organizing, and change detrimental policies and practices; 5) to teach stress management and stress reduction techniques.

An inside-out perspective might suggest: While it is important to change environmental conditions that appear to place a great degree of stress on people, because resiliency research has demonstrated that there is no direct causal link between "high risk" conditions and problem behaviors, some other variable must be present. The inside-out perspective would agree. The resiliency literature finds two primary interceding variables: 1) an environment that creates conditions fostering resiliency, or 2) a strong, individual constitution or "resilient temperament." An inside-out perspective would suggest that an even more fundamental variable stands between a healthy environment and behavior, and between one's constitution and behavior: *Thought.* Unless the thinking changes of people who act in abusive ways, they will continue to act that way. Thus, it is not the environment that "causes" people to be stressed, it is the way people think about their environment and themselves in relation to it that causes their stress.

As indicated earlier this is a huge wrench for most of the prevention field, and it is difficult to accept. On the surface this sounds suspiciously like "blaming the victim." Yet, the most empowering thing that can occur for people is to recognize how their own thinking determines the amount of stress and distress they experience. A close examination of human behavior reveals people are affected differently by the same so-called "stressors," and the same person is affected differently at different times. The difference is *Thought.*

Community development is a fine approach. Its flaw is that people will get together to organize or better themselves only when they feel worthwhile and capable enough to want to change their conditions, or when they feel hope that things can change. This internal feeling is really a way of thinking that drives people either to tacitly accept their lot in life, or to take action to change it.

As indicated earlier, stress management assumes stress is a given and, therefore, people need to be helped to adjust to it in a way that will not adversely affect them. A look from the inside-out suggests that stress is no more a given than is, say, violence. Both stem from people's thinking. When people gain new perspective on the thinking causing their stress, their stress diminishes. Stress management or relaxation techniques that would otherwise serve to release pent-up steam (as from a steam valve) are no longer needed.

Roger Mills entered the Modello Housing Project with a strong community development background, yet he chose not to use a traditional community development approach. Rather than organize residents to change the destructive conditions around them, he set out to help people realize their inner Health. Once they began to see themselves and their circumstances in a new, healthier light, they found the inner resources to organize to change their conditions. Further, the stress the residents felt in their day-to-day living reduced markedly. Circumstances that would have stressed them out—such as the housing authority not fixing their leaky roofs, or neighbors coming at them to fight—were no longer taken personally. Thus, they had access to more energy and wisdom to take constructive action.

3. Organic Factors That Become Problems

Research shows the more people are subjected to organic factors such as the Fetal Alcohol Syndrome (FAS), premature birth or low birth weight, brain damage from traumatic head injury, ADHD or genetically or chemically-caused problems, the more they will act in troubling or troubled ways.

The grain of truth: Organic problems do appear to affect people's behavior and need to be addressed.

Some generally accepted prevention solutions are: 1) to educate and teach skills about safety issues so people will, for example, refrain from drinking or drugging during pregnancy, wear seat belts and helmets, protect themselves during sex, stay away from harmful chemicals, etc.; 2) to educate and help people learn skills to adjust to organically caused problems; for example, how to handle a child with FAS, ADHD, or brain injury, or if a child appears to have a weaker constitution; 3) to organize to create healthier physical environments, including cleaner water, air and land. A solution generally not accepted by the field is to blame people's behavior problems on genetics, yet some people actively push this approach. (It is scary to imagine what it would it take to prevent "bad" genes.)

An inside-out perspective might suggest: Of course we should do everything we can to prevent organic problems. However, although evidence suggests organic problems do affect behavior, an intermediary still exists. Although less apparent here, the intermediary is still *thought*. In other words, two individuals with the same organic condition may not experience it in the same way and therefore may not act the same; the same individual may not act the same at two different times depending on his or her moods. An inside-out approach might examine how the different thinking associated with different moods seems to alter responses even within a given organic problem.

This is another controversial point. Am I implying that ADHD, for example, does not affect people, that it is all in the mind? No! Whether the condition exists is not the issue here. Empirical evidence suggests that when people with organic problems are in a calm state they have more access to whatever faculties they do possess. An inside-out view helps people explore the power of a calm, clear mind and what it brings us, and this understanding can be superimposed over whatever else these practitioners do.

Further, what appear to be constitutional variables—one child having a stronger constitutional make-up or a more resilient temperament than another—upon closer examination is really just a different use of thought. The reason, for example, the same harsh words will cause one child to fall apart and will not affect another is because of a different way of thinking—they take it differently—and such thinking can change.

In Modello, many residents and their children behaved in ways that, had they lived in a White, middle class neighborhood, would have caused them to be labeled ADHD or a host of other labels. No matter what their presenting problem, however, when residents were helped to realize how they thought, felt and acted largely depended on their views and moods, they were able to make adjustments when in low moods and not act out of low-mood thinking. No matter what their presenting problem, they saw when they calmed down they had more access to clear-headed thinking and common sense, so they learned to calm down before acting, thereby avoiding many problems. It is not that the organic problems disappeared, but *the way those conditions affected them and the way they interacted with those conditions changed.* The way people experience an organic problem is through their own thinking coming into their consciousness in the moment, and this varies considerably.

4. Lack of Opportunity

Research shows the more people perceive that because of their lot in life they lack the opportunity to achieve what society values, the more "strain" they feel, the more they feel hopeless or helpless, and the more they act in troubling or troubled ways

The grain of truth: When people perceive they lack opportunities and feel hopeless they often lack the desire to move themselves out of their plight.

Some generally accepted community-based prevention solutions are: 1) to provide opportunities such as adequate jobs and/or training programs; 2) to engage in community development; 3) to provide alternatives.

An inside-out perspective might suggest: While it is certainly important to have jobs and training programs and to help people come together to solve these problems, these strategies neglect an important variable. When a "skills center" sat directly across from the Modello Housing Project, no residents took advantage of it. When community development efforts were attempted there, only a few residents took part? Why? The answer is that "lack of opportunity" is often a perception, and a perception is a thought picked up by the senses. So long as people think, for whatever reasons, that there is no point in trying to better themselves, they will not take advantage of whatever opportunities do exist.

In Modello, once residents realized their health and saw how their own thinking kept them down and held them back, they began on their own to complete their education, take advantage of job training, become employed, and create their own healthy alternatives.

5. Family Problems

Research shows the more people are subjected to family abuse, family "dysfunction," and/or confusing family roles, the more they will act in troubling or troubled ways.

The grain of truth: The more difficult a family situation, the more children's thinking and subsequent feelings and behaviors are affected in negative ways.

Some generally accepted community-based prevention solutions are: 1) to train parents to create healthy environments from the earliest moment, such as home visits for pre- and post-natal care, through parenting skills education; 2) to provide early intervention through counseling to children and families from high risk families; 3) to teach children social or coping skills to counter family "risks."

An inside-out perspective might suggest*:* While home visiting and parenting education are very important, what is taught within them can be even more important. Traditionally, parenting courses and home visitors teach techniques. Unfortunately, when parents need techniques most they often do not have the presence of mind to use them, and when parents have the presence of mind they don't need techniques because their own common sense kicks in to guide them. *Parenting from the Heart* (Pransky, 2000), an inside-out approach to parenting, points parents toward understanding how their children and they themselves generally function, from within, and how they can disengage from the presenting problem to be guided by their own wisdom and common sense.

In Modello, Mills and staff taught a "parenting course" with no set curriculum. In each class, parents would bring up issues of concern about their children. As in *Parenting from the Heart,* Mills would help them see those issues through, for example, the lens of calming down and engaging their innate wisdom and common sense, recognizing the difference in how they and their children see the situation, how to avoid taking things personally, how their moods and feelings were guides, how to bring out the best in the child, etc. Mills never taught a parenting technique, yet for nearly all parents who went through this informal "class," family relationships and children's behaviors greatly improved.

Healthy Environments that Build Healthy Self-Perceptions

Everything stated above for families also applies to the other major influences on young people: school, the peer group, and the rest of the community (church, the work environment, a community group, an individual mentor, etc.). Thus, similar preventive approaches hold true for these settings as well. <u>School</u>: 1) to create a healthy, caring, supportive school climate that includes teaching and disciplining with respect; 2) to institute a comprehensive health education curriculum, as well as law-related education and "Character Education," 3) to ensure that lessons related to real life experience. <u>Peer group</u>: 4) to turn negative peer pressure into positive peer influence; 5) to ensure positive youth development. <u>Community</u>: 6) to create meaningful work and community service; 7) to ensure healthy workplace environments; 8) to build neighborhood involvement and pride; 9) to create community support groups; 10) to connect people to religion or spirituality; 11) to ensure "significant others" mentor or positively influence children's lives.

All are important prevention strategies. Conducted well, all build resiliency. Research shows that, to prevent problems, people in all these environments must be treated in ways that build the critical healthy self perceptions consolidated by H. Stephen Glenn (in Pransky, 1991). To embellish what was stated earlier in this chapter, these are:

- *capability*: feeling self-worth and competence enough to go into changing circumstances and feel capable of making it without forming dependencies;
- *importance*: feeling that one is an important contributing part of something greater than oneself; that one belongs or has a stake in something; that life has meaning and purpose;
- *power*: feeling that one can affect what happens to oneself in life, that one has some power or control over his or her own life.

The terms change with the researcher and by problem-specific field, but no matter what one calls them, according to research these perceptions are what make the primary difference in people's behavior.

The grain of truth: People who have healthy self-perceptions are far less likely to engage in problem behaviors and far more likely to experience well-being. People appear to gain these healthy perceptions from being in healthy environments.

An inside-out perspective might suggest: All this is true! However, most of the suggested implementation strategies conveyed in the resiliency literature implies something must be done *to* or *with* or *for or around* people for them to be resilient. The inside-out resilience perspective insists all people have innate resilience or Health within. To experience it, we have to realize it and understand how to get out of its way so it can emerge and blossom. Without this understanding people do not have access to an awesome resource in which they can have faith and hope to guide their lives toward well-being, even in dire circumstances. People can be helped to see how their innate resilience emerges naturally when the mind is quiet.

In Modello, the school, peer group and community all became vehicles through which the inside-out perspective was "taught." Educators were helped to see students in healthy ways and to draw out the Health in their students. From a common sense perspective peers were helped to see where their lives were heading. Mills's staff served as informal counselors and mentors with neighborhood residents and their children. Most of this counseling—based on this inside-out understanding—was conducted under a tree or on people's steps or on picnics or outings or where otherwise having a good time. Once residents realized their Health they took a new sense of pride in their neighborhood; for example, they no longer tolerated the drug gangs that had overwhelmed the housing project and whom they used to shelter during drug busts. The residents' perceptions of capability, importance and power naturally emerged out of realizing their own Health.

This leads us to the difference between a reliance on "skills" and a reliance on inner wisdom. A set of "life skills" also makes a difference in people's behavior: *intrapersonal skills*, such as self-discipline; *interpersonal skills*, such as communication and listening; *systemic skills*, such as responsibility and adaptability; *judgmental skills*. Various combinations of these often are called "responsible decision-making," "problem-solving," "conflict resolution," etc.

One mistake often made in the prevention field is to teach skills independent of building healthy self-perceptions. A person can have a great many skills, but if he thinks, "I am worthless, insignificant, and powerless," he still will say, "Why should I bother trying?"

The inside-out approach goes a step farther. Skills are no substitute for wisdom and common sense. When people clear their heads, and realize the vast, untapped resource within, they tend to gain insights that help them know what to do in a given situation, regardless of skills. Then, when skills are built on this foundation, they have far more meaning and efficacy.

In Modello, residents who caught on most to Health Realization were selected to receive additional training and grounding in this perspective to help other Modello parents, and spread the effort into the Homestead Gardens Housing Project. They ended up having a great impact on others, yet in the training they were not taught skills in how to get these ideas across. Instead, they were told to speak from their hearts and from their own experience. Their own wisdom guided them, and they were very effective in helping others' lives to change.

Self-Esteem?

Many in the prevention field have confused "self-esteem" with "healthy self-perceptions." People also confuse "self-concept" (one's image of oneself) with "self-esteem" (pride in oneself for who one is, inherently). Further, most tend to believe that self-esteem, like resiliency, is something to be given to people. Thus, many self-esteem curricula have cropped up suggesting, for example, that if people give themselves positive affirmations and visualize being successful they will gain more self-esteem. While there is nothing wrong with this type of positive thinking (and it is certainly better than negative thinking) it creates subtle internal pressure to keep thinking that way and to succeed in order to attain self-esteem.

An inside-out perspective suggests that everyone already has self-esteem naturally, without having to do anything to get it. It is part of our innate package. *We can only think ourselves away from it.* In other words, but for our thinking we would always automatically and naturally experience it.

Motivation?

Many prevention practitioners and others frequently say people need to be motivated before they will do anything. Therefore, they must somehow learn how to motivate others. Some create clever ways to get people excited about or interested in what they have to offer. The more astute prevention workers know what research shows: when people feel genuinely needed, when they have meaningful roles and are valued, they are more motivated to become involved. When people define their own needs and create their own programmatic responses, they become more involved.

The grain of truth: For people to do anything, motivation is necessary. People have a far better chance to be motivated if their thinking is affected by what is suggested above. Current thinking on motivation, however, neglects an important fact. Teenagers, for example, are already quite motivated to do lots of things—only not the things many adults would like them to do.

An inside-out perspective might suggest: Motivation already exists within everyone's innate Health; it too is part of the entire package. When people operate out of their Health they automatically love what they do. They are exhilarated by the prospect of new learning. They feel compassion for others so they are naturally motivated to do no harm and help them out when needed. It is unnecessary to motivate via fear or rewards because they *naturally* want to be helpful to humanity. People's naturally healthy feelings are what move them to healthy behavior. Little children are good examples. They are naturally motivated to learn—until they listen to people who mess with their natural motivation. When people aren't functioning in healthy ways they often have little motivation because they are fighting against their own thinking.

In the Modello Housing Project before Mills arrived, many service providers tried to motivate residents to take advantage of their services. They were unsuccessful. Residents were motivated to take advantage of a new community store, because the store met their needs, yet they did not generalize that motivation to other areas of their lives. When Mills came, at first the residents resisted all his efforts, although he based his programming on their own expressed needs, and he valued them. It did serve to warm them up to Mills somewhat, so they could at least listen. But they did not become motivated to change until they realized their own Health by: 1) having their own insights about their own lives from what Mills and staff were saying; 2) losing themselves in having a good time until their programmed, unhelpful thinking stopped and they were able to see and understand the difference between that and their wisdom. It was all they needed. From that point, their healthier thinking naturally motivated them to do what they needed to better their lives. As their levels of consciousness rose, they felt motivated to improve their family lives, to get their own lives in order, to pursue education or jobs, to improve their community—all through natural motivation.

Providing Information?

"Providing information" or "building awareness" is another approach often applied in prevention, particularly for substance abuse, sexual abuse, teen pregnancy, and sexually transmitted diseases, including HIV/AIDS. Often the type of information provided falls under what to do and what not to do, and how what we put into our bodies affects us.

The grain of truth: It is wise for people to have accurate information before they make decisions. Around the mid to late 1980s this approach to prevention became suspect, but it is still practiced often. Astute prevention practitioners have concluded, by paying attention to research, that solely providing information to people does not prevent problems; it works only in conjunction with providing skills and building healthy perceptions.

The inside-out approach of Health Realization appears to throw a monkey wrench into this research by asserting that providing information about how human beings function psychologically and spiritually to help them live in well-being is quite efficacious, so long as people are open enough to hear it. The two views, however, only conflict on the surface. Health Realization practitioners recognize that no outside information will make any difference unless it connects with what people already know deep inside. In other words, it is not that Health Realization practitioners convey information that others don't know; rather, what is conveyed appears to strike a chord in many people that yields insights, and *the insights, not the information, is what makes the difference.* Without insight, no change occurs. In outside-in prevention the information conveyed does not often produce insights.

Feelings?

The prevention field is very feeling-oriented. Borrowing from Humanistic Psychology, it takes people's feelings very seriously. It recognizes that feelings drive behaviors. *The grain of truth* is that feelings do drive behaviors. *In inside-out prevention*, however, feelings do not have a life of their own. All feelings arise from thoughts. This requires a lot more explanation and will be discussed further in Chapter VI.

Conclusion

The conceptual framework presented in *Prevention: The Critical Need* is really a conceptual framework for outside-in prevention. As such, for outside-in prevention it still holds true. However, to cover the entire spectrum of prevention—to cover the inside-out as well—a critical dimension must be added. The entire picture of external influences must be filtered through the individual's own thinking [Figure 3]. Everything external is always filtered internally through the interplay of Mind, Consciousness, and Thought. This is what most of the rest of this book is about.

The Different Directions of Inside-Out and Outside-In Prevention

Figure 4 illustrates the difference between outside-in and inside-out prevention in action.

The prevailing, outside-in model can be viewed this way: Within an environment filled with risks, we can work to reduce those risks and build resilience-fostering environments that protect people from risks and yield healthy self-perceptions which, in turn, give people internal Health and strength.

Inside-out prevention reverses the direction. Initially unveiling people's innate Health and natural, inner strength automatically brings them healthy self-perceptions. In turn, they create resilience-fostering environments around them that yield healthier relationships. Then, when a critical mass of community people has caught on, they will naturally work together to reduce the community risks.

Again, so long as people's feelings compel them to act out, they must. Until their feelings change, no matter what sanctions we thrust upon them, no matter what programs we serve them, no matter what education and skills we give them, no matter how good our community development process, people will feel compelled to act out in troubling or troubled ways. And until their thinking changes people have no choice but to feel those compelling feelings. Inside-out prevention attempts to "go after" the very point where change truly occurs: Thought and Consciousness and Mind.

In sum, to change unhealthy conditions to healthy conditions is a wonderful thing, and we should not stop doing it. What has been missing in the field, however, is the recognition of the profound internal power of *Thought* and the profound internal resource of *Health* that can be unveiled or drawn forth. To have the best chance of helping people move away from problems and toward their well-being, the field of prevention would do well to look to the *source* of change. To realize this, and to act from this perspective, would create a renaissance in prevention.

Jack Pransky

Figure 3

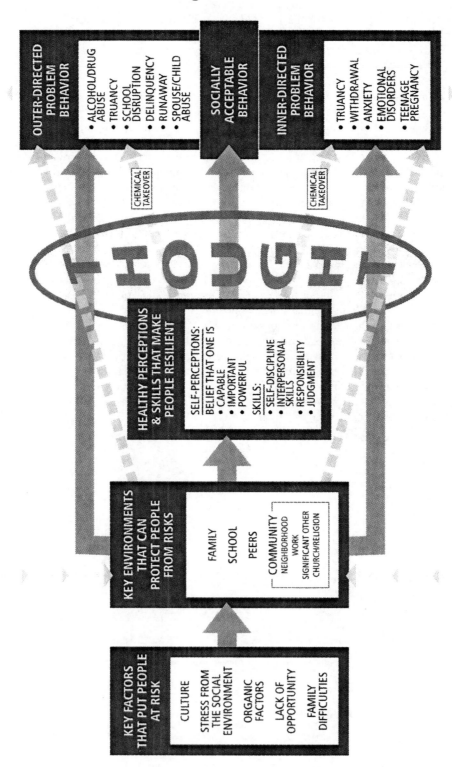

NEW CONCEPTUAL CHART OF "PREVENTION"

40

Figure 4
Outside-in and Inside-out Prevention

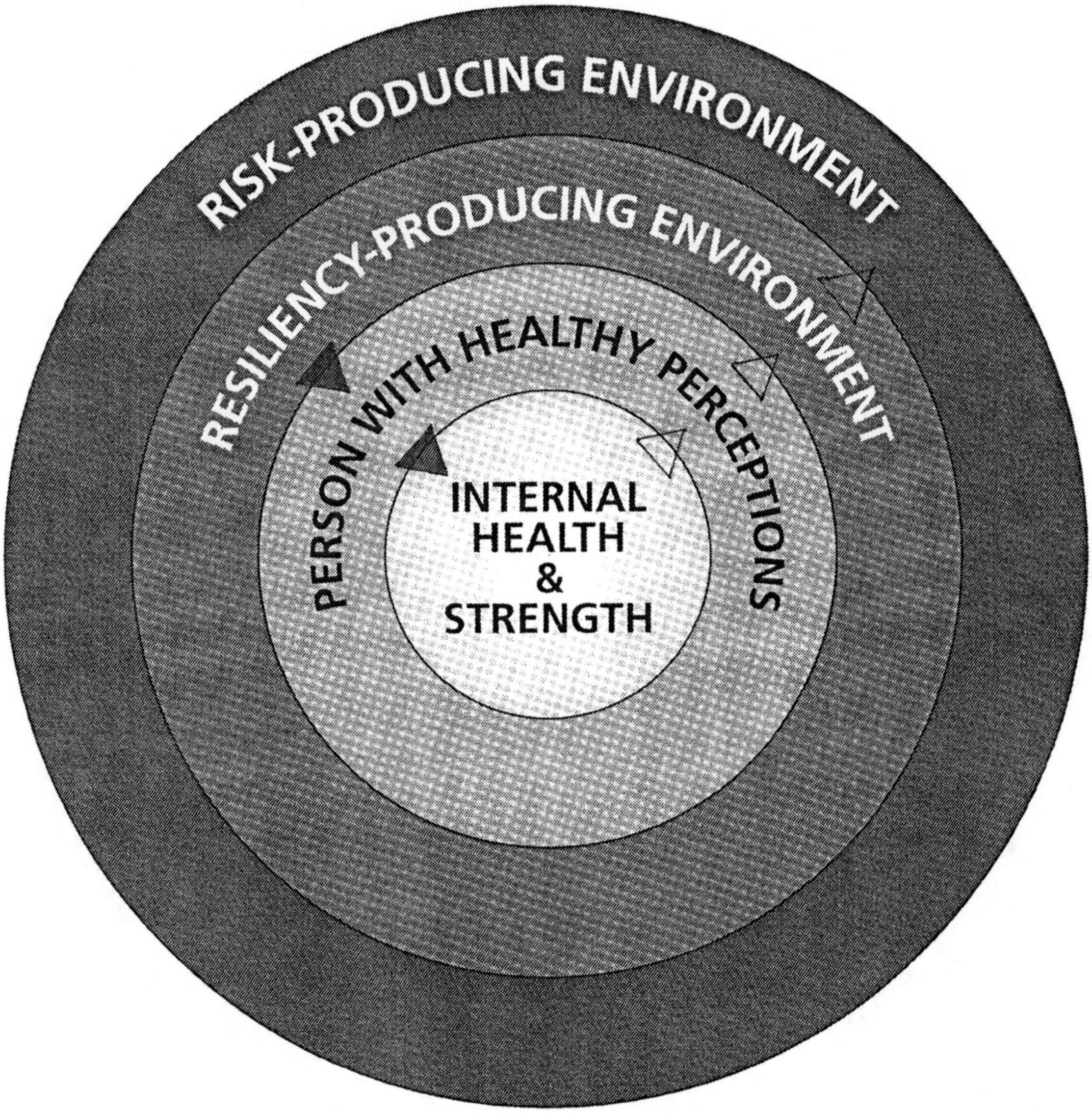

RISK-PRODUCING ENVIRONMENT

RESILIENCY-PRODUCING ENVIRONMENT

PERSON WITH HEALTHY PERCEPTIONS

INTERNAL
HEALTH
&
STRENGTH

IV. MISS BEVERLEY

Interview with "Miss Beverley" Wilson. Beverley Wilson is one of the most powerful people I have ever met. She has a look that can cut through you like a razor. Beverley became one of the best at doing whatever she felt she needed to do to survive on the streets. She became one of the best and meanest of addicts. She became the one of the best at throwing herself into recovery. She became one of the best at seeing from the inside-out, then in conveying this understanding and drawing it out of others. In a way, this interview contrasts the difference between what often occurs when traditional programs affect people from the outside-in and what can happen when people are affected from the inside-out. Miss Beverley never ceases to touch my heart. I interviewed her at her home in San Leandro, California in May, 2001.

JP: What were you like before you got into Health Realization?

BW: I guess a good word would be *intense*. I was three-and-a-half years sober, going to a lot of AA meetings and just doing that 110%, and part of the AA program is that you get a sponsor. So for me, being the oldest in my family of seven siblings and always having a lot of responsibility and being kind of a leader all my life, this was a time when I really surrendered my life and kind of allowed this woman that I was with to show me some things about life.

JP: The woman you were with?

BW: Her name is Jewel—my sponsor. We had a job working for the County in the community trying to get people into recovery. We'd go up under the bridges and out to the public housing developments, on the streets, on Skid Row—we'd go everywhere. I knew all the people because I was born and raised in the town. Jewel had been sober, like, ten years, so she had the sobriety, and I knew all the little cuts and the underground paths to the community. So I really got into the mode of following, and I needed to do that because I really had never did that. I followed this woman, Jewel, for a long time, but about three years into it, I just started getting this feeling like, "This is too hard!" We were working seven days a week, from 7:00 in the morning often until 11:00 at night, every day of the week. And our work life and our volunteer work life was enmeshed, and it was non-stop. You get on this drive of helping people, and it's *intoxicating*—just keeps your adrenaline pumping. You're always looking out for people to help. You always carry a bag with stuff to give them. I mean, it was just intense [laughs].

I just kept getting this little gnawing feeling in my gut, like something's wrong with this picture, but I didn't know what. I was staying sober, coming from experiencing heroin addiction, twelve years on methadone and all that stuff. To be living this life was certainly much better than what I had, right? So I just put my heart and soul into it, but after a while I noticed when I went to the gas station early in the morning, I'd give the woman my money, and she'd throw money at me in the change machine. And one of the things they teach you is to act as if you're okay, especially in trying times, so I had gotten to be pretty good at this, but on the inside, I'm like "Rrrrrrrr!" I'd be wanting to bite her head off. So, one day it was like, "I don't like this feeling. I'm tired of acting as if I'm okay." I'm looking good on the outside and I'm doing all these wonderful things, but on the inside I'm taking all this medicine for my stomach, and I'm just all like full of knots. And I was asking people about it. And it was like, "Well, Beverley, you're going good. This is great," and dah de dah de dah.

So I had formed a habit of praying and meditating, so I got talking about this with God that I was tired of looking good, I wanted to *be* good, you know? It's something wrong with this woman in this box at seven o'clock in the morning throwing the money at me—how do I deal with that? How do I deal with when I'm in the supermarket and I specially picked out all these luscious nectarines and some really soft bread, and I get to the stand and they throw stuff in on top of it? How do I deal with this? And so to me it was presented in my mind like a big old question mark in the sky. How do I reach the people that don't even want to hear about God, because everybody doesn't want to hear about Twelve Steps and your Higher Power? And I resented—but I could never admit to it—the fact that I needed a sponsor and I needed to go to meetings all the time. For me, there was something wrong with that.

JP: It was like a dependency on it?

BW: Well, it just didn't seem right. It seemed kind of like being a Catholic the first five or six years of my life, you couldn't talk to God directly, you had to go through a priest, and I didn't like that. I wanted to know how could I do this on my own. Another thing that popped in my mind was I get good feelings from going to meetings—don't get me wrong, I had nice feelings—but what I wanted to know internally, how do I create this feeling that I get in a meeting on my own? And that was the same question I was asking the priest in catechism a long time ago in church. "I want to talk to God my own self. How do I do this?" [voice deepens] "No, no, you can't talk to God. Who do you think you are?" It's always like you go through a middleman. Even on the street with the drugs, I hated middlemen. I always tried to get around them. And, like I said, the question in my mind was, how do I reach the people that don't want to hear it?

About six months I had this with me, but I didn't have no solutions. I'd got sober and moved to a nice neighborhood, but where I grew up at there was no services for people coming out of treatment. So I asked my agency, could I start a group out there? I had this ex-convict guy that was tattooed from his neck all the way to his ankles. He drew me this beautiful picture of a horizon, with the sun and this beautiful sunrise, just before the sun comes up, where the rays peek up over the hills. And that's when I named the classes, "The Sunrise Look into Reality." This group became very, very popular. It was like a wellspring to the people in the community. People was waiting for me at work. They'd be sitting there like it was a haven, because they knew on Tuesday, at 12:30, I would be there.

JP: Besides, you always had a way with people.

BW: Oh, I always did, yeah. I went on to another job but I kept doing that group, and my boss who I worked for at that time never forgot that. So Stockton, where I lived at this time, they had twelve international visitors from South Africa come who were on a tour around the United States. So the mayor and the community activists had, like, a town hall meeting for these visitors, and one of the places they wanted to take them was to a grass roots effort, and guess where they chose to bring the international visitors? To my group! So, man, I'm getting all this attention from the people over at Department of Drug and Alcohol Services, my ex-boss and stuff. So when they got to my class, I was really kind of nervous, because it was so important, and who am I? I'm just this little peon out of the community doing this stuff that I'm doing. But here they come! I asked the class permission for them to sit in. I told the visitors that they could stay on one condition: "You have to participate in the class." So the same assignment that I gave to the class that day I gave to them, and it was some kind of handout that talked about how we shrink when we get in front of people and don't say the things that's really on our mind because we feel intimidated by this or that person, and how to really look inside and envision yourself moving past that—something to that effect. And one of the women had a life-changing experience in the class—

JP: One of the women from the class?

BW: No, one of the international visitors had it! And let me tell you how it looked to me, Jack. When they got through with the assignment, it was their turn, if anybody wanted, to voluntarily share what they had found out. Well, a few people was real enthusiastic. They just shared what they got and they were so gut-level honest. And one of the visitors raised her hand and I saw tears streaming down her face, and, oh my God, inside, I got so scared. I was like, "Oh no, she's crying!" When people cry, it meant to me that I had did something to them, you know? So I was *nervous*. She raised her hand, and I'm just holding my breath, but on the outside I'm looking cool—because I know how to act. And this woman, she begins to talk in broken English, and she said she was a pharmacist, but all of her life what she really wanted to do in her heart was work as a public servant in the community with people. But because of where she came from, everyone was in the field of medicine and professionals in her family. Even before she said it, you could feel the power coming from her. So she said, "I'm going to speak to you, I have never spoken before." The way she said it, you couldn't understand what she meant, because she spoke broken English. So she took a deep breath, and the tears were still streaming down her face, and she said when she gets around her father and her two brothers, all doctors, she never, ever has spoken that she really wanted to get out into the community and work with people. But she looked inside herself and saw that when she got home she was going to see about changing and working in the community. It was just powerful. And so, they left. The class was good, we all had a good time, but I was glad it was over, and I went on about my life.

About a week later, I get a call from Robert Graham—he forms small businesses in foreign countries like Honduras, and he was one of the people that was on that committee with the international visitors. I had told him that I wanted to start a consulting business but I didn't know how to start it, and could he help me? So he contacted me and he said, "Beverley, I wanted to tell you what happened the other night with the international visitors." I said, "Really?" "Yeah," he said, "they had a big dinner that night, and all of them met back up and told what they had experienced in our town." So that African lady told about what she'd discovered about herself in that class. Another African lady jumped up and says, "All we want to know is, why do you have Beverley Jones [my name at that time] out here in this little, small building, doing this work that she's doing? Why don't you have her somewhere where she can effect world change!?" And everybody was, like, whoooo, what happened? They was just saying all these things about me. I didn't know none of this was happening. So he told me he thought that I was doing a thing that they was calling, "Psychology of Mind," and he wanted to send me to a six-day conference. He had talked to my boss about it, and if I was willing to go, he would sponsor me to go there.

JP: He said he thought that you were doing that?

BW: He said, "There's a conference where I think what you're doing naturally is the thing they're calling 'Psychology of Mind.' I'd like to arrange for you to go check it out." That's where I met Roger Mills, Elsie [Spittle] and the girls from Florida [the Modello project], and that's how I got into what I'm doing now. That was my beginning.

JP: Do you remember what your experience was at that week-long conference?

BW: Well, this was 1991. I went up there with Manzell Williams and we missed the first day of the conference. So on the second day I'm trying to be all inconspicuous and find out what this is all about, because I'm suspicious as hell. I just was checking everything out.

Then an interesting thing happened for me when Roger spoke about a quiet mind. I started hearing scriptures out of the Bible. Like he would say, "We've got to have a quiet mind and connect with this thing inside of us," and I would hear, "Be still and know." At this time I didn't know anything about scriptures, but he would say one thing and I'd hear something coming from inside of me—something else. So I'm wondering, how did he do that trick? I thought it was some kind of trick. So I'm sitting like in the back, and I said to myself, "I got to get up here closer so I can examine him." So I got up there closer, and then he appeared to me to be cutting up everything that I believed in, because he was talking about Twelve-step programs and how you could peel the onion layer by layer if you wanted to, or you could learn this and it was like having a knife cutting in you straight to the core. So I was, like, "Who in the hell does he think he is!?" Because I'm 110% into AA and NA, and he's telling me stuff that's shaking everything that I believe in. So that was the stuff that I had to get through the first day or two.

But the interesting thing was, I was sharing a room with Laura Graham, Robert's daughter. And they were saying, "Just start playing around with this right away," so I started playing around with it. The thing that really got me was what they called "quiet listening," but when they said "quiet listening," I heard "listening softly." You know that song? [sings] "Killing me softly with his song, killing me softly," and I would hear [sings] "Listening softly to this song," and it was just like something magical was happening inside me about the listening piece. And I started trying it out on Laura in the room, and we got to be really, really good friends, and she got some insight about some stuff that had been troubling her a long time. And I knew I was onto something, because that question mark that I had in the sky about something that would help humans that was not restricted to just one little group, it answered that question for me. So that was very exciting to me. It was like, "Now, I want to know more about this!"

Plus, I wanted to start a business, and I was in a thing called Women Entrepreneurs, and one of the things my teacher had talked about, Roger kind of validated. She was talking about working smart as opposed to working hard. Some people are taught to work hard, and they think the suffering and the hardness all that hard work is good. I'm always looking for a way to get stuff accomplished, but I really would like to know how to get it accomplished in a smooth way, you know? So when they was talking about how we stay so busy, and we run so much, that we can't even see how to make our lives work—and I learned from that conference that that was true. Because I had been so busy—I was on a hot-line list for five years that was twenty-four hours a day, so I'd get suicide calls in the middle of the night—plus I had four kids still at home. I just had this crazy, no-stop world, and I wanted to get off this world, even though I didn't know where I would go from there because it was the best thing I had. But I started getting an idea that if I learned more about this Health Realization, that I'd be able to accomplish some goals that I had. And around this time that I was learning Health Realization, I was developing my idea about being an international motivational speaker. I wanted to do that for a living. And Jewel had an idea that she wanted to open up halfway houses. So something in me told me that whenever you want something to happen good for you, help your friend. So I helped her start this house, and that took seven years to get the house really established. In my heart of hearts—I didn't speak with no humans about this—was when the house got established and was self-sustaining, I'd go pursue my little idea about starting this consulting thing.

So I started following Roger around. Wherever Roger was having a training that was in California, I'd ask him, "Could I come?" Or I'd just show up. I had back surgery around this time and I was off from work for a year. So that year I'd just followed Health Realization around and cut loose a lot of the work because my back was hurt. I was really slowing down a lot and deciding to do some things on my own.

JP: Did you feel differently at all during that time?

BW: Yeah. I felt scared. I felt real scared.

JP: How come?

BW: Well, you get dependent—but you don't know you're dependent—on a system. In AA and NA they're telling you that if you don't do this system exactly the way it's laid out, you're going to get drunk again, you're going to die. I had all this conditioning. I really believed, and it was working for me a long time. But this other thing was springing up in me—that I didn't really trust—telling me there was another way. This other was good, but it wasn't really me. I was going along with something. I lived in this real protective world of AA for four or five years. I met Roger when I was about three-and-a-half years sober, but I stayed in this world. I didn't do no functions outside of this world until I took that course in Women Entrepreneurs and went to that conference where Roger was at. I was afraid—but he was teaching me how to recognize my thoughts, and pay attention to that, and then quiet myself. So I saw that I had this fear that they was going to make me think something that would get me drunk. I kind of always walked with that trepidation, you know? I'd do it, but I'd have to walk through *trembling* inside. I'd be trembling inside, but I couldn't *not* do it. Something was drawing me to this. You feel me?

JP: Yeah, I do.

BW: So I couldn't really talk to nobody about it, because everybody I talked to believed like I did. The motto was, "Meeting makers make it." I still was doing a lot of meetings, but now I had these two worlds going. After I went through Women Entrepreneurs, I decided on a salary that was double what I was making. At that time it was audacity to even *think* that I could make $15 an hour, but that was my ideal salary. I was grateful for the $8.16 I was making, but while everybody else was happy to be driving County cars, that wore off for me in about three months. I mean, let's get real, we're still on poverty level, we still need food stamps, we still aren't making enough to even live. This is *poverty level*! So I saw that I needed to make $15 an hour, and I stuck to it. I'm a stubborn old fool! [laughs]

And another interesting thing that was happening, Jack—and this is the part I really want to somehow blow up because one day I'm going to write a book about it—I was a heroin addict of the worst kind. I had been on methadone for twelve years. Most people that stay on methadone that long never get off. They're deemed doomed! And they kind of get this thing in their head that they're going to do this "'til the wheels fall off," because it's legal, you can stay loaded, and all this stuff. But one day I looked around, and I was like, "*Hell, no!* I don't want to do this 'til no wheels fall off. I'm sick of this!" I just got tired of it. Something happened and I got off the methadone, and I went into a program and stayed sober for a year. But at that time they had all these incredible hurdles, and my four kids were in foster care, so you had a reunification thing but it was so tough hardly nobody made it. But I made it! I wanted to get my year pin, and I wanted my kids back. I loved my kids, even though my actions and behaviors along the way didn't always reflect that—but in my heart, you know? So whatever they told me to do, I did it.

And when I came back and got my year pin, this got the attention of the Welfare Department and the Methadone Clinic. They sent the top administrator to have a little meeting with me: "How come you're the only one out of eighty people in your class that came back to get your year pin? What could we have done to make that easier for you? If you could design a program, what would it look like?" I said, "Number one, I wouldn't have it so you have to go so many different places"—you had to go to a parenting class for your reunification, you had to go to four meetings a week, you had to get a job because you didn't have no welfare check anymore and the job is going to be minimum wage, you had to go and find a place to live that you could afford, you had to get back and forth to work, and you didn't have a drivers' license. So I told her, "If I was going to do it, I'd have all those services set up in one place, and I would really want the people to get training *with* their kids—provide a way that they could come and bring their kids, because they was teaching me stuff in parenting that I had never learned." I was honest, and I was able to put words to feelings—raggedy, it was rough—so I was straight, direct, to the point, but it was knocking people's socks off.

I started crying in one parenting class—they was talking about teaching your kids socialization skills. Usually when I start crying I'll get mad about something and I would leave because I'd be embarrassed that I didn't know, because something in me thought I'm supposed to know all this stuff. So one night in the parenting class, I just got overwhelmed from what they was teaching us, and I'm supposed to remember it and do it when I get my kids back! I realized that they was telling me to teach my kids something that *I* didn't know, and that angered me. I was also learning that anger was motivated by fear—and I was afraid I was going to learn all this stuff and *still* be inadequate at parenting. And I told that to the teacher. And when I said it, about four or five women and men started crying and said the same thing. Some of them was ready to exit but had been feeling these feelings for months and never spoke. I was new.

So big things started happening for me. People started coming asking my advice and asking me how to put something together. The very first program they opened was FOCUS—Families Overcoming Drug-Using Situations—where they had everything that me and Bonnie Butz had talked about in place. And they hired me as the first drug counselor to come there and teach the classes. So that was my first experience. This was like my dream job, because it was working with women who were drug using, or who had babies and got those babies taken because they had been under the influence.

About four or five times I'd be asked to help them design these programs, but I'd still be the lowest person on the totem pole. I'd still be the drug counselor. Roger pointed out to me in the Health Realization classes that something's trying to tell us something on the inside, but we're so busy we can't even hear it. And when I slowed down and had that year off from work, I was able to really start considering some things. One of the things I was feeling was, it looked like injustice: They was asking me a lot of questions, taking my ideas and formulating them into programs and giving me a little slot in that thing. I had a funny feeling, like, if they're asking me all this stuff, maybe what I know is important.

By the time I was work-ready again, the County called me back: "Beverley, we want to start a program called AIM—Allegiance of Infants and Mothers. Can you show Janet how to start this program?" I said, " I don't know. What would my job title be?" "Oh, you'd have your same job back as a drug counselor, but she doesn't have any idea how to start this thing, and you know everybody. They're going to come if you're there. Can you start it?" And I said, "I don't think so. If I do this, I want to earn $15 an hour. Can you pay me $15 an hour?" She caught her breath. She was like, "I barely make $15 an hour." I said, "Then I'm sorry, I can't take your job." And I'm telling you, at this time I didn't know *nothing*! I was, like, crazy, but I hung up the phone, and I felt weird. But I just had made up my mind that I'd just stick with the unemployment and the workman's comp until I got what I needed. Here I am telling people that they can come out, but I'm really living and working on poverty level. So that was screaming in me.

About two or three days later I get a call from Marta Obekowski at East Bay Community Recovery Center, and the mayor wanted them to start up a Health Realization Project in a place called Sixty-ninth Village in East Oakland, and she wanted to know could I come there and help them start this program. I said, "I'll come if you'll pay me $15 an hour." She said, "We were prepared to pay you $13.20." I said, "I'm sorry, I can't take it," and I thanked her for considering me, and I hung up. About twenty-five minutes later, she called me back. She said, "Beverley, I talked to my bosses. If you come, we'll pay you $15 an hour." I said, "I'll be right there!"

I was scared of driving on the freeway, but I was tired of being afraid of driving on the freeway without alcohol or drugs in me. So this job gave me that opportunity, because I knew if I ever got a chance to drive on the freeway that I could learn, and that if I kept doing it I would do it well. That was my thinking. So I did. I took the job in Oakland, and the rest is history...

[This interview with Miss Beverley continues in Chapter XIV, page 203, where she describes her work in the Coliseum Gardens Project in Oakland. The interview then finishes below.]

JP: During those five years you worked at Coliseum Gardens, what was happening inside you?

BW: Oh, I was beginning to dream great dreams—that dream of being an international motivational speaker was really, really in me. Because now I'm making enough money to go in the store and put stuff in the shopping cart and at the checkout stand not have to put six things back. I'm feeling good. I'm long hours on the freeway, because I had a three-and-a-half hour commute round-trip some days, but I'm making my life work. And by me getting away from Stockton working for East Bay Project—nobody who worked there was in recovery. Nobody! Matter of fact, the first dinner we had, everybody ordered drinks. So I really had to make up my mind what I was going to do, because I was outside my web of security. So I'm getting stronger and stronger, and not so much into this life that I had known. I'm exploring new territory. I'm starting to build friendships here. I plugged into AA down here, but it wasn't no-ways like when I went to seven to nine meetings a week. When I got here I would go to a meeting because I'd be shaken up from driving on the freeway, so I'd go in and get centered.

But I still had that big question of how do I create what I get in the meetings when I'm in the car or in the gas station or in the grocery store? I was starting to get a sense of how you do that, because I got none of these safety nets over here that they said I was dependent on. I had to learn to be there for myself. And then what I was learning—and the more I taught it, the more I learned it—was that our wisdom is inside of us. The piece that was missing that they never really talked about was *that we think*, and that *our thoughts create our reality moment to moment*. And *being okay when I'm in a low mood*—I don't have to be terrified about that and run nowhere—that I could be okay if I just had the understanding that I was just in a low mood, it would pass. I didn't have to be frightened by it or terrified by it—just be still for a minute, reconnect to myself. Because the help is in the understanding that I'm in a low mood. I don't have to be in a high mood all the time, or way up there. The fact that you're in a low mood, enjoy it. I really was learning all this stuff and I was sharing with people, you know? I was real open about the times I wasn't in a good mood. I made up a little signal with them. I said, "When I get to working and I'm off-base, I'm going to let you know. I'm going to tell you, 'Lilly's loose.' Just give me a little time, I'll make my adjustments as I move around." Because I would get off balance; it was like I was crooked, you know? But if I just acknowledge that and let everybody know to give me a little space, then I could feel myself self-correct somewhere.

JP: Was there any point, either during the Coliseum Gardens phase, or afterwards for you, where you really felt like you made a major shift?

BW: Yeah. It had to do with a tragedy. In February, two important things that I had always dreamed of happening were about to occur. I got asked to speak at the annual conference in Burlington, Vermont.

JP: Where we met.

BW: Yeah, where we met. That meant I was going on a big airplane. And at the same time I was asked to do a world conference meeting at a thing called a "Mountain Miracle" for NA World Service. So that was going to be taped, and the tape would be distributed around the world. That was two major things leading me to my goal.

And they were, like, scheduled three weeks apart—both in the same month. And I had been telling Vivian [a co-worker/resident in Coliseum Gardens] and Jerry [Williams, a community police officer] too, "Oh, we got to keep learning this, because there's no telling where our life is going to go." So the day I came and told Vivian that we were going to Burlington, Vermont—she was doing outreach, and I went and found her. "I have our tickets to go to Burlington, Vermont." She said, "What?" I said, "Girl, I got our airline tickets right here!" She just fell over backwards on the grass, because I had been telling her for months to hold on to her seat belt, because we was going somewhere. This was big, because I could just *feel it*.

But let me tell you what happened, Jack. I was excited. Everybody in my family was excited, because I got asked to talk at the Vermont conference for Psychology of Mind. And my mother, who I had a new relationship with for six-and-a-half years—I'm six-and-a-half years sober by now—my mother was excited, because I'm telling her I'm going to be an international motivational speaker. I don't know how it's going to happen, but I'm dreaming. I'm saying stuff and it's coming out of my mind into reality all the time—little bitty stuff, then big stuff, then bigger stuff. Going to Vermont is like flying all the way across the map! I had a map showing them how far I was going to fly. Everybody was excited. I had my bag packed for weeks! And my sponsor bought me a camera and three rolls of film. So I said, "Hmm, I got two trips planned, and she bought three rolls of film, I guess one event is a surprise." I knew intuitively that something else was going to happen that was unexpected, and I never thought anything more about it, and pretty soon it was July.

And on July 10th, my sister Elaine called. She said, "Beverley, they say Mama's at the hospital, and she can't talk!" And I don't know why, I just felt this paralyzing, gripping fear run through my body like a cold, icy finger go down my back. I just fell on my knees, and I laid flat on my face on my bed. And I just started praying again that God's will would be done in me, that I would be still, quiet. And for some reason I had calmness about it. And I got up and my daughter, Mary, went with me. And I was kind of driving a little bit fast, but I was real still inside and driving with precision. Then all of a sudden something occurred to me, and it said, "Drive the speed limit. It's over." So I was, like, "Hmm," so I slowed down. I got to the hospital, about eleven miles from the house, and one of the nurses I had went to grammar school with saw me, and knowing I'm the oldest in the family she said, "Beverley, go in there and tell your sisters and brothers to quiet down. This is a hospital. And tell them to stop beating your mother and shaking her like that, because the mortician is going to think that somebody beat her!" So I can't believe what she's telling me. I said, "What are you saying?" She said, "Your mom passed away."

Now my normal response to that, Jack—I really need to tell you this because this happened to me in 1975: My brother died, and my ex-husband—my husband at the time—came to me and said [gruffly], "I just came to tell you that your damn brother is dead." And I just went *off*! And that's when I had started on a downhill spiral in life at that time, because of my inability to accept reality— especially the way he told me. In my mind it was like, "If you were going to tell me that, why didn't you tell me in a nice, calm way?" Well, people tell you in a way that makes sense to them in that moment. And again, here was this woman telling me the biggest thing that could ever happen to me—my worst fear in the whole world was the death of my mother—and she is telling me to go in and take care of my sisters and brothers. I felt just assaulted. I just felt hurt. [emotional voice] Right away I wanted to get so mad at her, but I realized—because I knew Health Realization—that wasn't the real issue. So I asked myself, "Beverley, baby, what are you afraid of?"

And I walked down there where my mother was, and I walked in the room, and my seven brothers and sisters was in there and some of my nieces—and at this time everybody was still on drugs; I was the only one that had gotten out. It was like I was the survivor off a wrecked ship. And there I saw—my niece was beating her head up against the wall, my other brother was standing at my mother's feet, just shaking her, trying to wake her up, and my little brother who's 6'9" had called the doctor and told him with a look of death, "You better wake her up!" And I'm looking at everything that's happening in this room, and then I looked inside me, and I understood the meaning of the Serenity Prayer so deep that day. I'd been saying it for over six years, but that day I *saw* it with a striking clarity. It said, "God grant me the serenity—to accept the things that I cannot change—courage to change the things I can—and the *wisdom* to know the difference." For some reason that prayer *split* from me that day, and I understood that this was a situation that I could do nothing about. So something inside me said, "Just quiet down, calm down."

So I had the most beautiful thought in my mind, and I couldn't tell nobody in the room this thought, but I imagined my mother in a spirit form just floating up in the air, turning flips backwards. She was so free. My mother was crippled and had diabetes, she was very sickly. And in my mind's eye I saw that she was free. And something in me said, "She done shed this body and jetted up on out of here, on to a new adventure." And to me that was a warm, comforting thought. But the reality was that my mom, when I went over and looked at her, I could see something was missing. My mother was not there, and it was so final for me. It was in that moment I just embraced that reality. It was, like [softly], "Bye, Mama. You're gone." And I turned around and looked at my sisters and brothers, I said, "You guys, she is not here! And this is a hospital. Deal with your hurt the way you got to, but there's other people in here that need help"—or whatever I said to them. And then, I knew what to do. Something told me to go call Jewel, and go call my daughter who's waiting at home, and make a couple of phone calls. That's what I did. The next thing I knew, two or three people from the fellowship of Alcoholics Anonymous came into my mother's hospital room and sat in there with me until the coroner came to take her body away. But me having that calmness was like a tuning fork to my brothers and sisters. What I said to them was in such a quiet, certain way, and at the same time it was so respectful of where they were at that they just responded to it, you know?

Anyway, that was four days before July 15th when I was scheduled to go to Vermont. I had never done a funeral before. And I walked in a kind of quietness, because I knew about this inner chamber in me, this innate health, and I kept telling tapping into that. And I was able to make my mother's funeral arrangements, got my crazy brothers—my seven brothers and sisters who were drug-addicted at that time—to sign over parts of their insurance money, because we didn't quite have enough money. They all agreed to give up $150, $100, $50 off their insurance policies! These people were *hooked* and alcoholic, and they didn't ask for no money! They didn't even think about it because there was such a hush and such a quietness surrounding this whole thing. And we buried my mother that Wednesday. And that Thursday, at 4:00 in the morning, I drove from Stockton to San Francisco and caught the biggest airplane I ever caught in my life and went to Burlington, Vermont with the freshness of my mother's burial and death still in me. But I knew that this was one of the price tags, or one of the omens or challenges in life that I had to walk through to get to my dream. And how I knew that I'll never know. But I went there and did that. I was there for four days. I came home, and then got ready for the Mountain Miracle picnic where I was supposed to speak. And I just had a strength, an inner-knowing—an inner strength that I had never experienced before—

JP: You moved me big-time that day when you spoke at the conference.

BW: Oh, really? Well a tape came out of that other experience, the name of it was "A Mountain Miracle," and to this day it is the most widely sold tape in Narcotics Anonymous. That tape almost got me to Paris, but I didn't make it. The tape went to Paris; I didn't. But it was a masterpiece—I knew when I was doing it that *I* wasn't doing it, but I knew that it was deep. That was the time when I knew, when I walked in the death of my mother and I wasn't in my conditioned habit of being in my AA meetings supported by the people, because when I went to Vermont I was around no one. And I knew that something wonderful and powerful was happening inside of me. It was with me 24-7—and that was the best news I had even gotten in my life—that I was very capable of dealing with life as it unfolded, no matter what happened. Because if I could walk through the death of my mother and stay sane and lead my brothers and sisters through that, then I could do anything!

JP: So, in the few minutes we have left, what else do you want to make sure I get in here?

BW: Well, I just want to speak to the people that look like they're caught up in a cycle. I'm a behind-the-scenes person, and I like that role. I like when there's something that I can teach people that when they learn it they feel like they got it from inside of themselves. It's almost like I'm invisible. But it carries a certain weight when you're working in a community or when you're doing work in a thankless job. The main thing I want people to know is to look for the hidden justices in life. Look for hidden justice! Because the hidden justice carries the payment. It's the thing that *lifts* you up when you want to give up, or it *lifts* you up when someone else might get credit for some work that you feel like maybe you should have been at least mentioned in. And it's always present if we look for it.

JP: What do you mean by hidden justice?

BW: I mean that every time something happens, and it may not look like it's right, *know* that even though it looks like it's out of order, it's in order. There's a bigger picture. There's a bigger message. There's something much bigger going on than what our sometimes-finite mind can see. There's infinite possibilities of reward, but they may not come in the way that you think. And if you keep your mind focused on the way you *think* it should look, you'll never see the reward that's there, every step of the way, all the time! Because the greatest gift I've learned out of every time I thought there was an injustice—even when I was starting all these programs and they was still giving me the same job and it gave me a feeling that I didn't like that. And when I learned Health Realization, they let me know that people wasn't doing things to me, that I had the power to let life go *through* me—not happen *to* me! And if I feel I was being victimized, it couldn't happen unless I participated. If I felt like I was being stepped on, then I needed to stand up! There's a bigger picture than what we can see. Always! Especially when it's something that feels like it's not right. When it feels like it's not right, *know that it's right*. The way I'm looking at it can be seen so many different ways. If I know that, even if I can't see it, just knowing that there's a different way gives me leverage in life, and it gives me the ability to navigate through life. And even if I can't *see* the hidden justice, I know it's there! So having the ability to just know that it's there and move on—go on and do what makes you feel good and let peace of mind—having real peace of mind and feeling good from the inside-out—be your reward. And then what you do is you turn around, and you look one day and you see countless things that sprung up out of that, that you never would have been able to see if you hold on to the idea that people are doing something to you. And a lot of people walk with that feeling of injustice, like they can't get anywhere because somebody's got their thumb on them. The only person that has their thumb on me is what's going through me in my mind and working through me, coloring the world that I see. You feel me? So the most powerful gift I've been given is having the ability to know that I could have anything I want. I'm Beverley Wilson. I can do anything I want!

The last thing I'm going to show you is what the lady that knew me the longest—one of my sponsors, who was also my methadone counselor—at my going-away party when I was moving to the Bay area, she wrote this poem about me. I want to read it to you. It's called, "Why did you call her a lady?"—because they called me *Miss* Beverley. That's my new name. It says:

> She lives in the darkness. She's OUT of her mind.
> Obsessed with drugs. Surrounded by thugs.
> She SCREAMS, yells and curses with a stare in her eyes.
> She despises the world, pegs in her head

(That was me she's talking about!)

> She's CRAZED with no rhyme or reason, no purpose, no plan.
> NEVER a kind word or gesture in mind.
> She's sad and she's lonely, CONFUSED and out of control
> Her children are scared, all tattered and torn.
> She's LOST and astray, Most said she will never find her way.
> But I said to myself, No addict is without hope.
> So you can say, then, Why do I call her a lady?
> Because today she's REBORN. A bright, shining star.
> GLORIOUS, a winner. Spiritual and fine.
> She's clean and she's sober. God's in her life.
> She's got dignity and pride. Friends all around her.
> She's talented and blessed. Her children have blossomed.
> They're happy, they're wholesome. Their mother's a mom.
> She's black and she's beautiful. She's one of a kind.
> She's joyous and free, and best of all, my sponsee.
> A gracious lady, Miss Beverley.

Written by Pam H. [laughs] Whooo! Every time I re-read it I'll be, like, dang, she really saw that in me. Because this was really who I was! She was my sponsor the twelve years I was on methadone, coming in and out, crazy as hell. She knew me good! You feel me? [laughs]

JP: Ah, that is really beautiful.

BW: You want one more thing somebody else wrote? My daughter just wrote this to me. I got to read this to you. My daughter's twenty-five. She wrote,

> As I write this letter, a sense of self-trust overwhelms me. That self-trust assures me that no matter what I write here, or decide to write, God's will and His favor accompanies me wherever I may go. It leads. I follow. And who taught me that truth? You, Mom. Who taught me to soar when I left the nest, unsure and afraid of the fall? You left the house with wings. I know it's true, because as I teach my two kids to soar, what you have taught me comes up more and more. If you felt unappreciated on Mothers' Day, know that the appreciation is in the day you received your first breath. You have been a counselor, a mediator, a devout mother, a father, a friend. There are just so many things to me that you have been. I could go on and on, telling all these nice things, because you are worth it, but I truly need to thank you for following God's words, hearing His voice, heeding His call, oh, because by your example, you have taught me it all, just by saying Yes to the Master's Will. I understand that you are at a place where the last child is leaving the home, and thirty-two glorious years of mothering is about to be done. But as you experience that, know that I truly believe I stood on the edge of time and chose you

53

as my mom. Only you could have executed, from the ups and downs of life, a landing so smooth under the command of God. Mom, you did that. I love you, you strong, beautiful, spirited mother. I salute you. Your daughter, Monique."

JP: Brought tears to my eyes.

BW: [laughs] That's what my girl wrote. Ain't she something? Ain't this girl something!? That's my *girl*! She read this to me. I spoke just this last Saturday night in Stockton for the treatment center that I went through fourteen years ago, at their annual dinner, and she had arranged with them to read me that after I spoke the other night. There wasn't a dry eye in that place. She knocked me out. That is my girl. And *all* my kids are like that.

V. MAKING A CASE FOR PREVENTION FROM THE INSIDE-OUT[6]

In this book we're after a balance of heart and science, at least as close to science as we can get at this time. In the previous chapter we experienced a dose of heart. We now turn to a combination of context and science. This chapter is written from a more academic perspective than most of the rest of the book. This is intentional, for it examines where inside-out prevention fits with what we know about prevention today.

A Brief History of the Modern Prevention Era

To place inside-out prevention within a historical context, an argument could be made that the "modern prevention era" began with the initiation of programs in the Kennedy and Johnson Administrations of the early to mid 1960s, or perhaps with the commissions and reports that contributed to the Kennedy Administration's interest in preventive mental health (Albee, in Pransky, 2001). This is because the government programs created under those administrations provided an overall structure for prevention in its various forms to operate on a national scale, and many of these structures still exist today.

First came the Community Mental Health Act of 1963, which established community mental health centers. Then came the Economic Opportunity Act of 1965, which established community action agencies and other arms of "the war on poverty." Then came the Omnibus Crime Control and Law Enforcement Act of 1968, which provided funding for youth service bureaus to prevent delinquency. Later legislation established the National Institute on Drug Abuse (NIDA) in 1972, the National Center for Child Abuse and Neglect (NCCAN) in 1974, and the Office of Juvenile Justice and Delinquency Prevention (OJJDP) in 1977. All of these together (plus public health) direct much of the national preventive effort at the beginning of the 21st century.

From the start, each of these federal agencies and their respective state agency counterparts operated independently of one another, with separate categorical funding streams. Until the early 1980s they had little contact with one another, despite accumulating evidence that all social-behavior problems were related to the same contributing factors, and the same practices worked to prevent them all (Pransky, 2001).

Early in this period a few university-based psychologists such as George Albee (1980; 1983), Emory Cowen (1977), James Kelley (1968), Richard Price (1980), Bernard Bloom

---

[6] Note: A small portions of this chapter also appeared in the second edition of Prevention: The Critical Need (Pransky, 2001), although it was intended originally for this book.

(1986), Martin Bloom (1981), psychiatrist Gerald Caplan (1986) and others—and Stephen Goldston within the federal government (Klein & Goldston, 1977)—began to extol the virtues of primary prevention. They drew from practices within the field of public health, but primarily from "community psychology," a new branch of psychology that sprouted in the mid-1960s (Bennet et al., 1966). Proponents of community psychology believed the field should counteract "harmful circumstances before they have a chance to produce illness, thus reducing the risk for whole populations…" (Bloom, 1988).

Around the same time, Community Action Programs and VISTA Volunteers were engaged in community organizing to reduce poverty and its resulting problems. A "positive youth development" movement also began within youth service bureaus (Polk and Kobrinm, 1972). Meanwhile, from the fields of community psychology and mental health, delinquency, substance abuse and child abuse came theories and research about the causes of these problems and what might prevent them. Some of these were Hirschi's social bonding theory (1969), Elliot & Voss's (1974) research on delinquency and dropout, Kempe & Kempe's (1978) study of child abuse and neglect, Kelley's (1968) ecological approach and, later, Hawkins & Weiss's (1985) "Social Development Model."

As this new field largely was ignored by politicians and the general public, an NIMH-sponsored conference heralded the coming of prevention with the important report, *Primary Prevention: An Idea Whose Time Has Come* (Klein & Goldston, 1977). Another milestone for prevention came when President Carter sponsored a White House conference that led to the establishment of a new Commission on Mental Health, which recommended federal funding for prevention and that an Office of Prevention be established within the National Institute of Mental Health.

How did these government and nonprofit agencies know what approaches would work best to prevent or solve these problems? Primarily, it was guess-work, a hit-or-miss proposition, guided by good intent. University-based researchers and others, primarily from the mental health field, did produce some research evidence, but rarely did this evidence make its way into the field where prevention practitoners operated.

In the late 1970s-early 1980s the field of prevention took an important turn with the publication of three major sets of research that guided the direction of many practitioners. The first was a major longitudinal study on problem behavior and psychosocial development (Jessor & Jessor, 1977) that H. Stephen Glenn (1983) largely drew upon to identify seven healthy perceptions and skills that made the primary difference in the behaviors of young people [Chapter III]. These were the result of how children and young people were treated, primarily, within the family. OJJDP then published *Delinquency Prevention: Theories and Strategies* (Johnson, Bird & Little, 1980), which identified contributing factors for delinquency similar to the Jessor study. It also found little evidence that most delinquency prevention strategies worked but suggested school improvement would potentially have the most promising effect.

Research evidence about what did work began to accumulate (Price et al., 1988; Benard, 1988). Such was the state of the field at the time *Prevention: The Critical Need* (Pransky, 1991) attempted to pull together all the existing evidence for practitioners. Since its initial publication, the prevention field has been involved in a number of different trends.

Prevention Trends in the 1990s

Four or five major trends emerged in the field of prevention in the 1990s. The first was an emphasis on *risk factors* (Hawkins and Catalano, 1992), the second an emphasis on *resiliency* (Benard, 1991; 1993), and the third, closely related, an emphasis on *assets* (Bensen et al, 1995). Overlapping these were emphases on *outcomes* (Williams & Webb, 1992; Schorr, 1997) and, at the very end of the decade, *research-proven programs* (U.S. Department of health and Human Services, 1998).

This book is not the place to examine all these trends [For that, see *Prevention: The Critical Need* (Pransky, 2001)]. What is important is these trends were an attempt to bring improved efficacy to the field of prevention, to bring focus to what people considered important. Arguments arose only over what people considered most important.

In this book I talk about only those trends that help point to the need for inside-out prevention.

Protective Factors, Resiliency, and Assets

In the 1990s interest in resilience surged. Thanks largely to the work of Bonnie Benard (1991) and, later, Nan Hendersen (1997) and others, most prevention practitioners now have been exposed to research-identified factors that helped people "make it" in spite of growing up in high-risk environments (Garmezy, 1974; Rutter, 1979; Werner & Smith, 1982; Wolin and Wolin, 1993; O'Connell-Higgins, 1994).

Resiliency research proved we could no longer assume that high-risk conditions *caused* problem behaviors. An intermediary existed. While research showed that the greater the number and more intense the risk factors, the more they correlated with higher rates of problem behaviors (Hawkins, Catalano, & Miller, 1992), correlation does *not* mean cause and effect. Clearly, it is helpful to reduce high-risk conditions, but we cannot assume behavior will be changed by doing so.

The notion of resiliency was a huge step forward for the field. However, many resiliency proponents appear to have assumed their own cause and effect, assuming if the research-identified protective or resiliency conditions were built, it would result in changed behaviors and healthier people. Again, while again true as a correlation, cause and effect cannot be assumed; another intermediary exists still. I submit this intermediary is *Thought*. We can build the most wonderful resilience-producing environments—which clearly we should do—but, as I keep stating, if someone's thinking does not change, behavior will not change. The only true cause and effect we will ever find in this field is between one's thinking and one's behavior.

Also interesting is that research identified *both* external *and* internal factors that protected people from risks and produced more resilient people. Enter the notion of "assets." Because of the Search Institute's work, most of the field is quite familiar with assets. Their huge study found when young people experienced a greater number of assets they were less likely to engage in behaviors such as sexual activity, violence/antisocial activity, school failure, illicit drug use, depression and/or attempted suicide, problem alcohol use, tobacco use, and vehicle recklessness, and were more likely to engage in volunteer service, and succeed in school (Benson et al., 1995, p.10). Calling their 40 identified assets "building blocks of healthy development," they concluded if communities went out of their way to build a greater number of assets, young people would do better. This reframing of resiliency into assets captured the imagination and interest of the prevention field and began to guide much of its direction (until the notion of "research-proven programs" took over at the end of the 1990s). Unfortunately, this huge study provided no indication whether some assets had more of an influence than others, or whether when certain assets are in place the need for others is countermanded.

Further, the lists of external and internal protective/resiliency factors/assets could be boiled down to a few key *external* factors that appear to make the most difference (bonding to family, clear standards for behavior, opportunities to contribute) and a few key *internal* factors (often called individual characteristics, such as a resilient temperament, a sense of purpose and meaning, healthy beliefs).

While the Search Institute's research focused solely on the total quantitative number (the more assets, the better), a major national longitudinal study on adolescent health did examine relative importance. Surveying 12,118 adolescents in grades 7-12 from 134 high schools including feeder schools, eight areas were assessed: emotional distress; suicidal thoughts and behaviors; violence; use of substances; age of sexual debut; pregnancy history. Results showed that perceived "parent-family connectedness" and "school connectedness" were protective against every health risk behavior measure (p.=<.001) except for history of pregnancy. In conclusion the authors stated, "We find consistent evidence that *perceived caring and connectedness to others...*serves as a protective factor against a variety of risk behaviors" (Resnick et al., 1997, pp.830-831).

No doubt caring and connectedness clearly are extremely important, but another perhaps even more important finding from this same report was overlooked in most circles and received very little coverage. "*Individual characteristics*"—which in the study included factors such as "self-esteem," "religious identity," "self-report of physical appearance," "repeated a grade," "grade point average," and "paid work"—often proved *even more significant* than connectedness. For example, regarding "emotional distress and suicidality," while parent-family connectedness explained 14%-15% of the variability for 7th-9th graders and school connectedness accounted for 13%-18%, individual characteristics accounted for 21%-22%. Regarding violence, while family connectedness accounted for 7%-5% and school connectedness accounted for 6%-7%, individual variability accounted for 44%-50%. Regarding alcohol and marijuana use, while family connectedness accounted for 6%-9% and school connectedness 4%-6%, individual characteristics accounted for 5%-7% (Resnick et al., 1997).

Despite equal attention paid in the research to both external and internal factors and despite the implication that both are equally important, most resiliency and asset-building approaches have focused on the external. Why? Perhaps the reason is working with external forces is easier to grasp and to plan strategies around.

Let's explore this further by examining a program that gets results. Research similar in a way to the Search Institute, but better constructed, comes from Russell Qualia's National Center for Student Aspirations (NCSA) at the University of Maine in Orono. They found that students with "high aspirations" do better, and that high aspirations can be fostered in students. They define student aspirations as "the ability to set goals for the future, while being inspired in the present to reach those goals" (Qualia & Fox, 2000, p.12). Unlike the Search Institute (as of this writing) the NCSA *has* documented results of its implementation efforts. Generally, their process is this: a school takes its "Student Speak" survey, the NCSA provides data analysis, then works with all parties in the school (including students) to help them determine the best ways to help students develop high aspirations, given the culture of that school. Two independent organizations, Acu Poll and Eureka Ranch, independently evaluated this effort and found children with high aspirations are significantly 1) more excited about learning; 2) happier, with greater ambition; 3) less likely to do drugs and alcohol and cheat; 4) better able to resist peer pressure. NCSA's School Aspirations programs showed a-

- 150% increase in national proficiency test scores
- 50% increase in grades, with a 43% increase in A's and B's
- 72% reduction in discipline problems
- 25% reduction in absenteeism
- report card increases in demonstrating self-control, cooperating with others, following directions, and showing respect.

NCSA research identified *eight conditions that affect student aspirations and make a difference in the lives of all youth*, which is what the NCSA helps schools develop in students:

- *Belonging* — the experience of being a valued member of a group, characterized by a sense of connection, support, and community
- *Heroes* – having someone to look up to, admire, and appreciate and who models a constructive way of relating to the world
- *A Sense of Accomplishment* – not only through recognition of academic, athletic, or creative achievement, but also of effort, perseverance and citizenship
- *Fun and Excitement* – ability to make or find anything fun and exciting (even school)
- *Curiosity and Creativity* – eagerness and strong desire to learn new and interesting things and to search for and find answers; to seek new discoveries
- *Spirit of Adventure* – willingness to take risks and receiving encouragement for taking them
- *Leadership and Responsibility* – responsible decision-makers
- *Confidence to Take Action* – believing in oneself enough to act

I think it would be safe to say that the majority of schools do not go out of their way to foster these conditions in their students, yet this research shows when they do, they get results. The point is, in each of these categories, schools can reconstruct themselves so their students have a better chance of feeling belonging, having heroes, having a sense of accomplishment, etc. It is great to know this! However, no matter what the school does to foster high aspirations, *only* if an individual student adopts this thinking *internally* will he or she change. Ultimately, whether or not students have high aspirations comes from their own minds. No matter how well a school builds the conditions that foster high aspirations, some students won't develop them. Other students will have high aspirations no matter how poorly a school does.

Does this mean schools should not take on NCSA's approach? Of course not! I would encourage every school in the country to do so. I love their work. They have proven success. I am only suggesting *the external isn't all there is to it.* I would suggest that when students are connected with their innate Health and wisdom, they automatically have high aspirations. If we could help students see this in themselves, we could accomplish the same thing. And if we could meet half-way and do both simultaneously, we could be even more effective. That is an exciting proposition! And it holds real promise—not only for the NCSA's work but for any of our existing prevention efforts. I am talking about *superimposing the internal over what we are already doing—adding that extra ingredient of helping students realize their Health and wisdom and what keeps them from experiencing it.*

Unfortunately, working from the outside-in, traditionally, most of us have not seen kids as whole and complete. To me, the crux of it is portrayed in Benson's (1995) statement: "Unless we begin *providing* [my emphasis] all youth with the assets they need to thrive, we will continue to see many children and youth struggling to find their place" (p.4). On the surface this is a true statement, but looking more closely, to Benson *even the positive internal assets appear to assume a lack within a young person; the implication is that it is up to others to provide or build what it is believed they do not have.* And Benson is only an example of how most of us in this field inadvertently have been thinking, myself included; for example, when we have the notion that kids will do well *if we* give them skills or provide healthy environments.

Emmy Werner (1996) reminds us, "We need to look and see what [resiliency] researchers found in the first place…It wasn't just that the children behavioral scientists studied were empty boxes into which someone poured 'resiliency'" (p.19). In the pubic health model of prevention, we focus on the host, the agent, and the environment. All three are supposed to receive equal attention for a whole preventive effort. In traditional prevention most emphasis on attempting to strengthen the host has occurred through the teaching [pouring in?] of skills. Werner is pointing to a notion beyond this: Something within the host makes it vulnerable to the agent or not. I suggest *what internal resilience or internal assets really means is that something resides within the individual [host] that in and of itself makes people resilient.* As we shall see later, this alternative view has become the view of a growing number of resiliency proponents (Benard & Marshall, 1997).

In its draft paper on science-based substance abuse prevention, the U.S. Department of Health and Human Services (1998) reported what it believed preventive interventions should focus on. It listed both the external and internal factors found by research. The key individual factors found were "biological predisposition," "shy and aggressive temperament" at a young age, "irritable temperament" at a young age, "mental disorders such as clinical depression and anxiety," "sensation-seeking personality and behaviors," "low sense of self-efficacy," "alienation, rebelliousness, and anti-social attitudes," "early drug use," "underestimation of the consequences and harmfulness of drug use," and "expectancies about substance use and abuse" (pp.4-5). What does this means for us programmatically? First it is important to separate out those individual factors that prevention practitioners *can do something about before the fact.* There isn't much we can do before the fact about "predisposition" or fixed "temperament" or "personality" or a previous "disorder," given that these are said to already exist within certain individuals, and pretty much all we can do is respond constructively to these conditions. We could certainly try to prevent "early onset of drug use," but that is what we are already trying to prevent, so that is not particularly helpful. What, then, are we left to focus on? Self-efficacy, attitudes, and expectancies. All have their foundation in *thought*. Even what we call "temperament" or "personality" may be rooted in thought. *Most of the prevention field and most resiliency/asset proponents have not directly and purposefully attempted to affect thought as a primary goal.*

The same study also reports, although it says there is less research on this: "Individuals may turn to different drugs with the expectation of reducing undesirable feelings or conditions such as tension, anxiety, loneliness, boredom, depression, fear, impotence, appetite or weight... [therefore] effectiveness may be further enhanced when they address the needs and motivations behind the substance use and abuse of a target population, when they address cognition related to substance use, and when they encourage or provide safe and healthy alternatives to substance use" (p.6). Perceived needs, expectancies, and motivations are all thoughts. An implication is that prevention may need to focus directly on *thought* to provide a complete approach.

This idea is not completely foreign. Seligman (1991; 1996), who initially researched "learned helplessness," began to research "learned optimism." This means, basically, the ability to shape one's thoughts and beliefs to forge ahead despite setbacks. He found what people tell themselves about an event or circumstance—whether people have optimistic or pessimistic thoughts—in large measure determines how well they do in the face of it. He found when people learn to assess and dispute their pessimistic thinking and gain more optimistic thinking they are less likely to get depressed and more likely to succeed at work and in relationships.

These data suggest a need within prevention to help people gain new perspective on themselves from within. In so doing they could strengthen themselves and move toward well-being and away from problems. The job of prevention would be to have people realize a new, healthier perspective. This could be a goal within any of Lofquist's (1983) four "arenas of human service activity": I) "community development," II) "personal growth and development," III) "community problem-solving," and IV) "personal problem-solving." "Building on people's strengths," then, would mean a lot more than discovering what people already do well and finding a way to capitalize on it to help them get where they want, or offering their resources to others as suggested by McKnight (1997). *The greatest strength people have is what already resides within them.*

Resiliency, then, pointed the prevention field in an important direction. Rather than only take the factors identified in resiliency and protective-factor research, provide those skills and supports, build the right relationships and create the right conditions, however, *it may be even more important to help people recognize their own internal source of resilience.*

Werner (1996) spoke of "cognitive competence" being "one of the hallmarks of resiliency" (p.22), and of a "self-righting mechanism" inherent in all people. These are clues. The notion of a self-righting mechanism assumed far greater importance for the field when the editors of *Resiliency in Action* (Benard, Henderson, Sharp-Light, & Richardson, 1996) took a major philosophical stance by essentially redefining resiliency as *"an innate self-righting and transcending ability within all children, youth, adults, organizations, and communities."* "Innate" means inherent, possessed at birth, within all human beings. Resiliency, then, is something more than the commonly accepted definition, "the capacity to spring back, rebound, successfully adapt in the face of adversity." The new interpretation brings the definition in closer alignment with the other dictionary definition of resilience:

"the property of a material that enables it to resume its original shape or position after being bent, stretched, or compressed" (The American Heritage Dictionary). Resiliency is more than a "capacity:" it is inherent within the very *property* of the material—within our very fabric as human beings. The implication for understanding internal resilience is this: *We do not have to do anything to anyone to make them resilient; they already are!*

Benard and Marshall (1997) and Marshall (1998) speak of tapping the natural, innate health or resilience of people, defined as the human capacity for transformation and change (Lifton, 1993). We are all born with the innate ability to transform the way we experience life from the inside-out with our own thinking.

This innate self-righting mechanism appears to be a force that can keep people on an even keel. *People only need to not interfere with this natural tendency.* To begin with this as a starting point in our prevention efforts changes everything. We are no longer "building" resiliency or even helping people acquire it. We are simply helping to draw out what they already have. In sum, instead of beginning with an incomplete person who becomes complete if s/he is in the right environment or learns the right skills or gains the right supports or gets the right information, we begin with a wholly complete person who has the innate capacity to realize his or her own internal health and strength and how it becomes obscured.

Another major theme identified in studies of internal resilience is religion or spirituality or faith (Resnick et al., 1997). Werner (1996) states, "...shortchanged in scientific studies is that these children had some faith that gave meaning to their lives..." (p.24). This does not necessarily mean denominational faith. "The ones that were able to use this faith to overcome adversity were the ones that saw meaning in their lives, even in pain and suffering. It wasn't church attendance, but it was a belief that life, despite everything, made sense and that even the pain they experienced could ultimately be transformed" (p.24).

This evidence suggests that to be wholly effective the prevention field must find ways to affect these yet-untapped realms.

> The starting point and key to effective prevention is the deep-seated belief ...that every youth has innate resilience..."the human capacity for transformational change"... According to Roger Mills, whose Health Realization approach is the most powerful prevention model I've witnessed, the capacity for mental health, resilience, wisdom, intelligence, common sense and positive motivation...is in everyone despite their 'risk factors,' is potentially available at all times, and can be realized without reliving and working through the past and without direct teaching of life skills... It is time for the prevention and education fields to acknowledge the important findings from cognitive science, psychoneuroimmunology, and brain research about how human beings learn, as well as the power of our thoughts, attitudes, and beliefs to affect our mental and physical health.... All of this research, as well as that of the longitudinal developmental studies of "high-risk" youth, clearly document human beings' innate self-righting mechanism, the developmental homeostasis that is genetically encoded in all of us and propels us toward healthy development (Benard, 1996a, p.3).

At the end of this chapter we revisit the relationship between inside-out prevention and resilience.

We could look in the direction of social-ecology, from the perspectives of James Kelley (1968), Urie Bronfenbrenner (1977), Belsky (1980), or to chaos theory (Wheatley, 1997), and try to unravel all the complexities of all the contributing forces to behavior. But this direction has a drawback. As Tom Kelley (1990) stated about the proliferation of theories and approaches in the criminal justice field:

> [T]he variation that exists both within and among our theories appears to have become as great as the variety of factors those theories are attempting to explain. Instead of seeking some common factors that would break down the variation into some comprehensible design, it has become commonplace for the field to focus on the variation itself" (p.3).

To find simplicity—boiling down all the complexity to its essence—is the direction we might seek.

Interestingly, Roger Mills had been a protégé of James Kelley, and had begun to add into the complex ecological mix a focus on "belief systems," where participants would be helped to "become aware of the subjective nature of their own personal perception of the world" (McCullough, 1980). Thus, Mills would attempt to explore each individual's belief system, "noting the cultural context and various levels of influence which affect this belief system." Mills would use experiential exercises "to help illustrate how an individual's internal frame of reference shapes his experience of life"(p.39). Once Mills became exposed to the deeper view of *Thought* as the source of people's experience, however, he turned away from the specific content and variety of individual belief systems and, with it, from all the complexity.

The Fundamental Flaw, and a New Direction

Marilyn Bowman (1997) made a startling discovery.

In a quasi-meta-analysis of well over 500 research studies Bowman found that "event-related factors do not represent the most important component in any useful conceptualization of event-attributed clinical distress" (p.39). Counter to the prevailing model employed by the mental health profession that "toxic events will normally trigger clinically significant distress symptoms..." (p.135), she reports that after toxic events "only a minute fraction of people" develop chronic, persistent fears and life impairment defined as post-traumatic stress disorder. "Most people traverse these events with resilience after a period of initial distress, owing to combinations of personal factors that are significantly unacknowledged in the clinical literature concerning diagnosis and treatment" (Bowman, 1997, p.145).

Bowman found "considerable evidence" from longitudinal studies that "happiness or the subjective experience of well-being is remarkably independent of significant life events, whether these events are positive or toxic in nature" (p.110). She found that *whenever* data are collected comparing individual qualities pre- and post-event with event characteristics, individual qualities are found to be more powerful in accounting for distress. These individual qualities include "cognitive competence, ... personality traits of emotionality and attraction to risk, as well as beliefs about the self, the world, sources of danger, and the appropriateness of emotional displays" (p.89). Of these, the most important were found to be "long-standing traits of emotionality and general belief systems…" (p.136).

Bowman concluded that the stress response is internally generated. *"Individuals structure the meaning of the event…and help shape the kind of emotional response the individual shows"* (p.76).

Her findings, drawn primarily from a treatment perspective, run counter to most prevailing efforts, but they also may have profound implications for the future direction of prevention.

In light of her findings, Bowman proposes what she believes to be the most efficacious strategy for treatment: In short, she says therapy should "educate…individuals in the ways in which their characteristic thought and reaction styles can contribute to prolonged distress," and "help…individuals to understand that blaming an external event for their emotional condition will not contribute to long-term well-being." She asserts that "changes in the way an individual thinks about events and about their emotions and thoughts will be at the core of effective treatment" (p.142).

The same applies to prevention. In fact, Bowman draws an astute distinction between what she calls "incorrectly focus[ing] on thought contents as the valid guide to causation" (p.102), and properly focusing on "personal agency." [see below]

Thus, instead of looking toward the complex array of external factors as an explanation for and as a point of intervention, this direction points people within themselves. But, further, Bowman is pointing beyond cognitive skills, beyond cognitive content, to an even more powerful notion: to the cognitive self as agent, or *"self-efficacy."*

Bandura (1989) calls self-efficacy "a major function of thought." and states, "There is a growing body of evidence that human attainments and positive well-being require an optimistic sense of personal efficacy" (p.1176). He found that *people's perceptions or beliefs about their capabilities and behavior influence their behavior even more than their "true" capabilities* (Strecher et al., 1986, p.74). Bandura argues that perceived self-efficacy influences all aspects of behavior. It affects people's emotional reactions, such as anxiety and distress; it influences their thought patterns. Thus "individuals with low self-efficacy about a particular task may ruminate about their personal deficiencies rather than thinking about accomplishing or attending to the task at hand; this, in turn, impedes successful performance of the task… People with a high sense of self-efficacy may attribute occasional failures to chance or to some temporary condition and thus maintain their success orientation" (pp.75-76). For all health-related areas—including contraceptive behavior, alcohol abuse, and exercise—self-efficacy appears to be a consistent predictor of short and long-term success.

Bandura asserts that much human depression is "cognitively generated" by "dejecting ruminative thoughts" (Bandura, 1989, p.1178). Yet, "perceived inefficacy to exercise control over" such ruminative thoughts figures prominently in the duration and recurrence of depressive episodes. In other words, *having problem thoughts is not the problem; it is what one thinks about those thoughts once one has them. The crucial factor is whether people believe they can exercise control over these potential threats to themselves.* If they believe they can exercise such control, Bandura states, they "do not conjure up apprehensive cognitions and are therefore not perturbed by them. But those who believe they cannot manage potential threats experience high levels of stress and anxiety arousal. They tend to dwell on their coping deficiencies and view many aspects of their environment as fraught with danger. Through such inefficacious thought they distress themselves and constrain and impair their level of functioning…" He sums up with this proverb: "You cannot prevent the birds of worry…from flying over your head. But you can stop them from building a nest in your head." "It is not the sheer frequency of aversive cognitions but the perceived inefficacy to turn them off that is the major source of distress…"

Thus, Bandura looks beyond thought content in a direction corroborated by Bowman (1997). While we all generate thought content, more important is that we make something of that thought content by the way we see it. Here a larger pattern emerges. Self-efficacy affects thought patterns that may be self-aiding or self-hindering. But *self-efficacy itself is thought! And therein lies our power to determine whether our generated thoughts will have power over us or not.* The question becomes: How does this larger thought context become generated? Where does it come from? Bandura takes a huge step:

> … understanding the brain circuits involved in learning does not tell one much about how best to present and organize structural content…and how to motivate learners to… cognitively process…what they are learning. Nor does understanding how the brain works furnish rules on how to create social conditions that cultivate the skills needed to become a successful parent, teacher, or executive. The optimal conditions must be specified by psychological principles… Were we to embark on the road to reductionism, psychology would be reduced to biology, biology to chemistry, chemistry to physics, with the final stop in atomic particles. Neither atomic particles, chemistry, nor biology will provide the psychological laws of human behavior… The construal of cognitions as cerebral processes raises the intriguing question of how people come to be producers of thoughts that may be novel, inventive, visionary, or that take complete leave of reality as in flights of fancy… Emergent cognitive events draw on existing cognitive structures but go beyond them (Bandura, 1989, p.1182).

Go beyond our cognitive structures? Bandura is pointing to a mysterious process that cannot be understood by heading down the reductionist road (as indicated above), no matter how good science becomes at navigating it. He is pointing to people's own *act of creation*, the ability of people to create what they ultimately experience. Though not expressed precisely in those terms, and perhaps not knowing exactly what to do about it, Bandura implies that the answers to behavior lie somewhere within that realm. He then makes this profound statement:

> In the model of reciprocal causation, people partly determine the nature of their environment and are influenced by it… Through their capacity to manipulate symbols and to engage in reflective thought, people can generate novel ideas and innovative actions that transcend their past experiences. They bring influence to bear on their motivation and action in efforts to realize valued futures. They may be taught the tools of self-regulation, but that in no way detracts from the fact that by the exercise of that capability they help to determine the nature of their situations and what they become. The self is thus partly fashioned through the continued exercise of self-influence (Bandura, 1989, p.1182).

In other words, *people as thinkers actually participate in creating what they experience of their environment, and what they become.* We are not simply subjected to the ravages of our environment. We *shape our experience* of it. And therein lies the essence of the flaw in the argument of those who point to the outside world—to the environment, situations, events, other people—as being *the* important influence on people's behavior.

This flaw may be best summed up by a line from Ben Harper's song, "Oppression":

> Oppression
> I won't let you near me
> Oppression
> You shall learn to fear me
> — Ben Harper, "Oppression," *Fight for Your Mind*

If people saw the oppressive conditions to which they are subjected as expressed in Harper's song, they would have completely different thoughts, feelings and behaviors than if they saw themselves as victims of, or helpless in the face of, those same conditions. *To look inward instead of to the outside world is to see one's own power to create either view or belief.*

Metacognition

This brings us to what some have called metacognition (McCombs, 1991). Mills (1991) defines metacognition as "the ability to recognize and experience a higher and more natural condition of mental health, that is outside the framework of conditioned ways of thinking" (p.80). In essence, this means the ability to see facts about one's own thinking (Mills, 1996).

Higher level processes such as insight, creativity, wisdom and common sense operate outside our usual cognitive system "and are accessed at higher levels of consciousness; they involve seeing beyond our conditioned belief system or personal frame of reference" (McCombs, 1991, p.7). By looking at where thought content originates—in the knower or person as agent—we see that *thought* is the common denominator for understanding human functioning, not the content that is the product of thought.

The metacognitive realm is one of "a basically healthy, already actualized self as a source of intrinsic motivation" (Mills, 1991, p.68). It is a state that is "not only natural, but is unchanging in that it engages these same capacities or attributes in everyone…, everyone has an innate propensity toward intrinsic motivation…These attributes exist at the core of one's psychological make-up" (p.69).

This coincides with Maslow's (1968) notion of self-actualization, in which intrinsic motivation is a natural occurrence, and is akin to self-realization, integration, psychological health, individuation, creativity and productivity. Maslow and other Humanistic psychologists such as Rogers posited that individuals began life with a biologically based, intrinsic, inner nature which is inherently good or at least neutral (not evil). Less commonly known is that Maslow also found that the characteristics of "self-actualized" people were the same qualities displayed by normal, everyday people in moments of what he termed "peak experiences." In other words, all people in their healthiest moments display the same characteristics as self-actualized people generally do. Both naturally display what Maslow terms "Being-values" ("B-values") such as wholeness, justice and fairness, aliveness, richness, simplicity, beauty, goodness, effortlessness, truth, and self-sufficiency. Also not commonly known is that toward the end of Maslow's career (1968—3rd edition) he saw what he called "self-transcendence" at the pinnacle of his hierarchy of needs, even beyond "self-actualization."

A key difference, however, remains in whether when one sees self-actualized or self-transcendent states as inherent within all human beings—that is, naturally residing there—or whether one thinks people have to go out of their way to achieve those states.

The End as the Beginning

Thus we have come full circle to the very origins of American psychology itself, in the late 1800s. William James stated, "The only thing which psychology has a right to postulate at the outset is the fact of thinking itself... The first fact for us, then, as psychologists, is that thinking of some sort goes on" (James, 1981, p.219). He offered five important characteristics of thought:
- Every thought tends to be part of a personal consciousness.
- Within each personal consciousness thought is always changing.
- Within each personal consciousness thought is sensibly continuous.
- It always appears to deal with objects independent of itself.
- It is interested in some parts of these objects to the exclusion of others, and welcomes or rejects—chooses from among them, in a word—all the while (p.20).

James thus linked our continual stream of thought to our stream of consciousness. They are *inseparable*. He proposed the primary direction for psychology was to better understand this process. While the history of psychology shows his plea has, thus far, gone largely unheeded, James went even further. He considered something he called the "spiritual self" and saw its link to thought:

> ...our considering the spiritual self at all is a reflective process, is a result of our abandoning the outward-looking point of view, and of our having become able to think...of ourselves as thinkers... We can feel, alongside of the thing known, the thought of it going on as an altogether separate act and operation in the mind (p.299).

James saw "an hierarchical scale, with the bodily Self at the bottom, the spiritual Self at the top, and the extracorporeal material selves and the social selves between" (p.299). Further, he saw this spiritual self connected in some way to what he called "Absolute mind...the essence of which we know nothing." (p.329). He posited that "the consciousness of Self involves a changeable stream of thought... a Thought [that], at each moment, [is] different from that of the last moment..."(386).

Thus James appears to have anticipated many of the elements involved later in Sydney Banks's discovery of *the three Principles*" [Chapter VI]. But from my reading of James's work it seems to me he did not quite understand how they all worked together to give people their experience of life. This is the breakthrough Banks provides.

James himself began to look in a more spiritual direction. In *Varieties of Religious Experience* (2000) he suggested that the natural state of mind is positive until it is contaminated by self–defeating patterns of thought.

The Focus on Health and its Relation to Spirit

While most psychologists did not follow James into the realm of Spirit or Absolute Mind, what is the prevention field to make of this? Interestingly, unlike traditional psychology, prevention has already begun to embrace the notion of spirituality. In part this may be because Alcoholics Anonymous, on the treatment end of the alcohol and drug field, has effectively used spirituality as an integral part of its approach. The prevention end of the substance abuse field has slowly begun to embrace its power—it has been tougher-coming in other prevention-related fields—but a clear idea about how to approach it has not yet emerged.

Prevention: The Critical Need (Pransky, 1991) was the first book to give credence to the importance of spirituality in prevention, pointing to empirical evidence that some people who have had spiritual or religious epiphanies have completely turned problem lives into healthy lives. Such a life-altering epiphany is vividly apparent in the life of boxer George Foreman. The happy-go-lucky George Foreman of today bears almost no resemblance to the mean and nasty George Foreman of his early boxing days. It happened after a spiritual experience that occurred out of nowhere after losing a fight, as he lay on his dressing room table (then the floor) (Forman & Engle, 1995).

This theme was later echoed and expanded upon by the Canada- and New Zealand-based *People-Centered Health Promotion* (Raeburn & Rootman, 1998), which posited that the goals of health promotion should properly be concerned with "a better life for as many people as possible, a reasonable level of good health in society, and the enhancement of well-being, life satisfaction, happiness and 'spiritual strength'" (p.38). While the focus is improved quality of life and well-being, they take it further still by stating that the fundamental goal of any true health promotion activity has "something to do with the state or nature of the human spirit, soul, essence, Buddha Nature, godhead, ground of being, and so on" (p.43).

Delving into the spiritual realm is not for the faint of heart, because of so many differing views and highly charged emotions. But Raeburn and Rootman tackle the issue head-on, stating that "numerous health promotion workers, as well as many 'ordinary community people,' have strong interests in this [spiritual] area, but there is not yet the language, the professional permission, or the academic base to put this subject "out there" in the public domain (p.111).

Citing the "Perennial Philosophy" popularized by Huxley (1944), which also is used as a foundation for Transpersonal Psychology, they boldly state that "until we come to a realization of our 'true nature,' to use the Buddhist term, we will not have fulfilled what we are here for, and will therefore remain in a fundamental state of discontent or 'unwellness'" (Raeburn & Rootman, 1998, p.117).

In a review of *Community Building: Values for a Sustainable Future* (Jason, 1997), which speaks of the need to incorporate teachings from "the wisdom traditions" into prevention practice, Berkowitz (1999) states, "What is ultimately preventive and community-enriching is personal transformation, our own transformation, and the full implications of that argument cannot be underestimated" (p.253). This is because "only a transformation of our values will provide sufficient motivation and willingness to work on the forces that cause unequal distribution of the world's resources," and presumably the social problems that accompany them (p.251).

In her review of effective preventive programs Schorr (1997) states, "A growing number of observers and people at the front lines are calling attention to a spiritual dimension to the relationships that seem to foster change" (p.15).

Thus some are beginning to acknowledge the importance and use of the spiritual realm in effective prevention practice. What we ultimately make of this and where it will lead the field is anyone's guess, but it suggests that inside-out prevention—which points in the direction suggested above by Bowman, Bandura, Maslow, James, Raeburn and Rootman, and Jason—could move the field forward a critical step. Accumulating evidence suggests that for prevention to look in an inside-out direction would be both viable and beneficial; Bowman would say, essential.

As of the year 2002 the prevailing trend still moves otherwise. Yet, as Bandura (1989) states, "Scientists often reject theories and technologies that are ahead of their time. Because of the cold reception given to most innovations, the time between discovery and technical realization typically spans several decades" (p.1177).

As Thomas Kuhn suggests, just when we believe we know something for sure, "anomalies often emerge that throw our certainty into question and stimulate new discoveries in science" (in Bloom, 1996, p.90). For example, it was not until the emergence of cognitive theory in psychology, long in coming to the United States, that "what happens inside a person's head finally was recognized as a part of the set of events that leads to behaviors" (Bloom, 1996, p.92). In prevention, a new discovery may emerge in looking beyond even the cognitive to the power that lies behind changes in people's thinking which then results in thoughts, feelings and behavior.

The Trend toward Research-Proven Programs

While very well-intended, the trend toward research-proven programs inadvertently may have inhibited the growth and development of inside-out prevention and other worthwhile prevention efforts. Why? Because when emphasis is placed only on those programs proven by rigorous scientific research (mostly because those programs had large research grants behind them) innovation and creativity in developing new prevention models is stifled. Directors of numerous community-based agencies have told me they would love to become trained in Health Realization, but because it was not on some government list of research-approved programs, they could only receive funds for those on the list. I have suggested that the government test the inside-out approach against other programs already considered "research-proven" to see which ultimately shows greater results, but no one has taken me up on it.

Chapters X & XII demonstrate that enough evidence exists to show Health Realization is at least a "promising" if not "effective approach." I believe it will not be long before more such programs are accepted for funding.

Many seasoned prevention practitioners have realized another flaw in the research-proven model focus. Such models can be implemented perfectly on paper, but if the relationships aren't right among the people running the program, the program will not be effective. This caused many preventionists to realize, if they hadn't already, that prevention is (and should be) more about developing healthy relationships than it is about programs. The same, of course, is true for resiliency.

Revisiting the Relationship Between Resiliency and Inside-Out Prevention

We now return to resiliency and strength-based prevention and make clear its relationship to inside-out prevention. As I implied, "internal resilience" has been the least understood and least well-practiced aspect of resiliency.

A number of my colleagues who have knowledge of both resiliency and Health Realization, as an example of inside-out prevention, emphasize that Health Realization is the embodiment of what resiliency is ultimately pointing to (Marshall, 1998; Benard & Marshall, 1997), or Health Realization is the best example of an effective approach to resilience that they have seen (Benard, 1996a). I agree with these statements, and I have the utmost respect for these colleagues. I fully understand that Health Realization would be more readily acknowledged and accepted by the field if it were considered *a part* of the already accepted resiliency picture. In my own view, it is more important to draw the distinction between outside-in and inside-out approaches than it is between risk-focused and the resiliency-focused approaches. By saying this, I do not mean to divide. I draw this distinction because I see such a critical difference in both the starting points and direction of movement of the outside-in and inside-out approaches to prevention and resiliency. Because my colleagues have such a deep understanding of resilience that they see it primarily as an inside-out affair, this is why they draw the distinction where they do. To date, from what I have observed the majority of resiliency practitioners still do not see as they do.

In my view it would be wise for people not to see Health Realization as simply another resiliency strategy. Rather, the three Principles behind Health Realization are what allow or cause people to be resilient or not [Chapter VI].

Why did those children on the island of Kauai—who grew up in high-risk conditions and were studied and followed longitudinally by Emmy Werner for many years—make it out and do reasonably well? It is well-known that Werner's research found high correlations between those who had at least one caring adult in their lives and those who "made it" (Werner & Smith, 1982). This is an external factor. Many practitioners then jumped to the conclusion that, therefore, a caring adult is *necessary* for resilience to occur. While having a caring adult or mentor in one's life, however, is extremely important and valuable, I would submit it is *not* absolutely *necessary*. It helps a lot but it is not essential. Why? Because some people without a caring adult in their lives make it too. This is far more rare, but it happens. Even if it happens even once, there can be no cause and effect.

How can a few people make it even without a caring adult in their lives? Because they had it within them all along! Somewhere along the way those people who made it *saw* their own internal capacity to rise above their circumstances. They realized it. They *knew* it. They felt it. A caring person in their lives helped greatly, but somehow they had to see it for themselves.

Everyone has this quality within them. It is innate. It can never disappear. It is available to reveal itself at any time, even for a moment, as soon as one's typical thinking lets go. Resilience itself is innate and inborn. If people did not have this quality inside they would never know it if it were shown to them. A huge difference exists between thinking one does *not* have internal resilience *unless* we do something to them from the outside, and thinking that one has *everything s/he needs inside* to live a happy, mentally healthy, productive life.

I see this internal, innate state as more than a tendency, even more than a capacity or capability. All those words carry the subtle implication that it isn't there yet but can be at any moment. This explanation works for some people, but to me it is deeper. To me it looks as if our spiritual essence is always present, only not realized in any moment. *We are pure resilience at our very core, and when we realize this fact, we are!* We feel it! And when we realize *thought* is the power allowing us to experience this resilience or not, we automatically experience it. [This will be explained in more detail in the next chapter.]

This offers a more pure approach to internal resilience. Resilience occurs when people gain new perspective on themselves from within. In so doing they strengthen themselves, and move toward well-being and away from problems. Our job as prevention workers, then, becomes to help them realize a new, healthier perspective—which they really already have, they just don't know it yet.

I offer four premises for finding internal resilience:
1. We all have internal resilience within us naturally, or at least the capacity to experience it at any moment.
2. It would be present for all to see if we didn't get in its way (with our own thinking).
3. It can be unveiled at any moment
4. It naturally emerges when we realize this, or when we realize how our experience is created within us moment-to-moment [Chapter VI].

Gaining new perspective on ourselves from within arises from new understanding. We see ourselves in ways we never saw before. To begin to come to grips with this, we could ask ourselves some questions:

- Would I rather be guided by my wisdom and common sense, or by my habitual, programmed thinking?
- Would I rather talk and act and make decisions when I am in an insecure, reactive state of mind, or when I am in a secure, responsive state?
- Would I rather take things personally, or see how people's attitudes come from their own, personal ways of seeing things, or from their moods?
- If I keep running into the same kinds of difficulties again and again, do I realize what keeps getting me stuck so I can transcend it?
- Do I realize that there is always a higher or deeper perspective from which to view any situation I encounter?
- Can I function at a more optimal level than I am now?

If we reflect on these and other similar questions and can conceive of moving beyond what we see now to reach deeper levels of understanding and well-being, we might gain new perspective, new insights, experience an internal shift. We might realize new things about ourselves and our lives we do not now see. We may change our view of ourselves or others or our circumstances. If this happens, how we feel and how we act will change, accordingly, and will flow naturally from there.

Can anyone make this happen in us? No! It must happen from within. What role, then, could prevention workers possibly have in getting this to happen in others? Our role becomes learning how to point people in a direction where they are more likely to experience new insights [Chapters XIII and XIV].

A Magic Bullet?

Contrary to popular opinion, I would submit we do have a "magic bullet" in prevention. The problem is we don't have a "magic gun" to shoot it in with. This is because the answer already lies within each of us. The magic bullet is already there! There can be no magic gun because it has nothing to do with anything we do; it can only be realized through insight and, as I repeat again and again, no one can make insight happen in another human being. But it is always there, waiting to be uncovered, unveiled, even in the most troubling or troubled individuals.

A power deep within allows anyone to transcend what they now realize. Some would call this spiritual. No matter what one calls it, its possibilities are limitless and carry automatic hope for all. This is perspective from the inside-out. Hopefully, this will become more clear as the next chapter unfolds.

We now turn our attention to an exploration of the Three Principles that underlie inside-out prevention, and what this understanding can mean for people's lives.

VI. THE THREE PRINCIPLES

In the last chapter I asked whether, in prevention, we wanted to look in the direction of complexity or to look in the direction of simplicity in an attempt to discover the underlying essence of all human behavior. Looking to the simple, underlying essence is looking inside-out. This is the direction we explore here.

To discover this underlying essence would be like finding the key that unlocks the secret to all behavior.

Many people scoff at this notion. Skeptics say, "Impossible!" "You're kidding yourself." "If it can't be proven by research it is all speculation, and what you're talking about can never be proven." "The field of psychology hasn't been able to come up with underlying principles; it's ridiculous to think you can." A few even get offended and say, "It's an insult, a disgrace" or worse.

Are the skeptics suggesting there can be no common basis for human behavior? Are they suggesting that all human beings cannot possibly function in the same basic way? Biologically, we know every human being functions in the same basic way. For example, despite fantastic variation everyone has a heart pumping blood through a circulatory system that nourishes the entire body. This is the simplicity. Despite phenomenal variation we all have a nervous system with a brain that allows us to feel pain and pleasure and have memory and lots more. That is the simplicity. A fairly recent discovery taught us our bodies have a system of tiny neurotransmitters and receptors that communicate with each other and have a "mind" of their own, which cause molecules to move and trigger chemical changes that can lead to various emotions (Pert, 1997). That fact is the simplicity. Before this was "discovered" by science, did that make it untrue?

Are scientists suggesting there cannot possibly be some common basis for human psychological functioning as well? Or do they think common basis can only be physical, such as understanding the structure and function of the brain or, in physics, reducing matter to its tiniest possible particles? Even if we went down that road, would we ever know what "powers up" the entire system? Would we ever know what gives the entire physical structure its life, so to speak? What is this "life force?" Science seems able to take us only so far.

What can we rely on besides science? Our own observation? What do we see when we truly look within?

What Lies Within?

As suggested in Chapter III, at the deepest depths of prevention everything turns inside-out, and we are faced with an entirely different world in which to operate. At first this new world looks and sounds strange. Because we are not used to it, it does seem odd and somewhat unsettling, which is why, I think, some people take issue with it. At first they cannot fathom it. Or, it seems too simple to be true.

If it is too simple, why would it have such a life-changing effect on so many people's lives when they do see it? The interviews in this book are examples. I believe the reason it has such a life-changing effect is because it shows people the "mechanism" behind their experience of life—how their experience of life gets created. What do I mean by "mechanism?" Ironically, I do not mean it in a mechanistic sense. I mean it only to imply the inner workings of something; how something really works. Once people see how something really works, they have the capacity to use it to enhance their lives.

We run a summer camp out of our home, so during the summer many kids run about. One day I heard commotion outside my office in the hallway. One little six-year old was apparently stuck in the bathroom. (She wasn't supposed to be there). She couldn't get out; she became increasingly frustrated. Another little girl stood outside the door trying to give her instructions. "You see that thing there on the door?" "What?" "That little thing holding down the handle." "No. Oh, yeah!" "You've got to push down on it." "Oh! [struggling sounds] I can't!" "You've got to turn push down on it with your thumb really hard." "Okay." The latch clicked. "Oh!" She was free! It was so cute.

This is what I mean by seeing a mechanism at work. Now that this little girl *saw* how it worked, she will never again be stuck in a bathroom with the same kind of latch; she will always be able to free herself when stuck like that. Once we see how a mechanism works, we can free ourselves. The same holds true for our minds. Once people see the inner workings of how they create an experience of well-being—or not—they seem to gain a handle on life that protects them internally from the ravages of the external world.

What is the "mechanism" behind human mental functioning? How does it make us function as human beings?

The mechanism behind human mental and spiritual functioning consists of three Principles that, together, create our experience of life: Mind, Consciousness, and Thought (Banks, 1998). As words, these mean nothing. As a theory, it means nothing. As forces in the universe, acting upon us or within us, they mean everything for our lives.

An understanding of the three Principles and how they work is at the very heart of transformational and transcendent change. It is therefore the foundation of prevention from the inside-out.

These Principles are not "new." They are universal, common sense, basic human nature, akin to some of the great teachings throughout history and across many cultures. Any attempt to describe these Principles in words is a nearly meaningless exercise. Unfortunately it is all we have. So some preparation is in order.

Preparation for "Hearing" the Three Principles

Perhaps the most difficult thing to comprehend about *the three Principles* is that they cannot be understood by the intellectual mind. They have to be *realized* from beyond the intellect. This can be disconcerting. How can people relate to something they have not yet experienced? The whole idea is to have a personal experience of the Principles—seeing the Principles in action in one's own life. This means having an insight about the meaning of the Principles for one's life. This means your life, my life, and all of our lives.

This is why it is inside-out: It must be realized from within. An insight—a sight from within—is a realization of something we really already know deep inside. Something clicks. A light bulb comes on. We see something we never saw before. Yet once we see it, it feels like certainty, as if we knew it all along deep inside; we just didn't realize it. At that point it is no longer a theory or belief; it is *fact*—to us. It is *truth*—to us.

As stated, an insight is one thing we cannot *make* happen either in ourselves or in others. This is inconvenient. All we can do is enhance the possibility of it. We can get people to the doorway; we cannot make them go through it. But they have a far better chance of going through the doorway if they are standing at the door.

What is our doorway for insight? A relaxed, calm, quiet mind.

For example, while attempting to read this chapter if our minds are distracted, we minimize our chances of having an insight about these Principles. If we're thinking about all the things we're not getting done because we're reading this, we are unlikely to have an insight about it. If we're comparing what we read to various outside-in prevention approaches, or to our own views of what we think inside-out prevention is supposed to mean, or to various spiritual approaches, we diminish our chances of having an insight. If we are judging what we're reading as worthless or useless for prevention, we diminish our chances of having an insight. All such inadvertent mental activity clutters the mind.

A cluttered mind is like a bridge packed solid with cement barricades. It is awfully tough to get through. We need a bulldozer to clear the path. Then we can pass with ease. Forgive me for this metaphor, but we need the toilet of our minds to flush. We need to be clear-headed; we need to have nothing on our minds. Our typical thinking needs to quiet down. That allows us to be in a state of deep listening. Being in a state of "not knowing" allows our heads to clear so we *can* listen deeply.

Now that you are in such a state ☺, we can talk about *the Three Principles*.

One more caution: I am going to use terms we have all heard before. As such, various meanings arise when reading them. To understand the meaning intended here, it is best to forget what we think we know about them, to read with fresh eyes or hear with fresh ears. Old meanings can get in our way. We want to understand something beyond the words, beyond the terms. We want to hear the essence of what is being said or written. No words are capable of describing the spiritual. Words are forms, and we are attempting, feebly, to describe the formless. So the words don't count, but they are all we have. If I could draw it in a picture, I would. But a picture is also form and therefore inadequate. Pictures also hold different meanings for different people.

What is a Principle?

One of the words that often causes confusion is the term, "principle." I do not mean it the way it is often used; I do not mean it the way I used it in *Prevention: The Critical Need*. There I meant something like "guidelines" to live or work by. Here, "Principle" (with a capital "P") means something akin to a universal law. The term "Principle" as used throughout this book means some force that exists in the universe, whether we recognize or realize it or not.

Before some point in history (before Newton, I think), people did not know about gravity. Yet gravity existed. People were still held to the earth by some force, whether they knew it or not. Gravity as a force, as a *Principle* of the physical world of nature, was acting upon them, even when they knew nothing about it. Gravity didn't care whether people knew; it was still doing its thing.

The definition of "Principle," used herein, is *a force in the universe that always exists and is always at work, irrespective of people's awareness of it.*

Principles at this level may not be so easy to grasp. As Judith Sedgeman of the West Virginia University Medical School writes (1998):

> ...to grasp the difference between seeing Principles and learning theoretical knowledge is unsettling for disciplined academics. It requires them to examine something "new" or "different" in the context of insight and discovery-based learning...and...reflection as opposed to analysis... As long as the learners' minds are focused on whether things are alike or different, revolutionary or evolutionary, new or derived, learning stops at the boundaries of the already known, at the edge of the past. That is, we can only compare and contrast known information with other known information... The study of the Principles...is about what happens before there is any content — that is, before the formation of thought. It opens the door to the spiritual — that is, to not knowing in faith that one can see beyond one's knowledge (pp.1-2).

The Principles we refer to are universal Principles of how the mind works, or what is behind human mental functioning. To underscore their importance, again, *these Principles underlie and form the basis for anything we can create and experience.* I did not make these up. They are not theory. Sydney Banks (1998) calls them spiritual facts. He *saw* them. I did not. But I have felt the truth of them—for me—and I know many, many other people who also have felt the truth of them—for them—and as a result our lives have improved, some so dramatically it is almost unbelievable.

I know some readers will scoff at that last paragraph, but what am I to do? I know it doesn't make sense to the intellect. We say, "It can't be" or "It can't be that simple" or "No matter what you call it, it's still a theory" or statements less kind, but it is what it is. I don't expect anyone to "believe it" because, as I've said, as a belief it means nothing. People will either have a personal experience of the Principles through their own insight or they won't. And if they do, they will know it like I do (or better), and if not, they may experience it later, or they may never.

Truth be told, when I first heard *the three Principles* described I could not fathom them. It was listening like to a foreign language. When I first listened to a tape by Syd Banks—the first I heard of the Principles—it sounded to me like he was from outer space. I had no idea what he was talking about.[7] I can listen to that same tape now, and I can't imagine what I was thinking. Now I think these Principles must be this obvious to everyone. Yet I also know *the three Principles* are obvious to me only at a certain level. At an even deeper level I still cannot fathom them and never will. They are completely beyond the intellect.

So here we go. Sit back and relax, and enjoy.

The Three Principles

Over the years, a number of people have expressed the need for unifying principles in the field of psychology. Cottier, for one, writes, "We do not need more theories of psychotherapy; we need fewer of them. We need unifying principles of helping that simplify the confusion of competing concepts, that describe the essence of effective psychotherapy, and provide generally accepted principles that most clinicians could subscribe to" (in Pransky, G., 1998, p.30).

In prevention we could look to the same unifying principles psychology hopes to find about what creates behavior. I believe we have found these Principles—for both psychology and prevention: "Mind," "Consciousness" and "Thought."

I will attempt, first, to briefly summarize these Principles and how they fit together (as I see them at this writing). I then will delve deeper into each Principle, partly drawing upon the work of others.

Mind refers to the universal, formless energy or intelligence behind life, the life force that is the source of All things.

Thought, in essence, is the power to create.

Consciousness, in essence, is the power to experience.

The kicker is, we can have no experience that is not created by our own thinking. We are capable of experiencing *only* what our thoughts create.

This could not be more profound. It means everything for our lives! It means that *when we look out at the world and see what we call "reality," we are really only seeing "a reality"—our own reality that we have made up with our own thinking. And, everyone's "reality" is different. And, our own reality is as fluid and changeable as our next thought.*

This statement does *not* mean that with our thinking we make up what happens out there in the world. It *does* mean that we make up what we *see* of whatever is "out there." It means that we can never know what is really "out there." The only thing we can ever know is *our own thinking* of what is "out there." This includes how we see ourselves.

The implications are enormous. When it looks as if we are stuck, we only *think* we are. When it looks like we have a problem, we only *think* we do. When we're in a bad mood and it looks as if we must take action right now, we only *think* we do.

We can often see this with teenagers. They may be convinced that to be accepted or cool they have to smoke cigarettes or drink or join a gang. We know they don't really have to; it is only their thinking. We can often see this with sexual predators. They are convinced they must have the object of their sexual fantasies, no matter what. We know this is not really *true;* they only think it is. We can often see it with others. We hardly ever see it with

---

[7] I am not saying it was that way for everyone; I'm not saying it would be that way now. I am only talking about myself back in 1991.

ourselves. We are absolutely convinced the way *we* see it is true or real. This is because Consciousness makes whatever we think look real—to us.

It looks as if we experience the outside world directly through our five senses. We would swear to it! We don't realize there is an intermediary between the world out there and what we sense of it or experience of it. The intermediary is our own thinking. We can never know the real world; we can only know our own thinking of it. What we see is not "reality." It is something we have, essentially, inadvertently made up. Whatever experience we have—be it a perception, a feeling, or something we would swear is real—it is really only our own thinking being picked up by our consciousness. Out of this "reality" we've made up, we then think, feel and act based on it.

Fortunately, fortunately, fortunately we are not entirely at the mercy of our own thinking. Within us we have wisdom or "innate Health." We have access to it when our minds are clear. Luckily, we don't have to think our way to wisdom. On the contrary, when the busyness of our minds quiets down, our Health and wisdom appear. This Health is more than we can ever conceive "health" to be. It includes mental health, peace of mind, natural self-esteem, deep feelings such as love, compassion and gratitude, and common sense (sense common to all). We can only lose touch with our Health by thinking ourselves away from it. Yet it is always accessible and can be unveiled or drawn out in anyone.

When people realize that through their own creative power of Thought they can either experience their Health or its opposite, they seem to gain greater equanimity. *When people realize their own freedom either to live allowing their healthy thinking process to flow through them, or to live controlled by their unhealthy thoughts, they begin to see problematic experience for what it is—something created in their minds. Thus, their problem behaviors diminish* because what drove those behaviors simply doesn't look as "real" any more. From this new psychological vantage point they then naturally and more effectively work to better themselves, improve family relationships, and affect friends and neighbors and even community in a healthy way. It is the essence of prevention from the inside-out.

When people are helped to see how the three Principles are continually creating their experience anew, when they see a new experience can and will be created with the next thought, they can rise out of situations they previously saw as insurmountable. This is because the real problem is that, inadvertently, they have used their power of Thought to limit themselves or against themselves.

This is not to say that terrible things don't happen to people. It is to say that how people *experience* what happens to them is completely dependent upon their own thinking. Because thinking can and will change, there is always hope. Because people can come to understand that as their thinking quiets down their Health or wisdom returns, there is always hope.

Conversely, the path to an unhealthy existence or dis-ease and problems is a mind full of muddied, agitated, compelling thinking, taken seriously, that accompanies low moods, highly charged emotions, or a busy mind—unless people realize these are only passing thoughts.

When people realize that life happens to them "in their heads" and not "out there" in the outside world, their life experience seems to improve.

Ultimately, change occurs within people's consciousness, which is the same as saying that change occurs as people's thinking changes. That's all there is to it. If it sounds too simple, remember, there is no limit to its depth.

A Deeper Look

What follows is an attempt to look deeper. Again, remember, it can't be figured out. The idea is just to get a sense of it, a feeling for it, an experience of it. Sydney Banks (1998) expresses it this way:

> Mind, Consciousness, and Thought are the three principles that enable us to acknowledge and respond to existence. They are the basic building blocks, and it is through these three components that all psychological mysteries are unfolded... Mind, Consciousness, and Thought are spiritual gifts that enable us to see creation and guide us through life. All three are universal constants that can never change and never be separated... All psychological functions are born from these three principles. All human behavior and social structures on earth are formed via Mind, Consciousness, and Thought. In chemistry, two or more elements create compounds. It is the same with the psychological elements... (pp.21-22).

MIND

We are blessed with Mind.

We are not talking about our own little minds here, but of Universal Mind.

Universal Mind is the supreme intelligence behind all life, the formless energy behind life itself. From it, all things spring. Mind is impossible to describe. Different people, different cultures, different religions all have different names for it—all of which carry their own meaning, to every different person—such as Spirit, The Creator, Master Mind, Allah, God, to name only a few. No matter what it is called, it is the same thing. It is the Source of life itself.

Because Universal Mind is All things, It is impossible to get away from. We are never apart from It. We only *think* we are separate. If we could truly realize this we would realize we are always safe, always protected, for there is no way to be separate from It. There is nowhere to go, there is nowhere to fall.

At the same time, each of us is merely one little teeny part of Mind, one tiny, miniscule part of the All. In one sense we are extremely insignificant; in another sense if *we* change, then what *Is*—what exists—has changed. What could be more significant than that? I have heard Sydney Banks liken it to a teardrop in the ocean. One little teardrop has no power, but if it falls into the ocean it has the power of the entire ocean. Although we are merely a part, we are never separate, no matter what we do. Any separation is an illusion.

Because Mind is the life force itself, It has not been and never will be measured by any scientific instruments. Yet most scientists do not deny its existence. One could say the human heart and other organs merely make use of the life force, and in so doing access "an intelligence...so profound that it has not yet been fully grasped by science..." (Pransky, G., 1998, p.36).

CONSCIOUSNESS

> Consciousness allows the recognition of form, form being the expression of Thought. Somewhere in the innermost recesses of our consciousness lie the answers

79

> to the questions all mankind seeks. As our consciousness descends we lose our feelings of love and understanding and experience a world of emptiness, bewilderment and despair. As our consciousness ascends, we regain purity of Thought and, in turn, regain our feelings of love and understanding... Mental health lies within the consciousness of all human beings, but it is shrouded and held prisoner by our own erroneous thoughts. This is why we must look past our contaminated thoughts to find the purity and wisdom that lies inside our own consciousness. When the wise tell us to look within they are directing us beyond intellectual analysis of personal thought to a higher order of knowledge called wisdom... Wisdom is an innate intelligence everyone possesses deep within their souls, before the contamination of the outer world of creation (Banks, 1998, pp.39-41).

Out of the formless, intelligent energy of Mind, somehow we come into form and are given the gift of Consciousness. Again, we are not talking so much about our own, little consciousness as we are of Universal Consciousness. Universal Consciousness is the force that allows us to have our own individual consciousness. Without that force, we could never be conscious of anything; we would never know anything existed. We would not even know *we* existed. Without Consciousness, we would have no experience because we would not know any experience was happening to us. Without consciousness we would not be aware of what we call "life." Without Consciousness, we could never know Mind or God. Consciousness is the only way we can have an experience of God. Consciousness is the only way we can have an experience of a cut finger. Consciousness is the only way we can have an experience of love. Consciousness is the only way we can have an experience of hate. Consciousness is our power to experience.

Our consciousness is capable of experiencing both the pure—pure spirit, so to speak, and everything it can bring us, and our consciousness is capable of experiencing misery, pain and terror, and an infinite variety of levels in between. Whether we have an experience of the pure (if that is even possible in this form), or whether we have an experience of complete separateness from Mind, or whether we are oblivious to it all, it is all Consciousness at play, neutrally taking in whatever thoughts come its way and giving them life.

Consciousness is the only way we can experience experience.

So, we can either have an experience of our spiritual essence, or we can have an experience of our ego lost in itself—or many levels in between. At any time we can be at higher or lower levels of consciousness.

Some people say, "You shouldn't say 'higher' and 'lower.' Hierarchy is no good." But as Ken Wilber (1996) masterfully points out, we can't get away from hierarchy. The people who say hierarchy is not as good as some other way are setting up their own hierarchy, one thing being better than another. What is important is, whether we like it or not, at any given moment we are closer or farther from our spiritual essence or pure Consciousness.

Another way to see this is that our consciousness is always contaminated to a certain degree by the manifestation of the third Principle: Thought. Many people, among them Transpersonal Psychologists, have delved into the mysteries of consciousness. Consciousness would forever remain a mystery were it not for its connection to Thought. Thought is the ruler of Consciousness. Thought determines the level at which our consciousness is experienced. Most philosophers and theorists of consciousness, at least those I have read (Wilber, 1997; Dennett, 1991; Searle, 1994) appear to have completely missed the relationship of Consciousness to Thought. At the other end, the physicist-philosopher of Thought, David Bohm (1994), brilliant as he is, appears to have missed the connection of Thought to Consciousness.

Thought and Consciousness are as inseparable as a light switch and light. Thought, the switch, is what turns on our consciousness, so we have an experience of the light. Without the light we would have no experience of what we turned on. Without the light switch there would be no light to experience. Without the source of electricity—akin to Mind in this metaphor—the light switch would have no power to turn on, and the light would not be experienced. All three are the critical elements through which we have any experience. Without any one of the three we would have no experience. Without Mind, we wouldn't even exist.

THOUGHT

> Thought…is the creative agent we use to direct us through life…Thought is the missing link that gives us the power to recognize the illusory separation between the spiritual world and the world of form… Thought is not reality but it is through Thought that our realities are created (Banks, 1998, pp.47-49).

The awesome gift of the power of Thought allows us to think anything we want—that is our *free will*. Thought is our creative force, the gift of creation. Every creation in the history of humankind began with Thought. We are thinking creatures. We have thoughts continually. Where many of our thoughts come from is anybody's guess. Some of our thoughts surprise the heck out of us. Others we are so used to thinking that they have become habits—habits of thinking. We probably picked up these thought-habits from what we were told and how we were treated while growing up. Now, if we listen carefully, they sound like old news that keeps reappearing.

Some of our thoughts zip by so fast we don't even notice we are thinking. No matter what we are thinking, the Universal flow of Thought allows us the ability to have whatever thoughts we have. Our consciousness then comes along (simultaneously, actually) and brings those thoughts to life, making them look "real," as if we are having a real experience. It is certainly "real" to us, but we don't realize we have inadvertently made it up with our own thinking. Like a vacuum cleaner, our consciousness sucks up whatever our thinking creates, and therefore whatever we think becomes our experience.

To illustrate this, most of us have had the experience of reading a book and suddenly realize that we just read two entire pages and have no idea what we read. This is because, but for our thoughts, the book does not exist in our consciousness. Our thoughts went elsewhere, and "elsewhere" is what we were conscious of at that moment—not the book. If we smell a flower, our experience of it—whether it is sweet or pungent or nasty—is determined by our thinking. In the heat of a fight we can be cut but not even feel it until later. Some readers seeing these words will think this concept absurd or worse; others will be so affected that life will never look the same again. The only difference is individual thoughts. In other words, for all intents and purposes, the "real world" does not exist for us except through our thoughts.

I find the best way to see this is through moods. In a low mood our job looks rotten and we wish we had another career. In a high mood our job is wonderful and we couldn't be

81

happier. And there are lots of levels in between. What's going on? Our thinking and our moods are directly tied together—they are two sides of the same coin—and whichever mood we look out of gives us a different "reality." And it changes. As our thinking changes, our "reality" changes.

This has profound significance for prevention. Most of us go about our lives believing that *our feelings and resultant actions* come from the circumstances of our lives or from conditions that affect us. Instead, *they come from our own thinking!* As George Pransky says, at every moment we are at a fork in the road: We either see our experience and our feelings coming from outside circumstances, or we see them coming from our own thoughts. If we feel depressed or angry and see those feelings coming from our circumstances, we often feel powerless. If we see the feelings coming from our own thoughts, we can at least do a little something about our own thinking. There is hope.

This suggests that some experiences (of Thought) seem healthier than others. The gift of Universal Thought is what brings us to one level of consciousness or another. The level of consciousness in which we reside at any given time is never left up to chance. It is completely dependent on how and what we think.

We can think up love, beauty, compassion and humor, and we can think up worry, bother, anger and misery. Either way we are making it up—but not on purpose. People don't realize that they are making up their own misery. If we know we're making it up, why would we be satisfied with making up misery?

To some this will sound suspiciously like "blaming the victim," or telling people to pull themselves up by their bootstraps. "Do you mean to tell me that getting beaten or getting raped is not a horrible experience that causes great harm?!" Of course it is horrible and harmful! Of course it is not the fault of the victim or survivor. But if we look closely we will see that different people experience the beating or the rape in different ways, and its effects on people's lives vary. To some it will ruin their lives, others will chalk it up to a very unfortunate experience in their pasts but not let it affect their lives, others will see it as a turning point in their lives, and a wide variety of ways in between. The only difference is their thinking. I put no value judgment on whether any particular thinking is good or bad, right or wrong. I am only saying that whatever we think about it is what we experience of it.

Again, I am *not* saying that our own thinking creates these situations. I am *not* saying that our thinking attracts such experiences to us. I *am* saying that whatever we make of these circumstances and situations—however we look upon them, think about them, feel about them, and see them—happens via our own creative power of thought.

Understanding how our thinking creates our feelings and our reactions or responses is the most empowering thing we can realize, because while we can't do anything about what thoughts pop into our heads, we can do something about what we do with them once they get there. We can take them seriously, take them to heart, take them personally, or we can ignore them. Anyone can do that—if they understand what is going on. People who believe the experience and feelings they're getting from life are coming from their own thinking have a tendency to function on a more even keel and not be thrown for a loop by what life throws at them. This is true resiliency.

Feelings As Experience

We can experience nothing that is not our own thinking.
One type of experience is our *feelings*. We think our feelings are "real" but really we get them from our thinking. They are "real" in that we thought them up and can feel them—we know this only too well—but they are not *real* in the sense that we inadvertently make them up with our thinking. If we had different thinking about a situation or a person, we would have some other feeling. This explains why a hundred people in the same situation will have a hundred different experiences. And it explains why we ourselves will have different experiences of the same thing (like our kids) at different times.

To truly see our experience is coming to us from the inside world—from our thoughts, not from reality out there—is to change everything. Why is this so significant? Because when we're upset with what someone is doing, we think it is because of what *they* are doing, when really we are upset by *our own thinking* about what they are doing. When we feel stuck about our lot in life, we are only stuck because of what we think about our lot in life. The significance is *there is nothing fixed about our thinking*. Thoughts can change, and they do, and with those changes we get an entirely new experience. *We are never stuck with the experience we are having right now. A new thought and therefore a new experience is right around the corner.*

This is most empowering! For example, if I know that if I feel stuck I am only creating it with my very own thinking, I also know, because my thinking continually changes, that I don't have to stay there. It will change with new thought.

Does this mean we can always go out of our way to think different thoughts? No! The power of Thought is too tricky to fall for that. If we try to think positive thoughts while still feeling negative, we can't fool ourselves. It means we are still thinking negative thoughts in spite of our best intentions (which of course are other thoughts but perhaps not as powerful at the moment). Instead, it is far more important simply to know we are never stuck where we are because our thinking can and will change. That is so hopeful! When sitting on our rocking chairs toward the end of our lives, many of the things that looked so important to us in the past, won't be. We'll have more perspective. All it means is our thoughts have changed. If they can change then, they can change now—if we do not take the thoughts we are having now so seriously.

Even if we use the phrase, "We create our own reality," we may not fully realize what it means or its significance. Why? Because much of our thinking is invisible to us. What we see really does *look* like reality.

A formula can be derived: *Thought + Consciousness = experience.* Or, *Thought + Consciousness = perception = "reality"* (Pransky, G., 1998, p. 42). This is where the inside-out view parts company with traditional psychology, sociology, and prevention. Most psychologists, sociologists and preventionists have found it difficult to embrace the notion that all our experience and "reality" derives from thought. To most of us it certainly looks as if external experiences cause reactions in people or cause people to think as they do. Traditional psychology, sociology and prevention are based on such "logic." Yet, as we have seen, Bowman (1997) concludes otherwise [Chapter V].

Even when some people have an experience of Health, they may not trust it. They'll call it a fluke. What makes us distrust our own Health? Our habits of thinking! We trust our old habits more than we trust our Health because we are so used to our habits. They have become the lens through which we see life. Without our habits we don't know what we'll see. To think we won't have our old habits to rely on any more can be scary (another thought). But after realizing this, we know innate wisdom resides within us, and to find it all we have to do is look in that direction and trust it will be there for us when our minds clear or become quiet enough. When our thinking becomes visible to us, we can see how it creates our lives from moment to moment.

Bringing It All Back Home

What can sound very mysterious, mystical, out of this world, from another realm, really isn't. It is as normal as everyday life.

I love to go cross-country skiing out my back door in Vermont. What I love most is seeing the bright sparkles on the snow caused by the sun. Occasionally, as I come out of the woods near a field, the sparkles turn suddenly into colors of the rainbow. This is special! One time I came over a hill around a bend to discover that the tiny rainbows had turned into extremely bright little rainbow crystals that were truly awesome. They looked like little, sparkling rainbow marbles scattered across the snow. I went to pick one up and it disappeared. I stepped to the left a few yards, and they disappeared. I stepped back where I'd been, and they were back as bright as before. I stepped to the right and they were gone again. A cloud came by and obliterated all the sparkles. At other times I have come by that same spot on a sunny day, at various times of day, and I have never seen rainbow sparkles that bright again.

Do the rainbow sparkles exist? Are they real?

We can't say for sure. All I can say with certainty is that they are real for me when I have a particular perspective. If my perspective changes, they do not exist for me any more. I then see some other reality. Sometimes I see regular, bright-white sparkles, and sometimes none at all. Whatever I see is the experience I have. There is no separating the two.

The same can be said for our thoughts. When I look out my eyes, whatever I see looks real to me. I don't realize I'm seeing whatever is out there through the filters of my own thought. I can never have a true view of the real world because my thinking is always in the way, and it changes. I can never see true "reality," because the "reality" I see changes with my next perspective, my next thought, so I can never know what it really *Is*. I can only ever see my own version of it. Yet, if I have a thought about something, it becomes real for me. I would call it "real" because it sure looks that way to me. And it *is* real—from that perspective. But it is only one of infinite perspectives. Just like the rainbow crystals in the snow, if someone were a few yards from me, s/he would not see what I do. If s/he had a similar perspective, s/he would likely see it. But it still wouldn't be "reality," it would only be our current perspective.

We get a "real" feeling from the perspective we have. In this case I had an "Oh wow!" feeling. Yet, even though we have similar perspectives, we would not have the exact same perspective. The other person might feel, "so what?" Someone else might not even notice. Someone else might think it was so gorgeous that s/he might not be able to move until it went away on its own. Which one is real? We cannot tell that any more than we can tell whether the crystals really exist at all. Yet they sure seem real to me.

What is the significance? What I feel is "real" may not be! If someone uses words toward me that many people would call "insulting," even feeling insulted is up for grabs. It is not reality that I have to feel insulted in those circumstances. No matter what words are sent my way, I would not feel insulted unless I took those words as insulting. This is different than cognitive psychology or reframing. Its practitioners would say, "Given the fact that I was insulted, how can I think of it differently so it will do me no harm?" The three Principles take us deeper. If we happened to think that the person yapping those words at us was off his rocker, for example, we might not be insulted in the first place. If we imagined the negative world this person must live in to do that, we might feel compassion. If I happened to think the person was just having a bad day so I couldn't take what he said personally, I would not feel insulted. It is only an insult if we happen to think it is.

A friend of mine—a good athlete—will not go downhill skiing because of thoughts (memories) from his past. He does go cross-country skiing and loves it, but downhill, no! This is because, years ago, when his "friends" took him skiing for the first time, after drinking a few beers they brought him up to the top of a mountain, and they took off. The last thing he heard was, "Follow us!" He wound up in the hospital with a broken leg. It happened in the past, but when the idea of downhill skiing is offered now it is as if he has a distorted lens across his eyes. The fear from his past experience is carried into the present—not that I blame him. But if my friend really understood how we function—how we all have a tendency to let fearful thoughts from our past get in our way in the present but that is really only a distorted view that we can't really trust—he would still have the thought of fear but may be able to dismiss it as simply a thought that has no basis in reality. Far less capable people have learned to ski downhill without harm—in a more common sense way. The only difference is, they don't have those thoughts.

Paul Gendreau (1996), a well-respected researcher and thinker in the corrections field, wrote an article, titled "Principles of Effective Intervention with Offenders." Within his presentation he mentioned cognition or thought as one of his "principles" of effective intervention. I humbly admit this is what I was looking for. However, he listed other principles that had nothing to do with thought. "What does that mean?" I wondered. Then it hit me. Whenever a cognitive or behavioral strategy works, it is because the offender's thinking has somehow changed. Whenever it doesn't work, it means the offender's thinking has not changed. Whenever *any* program or approach works, it means the person's thinking has changed. *Without knowing it, all of our programs are effective to the extent that they have changed participants' thinking* (in a healthy direction)! When measuring program effectiveness we really have been measuring how effectively any program is able to help change participants' thinking. But we have not known that is what we are doing! For the most part, we have been leaving it to chance.

What We See Is What We Get

Prevention and human services workers work with many people who live in circumstances they would say are detrimental to their well-being. If we look closely, however, we can see great variation in their behaviors even given very similar conditions. This would be puzzling if we did not understand the three Principles. If we look more closely we can see that people view the effect that life's conditions have on them in a variety of different ways.

Their responses might be seen on a continuum. What might we see if we looked into people's minds and saw what they make of life and its circumstances?

- Some people see themselves caught up in life, and they react. Life simply happens, and they don't give it much thought. It seems as if they act on reflex. A rapist sees a particular woman and he must have her, or he must teach her or all women a lesson, or something. Many people who cause harm to themselves and others fall into this category, such as child abusers and sex offenders and batterers. Most criminal and delinquent offenders would also be found here; those who see something they want or something they hate and just go after it without much thought. As the severity of alcoholism progresses some alcoholics would be found here, as well as many people who are mentally or emotionally disturbed.

- At a slightly higher level, some people see themselves at the mercy of the conditions in their lives. They see themselves stuck with what life has given them. Many welfare-dependent people see their lives this way, as does the teenager who thinks she needs a baby to make her life whole and meaningful.

- At a higher level, many people believe their feelings are affected by conditions in their lives. Most of us probably live at this level. At this level's low end are people in difficult marriages or difficult jobs or who see their kids as difficult. At the high end are most people who live normal, day-to-day lives, who move in and out of stress with their normal day-to-day problems.

- At a still higher level some people appear to live on a more even keel than most. They seem truly at ease with life. These people see that their feelings and actions are generated internally; in other words they know that they decide for themselves whether to be brought down. Some of these people understand that the conditions of their lives mean nothing unless their own thinking colludes to bring them down. Some of these people either largely ignore the circumstances that would bring them down, or they feel it but recover quickly. They tend not to dwell on problems. Many of these people know they don't have to take their thinking so seriously, and they certainly don't have to take personally the results of other people's thinking.

- At a higher level still are a few people who generally live in a state of grace and peace of mind. They are very wise and extremely insightful. Many of these people feel close to God. They see they have access to a deeper, transcendent wisdom that naturally guides them in healthy ways when their minds are quiet. Some of these people see more than "their thoughts create their reality"; they see that their thoughts *are* the only reality they will ever know.

People then think, feel, and act out of whichever way they see life.

What makes the difference in what level people find themselves? Only one thing: their use of their power of Thought. This is the reason people look and behave so differently in similar conditions.

Innate Health[8]

Despite the frequent use of the term "innate Health" in this book, it is not so easy to define. Inquiry into this area takes us into fascinating and deep realms. Is innate health simply the wise use of Thought? Is it Mind manifesting within? Is it the same thing as wisdom? Is it thinking from a clear mind? Is it a realization of the power of creation within? Is it an entity? What does Consciousness have to do with it?

At the outset we can say only one thing with certainty: Innate Health must be fully explained by the three Principles. If it cannot be so explained, it would be a stand-alone fourth Principle, and Banks (1998) *saw* there are only three Principles.

At the heart of this issue lies the question, "Where does Innate Health and wisdom come from?" "If Mind is the Source of All Things, and if Mind is neutral, formless energy, why is it that when our minds clear we get healthy, wise thoughts instead of evil thoughts?"

In the mid-1990s I posed this question to Syd Banks. Without batting an eye, as if it were the most obvious thing in the world, he answered, "Pure Consciousness."

I remember being startled by the answer, but it made perfect sense to me. However, at the time this was not the prevailing thinking among Psychology of Mind practitioners, because they reasoned that if Mind, Consciousness and Thought are completely neutral forces or powers or energies or elements, how could any of them also contain a property?

Yet this is part of the dual nature of life.

If Mind is All Things, it must include evil thoughts as well as our wisest thoughts. A metaphor may help: As light comes through a prism, the light breaks apart into all the colors of the rainbow. All the different colors of light are part of Mind. Yet, because Mind is All Things, Mind is also Oneness. It is One. Mind is also all the different colors of light combined; that is, pure white light. Mind is also the purest part of Itself. Take out the prism (because there cannot be a separate entity) and we have the Source being both the pure white light and all of its varying "broken up" colors. As individuals, we are "chips off the old block" of Mind, so to speak. Each of us is one little "piece" or color of the Total Source. We are both our own little "piece" of consciousness, and we are part of the Oneness in pure form. Consciousness in its purest form somehow becomes manifest in us. Banks has said our Soul and pure Consciousness are one and the same.

In human form our own "piece" of consciousness becomes contaminated—by the content of our thinking. In other words, but for our contaminated thinking we would be directly experiencing pure consciousness. We simply think ourselves away from it. Yet it is not a fixed state; it is a flowing through of the life force, so to speak, pure formless energy within us, which gets contaminated by *form*. To find it, as I heard Banks state in a September, 1999 talk in Richmond, B.C., "It is not a discovering, it is an uncovering."

It seems to me that Banks (1998) is saying that Consciousness is more than just the ability to be aware and to experience life but is itself a force that in its purest form contains *wisdom* and, if seen, will guide people well through life from within. For some reason, at least during the 1980s and 1990s many proponents of this understanding were reluctant to embrace the idea of "pure Consciousness," referring instead to something called "innate

---

[8] Most of this section was taken from Pransky, J (1999). What is Innate Health, and What does it mean to live it? One Person's View. *Communique. 11.*

health" which "results from a responsive thought process" (Pransky, G., 1998, p.133). Speaking personally, I have always subscribed to Banks's direct explanation:

> [T]he wisdom humanity seeks lies within the consciousness of all human beings, trapped and held prisoner by their own individual minds. Wisdom is not found in the world of form, nor in the remote corners of the globe. Wisdom lies within our own consciousness (Banks, 1998, p.127).

Ironically, we can only experience our purest states of consciousness through our thinking. If it were ever possible within the human form to have an experience of pure consciousness it would have to come to us via the very same power of Thought that enables us to think ourselves away from the pure. It is a paradox.

Does that mean, then, that innate Health is also a healthy thinking process? Yes. There is no separating the two. Does it mean that innate Health is also seeing the creative power of Thought within us? Yes. Does it mean also that we can experience innate Health even when we're down, so long as we know our state will change with another thought? Yes. It means all these. But how can that be? How can innate Health be pure consciousness, or wisdom unveiled, and also be the realization of the power of Thought within? Because it is a paradox! The definition of innate Health must be both.

A few years ago I had a discussion with a Christian Fundamentalist who could not accept a statement I made that we are born in an innate healthy state. Yet, he was also perplexed because he liked the other things he was hearing from me. "You've shown me that this approach works with people," he said, "and I believe that anything that works has a foundation in the Bible, but I cannot reconcile the two."

Naively I said, "Well, doesn't the Bible say that Jesus said, 'The kingdom of Heaven is within?' That's what that means to me."

He replied, "But that's only if you accept the Lord Jesus Christ as your savior."

It stopped me in my tracks. I had no response.

I woke up the next morning with absolute clarity. I realized it didn't matter! It does not matter whether we are born with innate Health or only have the capacity to achieve it at any moment with the next thought. This man could easily accept the latter, for that is how people become "born again." Beyond that, it is awfully presumptuous of me to think I know which of the two is Truth. I don't have a clue. My guess is none of us really Knows. I'm just stating a belief, and my belief is meaningless. My creative power of Thought to have any belief is what is important. What does it matter whether innate Health is inborn or simply attained when realized in the moment? Either way it comes to us via our thinking. The three principles encompass both—and all—views.

Yet, for me—and this is only my view—it gives me more hope to think innate Health or wisdom is within me already, and all I'm doing is thinking myself away from it. It gives me more hope to know my head needs only to clear to have wisdom revealed or mental health present. That gives me far more comfort than to think of innate Health or wisdom only as a capacity or a potential I might achieve or even will achieve *if* I have the right perspective on my thinking.

But that is just me. It is also the deep, unwavering knowing Roger Mills carried with him into the Modello Housing Project (Pransky, 1998), which in my view was the primary reason he was able to reach people and ultimately help them find the strength within to turn around their lives. Mills had absolute certainty they had innate Health that would appear automatically when their typical, everyday thinking calmed down and cleared. The residents felt it from him deeply. It gave them automatic hope because it was already in them. They didn't have to go looking for it. In fact, there was no "It." It was them, already! It *is* us.

In light of all this, I created my own definition of "innate Health." I share it here for whatever usefulness it may have: "Innate Health is a fundamental property of the three Principles that is an intrinsic, natural state of well-being or wisdom, arising from pure consciousness and accessed via a clear mind or from realizing the infinite capacity for formless creation of new experience via thought" (Pransky, 1999).

It seems we are better human beings in the moments we allow our innate Health to flow through us unencumbered by extraneous thinking. Some practitioners of this understanding speak of "Living the Principles." What does that mean? Here is another paradox. First, there is no way *not* to live the principles, because they are operating perfectly within us even when at our worst. But "living the principles" also implies living aligned with our innate Health, or it means living with the understanding that because we can create anything with our thinking we would be wise to live from our healthy creations—both for ourselves and others. It is wise to live from our creations that give us and others a good feeling. That is operating out of wisdom.

If terrorists operated out of their Health and wisdom it would be impossible for them to be terrorists, despite their invocation of, for example, Allah or the Koran. To intentionally kill an innocent human being is to operate out of hate, its opposite. To steal is (usually) to operate out of greed or desperation. To harm is to operate out of disregard and disrespect for fellow humans. None of this is possible when connected with our Health and wisdom. Had she understood about innate Health, it would have been impossible for that woman in Texas to drown her babies, despite hearing a voice she thought was God that told her to.

When we have our wits about us and operate from a calm, clear mind, we naturally see the Health in others. That is when we see innocence. That is when we see everyone doing her or his best.

For some reason it sometimes seems easier to see this in our clients, in housing project residents, in prison inmates, than to see it in our own colleagues. When we're aligned with our Health we treat everyone as we would like to be treated. When we are in our Health we treat others, including our colleagues, with kindness, caring, support, respect, compassion, humility, and with love, no matter how off-base we think they might be.

That's what living innate Health is really about.

Judith Sedgeman of the West Virginia University Medical School defines "innate health" in a slightly different way: "the inborn capacity of people to see things for themselves and redirect their energy and their thinking to create a different experience of life" (Sedgeman, 2000). In the end it amounts to the same thing. Either way one sees it is an equal source of hope.

There are two ways I know to be in our Health. The first is just being there—feeling good, sometimes in spite of ourselves—falling naturally into those moments indicated above. The second is being down in the dumps or angry but not taking it too seriously. Here, we have something in the back of our minds telling us, "This too shall pass"—which it will, guaranteed, even if we end up taking it to the grave. Why wait?

We can realize we don't have to be stuck in our emotions—even if we can't seem to get out of it at the moment. So long as we *know* it means nothing about who we Really are or about our lives but is just a temporary state that *will* pass once new thinking comes along, we are protected from the ravages of our petty little minds. We can use this awesome power of Thought to create such pathetic garbage for ourselves, given what it *could* create.

Why do we do this to ourselves? That seems to be the job of our little minds. At least one of its jobs is to trick us into seeing ourselves as other than who we *Really* are and make life look so serious, personal, petty, and filled with desire and want.

I have been a big fan of Bob Dylan since the early 1960s, and I used to think his music contributed to making my life happy. I now realize I was just using his music as an excuse to be happy because I was allowing my thinking to relax and forget about everything else—just be swept up in his words and the feeling his music conveyed. That's all that was going on. It was coming from within me. Some people can't stand Bob Dylan. Others feel it with classical music, others with rap, others with country, others with dance. We all pick our own excuse to have our extraneous thinking shut down and leave us with that pure connection that makes us feel good. Others do it with fishing, others with reading, others with Yoga, others with religion, and a zillion other things. We look outside of ourselves to give us an excuse to feel great, when we really are doing it to ourselves anyway.

Others think they need to get it through drugs, or from gambling, or from sex, or from porn, or from crime, or from putting down others, or from some other artificial means. They don't realize it is all there within them waiting to rise to the surface, and they wouldn't need to do any of that if they really *saw* their Health.

Some Native kids began to hang out in a mostly White residential area in Bemidji, Minnesota. They began throwing their garbage on the ground and causing enough of a ruckus that the residents became concerned. More than concerned, they wanted them out of there! Some residents harassed these Native kids. They called the police. Nothing worked. Julie Flathers, who had been trained in Health Realization, lived in the neighborhood. As I remember the story, she and her neighbor puzzled over what to do. She knew these kids had Health within them, only no one was seeing it. She and her neighbor then had the idea, "Let's bring them lemonade and cookies!" The Native kids were shocked and suspicious— at first. But when they saw the sincerity and friendliness of Julie and her neighbor, they became most appreciative. They all began to talk and make friends. Without even being asked, the Native kids started to pick up their garbage.

This is what can happen when people see Health and innocence instead of the presenting behavior. People rise to the occasion through that sight. It is another example of "what we see is what we get."

Is There a Difference Between Wisdom and Health?

Wisdom and Health, the way I mean them, are one and the same. Our Health seems to have an intelligence attached that emerges when our minds clear. It comes as an insight, popping up from out of the blue. We can't reason our way to insight. In fact, insights arise when our reasoning steps aside and gets out of the way.

Insights can occur at many different levels—from the mundane to the unfathomable. At the mundane level, any time we can't remember someone's name (but we know this person!) and wrack our brains to remember and can't, sometime later when our minds relax, suddenly the name come to us. Or we can't find our car keys and tear the house and car apart trying to find them, then we give up in disgust and suddenly remember we put them in our pocket. At a higher level we get an intuition—a feeling about something we know is right. Or we realize something we never realized before and see something new about life. At an unfathomable level we might suddenly experience an epiphany where life can never look the same, or we might suddenly *Know* Truth. No matter what the level, the same mechanism is at work.

When my friend Otto graduated from Yale and finished up a summer job by the ocean, suddenly he had no idea what to do with his life. For the first time he was no longer part of a "program." Like many of us, all his life he had jumped from school to summer job and back. His parents were in Europe and had rented out their house, so he couldn't go there. No one knew where he was, and no one cared. He was on his own, "without a home, a complete unknown…"

For lack of anything better, he took a temporary job as night watchman at the new Yale Art & Architecture building. One night he fell asleep at his post and was awakened by a student handing him a note. It said, since he was a German exchange student who spoke little English (not true) and was living in his car (true), a family associated with the school would offer him a room in their house in exchange for an occasional helping hand. He decided to take them up on it.

For two solid days Otto sat in his room, gazed out the window and ate tangerines. He pondered what to do next with his life, but came up empty.

With the bushel of tangerines devoured, at end of the second day he stepped outside. As he walked slowly along the sidewalk next to his house, in kind of a trance, he gazed down at a foot-high fence of white wire hoops. Suddenly, a thought burst through:

"Hey! Because you don't have to do anything, it means you can do *anything*!"

Tremendous relief and gratitude flowed into him. In that moment Otto realized he could define his own good work and call upon "our common endowment of curious intellect, inspiration and good-will" to create anything he wanted for himself. I have never met anyone who loves his work (and play) more than Otto.

Insights at a deep enough level change lives.

The Role of Feelings and Emotions as our Guides

What keeps people from being at the mercy of whatever thoughts come to mind?

Luckily, we have a built-in self-monitoring system, a way of knowing whether we are on or off track of our Health at any given moment: our feelings and emotions.

Banks (1988) states:

> Our feelings are the barometer of our thoughts… Our feelings are evidence of our mental well-being… Positive and loving feelings…will guide you through life…" (p.111).

Conversely, emotions such as anger, fear, insecurity, worry, anxiety, bother, resentment, grudges, jealousy, etc. are signals that guide people to recognize how far they are from their innate health or wisdom at any moment (Pransky, G., 1998).

This system is foolproof. If we're feeling agitated, the agitation is the signal we can't trust our thinking at that time. We don't want to follow it. The same holds true for anger,

91

fear, worry or any of the other emotions listed above and more. All those emotions are warning signals that tell us, "Wait! I'm feeling all riled up. I'd better be careful of my thinking right now because I can't trust it!" Our emotions are like warning lights on the dashboard of a car. They tell us, "You'd better stop what you're doing and take care of your car before something disastrous happens." All such emotions tell us the same thing: Our thinking is messing with us. We'd better slow down and take care of ourselves before something disastrous happens. We don't want to follow this faulty thinking until our emotions die down and a calmer feeling arises. This will tell us we are back on track and can trust our thinking again.

I used to get upset about what I considered great injustices and would write angry letters accordingly. If the bureaucracy did not allow someone to get help in the way I thought they should, I would get outraged, grab a paper and pen, and start writing furiously. It was okay to write the letters; it blew off steam. The mistake was sending them. They invariably got me into trouble, or they would just get the bureaucrats' backs up and nothing would be accomplished except bad feelings. Occasionally I may still get angry at what the bureaucracy does or does not do—old habits are hard to break—only now I realize my anger is serving a purpose. It is telling me my thinking is off-base. I may be right about what is wrong, but my anger is telling me I won't be effective if I act now. All feelings are good in that they all serve as signals. If I wait and let my anger subside, then if I choose to I can go in nice and calm and make my point, and it will be heard a lot better than if I had initially acted. Of course often when my thinking changes about what I'd gotten so upset about at the time it looks silly or no big deal—or maybe it does look important enough to act on but I'd better gather evidence first. That's an example of how this foolproof system works, if we realize and pay attention to it. Of course, sometimes perspective will tell me that I must take action, and how to do it constructively.

Sometimes an emotion like sadness can be very appropriate, such as in the death of a parent. Of course it is natural to feel sadness at such a time. The question becomes, "Is it serving me well?" At first, it is. Yet, do I want to be living in sorrow two years later? That would no longer be serving me well. Somewhere between the event and two years later, some line exists where it does not feel right any more. People must decide for themselves where that line is (and it can't be determined ahead of time), but people also know when they cross it—if they pay attention. Sometimes it just feels good to wallow in self-pity for a while, so long as we know it doesn't mean anything about ourselves or about life and these thoughts will change at some point when they're ready.

Thoughts Upon Thoughts

As I said, it is not our thoughts that get us into trouble. It is *our thoughts about our thoughts* that get us into trouble.

We have a thought and it means nothing. If after doing something stupid I have the thought, "I'm stupid," that thought will do me no harm. But if I then think the first thought really means something—"Whoa, maybe I really am stupid!"—that's when I get into trouble. If I didn't have that second thought that the first thought was somehow important, it would mean nothing.

What is worse is when such thoughts accumulate. Thoughts are not unlike trees being weighed down with snow. One little snowflake means nothing to a tree. Two little

92

snowflakes mean nothing. Ten little snowflakes mean nothing. One thousand little snowflakes mean nothing. Yet, at some point, enough snow accumulates to nearly cover it. If even more snow accumulates the tree becomes weighed down. It bends over with the weight. If still more heavy snow accumulates it can even crack and break. Yet it began with one little snowflake that meant nothing.

The same could be said about our thoughts. One little thought popping into our head means nothing, nor do two little thoughts or ten. At some point, however, if we don't allow those thoughts to simply melt or blow away like the snowflake, a critical mass of thoughts is reached, and it weighs us down or can break us.

Like snowflakes piling up, thoughts are insidious. They sneak up on us when we're not looking. We don't notice the thoughts building up and starting to weigh on us because the first few thoughts look so innocent and meaningless.

Summary

What is important about all this?

If we *think* our experience comes to us from the outside world, we will always look outside ourselves for answers.

If we *think* reality is what we see with our own eyes rather than being "true" only *from the level we happen to be seeing it at the moment,* we will act on that "reality."

If we don't realize that *in low or bad moods we have low-quality thoughts* and we can't trust our thinking at those times because it is giving us faulty messages, we will follow that thinking to our detriment.

If you disagree with all this, it is your thoughts coming into your consciousness and giving you an experience of disagreement. If you agree with this, it is your thoughts coming into your consciousness and giving you an experience of agreement. We can have no experience that is not *our own thinking.*

If we remember that pure Consciousness is always present within us and a direct pipeline to the oneness of Mind, and that it can only be hidden from view when contaminated by our own thinking, we would know we always have that Source to rely on. We would realize it is there *now, within* us, and we connect with it through *silence* of a quiet mind. When we do connect, it feels like *love.* We can't beat that. Thank God! Literally! That's where *gratefulness* comes in.

Inside-out prevention has as its basis Mind, Consciousness and Thought. These are its underlying Principles. These three Principles appear to unlock the secret to why people behave as they do, feel what they do, perceive as they do, and experience what they do. These Principles seem to be the essence of what is behind the human experience; in fact, these Principles appear to be what the human experience *is.* With inside-out prevention we want to get as close as possible to the essence of our own nature, and the three Principles appear to be as close as we can get.

Doesn't It All Come Down to Mind? Why Even Talk About Consciousness and Thought?

One could argue that if we are connected to Mind or Spirit or God or The Creator or Allah or whatever anyone wants to call It, we need not concern ourselves with Thought and

Consciousness. I do not dispute this. In those moments when we *are* so connected, we need nothing else, because we *see* exactly what we need to see. The problem is, I know of *no one* who is *always* connected in this way at every moment. Everyone, in moments, falls from the grace of Mind/Spirit/God/The Creator precisely because we are in human form. So yes, in those moments when we *are* truly connected with Mind, we need nothing else. But when we are not—which for most of us is most of the time—it is extraordinarily helpful to understand Thought and Consciousness.

Another difficulty is trying to help people understand the true meaning of Mind is a very difficult road. Because we can't describe the formless, in attempting to help people connect only with Mind/God/Spirit in their lives, we find ourselves resorting to rituals or techniques. We say, "pray, and here's how." We say, "meditate, and here's how." We say, "go to church" or synagogue, temple or mosque. We say, "listen to the stories of the Elders." We say, "Follow me." We say lots of things. But, the answers to finding Mind/God/Spirit do not lie in any of those. Why? Because those things are also forms in the external world, and Mind/God/Spirit can only be found within. This is not to suggest that many people haven't found a connection to Mind/God/Spirit by going through those rituals or techniques, because many have, but when it all comes down to it, they are using those as excuses or vehicles to find what is already inside them. Whatever they have done has brought them out of themselves, out of their typical thinking, and raised their consciousness to a closer experience of Mind within. Does this mean that I am putting down any of these paths? Absolutely not! *Everyone must find his or her own path with which s/he resonates.* All of the above (except "Follow me") can be wonderful, uplifting, beautiful experiences. But regardless of the path one follows, it leads to Mind, Consciousness and Thought.

Using a Form to Convey the Formless

Because no form we imperfect humans make up can ever truly convey the formless, what do we do? What form do we choose, knowing any form takes us "off the scent," so to speak?

Inside-out prevention itself is a paradox. Any attempts we make to communicate this understanding through form *must* be inadequate.

Health Realization is one such form. It is simply a name often given to the attempt to communicate this formless understanding through the purest possible form, in a way that it will be best heard when applied to prevention. As a form Health Realization has undergone many changes over the years and will likely continue to change. Why? Because as a form it is not perfect and never will be. Each evolution has attempted to get closer to its essence.

I remember at an annual conference in 1997 or 1998, at the end of a very eloquent talk about the then-latest evolution in this understanding, George Pransky said something like, "We'll probably look back on this sometime in the future and say, 'What could we have been thinking?'" I remember this clearly because at the time I couldn't imagine how it could evolve further. Within six months the way practitioners communicated this understanding underwent probably its most dramatic change [see Chapter VIII].

Figure 5
INNATE HEALTH

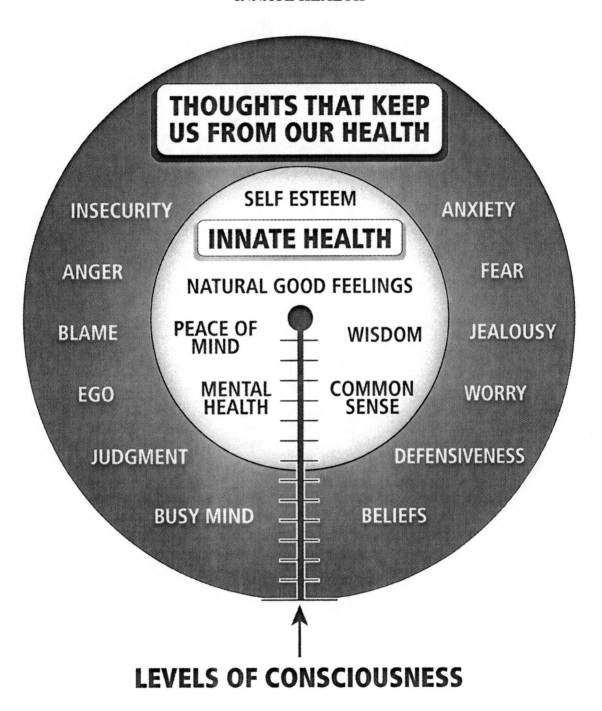

VII. KRISTEN

Interview with Kristen Mansheim. When I first met Kristen she looked mighty grim, tough as nails, impenetrable, her face hard as a rock. Everything about her looked hard. She never smiled. Today Kristen is soft and sweet. She has undergone a massive transformation. She had been addicted to alcohol and pills, and today she is free—not "recovering," but recovered and free. I have tremendous respect for Kristen. Unlike Helen, it took Kristen years, but the change is no less impressive. I interviewed her at her home in San Jose, California in May, 2001.

JP: What were you like before you discovered this understanding?

KM: I was working at a drug and alcohol treatment center for women, a very large facility. I had a huge caseload. I was overwhelmed, and personally I was functional in my life but not very happy. I felt like everybody else lived kind of up here [raises hand], and they would drop down if something really bad happened—a death, or a huge disappointment—they'd get sad for a while, and then they'd come back up. But I knew I wasn't like that. I thought I was somehow organically different, in that I was mostly down here [lowers hand], unless something really good happened outside of me—like if I met someone, got a new job, got a new car or something. Then I'd go back down again. And after struggling with being down for a long time—after working on myself, after reading 1500 self-help books and trying everything—I decided that the best I could do was accept that I was different than other people, that my home base was sort of down, and if that's the way God made me, I would just have to accept that that would be my lot in life.

JP: So you weren't happy.

KM: No. I would have temporary happiness, but it was always contingent.

JP: Did you know why?

KM: I would read books or I would go to therapy or I would go to support groups, and they would all say, "This is why you're unhappy." And by the time I looked at everybody's opinions about why I wasn't happy, I was studying so much unhappiness it's no wonder I wasn't happy. That's all I was looking at! But it seemed no matter how earnestly I considered that, I would be more informed about why I didn't feel better, but it didn't help me get out of it. So I had a lingering feeling that perhaps I wasn't getting to the bottom of why I was feeling bad.

JP: Can you give an idea of what your life had been like before this time?

KM: Well, as far back as I can remember, I thought I wasn't good enough, and I didn't know why. My strategy for dealing with that was to hope nobody noticed, and try to convince them by overcompensating, overachieving, being on the honor roll in school, getting involved in a lot of activities, trying to get outside acknowledgment. People would tell my parents how pretty I was, how brilliant I was, how gifted I was, how smart I was, but no matter how much people told me that, I had the feeling that if they really knew, they wouldn't say all those nice things. So now I had everybody fooled and I had all this tension around being found out.

Anyway, I got accepted to every college I applied to, and I didn't feel comfortable going to any of them. I just didn't have that kind of confidence or security to go out on my own. So I started working and went to a junior college and stayed in school and moved out on my own and just felt resigned.

And I found that by drinking I could get a break from all that. So on the weekends I would go out with my friends and get really drunk. And I didn't think that was a problem because I was the least drunk of all my friends. They would get so much more intoxicated that I'd end up taking care of them. I was the one who would clean everybody up and make sure they got home. But I couldn't get free of the alcohol—that would be the place where I could get a little break. It felt like the one thing I did *for me.*

As I got older my body started to hurt physically. I had been in a dance academy when I was young, so I had some physical issues. The older I got, the more physical pain I had, so I would go to the doctor and they would give me pain pills. I would drink on the weekends and take the pills sporadically during the week. I was not doing it in a way big enough to really catch much attention, but feeling more and more as time went by that if I didn't have those things I was in trouble. I knew more and more that I needed those things to be okay, and that made me feel even worse. Now not only was I not good enough, but I couldn't even be in the world without this help. I was in therapy, and I showed up one day at the therapy session, and it had been two days since I had taken anything, but I was still kind of really groggy and just out of it—

JP: What drugs are we talking about here?

KM: Opiates. Pain medication. I showed up at this therapy session, and she took one look at me and knew I was out of whack. And she said, "You really need help with this." And I said, "I can't give up the pills because my body hurts too much!" And she said, "Well, don't make any decisions about what you can or can't do." And she also said something really neat. She said, "Don't label yourself as anything. Don't make any permanent decisions about anything. Just go to this center and have an assessment and talk to these people. These people understand about chronic physical pain and they can help you with that. But they can help you do it without drugs."

JP: How long were you on these pills at this point?

KM: I went into treatment when I was twenty-two. I didn't get medication until after I was out of high school. But the alcohol started when I was—well, on occasion I used to sneak drinks at a very young age, about eight or so, but I started really drinking when I was a teenager. And again, the people that I'm checked in with at this hospital, their substance abuse was so much more exaggerated than mine that they kind of laughed at me. They thought I was cute. At that point I had the sense that if I let it get fully out of control, that would be one more example of how I couldn't do anything right, so I kept kind of a tight lid on it. But I was getting that feeling like, "I need it." I would make sure I had a couple pills in my purse everywhere I went, even if I didn't take them, just so I had them. And I would look forward to the weekends when I could drink. The physical piece was one thing, but the psychological insecurity was driving the whole thing.

So I had this assessment, and they said, "You need to check in." And I said, "That's crap! I'm not checking in. That's too big of a commitment." I mean, it scared me, really frightened me, because they wanted to take away from me the thing that I thought was helping me make it through each day or each week. So they called in the big guns, and this doctor shows up and he says, "So why don't you want to come in?" And I said, "Well I just don't think I'm ready. I need to think about this." And he looked at me out of the corner of his eye and said, "You know, you're the kind that'll probably go try everything else first, and then you'll be back," And he got up and walked out. I was so angry! Somehow I had the sense that he was onto me, and I really wanted to kind of stay in control. That was the thing I was holding onto, the idea of control, to compensate for all that insecurity. I didn't like that he saw me so clearly—somehow that made me feel like he knew, he had control and I didn't. I left the office in defiance and went home and called a friend and just started crying hysterically, "I don't know what to do. I'm a mess!" And she said, "It kind of sounds like you need a place where you can just sort of fall apart and chill out for a while and figure out how to feel better." And I thought, "Well, that's what this place is. Why am I not doing it? Life's got to be better *than this*." So I checked in.

That was actually a really great time, the five weeks or so that I was there. I felt better there than I had felt all my life. I had people teaching me how to deal with my body, and there were a lot of really fun people there, and I connected with people, and it was the first time I came out of my own head and was more connected to other people than to my own insecurity. I had this tremendous relief, but I was frightened to go home. And they made a big deal out of going home: That's when you have all this risk for relapse, and they have all kinds of labels for what I was going through and who I was now. Somehow, even though I had joined that recovery culture—where you label yourself as an addict or an alcoholic and do all this work on yourself and go to meetings—in the back of my head I still had those words from that therapist: "Just go see what makes sense, and don't identify with any one thing."

JP: How long were in that world?

KM: After I got out of treatment I went home and I crashed and burned. I mean I got swept right back into my head and was horribly depressed. I tried to work. I got a job, and I went to work for two days—and every break I got, and at lunchtime, I went out and slept in my car. I could not stay present. A couple of days later I walked into the human resource department and just quit.

JP: What year?

KM: 1990. And I ran to that doctor and said, "I can't function anymore. I can't work." He put me on disability. I was on disability for eleven months. Most of that eleven months I didn't get out of bed. It was a big deal if I could get up and do one thing. I would get up and go to therapy and come home and go back to bed. I would just lay in the bed and stare at the ceiling, lost in thought. I didn't know anything. I just knew I couldn't move. And the therapist I was still with at the time was very anti-medication. She wanted me to look at my past, look at my family, so I followed her recommendations for a long time, and after eleven months I still couldn't function. Eleven months sober and I was feeling worse and worse. So I went back to this doctor and said, "I don't know what I'm going to do because I can't function, and my disability is going to run out. I think I need to apply for SSI"—which is Federal disability. It's a more permanent disability status, meaning you'll probably need subsidy for a while, or forever. He said, "I think you should try to work before you do that. If you go on permanent disability that's going to be on your record for the rest of your life, and that may impact the way you want to live your life." And I'm really grateful that he said that. So I did.

99

I decided that I was just suffering too much, so I wanted to go check out medication. And at the time medication was still pretty controversial in the recovery community. "Don't take nothing, no matter what" was the attitude. I was very proud that I was off all pain medication and managing my physical issues holistically. But I kept getting that nagging feeling. "There's got to be something more to life. It's got to get better than this." So I went to another addiction medicine doctor who was a psychiatrist. He put me on Prozac. I had mixed feelings about taking a medication for depression, but it helped me. I could get out of bed. I could go to work. I could maintain a conversation with people. Before, even talking to anybody was too much effort. I remember driving over the Santa Cruz Mountains one day, and all of a sudden the trees were green. They had not looked green to me before. And I was relieved that I was depressed because at least I knew what it was now. People were giving me names for my problems, telling me, "It's because you have a chemical imbalance." In kind of a backwards way it got my confidence up that it wasn't my fault. I had so much insecurity that everything I did was an obvious symptom of my own inadequacy, and I couldn't do anything right, so to get these diagnoses in a way was kind of a relief.

But my body was still hurting and I was doing the best I could holistically, so I went to another doctor, and he said, "You have chronic fatigue syndrome." Again, another diagnosis, and initially, relief. I thought, "Maybe it's not me. I just have these things." So now I have this disease of addiction, and I have this disease of depression, and I have this disease of chronic fatigue syndrome, and it's not my fault. That took a lot of pressure off me.

I decided I would pursue my first love, psychology. I got a job working in a treatment center, and I got a degree in Behavioral Sciences with advanced certifications in addictions studies. I was still taking depression medications to help me, and it made a big difference. I could function. I could hold down a job. I could be consistent. But medications have side-effects and I suffered with those, and over time the medications became less effective as my body got used to them. So the doses would go up. At one point I got to a high enough dose on Prozac that I got really flat. While meds can take you out of depression, high doses can take you out of other feelings too. Then my dose had to go up again. All of a sudden I was angry. Finally I got so angry I wanted to run someone over with the car. I called the psychiatrist and said, "I wanted to run somebody over with the car today. I don't think that's good." At that point the dose was high enough on the Prozac that it would keep me up during the day, but I couldn't sleep at night, so then I had to take another medication for that—

JP: What year are we at now?

KM: Oh, 1993. So they switched me to a different medication. I was still reading self-help books, and I was going to support group meetings and getting more and more dissatisfied. It seemed like my whole life was working on myself, with this nagging feeling that it wasn't going to quite get me there, and that if I stopped all this working on myself, I was going to sink right back down. It was as if all the alcohol and the pills were replaced by this intensive work on myself, and I still wasn't happy.

JP: Were you still on pain medication?

KM: No. I was "clean and sober." I was taking medication for depression and high doses of antivirals for chronic fatigue syndrome. I got promoted to a position as counselor, and my job was to help the women on my caseload understand that recovery was hard, and they had a long road ahead of them. I couldn't understand why when they left treatment, they would get loaded again and come back. So I would tell them again, "Recovery *is* really hard and you need to work really hard on yourself, and we all have to do that." I was definitely in the popular recovery world, but it bothered me inside that over the years the same women that had previously received treatment returned again. I was discouraged. I saw they weren't happy either. I knew that I was only just a little bit ahead of

100

them. They were very hopeful about what I could offer them, because I wasn't relapsing. To them that was a big deal. But I wasn't happy. And I had been trained in a way of helping people with chemical dependency that was very confrontive, very in-your-face, so I was that way with them—

JP: I'll bet you liked that, too.

KM: I did and I didn't. I mean, that was what I learned, to be hard on people, confront them, break those walls down and get through to them. The training was that the disease of addiction is extremely powerful and the only way you're going to help people is to break through all that—really nail people. By then we were experiencing more and more women coming into treatment from the criminal justice system, and these women were even tougher and more manipulative. We learned techniques to get through all that criminal thinking. I proceeded to just get tougher and tougher. I prided myself on being a real bitch on wheels. And the more my clients disliked me the more I thought I was doing a good job. Nobody was going to get over on me! But inside I was not happy. I knew my clients weren't happy. And I just thought, "This is life. It's hard." And I watched my colleagues in the field and would sometimes hear things like, "So and so's back again," and people would sigh, "Oh, she's a tough one. Well, she never really worked the program, she doesn't work on herself, she needs to work her steps, she needs to go to meetings." But I was going to meetings and working on myself and I wasn't happy. I felt like we were blaming the clients for something that they were coming to us for help with, and underneath, it just didn't sit right.

So I don't know why but it occurred to me if we were still using the computers made in the 1970s, that wouldn't make sense. Technology evolves. Why is it that we're using therapies that aren't evolving? Why are we using therapies that are 40, 50, 100 years old with people? What's new out there? I decided to start looking around. I started going through the training catalogues, thinking there's got to be something else, and I went to a number of different things and dabbled in them, and then I went to a Health Realization training in the fall of 1994.

JP: How did you run into it?

KM: What happened was that, Bob Garner, who is the Director of the [Santa Clara] County Department of Alcohol and Drug Services, had encountered Health Realization. I was working for a private non-profit agency that contracted with the County to provide services. I loved what I did, but I was miserable. [laughs] So Bob Garner liked Health Realization, and he brought Mark Howard and Joe Bailey in. He thought, "Let me do a half-day orientation, and people can get a little feel for it and see if they want to sign up for this four-day training."

Some of my colleagues went to that orientation—I didn't go—and when they came back they were violently opposed to it. They trashed it because they listened through all their beliefs about addiction. I mean, one of the really important things for the recovery community is this idea of a power greater than yourself, something bigger than you are. We used to say things like, "Your best thinking got you here. Your best thinking got you loaded." So you didn't want to trust yourself. You didn't want to trust your own thinking. You didn't want to trust your head. You wanted to trust something bigger than you. So it was really important that you were connected to some kind of spiritual power bigger than you, and you could define that however you wanted, but it had to be more than just you. So my colleagues listened to the idea that people had Health in them and they could trust it and it came from within you—they listened to that idea through the lens of, "You can't trust yourself. You have to trust something bigger than you, or you're going to get loaded and die!" I mean, they had such a negative reaction to this overview, they felt like it was really dangerous for recovering people. And I can understand that, because we did lose clients. Clients would come in for treatment, and they'd leave and relapse and die. And when you're working around that, you start to

101

gather a lot of pressure in your own thinking about getting people well before they kill themselves, either directly or indirectly.

Anyway, I wasn't going to go to this training because I heard so many bad things about it, and the people who had mentored me and trained me thought this was the worst thing they had ever heard. Bob Garner had sent around this glowing, supportive letter introducing it, and I looked at it and I thought, "That's unusual." But couple of days before the training this clinical supervisor for the County came to our agency—Annette Graff. We had our meeting with her, and she was on her way out the door, and she said, "Oh, are you going to the four-day training?" And I said, "No. I heard really bad things about it and I'm not going to go." She said something like, "That's surprising to me. I've been involved with it for a while, and I've seen things from this approach that I never would have believed. I've seen people who are literally still under the influence sit on the edge of their seat, wanting to understand what this is, and I've seen people get well." And it wasn't so much what she said, but it was the way she said it. I didn't feel pressure to go, it was more like hope. I heard hope, and I got curious. So I said, "Well, can you still get me in?" She said, "Absolutely." So I went.

It was a huge training with about 150 of us, and Joe Bailey had come in from out of town and was teaching with Mark Howard, and the two of them had never taught together before. They did this four-day course. And I remember the first day, they spent the whole first morning from 8:30 until noon talking about how to listen. I don't know what they were doing, but in my mind at that time they were doing something to us. I didn't know what they were doing, but I knew I felt excited. They were going to tell us something, I had that feeling. And I just wanted them to get on with it. I was tired of hearing about listening. I felt like, "I got it already. Tell me what this is!" And the feeling that the two of them were in I had never been around anything like that. They were so light that I got giddy. I got high just being around them. And I thought I knew what they meant by listening, and I wanted them to just tell me what it was so I could listen to that, but in retrospect I realize I didn't hear anything. I wasn't listening to the piece about listening. But I knew I was excited. I loved what they said, and I wanted to be around them. I got such a good feeling those four days—that feeling changed my life.

I came back from those four days and I ran into my executive director after the training—because I would go to the training and I would go back to check on my caseload after hours—and she said, "What is with you?" And I said, "I feel like I've been on retreat!" Keep in mind though, because I didn't know how to listen I also heard everything Mark and Joe said through my own lens, which was the whole recovery culture, but I didn't hear anything that conflicted. I heard things that were the same, but the feeling was better, and I knew I just wanted to be around this. So there were maybe four or five of us that would meet every once in a while to read Joe's book, or watch a tape, or somehow try to keep what we'd learned alive. And pretty soon Bob Garner brought Roger [Mills] down to do more training. He sent out a flyer to everybody who had gone to the training that said, "If you'd like to stay involved in this, Dr. Roger Mills is going to come into the County and we'd like to get a nucleus of people together who'd like to stay connected to this."

So I went to that, and Roger started using us as facilitators for his training. I was willing to do anything that they wanted me to do. I just wanted to learn more. And everybody I met that was connected to this was in this feeling, and I wanted to be around them because I had never felt like that before in my life. I knew when I got around them it rubbed off on me, but I couldn't sustain that on my own. I couldn't maintain that feeling when I was away from them, so I just wanted to be around them. Thank God for Roger, because he wouldn't settle for that. He would not let that be okay. He would challenge us and talk about how the feeling didn't come from us being together. He would say it came from me, and I didn't understand that. And he would say things that at that point I didn't agree with. Roger would put it right out there. He said things that were very contradictory to what I believed in terms of keeping myself clean and sober and in recovery, and even though he said things I thought weren't true, and that he didn't understand addiction, I didn't care because I just wanted that feeling. So the feeling really hooked me.

So I followed Health Realization trainings everywhere. Anywhere Roger was going to be, I showed up. I didn't care if I was invited or not. I worked overtime like you wouldn't believe, just to be able to take time off. I used vacation time, anything. Later, Roger offered an advanced class and I didn't know how I was going to get the money to do it, but the money came through. I knew I didn't know how to live this, but I knew I wanted to. And because I wanted so badly to understand I would argue with Roger and Mark. I told Mark Howard he didn't understand women's issues, and I told Roger he wasn't an alcoholic so he didn't understand that. And the two of them were so patient with me, because I argued from my intellect about everything. But underneath I knew there was something that was true, and I wanted to understand it. Roger was the first person that told me, "Inside, you're not different than anybody else. You're just like everybody else, except for your thinking—except for the way you think." I thought I was different. I thought I had a chemical imbalance; I have these diseases. So I argued with him. But I wanted him to be right.

Roger would talk about Thought, and I didn't hear "Thought," I heard "thinking." So I would work on my thinking. For a year and a half I put everything I heard into my intellect, and I *worked* on my thinking, because that was what I knew. You work on yourself. Roger would talk about the difference between cognitive psychology and Psychology of Mind, and I didn't get that. In my own defense I see why I didn't connect to it, because one of the things that I felt, and what I've seen with other people who suffer with depression, is that sometimes thinking can be so heavy that it manifests itself physically—that's where there's a real disconnect. I was at one time so cut off from myself that I couldn't see myself thinking; all I knew was my feelings. It was like there was a wall. I didn't see myself as a thinker, creating. It was like fuzz. It was numb. I was not at all aware that I created a constant stream of thought. I just couldn't see Thought. So all I knew to do was to try to think right, try to think positive—I didn't see all the insecure thought that I created. I just saw myself trying to correct my thinking.

After a year and a half of doing that I was exhausted. I was so profoundly tired that I could hardly move. But it wasn't the same kind of lethargy that I had had with depression. I didn't feel hopeless. I didn't feel lost. I just felt tired. And right about that point Roger nailed me on my thinking about being "depressed." I asserted that I had chemical imbalance and did not have mental health the way other people did. I felt that this "innate health" concept was a great idea and if people could believe it it would be wonderful, and maybe people could talk themselves into it, but I did not have Health the way other people did. And he looked at me and said, "Why would you be any different than anybody else?" He nailed me. I don't know what happened, but I started sobbing in front of everybody. I just broke down crying. I don't know exactly what the catalyst was but right at that point, about a year and a half, I just felt too tired to work on my thinking any more. I didn't have it in me, so I finally let go. After a year and a half of being told, "You're okay, you have Health just like everybody else does, it will take care of you, you can trust it, if you start to understand the way you function and how your mind works, you'll be okay," I finally trusted it. Sometimes I felt a lot of fear that I was going to get horribly depressed again, that I was going to drink again. I mean, I just had all these fears—but somehow, eventually, I let them go. I started to see them as thoughts I created too. And I'm grateful that I was physically tired because I just didn't have it in me to do all that mental work. Actually, honestly, for a while I was so tired that I had to have people drive me places. I could not physically sit and hold still for more than fifteen minutes. If I drove for twenty minutes I was asleep at the wheel. I could not hold still without going to sleep. That's how tired I was.

JP: Were you still taking the medications at this time?

KM: Yeah. I was still taking medication for depression. And after I started to shift I slept for about six months. I would go to work and come home and sleep. I slept twelve to fourteen hours a day. I was absolutely wiped out, but for the first time I wasn't worried about being in bed. It wasn't the same kind of tired. I felt physically tired instead of mentally tired. So I rested. I knew to rest, no matter what anyone thought. People were worried about me. Cathy [Casey] was worried about me. Cathy was in the advanced class, and we didn't know each other very well. I had been a little insecure, because I saw other people getting healthier much faster than I did. Their moods were better. They had that feeling that I talked about, that Joe and Mark and Roger had, and I didn't have that feeling yet. And Roger was using them to teach, and he was taking them to Hawaii and all over. I was working and sleeping and working and sleeping, and I got a little insecure about that. But then all of a sudden *I started to see myself creating insecurity*. It was like the window opened and I started to see Thought. I saw the function of Thought, and how it created all the insecure things I thought *all day long*.

JP: Do you know what made you see that?

KM: I don't know exactly what it was, except I had been around this long enough and heard it, and I trusted the feeling of people I was around. I didn't always trust what they said, but there was something irrefutable about that feeling. So I started to get glimmers of my own thinking, and then I got curious about my thinking, and I started to see how much insecure thought I had. And at that point I did a lot of looking at the content of my own thinking, which is not something I encourage people to do, but that's what I did. And that was the proof for me. When I started to see what I thought all day long, I could see why I was so depressed. I saw why I thought I was never good enough, because all day long I thought I wasn't good enough.

JP: When you see what you're doing to yourself with your own thinking, that's helpful.

KM: Yeah, that's what I saw. It helped me tremendously, and that built up my faith that every emotion that I had was my own thinking. I used to think my thoughts and feelings were two separate animals. I thought my thoughts came from my head and my feelings came from my heart, and there was a world in between the two, and a lot of times there was a huge discrepancy between what I felt and what I thought. Now I know what that is—it's what people would call mixed feelings. Mixed feelings come from mixed thinking, and I had mixed thinking, and I didn't know that. So when I started to get those glimmers of how I created this feeling for myself all the time I went to Roger and I said, "I think I'm getting worse, because I'm making this insecurity all the time." And he laughed. He said, "You're not getting worse. You're just finally seeing what you've always been doing. It's always been there. You're just seeing it now." And I said, "Well what do I do? I don't want to think like this." And he said, "You don't do anything. Your own Health will take care of it. The fact that you see it is all." At that point I trusted him so much that I said, "Okay."

I remember one day that old feeling of depression came back. I started to go down, and I started to get scared. I thought, "Oh, God, here we go. It's coming back! Maybe it really is a chemical thing or a seasonal thing." But in the back of my mind I heard Roger saying, "You're just going into a low mood. Don't worry about it. Don't try to figure it out. Just try to relax and your Health will come back." And I thought, "I don't think he really understands, but I'm going to try this shit. I'm going to try what he says, and I'm going to see, I'm going to try leaving it alone and we'll see if it passes." So I got ready for a three-day depression where you don't get out of bed, you don't go out of the house, you don't go to work, you're down. I got in the bed and I got books and I got magazines, and I got food, and all the cats and the remote controls, and I was going to bunk down. I got ready for the big one. I watched some TV and read a book for about three hours. And all of a sudden I thought, "Well, I'm bored. I think I'll get up," and that was it. It was done! And I didn't even realize it was done until I was already up doing the dishes, which used to be a huge thing for me, even to do dishes. And I thought, "Oh, shit," and that was it! I tested it and it was true. It wasn't just something people were saying. It was the truth that we all function this way. This *is* how it works! It's just a matter of fact. And from that point, I took off.

JP: So where are we now?

KM: Maybe 1996 or 1997. We were still following Roger around, facilitating, and Bob was designing the training of trainers program, and I think Roger saw promise in me. So even though I kind of didn't connect as quickly as other people, he saw that I would connect eventually. He knew that the earnestness was there, that I really wanted to see it, even though I debated with him so long. So, then we started the training programs, got certified and started speaking. For a while, Roger would have me go in and talk to people about depression, addiction and alcoholism, and just tell my own personal story. That was kind of awkward because I never planned to be speaking in front of groups. I thought I would be a counselor in this rehab center until I died, I guess. I never saw myself being in front of the public, teaching, talking to the drug court, or a medical center. I didn't plan for any of this. In fact, ever since I really connected with this I don't think I've planned anything in life.

JP: So, when did you give up your medication?

KM: I don't remember, 1997 or 1998, somewhere in there. Actually, looking back, I think I could have gotten off of it sooner, but there was something I didn't understand. I didn't understand that as I stopped creating all this agony for myself that my chemistry would change—that my chemistry was coming from how I created my life through Thought. It was just the residue of my thinking in my body. I started to get some side-effects from my medication, and I didn't understand that as your own body begins to heal chemically you don't need as much of the medication, so you experience more side effects and less benefit. I was experiencing more side-effects, like my mouth was so dry I could hardly speak. When I told my psychiatrist that, he said, "Well, sometimes this happens after a period of years on a certain medication, so what we do is we change you to a different one." So I switched to a different drug, and actually I think what was happening to me was my own Health was coming up and I didn't know that. Eventually I started asking my psychiatrist. He said, "I think there's an integral connection between the mind and the body, and I don't know if you can separate them." So when I said, "I'm doing pretty well, what do you think about my medication?" he said, "Would you like to try lowering the dose?" And so we started kind of stepping it down, and I would leave it there for six months, then I would step down again and leave that there for four months, and step down, and eventually I just got off it.

JP: How did you feel when you finally broke free?

KM: I was a little frightened because I'd had so much thinking all of my life about needing something to be okay. I had that belief ingrained and didn't see it as Thought very deeply. I didn't know I had a belief about that. There was so much medical information given to me about chemical imbalances and reoccurrence and recidivism that it looked really factual to me that it might be more than my thinking. When I actually got off the medication, I had normal ups and downs like everybody else, but as soon as I saw them for what they were, they would shift.

JP: [laughs]. It's amazing how that works.

KM: And I've just never had a problem with it since. It felt like such a natural process. I didn't get attached to, "Oh, I have to get off these medicines." I made a kind of peace with medications. I just let it be okay that I needed to be on them, and when I didn't need them anymore I got off them with the help of my doctor.

JP: When did you start speaking at the annual conference?

KM: In San Jose. That was the first one. I was on a panel, and I just talked for maybe fifteen minutes.

JP: You were incredible!

KM: I was so inspired. I was helping myself, I was helping the clients.

JP: Not too long after that I think, or just before it, we first met at George [Pransky]'s, at his "rigor" session—and you still looked like a real hard-ass to me.

KM: It took time for me. I've seen some people jump! Like Cathy, when she heard the Principles, that was it! Day one! But it took me time. It just took time for me to see it, but I was slowly changing, and I was different with my clients in spite of myself.

JP: How were you different?

KM: Well, the thing that stayed with me first was the idea that *people have Health in them*, I think because that was so profound for me personally. Then, that *we created our life*. At that point we didn't talk as much about the Principles, we talked more about Thought. So I would talk about Thought, and at first I did more of a memorized, canned thing, and that didn't go over very well with my clients, so I dropped that. But *I remembered that if they had Health in them I wanted to look for it*. Even though I didn't realize it, I was hanging out with my clients more, whereas before it was more working on them. And early on I was still big into accountability and responsibility and all of that, but at least I was connecting to them, where before I was very disconnected.

[This interview continues in Chapter XVI, page 239, where Kristen talks about alcohol and drug abuse treatment using this approach—then it returns.]

JP: Do you see this as magic—how you got better, how others get better?

KM: Well, it's like it's magic, but it's science. It's like a magical science. By science I mean there are very specific laws that we now understand that can predict cause and effect. When people understand these laws, really feel them, it changes them in an amazing way that always still surprises me, even now. I had never before seen transformation like I've seen in myself or in my clients. It doesn't surprise me, but then again it does. I still kind of marvel at it every time.

JP: Do you remember at that next annual conference, when you spoke about rapture?

KM: Yeah. Rapture. It's just an amazing thing that somebody has gone to sleep inside, and then— [pauses, long silence]

JP: When you talked about rapture, it was one of the most moving things I've experienced.

KM: I remember not being able to find the right words for the feeling, and going through a thesaurus looking for the right word. And I found "rapture." I was so hesitant to use that word because it sounded Biblical, or it sounded weird. But it was the right word. [grabs a dictionary] This wasn't the dictionary I had, but it's still close. [reads] "Ecstatic joy or delight, expression of ecstatic delight, a feeling, especially in religious ecstasy of being transported to another place or sphere in existence." That's close.

JP: Did you feel that within yourself?

KM: Uh huh. I did. I would have moments of that. That's the place I had found in myself. I wouldn't say I was there every moment of every day, but for the most part, the world that I'm in is so light. I'm happy. And then I have these deep moments that just feel like they don't even belong to me. But in that feeling I feel so free, and I had never had that. I was surprised that my clients knew what that was. They would talk to me about, "Kristen, that's a natural high," and I just didn't know that. I mean, in my life I felt like I had gone to sleep or been in pain, that when you come out of that it's just an amazing thing. And to not only have that for yourself, but to watch that happen to other people. It looks like their soul wakes up again, and I know your soul is always there, but I don't know any other words for that. It's just, people come back! And I've seen that all the way now from people in jail, to people in drug treatment, to people diagnosed with catatonic schizophrenia—people who come back. I've even seen executives come back! [laughs] I guess it would be like—I've never had a baby or seen a baby being born, but you know when you talk to somebody who has witnessed a delivery, it's as if there are no words for it, except that it's an amazing, amazing thing. That's the only thing I know that might come close.

[This interview continues in Chapter XIV, page 217, where Kristen talks about her experiences in applying Health Realization at the Mariposa Lodge, a residential substance abuse treatment facility.].

VIII. THE EVOLUTION OF HEALTH REALIZATION

Health Realization is two things simultaneously: 1) the understanding of the three Principles [Chapter VI]; 2) and an approach to help people live more in well-being through seeing the three Principles in action in their lives [Chapter XIII].

Where did it come from?

The evolution of Health Realization began one day in 1973 or 1974 when an ordinary man had an extraordinary experience. Out of nowhere, Sydney Banks experienced a monumental spiritual epiphany.

Some people want to say this understanding evolved from some other philosophy or from a consolidation of other work. It did not. In that moment, for some unknown reason, Banks saw how all his problems were created from his own thinking. In fact, he realized this was true for all human beings. Over the following few days he came to *see* the spiritual basis for all psychological functioning and human behavior.

At least he claims to have seen this. None of us can ever really *know* because we are not inside him. All we know from eyewitnesses is that he went from being an insecure, troubled person to a peaceful, happy person. All we know is that when he began to talk with others about what he realized, those who *heard* began to change in a similar way. While most people who had known him before viewed him with ridicule, a number of others began to gather on SaltSpring Island, British Columbia to listen to him, and their lives began to improve dramatically. At some point Banks realized what he had seen could be helpful to humanity, and he decided to dedicate his life to sharing this understanding. Word began to spread.[9]

Sydney Banks spoke in very spiritual terms, and people began to come to SaltSpring Island from all over the world to listen to him—he didn't even know how they heard about him. For some reason he knew this understanding would be best conveyed in psychological terms and primarily through the world of psychology. A number of psychologists showed up to listen. In 1976, two of them, George Pransky and Roger Mills, heard something from which they could not turn away. Mills was the principle investigator under a National Institute of Mental Health grant through the University of Oregon to uncover intervention strategies that worked (Mills, 1996). He had hired Pransky to work with him on part of the project. After meeting Banks and being quite impressed with the well-being displayed by the people who had been touched by him, Mills and Pransky began to shift their work to study

---

[9] As I write this, Sydney Banks is writing the story of his experience. I don't yet know what the book will be titled, but it will be published through Lone Pine Publishing.

what makes mentally healthy people healthy. They began to work with Banks, then on their own, to attempt to turn his teachings into a new psychology.

Its use as a new, inside-out approach to prevention began in 1987, when Roger Mills applied the understanding in the low-income Modello housing project and achieved dramatic results. The story of how this effort unfolded from beginning to end is documented in the book, *Modello: A Story of Hope for the Inner-city and Beyond* (Pransky, 1998)—which I would recommend as a companion volume to this book. Later, Mills began to call the approach "Health Realization."

Communicating the Understanding

This inside-out understanding of how our experience of life is created through the interplay of *the three Principles* somehow must be communicated to others if their lives are to improve as a result. As I've said, it is not so easy to communicate formless understanding through some form; as a result, the communication of it has undergone a number of evolutions. Each evolution over the years has been an attempt to communicate it more precisely and more powerfully.

Initially when attempts were made to communicate this understanding to others, it had no structure. People whose own lives had been touched, such as Mills and Pransky, simply tried to convey their own good feeling and point people inside themselves for answers. To their surprise, their clients got better faster than they had through the traditional approaches they had learned and used previously.

George Pransky introduced this understanding to his colleague Dr. Keith Blevens, and Mills, Blevens & Pransky (1978) wrote the first papers introducing this new psychology to the world. These papers reported what its authors called "a breakthrough for the field of mental health...that we feel will fundamentally alter the manner in which psychology looks at change in individuals..." (p.1).

> We have discovered a deeper, more profound pattern that connects a person's individual thought process to their external reality... The key new dimension that provides a missing link to understanding change is what we are now calling "wisdom," defined as having or showing insight, intuition or common sense which does not emerge from a "figuring out" but from clarity or a perceptiveness that arises a state of creativity from which totally new understandings emerge (p.1).

The authors said that wisdom was linked to "formless emotional energy" that allowed people to focus their attention beyond the details of their behaviors, symptoms or emotions. They claimed this "higher order of wisdom" appears automatically when people "move out of their subjective reality." They called this a "second order frame of reference" from which people experience high self-esteem, a deeper common sense about life, and feelings of well-being about their future. In a "first order frame of reference" people literally are caught in their beliefs and emotions, and they are essentially prisoners of their own individual way of seeing, interpreting and judging life events. Once a person glimpses the power and accessibility of this second order, he or she experiences more energy, lightness, and confidence, which can be experienced at higher and deeper levels. The authors asserted that every individual is capable of living from the second order; in fact, people appear to gravitate toward it. The authors asserted that the "first and second order frames of reference" operate within each of us "to create our experience of life." They made the bold statement that psychology had been "looking in the wrong direction to attempt to understand change," instead of toward the dimension of "wisdom," which they said provides the missing link to understanding change in people (Mills, Blevens & Pransky, 1978).

Blevens telephoned his old college roommate, Dr. Enrique Suarez, to tell him what they'd discovered. Suarez, in turn, invited Mills to join him in opening the Advanced Human Studies Institute near Miami, Florida and co-author the book *Sanity, Insanity, and Common Sense* (Suarez & Mills, 1981; Suarez, Mills & Stewart, 1987). In an attempt to give structure to this understanding, Suarez conceptualized what he called "four psychological principles,"[10] which appeared in that book. The book stated that they "recognized and uncovered a deeper set of principles about the Mind that determines our experiences and behaviors as human beings" (p.i) that "will change psychology to become a more exact science" (pp. 31-32). According to these authors, "Psychology of Mind," as it had come to be called (or "NeoCognitive Therapy"), clarified how individuals and groups "become 'stuck' within the confines of problem-oriented ways of seeing reality without knowing that they are experiencing the end product of their thinking" (p.271).

In a review of the first version of *Sanity, Insanity, and Common Sense*, in an early issue of the *Journal of Primary Prevention*, well-respected community psychologist Donald Klein brought this understanding to the attention of the mental health field and prevention academics. He stated:

> I know from my own experience that the volume offers insights and wisdom which, once clearly seen, have the power to transform the individual reader and ultimately the field of mental health... Its authors hold out the possibility of going beyond theoretical formulation, setting aside preconceptions about origins of psychological distress, and transcending explanations of psychopathology that are rooted in external events, early upbringing, and life stress... What psychologists generally fail to grasp is the key underlying fact that the mind interposes its beliefs, perceptions, concepts, and expectations between each of us as experiencer and that which is being experienced. Therefore, the only sure way to improved mental health...is to help ourselves and others know that mind-created reality is illusory and that it is possible to move beyond the realm of belief to see and to celebrate the basic fact of experience itself (Klein, 1981, p. 203)

Klein articulated what he called "a central message" of Psychology of Mind: that insecurity itself was "merely an illusory made-up thought created from our own minds" that "obscures the deeper, more natural consciousness of the person." Further, "consciousness or experience of being—unimpaired by insecurity—is always accompanied by clarity of perception and natural good feelings" (p.203). He offered this observation:

> We all know that major breakthroughs in any field occur when some creative explorer cuts through complex, detailed, and often conflicting explanations in order to come up with a clear, simple description which, in effect, sweeps away much that has gone before. Not surprisingly, such discoveries are rarely welcomed by those

---

[10] These so-called "four principles" were later abandoned with a deeper understanding of what "Principles" really means—Chapter VI [See Appendix D for more detail]

who have been thoroughly immersed in refining, applying, or teaching the earlier explanations. In the past, images of self-importance have been tied up with propositions about the rotation of planets around the sun or the ability of humans to circumnavigate the earth. It would not be surprising to find that the mental health field too, will put up a considerable struggle to maintain its complicated status quo of methods and beliefs in the face of this simple revolutionary clarification. (p.204)... I know from my own experience that what this book has to say is true. It is grounded not in belief or theory but rather in direct experience and empirical observation. Once seen, the fact is apparent and the implications thereof are far reaching. Before it is seen however the fact is as elusive as quicksilver (p.205).

As I suggested, attempting to convey formless understanding is anything but an exact science. As a result its evolutionary road has been a bit rocky. For example, a deeper understanding revealed that the early conceptualization of "four principles" was off-base; instead, *three Principles* were the basis for this understanding. Later, six, then five "concepts" were introduced in an attempt to clarify what the three Principles meant, but these proved (in hindsight) to muddy the waters. It has only been since around 1999 that the articulation of this understanding has been based solely on *the three Principles*: Mind, Consciousness and Thought. [Note: More detail about its evolution is not particularly relevant for this book—that is, for understanding and applying Health Realization as an inside-out prevention model. However, interested readers can refer to Appendix D].

It could be argued that only since the late 1980s did Health Realization (and formerly Psychology of Mind) become reasonably formalized as a discipline, and only since 1999 did it begin to operate solely out of the essence (the three Principles) it purported to talk about. Thus, truly it is still a new approach. Even in its old concept-based form, in the world of treatment and psychotherapy, only since 1990 did a set of audiotapes formally define the practice of Psychology of Mind as a therapy (Pransky, 1990; 1994). Even in its old form, only since 1990 was it introduced formally as a therapeutic approach to the substance abuse treatment field (Bailey, 1990). Only since 1987 did Mills collaborate with others to present Psychology of Mind theory, in peer-reviewed journals, to the education and academic prevention worlds (Peck, Law & Mills, 1987; Mills, Dunham & Alpert, 1988). Not until 1990 did Mills report on his pilot project in the Modello housing project which showed the first impressive results on the efficacy of Health Realization as a community prevention-intervention strategy. Also, only since 1990 was Health Realization (under the name, "Neocognitive Therapy") first introduced to the criminal justice field (Kelley). Only since 1994, was it introduced to the field of social work (Polsfuss). Only since 1991 was it formally introduced to prevention practitioners (Benard & Lorio; Pransky).

Since then, in 1995, Health Realization was cited as a model approach by the Center for Substance Abuse Prevention (CSAP) Division of Community Prevention and Training, Training and Evaluation Branch, after consultation with a national "expert" panel, in its *Background Report for the Development of CSAP's Prevention 2001 Curriculum, Chapter III-12 and III-22.*

In September, 2000, the ***West Virginia University School of Medicine*** opened the ***Sydney Banks Institute for Innate Health*** (www.sbiih.org) under the leadership of Judith Sedgeman, to thoroughly research and promulgate this understanding [see Chapter XIV]. After more than two decades of attempts to create a form through which to adequately communicate it, this inside-out approach finally had gained acceptance by an established, presitigious institution. It is my prediction that this understanding and approach is now poised for acceptance by the fields in question. It is only a matter of time.

Finally, as of 2002 people can hear Sydney Banks directly by visiting his website: www.sydneybanks.org.

Despite a bumpy road, along the way thousands of people have been helped to find new, healthy lives for themselves. In my view, proponents of all incarnations of this understanding should be commended for being aware, forthright and flexible enough to abandon their created forms that did not prove as productive as they could be. It is not so easy to create something from nothing. Imagine trying to create an entirely new psychology based on someone else's spiritual epiphany, as George Pransky, Roger Mills, then Ric Suarez tried to do. But the "form" is not what matters. *Results* are what matters!

Health Realization, or whatever it has been called in the past or whatever it is called now or in the future,[11] has continually deepened its own understanding of how to communicate the three Principles. Through it all, Roger Mills and Elsie Spittle (2001) and others have continued to experiment with various models (forms) to learn how to best help low-income communities empower and revitalize themselves through Health Realization. George Pransky, Chip Chipman, Robert Kausen and others have taken this understanding into the world of business to affect changes in companies. Cathy Casey and others have taken this approach into prisons with very impressive results. It has been taken into substance abuse treatment centers [Chapter XVI]. It has been taken into a skid row drop in center (*Applications: Health Realization/POM in the Community* videotape, 2000). It has been applied in parenting (Pransky, 2001) and in schools (Pransky & Carpenos, 2000). This understanding and approach seems to be able to be applied generically with consistently impressive results.

We now examine these results [Chapters X and XII, plus all interviews in this book], and explore its practical application to achieve further results [XIII–XV].

---

[11] I, personally, refer to this understanding and approach as "Health Realization" because this term has begun to be recognized within the prevention field.

Jack Pransky

IX. ELSIE

Interview with Elsie Spittle. *As Elsie Spittle states in her new book, The Wisdom Within (Mills & Spittle, 2001), "Ken [her husband] and I had known Syd [Banks] prior to his profound discovery about the nature of Mind, and we initially found it extremely difficult to accept the incredible change that occurred in Syd. That a man with minimal education and no psychological training could have an insight so transcendent that he could describe the relationship between Mind, Consciousness and Thought with absolute certainty was beyond our understanding. I became quite indignant whenever he would make such statements—I had no idea that this discovery had anything of value to the world." Eventually Elsie came to see a bit of what he had discovered, and it changed her life. She began to work with Roger Mills in his community prevention efforts, then became an excellent inside-out community prevention worker on her own. Today Elsie is a deep and powerful conveyor of this understanding who has touched many lives. I interviewed her at her home in Long Beach, California in May, 2001.*

JP: What were you like before you ran into this understanding.

ES: [laughs] Oh, this is wicked! I was really a pretty unhappy person. I liked to blame other people for my problems, and so I lived in a lot of blame. I lived in a lot of dissatisfaction. I lived in a lot of neediness, wanting more, wishing I had more, and it didn't happen. I came from a religious background and I thought prayer would be helpful, so I would have this kind of wishful prayer that I would use on Sundays to see if that might help change my life, and that didn't work very well either.

JP: Well it did work; it just happened later than you thought.

ES: [laughs] A lot later! Many, many years later. So that's what I was like, I was generally discontented and didn't think there was any way out of it. I thought that's just what life was like, because, frankly, that was the environment I was brought up in. That was how my family was, and it looked pretty normal, but I didn't like that normality.

JP: Were you married at the time?

ES: Yes. I had been married for eleven years. I got married when I was almost eighteen.

JP: Could you characterize the reaction you had when you first heard this understanding?

ES: My first reaction was disbelief—disbelief that we created our experience. Then came anger.

115

JP: Anger? Why?

ES: Well, when I think back now—I mean, then I didn't know; I just felt angry and I didn't know why—angry because I thought it was nonsense; I was just hearing nonsense.

JP: What happened to change that?

ES: I had an insight about my anger, that *my anger was being created by the way I was thinking*. And that was really the start of my journey, where I realized, via insight, that it was an inside-out process that was creating my anger. You understand, when I was first introduced to the Principles, I had a lot of fear and resistance.

JP: Why do you think it scared you?

ES: Because it was the truth, and the message was pointing me to the fact that *we create our own experience*. If I bought into that, I would have to look at the fact that my life was a mess because of the way I was thinking and how I was living, and I didn't want to look at that. It was much easier, I thought, to blame—to blame my husband, to blame the children because they weren't behaving in the way I thought they should, to blame circumstances, the environment I'd been brought up in. It was much easier to blame everyone and everything else than to look at the truth, and that's what scared me. That's what really scared me.

JP: So how come you didn't run in the other direction?

ES: Where could I go?

JP: [laughs] Do you remember what you felt after your insight?

ES: I felt *such* relief. With the spontaneous release of the anger, I felt like there really *is* something to life, you know? There really is something to this understanding of how the Principles work to create our experience of life. And the overwhelming feeling I had was of relief.

JP: So from the point you had that insight, what started to happen to you?

ES: I started to listen more to my family. I started to listen more to myself, to the wisdom. I started to be more aware of my negativity and not go there—be wiser and not go in that same direction because I didn't like the feeling. When I'd experienced that spontaneous feeling of joy and relief, it was very strong and it lasted for a while, and I loved that feeling. So after that if I would start to go down in my levels of understanding and feel negative again, I wasn't so quick to move there. I had more perspective. And that affected my relationship with Ken, where I didn't take things that he said to me so personally. It affected my relationship with the children, where I didn't think they were doing things *to* me—I just recognized their innocence more. So I guess I was nicer to be around. I wasn't so judgmental. I wasn't so mean. I wasn't so critical, you know? I was gentler with the family, and with myself. And of course from time to time I moved back into the old habits, but they just weren't as strong and wouldn't last as long.

JP: Did anything different start happening since you started catching on to the understanding?

ES: For one thing, physically I saw the world different.

JP: Physically?

ES: Physically I *saw* the world, you know? The reality was brighter, the colors were more vivid, there was more dimension to the trees. I recall that distinctly on a drive through the countryside. It used to be just flat. Everything was flat in my world, and there was color but it was flat color. Truly it was like there was another dimension. The colors were deeper and richer. It was like filters were taken off my eyes. And the colors in the forest, there was another dimension to them. I could see another dimension to the trees. It wasn't just green. There were different kinds of green, and new green, that's the only way I can describe it. There was a different dimension of depth to the world I saw now.

And I saw people differently too. No matter what they were presenting to me. This wasn't all the time, but there were periods of time where I saw beyond what they were presenting to me, and I wouldn't get hooked by it—with my family, my siblings or my parents. Life was not always a good thing for them. Life was not a blessing. Life was a struggle. And I began to see that with compassion. I began to see them with compassion and with more love, so I wouldn't get hooked into their reality, into the way they saw life. Sometimes I still did, but at least this new level of understanding shifted that so it wasn't constant, where I lived there with them. That was kind of the before and after picture. That's what life looked like to me all the time. Now it no longer looked like that to me. Occasionally it still might, but even with those occasional times—and initially, there were longer periods of time where I would get hooked again, and I'd think, "Ain't it awful?" But even with that, this little voice would be saying inside me, "You know that's not so. You know there's something else now." But I may not have enough understanding at that moment to move out of it.

JP: As you began to have your own understanding evolve, do you remember any particular moments along the way when you remember being totally blown away by an insight of yours?

ES: More recently. I can't pin anything down over the years. They've just melded into a general understanding. To me, what was a watershed was moving back toward the Principles after realizing that "the core concepts" were taking us further away from the essence of this understanding. And when we were invited to work as part of the faculty with the Aquanimitas Foundation, there was a shift there—moving back to the Principles for the Foundation's programs—that was a real profound watershed for me, because it gently forced me to go deeper, myself. Although I'd been feeling that we were losing the power of this message by moving into the core concepts, I still didn't have a real deep feeling for the Principles yet. I didn't feel that I could talk about Mind and I would skirt the issue. And Consciousness was kind of a blur to me; it didn't mean much.

But however long ago it was, two or two and a half years, something like that, that was really powerful to me to move into the Principles, and my life has not been the same since then. It moved me more deeply into seeing the simplicity of how the Principles create our experience of reality, and how *we are the Principles in action all the time*. Before, I still was feeling that it was something that we applied—yeah, yeah, we're part of it, but we apply it or we practice it. I didn't have the feeling that we are the Principles in action. I never felt that so clearly as when I moved in that direction to be able to share it with others. And at that time, when I was given the opportunity to do the Foundation's program in Hawaii, and I knew the focus was on the Principles, I had substantial thinking about, "Can I do this? How can we possibly talk two and a half days on the Principles?" But I also welcomed the opportunity. It was a risk, I felt, that I might be left out there with nothing to say, but at the same time, I welcomed the risk. I wanted to go deeper. I just really, intuitively, wanted to go deeper.

JP: Do you know why?

117

ES: It was just a feeling I had. I felt I'd come to the cusp of what I knew then, and I just had this very strong feeling that I wanted something deeper inside, that there was more, you know? And I didn't know what it was. So it was moving into the unknown, and it was exciting at the same time—it was a little unnerving. And when I actually did the training with Rita [Shuford] and Chris [Heath], it was intoxicating as I heard what came out. New things came out of me—questions that were asked that I'd never answered before. Deep questions that had me reflective in the moment but answers came out and surprised me.

JP: Do you remember any of those?

ES: Well, there was a question that came out about duality.

JP: What was the question?

ES: What is duality? [laughs] Something like that. And Chris said, "You take it." [laughs]. And I thought, "Hmm, that's interesting. What on earth could I say about duality?" And I don't know what I said at that moment, but what pops into my head now was the duality of inside and outside, and at some point you see that duality is really One. And that, to me, was the whole essence of seeing "I am the Principles. We are the Principles." And in that, there is no duality. There's a duality when you "practice the Principles," then there's duality. That never had occurred to me before. I wouldn't even touch that. I would have passed that on to Rita. But I welcomed that question, because it allowed me to go deeper. And since that time I feel like I've been unleashed, so to speak. And I just continue to see the Principles deeper all the time, and I know that it's ongoing, but I see them simpler—the trainings I do are simpler, the feeling is stronger, I find the questions I get from people are deeper, they're a different quality of questions, and there are fewer questions. People are much more comfortable in just enjoying the feeling, where they don't question, "Well, is that all there is?" Because before, I'd say, "It's just the feeling." It's almost like I don't even have to say that, because the feeling is so deep, they go so deep, they intuitively know it. The audience becomes such a part of this connection of the Principles operating amongst everybody, that we enjoy it together instead of any one person being the trainer or facilitator. There's a real connection that happens, I find.

JP: I've noticed that myself. It's incredible.

ES: Isn't that remarkable!

JP: It's funny, I was always trying to teach that way, whereas it seemed most of the teachers were in "speaking" mode. I was always trying to teach by group give-and-take discussion, but I don't think I had the depth, originally, to be able to pull it off as well as I wanted. Now it just kind of flows, and I love that.

ES: What a gift! [whispers] What a gift.

JP: I remember the moment when you realized the connection to soul. We were sitting in an Aequanimitas Foundation faculty meeting, and you came in the next morning, and you talked about what you'd seen. Do you remember that at all?

ES: I do remember. I do remember. I saw more that Soul and Consciousness were the same. Because I'd been seeing Consciousness as something separate, as more of a capacity that allowed us to experience life. But all of a sudden that was more surface. I saw what was underneath that, at a much deeper level, and that was a lovely, lovely thing to see.

JP: When did you start to get the idea that you could actually be of some help to people with this understanding and actually do it for your work?

ES: As I started getting out there more on my own I just knew it was what I wanted to do, and I didn't know how to do it other than to do what I was doing. I'd volunteer my time and attend things. Then somebody might say, "Would you like to do something," and word just gradually spread. I tried to do something with a colleague in Vancouver to actually get into the colleges and offer programs, like continuing ed', or programs for adults that would come in the evening and wanted to learn something at college—kind of self-awareness programs. And I went to every college in Vancouver and submitted a brief program outline, and I got rejected, rejected, rejected. I did that a lot. I just put it out wherever I could. I would visit the administrator at the hospital and say, "This is something that I think would be of benefit to your staff and to the patients, and would you be interested in the program?" I did an enormous amount of cold calls in those days, and got turned down. And then finally, out of the blue, came an opportunity to move to Miami and to do work there with some psychologists, including Roger Mills, who had started a clinic there.

JP: So what year are we talking about here?

ES: That was 1984. So after due consideration and discussion with Ken and the family, we decided to do that. It was an opportunity to do this work in a way that I'd never had the opportunity before. And at the same time, a business client also had been introduced to this understanding and wanted this in his business. And he contacted my business partner and said, "Would you come and do a seminar for our executives?" And they enjoyed it so much that they invited him to move as well with his family. And because we were partners, he and I ended up working in that company together for about five years.

JP: Who was that?

ES: That was Reese Coppage's company, Duval-Bibb. They were our first business client, to that depth. We'd done a couple of other things with some other business clients, but it didn't take. With Reese it took. He had that deep commitment.

JP: Who was your business partner?

ES: Chip Chipman. So he and his family and Ken and our family moved at the same time to Miami. And I ended up working with the institute in Miami part-time and working with Duval-Bibb part-time. It was the first time that I actually got paid for doing that.

JP: So how did that feel?

ES: It felt wonderful. I remember Chip and I doing some work at Orlando for Reese's company, and that was the first company they wanted us to work with. And I remember he and I walking down the hallway almost skipping with delight, like "Here we are! This is our first client of any note, and here we are, going to do interviews and going to do training, *and* we're getting *paid*!" We were pinching ourselves, the two of us, because Chip, at that period of time when I was making all these cold calls to the colleges, he was doing the same thing. He was working and doing his best to implement his understanding in the company he was working for. So for the both of us it was an absolute delight that we could do this above-board, really go for it, that's what they were bringing us in for! It was absolutely intoxicating to do that.

JP: So when did you have your first opportunity to do community work with this understanding?

ES: When I was in Tampa. We moved to Tampa from Miami about a year-and-a-half later because we were doing more work then with Reese and his company, and other companies in Tampa were coming into the picture. Finally Reese said, "Why don't you just move here? It's cheaper than flying you back and forth and putting you up in lodging." And so we did. We decided that was the way to go. It felt right to us.

We moved to Tampa and ended up joining forces with Sandy Krot, who had a small clinic there. We became the business arm and offered leadership trainings and other programs. I became president of the Florida Center, and out of the blue—I know what it was, Jack—I had heard the Modello residents talk at the annual conference in St. Petersburg: Lloyd [Fields] and Cynthia [Stennis]and several of the other people. I was so taken with them, so struck by what they shared, by their presence, that I thought, "Hmm, I want to know these people." And then shortly after that came an opportunity with the Florida Center, to do some training in a disadvantaged community in Tampa. And, as luck would have it, nobody on our staff had the time to take it, and somebody on the staff, Sandy or Chip, said, "Well, Elsie, you're free right now. Why don't you take it on?" And I thought, "Well, I don't really know anything about communities, but what the hey." And so I went and met this community and put something together, and I picked Roger's brain, and I talked to Lloyd and Cynthia, and I thought, "Hey, this is really neat," and I did some training there, I think a six or eight-week program.

[Elsie goes on to describe the various community projects she has been involved with, which can be found in Chapter XIV, page 210]

JP: What's the most amazing thing to you about the Principles, from your own personal understanding?

ES: That we *are* the principles.

JP: Can you say more about that?

ES: Because I don't have any place else to look. No matter what is going on in my life, I always come back to me—the big Me and the little me, the universal Me and the personal me. I see that they are in partnership within me. And the more I see that, the personal is getting less and less and the universal is more and more. And what I see, then, is that my life unfolds. I'm so much more comfortable with life unfolding, that life is unfolding for me in a way that, personally, I was never able to experience before. I felt I still had to do much more planning and making things happen than I do now. And it's not like I sit back and don't do anything. I fan the flame. If somebody calls or says something like, "At some point we'd like to have you come," I will follow up on that. I won't wait for them to call me twice. I'll fan that flame, but I don't go out as such and try to market myself anymore. I just find my life unfolding so much gentler and easier and productively than I ever thought possible. That's what it means to me. That's what's awesome to me.

JP: Beautiful! And since the audience for this book is largely a prevention audience that doesn't know that much about the Principles—I mean I'm obviously attempting to describe them in this book—but could you say more what you mean by the "universal," as opposed to the personal?

ES: I see the "universal Me" in terms of being in partnership with this invisible power and wisdom that I'm made up of, that my soul is directly connected to. That's the "universal Me." The "personal me" is more the manifestation of my thinking.

JP: That's great. So one is the very power that you have to think anything—

ES: That's right.

JP: And the other is the result of the thinking, the manifestation of how we've used that power to create what we see of ourselves—

ES: That's right, yeah.

JP: Is there anything else that you haven't said that you would really like to say?

ES: I think the blessing of knowing that people are innately healthy, that under all the many disguises we use to hide this core of Health, there is this core of wisdom—that in itself has helped me enormously, you know? Whether people recognize the Principles or not, if they move toward recognizing that people do have wisdom inherent in them, and we don't have to fix anybody: What a relief! What a gift.

JP: How do you know that? What's your proof that you have Health and wisdom?

ES: Because when I look to that in people, it comes out. [laughs] That's the evidence to me! No matter what—no matter what language barriers are in place, no matter what cultures are in place, if you look to that, that's what comes out.

X. WHAT EVIDENCE EXISTS THAT INSIDE-OUT APROACHES ARE EFFECTIVE?

Most evidence on the effectiveness of inside-out prevention comes from Health Realization.[12] Most of this evidence, as of this writing, does not meet rigorous scientific standards. Does this mean Health Realization or inside-out approaches should not be considered effective prevention? It does not mean that at all.

First, abundant research evidence suggests that Health Realization shows great promise for improving behaviors. Secondly, I have never seen an approach where so much anecdotal evidence exists of major changes in people's lives as a result of exposure to it. The interviews in this book are examples, and these represent only a minute fraction of the thousands of people around the world whose lives have permanently changed for the better as a result of insights from exposure to this understanding—and the numbers continue to grow. If both types of evidence did not exist I would not be writing this book.

For those interested, this chapter presents all the available research evidence I could find. The reader will draw his or her own conclusions about whether it is enough.

It is important to remember that, unfortunately, we have the capability to measure only the *forms* representing this inside-out understanding. We are stuck with research measuring only the various incarnations of Health Realization, Psychology of Mind or Neo-Cognitive psychotherapy as they existed over the years. The earlier forms, in particular, contained explanations of the understanding that, in a sense, did not directly present or talk directly about *the three Principles*; instead, its practitioners generally pointed in that direction but talked around them—at least that is my interpretation—and, thus, these forms left something to be desired. We can say only that the research is measuring the form, the interpretation, the best its developers could imagine at the time, not the actual, pure inside-out understanding. Nonetheless, studies of even these earlier forms still showed promising results.

A book about prevention is not the place to examine effectiveness studies of psychotherapy based on this approach; however, for those interested I provide brief summaries of these in Appendix A. Here it will suffice to say that, although this was not stringent scientific research and many of the studies have design flaws, Psychology of Mind or Neo-Cognitive Therapy was found to show statistically significant effects on treatment with the following populations: chemically dependent adolescents in a residential facility (Minneapolis Institute of Mental Health, 1984); outpatients with symptoms of depression, anxiety, adjustment problems and chemical dependency (Suarez, 1985); outpatients with

---

[12] Some research evidence exists on the effectiveness of Transcendental Meditation; the question is whether Transcendental Meditation meets the criteria of an inside-out approach, as defined by this book.

anxiety, depression, relationship problems, child abuse, eating disorders, and alcohol abuse (Shuford & Crystal, 1988); outpatients with depression, anxiety or distress (Shuford, 1988); outpatients with anxiety and adjustment disorders (Blevens, Bailey, Olson, & Mills, 1992); outpatients with major depression, anxiety disorder, adjustment disorder, and substance abuse (Bailey, Blevens, & Heath, 1988); and prisoners (Epperson, 1993 in Mills, 1996). Two separate case studies also showed positive effects with sexual abusers in treatment (Crystal, 1988) and with paranoid schizophrenics (Ringold, 1992).

Results for Prevention and Education using Health Realization

Treatment or therapy is one thing; what about its use for prevention?

The first inkling that this inside-out approach might be effective as a preventive application came from the Looking Glass Youth and Family Services "Families in Transition" project in Eugene, Oregon. Its staff had been using a traditional approach, namely, providing information about life transitions and associated problems, teaching coping skills, and providing family counseling, parent education classes, and self-help support. The next school year, after the staff received training in the approach "based on the principles articulated by Suarez and Mills," the staff completely revised their program. In essence, this meant a focus on helping students "understand how insecure thought creates negative feelings and behaviors." This produced a significant change in program effect. Many student participants "developed a new level of security and maturity." Many of the more volatile students became significantly calmer. A school counselor at the middle school stated, "The Looking Glass group helped these kids look at life in a totally new way. Their attitudes became more positive and they began to feel in control of their lives. I wish we could have offered the group to every student" (Krot, 1983, p.207).

Next came findings from a private remedial reading clinic. Darlene Stewart (1988) measured the effect of feelings and emotions on reading achievement with students who self-referred or were referred because of low reading achievement. Most were delayed approximately two years behind grade level; the group was a mix of age, sex, IQ, and ethnic background. In this study 20 students were randomly selected for an experimental group and 20 for a control (comparison) group. The intervention consisted of 30 individual reading sessions of 40 minutes in length, almost daily for six weeks. All eight teachers used a variety of instructional methods, with no standardization of instructional materials. The experimental group's teacher had far less experience in teaching reading than any of the comparison group teachers. The only difference between experimental and comparison groups was that the seven comparison group teachers began their instruction immediately when the class session began, and the experimental teacher delayed interaction until the student was in a receptive frame of mind. In other words, if the student was in good spirits, the lesson was taught right away, but if the student was in low spirits or distracted the teacher waited from 5 to 20 minutes to teach the lesson—until the student's spirits rose. Sometimes if the student was hopelessly distracted they did not have a lesson at all that day. When this occurred, this teacher would simply try to elevate the child's mood level. This was the only difference between the two groups.

Results showed that the experimental group gained 14 months in reading level, compared with 7 months for the comparison group. Pre- and post-measures on the Gates MacGinitie Reading Achievement test showed a mean for vocabulary of 1.6 for the experimental group, and 0.45 for the combined comparison group, and for reading comprehension a mean of 1.4 for the experimental group and 0.7 for the comparison group. In other words, reading achievement doubled. Stewart's conclusion was that affective states affect learning potential, and learning is accelerated when students and teachers approach the learning process with positive, functional, stress-free states of mind. She suggested that training teachers to work with affect appears even more important than knowledge of instructional techniques. What does this have to do with an inside-out approach? It is one of the essential initial "steps" of an inside-out approach [See Chapter XIII]. Darlene Stewart approached her students this way because of her training in Psychology of Mind.

Roger Mills began to adapt this approach as a community prevention strategy in 1987 (later he began calling it "Health Realization"). He initially tested it in the low-income Modello and Homestead Gardens housing projects, in Dade County, Florida, which were replete with substance abuse, drug gangs, and violence (Mills, 1990). Results of this project, reported by Pransky, Mills, Sedgeman & Blevens (1997), indicated that for the 150 families and 650 youth served by the program in the two housing projects, after three years, households selling or using drugs dropped from 65% to less than 20%; the overall crime rate, which had been endemic, decreased by 70%-80%; the teen pregnancy rate dropped from 50+% to 10%; school dropout rates dropped from 60% to 10%; child abuse and neglect, which was endemic, decreased by 70+%; households on public assistance went from 65% to negligible; and the parent unemployment rate dropped from 85% to 35%.

I chronicled in detail the lives of seven of these residents for my book, *Modello* (Pransky, 1998), the story of how Health Realization changed their lives. One resident was a severe alcoholic who was severely abused by her boyfriend on crack and she was abusing her kids. She ended up stopping her alcohol dependency without going through treatment, completely turned her life around and ended her own physical abuse and the abuse of her kids. Another was a crack addict and violent woman who, through Health Realization, came to see enough worth in her life to go into treatment and completely change her life. Another was an extremely withdrawn mother of the project's main drug dealers and of a daughter so severely addicted to crack that she was prostituting herself to support her habit—her weight had dropped to 80 lbs—but through her new insights she helped her daughter break her addiction, and she became president of the project residents' council. Another was a suicidal woman with no self-confidence, welfare-dependent, continually being put down by her partner, who through her insights ended up living in well-being, which led her to get her G.E.D. and then to a good job in which she flourished. Another was a teenage drug dealer whose life changed to such an extent that he began a crime watch to keep out all drug dealers, graduated from high school (he had been failing and truant) and went on to college. Two other women who had been beating their children stopped that abuse and developed wonderful relationships with their children. These were merely a few examples of the changes in people's lives that occurred through their gaining understanding Health Realization.

Further, once a critical mass of residents saw their lives from this new, higher perspective, they began to work with the police to successfully drive the drug dealers, who once dealt on every entryway of the project, from their community. They worked with the schools to improve their relationships and connection with them. And they worked with the Housing Authority and on their own to improve their community and make it a much safer place, given that there used to be shootings almost every night. The residents had formerly viewed all these people and institutions as their enemies.

In his own study of this project, Mills (1990; 1991) reported, "At the end of the first year, dysfunctional school behavior, as measured by discipline referrals and suspensions, expulsions, drug-related incidents and referrals to the juvenile justice system had dropped by almost 75%. These decreases were sustained in Year Two and have been sustained through the third year of the program." Pre- and post-tests for 17 students involved in the first year of the program indicated that the number who reported doing well in school doubled, and 100% reported that they no longer skipped school. By the end of the third year only one student from Modello was failing at the middle school, and the student expulsion rate dropped to zero. In addition, 7 parents completed a Health Realization parenting Training of Trainers Internship Program and assisted 68 other families. Police reported that shootings and drug trafficking in Modello had decreased to such an extent that the Modello project was no longer considered a significant problem. Of 28 students who were assisted by the program social worker during the first six months, 30% raised their overall grade point average by at least one full grade, and the number of students who received failing grades (Ds and Fs) dropped from 63% to 46% in the second quarter, and to 40% in the third quarter—a decrease of 23%. Decreases were sustained in years two and three.

Attempts were then made to replicate this approach in other areas. The first occurred in Aurora, Colorado through the Mid–Continent Regional Educational Library Health Realization Youth and Community Empowerment Project. The West Middle School catchment area had a large population of low-income, minority students. Evaluation data showed that after the program began student suspension rates declined in both 1990-1991 and the 1991-1992 school years. Among the 30 students who participated, grades improved, absences decreased, and fewer discipline referrals were reported than for nonparticipating students. Teachers participating in the Health Realization training in turn were "able to change their perceptions of high-risk students, to see them in less judgmental ways and to begin to establish positive relationships, which reflected in their students taking more interest in school and achieving higher grades." All parents participating in the empowerment training sessions reported a positive impact of the training on their relationships with their children (McCombs, Bland & Shown, 1994).

Next came the Comprehensive Community Revitalization Project (CCRP) in the South Bronx, where Health Realization was put into practice. After 1½ years, 65 staff and resident leaders of six large community development corporations had participated in training. While to my knowledge no formal, final evaluation of this project was ever conducted, an early independent evaluation concluded: "Through participation in [Health Realization] group planning sessions and programs designed to enhance self-esteem and confidence, CCRP has enabled community residents to be involved in shaping their own future and that of their community's in a meaningful way… and to have more positive relations…" (O.M.G., 1994, in Mills, 1996). A later informal assessment showed that all six community development corporations (CDCs) reported substantially increased cooperation and improved working relationships within the organization. Residents felt more respected and understood by CDC staff, and there was a significant increase in resident participation in building tenant associations (Pransky, Mills, Sedgeman, & Blevens, 1997).

The Banyon Foundation supported a *Self Esteem is for Everyone* program (Timm & Campsall, 1994), based on this approach, in the Hillsborough County, Florida schools. After three years 375 students in grades 7-12 served by 36 teachers, 5 guidance counselors and 40 parents had received training in these principles. Pre-and post grade point averages were reported to increase significantly in all three years. The average increase in the first year was 64%, in the second year 56%, and in the third 57%. Students from the first year showed an additional GPA improvement of 24% during the second and third years, even though they were not still involved in the program. Absenteeism and disciplinary referrals decreased significantly, to well below school norms. By the third year participants overall showed a 58% decrease in absenteeism and 81% decrease in discipline referrals. Self-esteem, as measured on the Piers-Harris self esteem scale, improved from 49 to 64 in year one (+31%), 43 to 57 in year two (+33%), and 44 to 59 in year three (+34%). All scores moved from below the norm to above the norm (Banyon Foundation, 1992).

In a two-year study, Project Mainstream Hawaii served 55 Special Education students and their families in the Winward School area, Oahu, grades K-12, using Psychology of Mind counseling. The Mental Health Children's Team for Outpatient Counseling diagnosed these children as severely emotionally disabled, requiring both mental health and Special Education services. The students received counseling to help them understand the nature of their thoughts and feelings. Parents were involved in developing their children's treatment plan and they themselves received counseling to reduce stress and gain a deeper understanding of how they and their children function psychologically. This counseling emphasized helping parents see how to change themselves rather than how to fix their children. Teacher training emphasized learning how to live in a healthier, calmer and more positive state of mind. A five-point Likert scale by students, parents, and teachers measured perceptions of children's behaviors, pre- and post-treatment. At the end of two years, 6 of the 55 students in the program were integrated into regular classrooms, rescinded from Special Ed. and no longer needed counseling; 12 were still in Special Ed. but no longer needed counseling; 22 were still in counseling but "made progress"; and 8 were referred to other treatment services (4 had moved out of the district). Teachers reported that 44 out of the 52 remaining project students (85%) showed progress; they "noticed a large magnitude of behavioral improvement in each child." Compared to usual results with this population, the authors concluded that Psychology of Mind was "a very effective counseling approach for emotionally disabled students." No significant differences were found for age, gender, ethnicity, or duration of treatment (Heath, Emiliano & Usagawa, 1992).

The Center for Psychological Services at the California School of Professional Psychology at Fresno studied the effects of Health Realization training on city employees. Inter-departmental staff working with the resident leadership in five of the "worst neighborhoods" in Fresno were assessed for changes in their personal and professional lives as a result of participation in the training. Results on a five-point Likert Scale showed "much improvement" or "some improvement" in "not taking things as personally, including residents or others' initial negativity," "better able to maintain positive motivation and sense of direction," "understanding how to facilitate residents solving their own problems," and "working collaboratively with resident leaders." The report concluded that "common themes emerged: having better listening skills, becoming less judgmental, having more patience, moving away from old models, changes in views of residents, improvements in interpersonal styles, greater willingness to approach residents with openness, sincerity, empathy and understanding, facilitating rather than controlling, trusting residents' leadership." Participants stated they now recognized that citizens had the capacity to solve their own problems and that their job was not to go in and "fix" people, but to work collaboratively as equals and draw solutions out of people (Stokes, in Mills, 1996).

In 1997 The Health Realization Community Empowerment Project at Coliseum Gardens, a 200-unit public housing development in Oakland, California, received the California Wellness Foundation Peace Prize in behalf of police officer Jerry Williams and was cited by President Clinton and Attorney General Reno, after this housing project, once known as the "murder capitol," did not have one murder in the five years since the Health Realization program began. This housing project once had the highest frequency of drug-related arrests and homicides in the city of Oakland. Violent crimes were reduced by 45%, drug assaults with firearms were reduced by 38%, and gang warfare and ethnic clashes between Cambodian and African-American youth ceased (Pransky, Mills, Sedgeman & Blevens, 1997). Further, it was reported that "the drug dealers controlling the community have been dispersed, child abuse/neglect has dropped by 60%, drug and other criminal activities have dropped by 65%, school disciplinary actions have dropped by 70%, and 59% of dropouts have returned and graduated" (in Mills, 1996). In one of the most detailed analyses of a Health Realization/Community Empowerment project start-up, after widespread interviews with housing authority staff, residents, service providers and community police officers after one year of the program, an independent evaluation concluded, "The Health Realization Empowerment project has made significant impact on the quality of life at Coliseum Gardens in just twelve months. The results of the first year evaluation clearly indicate that continued development of the Health Realization Community Empowerment Project has the potential to stimulate and support deep, positive changes in both Coliseum Gardens and its surrounding social environment. Everyone agrees that something important has happened at Coliseum Gardens over the past year" (Roe & Bowser, 1993). [Also, see Chapter XIV.]

The Informed Families Substance Abuse Prevention Program was funded by federal Drug Free Schools grants to work in Dade County, Florida schools with "students-at-risk." Health Realization training was offered to students, teachers, school counselors, youth agencies, and parent groups in all twelve feeder schools. An independent assessment of effectiveness reported a "notable increase" in pre- and post-test scores on positive cognition and self worth. The evaluation stated, "This is a major change and one that will help insulate these teens from alcohol and drug use in the future. Importantly, the relationship between positive thoughts controlling our moods and self esteem not being related to alcohol and drugs is a significant change in the period between the pre test and the post test" (Cherry, in Mills, 1996).

The Glenwood-Lyndale Community Center in Minneapolis, Minnesota, located between two public housing projects with many problems, implemented Health Realization in all its community services and programs involving youth. Reportedly the atmosphere of fear has been replaced by trusting community relationships. Staff reported that police calls for gang and other community and family violence had been constant, but now fighting or conflict between residents is rare (Mills, 1996). Subsequently this center won the Nova Award. Another organization in the area, Life's Missing Link (formerly Professional Sports Linkage), founded by former National Football League Hall of Famers Jim Marshall and Oscar Reed, works with delinquent and incarcerated youth using this approach. After observing area results of both these programs, the Minneapolis Department of Public Safety reported: "Crime among juveniles has dropped to next to nothing, from the prior high rate more typical of public housing communities around the city. The dot map displaying the incidence and residence of juveniles committing crimes looks white compared to the concentration of black dots in neighboring areas" (Center for Drug Free Schools and Communities, 1996).

Although as individual studies none of these can meet rigorous scientific standards, as a cumulative body of research they offer compelling evidence that Health Realization warrants inclusion as a "promising approach" for prevention efficacy. It was not until Borg conducted the first rigorous, controlled study of Health Realization that a measure of scientific evidence could be offered.

Borg's (1997) study included 124 residents and service providers (63 in training group; 61 controls) living and working in six low-income housing developments in a racially and ethnically mixed population in Fresno, California. Training group participants received training in the Health Realization/Community Empowerment (HR/CE) model over six months, consisting of six three-hour training sessions provided by advanced Health Realization trainers certified by the California School of Professional Psychology. Training focused on understanding Health Realization core concepts and their application to personal and community development and empowerment. Pre- to post-test (after six months) measures of participant perceptions were taken on a standard mental health inventory. A multi-variant analysis (MANOVA) revealed that pretest to posttest the HR/CE program showed very significant differences (P.= <.0001) in anxiety, depression, behavioral/emotional control, general positive affect, loneliness, and belonging, with no significant changes in the control group on any of these measures. No significant differences were found in gender, ethnicity, income or employment, and the only age differences were nullified by the small number of participants (n=2) in the upper age ranges.

The latest research or evaluation I could find as of this writing comes from the Ke Ala Pono Program in Hawaii, The National Resilience Resource Center in Minnesota, the Visitacion Valley Health Community Resiliency Program in San Francisco, and the West Virginia University School of Medicine.

Ke Ala Pono Program

On Oahu, Hawaii, The Family Peace Center initiated an outcome study of the different models for perpetrators of domestic violence groups in 1997. Christine Heath and Louis Pavao of the Hawaii Counseling and Education Center in Kailua provided a 24-week group for batterers using the Ke Ala Pono Model for treatment, based on the three Principles underlying Health Realization. Twenty-five (25) individuals, mandated into treatment for domestic violence, participated in the study. The group was assessed using three different instruments that evaluated self-esteem, violence and depression with a pre-post test experimental design. Unfortunately, none of the comparison groups completed data collection, so results were unable to be compared with other models.

The results of the 1997 outcome assessment for the 24-week domestic violence group showed participants made significant positive change (p<.05) in both physical and non-physical conflict. Nonphysical conflict went from a pretest mean of 14.1 to a posttest mean of 2.5, and physical conflict went from a pretest mean of 9.8 to a posttest mean of 1.9.

In 1999, another evaluation was conducted on the Ke Ala Pono Program to find whether the program was effective in reducing the levels of depression and physical/nonphysical conflict among participants. The subjects of this study consisted of 25 court-ordered male adults who successfully completed the training (80% successfully completed). Each participated in 20 or more group sessions. A pre and post experimental design was applied, using the Zung Depression scale, and the Hudson non-physical and physical conflict instrument. The results of T-Test comparison scores pre- and post-intervention indicate significant decreases (p.>.001) for all three areas: depression, physical conflict, and nonphysical conflict. Mean scores for depression dropped from 37.84 pretest to 29.92 posttest, for nonphysical conflict from 15.70 to 4.60, and physical conflict from 10.62 to 2.67.

A six-month follow-up study was then conducted. All participants from the aforementioned study were contacted with a 32% return (n=8). A pretest, posttest 1, and posttest 2 design was applied, using the same scales. No significant changes were reported from post-test 1 to post-test 2, indicating a high level of maintenance of decreases in depression, physical and non physical conflict in the 6 months after completion of the Ke Ala Pono Program. These results provide preliminary evidence that the positive changes were of an enduring nature. A one-year follow-up was also conducted but only 4 returned surveys, so no conclusions could be drawn.

Visitacion Valley Community Resiliency Project

Visitacion Valley is a fairly new low income housing development in San Francisco, which replaced two old low income housing high-rise "towers." This evaluation data is sparse, because I was unable to obtain the latest research results for this project prior to publication, but the following results were presented at the June 2001 West Virginia University Releasing the Power in Health conference in Pittsburgh, Pennsylvania. From January 2000 to May 2001, instruction or training in Health Realization was received by 150 adults through Leadership/Empowerment classes, 50 elementary school children through class instruction or individual counseling, 60 middle school children through a Junior Leadership class instruction, 20 teenagers through a Youth Leadership class and/or projects, and 25 practitioners/service providers through Practitioner Training. Of these, 30 residents and practitioners participated in a Training of Trainers program. Plus, another 500 residents were contacted through outreach activities. Harder+Company Community Research conducted the evaluation.

Of the 45 residents surveyed who attended Leadership/Empowerment classes, 82% indicated that the adult trainings significantly helped them to feel in control of their behavior, thoughts, emotions and feelings, and 73% felt less tense and anxious and more calm and peaceful. Trends were observed between the following variables: belief in thinking positively and reduced feelings of depression; an understanding of the consequences of negative thinking and reduced feelings of isolation; an understanding of the causes of relationship conflict and improved interpersonal relationships; a belief that positive self-esteem is innate and increased feelings of happiness. In addition, a Middle school post-only retrospective survey administered to 11 middle school students after three months participation in the class indicated that the Health Realization class significantly helped them to get along better with most of their classmates and friends (N=8, 73%); make more friends (N=7, 64%), and feel better about themselves & the way they look (N=6, 55%). More research on this project is to come.

National Resilience Resource Center Efforts in St. Cloud, Minnesota and Menomonie, Wisconsin Schools

The National Resilience Resource Center (NRRC) at the University of Minnesota in Minneapolis assists school, community and organizational leaders in enhancing capacity to tap natural, innate health or resilience of youth, families, communities and systems. In schools they assist leaders and teachers to view all students and others as "at promise" rather than "at risk." Their work, developed by Kathy Marshall and Bonnie Benard, is based on the philosophy that "to successfully foster resilience, it is essential to focus on 'the natural, internal, innate capacity of young people and adults for healthy functioning,'" supported by resilience research. Their intent is "to help guide systems in bringing out the best in youth and adults." (National Resilience Resource Center website).

At North Junior High in St. Cloud, Minnesota, as a result of the combined efforts of good school administrative work and resilience/Health Realization training by the NRRC, from school year 1997-98 to school year 1998-99 suspensions were 70% lower, fights were reduced by 63.8%, and incidents of violence dropped 65.1%. In addition, school improvement surveys of faculty documented a 34% increase in faculty believing students respect each other, a 44% increase in faculty believing students respect adults, and a 40% increase in faculty believing positive interactions among students increased. This was an area where the North Junior High Building Reports data for 1996-97 had shown 2,975 incidents, mostly for disruptive behavior but also physical violence, fighting, harassment, destruction of property, insubordination, skipping school and others. Also, a Developmental Assets Survey completed at North Junior High in October 1996 indicated that 30% of all students had been physically abused or were victims of physical violence, 21% reported being in trouble with police once or more in the last 12 months, and 12% had attempted suicide (Marshall, 2000).

Other results of this effort are that the school climate reportedly improved. "Staff members began telling stories of students who were able to "quiet their minds and calm down with just a gentle reminder." Staff claimed, too, that being aware their reality was "just thought," and they could "let thoughts go," made a significant difference in "how well they could deal with the behaviors of middle-school students." Virtually all staff members involved in the effort report significant change in their personal lives. These data are not conclusive but certainly promising (Marshall, 2000).

This effort had begun with an interest in evaluating the Safe and Drug Free Schools program in 1994, which led to district-wide Student Assistance Team training, then a Resilience/Health Realization training pilot with 35 team members from North Junior High and the early childhood program. As of this writing, the initiative has reached more than 1,500 people from public agencies and small non-profits serving children, youth and families. (private communication from Marshall, May 8, 2002). Instruction in resilience/Health Realization began at North Junior High in 1996 with a pilot group of adults, and student instruction started in 1998-99. As of Marshall's (2000) paper more than 800 seventh- and eighth-grade students had been taught to tap their own innate resilience and common sense. Leaders at North believe they achieved a "critical mass" of faculty members whose insights into their innate health and resilience made a significant difference in the life of the school.

A similar effort occurred in the Menomonie, Wisconsin school district. It began in October, 1996 when school social worker Gary Johnson invited staff of the Menomonie Area Schools Pupil Services team to consider a paradigm shift, as Johnson says, to look at "what is right with kids rather that what is wrong, and see natural resilience—innate health—in everyone. " Similar agencies as in St. Cloud became involved, and more than 250 adults began a long-term training process facilitated by the NRRC. A focus group documented personal progress and found reduced feelings of distress and greater calmness resulting from "thinking differently about a situation" and increased support and cohesiveness among colleagues, among others. As an example of the change one participant reported: "It just scares me to think what I might look like if I hadn't been exposed to this. My daughter said, 'You know, we are doing pretty good.' Why are we doing pretty good? I am grateful. It's not some big mystery... you are aware of your innate health and kids are aware of their innate health. That's powerful." Similar results of school climate improvement and personal change occurred at the Downsville Elementary school (Marshall, 2000).

Research from the West Virginia University School of Medicine, Sydney Banks Institute for Innate Health

Classes titled, "Foundations of Human Understanding I" were conducted in various cities around the country to provide a first exposure to this understanding at this level for anyone who wanted to attend. Each class lasted 2½ days, and all were taught in the year 2000. Pre data were collected from 477 Foundations I class participants and matched with post data from 247 participants, then matched again with 6-month follow up data from 59 participants. The data show significant differences from baseline through 6-month follow-up.

It is important to note that this research represents only a preliminary step in conducting the first rigorous research into approaches applying the three Principles. The purpose of this first step was to develop a scientifically-reliable instrument—the Understanding of Experience Survey (UES)—that would be able to accurately measure the results sought by such approaches. In layman's terms, the real purpose of this research was to develop this instrument, not to measure results of this approach. As such, at this level it did not matter that the different instructors teaching these courses were at a wide range of differing skill levels, nor that all instructors were in the throes of making the transition to teaching solely by the three Principles [instead of through "concepts"—see Chapter VIII], nor that all participants were not tracked down to complete the follow-up surveys. Nonetheless, despite these limitations, at six-month follow-up statistically significant differences (improvements) were found at the .05 level for all factors measured: 1) "things people think are limitations to success", 2) "things people think are limitations to clarity", 3) "person's understanding of their own states of mind", and 4) "person's understanding of their own resiliency".

Here is the actual abstract of the finding as stated by the researchers:

This study explored how training in the foundations of human understanding affect participants' scores on a survey. The Understanding of Experience Survey (UES) assessed cognitive processes that are indicative of the principles of human understanding—mind, thought, and consciousness. The sample of participants completed this survey three times—before training, after training, and six months later. Using one independent variable (time), a one-way with repeated measures ANOVA with alpha=0.05 was conducted. The ANOVA reported that many of the items' means were significantly different, which indicated that there is at least one significance between the items' mean scores on the 3 survey administration. Pairwise comparisons were then conducted, revealing significant differences between the survey administrations (Shumway & SBIIH, 2001).

As of this writing the West Virginia University School of Medicine has now developed a draft instrument on which it is in the process of conducting reliability and validation studies. This is a necessary step in eventually being able to show changes that are scientifically verifiable.

Summary

Every study of Health Realization and its various incarnations, however weak or strong the design, has shown decreases in problem behaviors and internally experienced problems. This approach appears to reduce problem behaviors and to improve mental health and well-being. At the very least, this suggests the field of prevention should further examine the efficacy of this inside-out approach by conducting independent, rigorous, controlled, longitudinal studies, in comparison with other "research-proven" prevention interventions.

The totality of the studies conducted to date suggests that efficacy in the field may be enhanced considerably by exposure to and understanding of the dynamics of what makes people change, through this inside-out understanding. A step was taken toward ascertaining this in my own study [see Chapter XII].

These studies suggest that Health Realization provides a missing ingredient in the field's knowledge of prevention efficacy. While not emerging from it, the inside-out approach of Health Realization is aligned with the works of Bowman and Bandura [Chapter V] and appears to take both a crucial step further.

Jack Pransky

XI. JUDY

Interview with Judith Sedgeman. *Judy Sedgeman is director of the Sydney Banks Institute of Innate Health at the Robert C. Byrd Health Sciences Center at West Virginia University (WVU). WVU is the first prestigious institution to adopt Banks's Principles as an underlying foundation for service and education. Previously a successful businessperson and business consultant, after becoming exposed to this understanding Judy worked for nearly a decade with Pransky & Associates in LaConner, Washington and developed into one of the most respected conveyors of this understanding. She has written many insightful essays on subjects related to this understanding that can be found on the Sydney Banks Institute website: www.sbiih.org. I interviewed Judy at the Institute in Morgantown, WV in April, 2001.*

JP: What were you like before you got exposed to this understanding?

JS: [laughs] Well, you should really ask my daughter this question, because she does this fabulous description, but I was very successful and not very happy. I was a person who had achieved a lot of things—material success and business success and recognition, and it should have been "everything's great." But the more time went by and the harder I worked and the more I accomplished, the more empty I felt, and the less I felt that I was connected in any way to something meaningful. Now, looking back on it, I'd say that I was stressed way beyond anything healthy, and I was also depressed, although I wouldn't have called it depression. I would have called it "responsibility" and the way life is when you're a successful person and have a lot of obligations. I can remember getting up in the morning and standing in the shower crying, morning after morning, just because I had so many things to do, and I was never getting enough sleep, and I was so tired, and I was so conscious of my duties and my obligations and the people counting on me and all of that. I just wanted to crawl under something and stop, but I didn't know how to stop.

JP: When you say you were successful in accomplishments, what are you talking about?

JS: Well, I owned my own business, which was doing very well. I had a medical practice management business in Bradenton, Florida, which is how I stumbled into this, ultimately. I had a lot of clients. We were doing very good work for our clients. I was on a lot of boards. I was active in the symphony. I was on the board of trustees of the Florida State Museum of Art. I was on the Chamber of Commerce Economic Development Committee and on the board of the Chamber. I was on the board of the United Way. I was the first woman to do a lot of things in my community. When I first moved to Bradenton in 1970 there were very few businesswomen. Most women were taking a much more traditional female role, and I was kind of a pioneer in breaking new ground for women to be included in community activities that had been all male. So I took that on as kind of a cause, to open doors to an equal representation from all people. So I worked very hard.

And I had a child. My daughter was just getting into her teenage years, and I was married and had a very active social life. Anyone in the community would have described me as a prominent person and expected me to be deliriously happy. So then I had that expectation to meet, you know? I had to put on my happy face so I wouldn't let them down. I blamed myself entirely. I thought, "You have all this. You should be grateful! Why aren't you happy?" But I wasn't.

JP: So you would stand in your shower crying in the morning because you had an expectation of yourself?

JS: Plus, I didn't know what I was missing. I couldn't figure out what else could I possibly—I would ask myself, "What's left? What could I do? What should I be doing? Why can't I be satisfied? Why aren't I thrilled? Why aren't I happy? Why aren't I at peace? Why am I so driven?" I would look at everything I had and think, "Why can't I just be a happy, contented person? What's wrong with me?"

JP: And so, when you asked yourself that question—

JS: I had no answer. The answer was, "There's something wrong with you."

JP: That's a big answer.

JS: That's a big answer, yeah.

JP: So if you can reflect back to the time you first got exposed to this understanding, what happened, and how did it all come about?

JS: Well, I was in this state of agitation about what to do about my life and how to find some peace, and I decided I had to get out of my business. I was blaming the fact that I had taken on the ownership of a business and borrowed a lot of money and had a financial responsibility for my clients. And so I thought if I just get out of business, start over, maybe—everybody always changes jobs when they're unhappy, right? [laughs] That's, like, your first thought: "I've got to get a different job." And I was sitting in my office, trying to figure out how in the world I could do that, morally—when you had just put a lot of physicians' data on a big computer system in your office and they were counting on you. You just don't say, "Hey, we're not doing next week." It's not like you just shut down a production line. I didn't have the answer how to wind down something that I had started up in a way that was ethical, responsible and moral and in service to my clients, whom I really cared about. So I was very troubled by that, and I decided, "Well, I'm not going to take any new clients." So of course as soon as I said that, I got a call from a long-time friend of mine, Dick Connor, who was formerly an internal medicine practitioner in our community and he said, "I've got a client for you." And I said, "Dick, I'm not taking any new clients." He said, "No, I really, really, really want you to consider this, because this person really needs business help, and I think that you would really enjoy this person and get a lot out of being in a business relationship with him." I said, "No way. I don't want any new clients." And he said, "Judy, come on now, we've been friends for a long time. I've never led you astray. Trust me on this." I didn't have the courage to tell him I was trying to get out of the business. So finally I agreed to have lunch with him, and that proved to be Bill Pettit.

At that time he had been in Bradenton for a little over a year, I think, in private practice. So I go to this lunch, and I find out en route that I'm going to meet a psychiatrist. And I said to Dick, "You must be kidding me!" So we get to lunch and we had a very pleasant lunch with Bill, and I kept

136

asking him if he was really a psychiatrist, because I'm sitting there with a person who's talking about how much he loves his clients and enjoys the work he's doing, and he's excited about the future of what's possible for people. I was totally baffled by this; it's not what I was used to from psychiatrists. So of course in the state of mind that I was in at that time, I assumed that he probably had a drug—something really good [laughs]. So I'm trying to figure out what he's taking, and what he's giving to them, you know?

So we went back to his office, and I saw that he had a wall of files, which, for a psychiatrist who had been in town for a fairly short time—because psychiatrists usually see the same people for a long time, over and over again—I didn't expect. So I'm looking at these files and I'm thinking, "He mustn't be very good. He must have to keep getting new patients." So I looked at him and said, "Gee, you have an awful lot of files. You're a solo practitioner, aren't you? How do you see all these people?" And he said, "Oh, I don't." And in my mind I go, "Ah ha!" [laughs] And I said, "Where are they?" And he looked at me and said, "Well, I guess they're having a nice life."

I was stunned. I had never heard a psychiatrist ever suggest that a mental patient would leave treatment and have a nice life—I've heard them say things like "back to normal," "as good as they're going to feel," "stabilized," but never "having a nice life!" So I said, "Are you seeing people that are in the DSM description for all these things wrong with people?" And he said, "Oh yes. I'm on the staff of several hospitals, and I see everybody referred to me—the whole gamut of psychiatric illnesses." And I said, "And people get treated here, and then they have a nice life?" And he looked at me like a person would look at a two-year old, and he said, "Isn't that the point?" [laughs] And I said, "Of course it's the point, but nobody does it. What are you doing with these people, what are you giving them?" Then he started laughing, and he looked at Dick and he said, "You didn't tell her that I don't do traditional psychiatry, did you?" And Dick said, "No, I was just going to let her figure it out for herself." So Bill started to explain to me that he teaches people how to be healthy and teaches them how to find the Health that's accessible to all people, and that when they get in touch with that, they're able to have a nice life regardless of how they came into the practice. He said, "The state of mind they were in when I saw them really doesn't matter. It matters that they see it for what it is." Well, his certainty was overwhelming to me. I was blown away by it.

JP: What year was this?

JS: Probably late 1985. I was so suspicious that I said, "I'm just having a hard time grasping this, and I really can't represent a client when I don't understand his work," He said, "I'll tell you what, I do a group for my patients and anybody they want to bring, because frankly their families are often as baffled as you are that the patient goes back home and is in a different state altogether. So I do this public group—anybody can come—and I try to explain to the patients and their friends what this understanding that I've shared with the patients can mean. So you're welcome to come to the group." And I'll never forget this—I was so embarrassed—because I looked at him and, again, this probably tells you more than you ever wanted to know about the way I was living at the time, I said, "Don't you think I'd feel a little strange with all those mental patients?" And he looks at me, and he patted my arm, and he said, "Believe me, you won't be able to tell the difference" [laughs]—which was hilarious.

So I started going to these groups. I just wanted to interview these patients and find out if what he told me was true. I was waiting for the breaks so I could figure out who the patients were and ask them whether they really were having a nice life. Bill was a wonderful speaker and you couldn't help but be engaged, but I wasn't really paying much attention to the details, and then at the break I would start talking to these people. Well, after about three of these meetings it crossed my mind that these so-called mental patients had what I was looking for. They were much happier than I'd ever been. They took it for granted and it was a very ordinary thing, and they had no regrets about the number of years they had spent not happy until they found out how to be happy—they were just grateful for what they had. And they were all so matter-of-fact about it. It wasn't like some epiphany. For them it was like, "I used to think this, and now I see it differently, and I'm fine." And they had this very sweet—but not sticky-sweet or phony or weird sweetness—just a sweetness about them, a lovely human quality.

JP: How did it make you feel to think, "Wow, they have what I want?"

JS: I did want it! I was ready to just call myself a mental patient and go for it [laughs]. But I knew I didn't have to do that. I remember the first thought I had was, "Whatever he's talking about, I need to really pay attention. I need to come here to listen and be a student." So the first thought I had was to stop being so suspicious. When I did that I came with the right feeling, and I started to be touched, by everything—by what he was saying, by what the people were saying, by the questions people were asking. I just became a part of this learning.

And then—I'll never forget—this is like a turning point. One day, just in passing, he said, "You know, a lot of people live their life as though they got up every morning and wrote nasty notes to themselves and left them around the house, and came home at night and started reading them and didn't recognize their own handwriting"—which was kind of silly, but I thought, "That's what I've done my whole life. That's exactly what I'm doing. I'm setting up all these expectations: You should be this. You should be that. You owe this." And then I'd come home and take inventory at the end of the day, and it was like somebody else was giving me my marching orders. I forget I'm making this up. I don't have to do anything, and I could do anything! And I remember—actually this is almost embarrassing—this place where the meetings were was in this parking lot adjacent to the medical office complex, and I remember running out into the parking lot after that particular evening, and running around the parking lot screaming, "I'm free, I'm free!"—just so happy. I was, like, dancing in the parking lot, and it was so amazing to me to have that insight, which was the first of what I hope will continue to be a lifetime of insights, but that was the first time that I really knew what it was—to see what Bill was talking about: That when people see something inside themselves, and see it for themselves, they change. And everything changes, just like that! So I saw that.

Well then, we did take him on as a client and started working with his practice. So Bill called me one day, and he said, "Remember that book I gave you?"—*Second Chance* was the only book out at the time that Syd [Banks] had written—"Well, the author is going to be in my office next week, and I thought maybe you'd like to come in, since you're working with our practice and you're kind of part of our group. It's just going to be him and the people closest to him, and staff." And so I went and I sat there, and this was the first I'd ever seen Syd Banks, and it was a lovely way to see him. It was a lovely little meeting room that Bill had, and there were seven or eight people there and Syd. And Syd was just chatting, and I didn't really grasp what he was chatting about. I mean, it seemed like he was saying simple, straightforward things that I couldn't remember afterwards, but, you know, I was very drawn to the feeling, and very quiet. I mean, I felt like I was watching sediment settle to the bottom of the glass. I felt myself in those couple of hours that morning kind of settling to the bottom of my life, kind of—not bottom in a bad way, but as kind of "the essence."

And when I walked out of there, without giving it much thought at all, I walked over to the office of one of our troublesome clients—a surgeon who was very rude and mean to my staff—and I just fired him as a client. I was shocked, myself, at the certainty I felt about it, that it was no big deal to me, and I wasn't worried about what was going to happen. What I thought is, "We are indulging this man at his worst. We're not bringing out the best in him, or he in us. I don't understand why he's the way he is, but for us to accept it for money is a disservice to him. That's not right." And that's what I told him. And I then went back to my office and told my staff. Of course, people were a little bit frightened, because he represented a considerable amount of income to us. But at the same time they were grateful because I was standing up for a human value that they shouldn't just have to take any abuse because that's our corporate profit—which was a big lesson for me, how things work out.

Because when the word got out that I had done that, I had more business. So that was a big turning point. And I was very touched by Syd. I didn't really know too much about him, but I just thought, "What a lovely man. What a decent, kind, sweet soul I've just been in touch with." And it had a huge effect on me, although I wouldn't be able to say just what.

So then I went to Bill and I said, "I really need to learn this. I realize that in your world this is a therapy, but I'm a businessperson and this just rocked my world. Everything's changing. This is way bigger than therapy. It's way more than that, and I want to learn everything I can." So he made an arrangement with me that I could be, like, an apprentice with him, because there were so few places to go to learn it. I did go to a week-long program put on by the people in Tampa. It was Elsie [Spittle] and Chip [Chipman] and Sandy [Krot]. That's all they did was the week-long things, and infrequently at that, but really I just followed Bill around and listened to him talk—went to all the public things that he did, listening to him talk to other people. And I helped him set up a unit at a hospital for his practice to help him to realize the dreams that he had—

JP: What were you learning?

JS: I just found out that the way to be happy is to stop thinking about yourself and start thinking about other people, and just do what's obvious, and do the best you can, and not start measuring yourself against impossible standards and just, you know, be real. It was so simple, yet it hadn't crossed my mind before. So I got out of a lot of things I was doing without my full heart. I made the engagement of my heart the criterion of what I would commit my time to. And when I did that, it all fell into place, and I was doing everything I loved to do. So it didn't seem like a burden any more, and the things I'd been doing out of obligation or for external reasons just fell by the wayside, and I didn't even miss them. So things started to work out in my life, and from that starting point it was like a magic carpet ride, and the only time it's ever gone wrong is when I've tried to steer the carpet. As long as I just sit on the carpet and go with it, it's been wonderful.

But then, there was the bigger dimension to it, because I'd been working with Bill for about a year, I think, and my daughter had gone off to prep school, and then—you know, this is her story, so I won't go into detail—but she ended up running away from school. And I didn't know where she was for three days, and I went into this tailspin. I was told that she'd seen a psychiatrist at the school, and she needed to be committed. The psychiatrist said that she needed to be in a mental hospital, which I couldn't even relate to. And so in my heart I knew that I had to call Bill—but I didn't want to because he was my client and I was his student, and to be honest with you I realize in retrospect that I didn't want to admit that my family was so screwed up. But in the interest of my daughter I finally did, because I thought, "How crazy! If you do find her, who else would you want but Bill to treat her?"

So I called him up, and by that time I'd talked to all kinds of people, and everybody had an opinion about my parenting and why I was at fault, or why she was at fault, and I was so confused and upset. So I called Bill finally, and I told him what was going on. And he said, "How are you feeling?" I said, "Terrible. I'm a wreck!" He said, "Is it helping you to talk to all these people?" And I said, "No." "Then why are you doing it?" And I said, "Well, I don't know." He said, "Well, I just wondered. Well, when she comes home"—he was the first person that used the word "when"—"don't you think you'd want to be as rested and as calm as possible, to kind of be your best when you see her?" Well, that had never crossed my mind. I said, "Well, yeah." And he said, "Well, I think you should really take care of yourself, because if you can take care of yourself, then you'll have more resources available to you when your daughter comes home, and you can know what to do." And then he said, "Just page me and whenever she comes home, I'll see her. Don't worry about it. I'll be happy to do that." Well, when I got off the phone I was so relieved. It was like somebody had just poured some soothing balm on the turmoil of my life. And I went to bed and slept like a baby. And in the middle of that night I got a call from a friend who Sarah [her daughter] had called, and she was coming home.

Then of course I had this moment of panic. I called Bill the next morning and said, "She's coming, but I don't know what to do! What am I supposed to say?" I started going into trying to think ahead, and there was this long pause, and in one of those beautiful moments, he said, "You know, Judy, you're her mother, so just love her, and you'll know what to say." And that had never occurred to me either. And I remember when she walked in the door, and she was all wrung out and tired, and she'd been through a big ordeal too, and, you know, it was embarrassing for her. It's embarrassing to be fifteen and have to come home after you thought you were going to strike out and go on your own in life. And she started screaming at me, and all this stuff, and I remember looking at her, and I saw her in her crib. I saw—you know how babies start crying and they turn all blue and their little legs and arms are going. I could see that—I just saw her as this innocent little baby doing the best she could, trying to express her grief and sorrow. And I looked at her, and all I could think to say was, "Sarah, I'm really sorry. I'm so sorry it's come to this, and I'm so glad you're home." And she heard me, and she looked at me, and she went, "Mom? Is that you?" "Yeah, it is."

And she did see Bill. Of course I still had thoughts about this guy in Connecticut thinking she should be hospitalized and everything. After she'd been with Bill for about an hour and a half, he comes out to the waiting room and brings me back and says, "You know, she's really fine. Sarah's got a great sense of humor. She's a wonderful kid. She just got caught up in some thoughts that she didn't understand and she didn't know where they were coming from, and she's fine now. You can go home." And I said, "Well, what about the mental hospital?" And I remember he sat there and he looked at me, and he said, "Judy, I'm not going to hospitalize her. She can go home. If you want her hospitalized, you'll have to take her back to Connecticut to the other doctor. She's in my care. I'm telling you, she's fine. Take her home." And I said, "But, but, is she going to be on medication?" He said, "No." And I said, "Well, does she have to see you again?" And he said, "It's up to her." "What?" And he said, "It's entirely up to her. I think she understands what went wrong. I think she's fine, and if she'd like to learn more about it, then I think that's her decision." So Sarah looks up and says, "Yeah, I'd like to see you again. I'm interested in this, curious. I'd be happy to learn more." He said, "Fine. Then we'll make a couple more appointments." He saw her a couple times, and then she started going to the same group that I was going to, just out of interest. But we walked out the door and resumed life, and it's been beautiful ever since. It's the last bad experience I ever had as a mother. Just amazing! And after that happened, Jack, I really was committed beyond belief.

I remember shortly after that, one day I went to lunch with Bill, and I said, 'You know, I want you to really tell me, how did you find this? And how did you get over being a psychiatrist in the old school? And who are you? Where is this coming from?" And I remember we had this, maybe, three-hour lunch, and I looked at him, and I saw the soul of all of us. It wasn't a personal thing. I just saw what pure love was, and what faith in people really looked like. And it was the turning point—that was it for me. I went on a whole new path in life, and I committed myself to getting as much understanding as I could get for myself, and helping share it with other people. So that was how I got involved.

JP: What a great story that is!

JS: So as a result of that—and again, it isn't personal—I mean, of course, it's about Bill Pettit because he's the person—but *what I saw in him was the power of the impersonal, the beauty of love unconditionally given, without regard to the person's circumstances, and what this understanding could really mean for the well-being of all people.*

JP. So how did you get to La Conner [Washington]?

JS: Well, Sarah went to college, and I was alone. At that time I was divorced and I had this house, and I wanted to sell my business because I wanted to do this work. I had started doing this with my clients, who liked it, but it wasn't what the company was set up to do and it wasn't what the other people in my company wanted to do. So I ended up selling the company. I was going to go to California for no special reason except, why not? I had met George and Linda [Pransky] through Bill, and they used to have conferences in Florida fairly often. And George called me up one day and said, "Have you ever considered maybe coming out to La Conner? And I said, "No, not really." And he said, "Well, you could if you wanted to." So I did, and that worked out real well for a while.

JP: So, along the way, did you see yourself evolving in the understanding?

JS: It's so much easier to see it in retrospect. It's easier for me to see it in terms of what life looked like to me in 1990, 1991, 1992. When it's happening, it's so natural, you know? You notice it in either what other people say to you, or you find yourself doing things differently. Like the first thing I noticed is that I wasn't reacting to my clients' bad moods any more. I wouldn't do anything with anybody who was all upset and weird. I would look to get to a calmer state, and all of a sudden, it got very easy, because people function better when they're not upset, and so we weren't making so many mistakes and making fools of ourselves. I mean, I could go back to a month ago and say, "Gee, you know, I've seen things and learned things since then," as I think we all do. But at the time it's happening it's so subtle because when you see something different you just see it, and then you're looking out your eyeballs and it doesn't look like it just did. [laughs]

[Judy goes on to describe how the Sydney Banks Institute of Innate Health began at West Virginia University Medical School—Chapter XIV, page 221.]

141

XII. A QUALITATIVE STUDY MEASURING EFFECTS OF HEALTH REALIZATION TRAINING ON PARTICPANTS

In all the research cited in Chapter X, I could find no study that examined the internal aspects of people's experience after they participated in an intensive Health Realization training.

Through my doctoral program I was fortunate to have the opportunity to conduct such a study.

How This Effort Began

One day in October 1996 I received a call from Mary Marchel of the Violence Prevention Action Team in Bemidji, Minnesota, inquiring about my book *Prevention: The Critical Need* (Pransky, 1991). She had been searching the Internet for material on prevention for juveniles, found my book through the Texas Catalogue of Youth Programs and managed somehow to track me down.

The Violence Prevention Action Team had formed in Bemidji in May 1996 to "serve as a catalyst to initiate collaboration of community wide primary and secondary violence prevention efforts." In October of that year the Team worked with the local Family Services Collaborative to bring Arun Gandhi to Bemidji to speak on nonviolence. As a follow-up, Mary Marchel, Director of Beltrami County Public Health Nursing Service, volunteered to search for resource material to aid in writing a grant. I sent her my book.

After reading it, Mary called me back to ask if I would be interested in conducting some prevention training in Bemidji. I listened to what she wanted and suggested Health Realization training might meet their needs even better than a traditional prevention training.

"What's Health Realization?" she asked.

I tried to explain it briefly and sent her an article I had written called "Moving Prevention to a Higher Plane" (Pransky, 1994).

Mary called back again. The Action Team decided to take a chance on the training, even though they did not really understand what it was. Apparently they decided to try it because both Mary and Susan Smith, a local psychotherapist and another key member of the Action Team, had found the *Prevention* book to be "really impressive," particularly the chapter on "Spirituality in Prevention," so they decided to trust my suggestion.

Mary set up a training and invited Action Team members and other key community leaders to attend. I conducted a three-day Health Realization training in Bemidji on May 6-8, 1997. Both Mary and Susan were so impressed with the training that they arranged for another to be held in October, 1998 for other community members. This time I co-facilitated

two-thirds of the training with Cynthia Stennis, a former resident and staff member of the Modello/Homestead Gardens project.

The Bemidji trainings jumped into my mind for study because initially they had no idea what Health Realization was, nor what to expect. I called Mary Marchel to ask if she would be willing to have me conduct follow-up research on the results of the training. She agreed.

The Study

In this chapter I will present only the important results and say enough about the conduct of the study so readers will be able to relate to it. More details of this study for those interested can be found in Appendix B.

I decided to use a phenomenological[13] research design because I was interested in participants' detailed perceptions of *how* their lives had changed as a result of Health Realization training. I also wanted to know whether any effects lasted longitudinally (over time), in this case approximately one year after the two Bemidji trainings.

My study question was, "How do people perceive and describe their experience following Health Realization training?" I wanted participants' own descriptions of any major changes they had observed in their thoughts, feelings, and behaviors since the training. I wanted to know to what did they attribute those changes, what meaning it had for their lives, and what they were now doing with the understandings gained from that experience.

To the unknowing eye, phenomenological research might appear to be merely a reporting of anecdotes. It is far from that. First, quantitative research cannot possibly capture people's internal experience. Only by asking probing questions about people's own perceptions can anyone explore the internal. Not even brain scans tell us this. Secondly, the process of a phenomenological design leads to a scientific categorization and classification of data collected (Moustakas, 1994). The categories below came from this analysis. I selected an open-ended interview design, supplemented by a questionnaire to yield some quantitative data.

---

[13] Phenomenology asserts that a true understanding of the nature of mind can be achieved only by methods radically different from those that guide science generally (Churchland, 1993).]

> The concepts of physical science can never be anything more than the mind's constructed interpretation of the "objective" world. To understand the mind, by contrast, what we need to do is make a one hundred eighty degree turn...that will lead us back to the essential nature of the mind itself. It is possible for the mind to intuit its own essential nature, since, in contrast to its knowledge of the objective world, the mind has, or can aspire to have, direct and unmediated access to itself. Such...analytical and introspective research will produce a level of insight and understanding that is both superior to and independent of any possible understanding that might be produced by the essentially constructive and interpretive procedures of ordinary science (pp. 85-86).

Phenomenological and other forms of qualitative research are "all ways of saying that it is possible to get good information by asking people how they see the world, and how they feel about things" (Raeburn & Rootman, 1998, p.17).]

Participants

A total of 41 participants attended two separate three-day Health Realization trainings. Of these, 37 were found eligible to participate in the study, which occurred approximately one year after the two trainings. Of these, 23 returned survey questionnaires (11 from the May, 1997 training, and 12 from October, 1997), and 13 agreed to be interviewed extensively. This pushed the limit of interviewees for a phenomenological design, but I wanted to ensure that everyone was interviewed who wanted to be and had the time.

Most participants attending the trainings could be classified (with one or two exceptions) as white, middle-class professionals in the helping professions, primarily in the field of human services, with their normal everyday problems, concerns and stress in their personal and professional lives.

Results

From an extensive examination of the interviews and clustering these data I found that, one year after the three-day Health Realization training, participants experienced:

a. more calm and comfort in life
b. more lightheartedness, or a lighter feeling
c. fewer and less intense emotional reactions
d. less stress
e. better, higher quality relationships

To illustrate the meaning of each category, I will let participants speak for themselves by offering one direct quote from participant responses (sometimes with an additional quote or two if I thought another was particularly telling).

a. *More calm and comfort in life*

> DD: It has made me more secure. It's made me calmer. It's made me…feel better about things… Everything. Everything. Just my life. It's made me feel better about everything, my life at home and my family. All my relationships… It's just much calmer. It's more secure. It's more happy. It has a better feeling. There's more love. It's more peaceful. It feels healthier… This is my thoughts, creating my reality.

> MM: I don't know any other way to describe it but…to use the words "calm at my core." That's a new feeling for me. And it was amazing to me that regardless of what else is going on in my life or outside in the environment, that sense of peacefulness and calm like I've never known that before… I guess the word that just kind of pops into my head…is relief…, in the sense of, I don't have to know all the answers, I don't have to take on all the burdens that I previously had, whether it's at work or home. That's been big for me. It's obviously increased the quality of my life.

b. *More lightheartedness or a lighter feeling*

SS: I don't know, it's lighter, light, it feels lighter, more interesting, more fun [laughs]. I don't have the words. It's just more available... There are just so many more possibilities and opportunities than I would have acknowledged before... When I would get involved with thinking in limited ways I would feel discouraged, or I would feel lack of hope, or I would feel stuck, or those kinds of things... So I feel hopeful more of the time, and like, Whoa, why not try that?... Because it makes so much sense...I feel like my own personal growth just has been accelerated... Another thing is feeling more able to take risks, and that feels like another lighter thing. Not taking risks before was based in fear, and so there's not that fear...

c. *Fewer and less intense emotional reactions*

CA: When I use Health Realization I respond differently to things that happen between [my son] and I, because I don't just get this instant hurt, and I tend to look at it differently, look at him and where he's coming from...

d. *Less stress*

MM: For me I think it's been definitely more of a recognition that I'm creating my own stress, and that's been pretty nice to just know that I do it to myself and where that comes from. So I would say definitely my stress is lessened much since going through this, and again...it doesn't mean I never get stressed because I certainly do, but I noticed that I visit there less often, I don't stay there as long, and...and backing up from it and sometimes thinking to myself, "This too shall pass," I would say it's much less, much less stress. And I recognize myself as the creator of that stress.

e. *Better, higher quality relationships* (with spouses/partners, children, at work, people they found difficult):

GL: [Since the training] I've had some really great experiences with my wife..., some real high quality experiences...

MN: I've been telling just about anybody who will listen that this is some of the best training that I've ever had in my life, and I can't really pinpoint huge ways that it's changed my life, but in a lot of little ways it has—particularly at work. It's just been incredible in dealing with employees one-on-one, helping resolve disputes between employers and employees, and supervisors, etc. etc. It's been really helpful. A lot of their disagreements are just sort of disappearing now, where they used to continue fighting and dragging things out... The way I've been able to use the training is the indicator of its success. But I've also been through eighteen-and-a-half years of various human resources trainings, how to be a supervisor, how to train supervisors to be supervisors, how to deal with conflicts, and all of those kinds of trainings, and I have never, with all the techniques I have learned, had anything that worked anywhere as well as this does... Since I've had the training I haven't tried to be so controlling. And the amazing thing is that they are much more receptive to what I need to teach them how to do anyway, to what I try and tell them...[and] what I end up saying afterwards is usually more appropriate to the situation than much of what I would have said previously.

2. Why are they experiencing these results in their lives?

   a. *They realized their own power of creation—of their life experience*
   b. *They realized a source of "health" within, and to trust it*
   c. *They realized the pathway to their health, and what blocks it*
   d. *They recognized the signals that show whether or not they are in their health, so they could self-monitor*
   e. *They saw their choice to live in an outside, personal world or in an inside, nonpersonal world*
   f. *They saw their own habitual thinking patterns that kept them stuck, and their ability to transcend them by raising their level of understanding*

a. *Realizing the source of creation of their life experience: Thought*

MM: The whole idea of really seeing myself as the thinker...was huge, and in particular seeing myself coming to understand about my choices I make, and also...about changing my mind. That was particularly big. And I think that initial time when you came a year ago, at that time...I was in the process of a divorce...and we were literally days away from having that happen. And I can remember one morning taking a walk and thinking—and this was...about a month after the Health Realization [training]—thinking to myself about, "I don't love this man. Can I ever love him again?" And that's the point where I could see about changing my mind, and that I change my mind all the time, and that our feelings are a result of our thinking, and really seeing that, and knowing that, "Yes, I can change my mind." And as I was able to change my mind from loving him to not loving him, ...I could also reverse that... That was really big for me. Because I had previously thought...that I had made up my mind, that I didn't love him, thought that I didn't love him and didn't at that time. I thought that must be permanent now. And so really coming to understand that is a choice, and just like all the other choices I make all the time—many times in my life that I've changed my mind over all kinds of big and little things—that this was equally one of those times, and I could change it back... It was only the recognition to me that it was thought, that it's thought behind the feeling, the feeling of love... I don't think I went out of my way to change my mind. I saw some things that I hadn't seen before. I saw humility in this man that I hadn't seen before...and what those choices were in not taking things so personally... It was a relief to really see that that was all coming from my thinking... It was pretty incredible... So, you came in May and [my husband] was back home at the end of July... We [had been] all set, ready to go, and everything had been decided upon, agreed upon, ...just waiting for the court date...

DD: What's changed is my understanding that it's my thinking about what's going on out there that either makes me angry or uncomfortable, or however it is that I feel... It's not that stuff out there, but I can think differently, and it makes me feel differently...

b. *Realizing their unlimited capacity for innate "wisdom" or "health"*

SS: One of the pieces of truth is that when people are calm, they know what to do… That's a difference that I see is, in the…more common realm of psychology…when we get into that messy thought content like defensiveness or shame or guilt, you have to figure it out in order to get out of it. That's the common message, and Health Realization shows another way. Figuring it out just keeps you there longer. And you may get out of it eventually or you may not, but that I have—we all have—a healthier thought process that's just natural if we don't try to figure this out. If we just let it go and trust that we know what we'll need to know about it if we need to know something, and by letting it go we have better access to that understanding… I mean, we can analyze our thinking, and formulate the right thoughts,…we can be very deliberate about our thinking and still take ourself down a track that might be off for us. And going through all the work of affirmation—I can remember a time in my life where that is where I was…and so I would write out affirmations and read them and remember to tell myself these things and start to believe them. When the piece that Health Realization offers is that I don't have to do any of that stuff. It is already there! I mean, when I found the right affirmation and kind of probably linked up with what was already there, it was great. But I don't even have to do that. I just have to let…that…feeling come. There is no work to it. And that's a lot of work to take twenty minutes a day to visualize the perfect personality [laughs]. That's a lot of time—when it is already there! I don't have to do it, because it's in there. And in that whole framework of thoughts, somehow it's not there. You have to create it for yourself and put it in there. I mean, the fact that we can envision it says it's there, so it is like we're missing that whole piece of what's innate, and conjure it up, and put it in yourself to generate the good feelings about yourself. And the insight that I've had about that currently is that…still is me creating myself in some way that I think I'm not. And I already am! So it is like there is still a separation from the natural health that we have, and a lack of recognition of it, so I'm never going to let go and allow it to come through because I'm so busy thinking about how I want to be…And so it's like keeping people's minds even busier, rather than helping people learn how to just calm their minds so that can just be there for them, and allow. That seems a lot easier.

c. *Realizing the pathway to their health, and what blocks it: A calm and clear mind*

WP: Well, I guess the biggest thing is that I can enjoy the moment more… At one point in my life I could sit out on the deck and look out over the pasture and the pond and the flower bed, and I would see flowers to be weeded, a pond that needed cleaning out and needed fixing, I could see horses that needed their hooves trimmed, cockleburs taken out of their manes, and I'm sure they need shots again… Or you walk out through the garage and you see, "Oh man, I have to do this, this and this," and "that should have been taken care of," and "that has to be put away." And so you can either spend moment-to-moment getting stressed even in the most enjoyable moments on your deck, looking out over this beautiful—we have lots of acres out in back… and…taking out trees…you can see further and further… You can see a pond and you can see trees beyond…and then you can take out more trees…and see further…, and maybe that's a little bit like it is. You can clear away all this junk, and you just see more, and you see more beautiful, and the view is more grand. And I guess in a way that's kind of what's happened, is that you can sit out there, and you can enjoy the moment and you don't have to think about all that has to be done or should be done or could be done or would be done if I wasn't sitting here enjoying the moment. And so that's been big for me, too, is that moment—that must have been in the training, something about the moment... Clear your mind, and that works, and I think the more you do it, the faster it works and the better it works.

d. *Recognizing the signals of whether or not they are in their health, so they could self-monitor*

SS: The piece that was entirely new to me from the training was the whole revelation about moods. And that was something, in spite of all of the background that I've got in mental health and family relationships, I had never heard talked about in that way. And so for me moods was like a whole new piece, and I was fascinated by it. And that was one of the first things that I began to look at for myself in all my relationships...[and] the first thing that I started to help people with was my understanding of moods... And then at another level I seem to gain a greater ability to just be self-observant, so I would notice myself in low moods more often than I used to. I used to ignore and deny that I was in a low mood. So I think I've noticed myself there more often. I wouldn't say that I go there more often, I probably go there less often, but I see myself—I'm more aware of it, and at times get caught in it, but I still know that I'm caught in it. I'm aware of it now—almost invariably I know when I'm in it.

BC: Last fall BY was just in a...bad mood,...growling...like a rabid grizzly, and then all of a sudden he walked back into the room and he said, "You know, I'm just in a low mood, and I've taken it out on you, and it's not fair." And I went, "Awwww, [sigh]" [laughter]. And then everything was just fine. And he's really done that a couple of times, just stopped, and that's been wonderful.

e. *Seeing their choice to live in an outside, personal world or in an inside, nonpersonal world*

JF: When I first came back to the office after the training...there's a person there that always bugs me... We just don't really click. But when I came back from the training, she did the same stuff...to me, and it was like I had this shield... I could just see her, and...I didn't take it personally... It was, like, "Oh, you must be really insecure."...I mean, I could see so much clearer. [Before]...I was more into reacting. I was more into taking it personally...but...one of the thoughts that came to me is, "I wonder what it would be like to live with herself," so then I felt more compassion. Poor thing! [laughs] I should bring her brownies... I guess what I see now is...I don't have to get caught up—...there's just more perspectives and ways of looking at the experience of the moment than just one... It moves you into a different perspective where you can look at the situation from a different angle... Yeah, now it's, because I'm aware of it, I can choose it, where before I couldn't choose it because I didn't know there was another option or that I could control the way I looked at it, or that there were choices available to me...

CJ: Something just this past week...challenged me to this personal-nonpersonal thing... I have a son who has diabetes. He's been having a lot of low blood sugar lately. Now, the key symptoms of low blood sugar is irritability and not really being in your right mind, and some of these are in the middle of the night. And the other night at three a.m. he says to me, "You're the worst thing that's ever happened to me!" Now, I left his bedroom thinking, "Okay, CJ—that's about the worst thing that I could hear." I know he has low blood sugar…but I was faced with that reality of, what am I going to do? Am I going to sit here and dwell on that and start tearing up on that? No,…that would be the stupidest thing for me to do. There's no rationality into that. And then a couple of days later something else came out of his mouth. He had a 34 blood sugar—really low—and so I've just more really realized how here's a situation where in anybody's right mind they should never take that kind of thing personally. And so in my daily life when things happen to me…I have a choice… When you were a kid…people would say, "Don't take it personally." It's like, "Well then, tell me how else to take it! You know?" And I think that the training gave me that…

SS: The first snowstorm this year, I was going to go out to the store to get some groceries, and I went out to get in the car and I had to scrape all the windows. And as I went around the car scraping the windows one by one I somehow broke off all the windshield wipers, so by the time I got done scraping my windshield I had no windshield wipers on my car. And I just got progressively more upset and more upset, and by the time I got done, I thought, "All I wanted to do was go to the store, get some groceries, and here I have my windshield wipers in my hand and I can't go anywhere because I can't see out the windows!" And all of a sudden it dawned on me that I was taking this personally, and I burst out laughing. And it was the first time it occurred to me that I could take something personally from an inanimate object, in that I would just get stuck in that way of thinking and get upset. And that was just an element of my deeper understanding of personal and impersonal, and that it had more to do with personalizing something, and it had to do with just the kind of thought that I was going into—those two different kinds of thought that I could find myself in. The minute I started to laugh at the windshield wipers all coming off my car, I switched out of personal thought into that lighter, freer thought that doesn't take things personally.

e. *Seeing their habitual thinking patterns, and transcending them by raising their level of understanding*

JL: I put on a really nice party for my daughter's graduation at a distance in Minneapolis, so I had to do a lot of the planning in Bemidji and go down there early to my mother's, and try to get everything together and figure out how many people were coming. This is not a big deal, but in the past I would have had quite a bit of sense of stress about, "Am I going to get everything done?" and, "Are there going to be enough chairs?" [laughs]. Just all those things. But every time I found myself thinking that maybe I would get a little bit worried about something, I would just say to myself, "It's going to work out. Just enjoy the fact that right now you're cutting up celery. You're with your ninety-three-year-old old mom here, it's not going to be much longer." So every time I found myself wanting to fall into an old habit of fretting, I would instead say, "However it works out, it's going to be okay." So people will have a nice time. And it was the most relaxed getting ready and the most comfortably relaxed party that I've ever had. We had enough chairs, and it was supposed to be a bonfire-wienie roast-veggie burger cookout, and it was raining. Actually everything went perfectly…

MO: I…tend to be very judgmental, but I'm coming more and more to the realization of that not being necessary,…that it isn't necessary to judge everybody all the time, even myself… I've got some strong habits, some strong patterns that exist… [Now] I give myself a lot more permission to do things, to explore things…

BC: You…realize, all of a sudden, I could get in touch with myself. I could be one thought away from health… I was all upset about something one day, and we had just gone through the training, and I thought, "I'm frickin' twenty-nine ideas away from health!" [laughter] I mowed the whole damn yard, and it was October [laughter], because BY was going to tie the handle on the lawn mower to let it run at of gas, and I thought, "I'll go out and mow the lawn." Then I felt much better because the lawn was mowed, and I got my exercise and then blew off some steam. And I kind of knew…while I was doing it, "…Okay, so maybe I'm twenty-eight thoughts away from health [laughter]. But it's just the thought! And the real thought is, "Oh, I'm in a low mood." That's your one thought away from health…is that recognition. And then just go, "Oh, maybe now isn't the time to [take care of] everything, because I'm low mood."

3. How did they come to have this new experience in life?

a. Something "just clicked"

JF: The first day…when I went to the training, I was like, "So?" But the second day it started to sink in. And by the third day I remember a moment where it just all came together, where I had that place of understanding, where all the pieces kind of came together… I remember tears came to my eyes, I remember that feeling of, "Oop, I'm going to cry." I remember just a real sense of peace and understanding…It was the third day and…people were talking. I don't remember exactly. I just remember this sense of "Ahhh, I see it now. I see it now." You know, it's been kind of like to me…those pictures that you can look at at the science center, and you can't see it and you can't see, and where's the…[3D] horse or whatever in the picture? And all of a sudden, "Whooo, I see it!"… That to me is what this Health Realization is about, I mean the way that you learn it. It's not like people see it just because you said it… They had to see it in their own insight, and at their own time. And so when it comes up for you, it's going to be a different time than it comes up for me. But I remember that experience of, "Ahhhh, I see it now." I can see it with my own insight.

b. They gained new understanding or knowledge about their psychological functioning

BY: One of the contributions of the training is that I have that notion in my repertoire now, and I didn't have it before… that most of the time, or all the time, people are doing the best they can, given where they are and what they're thinking. And that's a real state-of-grace statement in words,…and it's happened to me a couple of times. You really feel it. There's a shift there, and I think that's part of the truth, that seems to feel like truth about the concepts.

c. *They gained new tools*

MM: I hadn't realized before what an awful listener I was, and how wonderful it is to feel the closeness in really listening to somebody explore their own thoughts, come up with their own answers, and that's kind of hand-in-hand with relief... I don't have to come up with your answers. And I know that if I listen, that that's still of help to you... Sometimes I visit my dad, and he's eighty-five, and I have heard some of the same stories for years and years and years—I thought! And suddenly...I decided, well, it might be just a good time to practice deep listening. And...I heard the same story, but it wasn't the same story. And I heard something I never heard before. And it was amazing to me to see that, and have that happen, and go away with a much deeper sense and closeness to him, of somebody that I love so much. And so just with the quality of what that can bring to the quality of my life, it's really exciting to think about

4. What meaning did this have for their lives?

JF: I have more hope because until this came along there just didn't seem to be any hope for society's ills. I hate to say that this is the panacea for all of society's ills, but it has a hopeful quality... It gives me a sense that my life has meaning and purpose... Health Realization has done a lot for me... What this has done for me is woke me up more. I think of Health Realization as a spiritual experience, I would say, and an awakening. And it does help the quality of my life a lot. And when I bring it back to my Christianity, it just fits so beautifully into my journey there, so it integrates into my whole spirituality so beautifully. And I think it makes me better able to become who I was created to become, you know? And get the barriers out of the way. And then that just springs out into the family and to friends and to people, and so it's been really great.

BY: I can just share a comment with you that...one of my colleagues said at one of our gatherings... She's recovering, and she said after going through Health Realization..., "Yup, that AA destroyed my drinking, and Health Realization destroyed my thinking." [laughter]

5. What have they done with this newfound understanding?

a. *They naturally used their own understanding within their own families and primary relationships to improve those relationships.*
b. *They used it at work to improve relationships and effectiveness.*
c. *Some then helped their friends gain new understandings.*
d. *Some conducted their own Health Realization training for others in Bemidji.*
e. *Many continued to meet periodically to work for community change.*

JF: [My daughter] just is strong-willed, and I think I was trying to really, like, make her not strong-willed, and then that would make me a good parent. So once I kind of let her be who she is and validated that "you already are perfect inside somewhere"—you know, it just kind of validated her and made our relationship a lot better... We had just kind of been struggling a lot. We just fought about little things, you know, not being nice to her sister. And I'm always, kind of, like, you know, yelling at her..., "I'm sick and tired of—knock it off!"...because...every time I'd see her it was like she was...doing something...that I didn't like, so I was always pointing that out to her. So I was always kind of in this struggle with her for a long time. And so when I just came home and came up to her and said, "You know, I think maybe I've been kind of doing this wrong. I mean I really feel like... I think maybe you already have it, and I just...need to help bring that out in you." And she just lit up...and she said, "I told you!" And...she was so glad I finally was enlightened... So it just made the parenting thing like a whole lot easier.

MM: There's...people all over the place [as a result of these sessions], as far as on the continuum of...seeing little bits and pieces, to people who have been kind of hit over the head with a two-by-four, really, and seeing it in a huge way... I had one other experience that...was pretty profound... CJ and I were doing a group of fifty kids,...so we spent quite a bit of time talking about moods. And at the end of this three hours around a circle of fifty kids we asked them each to go around, if they were willing, to share if they learned something new or had some insight about something that we had said...and there was this girl—I think she was probably a senior—she started to get a little teary. And she said, "You know, I've been on antidepressants for several years, and...this is the first time anybody has ever told me that moods were normal, that other people had moods, and that all it was was a mood. And...it makes me feel so hopeful that someday I won't have to be on medicine, and it's normal, and the rest of you here have moods just like me, and...that's okay." And...I thought, every second that we have spent talking and thinking and preparing and whatever, was worth it for me in that instant. I thought, "Yes, that's what it's all about!"

Summary

Participants perceived and described that, one-year after Health Realization training, they experienced improved lives. All those interviewed experienced higher quality lives with better quality relationships, to varying degrees. Further, Health Realization training appears to have had a ripple effect in the community. Individually, in their worksites, and collectively as a community group, they continue to experience the process of working together to improve the quality of life in Bemidji, Minnesota. Further, one year later the participants expressed in various ways how their own understandings have continued to deepen.

This closing quote sums up what Health Realization offers for improving health and well-being:

SS: The really clear piece that's different for me is, in the general realm of psychology, it almost always deals with what people are thinking, what people are feeling, and it just focuses on those things, and...on why people think what they think, and the exact nature of their thoughts, and oftentimes there's not even a connection made between thoughts and feelings in that whole realm. And what really stands out for me is understanding that...psychology stays in the personal thought system, the place where I would have gone, into that defensiveness or that trying to understand the way someone thinks and analyze it and pick it apart, make meaning out of it in some way. And this differs for me in that I don't even have to go there… And I think as I learned more from that first impetus of the training…my understanding of that piece has grown, because I don't think I grasped that immediately at the training,…and that stuff's phenomenal, understanding that. The other part that I need more of an understanding of is the natural intelligence of our impersonal thought or our innate health or wisdom, and that I can trust it, that it's there, and I don't have to think about it [laughs], and that I can have all kinds of messy thought content, and be upset and annoyed, and I don't have to figure that out to get…myself out of it. That's a difference that I see…in the…more common realm of psychology is when we get into that messy thought content, like defensiveness or shame or guilt, you have to figure it out in order to get out of it. That's the common message, and Health Realization shows another way. Figuring it out just keeps you there longer. And you may get out of it eventually or you may not, but that I have— we all have—a healthier thought process that's just natural if we don't try to figure this out. If we just let it go and trust that we know what we'll need to know about it if we need to know something, and by letting it go we have better access to that understanding.

Quantitative Data

The following is a compilation of results from a retrospective survey questionnaire sent to training participants (n = 23 out of a possible 37 responses, a 62% response rate), of their perceptions after the training. Of these, 10 participants who were not interviewed filled out the questionnaire, and 2 who were interviewed did not fill out the questionnaire.

The following are the responses of the 23 survey participants about changes in their lives one year after their exposure to Health Realization training [Note: For a full breakdown of responses on the questionnaire, see Appendix B(2)]:

Improved "Inner life" ("the feelings you generally carry with you and what drives you")*:* improved very much (2); improved (19); remained the same (1); got slightly worse (1); got worse (0)

General *feeling level at work*: improved very much (3), improved (16); remained the same (2). [Note: None got slightly worse or got worse for the rest of the survey questions].

Relationships with their kids: improved very much (1); improved (13); remained the same (5). **On average, before the training, participants reported they got into arguments or fights with their kids approximately 5.6 times per week, compared with 2.4 times per week now [at the time the questionnaire was issued], a 57% decrease.**

Relationships with their spouses or partners: improved very much (4); improved (12); slightly improved (1); remained the same (4). **On average, before the training, participants reported they got into arguments or fights with their spouses or partners approximately 3.5 times per month, compared with 1.8 times per month now, a 49% decrease.**

Relationships with friends, co-workers, and neighbors: improved (12); slightly improved (3); remained the same (7).

Relationships with boss or supervisor: improved (12); remained the same (6).

Relationships with people they found difficult: improved (17); remained same (5).

Level of stress: **On a 10-point Likert Scale (10 = get stressed "very little"), participants now gave themselves a mean rating of 4.2, compared with a mean rating of 7.0 before the training, a 40% improvement.**

General quality of their life or well-being: **On a 10-point Likert Scale (10 highest), participants now gave themselves a mean rating of 8.0, compared with a 6.8 before the training, an 18% improvement.**

Participants also were asked, through a series of questions on a 10-point Likert scale, to circle the number that best represented where they would rate themselves today, and then where they perceived they were before exposure to Health Realization training (Highest = 10). Mean scores are below:

1. *If I experience a problem that I can't seem to solve I almost always try to put it out of my mind and wait until my head is clear so a solution can pop up as if from nowhere.*
   Before the training 4.4; since the training 7.1 (improvement of 61%)

2. *If I am bothered by something I almost always wait until my mood rises before I say anything or before I act.*
   Before the training 3.9; since the training 6.7 (improvement of 72%)

3. *If someone yells at me or insults me or does something to me that most people would consider hurtful or disrespectful I almost never take it personally; I almost always chalk it up to the way s/he is seeing things, or to a low mood.*
   Before the training 4.2; since the training 7.2 (improvement of 71%)

4. *I almost always realize in the moment how my usual, habitual way of seeing things is affecting my tendency to get myself in trouble or to lose my bearings.*
   Before the training 4.1 since the training 7.1 (improvement of 73%)

5. *I am often aware that how I am seeing someone or something is affecting how I feel.*
   Before the training 4.7; since the training 7.5 (improvement of 60%)

6. *I almost always see beyond people's appearances or actions to the health inside them, and I act as if they are the embodiment of that health.*
   Before the training 4.2 since the training 6.9 (improvement of 64%)

7. *I am usually lighthearted or see things philosophically, even when things go wrong.*
   Before the training 5.2; since the training 7.7 (improvement of 48%)

8. *I almost always realize that at any moment I can see things differently and therefore don't take myself too seriously.*
   Before the training 4.2; since the training 6.8 (improvement of 62)

9. *When working with others or with a friend, child, or partner who experiences a problem, I almost always try to get them to calm down, to regain his/her bearings, and only discuss it with them once they do.*
   Before the training 5.1; since the training 7.5 (improvement of 47%)

10. *How would I rate my general mental well-being that I live in most of the time?*
    Before the training 6.2; since the training 7.7 (improvement of 24%)

Interpretation

Training participants reported being more peaceful, more clear-headed, more content and less stressed. Their internal quality of life and well-being improved. Their relationships with their children and partners improved. Generally, they experienced fewer problems. This is consistent with the results of other Health Realization/Psychology of Mind research cited in Chapter X.

For study limitations and concerns, see Appendix B(3).

While not the primary intent of this study, the quantitative portion establishes minimally that in the worst possible scenario—even if every training participant who did not complete the questionnaire experienced no positive effect from the training, the majority (56.7%) of participants in two separate three-day Health Realization training sessions reported improvement in their lives as a result of that training. This suggests that the reports of those who volunteered to be interviewed for the qualitative study were not isolated phenomena, that similar experiences were shared by at least the majority of training participants. Of those who did respond to the questionnaire, 91% reported improvement in their lives. All this suggests that Health Realization training is a valuable approach for improving well-being.

Because Health Realization is an inside-out prevention approach, it could be said that personal transformation is not the desired end result; rather, only if the change within is demonstrated "out," in the form of community change, would this be a viable prevention effort. In this case, community change did begin to occur. Because of the efforts of those who participated in this training, increasing numbers of people in the Bemidji area are continuously exposed to Health Realization and experiencing improvements in their lives. As of this writing it is approaching 10% of the entire Bemidji population. Also as a result of people's exposure, a Health Realization effort has begun in the low-income Ridgeway housing project in Bemidji, which is already showing some results. Future research is warranted to determine what ultimately occurs. However, this study suggests that a ripple effect occurs after Health Realization training, fulfilling the highest purpose of a prevention training effort, according to prevention researcher Barry Kibel (1996).

Implications

Arguably the most significant result of this study—and an unanticipated outcome—is an assessment of these data yielded six key variables that likely determine whether people's lives change through Health Realization. In other words, *the degree to which people have personal insights in the following areas appears to largely determine whether and how much their lives change toward well-being:*

1. the degree to which people realize their own power of creation of their life experience—through Thought
2. the degree to which people faith and trust in, and are able to access, an unlimited source of health or wisdom or common sense within
3. the degree to which people realize the path of access to their health—a free and clear or calm mind—and what blocks it
4. the degree to which people recognize the signals—their feelings and emotions—that indicate whether or not they are in their health, to self-monitor

5. the degree to which people recognize in the moment their life experience coming to them from an inside, nonpersonal world or an outside, personal world
6. the degree to which people see the habitual thinking that keeps them stuck, and their ability to transcend it via levels of understanding

This study raises the possibility that the extent to which a person has a personal understanding of these key variables may determine the extent that person is able to lift themselves out of problems and live in well-being.

Recommendations

The experiences reported by participants are sufficiently compelling to substantiate Health Realization as an effective approach to prevention, in that it appears to help people change toward well-being and reduces perceived problems. This study found that Health Realization training reduces perceived stress, a known precursor to many problem behaviors (Pransky, 2001). Because of this, it is recommended that Health Realization be included alongside other prevention efforts deemed at least "promising," if not "effective," and that sufficient efforts are made to further explore the efficacy of this approach.

Finally, this study suggests two hypotheses, recommended for future study:

1. *The extent to which people are able to see their experience being created by Thought in the moment determines their engagement in healthy or non-problem behavior.*
2. *The extent to which people have faith or trust in, and allow themselves to be guided by their innate Health or wisdom determines whether they engage in healthy or non-problem behavior.*

This study raises the possibility that the degree to which a person understands these and perhaps the other variables identified in the Interpretation section above may well *determine* the extent to which that person is able to disengage from problems and live in well-being. Thus, the key recommendation is for a controlled study that measures these variables for their impact on behavior and perceptions of well-being.

Other recommendations of this study can be found in Appendix B(3).

A Supplemental Follow-Up Study

Science requires that study results be replicated to have real meaning. With this in mind, after another Health Realization training in Bemidji, I conducted another one-year follow-up study.

In addition, I wanted to see whether differences would be found when comparing the new (Principle-based) approach to the old (concept-based) approach.[14] Health Realization trainers had been saying that teaching solely by the Principles yielded even better results among participants—that is, participants appeared to gain heightened understanding that had an even greater impact on their lives. I wanted to find out whether this was true.

---

[14] As stated in Chapter VIII and Appendix D, until the late 1990s Health Realization training focused on helping people understand certain "concepts" intended to help them realize the three Principles in action, and the two trainings in the original study were conducted under that model.

In March 2000 I conducted another training in Bemidji for new participants, this time solely through teaching the three Principles. This training lasted 2½ days instead of the earlier 3-day trainings. These were the only differences. Twenty-six (26) participants attended this training session. One year after this training I conducted another study to measure effects on participants' lives, employing the same quantitative instrument used in my doctoral study. I did not conduct extensive interviews or use the phenomenological portion of the design.

Fourteen (14) of 26 returned questionnaires (54%). Results after one year showed, after this training, similar changes did, in fact, occur in participants' lives.

The Principle-based teaching methodology also proved effective. Comparatively, at first glance, it appeared that slightly higher changes could be observed for the first two (concept-based) trainings, because participants' overall scores appeared slightly higher. A closer look reveals otherwise; that the Principle-based training yielded even greater improvements:

- Compared with participants from the original study, participants in this new training entered the training with more stress in their lives (a level of 3.6 [high stress] in this training group, compared with 4.2 in the initial training group), a perceived lower quality of life (6.1 compared with 6.8), and a lower level of well-being (4.7 compared with 6.2). Because their scores began at a lower level, if these participants improved at the same rate, their one year post-test scores would also have been lower, which is what occurred.

- Results showed that among this new group of training participants the percentage of improvement occurred at a higher rate in 10 of 14 categories, compared with the original two training groups.

- Among arguably the three most important categories (stress, quality of life, and well-being), improved change within the new training group occurred at a much higher rate in two of the three. Both "quality of life" and "well-being" ratings were twice as high for this Principle-based training group (Quality of Life ratings: +36% for this third group, compared with +18% for the first two groups; well-being ratings: +57% compared with +24%). Both groups showed an equal 40% decrease in stress level ratings.

- Results for the new training group were attained in one-half day less time (2½ days for the Principle-based training, compared with 3 days each for the concept-based trainings).

These results, then, were replicated across the training groups—across the two studies—and the new, Principle-based training group showed even more improvement in less time. [See Tables in Appendix C for comparison scores.] An interesting aside is that MM and SS from the first training sat in on this Principle-based training as well (they did not fill out a second questionnaire), and afterwards they said, "I felt like I was at an advanced training."

For issues and questions raised by these data for Health Realization practitioners, see Appendix C.

XIII. APPLYING HEALTH REALIZATION AS AN INSIDE-OUT APPROACH IN COMMUNITIES

> People have within them something so powerful—the power to change, to monumental degrees. People are walking potential to change at any moment. They can change their minds, change their thoughts. People have the power to have truly clear minds, and from that clarity to have insights they never before dreamed, insights so powerful the world never looks the same; their lives never look the same. Our innate Health and its natural intelligence is always dormant within us, just waiting to rise to the surface. All we have to do is allow what we think we know to drop away, or not take it seriously anymore, and it will speak to us. It is so close to us that we have forgotten it is there—like the air we take for granted—yet it holds the key that unlocks the potential in everyone. For everyone there is hope out of the destructiveness, out of the depression, the anger, the fear, the insecurity—out of every conceivable emotion and resulting behavior. To access it, all we have to do is let it come through us by recognizing its power in our lives and trusting it.
>
> - excerpt from Jack Pransky's forthcoming self-help book

If the goal of inside-out prevention or Health Realization is to help people gain access to their own internal Health and well-being and then ripple out to create healthy communities, the question becomes, "How does one do it?" or "How can this best occur?"

An answer emerges from how we see the causes of people's problems. When we do not look for causes in the external world, what does it look like when viewed from the inside-out?

Sydney Banks (1998) offers an answer:

> Cut off from innate wisdom a lost thinker experiences isolation, fear and confusion... The misled thoughts of humanity, alienated from their inner wisdom, cause all violence, cruelty and savagery in this world (p.83).

If we see the cause of people's problems as their own thinking, which has severed them from their inner Health and wisdom, *our solution would be simply to help people connect with their innate wisdom and see how their thinking obscures it, thus raising their level of consciousness.* The word "simply," of course, is both accurate and tongue-in-cheek. The simplicity is that people connected with their wisdom do not create problems for themselves and others; thus, problems are prevented. On the other hand, there is no simple, sure way to help people find their wisdom.

159

What we do know is this: When people *realize* that the source of *all* their experience is Thought combining with Consciousness, emanating from the infinite power and possibilities of Mind, they tend to become more hopeful. This combination of realization and seeing new hope seems to be enough to right people, as a tipping-over boat suddenly finds its equilibrium.

So many people *think* there is no way out of their lot in life, that they are stuck with their hopelessness. So many people *think* they have to continue to be beaten because they can't imagine how it could change. So many people *think* they need to harm others or be violent. So many people *think* they are damaged goods for the rest of their lives because they were sexually abused. So many people *think* they have to drink or do drugs to have a good time or survive. So many people *think* they can't get a job because they will fail, because they have always failed. So many young people *think* they need to join a gang to be safe and survive. So many young people *think* their parents will never understand them. So many parents *think* they will never understand their kids; that their kids are "good-for-nothing." Could anything be more empowering than for any of these people to *see* Thought from a higher level of perspective and consciousness? This is what the inside-out/Health Realization approach to prevention seeks.

How do we best help people see this? Practitioners have pondered this question and often struggled with it since they first tried to understand what Sydney Banks *saw* from his direct experience. What did he *see* that the rest of us didn't? What do we understand for ourselves? How can what we understand be best communicated to others? These are fascinating and often baffling questions. As inside-out practitioners, our answers have been continually changing as our own understandings have deepened and, hopefully, our answers will continue to improve.

The reason there are no easy or set answers is because, were we to look inside ourselves, to the times we had the greatest leaps of understanding or when our lives underwent major change, if we asked ourselves how we learned what we did at those times and looked closely, we would see that we changed when we had a major insight. Always! It may appear on the surface that something outside ourselves caused us to have this insight, but that is never true. That same outside event could have happened in the lives of thousands of others, and they would not have had the same insight. Further, we may not have had the insight if that exact event had happened at a different time in our own lives. Thus, massive change in anyone's life—a shift in the very way one sees life—*must* come from *within*.

The problem in working with people is we are outside their heads. We are attempting from the outside to somehow convey knowledge or truth about the way we function so it is experienced on the inside. How can we teach something from the outside that makes change occur within? We can't! This is another paradox. We can only point people in the right direction. If we can get people to look in the right direction, they have a chance of finding it. If they are looking in the wrong direction they won't find it, except by accident. Therefore, all of our "teaching"—and by this I mean attempting to draw out an understanding that is already inside but presently obscured—is geared to pointing people in the right direction. As George Pransky says, we can get people to the bus stop, but we can't make them get on the bus. If people are not at the bus stop, the odds of getting on the bus are mighty slim. We can lead a horse to water—we can't make it drink, but if the horse is not at the trough or some other water source, odds are against it finding a drink.

With this in mind we approach our task. It is an attempt to point people in the right direction—within themselves—and find some spark that will ignite an insight. It is an attempt to get under the radar of people's current mindsets keeping them stuck. To do this we sometimes have to talk around the point—tell stories, use metaphors, use other examples—do anything that might strike a chord in people, because we cannot simply tell people what we know and expect to have any impact.

The Inside-Out Community/Organizational Empowerment Process: Helping People Understand Inside-Out Principles

The intent of the inside-out community or organizational empowerment process, then, is to first help people see how they function from within. This is intended to trigger an insight of enough magnitude to shift their perspective to Health and well-being. Once there, people tend to create an environment around themselves aligned with their newfound health. This leads ultimately to constructive community or organizational change.

To get a sense of how Health Realization practitioners attempt to bring this about, we look to logic. The "logic model" has recently become popular in prevention, and without adhering to a specific "logic model" design, Health Realization applies a certain logic to create its community prevention strategy. To begin, most all prevention practitioners would agree that fewer problems exist in a healthy community, so we could begin with that assumption: If community conditions are currently unhealthy and we want healthy, constructive community change that will decrease problems, here is my take on the logic behind inside-out prevention:

- Constructive community change likely will not occur unless people work together to make it happen.
- People will not work to make it happen unless they want to and can see the possibility of change.
- Given where many community people currently are at, without a shift in perspective they will likely not want to try or will not see the possibility of making any change happen.
- People are most likely to have a shift in perspective if they have new insight.
- People either have insights spontaneously (which is unpredictable and unlikely) or they can be positioned to have the best chance of gaining insights.
- People will be in the best position to have new insights about themselves and their lives if they can see how they function from within (by seeing the three Principles in action in their own lives).
- People will best take in this new understanding if it is conveyed in a way they can *hear* it and is relevant to them.
- It will be conveyed in a way most relevant and likely to be heard if people are deeply listened to; in other words, the more deeply we listen to people, the more we know what to say and how to say it so they will hear it.
- We can only deeply listen to people if they let us get close enough and if they are open enough to say what is on their minds.
- People will be most open if their minds are relaxed.
- People's minds are most relaxed when they are having fun or when it feels good, so they want to be around.

161

- To best create a good feeling, we must generally live in a good feeling ourselves and be in that good feeling in the moment.

This logic of the inside-out/Health Realization approach holds pretty much whether one is assisting a community, an organization, conducting a training, or even individual counseling.

If we began at the end of this logic—with the last bullet above and work our way backwards—it would reveal an inside-out prevention "process." Were we to proceed through this process, logic would dictate we would have the best chance of achieving our ends.

The Process of Applying Health Realization to Prevention

Following the logic above, four "components" appear to be necessary to successfully apply an inside-out/Health Realization approach to prevention programming and community development [See Figure 6]. While the four components should generally flow from one to another in sequence, much overlap occurs, so there is much back-and-forth movement. The sole purpose of the four components is to move people to a fifth—a shift in perspective—which no one can make happen but is really the desired result. When people have an insight of enough magnitude that it changes their lives so they function at a higher level, they then reach out to touch others' lives, and community change ripples out from there.

What can be said in this book about each of these components or "steps" only scratches the surface. Deep understanding takes experiencing each personally, and having one's own continuously growing level of understanding deepen within each area.

These are not "steps" or even "components" so much as bases to be covered. As I have said, there is much overlap. On the other hand, remember, this sequence follows from the logic.

    I.   ***Living the Feeling/Living the Understanding***
    II.   ***Creating the Feeling/Creating the Best Climate***
    III.   ***Deep Listening***
    IV.   ***Conveying or Drawing Out the Understanding (Teaching)***

    V.   ***Insight: A Shift in Perspective***
    VI.   ***The Ripple Effect***

This is the simplicity of it. Yet, its practice is not as easy as it sounds. There is no set way to bring about each of these. Each practitioner must find her or his own way that naturally feels right. In so doing the practitioner must pay close attention to its effects, and know humbly that something more can always be done that has not yet been seen. Experience suggests that certain ways of proceeding are more effective than others. The ingenuity of the worker in the moment is the only limitation, and this ingenuity can be hindered by the worker's own limited thinking.

I. Living the Feeling/Living the Understanding

The Health Realization practitioner must be a model of the Health s/he is attempting to bring forth in others. Thus, the health of the helper becomes the first focus. This is quite practical, for if the worker does not really know what s/he's talking about, or only pretends to know, then whatever s/he tries to convey will be heard merely as words or beliefs or theory and will fall on deaf ears.

The first "step," then, is for the practitioner to be "well grounded" in the three Principles. To me, this means:

1. having a solid understanding of the meaning of *the three Principles*
2. generally living one's own life in well-being
3. responding to adversity, and to others, without getting reactive or being "brought down"

As Mills and Spittle (1998) state, "We all lose our bearings at times. Our level of understanding is measured by how we regain our equilibrium and composure…and…maintain a good feeling" (p.41). We have and maintain this good feeling naturally—if we do not get caught up in our personal egos. If we see ourselves in a state of service to others, our well-being is less likely attached to how well our clients (or we) are doing.

Simply put, this means *having and emanating a good feeling*, and knowing where it comes from and how we lose it. When hiring a worker for a Health Realization project, we first look for that "good feeling," regardless of one's experience. Some have this feeling naturally. Others can be helped to find it within themselves—for it always exists deep within everyone—through training and immersion in understanding the three Principles. Prospective Health Realization workers must get to the point where they can see how the Principles play out in their own and others' lives.

As I said, to live it is the only thing that makes it real; otherwise it is only theory and has a hollow ring. If they don't live it themselves it is a lie, and others can feel it.

How do we know we are well grounded enough? Let's look deeper at the aspects of grounding by asking ourselves some questions:

1. Having the understanding

Do I understand the meaning of the three Principles: Mind, Consciousness, and Thought? Do I see how they create my life experience? Do I see how they create others' life experiences? How well am I able to articulate the understanding of the principles with clarity? [Note: On the surface this item may seem more like a teaching issue, but I see it at this stage more as checking out one's own learning.] Do I see how the principles relate to all aspects of my day-to-day life experience?

2 & 3. Living the understanding and responding to adversity

How well do I see the three Principles operating in my day-to-day life? Would I say I am living my life at a reasonably high level of well-being? Would others say I am? Do I treat

163

others with love and kindness and my neighbors and colleagues like myself? When I am down, am I able to see the bigger picture and not take my thinking too seriously, know it will pass, and get back on an even keel fairly quickly? Am I able to not take personally what others say or do to me or what happens to me? Do I look upon others without judgment and see innocence? Do I see others' Health and know they are always doing their best, given how they see things? Do I keep my bearings when others treat me badly or when things don't go my way? How well do I avoid taking on stress in my own life? When I am stressed or angry or fearful or down, do I realize I have created it?

4. Ability to draw out the understanding in others[15]

How well am I able to help others unveil their Health within? How well am I able to help others see the three Principles in action in their lives? How well am I able to answer questions in a way that enhances understanding instead of breeding confusion? How well do I see stories or metaphors in life that show the principles in action? How well can I draw the understanding out of others? How well can I touch people's lives? How much do people's lives change for the better after my attempts to convey the three Principles?

To sum all this up, *effective Health Realization practitioners are those who generally live in a state of Health and well-being themselves, who walk their talk, and who can draw the Health out of others.* Their own lives are a testament to living in well-being because, after being exposed to this understanding, their own lives became less stressed, more calm, and more lighthearted, with better relationships.

How did they become this way?

They came to realize that no matter how they see something—no matter how bad things look at the time—they have essentially made up with their own thinking how they see and experience it. No matter what happens, no matter what problems they may encounter, they know it is all a thought-created illusion.

They realize that no matter how badly things seem in the moment, their thinking can and will change, and with it their experience.

They realize that when their feelings are "off," they have simply dropped in levels of consciousness. They know things look different now from where they were, and they will look different again from a still different level. Therefore they cannot take too seriously how they presently see things.

They realize that no matter what is happening or how bad things look at the time, they are protected, because they are connected to Mind, and Mind is the source of all things. It is All things, therefore it is Oneness. As they are all part of that Oneness, they know there is nowhere to fall.

They are not driven by ego. They take their ego and what springs from it with a grain of salt.

---

[15] This last set of questions deals with another aspect of grounding we have not yet covered: How well are we able to convey the understanding to others? But here we are not concerned about actually conveying the understanding, because at this stage we do not even want to attempt to convey it. Instead, at this stage our questions are about whether we feel prepared to convey the understanding when the time comes.

They do not cause harm to others (at least not on purpose), because they see others as special and precious. They take care with others' feelings and help others meet their perceived needs. [Note: In one sense this may seem like a contradiction: if we are all part of the Oneness and people can have an experience of harm only via their own thinking, how can we really harm anyone? While on one level this may possibly be true, it is also true that when people are aligned with their Health they would not even think about harming another.]

All this is a reflection of personal grounding. When these practitioners enter a community or organization or a counseling relationship, they have their own experience of Health to pass along to others. People can only pass along what they themselves have experienced to have it be felt by another. If any of the above is lacking, that person will not be able to teach that particular thing to others. In other words, if someone is able to live his or her life without taking things personally, s/he will be able to help others live without taking things personally. But if that same person is judgmental of others, s/he will not be able to teach how to live without judgment.

It is not surprising that our effectiveness in applying these principles to prevention is dependent upon how we see this understanding of life. For instance—

> If we see this all as "garbage" it will be of no use to us—we won't even listen.
> If we see it as "one of many theories," we will say, "So what?"
> If we see it as "I know this stuff already," we will close ourselves off to the new.
> If we see it as a theory that makes sense, we will find it interesting.
> If we see it as a philosophy of life with real value, we will listen carefully.
> If we see it as Truth—the way we truly function—we will know it in our hearts.
> If we live it, and find more well-being and peace of mind in our lives as a result, then we will naturally be able to help others see it in their lives.

Each item on this list reflects a deeper level of understanding or, if we were to turn this list upside down, each item would reflect a higher level of consciousness. No matter what the level, it emanates from within, and when it comes "out" of us to the extent that other people can see it and feel it, only then we are ready to assist others. With this feeling in our hearts, we are ready to enter a community or organization.

II. Creating the Feeling/ Creating the Climate

Once we are well-grounded in the three Principles *and* once we emanate a healthy feeling, we are now ready to interact with others.

As I see it, this stage has a few different purposes. These are-

- to create a good feeling around us
- to see people in their Health and innocence
- to allow people's current thinking to slow down or shut down
- to open people up so they can hear the new
- to give hope that there is something worthwhile here, which stimulates curiosity and interest

- to build connection within a group or community so people are more willing to share what is on their minds
- to draw out people's innate Health

A close look will reveal that all these purposes are directly connected. To accomplish one is to accomplish all. If we are "living the understanding" and "have the feeling," we naturally go out of our way to create a healthy climate around us.

What do I mean by a healthy climate? Simply, I mean an environment or atmosphere that emanates a good feeling. This feeling is no mystery. It is a feeling that we all like to be around: lighthearted, fun, warm, supportive, respectful. We need not make it any more complicated than that.

Why go out of our way to develop a healthy climate? Because in a healthy climate people are most open to take in new understandings. Each person we meet in our communities or organizations (or training or counseling sessions) will be at a different level of openness. Many carry around beliefs about themselves and others, philosophies of life or theories about how the world works. They carry what they "know" about what works, based on scientific research or their own observations or their past, and probably lots more. We all have a lot on our minds; the more we have on our minds about what we "know," the less room there is for the new. If we can elevate people's feelings or mood levels, they will forget about their own beliefs and ego for a while and will be more open to new insights. In inside-out prevention, by creating a healthy external climate around people we help draw out their internal Health, much as trees in a forest gravitate toward the light. An atmosphere that feels good also makes people want to be around us, want to hang out with us. It builds trust. It also happens to work best.

It seems to me there are four main facets to creating a fully healthy climate:

1. *Seeing people's Health, and how it gets obscured*
2. *Having fun with people*
3. *Building rapport*
4. *Building hope*

These obviously overlap with the "purposes" stated earlier, but here we are interested in what we can *do* to create a good feeling when we walk into a community or organization. These we can take one at a time.

1) Seeing people from a perspective of Health

No matter how badly people act, we want to see them as the Health they really are deep inside. We need to *know* everyone has this Health; everyone deep inside *is* this Health. We know this because we are talking about people's spiritual essence, so to speak, and this is what we are seeing. Or, if we personally do not believe in a "spiritual essence," we could instead see people as an unlimited, infinite capacity to rise above their presenting behaviors or above their circumstances and see anew. We see that people have innate qualities of natural mental health, natural self-esteem, and natural wisdom and common sense, no matter how badly they act, or we see they have the capacity to achieve these at any moment. When we look at someone, we see her or his potential. We see hope. We see them as having inside

166

themselves all the answers they will ever need. We know they have the capability to tap into this inner, healthy state for themselves, and this can happen at any time, no matter how bad things look at the moment.

Seeing people as healthy would never be in question if we see beyond people's presenting behavior, no matter how troubled or troubling it appears. When we truly see this Health in people they feel it. Even if we do not believe people have innate health in them, if we treat people as if they have it they generally respond better.

Another aspect of this is to see people's innocence; in other words, to see people as always doing their best, given their current thinking. If they saw it differently, they would do it differently. We are, in essence, our innately healthy Self that innocently gets lost. We *know* the only reason people are not in touch with their Health is because their thinking has obscured it, diverted them from seeing it. When people break the law, are violent, abuse their kids or partners, abuse drugs, are depressed, give us a hard time, it is only because their thinking is "off" and they aren't aware of it. They have no choice other than to act on what their thinking tells them. They don't know their thinking is off-kilter, skewed. They are only following what they see. In that sense, people are innocent; they can't see anything else.

If they're innocent, it is not difficult to see them with compassion, for it must be hard to live life the way see it. We can see them with humility, because we ourselves have done things in our lives that looking back we wish we hadn't but didn't know any better at the time. We can see them with forgiveness, "for they know not what they do." Thus we do not have to take personally what they do to us because it is just their crazy thinking talking. This insulates us.

When Roger Mills first started teaching his classes in the Modello housing project (Pransky, 1998) the residents did not treat him with kindness and caring. They wanted him out of there! They treated him accordingly. Yet, in Mills's mind was something like, "Of course they're going to treat me this way, given the way they see things now." That was his protection, the reason he didn't get brought down. He had faith that once they began to see their Health, they would eventually come around. And they did. In the meantime, the initial meetings were chaos. Yet it was Mills's own Health in this regard that insulated him from both the chaos and whatever the residents did.

One reason people lose touch with their Health is they don't realize everyone sees the world differently, they don't realize everyone sees a "separate reality." Everyone has had different experiences and has been taught to see the world in different ways. This forms a perspective—a lens through which they see the world—that makes perfect sense to each individual, given the way s/he sees things, just as our perspective makes perfect sense to us. When people's perspective takes them away from their Health, wisdom and common sense, their own constructed reality has given them a distorted view. They are simply swimming in their own thought systems they have created without knowing it. Within their worlds, they can justify anything they think and do. When people act disruptively or destructively, they are simply unable to see beyond their own creations that to them are "real" right now. But we know their creations are not real, and that is what protects us.

Seeing innocence does not mean denying someone is causing harm to another or displaying a lack of conscience by their actions. It has nothing to do with appropriate consequences. If they did harm, if they broke laws, they may have to pay, but that has nothing to do with the way we see them. If we hold grudges it only harms us, for those grudges are only within us. Forgiving and forgetting is letting go. It is our release. It frees

167

our mind, so we can regain our clarity, regain our perspective, and move forward with impunity. People are innocent because they aren't aware they've lost their perspective. We can see that people's worlds make perfect sense to them—as much sense to them as our world makes to us. When we see this, we take what others do and say less personally, and our egos are less likely to bring us down when people aren't responding.

To see people this way gives us a certain perspective and feeling that helps to naturally guide us in our interactions. With that feeling in our hearts we approach others; then we act.

2) Having fun with people

Nothing draws people out of their conditioned thinking more than being relaxed, lighthearted, having fun, and feeling supported, cared about and respected. At those times people seem to forget the way they normally think. Practitioners who go out of their way to create this atmosphere around them in whatever they do find people are drawn to them, because it feels good.

Having fun with people makes them want to come around. Simply hanging out with them and being lighthearted makes people feel good and their defenses start to break down.

We also can create opportunities for fun. In the Modello housing project Mills and his staff began to celebrate people's birthdays. They then went on picnics together, then to the beach, then on larger outings. Staff and residents were equal participants—no barriers. Lo and behold, the residents responded and began to open up.

What could be a better job than this!

The idea is to create a relaxed, light, positive environment where people will be most open to new learning, to have a good time with people so their barriers will naturally drop away. People's defenses and belief systems begin to break up a little. If people become immersed in good feelings they may inadvertently leave their entrenched thought systems behind. This is why this and the next related point are essential.

3) Building rapport

With a relaxed, positive environment and good feelings comes the building of rapport, which becomes our primary concern when dealing with anyone. In its simplest form, especially in the beginning, rapport is simply getting to know people and becoming friends. Lloyd Fields tells the story of when Roger Mills first hired him to work in Modello with him. Lloyd asked what he wanted him to do. Mills said, "Just go and be with the people, make friends with them. Lloyd asked, "And then what?" Mills said, "All I want you to do is go and be with the people." "I know I'm supposed to do that at first, but what do I do next." "*Just go and be with the people!*" In other words, don't even think about doing anything else until you have hung out with them to the point where you have developed rapport. Unless that exists, there is no sense doing anything else with them or saying anything else to them, because they won't be able to hear it.

When working with anyone, either one on one or as a group, a certain feeling exists within the relationship, a certain closeness or distance, a certain warmth or coldness. Without a reasonable feeling of closeness people's walls are often up. They are on guard. We would like people to see their lives with more perspective and understanding, but if they don't let us in then no learning can take place. Rapport breaks down the barriers so we can get in.

When working from the inside-out, practitioners who see rapport as their primary concern tend to get further with others than those who do not. Even when confronted or challenged people respond better if rapport is high. Without it people get defensive. We can see this in our own kids. Teachers can see it in their students. If we want people to learn from us, rapport must be at a high level. We can feel the rapport or lack of it. If we don't feel it, or if we had it but feel it slipping, we need to stop what we're doing and rebuild it.

For example, if I'm talking with my child about a concern and I can see he's not paying attention or is in a bad mood, I have to realize I'm not going to get anywhere with him at that time, no matter how hard I try. I either have to wait it out until he recovers on his own, or go out of my way to reestablish a warm, caring feeling before bringing up the concern again later when we are both more open. For the most part, rapport comes from the respect we feel for the other person, and having a warm feeling which comes from seeing the person's Health.

We must be dedicated to staying in rapport and enjoying our time with people because it leads to trust and mutual respect.

Rapport is easiest when we are in a positive state of mind. If someone is in a low state, we want to do what we can to help their mood rise before dealing with them.

If we want to be effective with anyone, people need to know we are there for them and they can count on us. Rapport comes naturally when people are grounded in their own Health and see the Health in others.

4) Building hope

Again, everything the Health Realization practitioner attempts to do initially is to open people to the fact that no matter what their lives have been to date there are always new possibilities. We can create the kind of climate where people will begin to feel the Health within them. Some haven't felt this for a very long time. For a seed to fulfill its potential as a healthy plant it must be in an environment that helps draw out or doesn't impede what is inside. When people begin to feel this Health, the thinking that has held them in place begins to break up and have less hold over them. When we see people as healthy, they begin to feel more healthy. It gives them hope. When they see hope, a world of possibilities opens before them.

It is curious why some people see hope and others don't, even in the same situation. For example, most prevention practitioners see hope and possibilities, while many of the people they work with do not. Why? Are the hope and possibilities not there? Of course they are! They are only obscured from view. Why? Conditioned thinking is in the way—maybe it was their parents telling them they were no good or would never amount to anything; maybe it was having all kinds of terrible things happen to them. Whatever it *was,* it is *now* incorporated into their thinking—blocking them from seeing hope and possibilities for their lives. The way out of this, or the way one can be helped to see beyond it, is to see this barrier for what it is—one's own thinking. Their own thinking is the only thing blocking hope and possibilities. So people begin to see they are constructing their own barriers, and when they see this the barriers begin to break up. Once the barrier disintegrates, what is left? The hope and possibilities that were always there in the first place! [Figure 8]

169

Without hope, people have nothing. With hope, possibilities abound that we can't even imagine.

The daughter of two close friends of mine, Walter and Valerie Crockett, gradually began to lose her coordination. She was diagnosed with an inoperable brain tumor, or so said a couple of brain surgeons. But after Walt and Val recovered enough from the shock so they could function, they held out hope and kept exploring until they found a top surgeon who thought there was a chance of helping her. He operated with his "magic hands," as Valerie sings, and was able to get most of the tumor out. All were overjoyed, but the long-term prognosis was not good. The doctors said it would likely grow back; it was only a matter of time. Emily showed tremendous bravery going through radiation treatments or chemotherapy or whatever it was, where her head swelled up to twice its size. She was in tremendous pain.

Valerie and Walter Crockett are excellent musicians and gifted singer-songwriters, and they had cut a couple of CDs, but because they had to stay home and care for Emmy they couldn't tour to promote them. Because they are such wonderful parents and their kids always come first it never occurred to them to do anything else. Meanwhile Emmy began to listen to country music, especially her favorite singer, Garth Brooks, on whom she had a pre-teen crush. She dreamt about him and was convinced she'd meet him. Her parents didn't see much chance of that.

One day when her condition began to look extremely bleak, with Emmy in tremendous pain, looking like she was losing all hope, it occurred to Val and Walt to contact the *Make a Wish Foundation* and *Dreams Can Come True* and *Why Me, Inc.* to see if they could arrange for Em to meet Garth Brooks. The Foundation said he was just coming off a long world tour and would be playing his last concert in New York City, and there was a slight chance they could meet then. A limousine arrived at their doorstep in Worcester, Massachusetts to bring them to New York City. They sat in a room waiting. The foundation could not guarantee he would show up at all, and if he did they said he would likely be able to visit for only a few minutes.

Suddenly, Garth Brooks bounded into the room. He became so taken with Emmy that he stayed with her for over a half-hour. Emmy beamed. As he was ready to leave he said, "So you're coming to the concert tomorrow night, right?" Walter said, "Gee, we weren't really planning on it. We're not even prepared to stay. We didn't bring any extra clothes with us. We just thought we were coming down and going right back." Garth said something like, "Of course you'll stay," and pulled out a roll of bills. He said, "You'll stay on me. Buy yourself some clothes. I won't hear of anything else." They were floored! Keep in mind, at this time Garth Brooks was huge—so huge that, worldwide, only the Beatles and Elvis had sold more records. And this incredibly popular man put them up in a hotel at his own expense and arranged for them to be at the concert in the set of box seats with his family. At the end of the concert, on his own, he visited with Emmy again, and they spent more time together. And as they were leaving, he gave Emmy his guitar, the one he'd had with him on this worldwide tour, and signed it personally to her.

The family went back to Worcester to resume their lives, but a miraculous thing began to happen. Emmy's spirits had lifted so much that she began to get better—not completely better (she is now legally blind), but enough to resume fairly normal activities. As of this writing, not only had she survived far longer than any doctors had imagined, she was thriving, having her best year since her illness.

Valerie wrote an extremely moving song about the experience, and Emmy herself wrote a great song about it too. Both can be found on the CD, *Emily's Angel* by Valerie and Walter Crockett (www.vwcrockett.com). Emmy even makes a guest appearance on the CD to sing her song. But it all happened because, through that meeting and all that ensued, Emily Crockett saw new hope for her life.

[Postscript: Emmy visited with her angel, Garth Brooks, again and played him their songs about the experience from the CD. Garth cried. I was not a Garth Brooks fan, but now he'll always hold a warm spot in my heart. My own wish is that he'd record one of Walter's wonderful songs on his own CD. But I supposed that's wishful thinking. One never knows, though. There's always hope!]

Hope is the most powerful thing in the world. Without it people give up.

How do we give people hope? The greatest hope in the world is the hope that comes from *knowing* that all people, no matter what their lives look like at the moment, have Health and wisdom inside them that can spring forth at any moment. It is *knowing*, as Syd Banks says, that people are always only one thought away from that Health. We just don't know when that thought will come. But it could happen in the next moment, because that has happened within many people. People's thinking has been known to change at the drop of a hat, and when it does their experience changes and, with it, sometimes their entire lives. Any of us who have seen this happen have a story to tell, and often those stories can give hope to others. We can tell those stories when the time feels just right. We can suggest to people that the way it looks right now isn't necessarily the way it *is*. We do have to be careful—the rapport and the feeling and the moment have to be right—but when it happens it can be very special.

This "step" in the inside-out/Health Realization process is similar to that used in any effective preventive effort because it builds healthy relationships. It is important to realize, however, that in inside-out prevention it takes on even greater significance. It becomes *the* emphasis, before anything else is attempted. Nothing else can even be attempted until rapport and a good feeling exist.

All this sets the stage for the next "step" in the process.

III. Deep Listening

If we want to affect people from the inside out, we must be able to see what is inside them (figuratively speaking). The best way I know to see or hear this is through what I call "deep listening." Other terms I have heard to describe it are "soft listening," "quiet listening," "passive listening," or when working with little kids "magical listening."[16] It doesn't matter what one calls it; it matters whether we engage it.

As I see it, deep listening has a number of related purposes, and each could represent a deeper level of listening. Some of these are:

- to feel a close connection to the person
- to not be distracted when listening by one's own thinking
- to understand how the person sees his or her world
- to hear the grain of truth in the other person's point of view

---

[16] This term was coined by Debra Crosby of Swampscott, Massachusetts.

- to hear what the person does not see about his or her own thinking, to know the best place to potentially have impact

In a workshop in Tucson, Arizona, as we were going around the room during the initial introductions, I watched one woman become so interested in what others were saying that at the break I approached her and said, "I couldn't believe how much you were listening to others when we were going around. I was impressed!" Matter-of-factly, she replied, "Oh I'm just really fascinated with what other people have to say." That is deep listening! That's the idea, to be fascinated by others.

When people feel deeply listened to, rapport improves. So this also helps with the second "step" in the Health Realization process.

Let's be very clear about something. Many prevention and human services professionals have been taught "Active Listening" or "Reflective Listening" or "Empathic Understanding"—all different terms for essentially the same thing. *Deep listening is none of these*; in fact, it may be its opposite. In Active Listening the listener concentrates on the content of the communication so s/he can repeat back or clarify what the other person is saying. In deep listening we do not pay attention to the content, we do not listen to the words, we do not listen for the facts or details, we do not pay attention to body language or anything else. In deep listening we have nothing on our minds. In Active Listening we fill our heads with what the talker says; in deep listening we want our minds as empty as possible. In deep listening we are simply *taking in the other person*, almost as if listening to music. Most of us when listening to music do not analyze it, we simply let it wash over us or sift into us and, if powerful enough, move us. In short, most of us *don't think about it*. This is what we are after in deep listening. Even the implication of "doing" is misleading. Deep listening is more of a "nondoing." It is completely natural. It is the way we were meant to listen to others without our own thinking interfering.

Listening for a Feeling

Many of us in the fields of prevention and human services believe we are good listeners. I no longer think so. I used to think I was a great listener. Once I learned deep listening I could not believe what a poor listener I was. It wasn't my fault. I never knew there could be another way. [I thank George and Linda Pransky for teaching me.] After all, this is not the kind of listening we are used to. Most of us have been programmed to listen for content. In deep listening, again, we are looking beyond the words to what the person is really trying to communicate—to the spirit of the message behind the words, to what is really going on within them. In deep listening, at least on an initial level, the idea is to be touched by the feeling of the other person.

We want to listen with soft ears the way a baseball player learns to have soft hands when fielding a ball. When a hard ball is hit hard at a fielder, the hands must give with the force of the ball; otherwise the ball bounces off the hands like it would off a wall. In deep listening, we want to take in what the other person is trying to say without it bouncing off our thick skulls.

The first "step" in deep listening is to clear our heads and allow ourselves to slip into a receptive, soft frame of mind. Again, we want nothing on our minds!

Here is what helped me most with deep listening: When I listened to others I never realized that while they were talking I would have thoughts. I might have thoughts about what they were saying, or what they were saying would remind me of something else, or I might get distracted, or I might drift off, or any of a million things. Then, without realizing it, I would follow my own thoughts while the other person was still talking, and sometimes I would lose the talker completely. I have run enough workshops in Health Realization and deep listening to know I am not alone. We all have this tendency. This is the opposite of having nothing on our minds.

What, then, are we to "do?" Again, it is not really doing, it is more of a *noticing*. No matter how hard we try we can't shut off our thinking. When listening to someone else we will have extraneous thoughts, guaranteed! All we have to do, though, is notice our thinking has left the other person and is now off in our own heads. As soon as we notice our thinking has "gone off," our mind will jump back to the other person, like letting go of a taut rubber band.

From running workshops, I have observed that when most people experience deep listening for the first time it feels wonderful to them. Simply by deeply listening to another human being they feel such closeness to that person, often a complete stranger. At the same time they are amazed at how often their own thinking leaves the other person and travels off in their own heads.

I have also noticed many people pick this up easily (although sometimes as easily slide back into their old listening habits), while a few run into problems because they think they need to "do" something. They try to concentrate on it, so they find it hard. There is nothing hard about it. It is simply being. The only thing that makes it hard is we get in our own way. With our own thinking we interfere with our natural way of being with others.

In a workshop in Western Australia, one young man caught the importance of deep listening until he realized that his mother-in-law, who drove him crazy, was coming over that evening, and I had the audacity to suggest he might want to try deep listening to her. He put his arms straight out—stop!—and shook his head vigorously. "No way!" Apparently his mother-in-law told the same stories again and again, and it drove him mad. I said, "Look, you're already having a lousy experience with her, what have you got to lose?" He shook his head some more. Everyone laughed. The next morning he came in beaming. He said, "I decided to try it, and it worked!" He said he heard things in what she said that he had never heard before—even in the same old stories—and it was really interesting. He felt a lot closer to her.

This is the power of deep listening.

Even with the most boring or repetitious person, wouldn't it be interesting to listen for what would make a person feel he had to do those things? This raises another point: Deep listening can occur at various levels.

This first level of deep listening is simply feeling a close connection with another human being. Because we are all part of the same river of life, this is the connection we would naturally feel if we weren't thinking extraneous thoughts while listening. In other words, if we didn't have the thought, "This person is boring!" we would not be bored. We would be naturally interested, if not fascinated, with whatever the person had to say. A close connection automatically has a nice feeling attached. When feeling it, we are listening in a deep, connected way. During this kind of listening we feel an ease float over us. If it is

173

effortful, we are off the mark. Our intent during this level of deep listening is simply to pick up a feeling—a good feeling that comes from truly connecting with another human being.

Listening to Understand Another's World

At a second, deeper level the feeling remains but we also pick up something else: an understanding of what the other person is seeing. We see something of the way that person sees her world. We are seeing why the person sees things as she does. We are seeing what makes sense to her. From this viewpoint, what she sees makes sense. We may not agree with it (later), we may question it (later), we may not see it the same way ourselves, but we understand why that person would see it that way, and her reason makes sense to us. "Oh, I understand how she could see that!"

At this level, we can pick up how the person makes sense of his world, and how he may be trapping himself—not by analyzing it, not by trying to figure it out, not by fitting it into anything we know, but simply by what occurs to us in the moment from what we hear. With a clear mind, intuition speaks.

An example: A woman in an inner-city housing project was being bruised and battered by her live-in boyfriend. Asked why she stayed with him, she said, "At least it means he cares for me." The Health Realization worker had difficulty comprehending the connection, but he kept his head clear and listened more deeply. Suddenly the idea popped into his head that she was insecure about being alone; that all she really wanted was someone to love and care for her. But something didn't compute. No matter what? A question came to him: "You mean he shows you how much he loves you and cares for you by beating you up?" She seemed almost startled by the way he put it, but didn't say anything. It occurred to him to offer, "My life isn't like that. That's not how I show my wife that I love and care for her. I think she's worth more than that. I think you are too." Within two months she booted the man out of the house and found a new boyfriend. It all started from the power of deep listening.

In deep listening, we might ask questions or, far less frequently, offer a viewpoint, but these arise directly out of a quiet mind. In deep listening, we are never analyzing or "figuring out." Our questions may surprise us as much as they surprise the other person. We also want to be a little suspicious of our question and perhaps hold it back unless we feel gut-certain it is right. It is far better to ask nothing and simply listen than to try to think up a question. Making comments is even worse. The comment in the above example came out of listening in the moment. It felt right to say it, which is the only reason it had impact.

Listening for the Grain of Truth

Our listening can easily get off track. Fortunately, we can realize it and get back on. Here is an example: On the first day of a Health Realization II (Applications) training, a man objected when I made the statement that everything is an inside-out affair, that no matter what experience we have, it is always the result of our own thinking. Khalil said something like, "Now wait a minute! I can't buy that. Some experiences are absolutely determined by the outside." He raised the example of, as a Black man, walking into an elevator and coming upon a White woman. He said he knows damn well she is afraid because he can see it in her eyes. Very forcefully he said that cultural and racial issues determine this reaction, based upon where we are in this society today, and neither that woman nor he is making it up.

I asked whether this always happens with every White woman he encounters in this situation. He said, "Always!" His answer surprised me. I can't remember exactly how I responded, but I remember feeling very solid and confident in what I said—something like, "That is certainly the way it looks on the surface. Clearly some people learn things like that as they go through life, but that doesn't mean the outside world determines how we think and that we're stuck with it."

I remember leaning back in my chair feeling very relaxed, even while he was still objecting forcefully—until the thought popped into my head, "I can't believe I'm sitting here discussing this emotionally charged racial issue with an African American man, when I've never had the experience and it has obviously affected him big-time." A killer thought! I believed it. I took the thought seriously. Big mistake! Suddenly I no longer felt on solid ground. He said I was polarizing the issue; that it was both the inside and the outside that makes a difference. He said with force, "It is *never* good to polarize and dichotomize!" The conversation became tense. All eyes were upon me to see how I would handle it. The feeling in the room dropped. In one respect I was kind of amused: This man was extremely intelligent, sharp as a whip, very tall, well-built, strong; I knew he had spent time in prison, and I had the thought that if he ever wanted to wipe me out it would be like flicking a fly off his arm. Fortunately, I then had the thought that this conversation was no longer productive for the group, offered some feeble closing comment, and we took a break.

During the break I pulled Khalil aside. Before all this we'd had a good connection; I thought we'd had good rapport and that he really liked what he'd been hearing about Health Realization. So I said, "I hope you didn't think I was putting down what you were saying or giving you a hard time or anything." Before I could even finish, he cut me off and said, "Oh, no, not at all! I really got a lot out of that conversation. I could tell that you were really listening to me, and I appreciated that." I was a bit surprised, but we talked some more in a good feeling. After the break, to be certain that no feelings lingered, I announced to the group that Khalil and I were cool; the feeling in the group rose again, and we proceeded on from there.

In the middle of the night I woke up realizing that as soon as I started to run scared in that discussion, I had stopped listening to him. My listening had been pathetic. Taking a step back, I realized I had been too caught up in my "position" to hear the grain of truth in his side.

I realized his view contained two grains of truth: 1) Dichotomies are dangerous because they polarize, and it is best to find common ground; 2) Social and cultural forces affect people's thinking. Both points are absolutely true. Had I been listening deeply enough at the time, I would have picked those up, and we would have had common ground from which to proceed.

On top of that I realized that my view had a couple of core grains of truth related to each of his: 1) Dichotomies do tend to polarize and are dangerous in that respect, and this is true within the outside-in world and perhaps even within the inside-out world, but *between* those two worlds we do in fact have a dichotomy, whether we like it or not. It is impossible to be in or think out of both worlds at the same time. 2) It is always and only our own thinking that ultimately determines our experience, no matter what social and cultural forces we are subjected to.

The next morning I explained to the training group what I had realized: how I had lost deep listening, and last night when I found it again I had seen the grains of truth in both our views. It elevated the entire conversation and feeling.

One of the morals of this story is that there is *always* a grain of truth in the other side, and if we listen deeply enough we can hear it. I could now see Khalil's world—at least as much as I could regarding this issue—and after I explained the "truth" I saw, he could see mine. We then we had common ground on which to proceed. Both our worlds were elevated. The point, again, is when we listen at an even deeper level we can hear the grain of truth in the other side, and this comes directly from seeing how the other person sees his world.

Listening for What the Talker is Not Seeing about How Thought Creates Experience

At a still deeper level, our listening can pick up what the other person is not seeing about how her own thinking creates her experience.

Even at this level, our minds still must be free and clear—we are still feeling the feeling, we are still picking up the other person's world. We are merely adding a new dimension. At this level of listening we want to be puzzled by what the person is saying: "I'm puzzled. This person doesn't seem to realize that his thinking has anything to do with how he feels and acts. I'd like to see more about what he's missing."

Here questions might occur to us. Again, we are not trying to *think up* questions; that only gets in our way. If a question does occur to us, by asking it we may begin to affect the understanding of the other person.

What do I mean by *affecting the talker's understanding*? Through our listening and puzzlement and questions that occur to us out of this puzzlement, we might help the talker enter a state of deeper reflection. This happens because *we* want to better understand. However, the questions we ask are not the kind that keep the person going further down the same road with what she already knows, such as "What did you do about that?" or "How did that make you feel?" or "What were you thinking?" The talker already knows the answers to those questions because the answers are in the past. Nor are questions about the future particularly helpful here, such as "What are you going to do?" because the talker will base her answer on her current view. Instead, we want a question that helps the person see more deeply in the moment, such as "What do you make of that?" [Note: It is tough to come up with sample questions of this kind because there are no standard questions; they occur to the listener in the moment.] It is a question that takes the listener out of the "rattling on" mode—talking about what she knows—and it brings her into unknown territory so the talker becomes surprised. She never considered that before. At an even deeper level of impact, the talker has new insights simply from our listening and questioning.

An example may help to clarify this: Barbara was rattling on in great detail about being frustrated by someone she felt was not being respectful to a group of kids and who appeared to be pushing his own political agenda on them. The listener asked, "What did he say? What did you do?" This caused Barbara to go into even more detail. I happened to be eavesdropping because it occurred during a listening exercise in my workshop, and a thought of curiosity came to me. I wondered what was behind her reaction. So I asked, "What makes you bothered by that?" It stopped her dead in her tracks. She had to go into reflection and consider it. She began to see that it had something to do with her own expectations for the meeting, and for the kids' needs not getting fulfilled. Then she wondered, "So what?" Why was that important to her? Then she realized she carried some beliefs about how kids should be treated and how bad it was for anyone to thrust political agendas onto others. Suddenly she had an insight that not only were her own expectations a killer (that is, they gave her a bad experience of that meeting), but *any* expectations are deadly. She then had an "ah ha!" experience, as she realized that expectations always come from beliefs. Her own beliefs, which were her own thinking, had gotten in the way of an experience that would likely have been a good one otherwise; furthermore, she ended up doing that to herself a lot! So did others. It was a huge insight for her. All this came from deep listening, puzzlement, and a question that arose from that puzzlement.

Questions such as "What did you say?" and "What did you do?" are horizontal questions. They yield more detail, while the person remains at the same level of understanding. Such questions take people further along the horizontal road. Conversely, questions such as "What makes you bothered by that?" are vertical questions. They come out of our own puzzlement and draw the listener into a zone of deeper understanding. They are vertical because they take the person deeper.

In a conversation between helper and helpee, if we engineered our minds, so to speak, to pick up deeper questions, then forgot about it all and cleared our heads, we would have a better chance of picking up the right questions. By engineering I mean simply pointing ourselves in a direction, setting an intention, to pick up what the person is missing. For example, if we are about to buy a car and ride down the street, it is very likely we will clue into the makes and models of cars. Normally we might not even notice, unless a car looked out of the ordinary or we loved a particular model or we were a car lover. When going to buy a car, however, our minds are "engineered" to be aware of cars. Without consciously thinking about it, we have pointed ourselves in this direction. In a similar way, we intentionally can engineer ourselves to pick up things in a conversation. Again, we are not consciously looking for these things or thinking about them, but our minds are geared to picking them up. For example, we could engineer ourselves to pick up, "What is this person not seeing about his thinking?" Again, we wouldn't want to have that thought on our minds at the time because we would no longer be deep listening. In fact, the only way to hear the answer to this question is for our heads to be clear, for if we carry any preconceived notions we will only be listening to our own notions and seeing whether things fit or not.

We want to listen for what doesn't make sense to us about what the person is saying, what does not compute. Our questions help us gain more clarity. "What do you make of the fact that you keep finding yourself in similar predicaments?" People, commonly, don't readily know the answers to these types of questions. If they did, they would tell us. We're looking to get touched, to get hit by a feeling through a clear mind, so an insight will pop into our heads about what the person does not see about how her thinking affects her life.

When the worker listens with an empty mind s/he is able to see how people have innocently become lost in their own habitual thinking. Therefore the listener knows what to zero in on to help the talker gain deeper understanding.

How would we know specifically what to teach people—how unbeknownst to them their thinking creates an insecure or fearful or angry or blaming or judging or anxious or stressed feeling in life—if it is also unbeknownst to us? The only way to discover what is going on inside them is through listening. Otherwise we're shooting in the dark, teaching about Health and thinking in general, in a vacuum, and expecting it to strike a chord or take hold.

Most of us have a tendency—I know I do—to be too quick to try to teach. This kind of listening slows us down.

One of the biggest drawbacks to deep listening is our own views. For instance, if we see a "client" or a housing project resident or anyone we're working with as a victim or a perpetrator or an addict or a delinquent or whatever, that is what we're listening to. If we have a tendency to agree or disagree with people based on our own views, we are listening only to our own views. If we see ourselves as having the answers (and they don't) that is what we are listening to. What we need to hear is blocked, for our minds are not completely clear. Our minds must be calm and quiet and clear to hear what we need to hear. What are they seeing? What is standing in the way of seeing how their own thinking is the real culprit? This is what we need to be listening for. But again, we're only pointed in that direction—that is our attention. When we are actually doing the listening our minds are as empty as possible.

What we're listening for is *the heart of the matter*. We're looking for the fundamental assumption keeping them stuck or in bad habits. With a clear mind we might realize, "Oh, I see what they don't understand." "I see what they're missing." This does not arise through analysis, but from insight. We can tell the difference. What pops into our heads from analytical thinking sounds like old news. What comes from clear-minded insight surprises us. And with that surprise comes an appropriate response. If compassion is in order, it automatically arises. If we see they're getting too serious we will automatically know to lighten things up.

Opening People Up

Not only do we want to listen to others, we also want to be sure people are listening deeply to us before we attempt to teach. It is not very productive to try to teach anything to someone with a closed mind. This is why at the beginning of a Health Realization training session, for example, I go out of my way to help people see the value of not judging at the beginning. I may suggest that they listen to the meaning behind the words and not get hung up on the words themselves because the words are inadequate. I may tell them to resist the temptation to try to fit what they hear into what they already know, because then they will listen only to what they already know. I may tell them to listen as if listening to music, without analyzing. No matter what I suggest, though, people will still follow what their thinking tells them. Bringing it to their attention up front, however, seems to help most people listen better.

Furthermore, I teach them how to deeply listen, pretty much as I portrayed the initial level of deep listening in this chapter.

IV. Conveying or Drawing Out the Understanding

Once we have listened deeply to people (not that this should ever stop), when the moment feels right we are ready to pass along our own understanding to others. This is not teaching in the traditional sense; this is *knowing* everyone already has within him or herself the understanding of how our thinking creates our experience. Our job is to help draw it out of them, to bring it into the light. After all, this *is* everyone's essence, this is who we all really are deep inside; we can't teach that! We can, however, help people see who they really are, and help them see how that is only obscured from view. Most people don't realize this, as we once didn't.

The field of prevention has long recognized the importance of information. If people don't know important pieces of information that might affect their lives, it makes sense to expose them to the information. Most information transmitted in the name of prevention, however, has been facts about, for example, the alcohol and other drugs and their effects; how child abuse affects children; the relationship between guns or TV and violence; warning signs of teen suicide or drug use; what puts people at risk; what creates resilient environments; what assets affect people's lives; how reading improves performance; what works according to research, etc. All this information is worthwhile, if coupled with skills and supports to use it. People can't make the best decisions without all the information they need.

The information imparted through Health Realization, however, is of a completely different nature. It is about the inner workings of the mind. It is about what makes people tick as human beings. It is about what makes people live in well-being. It is about how people create their very experience of life. To truly understand this information is to have the key that unlocks new worlds and new possibilities for people's lives. As this information is already known deep inside, the idea is to help them realize they know it. When people *do* see it, it comes in the form of an insight. Remember, an insight most often comes when the mind is relaxed—and people's minds are most often relaxed when they are in a good feeling. So when we are teaching, if people experience a good feeling we know we are headed in the right direction.

If we want real transformative change, a change in consciousness, we can help people see the three Principles in action in their own lives. In inside-out prevention this understanding is the foundation for change.

As inside-out practitioners we each have one thing that cannot be refuted: our own personal experience and understanding. This is the only thing we can convey with certainty. However, if what we are doing is drawing out what others already know deep in their souls, somehow there must be a convergence. What, then, do we teach? In this sense the word, "teaching" is really a misnomer. It is more of a "drawing out" or "unveiling." I use the word "teaching" only because it is easiest.

Teaching this understanding, it seems to me, has three primary purposes:

1. to help people see their experience of life comes from the inside, not the outside world
2. to help people see they can be guided by wisdom if their minds are calm
3. to help draw forth insight that will raise their level of consciousness and help them live more in well-being

Ultimately, Health Realization attempts to help people realize the power they have to see differently and therefore to create their lives differently. Could anything be more empowering than to see that they are not really stuck in their hopelessness? Could anything be more empowering for people than to see their lives anew, to see that such views are only thought-created illusions of the mind? To see this could set them free.

Teaching from the Heart

How do inside-out practitioners draw out what lies hidden inside? Unlike outside-in prevention, there are no "how to's." In outside-in prevention, especially in these days of set "research-proven" programs and curricula, many would have us believe we can almost follow a script: Here is the information and the skills that must be taught, and here is how to do it; here are the risks that must be reduced and the assets that must be increased. If we do these, we have been led to believe, we will produce fewer problems. As we have learned, however, it is not that simple. In inside-out prevention we cannot begin to approach teaching this way.

In fact, the way we approach inside-out teaching is akin to someone asking, "How do you build a close relationship? How do you make it happen?" Can we really give an answer? We could say things like, "Well, you want to meet people on their own terms, listen to their interests, be yourself, be supportive of them, treat them kindly, be lighthearted," etc., but a close relationship still may not occur. How a feeling of closeness develops is a mystery. All we know is, if we have this as an intention and are pointed in that direction, we may have a better chance of achieving a close, healthy relationship than if we were not intentional about it. This is similar to inside-out teaching. We want to point our minds in the direction of drawing out people's Health and helping them see how their experience of life is created and changes, but *we know we cannot make it happen.*

Therefore, we can't take responsibility for it one way or the other. If it happens, wonderful! If it doesn't, we have pointed the way and can only hope they will see it later. If they don't, there is nothing we can do about it. Here we do not have information that others don't have. Everybody has it already—they just don't know it *yet.* The emphasis is on the "yet." As a conveyor of this understanding all I can take responsibility for is my own life, and my own intention, and to give it my all. Anything else is ego-involvement, which does not serve anyone well.

Again—I keep repeating this because it is so critical—the entire idea of this teaching is to point people in the direction of realizing that at every moment they create their experience of life. By realizing this, their experience of life is created anew, becomes healthier, and they experience more well-being. If this were so easy, of course, merely telling people how it all works would be enough to change their perspective, feelings and behavior. But the understanding is elusive—until people see it for themselves. God knows why, but our own little minds often seem to try to protect what they've constructed for themselves and block us from seeing the role of thought [see Chapter XXI].

Unfortunately, all we have to convey this understanding are words (and pictures), and they have no power. Words need life behind them, a feeling behind them, to have a chance of affecting others. If we have felt the power of this experience ourselves that is what we convey, because it is part of us. Only then will others be able to feel it, but only if we feel it in the moment we're conveying it. Otherwise even our own experience has no power behind it.

Entry Points

In many communities it does not work well to go in talking "Mind, Consciousness and Thought"—at least at first. We could use that language, but few would listen. More likely, they would think we were crazy or from outer space and would turn off. The question, then, is how best to help people hear the message of *the three Principles* without (at first, anyway) using that language. What will people be open to hearing? What will be our entry, so ultimately they will see Mind, Consciousness and Thought in action?

For the first year or two, perhaps more, residents of the Modello Housing Project neither heard nor saw the language of "Mind, Consciousness and Thought," yet their lives changed dramatically. If they didn't see the three Principles, what did they see? In essence, they saw the three Principles in action in their lives without knowing specifically what they were called.

How was the understanding of the three Principles conveyed in Modello? To answer this, let's examine what the residents picked up. Remember, because the first three "steps" were in place—1) the workers living the feeling of Health themselves; 2) the creation of a healthy environment and rapport; 3) deep listening—the residents had begun to see-

- that they were cared about, no matter what
- that there is hope
- that they were listened to

In short, it felt good to be around the staff—they had fun around them—no matter what the staff were talking about. On top of that, through what the staff conveyed, they saw-

- their own Health
- how their thinking took them away from this Health, mostly through-
  - low moods
  - separate realities (that everyone sees the world differently)
  - taking things personally
- that in a calm state they had access to their Health
- that their feelings came from their thinking

These understandings reinforced their initial experience. For example, when people saw their internal resource of health and wisdom, it enhanced their hope. When they saw they were not at the mercy of their circumstances, they found even more hope. Though they did not necessarily hear much about "Mind" and "Consciousness," they certainly began to see "Thought" in their lives, so they began to see the manifestations of the three Principles in action. The residents didn't have to learn the three Principles, per se, but they did experience their essence. What they found was enough to raise their consciousness and lift themselves into a new life.

What, then, might be the *"entry points"* to learning about the three Principles. An entry point, as I envision it, opens the doors to hearing. What points of learning might be heard fairly early on? To answer this, it seems important to ask ourselves a few questions:

1) What do people see when they do *not* see the three Principles operating in their lives?
2) What *specifically* do we want people to see and realize?
3) *How* do we help them see these?

181

Let's consider these.

1) What do people see when they do not see the three Principles operating in their lives?

It seems to me people who do not see Mind, Consciousness and Thought in their lives see-

- – reality (the way things are)
- – circumstances (that the outside world affects them)
- – feelings (that often have a life of their own)
- – thoughts (but only when *applying* their thinking, as in planning, analyzing, figuring out, fantasy)

At least that's what I saw before I had this understanding. So this is what we are up against. People do not easily let go of these. After all, it is life as they know it. It is their world. It makes sense that people would resist. Resistance is not uncommon when people are first exposed to these new (for them) ideas. As soon as they see something new within, however, resistance begins to subside.

2) What specifically do we want people to see and realize?

While it may make little sense to talk to community residents about Mind, Consciousness and Thought, at least at first, it makes a lot of sense to teach (or to draw out the realization) that everyone has Health and common sense inside them that will arise when their minds are clear. It makes sense to teach that their minds are not clear in low moods or when they're angry or running scared, so it would be sensible to step back and calm down before acting. It makes sense to help people understand how everyone sees things differently, how people act based on the way things look to them, and how it doesn't help to take personally what other people do or say to us because that's just the way they see it. While it may make little sense to teach about "levels of consciousness," it makes a lot of sense to help people see that there are many different ways to see the same situation, and the way they're seeing it now will change when their thoughts change, and whatever they see causes them to feel whatever they're feeling, and sometimes what they see brings them closer to their Health than other ways of seeing it.

In short, we want people to see what they do not now realize that will help their lives. Here are some examples that come to my mind of the kinds of points we may want to make:

- that we all have wisdom and common sense within us that we can always rely on for guidance, if our minds are quiet enough to hear it
- that what we call "the way it is" or "reality" or our experience is really *our own thinking*
- that our own thinking is the only thing that can obscure our Health, inner peace and wisdom
- that our experience can (and will) change with our next thought; therefore, we are never stuck where we think we are

- that in low moods our thinking is off and can't be trusted, so we want to be careful of talking or taking action in low moods
- that it is always possible to see any situation or person from higher levels of perspective; that as our levels rise the "reality" we see changes, and the higher the level the more we see possibility and the more we are able to maintain our well-being
- that because we each live in a "separate reality" created by our own thinking we do not have to take others' realities so personally, nor our own way of seeing things so seriously
- that we all have habits of thinking that have power over us and rule us—until we know that they are only acquired, learned habits that don't mean anything; that our habits will be revealed to us when we need to see them and we're ready (but it doesn't help to go looking for them)
- that if we look closely we can see the difference in our lives when we act out of wisdom, rather than out of our habitual thinking or low moods
- that we are all innocent in the sense that we all get lost in our thinking at times, and if we can see our innocence we can see others' innocence, and if we can see others' innocence we can see with compassion, humility, humor, forgiveness and gratefulness
- that because we are all part of the same formless essence, the Oneness, there is nowhere to fall; we are always safe

The above is only my limited view in the moment. I'm sure there are other points. The key is always to help people look to the inside-out nature of their experience, to Mind, Consciousness and Thought in action. If we can point people in this direction, the life they experience can, and often will, change.

When people are exposed to such understandings, our hope is that it resonates with something deep inside them, leading to new insights that allow their innate Health and wisdom to intervene and guide them in healthier ways. To make any difference, they must see it operating in their own lives. This is its only relevance. Once they see the three Principles in action in a way that makes sense to them, life never looks the same. We all get off track and lose sight of it at times, but once we *see* it, in the back of our minds it is always there. Everything we do as practitioners is to help people see how the answer lies inside them. As people quiet their minds and clear their heads, they are better able to hear and tune into their own wisdom; then they will have even more insights.

3) How do we help them see these?

How do we know what specific points to try to convey at any given moment? This comes from deep listening with a clear mind. What we teach comes out of the present moment as things naturally arise. This keeps our teaching fresh and relevant.

Again I repeat because it is so crucial: Before trying to convey anything, before trying to teach anything, before trying to draw out anything, it is critically important for us as practitioners to ***be in a good feeling in that moment***. If at the time we are insecure or reactive it makes no sense to try to convey anything because it will not be heard, even if we generally live in a state of health. It is equally important for the hearer to be in a receptive state. If the person we are working with is in a low mood, forget about teaching. Instead, do whatever we have to do (without being obnoxious) to *elevate their mood level*. Remember Darlene Stewart's (1988) study of reading receptivity [Chapter X]? This isn't being "touchy-feely"; this is what works!

Next—still before attempting to convey anything, especially if people are riled up about something—we want to help them disengage from the situation and quiet their minds. We want to *help them calm down*. Then we can help them see the difference in their thinking, feelings, actions and results when they're calm.

Now we are ready to teach. Then we can take any opportunity to help them look in this inside direction. This can happen in a nearly infinite variety of creative ways, limited only by our own imaginations (thoughts) as practitioners.

Mills, for example, used community conflicts to point people in the direction of Thought. As he described it, "When meetings would start to get negative or conflicted we could point back to how people were thinking about things at that moment" (in Pransky, G., 1998, p.226) and how different the thinking was on each side. This was not a set, canned approach. It occurred to Mills in the moment—not by listening to the different sides of the conflict but by *listening deeply to what was behind the conflict*; that is, to the differing thoughts each side believed were real.

I once taught a course at the New England School of Addictions Studies called "Deep Listening, Conflict Elimination and Peace." In the middle of the session, out of nowhere, a Puerto Rican student pulled out a camera and snapped a picture of another Puerto Rican student across the room. The second student flipped out and started yelling at the first student. A heated argument erupted. I and the other students were taken aback. Then I remembered the title of the workshop. I realized, "What a gift! Here we have a conflict right in front of our eyes!" Clearly, these two fellows were not listening to each other. So I calmed everyone down and said, "This is great! Let's turn this into a learning experience." I talked a little about how sometimes we all get so caught up in the way we see things that we can't see the other side. So I asked the fellow who'd flipped, "What made you get so upset? What was behind that?" He said where he grew up in Puerto Rico he was brought up to believe that if someone took a picture of you, they were taking away part of your soul—so he expected his permission asked before anyone took a picture of him. The group was stunned, including the Puerto Rican photographer. So I turned to him: "What made you want to take his picture? What was behind that?" He said, "Hey, I just wanted to take a picture of mi hermano, my Puerto Rican brother, you know?" He said he just appreciated having him there and wanted a record of it to take home. Again, everyone was surprised. Just by listening deeply to the other side the conflict disappeared. They could appreciate and respect each other's sides, and their own views became elevated. It was a tremendous learning experience for everyone. The teaching came from the listening; I hardly had to say a word. (My other option was to run scared and try to stop the conflict.)

Deep within ourselves as workers we have answers for how to help any individual, organization or community, *if* we quiet our own minds and stop trying to figure out what to do or say.

Vehicles Through Which the Understanding Can Be Conveyed

Since we can't often go up to people and out of the blue start talking about any of those points above, we usually need some *vehicle through which to legitimately convey this understanding*.

Obviously, if we are engaged in a counseling or training session, or if someone comes to us for assistance, those are automatically legitimate vehicles. But what if we are working in a community?

In Modello (Pransky, 1998), at first Mills attempted to establish a Leadership Training course as a vehicle. This gave him legitimacy to talk about Thought and common sense within the context of leadership. While it served the purpose of a legitimate vehicle, it did not work well. In my view, this was because the people did not ask for it. A few months later, through a survey questionnaire, he and staff did ask the residents what they wanted and what their and hopes concerns were. This requires listening so we are able to see the places we might best have impact. What are people interested in? What do they care most about? Through what venues would they most likely show up to hear something new?

Modello survey results indicated residents were concerned about their kids' behavior, so Dr. Mills and staff set up an informal parenting class. They did not use a traditional parenting curriculum but instead used the class as an opportunity to talk about their kids in relation to Thought and common sense and moods and separate realities and taking things personally (Pransky, 2001). It took hold. It began to make a difference in people's lives because it hit home. But the residents still did not show up in droves; they were still skeptical, still angry about other times when other service providers and politicians had come in and let them down, still fearful. So it didn't happen all at once. But having only a few people show up was enough for Mills and staff, for they knew once people had a good experience there and their lives with their kids (and their own lives) began to improve, word would get out. Once word got out they knew other people would come. "If you build it [right], they will come."

Other vehicles also were developed from the results of this questionnaire. It showed residents concerned about the way school treated their kids, so the staff helped them set up a Parent-Teachers Association (PTA). They were concerned about the Housing Authority not fixing the problems in their apartments, so the staff helped them set up a Residents' Association. It didn't matter that most of the same people were involved in each, each vehicle served the purpose of meeting people where their interests lay, and all those vehicles became the venues through which most of the Health Realization teaching occurred. For example, the staff helped the residents to see that the nasty woman behind the desk may have had a bad day, perhaps a difficult life. This enabled them to see her with new eyes, so they became less confrontive. It is hard to fight with someone for whom you feel compassion.

At the same time, Mills and staff would hang out around the projects, and when residents began to feel comfortable enough with them, they began to share their problems. Thus, informal, friendly counseling became still another vehicle to help residents see their problems in relation to the principles. Further, the staff played the role of social workers, their first intent being to help people with whatever they wanted or needed. When those residents felt comfortable enough, as issues arose they would use this connection as another vehicle to draw out this understanding.

Jack Pransky

The proper vehicle for teaching is whatever the community process yields or whatever the prevention program is. People learn in different ways; some are more open to particular things than others, so each vehicle provides a different opportunity to convey the understanding in ways connected to day-to-day life. We can use educational settings, cultural settings, religious settings, parent-child settings, youth programs, community prevention partnerships, etc., as opportunities to provide information to their participants that might bring about insights about how one's experience of life is created.

Teaching from the Impersonal

When we talk with folks it is important to remember *we are not dealing with their personal issues so much as with how everyone gets caught up in the same ways yet has access to the same Health and wisdom to rise above any circumstances. We are after the universal connection, not the personal.* We can use the personal as examples of what we *all* do.

Sometimes, ironically, when we hit too close to home people's walls go up, and they will not hear what we have to say. When Health Realization practitioners counsel alcoholics, for example, they often try to avoid examples that pertain directly to drinking. It is too close. Defenses are summoned to protect. On the other hand, they may be able to hear something about people who, for example, have gotten caught up in other addictions such as food or heroin. In other words, because we don't want them listening through their defenses, we may not want to use examples about their specific problem. For example, in speaking with a problem drinker, we might talk about how some people's thinking tends to get them to see food or their bodies in a skewed way so that their food intake gets messed up, and the way they eat makes sense to them but to no one else. [Note: I do not like giving such examples because people may think this is *the* example one should use with someone who has a drinking problem. It is not; it is just something that came to me. All I'm suggesting is that people can sometimes see things better when their defenses and denial are not directly attached.] If they see it, it may strike something in them about their own lives, but it happens inside their own heads. They reach their own connections.

People can be helped to realize, when they experience a problem, that the problem has something to do with their own thinking. One can see where this might be a touchy subject. When people have a problem they don't often want to look at themselves; they don't want to see their own thinking as the culprit. People tend to see the causes of their problems residing in the outside world. When faced with the possibility that their problems may emanate from within, defenses abound. It may sound at first as if we're saying what happened to them is their fault, or they attracted the problem to themselves somehow, but that is not at all what we are saying. We *are* saying what they are now seeing as a problem might be seen by others—or by themselves at some time in the future—as an opportunity, for example. If so, they wouldn't be seeing a problem. They're the ones who decide, with their own thinking whether something is a problem or not. Again, we're not talking about what happens to them; we are talking about *how they experience* what happens to them. This does underscore the care we might take to teach this understanding as impersonally as possible, because it can be heard wrong.

Besides, we are not so much interested in helping them solve one particular problem as we are in helping them see how they get themselves into these types of problems in general;

in fact, how people in general tend to get themselves into such problems. A bigger picture exists than their individual problems. The larger the perspective, the better. They will make the connection to their own problems by themselves.

A Spiritual Connection

Remember, we don't want to lose sight of the fact that no matter how it is conveyed our intent is to touch people on a deep, spiritual level, to help people transcend their analytical thinking and jump directly into that deeper intuition that holds the answers. We want to help people see how they have a built-in, natural tendency to move toward their Health without needing to rely on anything external. We need only get out of our own way. In certain states of mind we have thoughts that interfere with our natural healthy state, but we can discount such thoughts. We don't have to listen to those thoughts; we don't have to follow them. In so doing we strengthen our psychological immune system—our natural, internal resilience. As Mills says, "People's lives become what they think is possible. Take the blinders off and their own natural wisdom and common sense will rise to the surface." (Today Show, 1990).

Again, we don't know anything they don't; we have only realized something for ourselves that they have not yet realized for themselves. Our job is to help uncover it or unveil it, so it comes into the light.

Why don't we simply come right out and describe *the three Principles* and how they work? Sometimes we can; sometimes we do. But many people won't hear it. Some will, but many won't. As we have said, to describe the formless is a contradiction in terms. If words are inadequate, pictures or diagrams aren't much better, for people have their own interpretations (thoughts) of what the pictures or diagrams mean. With some people they will resonate, and with others they won't. Many people have found the diagram in Figure 7, which I first saw used by Mills, very useful to illustrate separate realities and how to transcend them. Others have not found it particularly helpful. The idea is not to rely on other people's diagrams or the way they say things (unless it particularly resonates) but to use illustrations that arise from one's own insights. This happened to me when I envisioned the diagram that illustrates Innate Health and the thoughts that keep us from experiencing it, with levels of consciousness [Chapter VI, Figure 5]. Many people have found this diagram so useful that I find myself using it again and again, which is rare. The drawback in using any illustration is that it becomes fixed and often stale. But I have used it in many different ways, depending on what feels right in the moment. I do not encourage others to use it in their teaching, unless it really speaks to them deep inside. The use of diagrams or other pictures in teaching isn't necessary. Some will appreciate them, and others won't.

If words and pictures have limitations, what are we left with? Metaphors and stories and experiential exercises—or whatever else anyone can come up with.

Metaphors can help bring our points to life by stimulating visual images that are not easily forgotten. George Pransky is king of the metaphor. When I was first learning this understanding, listening to him in person and on his tapes (most of which, unfortunately, he has taken off the market) I never ceased to be amazed at the connections he saw to illustrate his points. For example, when describing how we give thoughts power, he likened a thought to a seed that blows in on the wind. Without nourishment, he said, that seed would simply blow away with the wind. A seed's nourishment is water. Give that seed water, and it begins to take root. A thought's nourishment, he said, is attention. Give that thought attention—take it seriously—and it begins to take root in your head. Otherwise it is just a harmless thought that blows out of your mind; it blows in, it blows out. That image has never left me and is now part of me.

Metaphors can be used to convey meaning. For instance, a metaphor came to me about how our habits of thinking begin to look normal to us and becomes our "reality." I realized when we put on a strangely colored pair of sunglasses, at first everything looks weird, but if we leave them on for a while everything begins to look normal. That's how our belief systems work. When we look out at the world, without realizing it, we are filtering whatever we see through our own self-generated belief systems, and whatever we see looks real.

Another image I got was picturing an anorexic looking in the mirror thinking she is fat when everyone else considers her bone-skinny. This illustrates how the world we see out of our eyes, created with our own thinking that we have made up, regardless of whether it has any basis in so-called reality, determines how we feel and act. But that person can't see it! We can see it with an anorexic, but we can't see what we have made up about ourselves any more than an anorexic can about herself.

When people are attuned to pick up metaphors they begin to see them everywhere. The metaphors we ourselves see are the most powerful when talking with others.

Stories can also be useful—if they are relevant to the point and help illustrate it. For example, one day I realized that with our thinking we make up what is important to us at any given time. One slippery winter's day in a town near Boston, with snow falling, I had driven down from Vermont and parallel-parked my car on the street. As I picked up my notebook and papers for a meeting and half-opened the door to get out, I put my left foot on the ground and happened to glance behind me for a split second. I saw a car sliding toward me, out of control, wheels locked, on the slippery snow and ice. I leaped back into my car—I have no idea how—just before the other car slammed into my half-opened door, smashed and bent it nearly off its hinges, clipped my left elbow in the process and threw the notebook and papers in my hand out into the street. As the car skidded by, miraculously missing the main body of my car by less than an inch, I somehow rebounded back toward the door and ended up hanging upside-down with my head nearly on the ground. My arm was slightly cut and bleeding, but that's all! It had all happened so fast, I was stunned. When I recovered, I realized I could easily have been killed, and only by the grace of God was I not. Suddenly life looked different to me. All the things I had been holding onto, thinking they were all-important one moment before, I suddenly saw as the trivial, petty things that they were. Although at that point I had been talking with people for at least five years about how Thought creates our experience, I never realized how much Thought really, truly did, until that moment. Life suddenly seemed very precious, and I no longer felt like wasting my time or energy on trivial garbage.

This, of course, is not unique to me. I am writing this not long after the terrorist destruction of the World Trade Center, where many people suddenly realized what was important in their lives, and it didn't have much to do with what they considered important moments before. Even more fascinating to me was the fact that, over time, I found myself sliding right back into my old routine, getting caught up in the usual pettiness—because it was such a habit! It blows me away. This, too, has now happened with many people as the terrorist attacks faded from immediate memory. Yet, what we glimpsed then, even though it faded, was a lot closer to the truth of our inner selves, and when we remember it comes back.

Figure 7
SEPARATE REALITIES

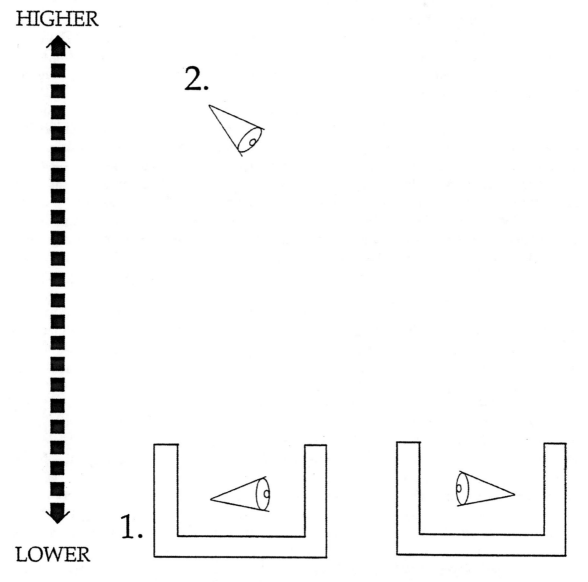

1. People seeing out of their own belief systems or separate realities.
2. A person seeing from a higher perspective that transcends belief systems; a person seeing oneself and others in their separate realities.

More important, that truth of what's really important can be accessed at any moment because it *is* who we *really* are!

Telling other people's stories can be powerful as well, but only if their power is present in the moment. This is why in this book I included other people's stories in their own words through interviews. It makes this understanding come alive.

Some people, of course, can tell stories and use metaphors and give talks as if it is second nature. This is George Pransky's gift. Syd Banks talks at such a deep level in such a quiet way that people listening are usually on the edge of their seats. Because Banks and Pransky could do it so well, somewhere along the way "giving talks" became *the* way to deliver the message, and this proved to be as much of an "activity trap" as anything else. Practitioners have to use whatever means of communication resonates with them most.

This brings us to the use of ***experiential activities***, which are highly regarded in the field of prevention. In the past, they have not been so highly regarded in Health Realization, but I for one like using them. For example, at times I have asked people to pair up with someone to reflect on and talk about what they picked up from their parents that may have developed into their own thinking habits. Such activities help people relate things to their own experience, rather than merely listening to someone else. Yet this, too, can be a trap. The more "canned" approaches we bring in, the less in the moment we are. Something that worked once won't necessarily work again if it doesn't have the same energy behind it. In fact, I find myself not using that question much anymore. Besides, when working in a community it is very unlikely we would use experiential activities, except possibly as part of a formal training.

Interestingly, metaphors and stories and examples and activities all talk around ***the point***. Going too far into illustration or examples may obscure the point. On the other hand, if we simply state the point, people will likely not get what we're talking about. They will hear the words but will not connect in any meaningful way. It is wise, then, to strike a balance between the point and the illustrations.

One of the trickiest yet potentially most impactful ways of teaching is through participant ***questions***. Here is where the presenter, trainer or practitioner must have a solid grounding in the understanding. Some people's questions can be downright challenging. Personally, I teach best through having people ask questions, because it keeps me fresh. I love it! It takes me out of myself and requires being in the moment.

As an illustration, when I was running a training at the Red Lake Reservation in Minnesota, I was talking about how we create our reality with our own thinking. One Native man, who apparently had always dreamed of becoming a professional baseball player, raised his hand and, with kind of a smirk on his face, asked, "So, are you saying that if I think I'm a great baseball player, then I will be?" The question took me by surprise. It was a brilliant question that at the time I had never considered. I paced around for almost 15 seconds in deep reflection. Then it came to me! I said (something like), "What I'm saying is this: If you go to a baseball tryout thinking that you're a great baseball player, and you're in the field and you make brilliant plays, you'll walk away confirming the fact that you're a great baseball player. If you go to that same tryout and make a bunch of errors, you'll walk away thinking you had an off day. Either way you still think you're a great baseball player. But this has nothing to do with whether you are or not. Our thinking determines what we see about ourselves. The notions about ourselves that we carry with us are self-validating and self-consistent. In other words, no matter what happens, either way we will make it fit our view. Either way, we validate what we believe to be true, and it keeps our view consistent. It's just another way our thinking tricks us. But the way we see it doesn't necessarily make it true or 'the way it is.' It's only true for us, according to the way we see it."

On the other hand, I remember hearing George Pransky say (something like), "People who have heart attacks and religious experiences change their world view." World views can change with a large enough insight. If that fellow went to ten major league baseball tryouts and kept making errors and being rejected, at some point it may sink in that he might not be as good as he thinks he is. That would be an incredible shift in thinking for him.

When I first realized this, I remember thinking, "Wow, we're never really stuck with what we see. It could change any time! We just don't know when." I remember thinking of the many people with whom I had worked over the years who believed they were stuck where they were, and it was *not true!* It could change at any moment. And people don't need huge epiphanies or religious experiences to do it. Any change of thought of enough magnitude accomplishes the same thing, because it is the same thing. In Modello, for example, many of the teen drug dealers suddenly realized (something like), "Hey wait! This is a dead end. I could be somebody!" Suddenly they saw that no matter how much illegal money they gained, it never seemed like enough because they would go through it like water; if they worked for it legitimately they would appreciate it more. Partly because they made far less money legitimately they would spend far less, and they realized they actually ended up with more in the long run. Plus, it felt better. This change could not have come about if their world view had not changed. One moment they're drug dealers, and the next moment they're kicking the rest of the dealers out of the neighborhood and keeping it safe. Why? They had a new thought, a new thought about their lives, a new thought about who they were, a new thought about what should be. *Only a new thought,* and the world one sees changes. Only a thought! That's all! That's the amazing thing about it.

Still, they have to see that they are the ones with the answers, not us.

Again, once people begin to see that it is not the circumstances of their lives that cause their problems but the way they *think about* the circumstances of their lives, life can't look the same. It simply can't! Even abusers and victimizers can begin to see that what has seemed so real and compelling maybe isn't so real and compelling and can be questioned.

It often takes a couple or few days of training for people to truly see the Principles in action in their lives and to understand how the three Principles can be used to help others. Or it takes hanging out with people in a community or organization over the long haul. Some see it right away; some never see it. It cannot be found through the intellect, only by being struck by the feeling of it, so one knows it in his or her heart. None of this can happen, none of it means anything, without the next "step" in the process.

V. The Ultimate: A Shift in Perspective

As I have said repeatedly, intellectual beliefs about the three Principles mean nothing; it only matters whether people discover these for themselves. This can happen only through *insight.*

Again, we cannot make an insight happen in anyone else, yet it is *the critical point of change.* An insight is a sight from within, a moment of understanding. An insight is a vertical jump in one's "level of understanding" that lifts people into a new "reality" where they see more of the big picture and see things less personally. *Understanding* here refers to

191

the degree to which Thought is recognized as the source of one's experience; where the person "actually sees the connection between his/her thinking and his/her experienced reality, and having seen that connection, is able to change from within" (Pransky, G., 1998, p.51).

Very little can be said about how to help spawn insight, except that it takes a clear mind. Sometimes this happens when the mind quiets down, sometimes when one forgets what one knows; sometimes it comes from dropping into a feeling of momentary Health from out of the blue, sometimes from having one's world shaken up when the mind is so scrambled that it goes "tilt" as in a pin-ball machine and the world one is seeing no longer makes sense. Again, we can get people to the portal, but we can't make them go through it. We can't take responsibility for whether someone has an insight. No one can change anyone's thinking except the person herself, and most often it doesn't happen on purpose.

People either connect with this or they don't. We may never be able to reach everyone. But anyone can be reached! If we see people are not connecting, not having insights, there is not much we can do—except *make adjustments* to what we are doing. We might go back through all the steps or components above to see if we are on track. We might ask ourselves, for example: Am I in a good feeling? Am I creating a lighthearted feeling around me? Am I seeing the person's Health? Do I have still have rapport? Is my mood right? Has the other person slipped into a reactive or negative state of mind? Am I listening deeply enough? Am I being judgmental, or am I running scared for some reason? Am I really connected in the heart to what I am conveying? Am I being creative enough in how I'm attempting to help them see it? I don't mean this as analysis but as reflection. We don't want to be impatient. People have insights in their own time. If they experience a good feeling they are on the right track, and that is all we need to know.

All the above may help us see where we are off-base, but we still cannot make insight happen. We may have to become even more creative in helping them see it—even in ways we've never thought of before. Once while conducting "an intensive" weekend counseling session, my client and I had spent the entire first day getting nowhere. This man was scared to death of getting married to a woman he'd been living with for a long time who, by all appearances, was perfect for him. He was even more afraid of having kids because he didn't want to mess them up like he felt he'd been. He couldn't commit. He didn't want to chance tampering with his life-style (which included having a lot of women after him). That night reflecting on it I realized, great guy that he was, he didn't really want to change. He wanted life to change around him. I realized I needed to shock him out of it. An amazing thought then came to me: "I should kick him out—give him his money back and show him the door." The thought unnerved me; I really didn't know if I had the nerve. But the thought kept coming back. It felt right. Besides, we had good rapport. So the next morning that's exactly what I did. After explaining what I felt, I said, "There's the door" He was stunned—shaken. "Or," I said, "you could really commit to opening your heart to change. Take your money and run, or commit for the rest of our time together and pay me the full amount. It's up to you." He was scared. He broke down. Something shifted in him, he decided to stay, and we got further in the next hour that we had the entire first day. I wouldn't recommend this. I never have done that again; I never had that thought again—thank God! It was scary for me. Sometimes thoughts that we can't believe we're having are our best—in that moment, if they *feel* right—because our wisdom knows more than we do (or we think we do).

If someone is stuck, and we don't know how to reach him or her, we could say to ourselves, "I don't have a clue how to reach this person, but I know the answer is there." Then put it on the back burner and wait for something to occur. If it doesn't, it may simply mean the person is not ready to see it yet (or we aren't), and that's okay.

All we can say is, insights happen more when our typical thinking is disengaged, and the mind is disengaged more when people are in a good feeling.

People, of course, can have insights anywhere, not only in a Health Realization effort. Insights among participants about what creates their behaviors and emotions may occur within any prevention program. Most prevention programs, however, have left this to chance, and Health Realization appears to move more people more closely to having such insights because in this approach it is intentional.

VI. The Ripple Effect

When people see the three Principles play out to the point their lives improve, they automatically want to give away what they learned to others, because it feels so good to them. Because of the contrast with their former lives, they have some real experiences to offer. Their own lives reflect more well-being, and they are so excited by it that they want to give it away to others.

Once their own lives improve, a natural process seems to unfold. First, they act differently in their relationships at home, so their family relationships improve. They begin to emanate a better feeling. Others like being around them more. They begin to see value in applying this in their work, so their work relationships improve. They begin to listen more deeply to others. They may then try to teach this understanding to others. Sometimes they find this is not so easy because they cannot find adequate words, but by simply living the feeling and talking about their own experiences they can begin to impact others. Note, these are the very same steps in the process as outlined above, yet they have begun to occur naturally—living the feeling, creating a good feeling around them, listening, and passing along what they know.

Some begin to have an impact on others, so the improvement becomes exponential, as ripples in a pond. If a number of people in a community or organization who have been affected, then begin to meet together as a group, they have a natural inclination to use their understanding to improve their community or organization.

To sum up this rippling process, first their own lives improve, then they reach out to others, then they improve the relationships around them and change their immediate conditions, then, when a critical mass of people with this new perspective come together, they naturally work to create community change by changing community conditions. Hence, prevention from the inside-out.

Teaching Maintenance

Once people learn this understanding—just when they think they've got it nailed—almost inevitably they bump into their old habits and lose their good feeling.

As I've said, habits are often hard to break, and even though people may see something new, they sometimes find they slide back into their old habits of thinking. After all, that's what they're used to. They're ingrained. The deeper the insight, the less likely this is to occur, but it still can. This is where it can be helpful to teach maintenance.

By this I mean people have to be reminded that their old habits of thinking will likely return, and the lower their mood the more "real" this thinking will seem. They need to know such thoughts are just trying to trick them at these times, and they don't want to be fooled by them. We can turn our backs on *our own* habits of thinking. We can help people remember, if they are fooled by old habits, all they have to notice is, not *what* they are thinking but *the fact that they are thinking*. I'm not saying it isn't helpful sometimes to see the old habit kick in, but, more important, we want to help them see that if their thinking is riled up it is also giving them faulty messages, and they can follow it if they want but it won't lead to peace of mind. Instead they could use their uncomfortable feeling as an indicator that their thinking can't be trusted at that time. It is a signal to get calm, to clear the mind or, if they can't clear their heads at the time, just don't believe the thinking. The job of Consciousness is to make it look very real. But what they really are seeing is their messed-up thinking creating a messed-up experience.

Of course, it is helpful as a reminder to have other people around who also have this understanding. It is nice to be reminded that our minds are too busy, or that we're caught up without realizing it. But it is not necessary. Sometimes it seems we are alone and isolated, because to date comparatively few people have this understanding. [This is why I became a "personal well-being coach," so people could always have someone to talk to only one telephone call away.] But really we are not alone because we have the power of Mind behind us. It is always present for us, though we sometimes forget. Once we have glimpsed this at a deep enough level, however, our forgetting is usually temporary. Even when we forget, it seems something in the back of our minds is saying, "This too shall pass," or "I know my thinking is off right now and I can't help it, but I know somewhere down the line my thinking will change and I'll be back on track."

If a problem arises that we don't know how to solve, our habit will be to analyze our way out of it. Our minds grind away and go over the same things over and over again. But we need new, fresh ideas, and so long as we keep our minds cluttered with all that wheel-spinning, we leave no room for a new, fresh solution to arise as insight from a clear mind. So part of teaching maintenance is to help people know what to do when that inevitability arises.

When we think we have a problem, some reflection might aid us:

1) Admit we don't have a clue how to solve this problem
2) Know that a solution exists and we will see it when we are ready, have faith in it and hope to see it. Here we are setting an intention to see a solution.
3) Forget about it! Clear our head. Go about our business, and when we least expect it (when our mind is relaxed) a solution will pop into our head.

Of course, another part of our mind is saying, "You have to solve this—now! You need to bear down and get to it!" The lower the mood the more immediate it looks. To just forget about it seems too passive. This is another of those paradoxes. To forget about it seems too passive to find a solution. But to find it we have to forget it. Knowing this is part of maintenance.

Even the most practiced Health Realization professionals at times forget what we know and disconnect from our Health. Then we think we should know better, and can get down on ourselves some more. But, God knows, we're only human like everyone else. Yet if we held it as our intention to keep our Health and others' Health in view, if we engineered ourselves to see it and act out of it, we would be more likely to do just that. And we would be able to help each other with gentle, loving reminders when any of us slipped away from that state. Then we would really walk the talk and become the model of a healthy way of being in the world. So I invite us all to use our creative power of Thought to see anew, and to start afresh with anyone we may need to, and work in harmony for the common good.

After all, only three things really count in the work we do: 1) the feeling we have in our hearts; 2) understanding how things work (the three Principles); 3) the results we achieve with others and with ourselves. Everything else is an illusion. (This, too, may be an illusion, but at least it's a healthy one.)

Four Options for Community Applications Based on Health Realization

Communities or community-based organizations considering a full-blown Health Realization effort might consider different options. Four options are presented below. Remember, any application of Health Realization in a community or an organization is a form, and as form it is not perfect. Each has its advantages and disadvantages. The option selected should best meet the needs of the community, and best fit the community or organization.

I have seen the following applications in action. Combinations of these also have been applied. There may be others as well. The titles below are used only for convenience.

Option # 1 – The Bemidji model: One (or two) trainings for many different groups

Brief Description: A 2 or 2½-day Health Realization I training or training in *the three Principles* is provided to a group of 10 to 30 people, possibly followed by another 2-days equivalent to a Health Realization II or Applications training. This training (or set of trainings) is then repeated periodically over the next year for two to ten other groups of community or organization members. The trainers then leave and allow whatever happens to occur on its own.

Rationale: People who catch on will work on their own to create whatever can be created for that community. If they think it appropriate, on their own they will arrange more trainings or create a community process to yield community change.

Resources Needed: One or two trainers for each group trained.

Advantages: This option allows for the most natural propagation because it evolves completely on its own. It is probably the least costly. So many people receive training over time the odds are high someone will catch the feeling enough to take the responsibility of creating a constructive community response.

Disadvantages: This option relies on at least one and preferably a few people being affected strongly enough and, on their own, without much training and only because of their goodwill, taking the responsibility to make something happen.

Figure 8

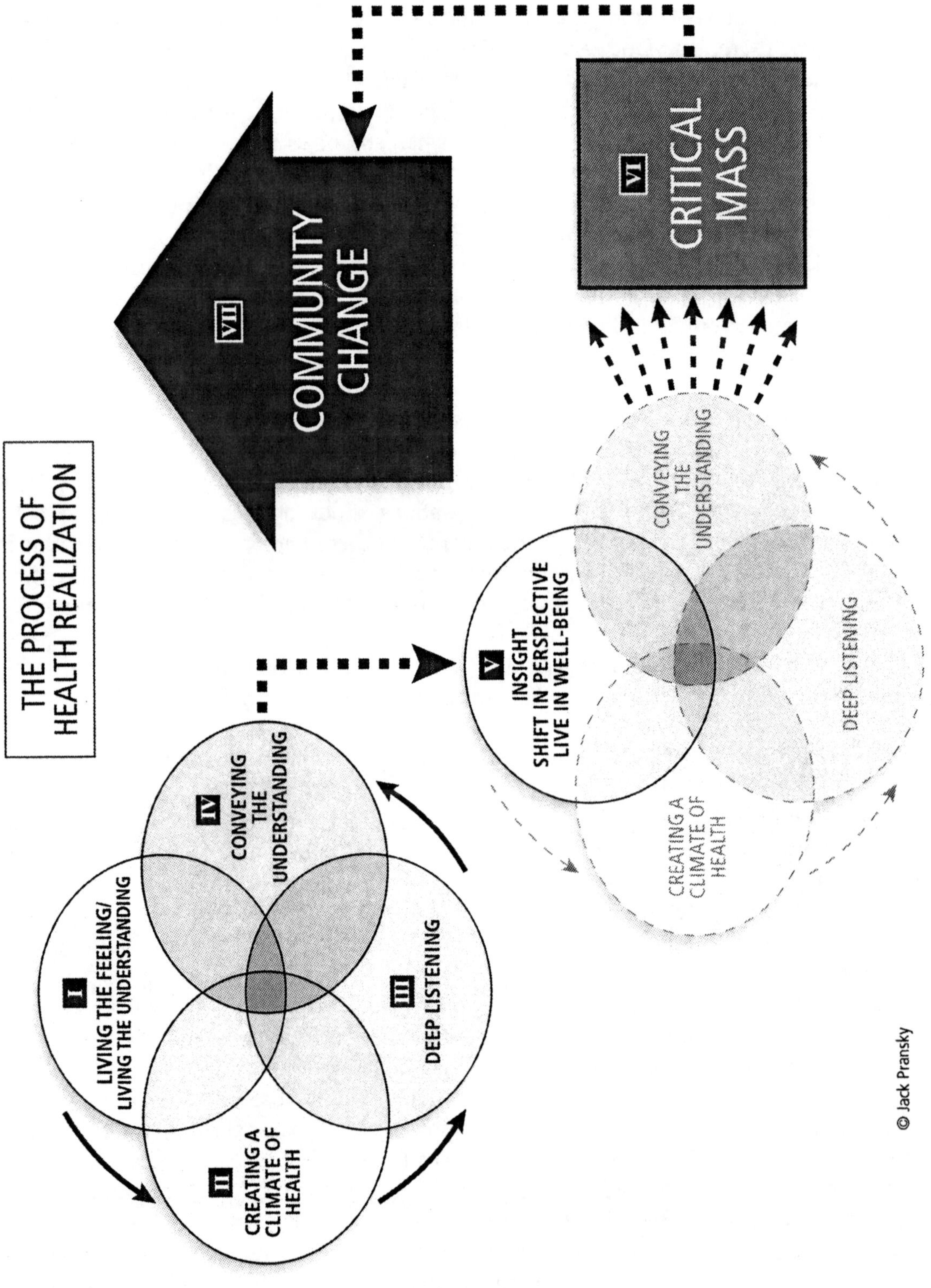

THE PROCESS OF HEALTH REALIZATION

VII COMMUNITY CHANGE

VI CRITICAL MASS

I LIVING THE FEELING/ LIVING THE UNDERSTANDING

IV CONVEYING THE UNDERSTANDING

III DEEP LISTENING

II CREATING A CLIMATE OF HEALTH

V INSIGHT SHIFT IN PERSPECTIVE LIVE IN WELL-BEING

CONVEYING THE UNDERSTANDING

DEEP LISTENING

CREATING A CLIMATE OF HEALTH

© Jack Pransky

Option # 2: The Long-Term Training model: Six to twelve trainings for one group

Brief Description: One group of 8 to 30 people meets for 2 days once a month for 6 to 12 months. This training is designed to deepen understanding and personal grounding in Health Realization to the extent that participants "live it," and to learn and practice how to apply it with others and in communities. The trainers then leave and allow whatever happens to occur on its own.

Rationale: Same as above, except it intends to provide much more intensive training over a longer period of time to fewer people, in hopes people will be affected so deeply they will have no choice but to create community or organizational change.

Resources Needed:: Two trainers are preferable for a long-term training. Therefore, it may cost a little more than Option 1, depending on the number of trainings.

Advantages: This training goes much deeper for fewer participants, increasing the likelihood that someone will create, or work with others to create, community or organizational change. This model still allows for natural propagation.

Disadvantages: Comparatively few people attend the training, thus lowering the odds that someone will pick up the ball on their own. It still relies on people taking the responsibility on their own to make something happen, which may lower the odds of it actually happening.

Option # 3. The Training of Trainers model (used in Santa Clara County, California):

Brief Description: This is an extensive, on-going training system where Health Realization trainers train others who then become qualified or certified to train others, who then train others, etc.

Rationale: Community or organizational change most likely will occur if a self-perpetuating, ever-expanding system is established that continually beings in new blood and ensures ongoing training of new people.

Resources Needed: High cost, because many trainers keep needing to be paid, unless they are able to do trainings as part of their existing job descriptions.

Advantages: This model keeps an ongoing cadre of people continuously trained and increasing their grounding and skills, which allows for an ongoing community presence. New people are continually being trained, which spreads the understanding. This is the most systematized of the models. It possibly turns out the most "well-schooled" trainers.

Disadvantages: This model forces people to sit in judgment of others' capabilities or readiness. If training styles don't mesh or a trainer finds fault with a trainee, that judgment could be compromised. It may encourage an "I know something you don't" mentality, and subtly imply that someone is not capable of finding one's own wisdom to improve others' lives in one's own way. It carries a higher price tag than the first two options.

Option # 4. The Modello Model — Trained community-based staff

Brief Description: At least two Health Realization-trained staff are hired for every 150-200 housing units or 300-400 people, with at least ¼ time of a skilled Health Realization supervisor familiar with community work (who may or may not need to be on site). Preferably, half the staff should be from within the community. This is coupled with large community trainings for community leaders and providers who serve the area. Staff could be hired under a new grant, or job descriptions of existing staff from agencies currently serving the area could be revised for this purpose. The staff role is to build rapport, build hope, deeply listen, provide informal counseling as needed, help out residents as needed, create vehicles to convey the understanding based on perceived community needs, assist residents in creating community change, work with schools, and provide or arrange for Health Realization trainings. Before hiring staff, this effort can begin with a small community group meeting once a week (with a volunteer or two facilitating) on whatever topic would attract people. This option probably is most effective when later combined with extra training for community people who have caught on most, who then help others in their community.

Rationale: Community or organizational change will most likely occur if an ongoing presence is assured. In other words, people who "live the feeling" and are trained in Health Realization are available on an ongoing basis to help community members deal with difficulties and help them join together to improve their community.

Resources Needed: This is the most costly of models because of hiring staff—unless existing job descriptions are changed for this purpose.

Advantages: This option ensures an ongoing staff presence in which community members (both individuals and groups) are worked with from a Health Realization perspective. This option may have the greatest potential to touch the most people's lives in a community. It provides direct service to community members and guides them to make the community changes they desire from a perspective of Health.

Disadvantages: With paid staff it is easy for the community to lay the responsibility (and blame) on them and not take it themselves. It is possible that if people from within the community apply unsuccessfully for the staff positions jealousies could develop that would run counter to Health Realization. It is also possible for jealousies to develop among other agencies if they see this program as competition. It is potentially the most costly option.

Again, combinations of these options are common, and the situation will determine which is most appropriate. There may also be other options that I have not experienced.

XIV. APPLICATIONS IN ACTION

This chapter is intended to make the Health Realization community empowerment process come alive, to demonstrate how it works in action. The interviews, continued here from previous chapters, present four stories of how the inside-out/Health Realization approach has been applied in different settings: 1) Coliseum Gardens housing project in Oakland; 2) various other community empowerment projects from Florida to California, 3) Mariposa Lodge and Santa Clara County, California, and 4) the Sydney Banks Institute of Innate Health at the West Virginia University School of Medicine.

Miss Beverley Wilson on her experience in developing the Health Realization project at the Coliseum Gardens Housing Project in East Oakland, California [Interview continued from Chapter IV, page 51.]

JP: How did you end up working with the Coliseum Gardens project, to start it off?

BW: Well, they was paying me $15 an hour, number one [laughs]—I didn't care what they wanted me to do. That was a dream come true. How I started working with it, it was me and Ron Pellum, who was an African American male—Ron, he's a knowing person about street stuff, but he's not really a street person. He's what street people would call a square, but he's hip—he's a hip square, but he ain't really been out there. And Lisa Allen was a White woman—me and her was about the same age. She had the prettiest green eyes, and she was full of spunk. She was real intense, real intense. She was always moving, always going, and she loved people. That was her gift. And Ron could fit in anywhere. He was just a mellow dude. Lisa was a real go-getter, just finished her Masters in psychology. What I brought to the table was that they needed somebody that was African American and knew Health Realization, and also knew the language of the people.

JP: These two other people didn't know Health Realization?

BW: No. Well, Lisa knew Health Realization; she was at that training in Vallejo with me. But I had followed Roger [Mills] around for a year, so I really had the most experience out of anybody there as far as knowing the model. And Ron had little or no experience.

JP: What year was this?

BW: This was in '92. So we started going into Coliseum Gardens in East Oakland.

JP: Did you get any direction about what you were supposed to do?

BW: We flew by the seat of our pants—that's what we called it—but what we were supposed to do was go and see the Health in the community. That's what we were looking for. We was looking for the Health in the people that we knew was there. So our first six months was basically going from door to door, getting cussed out, slammed doors, sometimes making a hit, and doing the same thing over again the next day. So that's what we did. We built rapport one person at a time for six months. Lisa had a passion for the adolescents, and I liked the adults. And Ron just kind of got along with everybody.

The agency that I went to work for, they wrote a simple proposal for some grant money, and they got it. That made a big difference, because it kind of gave us free rein to go in and assess the situation and find out what we could and could not do. At that time at Coliseum anybody just couldn't go up in there. It was like a desert. They had no services. If a person had a heart attack and needed an ambulance, if that ambulance couldn't get police escort to go in there to serve that person, it was tough-titty. They just couldn't get services. They didn't have maintenance services. They didn't have cabs—that was unheard of—cabs did not go in there. Pizzas, cable TV, none of that stuff was in there. And the place was guarded by sentries—little kids. It's one way in at Coliseum and one way out, and the little kids would stop you and ask you what was your business there. "What are you doing here?"

So, when we first went out there, our first day we were received like, "You guys got to be crazy, coming out here! These people don't want no help." That was an Oakland Housing Authority police officer speaking to us. "You guys are crazy. You done lost your minds!" "What, you think you're going to come up here and set out a table and hand out little pamphlets?"—we had little papers about health issues. We just started with whatever we could, and try to get in and meet the people.

But first we had to get through these little kids blocking the entryway. So I handled that situation when we got up there. They said, "Who you coming out here to see?" I looked at the little boy—I looked him up and down and I said, "I might be coming to see you! You sure got on some cute tennis shoes." He looked at me, and he looked at the other guys, and he said, "Oh, man, she crazy!" See, I knew it was a good thing to be considered crazy in the ghetto. So they let us come on in.

We told them we was coming out there to work, and we just was going to try to start some empowerment classes and get to see if anybody was interested in going. We set up a table. Some people was curious and came by and talked to us, and stuff like that. And after we went around the whole development and kind of talked to people for about two or three weeks, we decided to start a class.

The first class we had was, "Girl, Let's Talk!" We set it up for women to see if women will come out. We just got a handful of people, and that went okay. Nothing was going real fabulous. We still had to go back and back and back, over and over again, back and forth to them doors, and every time we see the people, just treat them kindly and really ask them important questions like, "How are you today?" and remember their names and stuff like that. We just chatted with them. We got the kids interested in Girl Scouts. I was a Girl Scout leader, but my task was to teach Health Realization in the Girl Scout classes. And I was good—

JP: I'll bet you were!

BW: The kids, they catch on so quick. But at first it was real trying. One day, I asked them to draw something, and what they drew was tombstones and guns and Uzis—all kind of stuff. It was just sad—that was sad to me. When I drove home that night I was thinking about it. I didn't understand what I needed to do, but having that hour-and-a-half commute was really good for me because I could kind of sort stuff out. And it occurred to me that instead of asking them how their community was, maybe I should ask them to dream of what they wanted their community to be like. And that changed the whole flavor of the class. And this time when they did the drawings, they drew fruit trees. What the kids wanted was, they wished there was trees out there that had fruit, where they could just go in their yard and pick the orange or a plum or a peach or something like that. And they wished that they had equipment where they could play on. They had sandboxes and stuff, but all the toys had been tore up years ago. Some of them wished they had grass and flowers in there instead of the dirt. It was just like barren dirt. You ever been out there?

JP: I never have.

BW: Oh, I wish I could take you out there one day. Anyway, so that's what they dreamed of and that was a good thing, because later that came true. It really happened! If you go out there now, it's trees, fruit trees. It's still got patches of dirt, but it also has grassy areas, too, where before there was none. But that's kind of how we got in with the kids. So the kids started to go home and do their homework, and they would voluntarily ask to wash the dishes, and their mothers' got interested in what we was teaching them. And finally we got a big class started, for big people.

Coliseum was mostly Asian Americans and African Americans, but what happened was, I found out from doing the door-to-doors that the Asian people were already organized. They met in family circles and group meetings in their homes all the time, so it was about finding out who was the leader. They won't really say there was a leader, but it was this one guy named Chi. And Chi had his people organized. When I met him, we ended up becoming close because he told me a story that was so powerful I was stunned. I was just stunned. He told me about his journey from Cambodia to here, what he went through, what it was like for him growing up. He told me stuff that just really opened my eyes, because I never personally talked to anybody—I'd seen a lot of immigrants in my town, but I never really, personally talked to any. And he told me a story that was so moving that it just stunned me. I mean I was in a daze for about a week. So I was telling Ron and Lisa, "We got to figure out how to get the African American people together, just to tell their separate stories!"

So what we discovered from doing our outreach was that the Asians had some preconceived ideas about the African Americans, and the African Americans had some ideas about the Asians, and everybody's assumptions were off, you know what I'm saying? So it was so good when we first got this little core group of people. We had twelve Asians, because Chi would organize the Asians. It was so sweet, because he'd come and his people would come. The African Americans, on the other hand, were filled with apathy and mistrust, because so many times people came out there to work and they said they'd stay for five or six months, and it looked like they just left in the middle of the night. So they were reluctant to join anything because they had always saw that people would bring them a false sense of hope, and they'd be telling them what they should do, and then they'd leave. But we wasn't telling them what to do. We was actually telling them that we was there to listen to their ideas and to be the bridge between them and Oakland Housing Authority. And I told them I was out there to work myself out of a job, because I really wanted to be an international motivational speaker, and I really meant that. I'd just tell them that all the time.

And it was so funny, after a while we got a little core group of African Americans, maybe ten, and four of them was out of the same family. But the people that we got was so key, because they were like the matriarchs of that community, you know? Because we got Mama Smith and her two daughters, Adelle and Ruby, and then maybe one of Ruby's daughters would come every now and then, so we had like four generations out of one family. Then we got this other lady named Alice that liked to feed the homeless, so she was like a powerhouse in their community, and she would come. And then we got a few other people that were just interested in getting things for their kids—the kids that had been in the little Girl Scout classes.

JP: Did you go out of your way to go after folks like that, or did it just kind of happen?

BW: In a way, yeah, you're looking for leaders. My ideal was that we were going to go in and this was going to become a self-sustaining community, but I didn't know how long that was going to be—if it was two years or five years, or how long, we didn't know.

JP. How long did it take you to even get this core group?

BW: The core group probably took about six to seven months. Yeah, we had just the little group of people and that built over time, because that core group really bought it, you know? We taught them about separate realities. And at this time, the relationship with the police department and the relationship with Oakland Housing Authority was torn, it was ripped, it was really bad. The Oakland Housing Authority police could not come in Coliseum without being escorted by the Oakland PD. They could not come out there, because the people would rock them and bottle them, and the way the Coliseum is set up, it's like a fort. It's one way in and one way out. It's only two entrances and exits, and it's a high-rise, and they would get on top of the buildings and rock and bottle the police, and they couldn't see who was attacking them so they wouldn't go in there.

So through having the classes the people bonded. They told each other their stories and found out they had a lot of misconceptions, and they were laughing at them. An example of that is that African Americans thought that the federal government had a warehouse where they was giving the Asian people new cars, so they was mad at them—every time the Asians got a new car, when they come outside they cut all the tires. In their minds, they're thinking that these people are being treated privileged, and they've been here all their lives and they ain't never gave them *nothing*! So what Chi was able to do was tell them that when Asian families wanted a car, five families would get together, or three families, and what they'll do is buy a hundred pound bag of rice. Wherever Asians have dirt, they're going to make vegetables, they're going to plant stuff. So they said they plant their vegetables, and they buy these big, large bags of rice and big bags of potatoes. They buy in quantity, and they split this stuff up among the families, and they stay out of the grocery stores as much as they can so that their money don't go for food, and they save their money. In three months' time, they can go and purchase a car. All five families will use that car, and they'll repeat the process until the next family gets a car, then they'll do the same thing until everybody in their group has a car. Then they'll start eating. So when they was talking, Ruby asked, "You mean you don't eat no meat?" And Chi said, "Very seldom." And she looked over at Adele and she said, "Girl, we ain't gonna do without no meat!" It was like they never imagined that these people had a system—they was systematically accomplishing these things.

And the Asians' misconception about the African Americans was what the general society thinks, that these people are lazy and shiftless, they been here all their lives, and they don't want nothing, they ain't gonna never want nothing, and that's why they ain't got nothing. So they told some of their stories about how they came from the South, and it never occurred to the immigrants from Cambodia that African Americans have migrated from Alabama and Louisiana and all this stuff and came here and thought that they was going to get—to them California was the land of milk and honey, not just America. They wasn't free where they came from. They told about living where Blacks didn't drink out of the faucets. They just told their stories, and it was just bonding. We had an interpreter in those classes. These classes, they were very slow, because the interpreter would interpret what the Cambodians who couldn't speak English would say to us. After a while, we got so good, we were so in tune with each other that they would be telling a story, and we would be crying, and we don't even know what they was saying yet. We were so connected we could feel the emotion of each other, and it was happening the other way around, too. That's the invisible stuff that's happening within the group.

One day I was teaching about separate realities—and when we're connected to our intuition, we know what to teach—and one of their big barriers was going to the welfare office. The Asians and the African-Americans would have this trouble, because they always felt talked down to. So they go in there with an attitude. The attitude was like, *"I need these food stamps!"* or whatever, but it was always meeting this resistance. So we was telling them about Mind, Consciousness, and Thought—how our thoughts create our reality—and helping them see that behind that desk this welfare worker is just a human being. They function just like you do. They have high moods and low moods and all this stuff. And the judge, behind that robe, is a human. They function just like you. But that day we was talking about a judge and a police officer, seeing beyond their roles, their roles in life, and seeing that a person really existed in there, and to stop approaching the robe and instead approach the person—go to the heart of the matter, and kind of talk about what comes from the heart reaches the heart and ways that we could do that. And some of the ways they had tried that didn't get them the results that they wanted, like cussing the woman out—"You just think you something because you working in this office. You could be out here in this line!"—and all that stuff that didn't work. And we was taking a look at it, just knowing that if they quieted down when they felt themselves getting angry, maybe step back from the situation, and then approached it different, they might get different results.

So the day that we was talking about the judge and the police officer, in walks this little, frazzled police officer! And right away, when he walked in the room, you could feel the energy shift. Just for a moment, there was a dead silence. But around this time we had been having a class of about eight or nine weeks now—

JP: Meeting once a week?

BW: Once a week. But we see the people every day, you see what I'm saying? So we get personal contact with people every day, but we had a formal class once a week. So in walks this police officer. And he looks like, I swear, you know how the Indians, when they had the forts and the messenger would come with the mail and he had arrows sticking on his back, and he'd rush in the door? So this police officer, he just looked like he got arrows sticking out of him and everything [laughs]. I turned around and I look at him, and I'm fascinated because I can't believe my lucky stars. Here I am, teaching the class about taking the uniform off the police officer and the judge, and getting to the heart of the matter, really finding out who this person is and, like, out of nowhere, in drops this frazzled-looking police officer. So just for a moment, there was a little stigma. And I looked at him, and I said, "Welcome. Hi, my name is Beverley Wilson, what can we do for you?" And he said, "Well, I'm here because I got to do some community policing in this area, and I need to learn to work with the community." And he was just saying all these things, and so it was like, *wow!* I said, "Well, it's good that you came because our class today is about separate realities." And because I had listened to them very softly, and I could hear the things that troubled them, I was able to articulate to him what they was saying, and they was just sitting there nodding their heads.

One of their complaints with the police department was that their kids and grandkids would be sitting on the porch—it didn't look like they would be doing anything—and all of a sudden a police car would pull up and they'd arrest him. And when they came out of the house to ask them what was going on, they'd tell them, "Shut up! Go back in your house or I'm going to arrest you too." And that made them very mad, made them want to throw bottles at them and rock their cars, and run them out and protect their kids, because it didn't seem fair. So I said, "Maybe this is what they're concerned with." I spoke for the people, because they had just told me all this stuff. So then I said, "Maybe you could give us the separate reality for the police officer. What does it look like for a police officer coming in here?"

And Jerry [Williams], he looked around—I mean, this took him so back, number one that people was on the edge of their seats waiting to hear his response. It was dead quiet. So he said, "Well, one of the things that happens is that we get insecure"—because he had heard me talking about insecurity. He said, "When we're making an arrest there are certain things that a police officer has to do to secure his area—it's a procedure that we have to do to make sure that we're safe and that what

203

we're doing is safe." And he just kind of laid down everything that a police officer goes through. And so Miss Smith, one of the matriarchs of the community, she said, "Well, some of the police officers are really rude!" He said, "I know that's true, but I'm here hoping that if you can tell me some of the complaints, and that you could tell me some of the problems, and that I could sit down and listen to more classes like this, what you guys are doing here—if you just allow me to come in and just learn, hopefully I can do something about it." So they considered that. It still was a little tense.

And at the end of class that day Miss Smith asked, "Could we end the class in prayer? That we could pray for peace in the community, and for better relationships with the Oakland Police Department." And that's what the prayer was. So the next thing you know she held out her hand and she grabbed Jerry's hand, and it just hit her. She said, "I can't believe it. Here I am holding the police's hand." They *hated* them! And that was like the beginning of a long process.

JP: Jerry must have felt like he was walking into a gold mine.

BW: He did! Well, it was interesting. What we didn't know, he had just left Lockwood Gardens. Coliseum and Lockwood are across the street from each other. They're two different communities and Lockwood is, like, the better of the two as far as society is concerned—and Coliseum is like the stepchild. So he had just went to Lockwood, and he walked in on a meeting where they was getting all their frustrations out. They was talking about the problems in the community and they needed to get their anger out and discuss the problem. Then he walked in, and they turned around, and they said, *"There's the problem there!"* [laughs] And the lady that was having the meeting said, "You better leave." So he got run out of there. That was his frazzled look. It was like, "How am I supposed to work with this community? I've been working on them all these years, now you want me to work with them?!" He felt like somebody had given him a bad injustice, like somebody didn't like him in his department. He thought he was a good cop! And then he got to walk into this other meeting, what we was doing. And we didn't have no way of knowing that, but that's what happened.

So what I suggested to him was that he come and take the class. Everybody agreed that he could come if he wanted to. So for about the next six months, Jerry came into the Health Realization class on Thursdays. And he gave everybody in there his pager number, his beeper number, and they started paging him and all kinds of stuff. He really made my work a lot easier. And I made his work a lot easier, because the gift he said that I gave to him, and I know it's true, is that I taught him to look beyond the role that the person had chosen—because people in the community have roles, too, you know? And to be able to see that.

Like, one of the things he thought was that heroin addicts were just sitting up nodding, that they just sitting there doing nothing. And I told him, "Oh, no. Why don't you go ask her what she been thinking about when she's doing that?" I said, "She could be tap dancing, she could be dancing with Fred Astaire, she could be on a slow boat to China. Because a person on drugs—I know this from my own personal experience—you'd be dreaming about stuff, but you don't call it dreaming. You think that you living in an unreality, you know? You just create a world inside your head, but it's very real. That's why you want to go back there so much." So he got so curious as to what was really going on with people. And he was so humble, because he didn't get it. It took Jerry about six months before he ever understood our thoughts create our experience, and his thoughts was creating his experience too with the people. But because he had decided to come to the class he had kind of suspended his judgment. He was trying to create something, so he had to abandon everything that he knew.

Then one night I did a talk down at a college for NA [Narcotics Anonymous], and Jerry came. It was like he was looking for answers wherever he could. At that time I probably had been sober five years, and Jerry had just came out of being an undercover cop five years before, and we was the two most unlikely people to team up: An ex-undercover cop and an ex-recovering addict, you know what I'm saying? [laughs] But we was so good for each other, because I could tell him things he would never think about, and he taught me stuff that I would never think about that gave me empathy and compassion for the role that he chose in life. Police officers have a hard role, and their lives are always on the line, you know?

And so he came to this big old thing I did down at this college. I was, like, the Unity Day main speaker, and Jerry sat there and counted two thousand people, and when it was over he waited for me. And he had to wait a long time because it was lines of people waiting to talk to me. And he said, "Beverley, why isn't the media here?" He was so excited. He thought that people was on drugs and didn't get off and they was bad people and they died or they went to prison. He didn't know that there was this whole other world. So that made me very rich. I introduced him to stuff that he didn't even know about, which gave him a lot of hope. He started seeing hope in the people, and it was a fun thing.

JP: So did you feel the understanding coming alive in you during this time?

BW: Oh yes! All the time! We didn't have no set agenda for our work. We created the agenda at the end of the week. We looked back and saw what happened, you know what I'm saying? [laughs] We didn't never know what was going to happen. But we knew that if we were quiet, that intuitively we would know. And we knew that our job was to find the Health in the people—that's mainly the main thing—and to hold it up so that they could see it. We couldn't give it to them, but we could hold it up so they could see it, hold it up in a way that they could see it their own selves. And that's what we were able to do. Sometimes Roger [Mills] would come. I think Roger came up there about three times, did about three two-or-three-day classes during this period, and I ended up working out there five years. But in two-and-a-half years so many changes had happened between the African Americans and the Asian Americans and the relationship with the Oakland Housing Authority Police Department and some of the relationships with Oakland Housing Authority that people start coming from all around the world to find out what was going on there.

They sent these two reporters out there, and this reporter, she stayed for two months interviewing all the people. She wanted to know what had happened that was causing the peaceful times that was happening out there, so she interviewed the people, one by one, for two months. And when she got through writing up her story, the editors named it, "A Miracle on Sixty-Sixth Avenue." It was a twelve-page article in the *Oakland Express,* October of 1994. And I tell you, after that article went out, people started to come out—even before that people started coming, like John Wood from Australia, and Linda Washman from Minnesota who works at the senator's office. They came out. They wanted to see the people and talk to the people and find out what happened that brought about this change, where people were planting seeds, flower seeds, fruit trees. And you'd see an African American digging the dirt, and you'd see an Asian person putting in the seed, and an African American watering, you know? They was just like, "What brought about this unity in the community? What happened?" What happened was, we just talked to people about their thinking, taught them Health Realization.

JP: That answers what I was just going to ask you: What do you attribute the change to?

BW: And I attribute the change to a bunch of people that I worked with, like Lisa and Ron and myself, and then Jerry coming on board, and then us being able to recognize a couple of residents like Vivian and this other guy that we got on as part-time employees and taught them the Health Realization model. And Chi, the Asian guy. Those people loved us. I mean, they loved us! You see, I didn't know when I first went out there that African Americans wasn't supposed to talk to Asian people. I didn't know that. That was good, because I just talked to them. Even though they didn't speak English I just talked to them. I said, "Well, you know 'Hi!'" I was just speaking to them, and shaking their hands. And, if something really happened good—like I had three Asian girls in my class, and them little girls loved me, and so their parents started loving me because the kids didn't want to go home, you know? There'd be all this different interactions, relationships-building. So it was just a good thing.

[This interview with Beverley continues in Chapter IV, page 51] As of this writing, there has not been a murder in Coliseum Gardens for six years, and before this effort Coliseum Gardens had been known as "the murder capital."

* * *

*Elsie Spittle talks about her experiences with various **community-based Health Realization projects**. Her interview in Chapter VIII page 122 ended with her asking Roger Mills, Lloyd Fields and Cynthia Stennis how they achieved their impressive results in the Modello and Homestead Gardens housing projects.]*

JP: What did you hear from Lloyd and Cynthia, when you were picking their brains, that struck you about the way to go about working in a community?

ES: To listen to the residents. Rapport and listening. That the residents were the experts. And that helped me feel relaxed, because then I knew: Hey, it's not about me. It's about them, and they know what they want. They're the experts in their community. And what I can share is the understanding of creating an internal reality that impacts the outer reality, and there's the partnership. But they know what they want, and if I can listen to them, that's how we can work together—and rapport. Rapport, intuitively, I just knew that was the way to go.

JP: What was the name of this community?

ES: The very first community that I did that brief program for was Tampa Heights. It was six weeks, and then I think I did maybe another six weeks, just strictly training. It was not a comprehensive program where you go into the community and hire staff. That came later.

JP: So you just basically entered the community and did the training, or did you hang out first?

ES: No. I just basically went in and did training.

JP: How did that work?

ES: It worked fine, because the kind of training I did was really group training, drawing out from them, because I've always liked that. That always has been food for me. So I would introduce something, probably in those days more about Thought and Health, that people are innately healthy, and then would draw out of them, like, "How does that sit with you? How do you see that? Have you ever considered that?" So it was a lot of dialogue, and in that dialogue, rapport was being built. So it was that kind of training. In those days I didn't do much [writing] on the board, and I've almost come full circle, where I don't do much on the board now. It was more dialogue and, "How do you see this? What do you think this might do in your life? If you saw your partner or your children as having Health inside them, what do you think that might do?"

JP: Did you find that they responded to it?

ES: Very much! The person who did not respond was the person who brought me in. [laughs] She got nervous because she saw the residents growing and changing, and she wondered whether she'd have a program left and was most unnerved by it. The residents themselves really took to it and would share great examples, where they would be more thoughtful when they would go back home. I remember one woman in particular, she was really tough, she'd been on drugs and alcohol, had no teeth, but she somehow resonated with the idea that people had a core of Health inside them. She'd knifed her husband at one time and he ended up in the hospital with eighteen stitches—that was the kind of domestic, violent situation between both of them. And when she started to see the Health in him, she came back in and told this story about where he'd come back home drunk, and instead of her taking after him with a frying pan full of hot fat like she had the feeling to, she stopped herself, and she put on her shoes and she went out for a walk. Stories like that would pop up from people. She stopped this thinking where she was getting "het up," and she realized, "Here I go again, I don't want to go there," and she caught herself, and she put on her shoes and walked away.

JP: So she learned that in the training—meeting once a week for a day-and-a half for six weeks. The same group went through the second six weeks?

ES: Pretty much the same group. You know how it is. There'd be some come and go, but there was essentially a core group there.

JP: Was it an African American community?

ES: Primarily.

JP: Did you have any trepidation about being White?

ES: No. I really didn't. I had done some work with Roger as well. He'd invited me in, whether it was before then or around then I'm not sure, where I'd gone to New York with him, to the Bronx, and done some work there. And I got over the fact that I was White during that time period, and I was just seeing people as people and really grateful for the opportunity. So I didn't feel any qualms about that, just delighted that that was happening—

JP: So when was this?

ES: 1989. Then I think it was 1990 when I got my first opportunity to develop and find funding for a three-year program that was more comprehensive in Riverview Terrace, in Tampa.

JP: So that was where you were pretty much functioning as staff?

ES: I was the project director, and I hired a part-time staff person to actually be in the community, to have an office, so we had visibility in the community. Then within a couple of months we hired some part-time outreach workers, and hired a couple of people to work with the youth as well. All of that was resident-driven.

JP: You did that for three years?

ES: Two-and-a-half years. Then I got the opportunity to move to California to start a business with Roger. So I turned the project over to the community and other people, and I would consult with them long distance. I went in at the end of the third year to help them give out certificates and complete the program, but the last six months they really did on their own. We probably started Riverview Terrace in 1992-1993, something like that, and it ended three years later.

JP: What ended up happening in Riverview Terrace?

ES: It ended where half the community was getting torn down, and they were already starting to tear down some of the homes. It was a really old community, and they were going to rip it down and build new units on it. So a lot of the residents got dispersed, and where it is now I don't know. So in terms of community revitalization, I would say really nothing happened because that community is no longer. Again, it was individual changes. There were a number of people who individually changed, moved out of the community—some of them moved out even before the demolition, and others moved out due to that and started new lives. So a couple of them continue to keep in touch with me.

JP: Did you feel that project was a success?

ES: Based on individuals, I would. Based on community revitalization, no. What the resident council brought me in for was leadership empowerment, to get the residents out of apathy so that more people would sit on the board, on the resident council. They also wanted a youth leadership program—which we developed and worked with the youth—that could get the kids off the street. And that also was successful for that period of time. From what I understand, some of the youth that were really impacted continue to have nice lives today. So on an individual basis, that's how I see it. That's why, frankly, I don't know that I would do a community project again in the way that we have done it, where we develop such visibility in the community, hire staff, work with residents to go away on retreats and do action planning meetings and all that.

JP: Why is that?

ES: Because I think you, in essence, can put pressure on people to follow up with the action planning—all the goals and objectives that come out of that action planning. In the spirit of the moment a lot comes out, but the actual fruition of the action plans are few and far between. So I think a lot of money gets spent on areas like that, that don't necessarily come to fruition. I'm leaning more and more toward training, and then getting out of the way. Just train people and turn them loose, and let them do what they see to do in their own time.

JP: You must have had some experience with that. Where was that?

ES: Avalon Gardens. I've seen that in Avalon Gardens in south central Los Angeles. When we moved from Tampa to L.A. Roger asked me to take over that project.

JP: Had he started there already?

ES: Yes. He'd been there for two years, and I came in for the third year to supervise it. Again, that was to be a revitalization of the whole community, and a lot of goals and objectives, a lot of money spent, and I saw individuals change and not the whole community change.

JP: What had happened in the two years before you got there?

ES: A lot of training, and there was action planning that went on with some, frankly, grandiose ideas about what to do in the community that did not pan out. Then when I came on board, there was another action planning where the ideas came down to earth more, and nothing really happened there either.

JP: Interesting. And do you attribute nothing really happening there to the action planning?

ES: No, I attribute it to that people hadn't gone deep enough, so that wasn't what they really wanted to do on their own.

JP: Oh, that's very important!

ES: You know, all of this is in hindsight. In the heat of the moment during those action planning retreats where you'd all go away, where these wonderful brainstorming sessions would take place, these ideas would emerge, committees would be formed, they'd go back home and the ideas would just slowly sit there—where few people, if any, really owned them and said, "This is what we're going to do." It would require, to no avail, frankly, in my experience, calling: "Have you had your committee meeting? What's the outcome? How can I help you? Is there any way I can help you move this along?" Lots of words spoken; bottom line, nothing happened.

JP: You know what's amazing to me? What you're just describing did not happen in Modello. And it sounds to me that what happened in Avalon Gradens was there was an attempt to take a traditional outside-in approach—an action planning approach—and intermingle it with Health Realization, an inside-out approach. Does that sound right to you?

ES: I think there's a quality of depth where things unfold from, where you can't have the project director saying, "Okay, now it's time—we're looking at our goals and objectives, and within the time frame of the program, now it's time to have our action planning." And it's driven via that, as opposed to the residents coming up with these ideas and driving it themselves.

JP: It sounds like what you're saying is, the idea of traditional action planning is not something that moves this effort along, and it may inhibit it.

ES: Yeah. That's what I'm beginning to feel—because it's not resident-driven.

JP: So it's somebody else's idea to do that, and they don't have the buy-in.

ES: That's right. That's what I'm feeling.

JP: That makes sense to me.

ES: Although, even in the moment, as I say, in the retreat setting where the brainstorming is rich and fertile, it doesn't seem to pan out.

JP: I've noticed that just with traditional action planning. It almost never pans out, but people do get very excited at the time. And I always left those sessions—because I used to do those things—with a feeling that nothing is really going to come of all this. And I also noticed that it was in the people-taking-responsibility-to-follow-through phase where the energy would drop. Vision? Great. Energy's high. Desired results? Energy's high. Goals? Energy drops slightly, but it's still up there. Objectives and what we're going to do. Drops more, but still okay. Then as soon as you get to the, "Okay, now specifically, how are we going to make this happen?" and "Who's going to do what?" Boom. It drops. That's just from my experience.

ES: That's right. Exactly, Jack. And I see that continuing to happen, because that's become the model for community work. I continue to see that happening.

JP: You mean it's become part of the Health Realization model of community work?

ES: Uh huh.

JP: Really? Whose model? Not from what I've seen and done personally. It never would occur to me to do that. That's very interesting to me. Coliseum Gardens, to my knowledge, was another place they did not do action planning—which may be why it was so successful. So after Avalon Gardens, where did you really start feeling like you were having an impact on a community?

ES: I guess it would be in the Bronx and in Visitacion Valley [in San Francisco]. But again, not on the community as a whole, although I suspect in Visitacion Valley there is that ripple effect happening, probably, with some of the drug dealers not being on the streets. But I would say in regard to the training of individuals in both those communities, Visitacion Valley and in the Bronx, the people that we've touched there, many of whom have gone their own way and gone into other organizations in the last five months even, we have seen some wonderful, wonderful changes with individuals, with people there.

JP: When did that project start in Visitacion Valley?

ES: September of, maybe, 1999? I think Roger went in September to start the rapport-building, and January's when we actually hired LaThena [Clay] and Barb [Glaspie] and other staff, and that probably will be two years this January [2002].

JP: What role have you had in that?

ES: I worked with Roger on the actual proposal and developing the model for Visitacion Valley.

JP: How does that model look different than some of the other models?

ES: It's more extensive in terms of time. It's a five-year project rather than a three-year project that we've done before—and there's more action planning in it [laughs]—retreats to do action planning with the residents and service providers to see how to implement and move things along. I think that the grant proposal built on what Roger developed for Avalon Gardens.

JP: What have you learned from this latest project?

ES: I am leaning much more toward just training, and letting people do what they're going to do with their wisdom in their own way and their own time. I think we'd save many dollars that could be used for more training in other communities, rather than hiring staff like we do. It just sets up a lot when you move into a community like that, that already has other programs—even with the rapport, there's always going to be some programs that are already in place that take umbrage at the new folk coming in. And I know that will happen anywhere, but that's why I think the simplest, cleanest way to introduce this in communities, organizations, what have you, is to train people to the best of your ability—as long as it takes to get them to some depth—and turn 'em loose. That's what happened to us.

JP: The only thing I wonder about here is the staff issue, a staff presence. It would seem to me that if you had people as a daily presence in the community—like in Modello as Lloyd and Cynthia did, or in Coliseum like Beverley did—who are just there to help people out in whatever way they can, and just keep a good feeling and do whatever they have to do, it would seem to me that it would have more potential to have impact than just doing the training and letting the chips fall where they may, so to speak.

ES: Yeah. But we are training service providers to do that, who are already in the community. Like in Visitacion Valley we trained residents *and* service providers—service providers that have programs that work, that service youth, that do job training, that work with welfare-to-work recipients, just to a name a few. We're training them, those that have been interested. And that was part of Avalon Gardens as well. To me, the best would be to have those people trained. They're already visible and working in the community. They're already accepted, only now they have this added wisdom and understanding that they contribute. And they're already part of the community, rather than possibly introducing a whole 'nother kind of entity that oftentimes can create some resentment with some of the other providers. In Visitacion Valley there are still a very small group who are saying, "Well, we were already getting some of these results before Health Realization came along." Now, again, I think you're going to have that no matter what. There's always going to be some dissension, but I think that would lessen it.

JP: If you had the opportunity to go into a community now and do it exactly the way that you wanted to set it up, what would it look like from beginning to end?

ES: As much as I can see now, I would do resident training and service provider training. That would be it.

JP: That's all.

ES: Yeah, and I would just see it unfold from there.

JP: How often would you do the training?

ES: I don't know. I'd have to look at that. It may be that we'd do two days a month, to give them maybe ten to twelve days over the course of seven or eight months or something, and then reassess and see where we go from there: Do we pull back a little bit and let them just try it on and do what they want to do, and see how things work out for them? What ideas occur to them at their own pace? And be on board as a consultant for a period of time. But when people are hired in a community and are employed, that also sets up some resentment with other residents. It sets up, possibly, some prima donnas, you know? It sets up a dependence on the grant. It sets up some things that I think aren't healthy.

JP: What do you think about the training of trainers model like they do in Santa Clara county, where they give a certification—

ES: I do a training of trainers, but I don't give a certification—other than a certificate of completion. And they write a paper or submit an audio or a videotape. I love to see what they've learned. I think it's good for people to actually write down, "What I've learned in this program. How it's changed my life." And I like to do two programs concurrently: a Principles program which is basically an introduction where people don't know anything or very little about this, and a training-of-trainers, so the TOT group helps me train the newcomers, and they make a videotape before the third session of them training before an audience, and get feedback.

JP: They still get their certificate, no matter how well they do?

ES: Absolutely, because they've completed the program. Now in Vis' Valley, I went in there a day-and-a-half every month, and out of ten sessions the first three I really work with the group, then I have them train each other. We take a day where I actually assign different topics to the group, in teams, and then for the other half-day they would come back in and present. I had one team present the Principles to the best of their ability, with examples. Then, I would have another team talk about how the Principles relate to rapport. I'd have another team talk about how the Principles relate to listening. I would have another team talk about how understanding the Principles helped them in their work, in the community. So although they wouldn't necessarily say, "These are the Principles and what they mean to me," they always have that as their basis…

JP: When you look back at the community projects you've done and all this kind of stuff, are there a couple of people whose changes stand out in your mind most vividly?

ES: Yeah, I would say Helen [Neale-Pore].

JP: I'm interviewing her [Chapter I]. Anybody else—a story or two that comes to your mind?

ES: Well, a woman from Riverview Terrace in Tampa, who, when I first met her, when she just came in to sit in our training program there in the community—a big woman—had three little grandchildren just clustered around her, hanging on and agitated and crying and unhappy. She was wearing a green smock that you get when you're in the hospital as a patient. She looked psychotic to me. She just looked so out to lunch. And I thought, "Hmm. That's interesting. Why is she even here?" And she was even rather disruptive in her care of the children, and noisy and very vocal, and I thought, "Hmm." But we just went along anyways, because you get used to that a lot when you're working in communities. And we just carried on with the dialogue. And over a period of time I found out more and more about her, and she just was drawn to this, with her little grandchildren. I found out later that she had some bookkeeping experience, and the more that she regained her health, the more she was inclined to get out and about in the community, and the more she dressed nicely. Sometimes she had her grandchildren, and sometimes she didn't, but when she did have them it was noticeable that they were also quieting down and were more well-behaved. And she was looking happier. And her daughter started to come in. I don't know exactly the story of her daughter, but her daughter, whose little children these were, started to come in occasionally with her too. And it turned out that she ended up going back to school, night school, and getting her CPA for accounting. She stands out in my mind—and she continues to e-mail me occasionally and is still doing well—because she just looked like she would never make it. And here she is now, a productive member of the community.

Another woman that I remember, again from the same community, when she first came in I thought, "I don't know about her." But there was something about her also that I liked. And when we had to hire someone to work with the children in the youth leadership component, she kept coming to mind. Yet at the same time I saw that when she would get upset and frustrated she would take it out on the kids, and she would threaten them with the belt, because that's just the way she was. And I thought, "I don't know about this." Yet my head said one thing but my heart said, "Hire her." And so I hired her and someone else who I felt would be a really good team with her. And the two of them started to work with the kids. And she was blossoming and growing. Then she was hired to work at the school as a teacher's assistant, and she was really growing. And then I started to hear from some of the staff I had hired in Riverview Terrace that she was threatening the kids in the Health Realization program—that if they misbehaved she'd take the belt to them. She never did, but she would threaten them. And I really felt a little intimidated by her. She had three children, all of whom were in jail, and she had the two grandchildren—she had been appointed the guardian for the children. I was a little intimidated by her, because she was pretty tough. But finally I could no longer ignore it, and I ended up inviting her to lunch to talk to her about what I'd been hearing from the staff, to say, "Could we talk about what's going on?" And I hemmed and hawed and hemmed and hawed and finally just cut to the chase, and we ended up having the most productive, warm-hearted talk that you could imagine. She was in tears, I was in tears. And we left almost holding hands. There was such warmth between us. Because I finally said to her, "You know, you intimidate me. I'm intimidated by you, and if I'm intimated by you, imagine the kids." She didn't realize that! That was such a habit of thought to her to threaten the kids with the belt. She said, "I'd never use that, Elsie, I'd never beat these kids. That's just my way, and I'm doing it because I love them and I want them to behave." Well I never realized that she didn't know how intimidating she was. I didn't realize that she was threatening out of love! So it was a revelation for me. And she didn't realize that I was intimidated, and if I was intimidated, who she respected—and who she felt intimidated by—then what could those kids or other staff members be feeling? So it was a revelation for her. It was a revelation for me, and we became really close in that time. And she became much gentler.

[This interview with Elsie finishes in Chapter IX, page 122.]

* * *

Kristen Mansheim *talks about her experience in developing the Health Realization approach at the Mariposa Lodge alcohol and drug treatment facility, and her perspective on how the Health Realization effort began at the county level in Santa Clara County, California. [This interview continues from Chapter VII, page 109]*

JP: How did it all get started at Mariposa Lodge?

KM: Well, I came back from that training with Joe and Mark, and I was different. I was not the same. I didn't understand the Principles, but I heard something that changed me, and I was in a better feeling, and my clients picked up on my mood because I was not in a great feeling before. I noticed they wanted to be around me.

JP: That was a switch?
KM: Yeah, well, they normally wanted to run from me. I mean, when clients came in, the first thing they would do is find out who's who and what lodge they want to be in and who their best counselor is, and you didn't want to get assigned to me because I was tough. I nailed you on everything, didn't give a lot, withheld passes and privileges. I was big into the "being accountable" thing.

JP: So that's where you were working, at Mariposa?

KM: That's where I was working, and I changed with my clients. They stopped feeling like my clients and they started feeling like my girls. I just wanted to go hang out with them. And I stopped trying to do a big clinical thing when we did group. I really didn't even want to know how they were doing and what was up. I just wanted us to get to that feeling. At the beginning I was still teaching some of the old stuff, and I tried teaching some new stuff but they just don't mix. I loved the idea that people had Health in them, and even if they couldn't connect to it they still had it. I loved that. And over the course of a couple of years, I kept going to trainings, kept going to trainings, and Roger

213

used to tell us, "Don't worry about teaching this. Just talk from your heart. Just say what you know. Say what's real to you." So I guess I was just doing that, and I didn't really realize I was being different that much, because it wasn't something I was *trying* to do, be different. One day I got a call from my boss at our work, a "Come to my office" phone call. So I walked up to her office thinking, "What'd I do? I don't even know what I did." And I sat down and she said, "You know, I have noticed that your Lodge doesn't take a turn anymore."

JP: A turn?

KM: At Mariposa the clients live in these lodges, and there are three primary lodges and a detox lodge. There were three counselors, and every counselor had a lodge. Every morning we would sit at staffing, and staffing consisted of the night shift reviewing everything that had happened since we left. On Monday morning that was a long thing. They'd tell us who did what, and everything that was happening. Of course the clients would spend their time acting out as soon as the counseling staff went home because nobody was on them anymore, so they would gear up. We used to spend our time containing them, and as soon as we'd leave they'd explode. So morning staffing was the report out of who did what to whom, who's fighting with who, who had a breakdown, who got suicidal, who came back loaded, and who was in the bushes with whom—all that happens at every residential facility. There's this contagion effect. For example, if one person started stealing in the lodge then everybody became suspicious, which bred hostility then anger then fighting, and then somebody was drinking or loaded—it was like a nuclear bomb would go off in the lodge. It would take maybe a week or so and you'd finally get the whole thing settled down. Then the same thing would happen in somebody else's lodge. So it just rotated. It was kind of like, "Whose turn is it now?" And your job as a counselor was to try to get that under control. So when my boss called me up to ask me about my lodge, that was a big deal. She said, "Your lodge doesn't take a turn anymore. I don't hear about your lodge in staffing anymore. They're not fighting. They're not sneaking their boyfriends in. Their tests are coming back clean. They're completing treatment. I just realized your lodge hasn't had a turn in a long time. What are you doing down there?"

I remember I was in a horrible mood that day, and I knew I was in a low mood and so I thought, "Oh, my God. They want to know what I'm doing, and here's my opportunity to say something about Health Realization, and I feel like shit." And I thought, "Well, you know, Kristen, it doesn't matter. The door is open, just walk through it." And so I said, "Well, I learned this new thing, and it's called Health Realization, and it's based on the fact that everybody is healthy, and that sometimes we're connected to it and sometimes we're not, and whether we are or not depends on how we're using our own functioning, and once you know about that, you can navigate it better." I don't know if I said it like that but it's an approximation of that in my own simple language at the time. She said, "You're kidding." I said, "No." She said, "You've got to tell Shirley [Wilson, the executive director] about this!" So she kind of drug me by the hand and put me in front of Shirley and said, "Shirley, you've got to hear this!"

And I remember I was feeling so bad that day, I thought, "I just don't have it in me to do this again," but I did it again. And Shirley got so excited. She got so excited! Shirley is an incredible person, because she is always only interested in what is best for the clients. And she said, "This sounds like it's really good for the clients." And I said, "Yes, I think it is." She said, "Well, do you think you could teach this to the other staff?" I said, "I don't know how to teach this to the other staff." And she said, "What if we get you more training?" And I said, "Well, I'll try." So she paid for some training for me. Then she created a position within the agency for me—I think I kept some clinical work at first, and I did a staff group at that facility, and then the next contract year she created a pure training position for me, and I traveled around to the different facilities within ARH Recovery Homes. I did some training at Mariposa, and I did some training at the other sites too and started working with staff. That came out of nowhere. That position did not exist. She created that for me. And then the County [Santa Clara] wanted to borrow me, so I split my time between the agency and the County. Eventually, Shirley asked me to train the executive management team for ARH Recovery Homes—so the Principles became a top-to-bottom understanding within the agency.

JP: So it kind of gradually took over the place?

KM: Yeah. Their position at the time I was still working there was that all staff were asked to check out Health Realization. They were asked to attend a core course. And a lot of the people after the core course would attend my ongoing trainings. Or sometimes they would sit in on my ongoing trainings and then get interested in going to the core course. And that's where the momentum came from. I learned a lot doing that. It was a huge transition for me to go from working with the clients to working with staff, because in my mind staff were different. I could see the utmost innocence in a client that threw a hissy fit or stole food or got loaded or hit somebody else—I mean, that was very innocent to me—but when my boss would ask me to sit with a colleague who had been screaming at clients and telling the clients to "fuck off" and "go pack your fucking bags," I didn't see that as innocent. I had a lot of judgment about my colleagues because I had an idea in my head that they ought to be in a certain place, because they were staff.

JP: That seems to be true for a lot of us.

KM: I didn't know how to be with that, and I struggled with it for a while, and I remember kind of running to Roger. "Roger, what am I going to do? Some of them are hurting the clients and acting like idiots!" And he said, "Well you've just got to see *them* as your clients. You've got to see them the exact same way you see the clients." Pretty quickly that part became easier because I realized, "Well, they're human just like the clients. It would be nice if they knew better, but sometimes they don't. They lose their bearings just like the clients do." So they became my new clients. Then I got frustrated with some people in my personal life. And then I saw, "Oh, this is the same thing." And the insight was kind of like, "Oh, everybody's a client!" But not like I'm walking around doing therapy on everybody; it was like, "Oh, *everybody's just human!*" It's across the board, the human thing. You don't change up when you change roles. The rules are the same, and you stay the same no matter where you go.

The next big one for me, was seeing Health in systems, seeing the innocence in systems—because the systems didn't work the way I wanted them to. But when I sat and looked at it, a system is made up of people, it's group thinking, it's layers of thinking, and that's why it can get bogged down. When I would try to fight the system I would get nowhere. I would make enemies. I'd lose my good feeling. And I saw, "*Oh,* this is the same thing!" You don't go into a system and challenge the system and fight the system and take on the system—you look for the same Health that you look for in your clients and your colleagues. Then you draw that out and that gets the system moving. You don't work against it. So I saw that in kind of gradual layers.

JP: So is that pretty much how it evolved in Santa Clara County?

KM: A lot of it was from the ground up. Some places you go, you go in top-down, but Santa Clara County has been more bottom-up. The first people to really appreciate what we were saying were the clients and the inmates.

JP: Is that how Bob Garner [County alcohol and drug abuse director] ended up hearing about it, and got turned on enough to want the training?

KM: No. Bob Garner heard about this from his partner, Penny. Penny was into this, and she works for a business; she'd been into it for a while, using it in business as a leadership paradigm—

215

and she kind of dragged him in one day and said, "You really have to listen to this." And he got turned on. Some of the stats from Modello got him curious. He talks about how he knew that the alcohol and drug system did the best it could by people, but the results weren't great. Bob is amazingly visionary. He was looking for something that would get results, more than something safe. That's why he threw this out in that huge training in 1994, and there were a handful of us that stayed with it. He brought Roger in, and we stayed with Roger, and he kept providing trainings, and we got enough of us that we started to be able to teach the clients. I was at Mariposa, Cathy [Casey] was in the jails, various other people throughout the County within little, tiny pockets that you would think wouldn't impact a whole County, but we hit enough clients and enough inmates that they started saying to the judges, to their social workers, to their counselors, "I'm into this Health Realization thing. I see it's my thinking now. I know I'm okay now." And then the social workers and the counselors would come, would want to know what it was, because their clients were talking about it. We'd have people come to our core courses and say, "My clients know more about this than I do. I need to know what this is!" So it really went up from the bottom, and now we're at the point where the board of supervisors has heard about it, and some of them have participated in the training themselves and see how helpful it is, and support its use in different agencies. Social Services is now involved. It's really mushroomed.

JP: Was Beverley involved at all in training in the County?

KM: Absolutely. The first time I met Beverley, Roger brought her in to speak at one of those trainings, and she was really helpful for those of us that were in recovery because she could speak so powerfully. So that made us all feel safer—there was somebody that understood. Beverley has so much presence. She's so dynamic that you can't be around her and not hear something. It doesn't really matter what Beverley says, you just change after you've been around Beverley. So, yes, Beverley was one of the people when I got ready to present this to the staff—we did a big presentation at Mariposa—Roger came and she came, and she was hugely instrumental in people being willing to listen, because of the way she spoke. She just has that. She's still working miracles here, teaching in the jail.

[This interview with Kristen continues back in Chapter VII, page 109]

* * *

Judy Sedgeman *speaks about how the effort began at the West Virginia University [WVU] School of Medicine in Morgantown, which culminated in the establishment of the Sydney Banks Institute of Innate Health. [This interview continued from Chapter XI, page 143.]*

JP: How did it start here, at West Virginia University?

JS: I met the dean, Bob D'Allesandri, when he was a participant in a Health Care Forum physician leadership group. Although my part in it was fairly brief I was very struck by the depth of his interest, as opposed to everybody else in the room. There were nine physician leaders, and the other eight were filled with intellectual questions, like, "How does this work? How does that work?"-type questions, and he wasn't. He was reflecting. He didn't say very much, and when he did say something, it was different. George [Pransky] and I were just one event within this whole Forum. George did the beginning, and then I did the last part of it, because our schedules didn't work out. So D'Allesandri said that he was going to follow up with this. At that time I was working all over the country doing a lot of public speaking to a lot of health care people, and they give you a card and you never hear from them again. But in this case, he did. He called. He started looking to find ways to get his leadership group exposed. At that time the only way he could really do it was to send them out to workshops, which he did.

JP: This was the leadership group here [at WVU]?

JS: Yes. And Bob came with every group that came out [to LaConner, Washington, Pransky's base of operations]. Then he was trying to find a way to do things on campus, because you can only afford to send so many people across country so often. And Bob would say, "Why don't you join us for dinner?" So I frequently had dinner with the groups, and towards the end of that time one night, Bob said, "I'd love you to think about coming to West Virginia for a visit." I had never been to West Virginia. So I said, "Sure." And I came out, and we talked, and I was here for, like, five days, and at the end of that time he said, "What would it take to get you to move here?" By that time, I'd so fallen in love with this place and him and the people here, that I said, "Just send a truck, and I'll be here."

JP: How much exposure to training in the three Principles had he had at the time?

JS: Well, maybe four or five workshops of two or three days each, and then whatever else he'd pursued, I don't even know—like reading Syd's books or listening to tapes. But to me, as I reflect back on it, Bob was a person who naturally was drawn to the common sense of bringing out the best in people, and this institution was—before I ever got here—committed to service and love and very respectful interaction with people. So it wasn't, like, shocking that he would be so interested. And when I came here the thing that really got to me was—I went to the new faculty orientation, and he had put me on the program at three different spots so I couldn't leave. I had to stay and listen to everybody else. And I was so moved by the sincerity and the genuineness and the simplicity and the caring of every person that got up to speak—whatever aspect of the university they represented—and I thought, "This place is very lovely. This is not what I thought an academic institution was going to be." So I fell in love with it—I really did—and the people that I met. So then I moved here, without any real understanding what my job was going to be.

JP: So there was no official position that you were coming into?

JS: Not really.

JP: Did he guarantee you a salary?

JS: Yeah. It was a salary of a part-time adjunct assistant professor, which I did get an appointment to be. You have to have a faculty appointment to work here, but an adjunct assistant professor might or might not ever teach, and the suggestion of that position is that you will find a way, if you're responsible, to integrate your service into your department and offer something. So the first thing I did is design this course called "The Resilient Health Professional," which I've only taught once, actually, because then after that they needed somebody to teach the management class, and I was kind of a natural fit because I'd been a management consultant my whole life before I got involved in this and had been the CEO of my own company and obviously knew something about health care. But I didn't even have an office for the first six months. I worked from home or my car or just met in other people's offices. And Bob said, "What I want you to do is spend time with people and see where you can be of service, and if you feel there is something you can offer, then it'll work out." He said, "I trust you to create what needs to be created here to bring this into the culture." Then he set up a certain number of things that he wanted me to do for the leadership group, so I did leadership training. But really, when I think back on that time it was very magical because it's the only time in my life I've ever been in a position where I didn't have to do anything, but I could do anything! So it was totally open.

JP: What year was that?

JS: 1998. And I didn't see that much of Bob, either. I mean, it's like he really just said, "Be who you are and this will work out."

JP: Did he say why he wanted you there?

JS: No, he didn't. I mean, I would never, in a million years—Jack, I have to tell you that when this thing [The Sydney Banks Institute of Innate Health] opened last September, it was as unbelievable to me as it was to everybody else. [laughs] I mean, I couldn't have imagined when I came here that it would come to that. I mean, what I wanted to do was just see how helpful I could be, and because I was still part-time I was still doing other consulting and traveling, and I just created my own life here in a sense. And then I started giving up a lot of my old stuff, and I went through this period of time where I thought, "Financially this isn't such a wise thing." And then I thought, "It will work out," and I stopped thinking about it. And it worked out.

JP: Did you ever have a grand design in your mind about what you would like to see happen?

JS: No, I didn't. What inspired me when I came here was two things: Within the Health Sciences Center I wanted to talk to people about what was underneath their natural goodness and their instinct for service, and underpin this so that it could get communicated to students more effectively. This was a traditional medical school with all the problems of a traditional medical school, in terms of the pressures students are under and the stress they experience. Yet the people here had this desire for things to be different. What I realized was that a lot of people walk around in service to others and in a beautiful, loving state, but it's easily lost and not easily transmitted if they don't have the understanding of the Principles underneath it. So when they lose it, it looks like it was a dream, and then when they get it back, they don't know how it happened and they don't know how to talk about it. So what I saw was kind of a fragile state, uninformed by knowledge. So within the Health Sciences Center I saw the value of the Principles in that regard.

Within the state of West Virginia I saw wonderful people with huge resiliency. This is a very difficult place for people to have a life. I mean, the infrastructure isn't very strong. People live in these rural, remote areas that are almost inaccessible in the winter. People have to get by with very little. There's a lot of poverty. It's just a very poor state. But the people are so nice, and they're so wonderful, yet they have this thinking of resignation and poverty. It's like, "Well, this is West Virginia." They have this kind of overlay of thought that, continually, is like a big, thick coat of dust on their resiliency. If they would just dust it, it would shine, and then it would be something. So the two things that struck me is that this medical school and this Health Sciences Center had all of the goodness and the capacity to bring this beauty out in the people of West Virginia, and had everything going for it. And given the knowledge of how to awaken people's Health, this could be a model for what could happen in a whole state. I saw that. So that's what inspired me, but I had no idea how that was all going to work. I just was inspired by that idea.

JP: You know what's interesting to me? In a sense that was your grand design. You wanted people to feel that, to see the underpinnings—

JS: Yeah, and then share it—bring it out in other people.

JP: What didn't matter was *how* it happened, but if you didn't *see* that as your grand design—

JS: It's probably true. And also I had come to a point in my own understanding where I had faith that if you just trust, if you keep yourself in a good state, if you stay rested, stay connected to people and you care, and you stay in love with life, that things will work out however—who knows how? So I just kind of came in every day and hung out with people. But one thing I discovered was that before I got here people had made a big deal about George [Pransky]. They made him into something. And it occurred to me that they may have lost sight of the fact that the idea was that *everybody has Health*. They were thinking, "You have to keep going back to the source, to the well, for the clear water." So my first job when I got here was to put an end to that, and not let that happen to me. So I was really glad I didn't have an office. I just came and went. And if I formed a group for a task and we finished the task, I would disband the group. People would say, "Well, let's continue to meet," and I said, "No, you make up your own group." And it was a tremendous learning experience for me. People do that with Syd sometimes; people do that with Roger. It isn't because these guys are trying to make it happen. But I wanted to be invisible. I didn't want to be "a thing." Even now my office is way far from community medicine, way at the other end of the building. And I would go to faculty meetings, but nobody really knew where I went back to when I left. And I just wanted to listen and learn and share and let people blossom and wonder—I mean, the happiest day of my life would be if they just couldn't imagine how this wonderful thing happened to them, and it would never even occur to them that they might have been to something I did three weeks ago. I really saw that that was important.

JP: So was that what you meant when you said you wanted to "put an end to that?"

JS: Yeah. For one thing I never referred to this as Psychology of Mind. If people brought it up I would, but I just referred to the three Principles. They'd say, "What do you call this?" I'd say, "Well, you don't need a name for it. It's whatever you see. Call it whatever you want to call it for whatever program." And people would name different programs different things that are relevant to the audience, which makes sense to me. I didn't want it to be "a thing," and I didn't want it connected to be "a thing-maker." People would ask me, "Do you think we should organize another trip to LaConner?" I'd say, "Well, there's an awful lot of people here that have their own understanding, why don't you just let people's Health do the work and see what we can do." I never discouraged people—if they wanted to go, they went, fine—but I was always trying to point it back to the person and their own Health, and not let them attribute it to anything else.

JP: At what point did you see that having "a thing" wasn't a good idea?

JS: Originally, I along with everyone else thought the way we were putting it out was a good idea, and I was behind it, and I was trying to help. And then I realized that this conceptual framework [the concepts] and all this intellectualization, people couldn't grasp it. And we're trying to say this is simple, it's in everybody. And people are asking, "Tell me again about the levels. Which levels?" And I'm going, "Something is wrong here." I just kind of got up one morning and I couldn't do it anymore. I didn't want to do that. I wanted to work with something much simpler, just talk about the Principles and just let people find their own voice, and that there wasn't a "right way."

JP: I remember at one point you said it occurred to you that you didn't have to look to somebody else to interpret what Syd Banks was saying. Would you describe that?

JS: Well, at one point I saw that there were people that thought Roger had the answer, and other people thought George had the answer, and I'm, like, "This is crazy!" And that was when it all fell into place for me. I'm thinking, "This is not right. We're all the same here, and we're just trying to do nice things for other people." I just didn't want any part of it. So I just started doing my own thing as a consultant, and I was doing pretty well, so when the offer came to move to West Virginia I was pretty ripe to go. But I realized that when this gets to be about people instead of about *all people*, then it's gone wrong.

JP: Somewhere along the line as this was evolving at WVU, it looked like you wanted to remove all "forms" that this understanding was put out as.

JS: Yeah, I did.

JP: And in a sense, I've always gotten the feeling that if you were going to start something here, it was going to start fresh. Can you say something about what made you come to that?

JS: Well, my biggest concern was that I didn't want to make "a thing." Well it has to be *something* in order to *be*, you know? You can't fund air. So it's still very unclear in my mind in a way. The biggest criticism I get when I'm out trying to help people to see how they could support it is, they say, "I'd love to support you, but I don't exactly know what to tell them they're supporting." Because I don't necessarily know what we're going to do exactly, but I do know what this does. I've seen it with my own eyes, and I've seen it for myself in doing it myself. That is, this understanding—when it's the foundation for education—creates a learning environment instead of a teaching environment. And whatever we do here we infuse a critical mass of people with this reverence for insight learning; for what it means to really *see* something as opposed to just memorize something; for what it means to be a partner in discovery with students rather than being the expert, filling their little heads. And there is no attachment to any particular system of learning implicit in all of that. There are so many dimensions to that experience; that's what we should be doing, creating something deeper than the subject, you know? This is why I love teaching management. They're graduating with competencies in management, but I'm not just teaching management. I'm teaching management in a way that's never been taught before, because no one has thought the students can discover what's good management without reading *The Seven Habits of Highly Effective People* and memorizing it. You know what I'm saying? And the same thing is true if I were teaching genetics or anatomy or biochemistry or whatever—as people begin to understand the mind at a deeper level, their level of respect for learning and the way they see the learning changes. And when that changes it creates a different kind of culture. So that's not a form. That's deeper than a form. So I'm interested in developing for the people who work with us here what Bob did for me—go out and see how you can serve, from what you know to be true about life and the Principles.

Then I wanted to draw influential thinkers to us, because I think the advantage of having a platform, of being part of a university, is that if you hold a conference, people come. It's like it legitimizes things, because when a university is behind something, people assume it has a little more credibility. And we can offer continuing education credits, and these are valuable. I'm not interested in structure, but I don't make fun of the structure I'm in, because that structure is what's provided the vehicle for me to propel this understanding to a new level of respectability.

JP: What made you and Bob [D'Allesandri] get to a point where you saw that this could permeate the institution?

JS: After the first several months that I was here I sat down with Bob, and we had this really nice conversation. He said, "I think this is working out. I think you've sort of become a part of the fabric of our life here." And I did everything I could to bring as many people as I could here—through the Aequanimitas Foundation faculty or whatever—so in the first year that I was here, I brought fifty-two people here over the course of that year, including you, Roger, Kristen Mansheim, Gloria Newton, Joe and Doris Boyle, the people from California, all kinds of people. Jim Marshall did a wonderful program for the kids. Any way that I could find a way to get people here, I would do that. I wanted people here to get the idea that this was just a regular, ordinary practice that many different people, with different personalities and different constituencies—coming from the same place—were putting out. And that really worked out, because people here were touched by their interactions with all these people. It wasn't just me, and it wasn't some special thing, and it wasn't like there's only one place you can get it, or one person. And I would show that "Applications" video [(2000)] any place I could. This is *before the form*, but work is still conducted *through* the form.

I have so much respect for how beautifully people do the thing they really know how to do well when they do it with a different spirit. And I should have known that from the beginning, because that's exactly what happened to me. It never dawned on me until years later, that I got sucked into this idea that if you had this understanding then that was the be-all and the end-all, and it really isn't. It's the beginning.

JP: Back to this meeting with Bob, how it started to become a vision for the medical school—

JS: Yeah, see, I don't know whether Bob may have had this vision. He might have had a thought about what he wanted to see happen, but he never said anything to me about it. At this particular meeting, Bob said, "What are you going to do with this?" He said, "You know, you're doing great. People really are responding, and a lot of people have been very grateful. You've done a lot of public service. I really appreciate the time you've put into traveling around the state and talking to people, but what do you want to do now?" And I said, "I don't know really."

JP: This was how long after you got here?

JS: Six or seven months, less than a year. So he said, "What do you think would make sense?" I said, "Well, I don't know. I guess it would make sense if it had a sort of a core visibility, but I don't really want a place, I don't want a building—just sort of a focal point. That would make sense." He said, "Well, why don't you think about that?" So what I started thinking about was the number of people over the years who I have met who said, "If there were ever an academic institution that we could provide money to in the future and we knew it was established, we would support it." I thought about all those people, and I thought, "Well, we could set up an endowment that would provide for Syd to be a lecturer, and to provide for a certain identity without too much form attached to it, and we'd provide for the future because if we have an endowment we could endow faculty positions where people would feel secure in undertaking longitudinal research." What occurred to me is that, besides teaching, we needed really good research. So I went back to Bob, and I said, "You know, I honestly believe that we could endow an institute, because I think there are people around the country—I know they're not in West Virginia—that would get behind it, if we do it responsibly, and if we do it without making it a big deal." So he said, "Well, do you want to explore that?" and I said, "Yeah, I think I do."

We had started that research project with the Aquanimitas Foundation, and I knew that people were dying for the results. They're still dying for the results, but we're working on it. But that was part of the reason you need to raise money, so you can process information and get things done. And I saw this big vision for research—I mean, that's really what struck me—that we could become a national data bank. We could give individual practitioners who want to research things that they're doing but who don't know how to set it up and get it published—I just saw a function for an institution to be a service to thousands of people around the country. Bob said, 'Well, if you can raise the money, if you believe in it and you think it's going to work out, let's see what happens."

So I wrote a little statement that became our original document that we sent out to people—and people responded! And the beautiful thing was that when people responded, everybody who gave money initially to start this—without necessarily communicating with each other—did not want to have it named after them. They all said, "We should really just call it what it is: The Sydney Banks Institute, because that's what we're doing here. So that's what happened. And in terms of the initial sufficient endowment to start, it happened within six months. So it was ready to happen. And then the more I talked to people about it, the more certain this vision became—that it should be education, research, clinical and service, which are the four missions of the medical school; that research should be the defining initial impetus because it will empower everything else. People care about results, and so many people for so many years have seen results but not documented them. And I wanted it to be something really beautiful.

JP: At what point did you talk to Syd about this?

JS: Right when I started to see that, and Bob talked to him, too, and then some our donors talked to him. And Syd was delighted. You have to ask him, of course, but for Syd, since I've known him at least, and I think before that, he's always said, "Someday when the time is right, this is going to be picked up by an academic institution, and it will change the world." And so I guess he just decided, "Okay, this must be it; it's happening now." So Syd has had not a very proactive role but a very helpful role in all of this. He's come in contact with a lot of people here, and they really respect him. But I think he doesn't have a big-deal feeling about it. It's like, "Well, now it's time for this, and we'll just see where it goes from here."

JP: So how would you characterize what his role is, in terms of the Sydney Banks Institute for Innate Health?

JS: He's a resource, and a teacher.

JP: Did he have any problems with his name being on it?

JS: No. He could have had problems with his name being on it, but it was focused more on the fact of him being a vehicle for the Principles, not anything special about him, so I think he thought it was okay. I mean, he's read our charter and our statement of purpose and all that very closely. Again, you should ask him directly, but I think he felt that it was done in a right spirit, just to be thankful to Syd as the person who articulated something that we are able to use, to take to go way beyond the initial articulation.

JP: So did you ever see what was happening here being a consolidating point for everything happening with this understanding?

JS: No. No. As a matter of fact I think that would be the kiss of death, actually. I think it would be very wrong. I saw it as being, hopefully, the wind beneath the wings of everything that was happening. And I'd like to see it that way, not as a consolidating point but as an uplifting force. Because if I were thinking about going into this field, if I were a young person now, it would be comforting to me to think that academic institutions are taking an interest in this, and that there's going to be a program, and that it will get legitimized, and that research is quoted and published in journals by people who do research and have published before on other subjects. I mean, it would give me the faith to know that it wasn't just some kind of an off-beat thing. And if there's anything I hope that we come to mean to people, it's faith that if it could happen here it could happen anywhere, and it should and can and will. And that the understanding is more powerful than our insecurity about it, you know? And so if it's an inspiration to people, that would be wonderful. As a matter of fact, I would do everything to avoid consolidation here of everything happening, because I think that would be a disservice to the creativity and imagination of so many people that are doing it their own way in different settings, and to the possibility that other institutions will find a whole other way to do this. It could be anywhere.

JP: That raises a really great question. What would you say are the critical elements that would make something like this be able to take hold in other places?

JS: I think faith that the institution will have the wisdom to see how to do it, and see how to work together with others. Faith in not caring about the form, but caring about the feeling—deeper than the form. So the first critical element is to know that, no matter what institution you're in or where you are or how dysfunctional it may seem, people want a higher level of functioning. People want stability. People want calm. People want peace of mind. And that the power of Health is phenomenal, and if they get a glimpse of it they'll find their way to it. And you don't have to do anything, except the glimpse. I think to a certain extent you need persistence. Just the ordinary, everyday little things speak more loudly than big things, like showing up where you said you were going to be, and not playing the political games, and apologizing if you're insecure and get off-base with people, and saying, "I'm sorry. I got insecure. It happens, we all get insecure sometimes," and being just a regular person, and living at peace within oneself. I think ultimately, in a big institution, you have to have the commitment of leadership. If Bob didn't want this to happen it wouldn't happen. So if there is one significant person, he is. There is always somebody that can say no, and if that person doesn't want to say yes, it doesn't make any difference how many other people want it.

JP: I heard a couple of other things, too, when you were describing how it all happened. One of them was, at the beginning you just hung out.

JS: Yeah. It was just kind of perseverance.

JP: And you listened, because you wouldn't have known what direction to go in if you hadn't.

JS: Yes. And of course I had to listen because I had never been in an academic institution before as a player—I mean I'd been a student, but that's a difference experience—so I was pretty humbled by ignorance. [laughs] So it was like, when you know you don't know, you just have to "not know" until you see something. And I had a good excuse for not knowing because I really didn't. And honestly, Jack, the other thing I realized is, in an academic institution people love to teach you. I was never thwarted from learning how things worked or from getting the help I needed, or from meeting the person I needed to meet, or from having somebody say, "Here, let me show you what you have to do to get from A to B here." If you asked me, "What's the Sydney Banks Institute going to be doing next year?" I've got a five-year plan, because you have to have a five-year plan, but I wouldn't be sure that I have any idea what we'll be doing next year. I do know that, whatever it is, we're not going to be doing it alone. We're going to be doing it as a part of something greater than we are—the Institute itself—and we're going to be doing it with a shared vision for the well-being of students and people.

JP: Can you recall some real stellar moments, things that have happened here that were really special, like when you saw a spark in people? You have stories?

JS: There are so many of them. One of the first things I did, even before I came here, was that I was invited by Hilda Heddy, who is the head of the Rural Health Education Partnership Program for

223

the State of West Virginia—she works with all the health sciences schools. They have eleven sites around West Virginia where they bring the students to rural areas to work with the rural population and work with rural doctors and learn about rural health. They have site coordinators in each of these sites, and I did a strategic vision retreat with the site coordinators. Hilda and I had talked, but it was one of my very first trips to West Virginia and nobody really knew too much about it [the Principles]. We got to this cabin out in this wilderness area with these site coordinators who tended to be young, driven, enthusiastic people with a kind of a Peace Corps mentality—in a good sense, that real dedication, and by God, we're going to get out there and help these people and do good things for these poor people. And I remember at that first meeting I started to talk to them about disempowerment versus empowerment. They were so mad at me—

JP: What did you say?

JS: The point was, if you really don't try to do too much *for* people except help them to see how much they can find within themselves, it works out better. But these were crusaders, you know? Their vision was to get out there and get things done for people. So when I started talking with them about it, "Find it in yourself first, and then you can see it in other people, and when you see it in other people, wake it up—and you have to accept the fact that they may know something you don't, and they might have a way of doing it that's better for them than what your best idea is—well, it completely undercut their whole idea. They'd had a retreat previously where they tried to refine their mission or their vision or whatever, and they had gone through this rather arduous two-day process with a consultant who led them through all these values-clarification exercises. So when I first started talking and saw how angry they were getting, I thought, "Well, they're going to have to experience it. I've got to stop talking about it, and we've just got to live it. They've got to see it happen here." So I said, "Look, I don't want to philosophize anymore. I gave you a little glimpse of just one way to look at working with people, but let's just get down to the task at hand here. We've got something to do." I just saw in that moment—I saw them as deeper than their ideas. I saw that I had to *be* what I was describing. I just stopped *telling* them how to be better at what they did and *let them see* how to be better at what they did. I took a big dose of my own medicine there, and it was a transforming moment for me because I saw the difference between teaching what I knew myself and *bringing it alive*. And we did. In an hour, something happened, and all of a sudden these people were just coming up with these incredible ideas—all of which had to do with releasing other people, setting them free to do more stuff. I mean, the stuff they were coming up with from their own wisdom without realizing it was what I had been describing that they were fighting when we were talking about it in the abstract. And so that was a defining moment for me, because it was a big, humbling learning experience for me. It's just to stop trying to tell people about it and live as though it were true [laughs]. So in a matter of a few hours they had their mission statement, and it was very different from the previous mission. And they were totally baffled and enthralled. And some of these people are now teaching our Stress Cure classes and everything. They have stayed with it. That Rural Health program has really taken on this understanding in a big way. So that was a defining moment.

And then another one was, I really was very anxious to get Bill Pettit here and involved, because I felt that, for doctors, it would be very comforting to meet another doctor. I think I'd been here about a year, and he was able to come, and we did a two-day leadership meeting on values—because I have this philosophical sort of logic that I follow when I work with leadership groups, which is, you start with values. They really have to have an understanding of what's important, what really matters, and that leads to vision: Given what really matters, then what's possible? And then vision leads to mission: Given what's possible, what are we going to do? And mission leads to strategy, which is the final step—which is where most people begin, but it should be the last thing and it should be obvious: Given what we're going to do, how are we going to do it? So we were at the values step in my program, "Bringing Leadership from Within" that I've done with corporations all over the country. This is with the chairs of the various departments of the medical school. The first day they were very grumpy, saying things like, "This is insubstantial!" "Why aren't we talking about strategy?" "We need to accomplish something, where's the agenda?" And Bill has such a deep faith, and we've worked together for a long time, and we just battled it out with them and hung in there. And we had dinner that night, and I remember it just being really pleasant, and then they all went home and came back the next morning. And Bill said to me that morning before they came, "You know, this group is going to be different today. I can feel it." I said, "God, I hope so because yesterday they just didn't want to see their own beauty—how beautiful it could be to really talk about what really matters first."

And they came back, and one of them said, "You know, I think that one of our values should be 'love.'" Now you've got to remember who we're talking to here. So we write "love" on the flip chart, and we talk about love for about an hour. We talked about what it really is, what's unconditional, what it means to express the love you have for people, how love is related to healing, what it would mean in a medical school for people not to be afraid to put that down on a piece of paper as a value—which now it is on our list of values as the first one! And it was such a beautiful discussion, and people were so touched. I mean, people were almost moved to tears, as they were saying things that really, really mattered to them. It really happened, and Bill and I were just there. We were there, but we didn't have to do much, and one of the Chairs, as we were getting ready to break for lunch, said, "You know, this is truth. This is the truth. We're talking truth here. This is wonderful." It was amazing! It was a beautiful thing. I'll never forget that as long as I live. And it's really sweet because we talk about it now, when student admissions people talk to students, they talk about our values, and they talk about love. Other deans from other medical schools are astonished, like, "How did you ever get a group of Chairs to use that word?" In honesty, it's true for everyone. And people start to feel that. And it has changed things here. They do remember that we love our students, and we love each other—not every minute, but a lot. So that was a big deal.

JP: That's beautiful. What about changes within individuals?

JS: Well, a really beautiful thing was that some of the people at student services got the idea that maybe it'd be nice for me to talk to some of the students that are experiencing stress and distress and struggling, rather than them either gutting it out without any assistance whatsoever, or making a big deal of it and ending up on Prozac or something like that. So students get sent to me—and I could tell you a lot of different students' stories, but one that stands out for me is a student who was really in danger of crashing and burning in the second year of medical school. This person was completely floored by the amount you had to learn, how fast you had to learn it, how many tests there were, how competitive it was. And what happened to the person, at one point, was to get sent to a psychiatrist, who then got them involved in a rather intense therapeutic process which involved medication, which made it very difficult to study. So the problem was exacerbating out of control, and the person was warned that they might not make it. So somebody had the idea, maybe the person should talk to me. The thing that had crossed my mind when I first talked to this person is, "It's amazing to me that you've made it through the end of the year, given all that's been going on. Don't you think that says something about the human spirit, and why didn't you quit?" And the person looked at me and said, "I don't know." I said, "Well, I'd look there. I would want to look there and ask myself, given that I was miserable, that I was depressed, that I was hardly able to study, that I was starting to fail, that I'd been seeing a psychiatrist, that I had persuaded myself that I'm a damaged human being inadequate to this task, that I'm on medication—I'm still in school. What the hell's going on there?" And I remember this person's little eyes just lit up, and the person looked at me and said, "That's what I want. I want to be a doctor." I said, "Well, why don't you just forget about the rest of this shit, then, and just be a doctor? The only way to get to be a doctor is to get through medical school." And the person said, "I know, but it's so hard to get through medical school." And I said, "Now, look around you. This building is crawling with doctors. They all went to medical school. What makes them so great that you couldn't be like any of them?" And the person looked at me and went, "Yeah." So I said, "What's really in your way? What do you think the problem is?" And I remember, there was this moment in time, and then this person just brightened up and said, "I guess the problem is that I just think about failure all the time, instead of thinking about just getting it done." And I said, "Hey, makes sense to me!" And within a few months the person was in good standing, had gotten through the crisis, had gotten off medication, still comes to see me occasionally mostly to celebrate good news—but it was one of those moments where you see raw Health, and how hard it is to kill it. I mean, you could look at a person like that—God, it would be so easy to just walk away from it, so easy to go shoot yourself, so easy to just go drink, you know? It would be so easy, but that love of people and desire to be their dream was so strong! And that Health in them was so strong, that despite all that shit happening, this person was still in school, still trying to see how to do it, and when the door opened, man, they went right through it! And I could tell you lots of stories like that.

JP: That's great! I just have two more questions. Aside from the Institute, how would you say that this has permeated the way the WVU medical school does its business?

JS: Well, slowly, in ways that's like water seeping through thick sand. There's still a lot of dry sand out there, but there's plenty of water, too. But I think because people—myself included—whose spirits have been touched serve on committees, go to meetings, lecture in classes, they're different. Jack, you know, every interaction is either a healing interaction or it isn't. So if I was a person who had kind of a dim view of students and didn't have a lot of faith in the learning process, and then I changed my mind and I started to see the thirst for understanding things for themselves and the different ways they find to express that, and I started to look at the learning experience differently, then I have a different kind of class. And if I have a different kind of class, maybe some of the students who might have been discouraged or disheartened in the other class come to life and stay with it. Just little, small things. It doesn't take very much.

JP: What percentage of your faculty has actually been trained in this understanding?

JS: Well, it hasn't been anything that I would call training, because a lot of what I've done is facilitated meetings, but in facilitating meetings I'm cognizant of making the point about why something is working. So I've facilitated a tremendous number of meetings in many different departments. I've since done public talks here, which have been attended by all kinds of faculty, but I have no idea what they took away from it. Thousands of Syd's books have ended up in people's hands, because we buy them and give them away. But there's never been something that I would call "a training." I have a problem with "trainer of trainers" and this kind of stuff; I have a problem with anything that looks like hierarchy. So I look at every opportunity I have to talk to people as an opportunity to touch their spirit in some way, and if it works out that's great.

JP: But it has permeated the philosophy of the way the school does business—

JS: Yeah, I think so. In the values and in the vision and mission, and in the way the Chairs interact with each other. I've lectured and I've facilitated some big committee things here that have to do with the educational process and our educational values and how we deal with students. But it's kind of opportunistic rather than strategic.

JP: Have any other universities or medical schools become interested?

JS: Yes and no. Bob D'Allesandri has been the dean here for more than eleven years. He's got a longer tenure as a dean of a medical school than most other deans in the country. So he's very highly respected among his peers. I believe that he has intrigued others. I think others are watching to see. Bob said, "You know, you've got to remember that we're in this for the long haul. We're not in this for a short term, and you can't push. You just want to keep working and doing the next thing." So people have visited. There's curiosity, but I don't think anyone's ever stepped up to take the obvious next step—yet—but they will.

JP: Is there anything else that you want to convey that I haven't asked?

JS: Well, I could say a few words about prevention, because one of the wonderful reasons that I feel lucky to be here is because the department that I happen to be in, the Department of Community Medicine, is focused on health education and prevention, and I think that we've been operating at the symptom end for the last several years. Most practitioners in this work have not been health educators, not been prevention people, but have been therapists, counselors, social workers—people who work with addictions, treatment—people who are working with the aftereffects. So one of the beautiful things to me—and I applaud you for staying in your field and for writing a book for people in prevention—and one of the things I love about working with my students here in the Masters' in Public Health program, because they're interested in social policy, health policy, prevention, education—is that it is a much better place to start the process. Anything that we can do that keeps people from suffering is much better than helping them to stop suffering, because in the meantime they've suffered. So I believe that the future of this work is in prevention. I really do! And I think that prevention education, and bringing this understanding alive in people before they have difficulties, will change the world.

XV. APPLICATIONS TO SPECIAL POPULATIONS WITHIN THE COMMUNITY

Inside, spiritually, everyone is the same; everyone functions in the same way. Thus, from the inside, there really are no "special populations." It would be wise, however, to understand the special culture (the collective thinking) where one is working.

Applications with Parents

Working with parents is no different than working with anyone in this approach, except they are very concerned about other little people running around them. Parents can be helped to see their children with new eyes.

Most parents don't realize some critical things about creating healthy relationships with their children, and how to bring out the best in them. Instead of teaching techniques (which most parenting programs do), parents can be helped to see what they don't realize.

I know from personal experience that if parents realized some key things, their lives with their children could be what they had always dreamed (before they had children). Here are some examples of **what parents don't realize:**

1. The feeling is everything! If kids are not feeling love from parents in the moment, discipline will not work; the kids will be too busy scrambling to protect themselves.
2. When parents' minds are calm and clear, they know what to do in nearly every difficulty because they can access their wisdom and common sense.
3. What parents *see* is what they *get*, and they will always treat their children the way they see them. (In other words, if parents see a kid as "up to no good," they get a kid who is up to no good, and if they see a kid who is well-meaning and doing his best but only doesn't know what else to do at the time, they get a well-meaning kid. Then they act toward that kid, accordingly.)
4. In low moods, their thinking can't be trusted, and if they follow it, they will get in trouble. (This goes for both parents and children.)
5. Kids misbehave for three reasons: 1) they are acting out of insecurity, 2) they are acting in a low/bad mood; 3) what the parents are requiring doesn't make any sense to them.
6. Most parents parent their kids as if their own parents were sitting on their shoulders barking orders.
7. Most parents don't really listen to their kids; they listen to their own thinking.
8. Most parents try to teach kids their conclusions, instead of what's behind their conclusions, so the kids don't "get it."

9. Their children are already learning plenty from what the parents are doing, only it is not often what they would like their kids to be learning.
10. Most parents think discipline means punishment or consequences, when it really means "to learn" (from the word "disciple")

This is not the place for details. For that, see the book *Parenting from the Heart* (Pransky, 2001). Suffice to say that when parents begin to realize the above, they begin to see their children with new eyes, and everything changes (For example, see the story of Lisa in Chapter XVIII). Many parents have had great success with this approach. One parent said, "This book saved my life, and it probably saved my kids' lives too."

Applications in Schools

School reform is essential. In my view it has gotten off track.

Testing is not the answer. Federal or state requirements for testing may force schools to transform themselves, but into what? To produce better test-takers? My guess is, these requirements will not turn out students who are better citizens, who care about ongoing learning, who better respect others, who are better qualified to enter the workforce. Furthermore, with everyone from the top down feeling pressure to produce higher test scores, no one functions at their best, and the quality of teaching and therefore learning may even diminish.

Instead, school reform could be about getting *all* students to love learning. Love of learning is an inside-out affair. Where does love of learning come from? From discovery! To see this, we only have to recall our own then-new, meaningful discoveries. When this happens we feel exhilarated; automatically we want to learn more. Students today are no different.

Most educators don't realize the same things parents don't realize (above). For example, what percentage of educators realizes that when students are "running scared" or are in low moods, they can't learn? What percentage realizes that when students' minds are relaxed and calm, they do learn?

What percentage of educators realizes and practices that when students are having fun, they learn well—precisely because their minds relax? What percentage realizes and practices that when students feel respected, cared about, appreciated in the moment, they learn well? What percentage realizes and practices that when students feel really listened to, they learn well; that when students feel hope, they learn well; that when students are helped to discover for themselves how things really work and fit together, they learn well?

Most educators don't realize that how they see their students is what they get. Just as with parents, if a teacher writes off a student as a troublemaker up to no good, this teacher will get an up-to-no-good troublemaker. That student's behavior will be filtered through this teacher's lens, and the teacher will treat that student accordingly. If that teacher saw this same student as acting out of insecurity and not knowing what else to do, the teacher automatically would act toward that student in a more constructive way. With their own thinking teachers inadvertently make up what their students are all about and then act toward them as if they really are that way. They can be helped to see their students with fresh eyes.

That many educators have not realized these things is not their fault. People can't realize what they don't realize. Most of those who train educators don't realize this either; therefore they don't teach it.

Students also don't realize a few things, and it is not their fault either. Students don't realize when they are in bad moods, they think dumb thoughts and tend to do dumb things. Students don't realize they don't have to believe or follow every thought that comes into their heads. Students don't realize they are really quite smart and sharp and will know the best thing to do when their minds are relaxed and calm.

Primarily, school has emphasized two things: 1) the pouring of information into students' heads, in hopes they will remember it; 2) problem-solving. More astute educators have focused on creative writing and critical thinking skills. We could take this all a step further: If we focused on getting all students to love learning, we could help students discover the new for themselves. We could help students see their own creative process at work. We could help them see their ability to create anything within their minds and to believe whatever they've created. When we give kids information, we are teaching about someone else's creations. When we teach critical thinking we are often (not always) teaching about analyzing someone else's creations. I am not saying some of this does not have to be taught in school, I am saying it would be most productive if we helped students to see creation at work within them, so they know can always go to the well and create anew.

We want school to be producing Einsteins and Edisons, not turning them off. Every student that gets turned off by school is a potential Einstein or Edison. How would we know? At the time they went to school, we didn't know those two difficult students were budding geniuses. Every student that gets turned off by school is a waste of human talent in some way—unless they happen to find the inner strength to prevail against all odds as Einstein and Edison did. If they do not find their own inner strength, our society is diminished, for their talent will be lost. More likely, they will become more candidates for the school of criminality. The percentage of dropouts in the criminal justice system proves this—and it is a crime.

In my view, a three-pronged approach is needed for applying an inside-out/Health Realization approach in schools:

1. *Educator training* about what makes students function as they do and what brings out the best in students (and in themselves). In and of itself, this would improve the classroom and school climate.
2. *An inside-out curriculum* or classes that teach students what makes them function as they do, and what brings out their best. As of this writing extremely few curricula are available that provide this. One is *Healthy Thinking/Feeling/Doing from the Inside-Out* (Pransky & Carpenos, 2000). Or, we want the educators trained in inside-out prevention to teach this to students in any way they know how.
3. *A student support system* for students having difficulty, with student supporters trained in this approach who, where appropriate, act as a liaison between the school and parents, the school and after-school programs, and the school and work.

It works even better when a # 4 is added, when the school offers parents the parenting approach suggested above.

Over time, this combination should lead naturally to school structure change or school reform aligned with student Health and learning.

Applications with Gangs

Manzell Williams, a counselor of gang members, was getting nowhere with them, trying to show them the error of their ways. Once he learned Health Realization he began to see each one's potential, who each really was deep inside. He began to see no matter how badly they acted, no matter how badly they felt, they all showed flashes of Health and wisdom at times.

Manzell began to concentrate solely on building rapport—just having a good time with them—and becoming attuned to the moments when he might be able to reach them.

When a negative feeling arose, he would listen deeply, and if he felt the timing was right he would ask questions to help them see that their own thinking was behind their feelings. He kept reminding himself that these young people were always doing the best they could, given how they saw things.

One day during a session he decided to take one of the gang members out to a park. They fooled around together and had a good time. In this relaxed state, they sat on a bench and saw some homeless people across the way. Something suddenly popped into Manzell's head. He said, "You know, most of those men gave up because no one saw them as being okay."

For some reason the kid heard something that connected with his own life. The next day he returned to school and began to turn his life around.

Many gang members began to change as a result of Manzell's work, but each happened in a unique way (Williams and Pransky, 1993). This is why there are no techniques in this approach.

Applications with Criminal Offenders

Tom Kelley (1990) offers this view of how this approach might be applied with criminal offenders:

> [The offender]…has no genuine ability to be responsible for his feelings, choices, or behavior because he does not experience himself (i.e., his thinking…) "as cause" in these matters. Rather, his experience is that his feelings and behavioral reactions are imposed upon him from some outside source. His experience is that other people and things, not he, are responsible for how he acts, his well-being and for what happens in his life; that he is at the mercy, or at the effect of circumstances—past, present, and future. Caught up in this experience, the offender has little or no sense of responsibility for his life, attributes the source of what he does, how he feels, and the events he confronts to outside circumstances, and generally feels victimized and helpless, persecuted, entitled, superior, etc. Thus, without first making the offender conscious of the fact that his reality is self-created through thought, any approach to changing him which focuses on altering some external condition (e.g., poverty, parenting, learning disability, punishment, etc.) will have limited power. For all such efforts will be filtered through the offender's rigid thought system and automatically manipulated and altered to support and maintain his personal pattern of self-righteous beliefs, insecure feelings, and deviant behavior (p.7).

It would appear, then, that the actual source of criminal and other harmful behavior is people blindly following thinking that looks real to them, that unknowingly leads them down a self-created, destructive path. They believe in the "reality" they see, without any idea their own thinking is creating it. To not focus on the fact of Thought and help them transcend their thinking is to miss the rehabilitation (or prevention) target. As Kelley suggests, the alternative is to "show him how to disengage from his rigid adherence to, and personal identification with, fixed thought and absolute views of his world, and, ultimately, how to identify instead with his thinking function... Only a change in level of consciousness can generate the possibility of significantly altering one's criminal orientation, and this is exactly what an understanding of these...principles...represents" (Kelley, 1990, pp.16-17).

A number of criminal justice applications now focus offenders on their "cognitive distortions," and this seems to work better than the norm (Gendreau, 1996). However, helping criminal offenders to see Thought as the creator of their experience is likely even more effective. If offenders only see "thoughts" instead of the "power of Thought" to bring them whatever experience they have, they will have to continually fight their negative thoughts, and this is hard to do. It may even add more stress. When we are feeling down or angry or driven, how easy is it to think other, more positive or healthier thoughts?

Cathy Casey and others have taught Health Realization with great success in the Santa Clara County, California correctional system (*Applications*, 2000), and it is happening in other places such as Las Vegas and Minneapolis/St. Paul.

Applications to Social Work

Health Realization is equally applicable to social work. Polsfuss (1994) states:

> If the power over our basic experience of life is 'out there' somewhere, it can toss one about at will! This alternative paradigm dares to assert that people not only need not be such victims, but are actually the creators of their experiences. This does not infer that real opposition and victimization do not occur, but how it is experienced and how it is responded to are in the hands (or more accurately: the minds) of the people! In other words, experience is created from the inside-out: It originates in our thinking! (p.3).

Conclusion

Where many prevention and human services approaches assume that new skills, information or attitudes are the key to changing feelings and behaviors, Health Realization asserts that to change feelings and behavior, people's thinking must change. Like cognitive-based approaches such as Relapse Prevention, Health Realization assumes that deviant and violent behavior stems from learned habits of thinking. Unlike cognitive-based approaches, in Health Realization people do not have to struggle with the content of learned thoughts or their conditioning. People can be helped to *see* how their own thinking creates their feelings and behaviors and their entire experience of life.

As Mills & Bailey (1996) state, "as people learn how their thinking works, they tap into an inner wisdom that not only allows them to take their own but others' negative habits of thought less seriously" (p.19). People's mental states tend to improve rapidly when they look within to what occurs before the content of their thinking, to the very power of Thought itself to create experience and to its source: Mind. As people regain their innate Health and wisdom, the habitual thinking patterns that keep them stuck tend to lose their grip. From this new, higher perspective both what they saw as problems and their problem behaviors tend to diminish.

At the same time, that people experience many problems that are quite difficult for them is to be respected and acknowledged. As Mills states:

> After 20 years of working in communities like this one, I'd be the last to imply that these perceptions and attitudes didn't seem justified. People endure horrendous conditions, suffering real prejudice and deprivation, often knowing no other world. We have genuine compassion for the depth of suffering that leads to violent coping styles. Yet, as we learned more and more about how the mind works in maintaining this world view, we realized that people could learn to free themselves from this hell. In fact, many of our clients have demonstrated that they are only a thought away from escaping that world entirely. The first step is understanding how thinking is influenced by the past, and how that past is carried into the present by means of a learned outlook… As we began to teach people the difference between conditioned thinking and original thought, we found that they could readily discern when they were caught up in conditioned thoughts that obscured their natural, healthy thought process… Once people see how their thinking perpetuates negative behavior, they become capable of doing even more than transcending those thoughts… [They] call on a common-sense perspective to solve pressing personal problems. This new perspective also helps people collaborate with one another to address the pressing needs in their communities (Mills & Bailey, 1996, pp.18-19).

The inside-out approach in the prevention and human services fields has potential to dramatically improve our effectiveness. Because of its potential to reach people who heretofore have not been reached, *I would recommend that everyone in these fields be trained in these Principles and how to apply them.* People then will draw their own conclusions. As in the Modello and Homestead Gardens housing projects, where Mills experienced such great success, Health Realization won't reach everyone, but those who are reached will be so affected that they in turn will reach others around them. This is how it seems to spread. The more people understand and help others understand this approach, the more we will increase prevention and human services efficacy.

XVI. A NEW LOOK AT ALCOHOL AND DRUG ABUSE FROM AN INSIDE-OUT PERSPECTIVE

*The relationship between Health Realization and the traditional approach to preventing and treating alcohol and other drug abuse, and AA, can be tricky and delicate and requires thorough exploration. I have met no one who has a better handle on this than Kristen Mansheim. She has lived it; she has been on all sides of the issue. The best thing I can do is step aside and let her speak. [This interview with **Kristen Mansheim** continues from Chapter VII, page 108].*

JP: At what point did you feel like you needed to switch what you did in your counseling?

KM: It was a gradual thing because, early on, I still believed there was a disease, a physical disease, and that's a big thing in the addictions field. It's almost blasphemous to say anything else. Initially I was still going to [AA] meetings, and I believed in that. At some point—I don't remember when, I think it was probably around 1996—I started to do some reflection about the business of addiction. What I noticed was, we called it "the disease," but it didn't start out that way. It started out as "the disease concept." And "concept" by now was a familiar word to me. It was clear to me that a concept is something you create through Thought. It's an idea—it's a way of looking at something. It doesn't mean that it's a fact. It's a way of holding something in your mind. And as I did some research, I went back and saw how originally it was "the disease concept," and there's a reason the field created the idea of a disease concept.

Before the disease concept, addiction or alcoholism was seen as a moral problem, a character flaw; people were put away in asylums, they were shunned, people would think they had evil spirits in them, and really bizarre things happened to people who couldn't stop drinking. And so the world came up with this idea of a disease concept, like diabetes—that there is this thing in you that happened and it's not your fault, but it does happen, and you can treat it, and you're not a bad person. That was helpful to the world when that happened, because people didn't feel bad about themselves anymore. They didn't have all that awful thinking about themselves as a horrible person. "I'm not a horrible person. I just have this thing, and I can treat the thing, I can deal with the thing, I can work on the thing." So that helped the world so much, and I found new respect for "the disease," but I stopped seeing it literally.

We used to have discussions in Roger [Mills]'s advanced class about what would happen to somebody who had really connected to their own mental health and saw the role of Thought—what would happen if that person who used to have an addiction problem had a drink. We used to debate about that. And initially I argued, "Well, if they have this disease, the disease is going to take over," and he looked at me—because that was my big fear, that I would take a drink again—and he said, "You have come too far. You can't go back. If you were to take a drink again, I think you would pretty quickly realize what was going on and turn away from it." And I didn't know about that, but it made me think. I did *not* want to check it out, but it made me think.

Over the years I've become happier and happier and happier, and now I don't need to be around Health Realization people to feel good any more. I feel good on my own, and I finally saw that this wasn't something you supported or worked on, it was just truth about how you function, period. I feel so good I really don't want to drink or take anything that would numb this feeling I found within myself. Actually, I guess what happened is that I forgot about the disease concept. I didn't feel opposed to it, I just saw it as an idea that was helpful to the world at a certain point, a way of looking at it. And we've now evolved and see something new, and despite the fact that it's controversial and difficult for some people it's still true, and it makes sense to me.

You know what really helped me? God, it was probably 1998 or so, and we were all having dinner at a restaurant, and they brought the dessert menu in. It was in French or something, and I couldn't figure out what everything was, so I said, "Bring me this one." I didn't know what it was. So they brought it and I started eating it, and I wasn't thinking about it; I was just eating. I didn't know that this dessert had a syrup on it that was just loaded with liquor, and pretty soon I start feeling fuzzy—you know that feeling where you feel like you want to come back but you can't? I asked, "Does this have alcohol in it?" And the waiter said, "Oh, yes, it's got"—I can't remember exactly what, but it had a lot of alcohol in it. I kind of started to freak out, because that's a big thing in the addiction field. You don't put any alcohol in your body because it triggers the disease and the whole thing will take over—and all those memories flooded back, and I was a little freaked out. So I had to get a hold of myself. I was like I was sitting there and kind of fuzzy, and the next thing that hit me was, "Kristen, I can't believe you ever wanted to feel this way." I felt *so* bad. I felt so fuzzy and out of it. It just felt bad. I felt numb. And that surprised me. That was a huge revelation to me: "*This is what you used to go through!?*" It made sense, though, because I was so low in my feeling that numb was an improvement. But now I was up a lot higher, so numb was a big step down. I felt this instant aversion to it then. So that was helpful to me, because all the fears about relapse, or wanting to drink, or the something waking up inside me and taking over again were obviously not true *at this new level of consciousness.* Right then I knew I was safe. And I've never worried about it since. Nor have I taken a drink. Why would I want to?

JP: So what do you say to people now who are totally into AA—whose lives are still not that great, but who can't bear the thought of giving it up?

KM: That's a tough one. I mean, I was there.

JP: Are you still going to meetings?

KM: No. I did go, but about six years into my own sobriety—like around 1995 or 1996—it didn't feel right any more. I just could not get into it. I noticed that most people—not everybody, but a lot of people—were in a bad feeling at meetings. But the thing I appreciate is, I think when Bill Wilson started Alcoholics Anonymous —see, Bill had what he called a spiritual experience, what I would call a huge insight. He had a huge vertical shift, and that changed him. And that's what he called a removal of the compulsion to drink—it was taken from him. And he knew that that was not something he did personally. He didn't will himself to stop drinking. He had this spiritual experience, and it was gone, and when he talked to people and worked with people, he worked from that insight, he worked from that feeling. And I think in trying to help other people, you can't manufacture a spiritual experience. You can't manufacture a jump in levels of consciousness. You can't make that happen from the intellect. And so in trying to help other people, what he did was kind of devise, "Well, maybe if you do these series of things you'll position yourself for a spiritual experience," and that's what the Twelve Steps are. If you read the steps, the last step says, "Having had a spiritual awakening as the result of these steps ..." In Bill's mind, I think he may have looked back and thought, "What happened to me before this experience? Maybe that was the groundwork, and maybe if people do that, they'll have the same experience that I did." The Twelve-Step programs came from that.

And over the course of years, I think the same thing has happened there that has happened to other movements: The further away you are from the original inspiration the more likely you are to find people following technique, following rituals that they don't really feel and understand. So I think there may have been a time where Twelve-Step was very different than it is today. I remember when I got sober the old-timers were different; they were different from the newer people. They had more of a lightheartedness. If you read the Big Book of AA, you hear some things in there that are very different from what modern Twelve-Step people talk about, but there are also some places where they were onto something. The old-timers were always really connected to the book, always really connected to how simple it is. They didn't do massive inventories on themselves where they looked at everything that happened to them and every feeling they ever had.

In the old days when Bill worked steps with people, they worked twelve steps in a series of hours, hours to days. It was like, "Okay, look. Do you realize that you can't control your drinking anymore? Are you getting that through your head? And what are you carrying around in your head? What are you carrying there? Who are you resentful of? Who are you holding on to stuff about, because you're probably drinking over that? Let's get that out. Let's get that out of your head. What do you need to do to get that out of your head? Well, you probably need to apologize where you were wrong, and let it be that other people have screwed you over, that it happened, and you're okay. And every day, why don't you try to live the right way, and get out of yourself and get out of your head and help other people." That's what the steps are. If you simplify them, there's wisdom in them. But now it's turned into *a thing*. People take years working the steps. They write small books. Bill didn't do that with it. It was a very matter-of-fact, kind of quick thing. Really what the Big Book of Alcoholics Anonymous says is that the point of getting sober is to go back to your life, go back to your family, go back to your community. They never encouraged you to spend your life in meetings and spend your life working on yourself. It's not about that. And the book even says that the spiritual power that's greater than you is inside you. It says that! It's deep in the essence of everyone.

JP: A lot of people see it outside of themselves.

KM: Yes. As you get further in time away from Bill who had the original insight, what you get are followers. And they follow the ritual and they follow the doctrine and they follow the dogma and they follow the technique, and they're not connected to what it meant. So it's different now than it was, and even as different as it is, it's still saving people's lives. The nice thing about Twelve Steps is that it's everywhere. It's almost "twenty-four, seven." And you can find other people who are sober anywhere, anytime. When you're in that much psychological pain that you need to take something to feel better, you're in *a lot* of pain. And you're very disconnected and very isolated. I mean, I love the idea that other people are around, that they want to help you, that there's hope that you don't have to do this any more. So I love those things. But I just don't know that they've seen the psychological function that creates the compulsion. They don't know about that. And in a part of the Big Book, it says science may one day discover a pill or some magic that will help us get past this, but it hasn't done so yet. Well, that was written when? Now we have that—not a pill, but this understanding—and I think that's just hard for them to believe, and they're frightened, and their life depends on not taking a risk that will take their sobriety away. I understand that. I've been there. I've seen people try to talk to Twelve-Step people about the three Principles and try to rip the way they see sobriety away from them, and they get too frightened to listen. So that doesn't make sense to me.

I know what appealed to me—even though I was listening through the whole recovery culture—was *the feeling*. And the fact that no matter what I said or how much I argued, people like Joe

[Bailey] and Mark [Howard] and Roger didn't lose their bearings, they didn't lose that feeling, and they didn't lose rapport with me, they didn't lose faith in me. They just knew I was in the middle of learning and I didn't see it yet. If somebody had taken what I thought was my recovery on with me too soon, I think I would have left. The clients, on the other hand, for whom Twelve-Step doesn't make sense, who are having trouble staying sober, who have tried that and are not having success with it, they get this like that! [snaps fingers] They're happy to give it up. It's the people whose lives have been saved by Twelve-Step that have trouble hearing.

JP: Is there anything else you would like to say?

KM: How this relates to prevention: I have never met anybody that works in the field of prevention that doesn't have a heart of gold, and really just wants to make a difference. Prevention people are so good-hearted, have so much good will, good nature. But I will be honest with you—I never saw myself working in prevention because, personally, I didn't have much faith in it—it hadn't worked for me. You see, I had been warned about the possibility that I could become easily addicted to substances. From that traditional prevention standpoint, people had warned me to be careful about that. They said, "These are the risk factors, these are the coping skills, these are the life skills. You want to watch out for this." People really tried to talk to me about it beforehand. This is just *me*, personally; I know there are prevention strategies that are proven effective. But what happened for me was that I still drank. The piece of it that was helpful was that, because people had talked to me about the fact that you could develop addictions, I knew that there were resources out there. I did know that, and I was connected to people in the community to get to those resources.

But *all the good information and skills in the world can't help you if you don't have the psychological functioning to support it*. I had really good information, I had skills, I was warned, but the level at which I functioned didn't allow me to make use of the good information and skills I had. When people are hurting, they just want a first step—they just want to stop hurting. And even if you know what you're going to use to help you stop hurting will hurt you even more, you don't really care because you just want to feel better. The worse the pain is, the less you care about the consequences and the toll it takes on you. It's a psychological survival issue. And the ultimate prevention can only be people understanding their own functioning, because it takes a healthy level of functioning to make use of good information and skills. And if people understand their own psychological functioning, they will be operating at a higher level and they won't need relief. But if you aren't connected to your own Health, if you don't feel well, then it's more important to feel well than to do the right thing. Think of all the people doing prevention work, intervention and treatment work, who are working so hard and feeling discouraged because it's hard work to make even a dent. This would be so helpful to them, because it would *move the clients into their own Health—that's the ultimate prevention*. And it would connect the providers to their own health more deeply. Professionals have to have their health too, so they can sustain their work. It's so important to me to have this understanding because I watch professionals wear down, and I've seen them discouraged, and I've seen them lose faith, and that's unfortunate. I'm so grateful for what I've found. I don't know how to express in words how truly grateful I am for what I know now.

[The interview with Kristen continues in Chapter VII, p.108]

XVII. A NEW LOOK AT VIOLENCE PREVENTION FROM AN INSIDE-OUT PERSPECTIVE

As with all problem behaviors, while research shows certain factors in the social environment contribute to violence or protect people from succumbing to violence, we still see vast differences in individual responses, even with similar environmental conditions. This suggests we need to turn to the crucial variable left out of the outside-in equation, and create a new inside-out equation that can achieve greater efficacy.

The key to understanding violence in others is to look at ourselves. If we ever committed one violent act, we may be able to understand what creates violence. If we have ever had thoughts of violence but did not carry them out, we may be able to understand. It would be helpful to take a close look at what makes human beings act the way they do at any given time.

To help a person change from a proclivity toward violence, or to prevent it in the first place, we must understand the internal ingredients that make one respond violently. Once understood, we are in a position to do something about them. Without understanding what is going on, this is impossible

Essentially, the internal ingredients that combine to create violence (or not) at any given moment appear to be "personal norm," "habit," and "anger." When people understand how each of these ingredients plays out in their own lives, and how they have access to and can tap a personal resource that helps them transcend their current response, they are able to turn in a different direction—away from violence and toward well-being.

I offer this inside-out formula for the prevention of violence, sexual assault or other aggressive acts. In my view this formula presents the missing components in violence prevention:

$$\text{violence or sexual assault quotient} = \frac{\text{personal norm} + \text{habit} \times \text{anger*}}{\text{understanding} + \text{perspective in the moment}}$$

*[Note: Instead of anger, we could substitute any other emotion or mood, but for violence anger is the primary emotion. Also, it would seem that after the word "anger" in the formula we could add "minus self-control (- self-control)." However, self-control is necessary *only* if one does not have an understanding of all the other components. Self-control comes *after the fact* of what this formula represents.]

First, I will define the terms used in the formula:

personal norm	=	the extent to which one thinks violence is an acceptable way to be
habit	=	the extent to which violence is one's habitual response
anger	=	the extent to which one is riled up in the moment
understanding	=	the extent of one's understanding of what creates each item in the numerator above, and where one is at in relation to each
perspective	=	the extent to which one can see where he is in the moment regarding each of the items in the numerator above

In essence, this means the more a person has understanding and perspective (in the moment) of where he is regarding personal norm, habit, and anger, the less he will engage in violence. This will become more clear as one reads on.

Here is what each of these does to people:

personal norm	-	puts them at the beginning of the road toward violence
habit	-	starts them down the road
anger	-	propels them down the road
understanding and perspective	-	takes them off the road

Below are some of the possibilities that exist within each item in the equation. Within each item in the numerator, one can be at many different levels of understanding and in-the-moment perspective. In the following, **read the statements in each section from the bottom up** (each level up represents a higher level of understanding and perspective). For each, these are some possible levels at which one might find himself.

Personal Norm about violence:

- Violence is horrible. Under no circumstances is it right.
- Violence is not good.
- Violence is not okay, but I slip sometimes.
- Something doesn't feel right about violence, except in these circumstances …
- Violence is okay under certain circumstances.
- Violence is the way to be.

Habit of violence:

- At peace. Violence is out of the question. I can't imagine it.
- I am absolutely committed to stopping.
- I really, deeply would like to stop.
- I would like to stop.
- I'd kind of like to stop
- I have no desire to stop being violent.

Anger (or other emotion) (example used here is for domestic violence):

•	gratefulness	I appreciate and respect my wife so much, no matter what she does.
•	humor	It's so funny how people see things differently.
•	humility	I probably annoy her sometimes, too.
•	compassion	I wonder why she needs to do that. Maybe she can't help herself
•	interest	Isn't it interesting that she would do that.

•	annoyed	She shouldn't do that. She made a mistake in judgment.
•	resentful	Why does she have to be like that?
•	angry	She's doing something she absolutely shouldn't do!
•	enraged	She's doing it to me just to get to me! It's a personal affront!

Regarding anger, the extent to which one attributes personal motive in a situation determines how angry one gets (Pransky, 1991). In other words, the same event can happen, but how one sees it determines whether he takes it personally, and to what extent. There are many, many ways to view the same event, and we essentially use our creative power of Thought to make up whatever we make of it.

So in looking at the entire formula, here are a few examples of what might happen. If a person believes violence is the way to be, has no desire to stop, and is enraged in the moment, that person is almost guaranteed to commit a violent act. If a person believes violence is out of the question, is at peace, and feels grateful, he is not going to be violent. These two extremes may be obvious, but if a person believes "violence is not okay but I slip sometimes," kind of wants to stop, but then gets really angry at something, for example, his wife did, then in that moment he will likely be violent. This would be good information for both the perpetrator and the victim[17] to have *before the fact*.

The point is, no matter what great things we do in the name of violence prevention, the way one sees the situation or person in general plus the *perspective* one has in the moment will determine where one falls on the scale at any given time. For all the above, in terms of *understanding*, the common denominator is that *it's all thought, not reality*. What a violent person sees about his wife (or whomever) only looks "real" from his point of view in the moment. What he sees is really only a thought-created illusion. At any given time people make up (with their own thinking) wherever they fall on these scales. If a person does not realize this, he will act on whatever "reality" he sees. If he truly understands or realizes this, he will not take what he sees so personally or his thinking so seriously, and will be less likely to follow it and act on it. *When people come to understand this and see it in the moment, their violence diminishes.*

This inside-out formula is equally relevant for sexual assault, sexual abuse, child abuse, street violence and more; the individual items need only be altered slightly to fit the particular act. *Unless* a perpetrator is helped to call into question what he would swear is a "reality" he must act upon, *he will have no choice* but to follow his thinking or be forced to continually fight against it.

---

[17] Note: I use this word here on purpose.

XVIII. COUNSELING FROM AN INSIDE-OUT PERSPECTIVE

This chapter is *not* intended to show people *how to do* counseling from the inside-out. It is intended to provide a glimpse into what might occur in an inside-out counseling session, and how it differs from traditional counseling.

In the field of prevention we are sensitive to the use of counseling as a prevention strategy, because traditional counseling has not proven to be a very successful preventive approach (Johnson, Bird & Little, 1980), the exception being some forms of family therapy (Kumpfer, 1997). But that refers to formal, traditional counseling. In inside-out prevention most counseling is conducted informally, and it is far from traditional. It may be helpful to view what might happen in an inside-out counseling session.

The process of therapy or formal counseling using the Health Realization model is really no different from the inside-out prevention process described in Chapter XIII; it is only more formalized, it is conducted with individuals (or groups), and it can be more intense. Yet, if some low-income housing project residents were White, middle or upper class, with some of their presenting problems they might be in formal therapy. As human beings we all function the same way. It is only a matter of extremes and context.

Thus, the components of inside-out counseling or psychotherapy are: First, the counselor has a deep understanding of the three Principles—Mind, Consciousness and Thought, lives generally in well-being and remains in a state of well-being throughout the session. Second, the counselor builds rapport and creates a good feeling, and nothing else happens unless rapport exists and is maintained; if rapport drops all counseling stops until it is regained. Third, the counselor enters into a state of deep listening. Finally, when insights occur to the counselor about what the client is not seeing, the counselor helps the client see how the three Principles work together to create her experience, with the intent that insights will occur that will unveil the client's Health. The Health Realization counselor or therapist does not take the client back into the past, nor deeply into her feelings or problems, nor into the content of her thinking. The idea is to for the client to see the three Principles operating in her life as the creator of her experience.

What follows are parts of a reconstructed transcript of a series of Health Realization counseling sessions. Actually, this transcript is of my first-ever inside-out counseling attempt.[18] I offer it here for the reader to get an idea of what this type of counseling might look like. As my first formal counseling attempt, I wouldn't exactly call it a stellar performance. I made some mistakes. Yet, as a result of these sessions—and surprisingly to me—this woman's life improved. As this is the only thing that really counts, I couldn't have

---

[18] Note: I happened to have the transcript because I had to submit it as part of one of my doctoral courses.

messed it up too badly. Because I conducted these counseling sessions as part of my doctoral program, I was fortunate to receive feedback on this series of sessions from two seasoned psychotherapists who have worked from this inside-out perspective for many years, Dr. Annika Hurwitt (now Schahn) and Dr. Keith Blevens. I have inserted their comments in the appropriate places. Their comments demonstrate where I got a little off track. I'm sure I would be even more effective now, because I have been.

The key portions of eight sessions follow. I have changed the name and initials of the client.

Background

I had conducted a three-hour Health Realization workshop for the staff of a family resource center. About six months later I received a call from the center director, asking if I would consider doing clinical supervision counseling for some of her staff. I said I wasn't really qualified, so I thanked her for asking but declined. The director asked, "Well, do you think you could?" I said, "I don't know. I've never really tried. I might be able to, but it would be an unknown." I recommended another inside-out therapist in the state. Within a couple of weeks I received another call from this director saying the staff person in question would rather try me. I said I'd be willing to give it a shot, but since I didn't really know what I was doing, she should feel free to back out at any time. She said, "Fine."

Session I, 9/98

C entered the session appearing very nervous. I tried to lighten her up. I then told her in the first session I would basically be doing intake and just listening to get an idea of the direction to go in. I asked C whether this counseling/supervision was her idea or her director's idea. She said, "Mutual agreement." I asked, "What's the main problem or issue you're seeking assistance for?" C said she worked with families with young children, and she was having difficulty getting through to two clients in particular. I asked whether she liked her job and received only a lukewarm response, though it appeared she liked the idea of what she was doing.

I asked about her kids. Both are grown and living away from home. She seemed to have a good relationship with the one who lived nearby but felt the other was clingy and needy. I asked, "What would you say your parenting style is like?" She said, "Wanting things to be right." She told me she was the youngest of nine children, but much younger than the rest of her siblings. For most of her childhood she lived only with her mother. They did not have a close relationship. She felt her mother blamed her for her father leaving. When she started to talk about this her spirits dropped, so I said, "We don't have to go any further in that direction."

Through deep listening it occurred to me that C had a head full of "shoulds." For example, she *should* be making sure that one of her clients (a teen mom) went back to school. I asked how her client would describe C as a worker. She said, "Probably as pushy." I suggested if that were true, it didn't sound like their rapport could be very high. She agreed. I said, "For the most part, people are wasting their breath trying to get others to do things without rapport." She said, "I need to work on that."

C said her client had stated that her (the client's) social skills weren't very good. I asked C how she had responded. She said she didn't; she didn't know what to say, but her inclination is to try to fix it or make it okay. I said, "It occurred to me when you were talking that if I had been in your position I would have asked her, 'What would make you say that?' C said, "I wish I could know to ask questions like that." I said, "The only difference is that I don't have my head full of having to do anything, so I was just deeply listening and it just occurred to me." But we can work on that in our sessions if you would like." She said she would. [Note: This was part of establishing an informal contract regarding what we would talk about in these sessions.] C said she wanted to feel like a success with her clients—for example, to get this teen mom to go back to school—which was apparently something similar to what she did with her own kids. I suggested to C that having things like that on her mind might block her from listening at the level she wanted, and we could talk about that, too.

She paused and said she was beginning to recognize that she may be treating this teen mom as if she were her third daughter. I offered that one possible way to help build rapport would be to admit this to her client and apologize, and say she now recognizes it was off base. She said, "I couldn't do that." I asked why? She said, "That's getting too personal." I said, "You're not supposed to share anything of yourself?" This puzzled her. I talked a little about how Thought can sometimes inhibit us, and the idea is to recognize when this is happening.

SESSION 2.

JP: So how are you doing this week?

C: I'm doing only sort of okay.

JP: That doesn't sound very good.

C: Well, I'm doing okay, but I'm thinking too much, and that isn't good.

JP: That's good that you're recognizing that.

C: You know, I read your parenting book, and I liked it a lot. But I had problems with some of it, like when you talk about what happened when you took your kid to visit colleges.[19]

JP: What problem did you have with that?

C: I was in that situation with my own kids, and I just think they should have been held accountable.

JP: What about what I wrote wasn't holding them accountable?

C: That he could get away with being nasty.[20]

JP: But C, the whole point of that was to see the insecurity behind his nastiness. As you recall, we were ready to leave, and that certainly would have been holding him accountable. But we needed to look beyond that if we wanted to really get through to him.

---

[19] For those who have not read Parenting from the Heart (Pransky, 2001) the scenario was that when my wife and I went with our son on a road trip to visit prospective colleges, he essentially treated us like dirt, insulting our driving and the like.

[20] Actually we had told him that we couldn't take his attitude any more and we started to head home without seeing any colleges—until he agreed to be reasonable.

C [wistfully]: I wish I could have done that with [my children], but now it's too late.

JP: Or, some people never get to see this, and now you have the rest of your life.

C: Hmmm. I guess so. You know, that client I was talking about last time told me that she had been doing bad things with her kid, but now she's changed. She was using the TV as a baby-sitter for her two-year-old. Then the kid never came out of his room, so she changed that.

JP: What did you say to her?

C: Something from your book. That we're always doing our best, and if we learn something new, then we do that.

JP: There's a subtle difference in what we're saying. I'm saying, we're always doing our best given the way we see things. That doesn't suggest we should be doing anything differently. There's really nothing to go out of our way to do. When we see things differently we automatically do things differently. But the real important thing for her to see is that her thinking changed, then she automatically did it differently. That would be a real valuable thing for her.

C: I'm afraid she's going to slide back. She's been making good progress. What should I do if…

JP: You know, C, I picked up from last time we were together that you have a head full of "shoulds" and "what ifs." Does this sound accurate to you?

C: Yes.

JP: So you don't trust the insights that would come out of a clear head—in this case in dealing with your client.

C: You're right. I don't.

JP: Have you ever had an insight that changed how you saw things?

C: [long pause] I'm not sure. Well, once when I was at college I had an "ah ha" experience. [She described it]

JP: What was it like for you to experience that?

C: I felt peaceful, like it was all right.

JP: Well, then you just told me you know how to do it.

C: Do what?

JP: Have an insight from a clear head.

C: But I don't trust that I'll be able to do it when I want to. Oh! I just thought of something else. I did it with smoking. I knew that certain thoughts were no good for me, and I let them go. It wasn't even all that difficult.

JP: See! That's what I mean. You have it in you to do it. How about when you are on vacation? Do you carry concerns about your clients around with you, or do you let them go?

C: Sometimes. But I carry work around with me a lot. I know how to put things on the back burner, but I can't do it if something is really on my mind.

JP: So you can do it sometimes and not other times.

C: If something is bothering me, if I don't grind away to get the answers what am I supposed to do?

JP: You just told me. When your head is clear, you have a better chance of having insights. Try it at work and see what happens.

C: I can't

JP: Why?

C: Because at work I always feel like I'm under pressure, and I process things real slowly.

JP: What's the pressure?

C: To come up with an answer for my clients.

JP: Who is the pressure coming from, your boss?

C: Not really.

JP: Well, there's no pressure from me. Who is it coming from then?

NC [long pause, then sheepishly] From me.

JP: Right! Then it's possible for it to change. That's the beauty of it. You could get quiet and reflective, and want an answer, and just see if it comes up.

C: I feel like if I did that it would be like sitting back and saying, "Pfft" [sidewise swipe of her hand], like it didn't matter.

JP: Is that what it feels like I'm doing here with you?

C: No.

JP: Well then?

C: If I really could do that, it would feel like relief.

JP: It does take a lot of pressure off, doesn't it? It's taking it off of yourself. You put it there. You could also take it off.

C: Something just came to me. My mother was filled with fear, and she filled me with fear, like about men and imagining the bad things that could happen

JP: See, that's what I'm talking about. Just now, your mind relaxed, and an insight came to you. That's how it works. Now that you saw that, you can just let it go, but at the same time recognize where those kinds of thoughts come from, those thoughts that pressure you all the time. And then you could not take them so seriously.

SESSION 3

C: You know, before we started this, I had a lot of doubts about the work I was doing with clients, but since I started talking with you I don't have those doubts any more.

JP: I'm glad you think it's been helpful.

[Dr. Blevens: The point is understanding. Did she know that it was her thinking that caused her to feel better?]

C said she'd had a nice vacation with her daughter's family (which was rare); in particular, she had a great time with her grandson.

C: When I was on vacation I found that I was not barraged by all these thoughts about my clients and what I needed to do with them. But at night I couldn't turn off the thinking.

JP: That's really great!

C: What?

JP: You noticed your thinking. Instead of being caught up in it, you observed it, and you knew that kind of thinking wasn't good for you.

C: But I couldn't turn it off at night.

JP: That's okay. You're noticing it now. Before you weren't. See the progress? The first step in changing something is to be able to see it. If you don't see it, you can't do anything about it. Besides, I can't turn off my crazy thinking all the time.

C: You can't?

247

JP: No way! But I know it's not good for me and it's just trying to trick me, and I know it will eventually go away, or diminish at least, and it does, instead of grabbing me and not letting go.

[Dr. Blevens: Teach her why we can't change our thinking. (My own note in response: We can't change our thinking because we can't stop unwanted thoughts from coming into our head. We can only decide, once they get there, whether we're going to take them seriously. Hearing that may have been helpful to C.)]

We talked about the fact that extraneous thinking can keep us from enjoying the moment, even when we're with clients.

C: I've tried this thing before about being in the moment. I've read about it. It's such hard work!

JP: What is?

C: Trying to be in the moment. Like I remember once trying to see all the colors in the trees and the textures of things. It took so much concentration. So I dropped it.

[In retrospect, I could have said, "See, you can drop some of your thinking," but unfortunately I didn't think of it at the time and said:]

JP: No wonder you don't want to go there.

C: What do you mean?

JP: Why would anyone want to do anything that hard? It sounds like you have somehow gotten it into your head that being in the moment is hard work.

C: Am I missing something? Are you saying it isn't?

JP: Didn't you tell me you were in the moment with your grandson on your vacation and you had a great time together? Was that hard work?

C: No.

JP: It was like it was the most natural thing in the world, right?

C: Right.

JP: That's what being in the moment is—natural. We would be in the moment all the time if it weren't for extraneous thinking.

C: I guess that makes sense.

JP: It doesn't matter whether we can see all the colors and shapes in the trees. *Trying* to see it is too much work. It takes the fun out of it. It actually takes us away from being in any moment because we've got thoughts of "trying" on our minds. But if we engineer ourselves to see the colors and shadows and textures, and then not think about it, we have more of a chance of seeing them. Besides, you already proved you could be in the moment and it was naturally easy—you could do it, as long as the extraneous thinking was not in the way. It can also be in the way when you're with your clients, too.

C: I know. I get into that. I see a lot of my clients getting into it.

JP: Into what?

C: Being so caught in their thinking that they're hardly even there.

JP: How do you deal with it when you see it happen with your clients?

C: I don't, really.

JP: That's interesting. I would have been inclined to say something like, "Wow, I get into thinking like that, too, and I can let myself go down that path but I know it's not doing me any good."

C: I'm not there yet. I couldn't do that.

JP: What do you see is wrong with it?

C: Not sharing something too personal about myself. I think I'm only half there with my clients. I only give half of myself.

JP: What would happen if you gave all of yourself?

C: I don't know. [She gave an example of a co-worker being torn apart because she couldn't find one of her clients a place to stay.]

JP: That's interesting. If I'm working with a client I have a few things in the back of my mind: 1) I can't change anyone; 2) I don't want to create a dependency on me. 3) I want to give it my best shot, but 4) I don't want to have investment in my success or failure. I don't want my ego tied up with whether I'm successful or not, so it feeds my ego if what I did worked, and I'm bummed out if it didn't. Yet I'm putting all of myself into it. Do you hear anything in what I'm saying that would cause me to hold back or be too emotionally involved?

C: No. I guess that's what I do. I didn't know whether it was right or not.

JP: I hear one important difference in what we're saying: I'm not giving half of myself, and you say you are.

C: Hmmm.

JP: Getting back to the client, why do you think I would have shared with her that I get into that kind of thinking too?

C: I'm not sure.

JP: Rapport.

C: Oh! [surprised]

JP: It shows that I'm a human being, and we all function in the same way. We can begin to relate to each other as equals, and that makes people feel relaxed and comfortable.

C: I guess I still have to work on rapport.

JP: Well, I don't know if you want to "work" on it. You just want to engineer yourself to build rapport with people, before you do anything else. If you don't have rapport they're unlikely to listen to anything you say anyway, so you may as well just relax and have a good time with them.

SESSION 4

C starting by saying she was lost and had been doing terribly lately. She felt like she hadn't learned a thing. She told me about a playgroup she used to love to run, and suddenly there were too many people. A problem arose with some of the parents, which she did not feel she resolved very well and left them in the lurch. She thought about it for the next two weeks, grinding away, and couldn't let go. She just didn't feel like this was taking hold with her. I saw she had lost hope, so I had to try to help her regain her hope.

JP: Everyone I know who has started catching on to what Health Realization is talking about, at first did well, thought they were doing well, and then ran into something where they went through something very similar, including yours truly. And we all came out of it. But, still, I couldn't get something off my mind the other night over some difficulty I was experiencing. I just couldn't get it off my mind. But the next morning as I was driving to meet the person in question, it occurred to me that I was seeing the problem as him, instead of seeing the problem as my own thinking. As long as it was on my mind that he was the problem, I kept thinking about it and couldn't let go. On my way driving there, I was listening to one of George Pransky's tapes, and I forgot about this guy being the problem. Then it occurred to me what to do. When I talked with him about what had happened to me, it worked out great.

I could tell C was taking that all in.

[Dr. Blevens: It's okay to be down, to go through negative feelings. We just have to realize that it's our own thinking doing it to us, not the outside world. And even when we're down, we can understand that the answer cannot be found in those negative feelings; the answer lies in understanding the direction that positive feelings point us to.]

JP: I find it interesting that you would take what's happening as a failure, instead of seeing that you were temporarily off track.

C: Yeah, that is puzzling.

JP: I wonder why, when you told me you failed, that I didn't take it as if I had failed as your counselor. I just thought, well, this is more information about what she still needs to learn. A setback is just a signal that there's still something you don't yet see about your own thinking. And that's the same with everyone. Everybody doesn't see some things about their own thinking that either brings them down or gets them angry or worried and caught up.

C: Hmmm. Why couldn't I let go of my thinking? I was trying so hard to? I tried putting it off my mind, and it didn't work. It didn't work!

JP: It's too hard to try to let go of our thinking when we think something is *real*. That's a flaw in traditional cognitive psychology, where they try to get you to reframe your thinking. "Given the fact that it's a real problem, how can I see it differently?"—as opposed to calling into question the whole notion of it being a problem in the first place. The fact is, someone else may not have seen the same situation as a problem, and you may not have seen it as a problem on some other day or at some other moment. So given all that, is it interesting to you that you would see it as "I'm the failure?"

C: I do that a lot.

JP: That's just one of those thinking habits. Somewhere along the line I realized I had a habit of worried thinking. You have a habit of failure thinking and tend to take things personally. But that's just stuff we pick up. Like I picked up a habit of worry thinking and didn't know it. We can't grow up with our parents for so long and not pick up their habits. But it rears its ugly head when we least expect it, in ways we can't see, and it affects us. Yet, the more we see it, the more we realize it's just Thought, when we recognize what's going on we don't have to let it rule us.

[Dr. Blevens: When she said, "I do that a lot," inquire right there: "Tell me more about that" Ferret out a little deeper and teach to that. How does she get into it? How could she let go of it? Inquire. Ask a couple of questions and listen.]

C: Actually, that kind of thinking that I was doing, I was able to get out of it in the last couple of days.

JP: How did you do that?

C: [long pause, embarrassed] I prayed.

JP: That's great! And that worked for you?

C: Yes.

JP: Ah, but you didn't tell me that at first. You just told me that you were a failure. Yet you already got yourself out of it—by yourself. You knew how to do it!

C: It was an act of desperation.

JP: Whatever works! One reason prayer works is because it takes you out of your own thinking, it points you in the direction of your wisdom, it clears the decks. But in prayer there's a subtle thing that goes on. In prayer, there's a difference between whether we see God as something outside of us, or whether we see God as within us.

C: I admit that a lot of the time I see God as being something "up there." I got that from my religion. But I really know God is within. I just lose connection with that sometimes.

[At that point I got the strongest feeling. I absolutely knew it was right. But I held it at the time and saved it for the right moment]

JP: You only trust that God is there for you sometimes. You only have faith sometimes, and not when it comes to having faith in yourself.

C: [Affected] You've got it! Sometimes I don't feel worthy of His trust.

JP: That's puzzling, isn't it? That you have faith sometimes when you pray, and other times you don't trust.

C: Yes.

JP: What do you make of that?

C: I don't know.

[I forget what I said in response—it was left out of the transcript—but C took it as a wise statement]

C: You can see that because you're a lot wiser than I am.

JP: Not so! It only looks that way because my thinking is less cloudy—about this issue, anyway—so I'm more in touch with my wisdom at this time.

C: It looks like even when we're having a problem, there is a wisdom in that problem.

JP: Wow! Now, that's a wise statement! That really struck me. I never saw it quite like that before. It is so comforting to know that wisdom is inherent in every situation—even when things go wrong. It is so comforting that, no matter what, we can always see something new! And that's why, when we are upset about something, there are always two roads we can walk down. One is, "There's something about the situation that is terrible," and the other is, "Something is off about my thinking." Each time we have a reaction, like you had, we are at that fork in the road. So we start going down one path, and it can take us to two very different places. But even when we're on one fork, at every step along the way we are at another fork, because at the very next step we could see that it's our own thinking—and then we're on the other road. Isn't that comforting?

C: Yes, it really is!

JP: It gives automatic hope that wisdom is always in your heart.

[Dr. Hurwitt Schahn: Instead of telling her what you think, ask her. In fact that's the one comment I have, really. In general, you could ask more questions to have her discover things for herself instead of giving her your answers.]

SESSION 5

C had been away for two weeks, then couldn't go to the next playgroup. The Head Start teachers who ran it in C's place called C's boss and complained that two day care center directors in town were bringing a bunch of their kids down there, and the parents were complaining because things were getting out of hand with numbers and control. C's boss called C in to say she was going to call those day care directors and tell them they would have to work out something else. C felt herself getting upset that her boss had not listened to her when she had said the same thing but was now listening to others instead. She felt herself getting annoyed with her boss and, worse, felt down on herself for not being worthy. But she "decided not to go there," and she felt better.

JP: That's great! Not only did you recognize your thinking, but you decided not to go in that direction, which really was deciding you didn't want to live in that feeling.

C: Another thing that happened was that a [social services] worker did not invite me to a team meeting for a client of mine that I had a lot of information about. The worker apologized to me later, but I could feel myself thinking, "She didn't think enough of me to invite me." Again, I saw myself going down that road and again decided I didn't want go there. Talking about the fork in the road last time we were together really helped. I could see it.

JP: That's great. See, you are doing it! But I can also tell from the way you're talking that you're still carrying around some nagging thoughts in your head about both of these issues. It doesn't seem like you have closure, almost like you're thinking that you're letting them off the hook by deciding not to go down that road.

C: You're right.

JP: Don't forget, we spoke before that your thinking causing your feeling state doesn't have anything to do with what you actually *do*. For example, you may have asked her, "So does this mean that you will contact me next time something like this comes up?" That would give you closure, but you could still remain in a good feeling state.

C: Hmmm. Yes. That's true.

JP: What about your boss? What lack of closure did you feel with her?

C: Why didn't she listen to me? Why did she have to wait for the Head Start teachers to tell her the same thing before she acted?

JP: So even though you kept yourself out of a feeling of despair, you are still carrying around some thinking that keeps you from feeling really good about it?

C: Yes.

JP: Well, how do you think you could get closure, and still remain in a good feeling?

C: I'm not really sure.

JP: Well, what if you just said what's on your mind about it? What if you said something like, "I've been having these thoughts, and I'm not sure whether it's me or you, but I'm wondering why when I told you about the play group problem you didn't seem to respond but now you did?"

C: Well, she did call me, and I really appreciate that. Maybe she wasn't really thinking that.

JP: When you say "maybe," you're just kind of guessing what's on her mind, right?

C: Yes, I am.

JP: So you don't really know, do you?

C: No.

JP: Isn't it interesting, we make up what other people are thinking. We attribute some motive to them—then we get a feeling from what we've made up. We are *making it up*, and then we are suffering for it.

C: Wow. [This really struck her—long pause] … But I still can't seem to let go of certain thoughts that I have. For example, when I am with clients, if they are complaining about something, I might be saying to myself, "Come on. Get it together!"

JP: Remember in my parenting book when I talked about the feeling we have in us at the time *is* the environment our kid is living in at that moment? One thing that strikes me is it might be that the only thing keeping you from having the kind of relationship you want with your clients is they are picking up that feeling from you—even though you are not saying it.

C: Hmmm. That is probably true.

JP: But it's only *thought*. That kind of thought is the only thing keeping you from feeling warm feelings toward your clients. And *if you were to see them differently, you would naturally have different feelings about them.* It's just like attributing motive. You decide what they're like, from what they say, then you get a feeling from them and react accordingly.

C: I don't trust that feeling—especially with my own daughter.

JP: That feeling would be there automatically, if it weren't for your thinking.

C: When I was at a Health Department conference recently, at first I was a little aggravated because it was such a boring conference, but then all of a sudden [embarrassed] I actually started seeing flowers around people's heads, and it totally changed how I saw them.

JP: Did you try to do that, or did it just happen?

C: It just happened.

JP: Well, let me take a wild guess: You liked that part of the meeting better than the other parts you described.

C: I did!

JP: See, that's the beauty of this. Our thoughts can change at any second. Sometimes we don't know what they're going to be, but our feelings change right along with them. And it's a beautiful thing to know that we are never locked into the way we happen to be seeing things in that moment. Another thought can come along, and we see everything differently, and then we get totally different feelings. And it's just *Thought*. All it is, is Thought, and Thought is not fixed in any way. That's the power of seeing thought in our lives. *[I actually felt moved when saying this, and it seemed that C really heard it.]*

A final issue had to do with an impending visit to her daughter in another state. This is the daughter with whom she does not have a very good relationship.

C: I think the problem is that we get expectations about what it's going to be like to be with each other, and then that sets us up for failure. So I was thinking of telling her that's what we do, and it gets in our way.

JP: Consider this: If you tell your daughter about her or "we," she will hear it differently than if you just talk about you. You want the feeling to stay warm, loving, and light. You don't want her walls to go up. But if you only talk about how you think your expectations have gotten in the way of the two of you, if it is true for her she will hear it. Otherwise, her walls will go up, and she won't hear a thing.

C: This will be the true test.

JP: Don't forget those thoughts of attributing motive—in this case, to her—they are like killer thoughts that take you away from that warm feeling you naturally have for your daughter, which have only been covered up by this kind of thinking. All you have to do is just watch those thoughts and swear off them, just like you did with your boss and that other woman.

[Dr. Blevens: This was your best session. I like the rigor in your thinking.]

253

The next two sessions I felt we didn't get anywhere new.

SESSION 7 - 1/99

C described a situation where when she received her paycheck, it contained a different dollar amount than usual. She went into blaming, then anger, and then she found herself taking it out on her daughter on the phone, an old pattern.

C: Then I saw a client do a similar thing. She got extremely angry and stuck concerning the fact that her ex-husband was not living up to expectations regarding their baby. She'd become frozen in anger, not able to move, and she really regressed from the progress she had made.

JP: What did you say to her?

C: Something that, in retrospect, wasn't appropriate. I wanted to agree with her and say "What a jerk!"

JP: What I heard was that she doesn't understand that her anger is coming from her own thinking. She thinks that *he* is causing her to be miserable. She also thinks that being angry at him does her some good.

C: I'd love to tell her what I've learned from George [Pransky]'s anger tapes, but I can't articulate it.

JP: None of that matters. You have something much more important to tell her.

C: What's that?

JP: Your own experience. What you realized about you and your paycheck. Something like, "Wow, I went through something similar recently."

C: [becoming teary] Wow! I am so glad to hear you say that.

JP: It's the only thing that counts. She won't be able to hear it if you talk about her. It's too close to her. But if you're talking about you, maybe she will make the connection.

C: [wistfully] I do really know this, but when I was growing up it was drilled into my head not to trust my intuition. "Don't trust it if it comes from you."

JP: Well, what if wisdom were greater than yourself? Something flowing through you, no matter what you call it.

C: I don't even want to go there.

JP: But you've told me times when you've prayed to God for an answer and it worked out. Why would this be different?

C: For some reason, it never occurred to me to go there for this.

SESSION 8 - 2/99

C: Last week was a horrible week. My daughter surprised me with a visit on my birthday, and we did not get along all week.

JP: How had things been going before that?

C: Pretty good. Good.

JP: So this was not your normal state of affairs lately.

C: No.

JP: And it's great that you were able to get yourself out of it.

[Dr. Blevens: Does she think she'll get to a place where problems won't happen?]

254

C: But I couldn't at the time. I got really depressed. I almost had suicidal thoughts. I wanted to see someone, to get on medication. I wanted to call you and say, "It's not working. Let's forget this!"

JP: So you saw this as a fixed condition, guaranteed to be true, instead of just a temporary flurry of depressing thoughts.

C: Yes, I did.

JP: What was the source of it, do you know?

C: As soon as she walked through the door, after the initial surprise, I found myself thinking, "Uh oh."

JP: And then you let that thought color the rest of your time together?

C: Yes, I did.

[Dr. Blevens: The question is whether she has knowledge that the source of her experience is her own thinking. Give her the understanding that makes her see that. Give examples or ask more questions, such as, "When you're down, do you remember that you felt differently at other times? What is going on that's different?"]

JP: What I'm hearing is you not realizing the power of your own creation.

C: Hmmm.

JP: That you created this incident with your daughter for yourself.

C: I know I did.

JP: But you couldn't see yourself doing it in the moment, therefore you couldn't create something new in the moment. Seeing something as fixed won't let the power of creation in. I just got this image of it being like a magnet. We have those kinds of thoughts, but they would just go flying off into the wilderness if it weren't for this magnet pulling them back— so they all stick there. And it just gets bigger and bigger.

C: That's true.

JP: You could create something new with your daughter.

[Dr. Blevens: We want to be careful about going in the direction of cognitive improvement.]

C: Yes, but when we're not together, like when we're talking on the phone or writing on e-mail, we're just fine.

JP: Well, you know, that's only an excuse.

C: Darn! [laughs] So how would I create something new with her? There's so much history.

JP: Well, history is only as real as the next thought. Does it puzzle you that you love your daughter and want to be with her, but this problem seems to happen almost every time you're together?

C: Yes.

JP: What do you make of it?

C: I don't know.

JP: You know, you mentioned before when you were in this uncomfortable state, you said, "I almost prayed." All that is, really, is asking for help in getting an answer. You could put yourself in a state of puzzlement about this, and see what arises for you. To do that is to create anew. In fact, you could go into a state of puzzlement with your daughter, be puzzled together about why you two seem to be able to talk on the phone fine, but when you're face-to-face you can't.

C: [reflective] I think I react to my daughter that way because it reminds me about what I don't like about myself.

JP: Well, that's an interesting thought. And now that you've had it, you could either dwell on it or use it to remind yourself that you don't have to go there. In fact, if you want to break the pattern with your daughter, you could talk with her about that.

C: That would be different.

JP: Or maybe over that weekend you were just in a low mood. A low mood is a more powerful magnet.

C: With my clients I notice that they get into moods a lot, and it affects how they are with me. When they're in a low mood I just back off. But when they're in a high mood, I don't want to go into their problems because I don't want to wreck it.

JP: If you want to teach them about moods, all you want them to do is to see the difference in their thinking when they're in one mood or another, and to know which thinking they want to follow.

C: Oh! Yeah, that sounds like something I could do. But, you know, with my daughter, it seems like she's in a low mood a lot.

JP: Your daughter thinks that it's real. She trusts that low mood thinking and goes down that road.

C: Wow! I just realized something big. I didn't really want my daughter to be there! And that's such a terrible thought to me that I went into denial about it.

JP: I've been there. Sometimes I just love my own space so much.

C: You have? I just don't want to have to deal with her low moods all the time.

JP: But see, that's the creation, C. You don't have to let yourself be dragged down by it. For example, if you were interested in what made her be like that, you wouldn't feel the same way. If you felt compassion for her being in low moods all the time, you wouldn't feel the same thing. We always are in the process of creating something new with the power of our own thinking. More and more I'm convinced that the name of the game is creation. Every moment is a new possibility. That's such an incredible thought.

C: It really is! It really is.

Postscript: C's life continued to improve, both at work and at home. She saw less "reality" and more creations of her own thinking. She attended a couple of Health Realization trainings, then joined a long-term professional training conducted by me and Lori Carpenos, which met once a month for six months. Somewhere in the middle of that training she had the realization—with utter shock—that with all she had started to learn about her thinking she didn't see her beliefs as thoughts. She saw them as "*real*"—the way things really were—and they had been ruling her. Once C had that insight, her life moved to a new level. Her face became lighter. She exuded far more self-confidence. Incredible wisdom started coming out of her. She became better liked by her clients and did better work with them. Her relationship with her daughter improved. As of this writing she looks like a new person.

Lisa

What follows is an example of how someone's life can change dramatically from the inside-out through seeing the three Principles in action in one's life. In this case it occurred through a combination of Health Realization counseling and training.

Lisa, a single parent, lives in a trailer in the woods of Maine with her two children. She had been on depression medication for twelve years. We met when she attended a course on Health Realization I was teaching at the New England School of Addictions Studies. Lisa describes what happened to her, in her own words:

I. The first time I took a class in Health Realization I really don't remember the content of what was said. What I do remember is that we did an exercise asking us about a time in our lives where we changed a belief, and what happened. My story was about when I decided to go to college. I always wanted to go back to school. One day I was driving up my parent's driveway, and I realized that it was an unspoken message I somehow picked up that I was not to succeed my parents. It blew me away to realize that this is how I was thinking. I assumed I must have picked this up from my parents so I thought about what I would want for my children. I discovered that I would want my children to be so much more than me, so there must be something wrong with my thinking. This was the only thing holding me back from going to college. I was then able to do what I needed to do to get in.

I was able to personalize this experience in relation to thoughts creating my reality and therefore experience. I also remember clinging to the idea of hope. There was hope I could actually be happy in life and be free to make my life my own. I loved this! I really needed this hope in my life. It's what I was looking for.

The other thing I remember about this time is something I will never forget. I left the conference with the most peace I had ever felt in my life. I was happy. I was content. I was free.

Instead of going straight home like I thought I was supposed to, I made arrangements for child care for another day. I drove home through the White Mountains. I remember at one point I pulled onto the side of the road and got out of the car. I gazed at the mountains and began crying. I was crying because I was totally in the moment and one with the mountains, and it was so beautiful. I thought, "What a gift to be given, to be so free from thoughts that I can actually see the beauty around me.

II. The very best thing that Health Realization has done for me is how it changed my relationship with my [seven-year-old] daughter, Bridget. I had my daughter during spring break of my second year of college. She was very sick as an infant. She cried all the time and was inconsolable. It turned out she was allergic to my breast milk, and I breast fed for six months. I remember it was a Wednesday that I stopped breastfeeding and put her on soy formula. Wow! She was a completely different child! That Saturday she cut her first tooth and had her first ear infection. By the time she was one, she had fourteen teeth and twelve ear infections. To say the least, it is very hard to bond with a child who is constantly crying. This continued until she was two. By that time we definitely had issues. She had learned to whine for whatever she wanted, and I had learned to give her anything just to have a little peace of mind for a moment.

I had talked to Jack many times over the past few years about my relationship with Bridget and how things had to change. I was in a group session with Jack and I was describing my relationship with my daughter to the group.

"She is a manipulative little brat, who does everything she can to make me upset and push my buttons." Pretty much from the time she was born I saw her as a manipulative and conniving little brat.

"Do you think there is any other possible way to think of her, Lisa?" Jack said.

I just looked at him and I was thinking, "Yeah right! I could think of her as an angel, an innocent child who doesn't even know what she's doing." I was picturing this temper tantrum in my head that she always does. I was thinking that I might be able to see her differently, but as soon as I saw the temper tantrum I would continue to see her as manipulating me.

Then something happened! I realized that if I thought of her differently, then the very same temper tantrum would look different!!!! Wow!! The only way I can describe this is like I was wearing a helmet with a red-colored face-shield and someone spun it around and it was, all of a sudden, a blue lens! Everything looked different. I bonded with my daughter that moment, finally! I realized that how I thought of her was what would determine my reality of her!! This was so big!!

My relationship with Bridget did change and has stayed wonderful. I have, for the first time in her life, been able to see the innocence of the sweet wonderful child that she is. (I feel like crying, tears of joy.) She no longer has the temper tantrums. If she does I just don't notice anymore; I see her as tired or having a hard day or needing my attention. Things are so different. She doesn't have to whine anymore or try to get my attention, because when she says, "Mom," I look at her and I listen, instead of thinking that she is just trying to bother me. She has brought me so much joy since then. I can't look at her without smiling at her expressions, or the way she acts, or the things she says. She is my wonderful, beautiful baby girl! If I never get another thing from Health Realization, this was priceless, and I am so very, very grateful.

III. In a private session, Lisa told me she waited up all night for her boyfriend to show up as he said he would. He never did. He never called. Whenever he didn't show up, she saw it somehow as a reflection on her. I asked Lisa what made her think his inconsiderateness had anything to do with her. She didn't know. Only one thing was clear: She felt abandoned.

Lisa told me when she was six months old her mother abandoned her—literally. Her father couldn't deal with a baby, let alone a girl, so she lived with a babysitter for the next two-and-a-half years. When she was three, her father remarried, and Lisa was taken to live with her father, stepmother and older brother, who all felt like strangers to her. She never saw her babysitter-mother-figure again. At the time of this writing she never met her real mother. Abandoned twice, Lisa said she had fought her whole life against the affect this has had on her life experience.

We talked a while about how the past no longer existed. The only thing that could keep it alive in the present was her own thinking. She simply was being ruled by her habits of thinking about abandonment that she'd picked up from growing up like that. That was understandable, given her circumstances, but if she really saw it for what it was, she wouldn't have to be ruled by it now. I saw that Lisa understood this, but only on an intellectual level.

Lisa said that when people gave her a compliment, it was like they were talking about a part of herself she couldn't relate to or touch. "It was like they saw something that I couldn't." While growing up she saw herself as a "bad child," and even now found herself self-sabotaging anything good in her life.

I had the thought that it was time to break through all this. I didn't care what it took. Here is what the two of us can remember about the dialogue that unfolded:

Lisa: My mother [stepmother] treated me like dirt. She hated me.

JP: So let me get this straight, your mother went out of her way to treat you badly?

L: Yes.

JP: She wanted to hurt you?

L: Yes

JP: So, like, she woke up each morning and said, "What can I do to hurt Lisa today?"

L: Hmm.

JP: When it comes right down to it, how do you know what was on her mind about you?

L: It was like I was in her way.

JP: How do you know?

L: That was the way she acted toward me. I couldn't do anything right! She told me I couldn't wash clothes because I would break the washing machine. I couldn't peel potatoes because I would waste too much of the potato. I've lived my whole life with that.

JP: But, do you know what was behind it?

L: What do you mean?

JP: I mean, what was her motive for saying things like that to you?"

L: I don't know.

JP: Wait a minute, you told me she deliberately wanted to hurt you. Isn't that what you're saying her motive was?

L: I guess, well—

JP: So you go around making up her motive, and then you get to suffer the consequences of what you made up.

L: Hmm.

JP: Okay, okay, let's say the absolute worst is true. Let's say that she really did get up every day and say, "How can I hurt Lisa today"—which I doubt, but let's say she did—do you think she knew what she was doing?

L: What do you mean?

JP: Could she have helped it, given her thinking?

L: I don't know—I mean, No—I don't—[great sorrow overcame her]

JP: I truly feel for you. It must have been so hard growing up with that. But can you see her innocence? And what about yours? Picture yourself as a little baby crying in your crib, and your mother can't stand it. Could you have helped it? Could you have done anything differently?

L: [sighing deeply, clutching her heart] I feel like I've got this deep pain in my heart.

JP: I'm so sorry. What are you seeing now?

L: [All of a sudden, something went whoosh] Oh my God! I just saw myself for the first time! It was like part of me was behind me, facing the other way, and I could never see her, and suddenly, Oh my God, I just turned around and saw myself for the first time! I just looked at myself, and I realized that I blamed myself for everything. I feel so sorry to have done that. I'll never see myself in the same way again. Just like with Bridget, I'll never see myself in the same way again.

Out in the parking lot, as Lisa was leaving, she said, "Goodbye, I'm going back to my hotel room…" Then she stopped, turned around, looked at me and, with astonishment, said, "…with myself!" She came running back to me, and said "Oh my God, Jack! I'm never going to be alone again! I finally have myself!"

After this, Lisa felt she could get off depression medication, which she did—cold turkey. She then felt she needed to go back on for a few months, then she went off for another six, then went back on temporarily during her usual worst seasonal time [on top of depression she had been diagnosed with "seasonal affective disorder"]. As of this writing, she is off her medication, this time, she claims, for good. In fact, during this past usually-horrible seasonal time, she described how fascinated she was by watching her emotions come and go, and she was no longer caught up in them.

A Critical Difference between Cognitive Therapy, Positive Thinking, and Inside-Out Therapy

In the middle of a conducting a training session, I heard participants talk about their "buttons getting pushed." Right then, I realized the key difference between cognitive psychology and inside-out/Health Realization-based psychology.

Cognitive psychology might say something like: "Given the fact that your buttons got pushed, how might you think about it differently so it wouldn't bother you so much?" This inside-out/Health Realization or Principle-based psychology, on the other hand, would help people see how they are making up their own "buttons."

In cognitive psychology the "buttons" are taken as a given, as real, and people are helped to think differently about them. In Health Realization, their buttons are merely illusions created inadvertently with their own thinking. To realize the latter places one in an entirely different world—the inside-out world, the world of creation of one's entire experience.

When someone is struggling with emotions, traditional psychology would have us take those emotions very seriously and deal with them—get to the bottom of them. In this Principle-based psychology, we would instead help people understand what emotions are: Emotions are what we get when we inadvertently make up with our own thinking how a situation looks to us, and then react to what we make up. All emotions are good because they are loaded with information we can use to get ourselves back on course. There is a huge difference between these two approaches, these two worlds.

The difference between Positive Thinking and Health Realization was summed up beautifully by a young woman named Meredith, who called herself "a recovering heroin addict." She had kicked heroin but was still unhappy and instead had developed a dependency on Narcotics Anonymous (NA) meetings. She attended a two-day Health Realization training and, with 15 minutes left at the end of the session, she began asking a ton of analytical questions. She seemed so confused. After the training I contacted her to see how she was doing, and she said, "I couldn't get beyond the fact that if negative thoughts created a bad experience, then positive thoughts must create a good experience. So I would go out of my way to try to create positive thoughts. But that was so hard! I couldn't believe how hard that was, and I was stuck on it. Then, right at the end of the training I realized, 'Whoa, wait a minute—if it's all an illusion anyway created by our own thinking, it doesn't matter what I'm thinking. Whatever it is, it will pass!' It was such a relief to realize that."

Two different worlds!

Working with Kids via Health Realization

Counseling young people from an inside-out perspective is really no different than working with adults. The only differences are that kids can see through insincere, ungrounded people who are not "real" even faster than adults, and they usually catch on to this understanding more quickly because they don't have as much habitual thinking in their way. Plus, one has to meet them on their own level, and rapport is especially important. The examples, metaphors and stories used, of course, have to be something they can relate to at whatever their developmental level, but that's really the only difference, except that some people have thinking about kids that makes it harder (or easier) to work with them. Most of

261

what I know about working with kids from this perspective can be found in *Parenting from the Heart* (Pransky, 2001) and the *Healthy Thinking/Feeling/Doing from the Inside-Out* middle school curriculum (Pransky & Carpenos, 2000).

One Final Note About Counseling

I don't pretend to know anything about psychotherapy with so-called serious mental disorders, but I once witnessed an inside-out therapist at work with a client diagnosed with a "multi-personality disorder."

The client was talking about the voices he kept hearing in his head. He said, "I heard that each voice is supposed to have a story."

This inside-out therapist said, "Naw, they don't have a story. Who told you that?"

"My former therapist."

"Well it's not true. Look, if you take their stories seriously, they'll be telling you their stories to their grave."

"Well, what am I supposed to do about them then? They are haunting me."

"What makes you think you have to listen to them?"

"What?!"

"Just because they're talking, that doesn't mean you have to listen. If you didn't take those voices so seriously, they wouldn't get to you."

Truth be told, I did not know what to say about this. I wanted to report it here because I found it so fascinating. In fact, I was going to remove it from this book because it sounded too far out—until I saw the movie, *A Beautiful Mind*. I realized this is exactly how the brilliant economist and mathematician, John Nash, overcame his own paranoid schizophrenia. Once he realized they really were only illusions, while he still could not stop them because they still looked so real to him, he could decide whether to take them seriously and whether to follow them. This is a profound example of everyone's innate Health and wisdom at work: our own capacity to see our own illusions for what they are. Many people whom society would call mentally ill have this same innate capacity—if they were only helped to see it. This is the hope!

What is the key that opens that door? How can we reach these patients or, better, reach them preventively? Another illustration provides an answer. This comes from an article about Dr. Bill Pettit—a psychiatrist [now with West Virginia University School of Medicine] who uses this approach—regarding one of his earliest cases:

> [It]…involved a 23-year old woman who had been diagnosed with schizophrenia, manic-depressive disorder, anorexia nervosa, obsessive-compulsive disorder and borderline personality disorder. She had become gradually incapacitated since she was 18.
>
> Over the course of her illness, she had been hospitalized for overdosing on Valium and her medications steadily increased so that by the time she saw Pettit, she was taking 30 milligrams if Haldol, 30 milligrams of Dalmane, 50 milligrams of Melaril and a milligram of Zanax at night in an effort to sleep. Despite all the medication, she continued to wake four or five times each night.
>
> She also received treatment at a well-known center where she was seen by a psychiatrist five times each week over a nine-month period. A former straight-A

student, she went from being a freshman at an Ivy League college to being someone who couldn't read a newspaper or hold a thought long enough to write it down.

When she got to Pettit's office, he said, she sat and cowered and was unable to move any further than the waiting room. After the initial visit, he said, she decided to stop taking the Zanax. On the eighth night, she discontinued all but the Dalmane. She returned to her hometown the next day and a few days later, cut the Dalmane back to 15 milligrams. In six weeks, she was off all medication and has remained off all medication since that time more than 15 years ago.

Shortly after discontinuing her medication, she taught men's cross-country at a small college, became a math major and graduated with a 4.0 GPA, then earned her masters in physical therapy from Columbia University in New York.

When Pettit asked what had allowed her to make such strides, she told him that she had seen hope in his eyes and that at some level inside herself, she knew he was right when he said, "You are totally mentally healthy—you just don't know it. You're living in a delusion and other people have innocently promulgated that." (Reitmeyer, 2001)

Is this magic? No! Does it work with everyone like this? No! I realize there is nothing scientific in reporting such anecdotes, but there is no denying the hope and possibility that exists in true stories such as this, with even the most severe problems.

Jack Pransky

XIX. SPIRITUALITY AND OTHER FORMS OF INSIDE-OUT PREVENTION

This book has attempted to show how an understanding of universal spiritual Principles—spiritual facts—changes people, reduces their problem behaviors, allows them to live in well being, and ultimately ripples "out" to affect other people and communities or organizations. It has concerned itself both with the *understanding* and with the *application* to affect change.

In this chapter we turn to the relationship between prevention from the inside-out and spirituality. This chapter is not about spirituality, per se. In this chapter I do not attempt to offer an explanation of the wide variety of existing spiritual practices and approaches. While these spiritual practices and approaches can be wonderful, uplifting and life-enhancing for the individual involved, most such practices are intended only to enhance that individual's personal growth and development. Such approaches and practices appear to fall within the "Personal Growth and Development" quadrant (Quadrant II) of Bill Lofquist's (1989) "Four Arena's of Human Service Activity."[21] Clearly, this quadrant is an integral part of prevention, but it is not necessarily the part of prevention with which this book is most concerned. It is wonderful to nurture one's own personal growth and development, but if the spiritual practice is not also intended to ripple *out* to affect others, organizations or communities, whether it would fall within the realm of inside-out prevention, as defined in Chapter II, is questionable. An argument could be made either way, but for purposes of this book I am more inclined to stick with those approaches that comprise both ends of the equation: the "inside" and the "out." On the other hand, an understanding of spiritual facts would be of equal benefit in all four of Lofquist's quadrants.

By "spiritual facts" I mean something within the spiritual realm that one truly *Knows* for oneself from within. In other words, it is not any spiritual theory or any spiritual philosophy or belief or any particular spiritual approach or technique. I, personally, see the *three Principles*—Universal Mind, Consciousness and Thought—as spiritual facts, because I see the Truth of them *for me* as they operate in my own life. All those interviewed in this book also see these Principles as fact. However, before people see them operating in their own lives, the three Principles may appear to be simply another spiritual theory or philosophy. As a theory or philosophy, though, the Principles mean little or nothing. Once people see them as spiritual facts operating within them, they mean everything.

---

[21] Quadrant I, according to Lofquist, is "Community Development," Quadrant II is "Personal Growth and Development, Quadrant III is "Community Problem Solving," and Quadrant IV is "Personal Problem Solving." The four quadrants or arenas represent four important parts of a balanced human services system.

Do other spiritual approaches, besides those that point directly to the three Principles, fall within the realm of inside-out prevention? Maybe. However, far more important than creating a distinction is this: I am suggesting that any inside-out prevention approach, or any spiritual approach for that matter, at its essence boils down to Mind, Consciousness and Thought.

Why do I say this? The reader will recall that Universal Mind is synonymous with pure Spirit or God or Allah or The Creator or pure formless energy or higher power or whatever anyone chooses to call It. Pure Consciousness is synonymous with Soul or higher consciousness or Christ consciousness or Buddha consciousness or higher self or whatever anyone calls it—and one's level of consciousness can rise toward that end. Thought is synonymous with creation. Are these not what most any spiritual view, approach or practice ultimately seeks connection with? I am aware my own view may be limited here, so I am certainly open to other possibilities.

Some might say, "What about the chakras?" The chakras have been described as "whirling vortices of subtle energies...The chakras are somehow involved in taking in higher energies and transmuting them into a utilizable form within the human structure" (Gerber, 1988, p.1). Are the chakras not spiritual facts?" They may well be—if they are *seen*. I, personally, have never *seen* them, but I also know others claim they have (Myss, 1996; Brennan, 1987), and I believe those people, but my beliefs mean nothing. Again, more important is this: Because the chakras are manifestations of energy centered in and around the body, would not the chakras be directly connected with Mind or pure energy flowing through us? And this pure energy flowing through us can be blocked—most often by inadvertently using the power of Thought against ourselves. When such blocks occur we find ourselves at lower levels or states of consciousness because we have inadvertently cut ourselves off from what pure Mind gives us. No matter what we talk about, do we not always come back to the essence of the three Principles? No matter what we talk about, does it not always come down to using these spiritual powers to our benefit rather than to our detriment? Is this not what spirituality is? Again, I am open to other possibilities but as of this writing I cannot see them.

Spiritual Practices

Many different practices are available to aid people in finding their spirituality or finding God or finding a higher consciousness. Many practices attempt to help people move closer to God, to connect with Spirit—from traditional religion to prayer to meditation to Yoga and many, many more. Many different practices attempt to raise people's level of consciousness. Many practices help people to reach their creative potential. Further, a connection to spirituality or religion has been found to help prevent problems (Resnick et. al, 1997; Shorr, 1997).

The number of spiritual teachings and spiritual healing practices now available is enough to make one's head spin. The number and type of spiritual approaches seems to increase with each passing year, most proclaiming their approach new or different or better than what has preceded it. Some are closely aligned with mind-body healing or energy-healing, such as Reiki, chakra balancing, cleansing, psychoneuroimmunology, mind-body integration, Emotional Freedom Technique, soul retrieval, acupuncture, Chiropractic, Contact Reflex Analysis, herbology, aromatherapy, essential oils, Four Element Acupuncture, Zero

Balancing, energetic balancing, crystals, and other kinds of bodywork or energy work—to name but a few. Some are aligned with alternative psychological approaches, most included within the realm of Transpersonal Psychology, such as past-life regressions, rebirthing, hypnotherapy, Jungian psychology, spiritual counseling, metaphysical counseling, and more. Psychosynthesis is an attempt to integrate the two. Some are aligned with ancient wisdom traditions, such as Native storytelling and shamanism; some with a connection to nature and the wilderness; some with a combination, such as Rites of Passage. Some are aligned with Eastern mysticism and meditation, such as Ayurveda, Chi Gung, Transcendental Meditation, Yoga, Tantra, T'ai Chi, Aikido or other martial arts. Some are aligned with psychics or clairvoyants, channeling, numerology, Tarot, astrology. Some are aligned with traditional Western religion, such as Christianity, Islam, Buddhism, Hinduism, Taoism, the Jewish Kabbala. And these are only a few, the ancient and the new.

One can cast the I-Ching or the Runes. One can read the Bible or the Koran. One can meditate. One can receive darshan with Mother Meera. One can listen to Gurumayi, the D'alai Lama, Krishnamurti, Maharaji, Sri Aurobindo, Eckhart Tolle, Ramana Maharshi, Nisirgadata, Poonjaji, Gangaji, Rajnish, Tich Nhat Than, Deepak Chopra, Carolyn Myss, Wayne Dyer, Barabara Brennan, Ken Wilber, Stanislov Grof, Carlos Castaneda's Don Juan, Neale Donald Walsh's *Conversations with God*, or Sydney Banks, or so many more. [Forgive me for leaving out so many and not giving proper citations for all the above.] There are so many different paths. There is so much wisdom everywhere. Everyone should listen to whomever they resonate with.

However, we often make a mistake. We often follow the person or the book or the practice, instead of realizing that whatever wisdom we get from listening to a great thinker or wise person or guru or swami or shaman or rabbi or minister or priest or the Pope or whomever, is really coming from within us. It must be, because the same words of these great teachers do not affect everyone in the same way, and the same words affect us differently at different times. If someone's words trigger something in us, it must have been within us all along; we are only using that teacher's words as an excuse to bring it alive and see it in ourselves. Another way to say this is we can find a connection to a higher consciousness but we can only find it from within.

Culture, religion, history or anything else can all inspire a spiritual connection, but this always occurs within one's own thinking. These sometimes can play a strong role in shaping one's thinking, but this happens only when we allow it to internally.

I can hear people say, "How could you put Christianity (or whatever) in the same breath as crystals (or whatever)!" But the point is, those who seek a connection to the spiritual part of themselves do it in their own way. I simply am not placing a value judgment on *any* way. Some people do place such a value judgment, and that is their prerogative; people have the power to do that with their thinking. To me, if anyone is searching for something spiritual, any path is beautiful, so long as it does not create a dependency on or do harm to anyone or anything. Many people want to be connected with something greater than themselves. Each person resonates with his or her own path. There is wisdom everywhere. If one looks closely beyond the words to the essence of any of these approaches they contain remarkable similarities. This is no accident! All are pointing in the direction of the Truth about the way things work—in their own ways and from their own views. The caution is, if we are on a spiritual search (like I was), subtly we are saying to ourselves that we don't have the answer within us already; we've got to find it "out there" somewhere.

Culture, religion, history or anything else can all inspire a spiritual connection, but this always occurs within one's own thinking. These sometimes can play a strong role in shaping one's thinking, but this happens only when we allow it to internally.

Health Realization is only one approach. I would not even call it a practice. Yet, Health Realization is both an approach and an understanding. As an understanding, it is the understanding of the three Principles in action, and how they work together to create our experience of life. As an approach, it is a means by which people are helped to find this understanding within.

The three Principles—Mind, Consciousness and Thought—show the way through all the tremendous variation to the simplicity. They point to the underlying essence of what all the above practices, approaches, and spiritual philosophies are pointing to. This is the remarkable gift Sydney Banks has shown us: how it all fits together. If we do not see how all parts work together, we are left only with great ideas, or we have to apply some spiritual practice to find what we are looking for. When we see how all three Principles work together to create our own experience of "reality" that changes from moment to moment, we have a key to help ourselves in our own lives any time we want, which we can then pass along to others. Plus, we find there is nothing to search for; the search is us—it is in us already. We can only forget. We forget with our thinking. We remember when our thinking clears.

When I now read or hear or see what all these great wise thinkers and teachers are saying, I now see Mind, Consciousness and Thought in everything they write, in everything they speak—everywhere. They all say it in different ways, which can often be very beautiful. The key is *seeing* how the essence of what they are saying works within us. And this same key also unlocks the mystery of what changes people toward well-being and prevents all the problems we are trying to prevent—if it is *seen*.

Criteria for Spiritual or Inside-Out Approaches to Prevention?

At the Spirituality of Prevention conference created by Prevention Unlimited (Namy Dickason, 1993), its 1995 participants defined principles of applying spirituality in prevention practice (Pransky, 2001).[22] Instead of repeating them word-for-word here, I took the liberty to consolidate and summarize:

- Spirituality is a connection to something greater than oneself, however people define it for themselves, and however it speaks to them.
- The spiritual dimension is an integral and essential part of the spectrum of prevention.
- The intent is to discover a state of inner peace, joy, happiness, fulfillment, wholeness.
- People are already perfect, pure and precious in their essence. Tapping into this essence creates positive change; coming from this core is prevention. Spirituality is helping people find their way home.
- Spirituality in prevention is seeing and helping others to see that everyone has something special to offer, and to find their creative expression, and loving enough to make a difference.

---

[22] The reader will note that the use of the word, "principle," here is not the same used in identifying Mind, Consciousness, and Thought.

- The more people are centered and grounded, open and nonjudgmental and walk their talk, the more others will be helped to find their health, well-being and peace of mind.
- Spirituality *is* prevention.

In the year 2000 at the Prevention Think Tank conference, interested attendees took a shot at defining some guiding principles for inside-out prevention:

- It comes from within.
- We are after a connection to a spiritual core; therefore, that becomes the beginning point.
- The quality of that core is Health, well-being, wisdom
- It is self-experienced.
- It is one thing that unites us all, a common thread across all people, ages and cultures.
- It connects us with purpose.
- It is not contrary to the separation of church and state.
- We are after spiritual qualities, such as peace, love, gratefulness, etc., and the purpose is to help people find these inherent qualities within.
- There are many different paths.
- Inside-out prevention must be considered an integral part of the entire discipline of prevention and health promotion.

Spiritual vs. Inside-Out Approaches?

Spiritual approaches to prevention may or may not be inside-out approaches. The question is whether the particular spiritual approach fulfills the meaning of inside-out defined in Chapter II. However, to me, these boil down to two:

- Does the approach recognize that change can only come from within?
- Is the intent of the approach to move "out" to affect others?

What would this mean for various spiritual approaches to prevention? These criteria would raise interesting questions:

- Does the approach suggest, however subtly, that the answer lies in following a particular technique or a particular practice or a set of rules or rituals in order to find the answer? If so, criterion # 1 above is not fulfilled, however subtly.
- Does the approach suggest that one's "higher power" (or whatever anyone wants to call it) is outside oneself? If so, criterion # 1 above is not fulfilled, however subtly.
- Does the approach have a clear intent to affect others, organizations, or communities beyond one's own personal growth and development? If not, criterion # 2 is not fulfilled.

I am not suggesting that this limit any prevention practice or that this be the last word on the subject. I am offering it as a view to consider.

Do Spiritual Approaches to Prevention Work?

The New England Network for Child, Youth & Family Services conducted what may be the first literature review on the impact of religious and "secular spiritual" practices on health and emotional well-being, particularly on children or adolescents (Wilson, 2002). It is obvious far more research is needed in this area, but there is some.

Regarding traditional religion, teenagers who considered religion important were less likely to use drugs and have a later age of sexual debut (Resnick et al., 1997). Teens who participated in religious services and other religious activities were found to be more willing to abide by the rules and expectations of society (Bjarnason, 1998). Twelve to fifteen-year-olds who prayed frequently perceived that they had more purpose in life than those who did not (Francis & Evan, 1996). For adults, active religious involvement substantially increased the chance of living longer, even when controlled for factors such as race, income, education, obesity and mental health (McCullough, et al., 2000). This is good information, but do these studies mean that if we encourage faith or religion or church in adolescents (or others) who do not have a religious background it will be helpful in ameliorating or preventing problems? No! We cannot draw that implication.

Regarding secular spirituality—that is, spiritual practices not rooted in traditional religion—youths aged 16-21 who scored high on the Spiritual Orientation Inventory (SOI), which measures such things as mission in life, material values, altruism, meaning and purpose, sense of the sacredness of life, were found less likely to engage in destructive behavior, more likely to report healthy ways of coping with crises, and more likely to be proactive, hopeful and introspective (Saunders, 1998). Youth who scored high in "spiritual interconnectedness," especially if they reported strong spiritual connections with friends, were less likely to engage in voluntary sexual activity (Holder, 2000). In a qualitative study, twelve former runaway or homeless youth reported having a relationship with a higher power was a significant factor in turning their lives around (Lindsey et al., 2000). Does this mean encouraging secular spiritual practices will be helpful in ameliorating or preventing problems? No! We cannot draw that implication.

Students in grades three through eight improved their standardized test scores significantly after practicing transcendental meditation (TM) during school for several months (Nidich et al., 1986). The practice of TM in prison populations yielded higher psychological and ego development, lower psychopathology, reduction in disciplinary reports and reduction in recidivism (Dillbeck and Abrams, 1987). Another study found TM more effective in consistently reducing recidivism than were prison education, vocational training or psychotherapy (Bleick and Abrams, 1987). Adjudicated youth trained in Yoga, breathing and meditation, after nine months of practice, reported that the program had a calming effect on their minds and helped them to recognize and control their feelings (Derezotes, 2000). Yoga yielded motivational change in substance abusers (Lohman, 1999) and improved attitude and behavior and decrease impulsivity in adolescent inpatients at a mental health center (Zipkin, 1985). Mantra chanting was found to reduce stress and depression (Wolf, 1999). Guided visualization (an introspective technique in which individuals are directed to imagine themselves in particular scenarios) was found to improve post-traumatic stress disorder, obsessive-compulsive disorders, childhood anorexia, drug addiction, and academic problems (Briscoe, 1990). When guided visualization was used along with standard treatment, depression scores improved significantly among hospitalized, clinically depressed teenagers, compared with those who only received standard treatment (Briscoe, 1990). Group drumming was found to stimulate the immune system to fight cancer (Bittman, 2001) and yielded people who were more energetic and confident (Segall, 2000).

Students who practiced Karate showed lower aggression and increased levels of self-reliance and optimism (Layton, et al., 1993); greater effects were associated with increased study and greater proficiency (Kurian et al., 1994). When juvenile delinquents received traditional Taekwondo training they showed decreased aggressiveness and anxiety, and increased in self-esteem, self-adroitness and value orthodoxy; however, when a similar group received a "modern" version of martial arts training without the traditional emphasis on philosophical dimensions they showed increased aggressiveness (Trulson, 1986). After 18 months, suspensions at a Kansas City school dropped 50% after an intervention comprised of a martial arts program called "Gentle Warriors," which included stories relating to the Bushido Code (emphasizing respect and compassion) along with coping skills, meditation, self-control, mentoring, and parenting classes (Smith et al., 1999).

Rites-of-passage—ceremonies or rituals generally meant to mark the transition from one stage of development to another, which often weave strands of religion and culture together and include gender-based rituals, myths, storytelling and initiation rites—were found to have a positive impact on coping and self-esteem among adolescents in a substance abuse treatment program (Mason et al., 1995). A drug prevention program for more than 200 middle-school students on an Indian reservation in the Southwest, which included cultural storytelling and cultural symbols, lowered drug use among Native American males; in Rhode Island, strengthening cultural identification of Native American youth was found to decrease use of substances (Sanchez-Way et al., 2001).

Does this mean if we apply these practices as prevention strategies that kids will do better in a variety of ways? Probably. That correlation seems to exist.

What do all these disparate studies really mean? In my view, they imply when young people (and others) connect with something that might be considered spiritual, a range of behaviors can improve.

What is the significance for prevention from the inside-out? To me, it is further evidence that preventionists would do well to see beyond the traditional outside-in approach, to explore and examine realms that appear to tap into something within that is powerful enough to change and improve behavior.

A Study of Spiritual Practices in Youth Work

Beyond their literature review, the New England Network for Child, Youth and Family Services conducted the first study of its kind: "Practice Unbound: A Study of Secular Spiritual and Religious Activities in Work with Youth" (Wilson, 2002). While not limited to prevention, the study sought to "identify and measure the kinds of spiritually oriented activities, both secular and religious, that social service providers use with adolescent clients ages 12 to 21," as a means of helping troubled youth with their problems." They defined spiritual activities as "activities designed to enhance a client's sense of awareness, wholeness and well-being and help them tap sources of inner strength"(p.1).

For this study, 191 randomly selected agencies throughout the United States were asked about their use of sixteen identified activities defined as spiritual in orientation (18% of these identified themselves as "faith-based" organizations). Specific religious activities asked about were Bible/prayer groups, clergy programs, religious instruction, religious counseling, religious rites of passage, and church attendance. Specific "secular spiritual activities" inquired about were education about spirituality, meditation, guided relaxation/visualization; musical expression, martial arts, yoga, 12-step groups, and rites of passage rituals. Blank lines were provided for "other." No distinction was made between prevention, intervention and treatment.

Approximately 60% of youth-serving agencies were found to use one or more secular spiritual activities and 34% were found to use one or more religious activities. The secular spiritual activities used most often were guided relaxation/visualization and Twelve-Step groups. Most of the secular spiritual activities were fairly new to the agencies providing them; conversely, half the agencies providing more traditional religious activities had been using them for over ten years and were part of the agencies' historical mission.

To me, the most fascinating finding of this study is "agencies offered remarkably consistent testimony about the benefits of the activities for their clients, almost regardless of the particular activity in question: spiritually oriented practices were thought to help youth relax, manage their anger and think constructively about their lives." Those who used secular rites of passage viewed this approach as probably the most beneficial.

Most agencies expressed the desire to expand or develop their spiritual programming (but only of the type—secular or religious—in which they were already engaged). The agencies surveyed indicated that their greatest needs in this regard were for training and funding.

Faith-Based Initiatives

In his 1/29/01 announcement, President Bush put a governmental stamp of approval on faith-based initiatives. No matter what one thinks of this, it is difficult to deny it would be wonderful to have greater involvement of the religious community in prevention.

The *Prevention Forum* magazine of the Illinois Department of Human Services devoted much of its Winter/Spring 2002 volume to this issue. It reported on many of the varying views that exist on the subject (as of this writing). Among the many items reported was a list provided by the Center for Applied Prevention Technology (CAPT) of what faith-based organizations could do to prevent problems. Their list consisted of typical things that private agencies now do that faith-based organizations could also take on, such as "provide important information to individuals so they can make healthy decisions about substance use and abuse"; "encourage and support substance-free social activities"; "teach young people to develop personal and social skills to resist pressure to use," and the like (Zoeller, 2002, p.7). A similar list was provided by the National Clearinghouse of Alcohol and Drug Information. An examination of these lists suggests that faith-based collaboration for prevention means, to many, telling faith-based organizations to take on what they (the secular organizations) already do, so the faith organizations can do more of the same. In my view, if this is the best we can do, we will be missing a golden opportunity.

I have not seen much opening from the traditional prevention community to ask the faith-based organizations what they do now that works, so prevention practitioners can learn from them. Faith-based initiatives will be ineffective if all they do is mirror what private and public agencies already do. Faith-based organizations have their own built-in strength, and it is not a strength many public or private organizations have. Their strength lies in helping young people to find faith or to get in touch with the spirit within, from which no problem behaviors are possible.

As Reverend Dr. Virgil Wood, Pastor of the Pond Street Baptist Church in Providence, Rhode Island explains (written specifically for this publication):

> Faith based mentoring is at the heart of the Black Church (and probably others) and its ministries of prevention and recovery. Faith is born at the point that persons teach themselves "the quiet mind," which leads to the "open (available) heart," resulting in the "restored soul," and issuing forth in the energized and revitalized body doing "the work of peace." Every Faith-Community probably has its own way of saying this, but in the Afro-Christian tradition, we say, "Hope unborn had died...when, with a steady beat, our hearts arrive at the place for which our Fathers (and Mothers) sighed." That is the point at which the mustard seed of faith provides the energy, and Hope as the pathway to a new future being born today, and becomes real, in overcoming stress and despair. The end result is a marriage of Love and Community, in which young folks' visions and old folks' dreams mix and match to become both prologue and epilogue to what Martin Luther King called "The Beloved Community."

To me, therein lies the real promise for faith-based initiatives: to work on the creation, beginning from within, of "the beloved community" envisioned by Dr. King. As Father Michael Pfleger of St. Sabina church in Chicago says, "faith and spiritual power are the cure" (in Zoeller, 2002, p.7). Reverend Charles Collins of the First Christian Church, Disciples of Christ, Rockford, IL says that [faith-based organizations] are uniquely able to "deal with and talk about prevention in relation to man's soul... They bring a very spiritual piece of it." (p.7).

Reverend Wood provides an example of what a faith-based initiative can do that has potential to make a real difference. He is the driving force behind the Ministers' Alliance of Rhode Island effort to create after-school programs for youth in need, based on the successful model employed by the Ministers Alliance of Boston in cooperation with the Boston Public schools. In Providence, however, besides creating an effective structure and process to bring this about as they did in Boston, they are adding an additional ingredient. Within this structure, their intent is to help point youth to their spiritual essence, to that place of Health and wisdom within, and Dr. Wood intends to use Health Realization to help bring this about.

It would be tempting for faith-based organizations to push their own sets of beliefs and morals. Most everyone agrees this would be improper for a government-funded faith-based initiative. On the other hand, it would be most interesting and useful to discover, among all the varying religious and denominational beliefs, what the common denominators are; what is common to all? It would be interesting to view moral and ethical behavior through this lens. Somewhere within these realms may lie the key to spiritual intervention for prevention.

Faith-based organizations have other strengths that the public and private sectors do not often have. Many have a unique understanding of their community. Many have the trust of the people [although some of this may have slightly eroded as a result of the sexual abuse scandals within the Catholic Church; a seed of doubt may have been planted about all religious figures]. Many have access to many volunteers. Many already have youth programs in place.

And what of the doubts about the separation of church and state? If nothing else, that statement does not mean "no collaboration"; rather, it means that religious goals and values should not be thrust upon others (Zoeller, 2002)

Some Findings In Support of a Spiritual Basis for the Three Principles

Let's go back to Sydney Banks's (1998) contention that if any spiritual or inside-out approach or any spiritual philosophy or any Religion were deeply explored, one would find at its essence Mind, Consciousness and Thought. In some we might only find an understanding of parts of this trinity; in others we would find them all—but they're hidden within the words and metaphors and parables and stories, and any techniques we find is intended to lead us there.

Can support for the three Principles be found in other spiritual realms? [Note: In Chapter XXI, we will see what science has to say about this, and there are remarkable similarities as well.] I do not pretend to have thoroughly examined spiritual or religious approaches. I examined only four different spiritual views as examples, from the ancient to the modern. Yet, those I read reveal close alignment with the three Principles.

I find it most interesting that three completely different spiritual traditions—Siddha Yoga (Muktananda, 1992) based on Hinduism; Vipassana meditation (Hart, 1987) based, it claims, on direct teachings from the Buddha; and the modern *A Course in Miracles* (Wapnick & Wapnick, 1995), based, it claims, on the direct teachings of Jesus—seem so closely aligned. Could Sydney Banks (1998) have borrowed his ideas from these traditions and approaches? Anyone who knew Banks before his epiphany would say that he was not a learned man who studied ancient religions (Pransky, 1998). It is also interesting that two recent independently "channeled" spiritual teachings, *A Course in Miracles* and Walsch's *Conversations with God* (1995; 1996; 1999), also bear striking resemblances. I use the word "channeled" to indicate that these sources claim that their writings did not come from them, rather through them, from some unfathomable source. Coincidence? Perhaps, but it appears unlikely.

First, some of these spiritual writings corroborate what we have learned from science [see Chapter XXI]. Walsch allegedly writes from the voice of God:

> All of life is a vibration. That which you call life…is pure energy. That energy is vibrating constantly, always. It is moving in waves. The waves vibrate at different speeds, producing different degrees of density, or light. This in turn produces what you'd call different "effects" in the physical world—actually, different physical objects. Yet, while the objects are different and discrete, the energy which produces them is exactly the same (Walsch, 1999, p.178).

Speaking as God, Walsch continues: "Every time you have a thought, it sends off an energy. It is energy" (p.115). No matter who is actually speaking, these are profound words for investigation.

> Emotion is energy in motion. When you move energy, you create effect. If you move enough energy, you create matter. Matter is energy conglomerated. Moved around. Shoved together. If you manipulate energy long enough in a certain way, you get matter… it is the alchemy of the universe. It is the secret of all life. Thought

is pure energy. Every thought you have, have ever had, and ever will have is creative. The energy of your thought never ever dies (Walsch, 1995, p.54).

Vipassana meditation states that every thought, every emotion, every mental action is accompanied by a corresponding sensation within the body, and that by observing the physical sensations, we also observe the mind (Hart, 1987, p.91).

This brings us to Mind, Consciousness and Thought. First we consider Mind. Buddhism speaks of Master Mind or Universal Mind. This is the Mind of which Banks speaks. Vipassana meditation says that the mind is everywhere, in every atom. "The whole body contains the mind" (Hart, 1987, p.29). Mind, used here, is another word for God. In *Conversations with God*, God allegedly says that He/She/It is All things. It is One (Walsch, 1995). Siddha Yoga says the following about God and its relationship with ourselves:

> The scriptures and the saints say that the individual self is not a separate entity but a part of God. It is completely pure and the embodiment of supreme bliss. Thinking that we are without God is like a fish thinking that it has never seen water. A fish would have no life without water; water is the element in which it lives. We are in the same condition. Our life is in God (Muktananda, 1992, p.2).

Life is spirit, they say in Siddha Yoga. There appears to be some life energy or "vital force" or "prana" that "permeates the entire body."

> The Upanishads also tell us that mind is united with the vital force... From the inner Consciousness originates *prana*, and with the help of the mind it moves in the body and carries out its functions (Muktananda, 1992, p.7).

This brings us to Consciousness, which *A Course in Miracles* calls the "first split" from God (Wapnick & Wapnick, 1995, p.17). Out of the Oneness of God comes a split of itself, or at least the illusion of a split, which is an individual Soul, within which is the purest of Consciousness.

Swami Muktananda (1992) quotes the *Pratyabhijnahridayam*:

> When universal Consciousness...descends from its lofty status as pure Consciousness and assumes the form of different objects it becomes...individual consciousness, or mind, contracting itself in accordance with the objects perceived. So the mind is nothing but Consciousness in a contracted form. That Consciousness is one with the Self, so the mind is simply that aspect of the Self which has taken the form of outer objects (p.27).

To be clear about the distinction, when "mind" is used in this sense, it refers to the little mind, our own personal little minds. When the term "Self" is used with a capital "S" it refers to the pure Self or Soul that we received directly from God.

Once this split occurs, and we enter the world of physical form, our consciousness tends to forget its divine nature.

> The mind is often compared to a mirror. If a mirror is dirty it cannot reflect objects clearly. In the same way, a mind that has become dirty by association with outer objects cannot reflect the inner Consciousness (Muktananda, 1992, p.14)... If the mind were to become pure, to discard all its thoughts and doubts, it would experience God everywhere (p.13).

275

Some Views on Spirituality and Prevention

I asked a couple of people I know, who in the last decade have been promoting spirituality in prevention, to briefly share their views:

Peter Perkins of Prevention Unlimited and Five Dimensions consulting, from Calais, Vermont:

My theme is awakening to all of who we are, helping people to become aware that there's more than what they're thinking or feeling or their behavior. In the human services realm or prevention those are what we spend our time on, and we really don't see that much change. Ultimately, until we go deep inside, and there's a shift deep inside—until you really embrace the total of who you are—change is limited.

In my workshops in the Five Dimensions of the Self, many people have an "ah-ha," and are surprised. "You mean, there really is a spiritual dimension to my existence? I never thought of that before. I never realized that's within my realm or my power." They shift in the way they think about themselves, in the way they feel, in the way they see their relationship to something greater than themselves. The Five Dimensions of the Self—Thinking self; Feeling self; Material self; Social self, Spiritual self—are all interrelated. Unfortunately, this compartmentalizes who we are, but it's a useful way for people to see how interrelated they all are—break it down and put it back together again. Mostly, through this process people see that they are spiritual beings.

The reason for being more in touch with the spiritual dimension is that it's the reason to care about who you are and how you are being in the world and the choices you make. It connects you to other people. Because it recognizes that everyone is of the same spirit, the same essence, and that gives people reason to care. Otherwise, so what if I kill somebody? It gives them more hope. People are hungry for more than the material world—more than "make money to buy things"—more than emote themselves through life, more than intellectual thinking and figuring things out logically. When people find that they don't only have to be there, there's hope for a more valuable life than what they've got in front of their face. This can be very meaningful to them.

I pose questions to kids to get kids to look and think and talk about this stuff. Something like, "What do you think it is to be who you are? What do you think it would mean to be a whole person?" We explore what each of the parts are, and share. But they always end up wanting to focus on the spiritual dimension. We talk about what the spiritual dimension is. We debate about it. We open up a bigger thought about it—what it is to be a spiritual being.

When kids and parents apply these dimensions to themselves, they have told me that it opens a new way of thinking about themselves, about their kids, about other people. They say, "I can really look at others or myself differently." Some people say, "I never thought about it that way. I can see how this would be useful in my work," or whatever. People want to know more about who they are. One pregnant girl in my workshops, who didn't want anything to do with spirituality, ended up realizing that there was a bigger side of herself, and she saw her baby in relationship to it. It was really profound for her.

Kids are endless energy and potential. The whole journey of adolescence is so similar to a spiritual pilgrimage or a discovery process that one goes through in their own spiritual discovery. It's about searching for identity. The ages of twelve to thirty is a search about "Who am I?" It's a huge existential question, the journey of adolescent spiritual development. It's an adolescent question that a lot of people keep carrying with them. Then, of course, when they hit a crisis, people tend to need something like the spiritual.

In inside-out prevention all we have are external tools, but they're focused on the internal shift. If meditation focuses on the practice—getting the thing right—it becomes an outside-in thing. The focus must be on the insight. If people have an internal shift, their thoughts, feelings and behaviors get healthier. Prevention has missed this. Since we started the Spirituality of Prevention conference, this shift has begun to happen for a lot of people. It's important for the field.

Jim Wuelfing, a private trainer and consultant associated with The Center, Hartford, CT[23]:

Fifteen years ago I heard John Wallace lecturing about alcoholism being a biopsychosocial spiritual disease. Over the years, those of us working in prevention and other helping professions have made advances in addressing the biological, psychological and social needs of the people and communities with which we work. Although there are exceptions, we tend to fall short in addressing spiritual growth as an integral aspect of wholeness. We tend to leave that to faith communities and 12-Step programs.

What is it that keeps us from speaking about and incorporating spiritual growth? My experience in training and working with literally thousands of helping professionals leads me to believe that the hesitancy generally falls into three categories. First, there is the belief that talking to others about spirituality would somehow violate the separation of the church and state. Secondly, many of us feel that to do so would be to impose our views on others. Finally, many us have our own unresolved issues with religion and other personal attempts at spiritual growth.

Trying to define spirituality is often an exercise in futility. It might better serve to describe our experience of it. When we do so, we are not imposing our view and allow for an openness to other experiences.

Many resources are available to help us explore spiritual growth. One of my favorites is *The Spirituality of Imperfection: Storytelling and the Journey to Wholeness* (Kurtz & Ketcham, 1992). The authors describe a journey of spiritual experiences that include release, gratitude, humility, tolerance, forgiveness and being-at-home. Those who have surrendered to any attachment—released from it—know that they were not alone involved–that a power greater than self is involved. This understanding leads to gratitude. Humility is the act of self-love—embracing all of ourselves, even those parts we hardly ever explore out of fear and shame. As we become more embracing of ourselves, we can more fully embrace and be tolerant others. Tolerance leads to an ability to forgive. Forgiveness becomes a gift that we give ourselves to free ourselves of old slights, embarrassments and resentments. We are set free. The experience of these spiritual realities leads to a "being-at-home" or spiritual integrity.

It seems there is a logical connection between traits of resiliency—such as autonomy, self-esteem, social competence, internal locus of control, healthy expectations, hopefulness—and the integration of spiritual principles into a way of being. Invariably, some people who come from the most trying of circumstances, have a strong sense of their spiritual selves and an ability to change the context of any moment to live in the solution. As Nelson Mandela said reportedly as he left the prison, "For 27 years I have been in prison. Never once was I a prisoner."

It seems folly to me to deny that all of our work within ourselves and with others is at its core a spiritual journey. We need only recognize it as such and embrace our work as a holistic endeavor.

---

[23] Sections of this were previously published in Adcare Advisor (Volume 7, Number 3), a publication of Adcare Hospital of Worcester, Inc., 107 Lincoln Street, Worcester, MA 01605.

In other words, as Mutakananda states, the sages compare the mind to water. Whatever color we put into that water is the color it becomes. "When the mind lights on an object, it becomes one with that object" (p.22).

A Course in Miracles suggests when we lose sight of our Divine Consciousness we enter an ego state where the perceiver and perceived "seem to exist as separate 'realities'" (Wapnick & Wapnick, 1995, p.17). Our consciousness then descends to having a concept of "a limited false self that is separate and uncertain, seeming to experience an opposite to the true Self as God created it" (p.17).

God (Walsch, 1999) says the same, that we incarnate as lower forms and can evolve to higher states of consciousness. "You are simply raising the energy... You are that energy (p.55)... The higher you raise the energy of life through your physical being, the more elevated will be your consciousness (p.151).

> What the soul is after is...the highest feeling of love you can imagine. This is the soul's desire. This is its purpose. The soul is after the feeling. Not the knowledge, but the feeling... The soul wants to feel itself, and thus to know itself in its own experience. The highest feeling is the experience of unity with All That Is. This is the great return to Truth for which the soul yearns. This is the feeling of perfect love (p.83).

God (Walsch, 1999) says that He/She/It has given us the ability to consciously have experience—to be aware of experience. The point of contact between ourselves and whatever is experienced in our consciousness is through our senses. Consciousness creates experience. "You are attempting to raise your consciousness... (Walsch, 1996, p.49). "My purpose for you is that you should know yourself as Me" (Walsch, 1995, p.26).

Vipassana says that unless something comes in contact our senses, it does not exist for us. The senses are the gates through which we encounter the world, and the bases for all experience. Vipassana teaches that since the deepest level of the mind is connected to sensation, meditating on the sensations is what liberates the mind. Here it is important to make a distinction, because on the surface it may sound as if Vipassana is saying that sensation is more primary than Thought. Clearly, sensation is more primary than what most of us think of as thought, and that is the level of thought Vipassana appears to be speaking of here. It makes perfect sense that meditating on sensation without any intervening, distracting thoughts could bring people to be one with the moment. Yet, a deeper level of Thought [Chapter XXI] is even more primary than sensation, because we would not have any ability to experience sensation in any way if not for Thought. We would not know that we were sensing anything if not for Thought. The vehicle of Thought must be used to experience any sensation. The vehicle of Thought must be used to take in any experience through our consciousness.

> The process of creation starts with thought—an idea, conception, visualization. Everything you see was once someone's idea. Nothing exists in your world that does not first exist as pure thought... Thought is the first level of creation (Walsch, 1995, p.74)... We are constantly in the act of creating our Selves (p.65).

The power of Thought is recognized in Siddha Yoga: "Thought has infinite power. That is why the sages pray, 'O my mind, always think well of yourself and others.' When your mind is restless and turbulent, when you think negatively all the time, you harm not only yourself, but others as well... It is our thoughts that create our heaven and hell; by our thoughts we can make our cells experience divinity or we can put ourselves down until we feel like hellish insects" (Muktananda, 1992, p.12).

This leads us to a distinction made by both Jesus (Wapnick & Wapnick, 1995) and Buddha (Hart, 1987) about "right thought" vs. "wrong thought."

> This new mode of being asks us to become aware of the thoughts of our wrong minds, and to ask for help in switching to a correction that already exists in our right minds. In order to accomplish this, we must get our ego selves out of the way and let go... (Wapnick & Wapnick, 1995, p.54).

One of the things that brings us to "wrong thought" is attachment—to sensual gratification, to the ego, to possessions—and so long as this conditioning remains in our minds, we cannot be secure or at peace (Hart, 1987). Yet, Hart also points out that what we need to stay in right thought is awareness of wrong thought, sustained from moment to moment. When we stay in this awareness, the nature of the thought pattern changes. Aversion and craving are calmed down by awareness and the mind becomes more tranquil, "at least at the conscious level..." (p.88).

Then we form a general way of looking at things, out of which we then think. This distinction between perception and thought can be tricky and appears to relate to different levels of thought [Chapter XXI].

> Remember, life is an ongoing process of creation. You are creating your reality every minute. (Walsch, 1996, p.10)...It is all a question of perception. When you change your perception, you change your thought, and your thought creates your reality (p.117)...Just know this: You are a being of Divine Proportion, knowing no limitation. A part of you is choosing to know yourself as your presently experienced identity. Yet this is by far not the limit of your Being, although you think that it is (p.65).

> You are the creator of your reality, and life can show up no other way for you than that way in which you think it will (Walsch, 1995, p.52).

A clear distinction is made about thoughts that come to us from what seems to be a different place than our norm. This could be called "insight" or "wisdom." In fact, "Vipassana" means "insight" in the ancient Pali language of India. It is the essence of the teachings of Buddha and the source of experience of the truths of which he spoke (Hart, 1987, p.6). Vipassana describes insight as "a sudden intuition" or knowing of truth (p.89).

A life without wisdom is a life of illusion. This produces a state of agitation, of misery. Our first responsibility, then becomes to live a healthy, harmonious life, good for ourselves and others. To do so, we must learn to use our faculty of self-observation, or truth-observation (Hart, 1987). Vipassana says that real wisdom brings about a change in one's life by changing the very nature of the mind. Its teachers teach that this comes about by observing the sensations. This is one way of stilling the mind.

The path to wisdom is by being still and quieting the outer world "so that the inner world might bring you sight. This In-sight is what you seek" (Walsch, 1995, p. 44).

Insight is the pathway to seeing our way out of our conditioned minds that see "the real world" and that "the way to live life is by contact with an external reality, by seeking input, physical and mental, from without" (Hart, 1987, p.5). But, as Vipassana says, "Unless we investigate the world within we can never know reality—we will only know our beliefs about it, or our intellectual conceptions of it. By observing ourselves, however, we can come to know reality directly and can learn to deal with it in a positive, creative way (p.6).

Creation is that at every moment something new arises as a product of the past, to be replaced by something new in the following moment (Hart, 1987, p.28). There is no real "being," merely an ongoing flow, a continuous process of becoming (Hart, 1987, p.29).

> External reality is a reality, but only a superficial one. At a deeper level the reality is that the entire universe, animate and inanimate, is in a constant state of becoming— of arising and passing away. Each of us is in fact a stream of constantly changing subatomic particles, along with which the process of consciousness, perception, sensation, reaction change even more rapidly than the physical process. This is the ultimate reality of the self with which each of us is so concerned. This is the course of events in which we are involved (Hart, 1987, 29).

If we were to listen closely, such spiritual teachings offer us healthy ways to live our lives. Here are but a few examples.

A purpose of *A Course in Miracles* is to teach us that we have a choice in thinking ourselves separate and special or in thinking that we are directly connected to and are a part of God, and that this choice rests within our minds. We can recognize our own free will in leading us in one direction or another—put simply, toward fear or toward love. Forgiveness often is what allows a change of mind to come forth. We ultimately learn and remember that our true will has been free all along; we simply had forgotten (Wapnick & Wapnick, 1995).

Both Siddha Yoga (Muktananda, 1992) and Vipassana meditation (Hart, 1987) also speak of this same illusion of separation with God. God or Walsh echoes this in *Conversations with God*: "Nothing is painful which you understand is not real" (p.143). We are encouraged to enjoy the illusion but not become it. Further, when we confront any difficult situation in life it is wise to inquire within rather than without, asking: "what part of my Self do I wish to experience now in the face of this calamity? What aspect of my being do I choose to call forth" (p.32). "There should be only one consideration when making any decision—Is this a statement of Who I Am? Is this an announcement of Who I choose to be" (Walsch, 1996, p.13).

Vipassana states that "the world will be peaceful only when the people of the world are peaceful and happy. The change has to begin with each individual" (Hart, 1987, p.30).

These are but a few suggestions for healthy living from these spiritual approaches. All are directly aligned with the three Principles, and with what we learned from science [Chapter XXI]. The most important difference appears to be that Vipassana meditation and Siddha Yoga both insist that their respective practices are *the* path to making the mind strong and becoming more closely aligned with Mind/Spirit/God. Banks (1998) suggests that no technique is really necessary to gain understanding of the three Principles from within.

What does all this mean? Simply that no matter what the spiritual teaching (the ones cited anyway, and the reader is certainly encouraged to look elsewhere), it always seems to boil down to Mind, Consciousness and Thought. The trick lies in seeing how they all work together, which is how they can be of most use to us.

XX. DESI GRAY WOLF LAUGHING ELK

Interview with Desi Shebobman. *I had the pleasure of meeting and working with Desi at the Hualapai Reservation in Peach Springs, Arizona. At the time Desi had not been exposed to Health Realization for very long, but his understanding was one of the deepest I'd experienced. He "lives the Principles" better than most, because he sees it so spiritually. I interviewed him at the West Virginia University-sponsored conference on the three Principles in Pittsburgh in June, 2001.*

JP: What were you like before you got involved in this understanding?

DS: [laughs] Oh man! That is a great question! Before I got into this understanding I was quite a lost person. I was an alcoholic. More than an alcoholic, I was a cocaine addict. More than that, I was a crack addict. I thought I was a product of my past. I am 6'1" and I eventually came down to about 115 pounds, if you can imagine that [laughs]. I have this picture that I used to bring to talks that I'd do, because people wouldn't believe it. It's the eyes. If you look at my eyes in this picture, my eyes show someone who is scared and lost and angry and filled with negative emotions and negative feelings, insecure. I was going to be going to jail for an assault charge. By the end of it I had lost my job, lost most of my friends—thought I had friends, but they weren't really my friends, they were just people I could pretend to be friends with or hang out with just so I could get more cocaine. I was very lucky and fortunate because I have an older brother who let me stay at his place, because I was living on his couch [laughs]. Do you want the reason why I felt I was like that?

JP: Yes. Absolutely.

DS: Like I said, I thought I was a product of my past. And being First Nations, my past is that I was taken away from my parents when I was two years old and placed in White foster homes until I was about six. So about four years of that, me and my brother suffered a lot of physical abuse and mental abuse, spiritual, the whole kind of deal, you know? And it didn't matter which foster home we went into—we were in several different foster homes, and in every single foster home we were abused. It was almost an everyday thing.

JP: Every day? Wow!

DS: Every day, yeah. I have certain flashes of other things as well, like being put in a crib on top of a table, and I'm two or three years old, and they are trying to potty-train me, so they want me to go to the bathroom at nighttime. Now, how the heck is a three-year-old supposed to get out of a crib that is on top of a table and get to the bathroom? So of course I'd wet the bed, and then the next day—I just remember this—they would bring in the whole family and friends, and I remember them

283

standing around and laughing and pointing at me and saying, "Ah, this kid wets his bed, and now he's three and he should be potty-trained—

JP: That's incredible.

DS: Things like that, yeah. I always had this nightmare. I remember I would be in this kitchen, kind of, and there would be all these women, all these Native women standing around, and all of a sudden someone from behind me would take my hand and start pulling me away from them, so I would start screaming. And I remember grabbing onto one of those islands in the kitchen, and as I grabbed onto that they actually had me off the floor, so I was being lifted up by my legs, hanging onto this counter. And when I met my family, I realized that this wasn't a dream. It was a memory. Because those ladies that were standing around were my aunts, and that is when the social worker was taking us away from our parents. So that was a bit of the past. And I was pretty much living that when I drank. I would become violent. It was like continuing the cycle. I would just become very violent and very angry, or when I would smoke crack I'd become very mentally abusive, and I would say things and do things to intentionally hurt people, and steal, and the whole thing—

JP: What kind of feeling level were you living in at that time?

DS: Oh man! I had no concept of what a good feeling was. I had no idea. Even when I was adopted there was no trust, absolutely no trust. Because me and my older brother pretty much thought that every big person is out to hurt you. So you just be quiet. You don't do anything. You sit there and just shut up and don't say anything. You don't ask for anything. You just be very quiet and try to be ignored, in a sense. And that kind of feeling kept on with me—except when I'd drink, where all that memory and all those feelings and anger would come out. I was at a very low level, a low state.

JP: What kind of violence are we talking about?

DS: Oh, like beating up people, or just freaking out on friends—family, even. Just going out and smashing cars and stuff like that. Very angry. We used to do things like that.

JP: Were you involved in any Native traditions at that time?

DS: No. And the interesting part about that is, for being Native I was very ashamed. And I think that's another thing the foster homes taught me. I wasn't proud at all of who I was. In fact I was very ashamed, and I wished I wasn't Native. I wished I was a White person. And my thinking in that was that maybe my life would be different, you know?

JP: Just for the record, where were you growing up and what was the tribe?

DS: I am Anishnabe. That is Ojibwe, from Thunder Bay, Ontario. That is where I was born and spent the first two years of my life. And from there it was all over Ontario, until I was adopted.

JP: So how did your life start turning around?

DS: That is another very beautiful question, because when I was, I think, twenty-one, a friend of mine's mom passed away from cancer, and she asked me to come over there and just be with her and kind of hang out. So I went over there. And she had invited this other friend of hers, Jen Wallace. And when we met it was so funny because it was such a quiet thing. I was so shy and insecure that I

284

didn't really say anything, and she was kind of shy as well so she didn't really say anything. But something kind of happened there, so we started hanging out. And one day her and our friend were in the kitchen, and they were washing dishes, and I was sitting at that kitchen table, and I happened to look over at her. And she had this golden aura around her. It was beautiful! It really blew me away to see that. I had never ever seen that before. And somehow the thought came, "I have to be with this person!" For some reason I felt very compelled to be with this person. So a little while after that I asked her if she would date me, and she said, "No." [laughs] And the funny part about that is that normally when somebody would say no, being the insecure person I was, I would be, like, "Whoa, okay, I'm out of here," and never in contact again. But with her it was so much different. I felt so compelled to be with her that I asked her four different times [laughs]. She said no all four times. Finally she ended up asking me. So next what happened was her parents wanted to meet me, and that scared the heck out of me because I was really insecure—

JP: You were still addicted at this time?

DS: Well, no, actually. I was an alcoholic. I wasn't addicted to cocaine at this time. I just drank a lot. This is very interesting because after that I met her parents and at that time also I was charged with assault. I don't want to get too much into detail about the assault charge. I was kind of wrongly accused. It wasn't me, but I was there. [laughs] But, the reason why I am saying I was going to jail is because I was so insecure that, because of my past I would have just sat there in court and said, "Okay, I did it, yeah, okay."—just so I wouldn't have to talk. Because I knew that I wasn't able to defend myself in any way.

So back to meeting Jen's parents. When I met them I walked up the stairs, and I walked over, and Jen's mom was lying on the couch, and she looks up and smiles at me with this incredible smile. The way she looked at me, I was just kind of taken aback because all of a sudden I felt this feeling inside of me, like a feeling that I could remember wanting back when I was two, like this feeling of non-judgment and love and unconditional love. Right away that is what blew me away. The love in the look she gave me, whoa, just blew me away, because I am used to people seeing the outside and the fear in my eyes, so they react to that. But she didn't do that. And then her dad came home, and the same thing! We just started talking, and that was the first time—because they had this feeling it opened me up, and then I was able to instantly feel comfortable with them, which was something that I never, ever felt before as well. So I ended up really wanting to hang out with them a lot because they had this beautiful feeling, and how do I get that? Or how do I do that? And they started telling me about Sydney Banks, who they were friends with. And eventually they started telling me about Thought. And we had these amazing conversations. And I must have heard something because I got to my court case, and I stood up for myself and I was acquitted. Because really there was no evidence. There was really nothing. It was amazing. I had grown a little bit, enough to hear something, and I was able to stand up for myself in court and not be so insecure. Still, all the while I was still drinking and I was still an alcoholic, so—

JP: Before you go there, what year are we talking about?

DS: Eight years ago, so 1992 or 1993.

JP: And where were you at this point?

DS: I was in Richmond, which is a suburb of Vancouver, in British Columbia, in Canada.

JP: So how did you kick cocaine?

DS: [laughs] That is actually the thing that is going to come up next. What happened next is funny because I realized that this understanding is so much deeper than the words we're using. Even though I thought I had this understanding, and even though I caught a glimmer of something that I've always wanted, I ended up getting addicted to cocaine. I started hanging around the wrong crowd again. And Jen and me, we kind of separated in a sense. Like she was exploring herself in her world, and I kind of went off into this cocaine world. It started off with just snorting coke, and my friend—or who I thought was my friend—showed me how to make crack cocaine. And so I got into that. And, whoa, that was an interesting time. Going over to people's houses, and there's lots of women. It is a whole lifestyle, and it is a very weird sexual kind of lifestyle. Yeah, I got addicted to it, and slowly I started losing weight. I would say I was 130 pounds before I started doing cocaine. If I wasn't smoking crack then I was shooting it in my arms. So I was stuck in that for about two years or so.

JP: So that was after you met Jen?

DS: Yeah, and the funny part about that, too, is that I had also gotten in contact with my family—my biological family—and so actually I went to Thunder Bay. I went back home and I met all my relations. I met all my cousins, my aunts and uncles and stuff. But people would say, "Oh, that is why you quit." No! Because when I was down there I found people that did cocaine, and I was still shooting up cocaine when I was down there, and I was still smoking crack. Really what happened was, I came back and I was talking with my younger brother, and I was telling him about this great understanding that I had [laughs] that I knew. And I go through the whole thing about Thought and everything. And he turns around and looks at me, and he goes, "You know, Des, that sounds really great, but when are you going to start living that?" And I said, "Whoa! Holy, man, he's right!" And that is when I learned that it is more than the words. You can talk this until you are blue in the face, but if you are not living it then it is just words; it is not anything to realize or anything. You've just got this kind of spiel, and you say it, and if you are not living it and you don't understand it, then it's just like any other words out there. That, for me, was very powerful. And right after that there was a Sydney Banks conference, and I went to that one.

JP: You hadn't met him yet?

DS: No. I went to that one, and a little while after that I was still thinking about cocaine. And I remember this one day—it was a beautiful day, and it was sunny, but I didn't have this good feeling inside me. I was thinking thoughts like, "Where am I going to get my next hit?" Or "Who can I pretend to be friends with so I can get more?" And the next morning I woke up, and I remember looking outside and thinking, "It *is* a beautiful day!" And for me that phrase has so much power. Because all of a sudden I was filled up with this incredible feeling of gratefulness to be alive, to look outside and have this beautiful feeling inside me—that it hadn't left me, you know? And that was the beautiful part. It was like all the things that I had talked about, all of a sudden they kind of sunk in. But it wasn't a conscious thing. They [the Principles] just realized all of a sudden. And it was just kind of a flow of insights into my past, and into what the past is, and into what the moment is, and into feeling and into Thought, and all of a sudden that was it! I was cured! And I didn't have any withdrawal. I didn't *want* to drink. I didn't have any thoughts any more about doing crack. In fact, what I did was enroll in school, and I finished off my counseling degree. It was just a complete three-sixty to a higher level. It was amazing. It was amazing! The amazing part was, because I had these insights the feeling stayed. Because these insights helped me and they came from inside me, and I knew that they were real! How could I not believe that! You know what I mean? It was amazing.

JP: Do you remember what some of these insights were?

DS: Well, the biggest one was the past—understanding really deeply where the past is really coming from, and what the past really is. And I realized how the past was affecting me, and I was letting it. I realized that, yeah, the past is sure in my mind, and it's got these feelings and emotions with it, but then I realized what these feelings and memories were.

JP: Which is?

DS: Which is thoughts. I realized that they were just my thinking. And when I realized that, it was, "Whoa, it's not real any more! *These people aren't hurting me any more! In fact I'm hurting myself in memory of that!*" I thought, "Whoa, what the heck have I been doing all this time?" It is such a beautiful thing. I realized living in the moment. I realized what the past is, and the past isn't real. I have heard so many times before that the past makes you realize who you are, but I realized that's not true. Because if only the moment exists—is real in this reality—and only in this moment, we actually have a choice. Then I can choose how I want to feel. I can choose not to take that path, not to take those thoughts, and just let them go. Because that is all they are, is just thoughts.

I also realized innocence, I realized forgiveness, forgiving. I realized here I was living in this low level of consciousness, unaware of the fact that it was my thinking, unaware that I had a choice, and I didn't have to go there. *I had the power and the gift inside of me to create a beautiful world, to create my reality, to create how I want to experience life.* I didn't know that. So I realized innocence. I realized that those people in the past that abused me are in the same state of mind I was in when I was drinking and a crack addict. *They're in the same low level of consciousness, unaware of the fact that it is their own thinking creating it.* When I realized that, I realized compassion, I realized innocence. And when I got that feeling it just empowered me so much more. These were the big ones that really helped me. And I realized the power of Thought, and I also realized the powerlessness of thought. I realized the neutrality of Thought.

JP: What do you mean when you say that?

DS: What I mean is that thinking, or thoughts, are neutral—*until* we give them action, *until* we give them power and take those thoughts into reality and put energy into them and make those thoughts real. So, the way I saw it was, a thought could be very powerful, or it can be powerless—depending on our choice of how we want to live. A thought is neutral, but it is powerful or powerless, and that is something that I realized, too.

JP: That's like a thought about a thought, right?

DS: Yeah! [laughs] And like I said before, the phrase came to me that it *is* a beautiful day. And that was the biggie for some reason—the biggest insight that I ever had. Because when I looked outside, that is what I saw. From then on, that is how I see life now. It is a beautiful day out—

JP: No matter what the weather is.

DS: No matter what the weather is! No matter what's going on around me. I realized that our gifts, the gift that we have inside of ourselves, is the power of creation. It doesn't matter what is going around outside of us. All that matters is our inside, is how are we going to react to these things, and we have a choice in it. Whoa, yeah!

JP: What year was this insight of yours?

DS: That was probably about five years ago.

JP: So that was 1997 or something like that?

DS: Yeah. And another thing that happened after that was I started realizing a lot about culture. I started meeting other Anishnabe people—and again, life is set up for us to grow. It is set up for us to gain a higher level of consciousness, a higher level of awareness. There are things out there that happen to us, opportunities that come, and if we take these opportunities then they will help us because that is what they are there for. I've met a few Anishnabe people, and they started teaching me things about the culture. It was funny because it seems to go up in levels as well. I met this other guy first and he gave me this gift of an abalone shell and an eagle feather, and that is what we use in our smudge ceremony. And that is a cleansing ceremony, a cleansing of the spirit and the mind of negative energies with medicines, and we burn the medicines and we take the smoke and wash it over ourselves and cleanse ourselves. So I learned that, and when I learned that I realized the truth behind that, and how doing that smudge ceremony actually is putting us in a quiet mind, because it is a preparation for prayer ceremony, because it is putting us in touch with The Creator, and ourselves, and opening that up into prayer. And prayer for me is just a silent mind, thinking really good thoughts about other people and wishing and hoping and praying for good things to happen for other people. And that is a quiet mind, for me.

And then from there I met this other guy who is still my teacher now, and he has been teaching me so much about the culture. And a lot of the stuff he is telling me I'm realizing is very beautiful because if you are listening for his words, for what he is teaching, then you miss it. But if you get what he is really saying underneath, you go, "Whoa," and you just grow.

I have been hearing a lot of teachings and realizing the truth in our culture, there's truth in it. This whole understanding, of prevention—of the whole thing—is in there. Our elders talk it. It's been our ancestors' teachings. It is amazing! And now I have such appreciation, and I am very proud to be Anishnabe. I am very proud to be who I am. I am very proud to be Native. I look around and I see other Native people walking down the streets, and a lot of them have their heads down. And I remember walking around like that; maybe I was walking around in shame. Now I walk with my head up and look up, and I feel like saying, "Be proud of who you are," and just sharing that. [long pause]

JP: When you are saying that the teachings that you are learning and this understanding are connected—can you say something about the connection?

DS: Yeah. Well, I realized the connection when I started attending ceremonies. And what I realized was that when we go to our ceremonies—just like in any other culture when you go to the church or something—when we go to ceremonies we gather together and we laugh and we get a great feeling. And we share and communicate and we dance and really celebrate and just have a great time. But when we leave the ceremony, it's like we go right back to our thinking again, right back to our habitual thinking. And I realized that these ceremonies, like the smudge ceremony and the sweat lodge and the Pow Wows and all these things are reminders for us. They were given to us to remind us to keep that feeling. When we go to these ceremonies it is a reminder for us to keep that feeling going, but we have lost that, we have forgotten that, but this is what the elders have been talking about. They have such beautiful words. Really, what they say is, look for the teachings. Elders, they *know*—just like this understanding—if you get a teaching from something, that teaching is coming from inside you, and it is a hundred times more powerful than if they were to tell you. Because they can't really tell you what the teaching is. Because it comes from inside, and they knew that, so they couldn't give you a teaching but they could say look for it. Again, they can guide you with words but that's all. Because the power of the gift is inside of us. So that is something else that I realized, too, is that there are many teachings out there, and what they are saying is that there are many, many insights out there for growth.

In our culture, in the wintertime was our time of gathering together the small families and separating and going off, but every family would have a group of elders, within their grandparents, and the wintertime was our time of learning and growth and sharing the culture. It was a time of storytelling. So every night they would gather together after dinner and the elders would start telling stories. But the neat thing about it was that they would tell the same stories that they told the year before, and the same stories that they told the year before that. But the interesting part about that is that the generations, the young children who hear the story, they hear something out of it, they get something from it, maybe something very simple and small, but they get something from it. The people who heard it last year, the older ones like the teenagers, they hear it again, but they catch something else from it this time, and go, "Ohhh," and get more from the story. The adults who hear the story go, "Whoa," because they get something different from the year before too, and it's a continual growth. They get the teachings from these stories that we tell, and it is a beautiful way to pass it on without giving a teaching, yet the teaching is in there. The teaching is beyond the words, and again that's exactly like this understanding.

There is a very beautiful teaching that for me really relates with this understanding, and that is the teaching of our wingashk, what we call sweet grass. The teaching is in the braid of it, because it is a braided piece of sweet grass. It's like a long kind of grass and we braid it together, and it's a very sacred medicine. We use it in our smudge ceremonies. And the truth is in the braid, because what it is is three different strands to make one braid. So one strand represents mind, one represents spirit, and one represents body, and when these are braided together they form one, and they all become the same. And that is the same with this understanding, is Mind, Thought and Consciousness—three seemingly different elements but all the same, all talking about the same thing. So for me, that was very powerful.

JP: What do you see is the connection between the three Principles themselves and the Native teachings? Like, Mind is comparable to—

DS: Oh, yeah. Okay. [pause] You know, I don't think that I can explain that. That is a really deep question. [laughs] For some reason it is like the Principles are working within the culture. The Principles are the basis of our culture, and we have built this culture around the three Principles, coming from it. This was our way of describing the Truth. That is the only way I could describe that, but that is a very deep question. [laughs]

JP: So what is your inner life like now?

DS: It is beautiful. Every time I share this understanding I just grow more and more. Because every time I share it I look around and look in people's eyes, and I see the Truth inside them, and I see they are seeing the Truth inside them as well—even if it is only a glimmer. And for me, that makes it so much more a fact. So when I know that it's a fact, I grow more. And I *am* living it now. I live this good feeling, and I realize that there is no reason not to [laughs]. It's like a lot of people in this understanding say that it's okay to wait in the stillness, and the feeling or the thought will pass and they will come into a good feeling again. But for me it is like, "Well that's just a thought"— that's *all*, and that is the *only* thing that is stopping me from being in my good feeling. And I know that. I truly know now what a good feeling is. I know this sounds really simple, but it is beyond the words, it is coming from a deeper understanding, a deeper level. So when I know that, I recognize a negative thought now coming, and I go, "Whoa, I don't have to go there. I am going to stay right in my good feeling." And it is having faith in that. And that is kind of where I am at today is living that good feeling, and trying to more and more live in that good feeling all the time. And for now, that is my goal, to achieve that. And it's a very realistic goal, because it truly is a Thought-created world, and it's our gift to do that. We have that power inside of us to do that. That is kind of where I am at now. My life is beautiful. People in my life are beautiful. Everybody I meet—and the elders tell us this, too—people are put in your path in life because you are to learn something from them, and they are to learn something from you. And then when you have learned that, you kind of go on. It's like I see that, and I do that. So I'm constantly growing and learning and really living this understanding and hearing a lot of Truth, and getting insights and sharing it.

This understanding is true prevention. Because this client asked me this question one time. He couldn't get his head around how I quit drinking and crack in just one day. He couldn't understand that. So he goes, "Okay, okay, let's take alcohol. I don't understand how you cannot say that you are not an alcoholic any more." Because in Alcoholics Anonymous they are constantly told that they are alcoholic, so they start believing that. He is kind of coming from that way. So he goes, "Okay, okay, what if you were to walk into a bar, order yourself a drink, now could you have that one alcohol drink and not have anymore?" And so I thought about the question, and I thought about it some more, and I realized I couldn't answer it. And I said, "I'm sorry but I can't answer your question." And he thought he had me there, right? But then I said, "And the reason is because I've never had the thought. *I've never had the thought of drinking again." And that is true prevention!* Because his question was coming from where I use to be at, and I'm at a different level now, it is impossible for me to think that way. I don't even have those thoughts any more—I can't. It is impossible. With this understanding it is true prevention because you don't even think the thoughts any more. It is amazing! [laughs].

JP: So once you had this understanding, you started using it as a counselor?

DS: Yeah, what I did was I went back to school when I got the understanding. I realized, "I've got to make changes. I've got to make some dreams come true." So I went in and I finished off my counseling degree. I am a Family Community Counselor now. I had this understanding while I was in school. And it was an incredible experience in school, because my professors were just blown away by me. Like, at the end of the year the program coordinator—she was also one of our professors as well—she was taking the students into her office and kind of interviewing them, and giving them last minute advice before we graduated. And my turn came up and I walked into her office, and I sat down on the couch and she sat down on a chair next to me, and she looked at me and she said, "You know, I have no idea what to say to you. The stuff you've written has completely altered my thinking." She was blown away. Like, she actually asked me, she says to me, "Are you Jesus?"

JP: You're kidding, right?

DS: No. She said, "Are you Jesus?" And I said, "No!" But I said, "That's what I have been trying to say, what we're talking about is Christ Consciousness, and it's something available to you, and it's something available to everybody." So I was really lucky because I had this understanding so I survived this school experience. A lot of my classmates didn't. We had a large class of about thirty or so students, and in the end I think fifteen or sixteen graduated. Unfortunately it was because of the psychology—the traditional psychology. With a lot of Native people, it is definitely our past, our immediate past, even our ancestor's past, that we've let affect us. So without this understanding, without this shield in a sense, without this prevention, they became victims of their own thinking. And unfortunately they couldn't handle it and ended up dropping out. Or other things happened in their family or something like that.

JP: And when did you start talking with other people as a group? Was it the first time that we—

DS: Yeah, the first time—okay, I did my practicum with the Selah group, and the Selah group is in West Vancouver in British Columbia—very sweet ladies. And every last Thursday of the month we do a talk. So I would do talks every now and then with them. But the best experience I had was when you asked me to come and do that talk with you guys. I mean, that was, for me—whoa! Here I am, this counselor, and these psychologists are asking me to come and present with them! It was such a beautiful experience. I was so grateful for you guys to—[emotional pause; tears came to eyes]—it really started me. Yeah, it was our talk when you had invited me to come and share with you guys with the Hualapai in Arizona, and I was so honored to do that. Wow! [emotional pause] And for me that was my first real teaching or sharing this. And it was such a great experience working with you guys that I just realized, "I've got to do this!" This is what I've got to do! I've got to continue doing this." So that's what I am doing, and I know that this is the way to do it. This is my path.

There's a lot of things in my life that, before even, like when I was eighteen years old, I was working in this warehouse, and I was with my co-worker and we were putting stuff up on the shelf. And all of a sudden he stops, and he kind of points with his head behind me. So I turn around, and there is this girl standing behind me. And the first thing she said, she goes, "Are you Ojibwe?" This is before I knew Jen. And I said, "Yeah." And she goes, "Wow! I felt so compelled to come in here. I was just passing by, and I felt really compelled to come in here, and now that I see your face I know why. I have something to tell you." And I said, "Well, I'm kind of working right now and I've got to get stuff done." So I got her number, and I phoned her that night. And she goes, "My father is a medicine man, and in our culture it's passed down through family, that is how our medicine people keep passing it on, because it's our clan totem." That is how they work. So she was gaining the knowledge from her father, and she said, "I have this dream. And in this dream, you were in it. But your hair was braided, and you looked a little bit different. You are suppose to lead people." And then she goes, "What do you want me to do? Can you lead me?" And I was, like, "Whoa! I mean, I'm drinking all the time. I'm hardly taking care of myself. How can I lead people?" So I hung up and never talked to her again.

And when I got my name, Gray Wolf, I got it in a dream, and I went to the elder and asked him to interpret the dream for me. And what he came out with is, "It is the ancestors giving you the name Gray Wolf." And he says, "That is a very powerful name. Because gray means wise. And the wolf is a leader. So your name means 'wise leader.'" So again, my life is showing me something. All my experiences have been preparing me for this. And here I am today, and I know how to braid my hair, and I do look completely different. It is because I have this understanding. I have this great feeling inside of me. And that's what we're all after. Everybody! Everything. Psychology. Mental health. Psychiatry. Culture. Religion. Every human being is after this one thing, and this one thing is a good feeling. That's our connection, and I think that thought is the connector between everything.

JP: You know what feeling I just got?

DS: What?

JP: There is no stopping you now!

DS: [laughs] There isn't.

XXI. SPECULATION: SCIENTIFIC BASIS FOR HOW THE FORMLESS COMES INTO FORM: ONE PERSON'S VIEW OF WHAT SOME OF THE LITERATURE SUGGESTS

The following is purely a speculative piece. It would never be accepted by most scientists. Nor is it necessary for understanding what is needed to improve one's life; it may even complicate matters unnecessarily, as most of what follows is after the fact (of the formless). Given all that, why do I include it? Because some people will find this possibility fascinating, as I do. My suggestion for reading this chapter is, if you find yourself getting into your head too much and losing the feeling, skip it and move to the next (the last) chapter.

I did not make up any of what follows. Every single part of it came from some other source. What I did do—and what perhaps makes it unique—is that I put it all together from pieces gathered from many different sources. I had been reading most of this seemingly disparate material for my doctoral study, and one day it all came together for me in a flash of inspiration. At that time only one piece seemed missing. That came a couple of months later when I discovered the work of energy scientist Valerie Hunt. Amazingly, this picture came together of how formless energy does come into form and manifest in the human body.

It would be wonderful if the scientific community took this "theory" of how the formless comes into form within human beings and conducted studies to see whether it could be proven true, or to prove parts of it false. Some of it likely will never be able to be proven either way. This does not make it untrue. I would call what follows "highly plausible."

It also provides some evidence for a quasi-scientific justification of the three Principles.

It was Carl Gustav Jung (1951) who predicted,

> Sooner or later, nuclear physics and the psychology of the unconscious will draw closer together as both of them, independently of one another and from opposite directions, push forward into transcendental territory... Psyche cannot be totally different from matter, for how otherwise could it move matter? And matter cannot be alien to psyche, for how else could matter produce psyche? Pscyhe and matter exist in the same world, and each partakes of the other, otherwise any reciprocal action would be impossible. If research could only advance far enough, therefore, we should arrive at an ultimate agreement between physical and psychological concepts. Our present attempts may be bold, but I believe they are on the right lines. (p.359)

To look within is a direction still largely untapped by science. Yet, science has provided some clues about the nature of what we call "reality." Sydney Banks (1998) asserts that it is possible for us to realize the inside-out nature of human experience. In so doing, we gain a handle on life that has heretofore been elusive.

It has already been reported that Banks came to this understanding through a spiritual epiphany he claims to have had. In other words, he did not deduce this; he *saw* it. Should the rest of us simply take his word for it? Or can any evidence be found within the broad realm of science that these underlying Principles actually do work together to create our experience, and, if so, how does it all work? This brings us to an exploration of how formless energy becomes manifest in form within human beings and thus affects lives.

Biologist Edward O. Wilson (1998) posits that a "webwork of causal explanation" can be found from quantum physics to the brain sciences. We only cannot see this all now because of gaps in our scientific knowledge. But it is attainable and profoundly important. Scientists have attempted to peer into the farthest reaches of the cosmos and reduce matter to its smallest possible particles (Lederman, 1994). All this substantive, tangible stuff can be seen or measured with the most precise of instruments, and is thus considered worthy of study, for it is a study of so-called "reality."

Mainstream science has not explored the opposite direction with as much vigor: the inner world of Mind and Consciousness and Thought, and the possible realm of "spirit." The field has found it difficult to take this direction seriously because it is so intangible and appears immeasurable. We must remember, however, that in the 19th Century mainstream science ignored surgeon Ignaz Semmelweis's pleas for doctors to wash their hands so their patients would not contract fevers and die. They scoffed and laughed at him because without any knowledge at the time of the existence of germs, his observations seemed to make no sense. Yet, as neuroscientist Candace Pert (1997) states, "absence of proof is not proof of absence" (p. 222). She reminds us, "Whenever something doesn't fit the reigning paradigm, the initial response in the mainstream is to deny the facts" (p. 162). Now, without scientific proof of a formless inner world, much of 21st Century mainstream science scoffs at the notion.

However, science may not know all there is to know about reality. Physicist Fritjof Capra (1997) insists that science always deals with limited and approximate descriptions of reality. Energy scientist Valerie Hunt (1996) states, "Classical concepts of reality have focused upon secondary manifestations—the unfolded aspect of things, not their source" (p. 51). Wilson (1998) speaks of "the humbling recognition that reality is not easily grasped by the human mind" (p. 31). Then he steps further: "...it is an empirical question that can be answered only by a continuing probe of the physical basis of the thought process itself" (p. 64).

The physical basis of thought!? This profound idea implies that thought makes something happen or is at least part of some process that results in physical form.

Evidence suggests that "reality" is not what it seems. For example, a table appears solid to us, yet if we examined it under a very powerful microscope and were able to see the atom, we would see that it is almost empty space (Bohm, 1994). This is an amazing enough concept to try to grasp, but suppose we had an even more powerful microscope and were able to actually see an electron. We might find that there is nothing at all to "see"—that it is merely a bundle of wave energy. Einstein proved that matter was simply another form of energy, but at the quantum physics level it appears that there may be no real separation between the two. Deepak Chopra (1990) states, "if you zero in on …bits of subatomic matter, they are not material at all but rather mere vibrations of energy that have taken on the appearance of solidity… Thus, matter is a fluctuation of energy dressed in a different guise" (p. 132).

Perhaps even more unfathomable, the further we probe in the direction of the subatomic world, just as we think we are about to isolate the essential building blocks of matter, sometimes we find particles and sometimes we find wave energy, and what we find depends on what we are looking for and how we look (Lederman, 1994), and whichever we find is a matter of probability (Wilson, 1998). This is because "at the quantum level of matter, things don't exist until they are observed" (Hunt, 1996, p. 41). It is all a matter of perspective.

Thus, it appears we form a constructed representation of reality that only makes us *think* it is solid. Quantum physicist David Bohm (1994) says it is "crucial" to see that "the representation affects the perception," and it is a "tremendous source of illusion" if we lose track of the fact that this is happening (p.110).

A "solid" object is an illusion of our minds? We only see it that way? And we would swear it's real! Bohm likens it to a television image, which is really nothing but a bunch of dots of light on a screen. If we looked closely we would see nothing but flashing lights. Instead, we see people, trees, characters, emotional conflicts, people in danger, anger, fear, pleasure. But we have essentially made it up from our thought interpreting the dots. Our imagination becomes infused onto the dots on the screen. What we experience in looking at television "must come from something like the imagination." (p.160).

How thought enters perception is becoming a bit more clear. Our thoughts get infused into all perception, just as our imagination gets infused with the TV image. Physicist Gary Zukav (1989) asserts that at each moment we are informing the energy that flows through us with each thought. Thus, through our thinking we infuse our imagination, our past, our knowledge, into everything we see. We don't know whatever we see is through the filters of our own thoughts.

What we have been missing, Bohm (1994) says, is that thought actually participates in perception. He states that while thought is continually affecting whatever we see, it *appears to be simply telling us the way things are*. We assume what we see is true. Thought does not tell us it is participating in and altering the very way things *are*. The information we receive through this filter then takes over and runs us. "Thought…is taking part in everything" (p. 5).

> …thought produces something which seems to be outside, and it doesn't notice that
> it is doing so. That's one of the basic mistakes. Thought produces something and
> says, "I didn't produce it. It's really there" (Bohm, 1994, p. 25).

Thus, the system of Thought has a built-in fault. When we bring thought to bear on a problem, we don't realize that thought is part of the system and therefore part of the problem. "It has the same fault as the fault I'm trying to look at…" (Bohm, 1994, p.19). Thought can produce experiences without our being aware they are produced by thought.

Descartes reasoned that the only bedrock statement he could make with absolute certainty, and from which all subsequent reason sprung, was, "I think, therefore I am." Without thought we would not exist. As with breathing, thinking is the most fundamental aspect of a human being. Thus, life and cognition are inseparably connected. Mind, or mental process, is imminent in matter at all levels of life. Mental activity appears to be the organizing activity of living systems at all levels of life (Capra, 1997).

Science-mathematician Sir James Jeans asserts that the mathematical pictures of nature disclosed by science are fictitious and do not represent ultimate reality. He concludes the world is more like a thought system than material reality (in Hunt, 1996). All we can perceive are illusions of the real world.

> [The universe is]...a unified network of events and relationships in which the mind and intelligence and then human soul are integral parts of existence, rather than products of nature... Many physicists believe it to be a fundamental event beyond physics—an act of consciousness and thought... As Jahns and Dunne put it, physical theory is not complete until consciousness is acknowledged as an active element in the establishment of reality (Hunt, 1996, pp. 47-50).

Thus, Consciousness is added to the picture. Without Consciousness, it appears we would never be able to experience the results of our thinking; we would never even be aware we were thinking in the first place. Zukav (1989) asserts that a thought is energy shaped by consciousness. Since no form exists without consciousness, there is only energy, or light, and there is the shaping of light by consciousness. This is creation. Perhaps it is the opposite: Thought gives shape to Consciousness. However, this may be only a matter of semantics because the two are inexorably intertwined, bound together, inseparable.

A system is an integrated whole whose essential properties arise from the relationships between its parts (Capra, 1997). Each of us is a living system. In summary, then, the human system appears to be propelled by its most fundamental property: *Thought*. Thought is somehow inextricably linked with Consciousness. "Reality" is not what it seems, precisely because Thought enters perception, without knowing it is doing so, and alters whatever we perceive.

We now turn to how this system seems to work to create what we see as "reality," and how it actually converts what appears to begin as formless energy into physical form.

The System of Thought into Form

After reviewing works cited below from particle physics, quantum physics, neuroscience, brain research, biology, energy science, health science, transpersonal psychology and the study of Consciousness, the conceptualization of a whole system began to unveil. What follows—the detailed breakdown of the system of how the formless comes into form within human beings—is a postulation based on this evidence. The components of this system appear to be:

1. a human being makes contact with the outside world;
2. formless Thought intercedes in such way that we can never know outside "reality,"
3. which likely occurs through the intersection or interaction between energy fields,
4. which is then picked up by our senses,
5. which then moves the molecules in our sense organs,
6. which then communicate with other molecules via Mind,
7. which stimulates cellular changes within the body;
8. simultaneously, a signal is sent to the brain,

9. where a second level of thought intercedes, which interprets what the organism sees or feels,
10. which stimulates other chemical changes in the brain and body,
11. which are experienced as an emotion or a mood or other feeling;
12. these affect a third level of thought that creates an intention where we decide what we are going to do about that experience,
13. which leads to behavior,
14. which affects the world "out there" and gives us a result in return,
15. which triggers the entire system to begin again so we can experience the result.

This is not to suggest that a specific transaction of this system works in so precise and orderly a fashion, because the movement of molecules and the electrical impulses that travel to and from the brain are completely diverse, simultaneous operations. This system does suggest how its components generally work to create what we experience as "reality." We then respond or react to the "reality" we create.[24]

1) A human being makes contact with the outside world

Logically, a person must somehow make contact with or interact with the world outside itself. It appears that the vehicle through which this contact is made is through our five—some would say six—senses, but what follows shows this is not so simple as it seems.

2) Formless Thought intercedes in such a way that we can never know outside "reality"

Contrary to popular opinion, thought informs the senses, not the other way around (Pransky, G., 1998). How can this be? Here are four possible views of how this might occur:

Reality Therapy psychologist William Glasser collaborated with scientist William T. Powers to offer one plausible explanation (Glasser, 1981). They posited that the only contact it is possible to have with the outside world is through a primary level of perception they call "intensity." In other words, some intensity of light hits our eyeballs, or some intensity of sound hits our eardrums, or some intensity of touch hits our skin, but that is all we can possibly know of the real world because from that point on interpretation (thought) takes over. This happens before the next level of perception is activated, a level they call "sensation." Some kind of intensity makes contact with our sense organs, but by the time the signal makes its way to our brain so it can interpret that intensity, thought has already altered it, and it is altered differently depending on the different interpretations (thoughts) people have of it. Of the real world, they conclude, we can really know nothing. We can only know our own interpretation. Sensation is already affected by interpretation.

Candace Pert (1997) suggests another possibility. Pert discovered that a signal does not have to travel to and from the brain for *mind*[25] to intercede. As we shall see later, when the outside world interfaces with our senses, molecules in the sense organs begin to vibrate and

---

[24] To be of assistance in everyday living it is not necessary to understand the detail presented here; a general understanding of how the system works appears to be enough to help people's lives improve (as suggested throughout the rest of this book). Yet, the detail may be important for those seeking to better understand the relationships involved in the various interactive components of the total system.

[25] Pert and others do not capitalize "mind" nor "thought," so when I quote or paraphrase their words I will not do so either.

somehow communicate with other molecules in other parts of the body faster than a signal can even make its way to the brain. Pert refers to this phenomenon as *mind* at work. As this communication via mind is found to occur independent of the brain, mind must therefore be separate from the brain. Before the brain even becomes involved, mind is at work communicating at some imperceptibly deep level. The vehicle with which *Mind* communicates can be said to be *Thought*, at a level far beyond what most of us conceive of as "thought." Thus, something "out there" may strike our senses, but by the time it comes out the other side of our sense organs so the brain would be aware of it, Mind or Thought already has altered the picture.

At yet another level, we have all had the experience of not seeing something that another person sees; for example, when writing then thoroughly proofreading and being sure everything is correct, then someone finds a mistake, or we find one the next time we look. Why would this happen? Is it not out there in "reality?" Are not our eyes looking directly at it? Yet we can't see it. Some filtering system must exist. Pert states, "The decision about what sensory information travels to your brain and what gets filtered out depends upon what signals the receptors are receiving from the peptides." We will see later how this works. "There is a plethora of elegant neurophysiological data suggesting that the nervous system is not capable of taking in everything but scans the outer world for material that it is prepared to find by virtue of its wiring hookups, its own internal patterns and its past experience" (p. 147). For example, the superior colliculus in the midbrain controls the muscles that direct the eyeball and affects which images are permitted to fall on the retina and hence be seen. This sometimes leads to a failure to see things. So we may well have selective perception because of some screening at an imperceptibly subtle level of Thought.

Finally, Valerie Hunt (1996), who successfully measured the existence of energy fields around the human body, asserts that some form of thought actually exists within the energy field surrounding the body. In other words, thought comes into play within the energy field that surrounds us—before it even reaches the senses. This astonishing possibility will be examined later.

No matter which of these four possible explanations is true, it appears that Thought—at an exceptionally deep level—has already irreparably altered anything we can pick up from the outside world *before* we can experience it. Thus what we perceive does not come to us directly from our senses; what we perceive comes to us through Thought. When we react to anything in the outside world that we would swear we're picking up directly from our senses, we really are reacting to our Thought.

Wilson (1998) asserts that outside our heads there *is* a freestanding reality, but inside our heads is a reconstruction of that reality. Philosophical postmodernists go to the extreme and insist there is no real, outside reality at all; that reality is only a state constructed by the mind, not perceived by it (Searle, 1994). I would suggest this philosophic debate is of no consequence. Either way, we apparently perceive only our own thinking, not any "reality" out there at all—because we are incapable of perceiving any outside reality directly. All we can know of "reality" is "our own reality" we have constructed—most often inadvertently, perhaps—through our own very deep and subtle level of Thought.

Another expansion of this view was brought forth by Chilean neuroscientists Humberto Maturana and Francisco Varela in what became known as "The Santiago Theory." Maturana postulated that the nervous system is self-organizing and continually self-righting, and that perception cannot be viewed as the representation of an external reality but must be understood as the continual creation of new relationships within the neural network as it attempts to seek some kind of dynamic equilibrium. He said, "the activities of nerve cells do not reflect an environment independent of their living organism and hence do not allow for the construction of an absolutely existing external world" (in Capra, 1997, p. 96). Perception and cognition, then, do not represent an external reality but rather specify *a* "reality" through the nervous system's process of circular organization, which itself is identical to the process of cognition. Varela termed this process "autopoesis," meaning, "self-making."

The Santiago Theory takes issue with the general view that "cognition is a representation of an independently existing world," that "the world is pre-given and independent of the observer." Rather, it says that cognition is a "bringing forth of a world" (in Capra, 1997, p.270). What is brought forth in a particular organism in the process of living is not *the* world but *a* world that is always dependent upon the organism's structure. Since individual organisms within a species generally have the same structure, they bring forth similar worlds. Even within human beings' generally similar worlds, however, our different thoughts bring forth different worlds. Thus, the Santiago Theory asserts that "'no things exist' independent of the process of cognition." For example, biologists know that birds see trees very differently than humans because they perceive light in different frequency ranges. Thus "the world we bring forth depends on our own structure" (p.271).[26]

"There is no physical universe without our thoughts about it," concludes Hunt (1996, p. 44). Pert (1997) asserts, "there is no objective reality!" (p. 146). To both of these statements I would add, "at least not that we can ever know," which is the only thing that really counts in day-to-day life.

In sum, *Mind* apparently acts upon us at a profoundly deep level. It takes the world "out there" and somehow allows human beings to be capable of picking up only a representation of that "outside world." Thus, the outside world becomes transformed through an internal process. It appears that what the mind acts with is a profoundly deep level of *Thought*. I will refer to this as *Level I Thought*—thought that occurs at such depth and subtlety that it is almost imperceptible, yet it alters everything that we can possibly experience through our consciousness. It is so powerful that it alters the very "reality" we see; it alters everything that comes to us in any way through our senses. There are no adequate terms to describe Level I Thought; the best I could come up with is *protothought*—thought in the process of becoming (as protostars are stars in the process of coming to exist within the physical universe). It is possible we may not even be able to affect this level of Thought, except to know, or to realize, or to recognize it is always there operating within us and affecting everything we can possibly know.

---

[26] Wilson (1998) illuminates this by pointing out that visible light is not the sole illuminating energy of the universe. But "because the human retina is rigged to report only 400 to 700 nanometers, the unaided brain concludes that only visible light exists" (p. 46). Varela observes that consciousness is the manifestation of a particular cognitive process; technically, "the synchronization of rhythmically oscillating neural circuits" (in Capra, 1997, p. 293). Capra concludes that the brain is not necessary for mind to exist. The simplest organisms do not see but nevertheless perceive changes in their environment. With perception comes cognition. Perception, emotion, and action are all involved with and therefore part of cognition.

3) Contact occurs through the intersection or interaction between energy fields

So we have "the outside world," which we can never really know, and we can only know it through Thought. How does it actually work?

Scientists accept that the human body generates electricity because living tissue generates energy, but medical intuitive Carolyn Myss (1996) claims to have observed, empirically, literally, that "everything alive pulsates with energy" (p.33). Barbara Brennan (1987) says the same, in different terms. Hunt (1996) offers scientific evidence in support of Myss's and Brennan's claims from her study of energy fields surrounding human beings. She reminds us that the most profound changes in the conception of reality came from Einstein's Unified Field Theory, which states that "all matter is organized energy..." Though Einstein never lived to prove this theory, he stated that "the only reality is energy organized into fields. If all matter were disintegrated, we would be left with a field, the primary source" (in Hunt, 1996, p.88). Hunt concludes that this "field reality is one of the characteristics of the universe. The deeper one probes material systems, the more one encounters field aspects or the substances' underlying electrical pattern, the very basis of the substance itself" (p. 47). Whether this energy is constellated as a tree or a human being, it has a field associated with it. No firm boundaries exist between these fields; fields extend as an open system, free to evolve and grow. Hunt makes the bold assertion that the most important level to understand both the world and human beings is at the level of field transaction, and that a human's field is primary to his or her existence. Chopra (1990) corroborates this:

> [All objects we see around us are connected by] infinite, eternal, unbounded quantum fields, a kind of invisible quilt that has all of creation stitched into it... The hard edges of any object, such as a chair or table, are illusions forced upon us by the limits of our sight. If we had eyes tuned to the quantum world, we would see these edges blur and finally melt, giving way to unlimited quantum fields (p. 131).

Does the human energy field have any qualities attached to it? Hunt (1996) hypothesizes that the energy field is the highest level of the mind of man, and it is through this level that we interrelate with the cosmosphere. She reaches this conclusion because of the following:

> Mind has energy since it causes things to happen... Other experiences and capacities such as thought, insight, imagination, and soul seem to be properties of the higher mind... The higher level mind seems to be outside the domain of material reality as we have been able to measure it. The mind is more a field reality, a quantum reality, or a particle reality... Basically, reality is neither fact nor fiction but is the emphasis we place on various parts of our stream of consciousness. My starting point was accepting that consciousness is a continuum extending from material awareness to higher awarenesses. I also knew that the mind experiences by means of its awarenesses... It began to look as though energy field patterns were related to streams of consciousness—a function of the mind. Along this line we discovered that when a person's field reached higher vibrational states, he no longer experienced material things such as bodies and ego states, or the physical world. He experienced knowing, higher information, transcendental ideas, insight about ultimate sources of reality, and creativity in its pure form... (pp. 87-94)

Hunt quotes Kurt Lewin: "At the deepest level, all things are composed of vibrations organized into fields that permeate the entire structure" (p. 109). Hunt says, "Thoughts...are structured vibrations—some fleeting and others which are recorded and become permanent" (p. 99).

A field is flowing; it flows within itself, and it flows into other fields. Hunt measured human fields with scientific instruments and found them to be separate from mass. In the future, she says, "we will be able to decode fields in other ways where relationships and patterns of happenings will not be looked on as cause and effect but as part of the transition." The unique human field, she says, does not merely react or interact; it transacts because it dynamically makes choices. Thus, she concludes, "matter and energy, mind and spirit, are not really different things, only aspects of an expanded reality" (p.50). Not all fields, then, are connected to substance. Some fields are connected only to thoughts and are called "morphogenic fields." The science of field constellations is too young to provide adequate answers, but it does seem clear that we live in a sea of force fields all being absorbed and altered by the human mind (Hunt, 1996, p. 67).

When an electron spins around the nucleus of an atom, a magnetic field is created. Might it be that thoughts are somehow already flowing in and through and around the electromagnetic fields surrounding our bodies, without our having much or any control over them, and whatever *Mind* propels them is sending signals to our bodies and brains? This is a difficult point for me, because I cannot grasp its full meaning or implications. But if Hunt asserts thought already somehow exists within our electromagnetic fields, it seems imaginable that before anything from the outside is perceived by our senses, *Thought*—the means of communication of *Mind*—existing within our energy fields, has already altered it.

4) Which is then picked up by our senses

Thus far we have seen that some profoundly subtle and deep level of *Thought* from our energy field that we don't go out of our way to think apparently sends us signals of some kind that act as intermediary between the outside world and our senses. Whatever we see or hear or smell or touch or taste is what Thought brings us from an already interpreted outside world. According to Bohm (1994), our senses pick up a representation painted by these thoughts in the same way an artist paints a picture that represents somebody but isn't that somebody. The senses take in information that is limited by these thoughts.

Hunt (1996) says the sensory information we get from the material world is always filtered. She found that each field carries within it its own resonating frequency or vibratory signature "that determines the energy it will absorb or by which it will be affected..." (p. 65).

5) Which then moves the molecules in our sensory organs

Bohm (1996) says it is important to see thought as a movement, a moving of one thing to another. "It may move the body or the chemistry or just simply the image of something else" (p.122). What thought does, it seems, is begin to move some crucial molecules, first in our sensory organs. Bohm insists that thought is part of a material process. It goes on in the brain, the nervous system, and the whole body. "It is all and everything; it's all one system" (p. 147).

301

Thus, formless thought comes into form and begins to be transformed into material substance in our bodies. Deepak Chopra (1990) gives us some clues into how this might occur.

> Physics informs us that the basic fabric of nature lies at the quantum level, far beyond atoms and molecules. A quantum, defined as the basic unit of matter and energy, is from 10,000,000 to 100,000,000 times smaller than the smallest atom. At this level, matter and energy become interchangeable. All quanta are made of invisible vibrations—ghosts of energy—waiting to take physical form. Ayurveda says that the same is true of the human body—it first takes form as intense but invisible vibrations, called quantum fluctuations, before it proceeds to coalesce into impulses of energy and particles of matter (p. 7).

Hunt (1996) showed the vibrational interaction between energy fields is likely what makes the molecules in the senses begin to vibrate. These molecules that vibrate are biochemicals called neuropeptides, tiny pieces of protein that consist of a string of amino acids beaded together (Pert, 1997).

6) Which communicate with other molecules via mind

These vibrating neuropeptide molecules are called neurotransmitters or "messenger molecules" because they distribute information to neuropeptide receptors that exist throughout the organism. An especially high concentration of neuropeptide receptors exist in virtually all locations where information from any of the five senses—sight, sound, taste, smell, touch—enters the nervous system. They are designed to be accessed and modulated by almost all neuropeptides. *Neuropeptides travel throughout the body every time we have a thought* (Pert, 1997).

When the neuropeptide molecules in our sense organs begin to vibrate, they somehow immediately trigger a vibration in specific receptor molecules in other parts of the body. Pert's astonishing discovery was that these signals bypass the nerves and brain in a direct, two-way information exchange, communicating directly from molecule to molecule. These "information molecules" communicate with other molecules through "some kind of coded language via the mind-body network" (Pert, 1997, p. 256). This communication is at least part of what I am defining as *Level I Thought*.

How can this communication, this thought, happen without the brain's or the nervous system's involvement? Pert says this is "mind" at work. The mind is different from the brain. "Your mind is in every cell of your body," she said to interviewer Bill Moyers, "…there are many phenomena that we can't explain without going into energy" (in Myss, 1996, p.35).

> …we can see that there is an intelligence running things. It is not a matter of energy acting on matter to create behavior, but of intelligence in the form of information running all the systems and creating behavior. [This has been called]…the wisdom of the body. Chiropractors refer to it as the body's innate intelligence… (Pert, 1997, p.185).

This proved a shock to biological science. The body has a mind of its own that has nothing to do with the brain? The brain and nerves have nothing to do with this communication between molecules because it happens far too quickly to work through chemical or neural signal transmission (Hunt, 1996, p. 93). Hunt concludes that it must happen directly through the body's energy field at some sort of quantum level—literally via a quantum leap.

7) Which stimulates cellular changes within the body

Neuroscientists had commonly thought of the communication between neuropeptides and receptors as like a key fitting into a lock, but this does not appear to be so.

> ...it is more like two voices—ligand and receptor—striking the same note, producing a vibration, which rings the door bell, which leads to opening the doorway to the cell. The receptor, having received a message, transmits it from the surface of the cell deeper into the cell interior where the message can change the state of the cell dramatically. This leads to a chain reaction of biochemical events which can manufacture new proteins, cause cell divisions, open or close channels, etc. What the cell is up to at any moment is determined by which receptors are on the surface, and whether those receptors are occupied by ligands or not (Pert, 1997, p. 24).

Ligand means "that which binds"—any natural or human-made substance that binds to its own specific receptor on the surface of the cell. Cells are constantly signaling other cells through the release of neuropeptides that bind with receptors through some sort of "feedback loop" (Pert, 1997). Pert says this is an inborn system of internal checks and balances that provides a relatively constant state of homeostasis within the body.

Thus the communication between molecules actually produces chemical changes in the cells. We sometimes experience these chemical changes as emotions or moods, which we will explore in "step" 11 because, simultaneously, a parallel process occurs.

Before going there, a review of *Level I Thought* is in order. Level I *protothought* might be seen as an extremely subtle level of "intelligent" energy that affects what we initially see or experience through any of our senses. At its primary depth this includes the most subtle communications of *mind*, a depth well beyond what most of us normally consider "thought." But its power cannot be overstated because it alters what each of us experiences of the outside world. At a less subtle depth, Level I thought gives us original insights that pop into our heads seemingly from out of the blue, which affect the way we subsequently see or experience life. It is also possible—though I have not seen any evidence for this—that at a much shallower depth, Level I thoughts from our memory also can alter what our senses initially pick up. Nonetheless, *Level I Thought* affects what we experience in our consciousness, and this appears to be what causes the molecules to begin to vibrate and move and communicate with the receptor molecules, which then causes chemical changes in the cells of our bodies. Another system, however, simultaneously is in operation.

8) Simultaneously, a signal is sent to the brain

While the neuropeptides are engaged in their vibrational communication, a signal is also being sent from the sense organ along the neural network to the brain via the firing of synapses. Thus, an entire other system is engaged (Kotulak, 1996). Sounds of words, for example, are received by receptors in the ear and converted into electromagnetic signals (p.16) and fired to the brain.

The brain apparently "reduces the world to its elemental parts—photons of light, molecules of smell, sound waves, vibrations of touch—which then send electrochemical signals to individual brain cells and store information about movements, colors, smells, and other sensory inputs" (Kotulak, 1996, p.19). These get established as patterns of connections, but they are quite changeable, not fixed. When triggered, these connections can "reassemble the molecular parts that make up a memory" (p.20). Each brain cell has the capacity to store fragments of many memories, ready to be retrieved when a particular network of connections is activated.

Within the brain, the thalamus functions as a relay center through which all sensory information other than smell is transmitted to the cerebral cortex and therefore to the conscious mind. While no part of the brain is the seat of conscious experience, most biologists believe "consciousness consists of parallel processing of vast numbers of coding networks" (Wilson, 1998, p.109). Searle (1992) asserts that "certain big collections of nerve cells, that is, brains, cause and sustain conscious states and processes" (p.89).

In this context use of the word "cause" is very puzzling. A brain is a lump of tissue with no life of its own. Can it possibly cause or produce consciousness on its own? With no life of its own, can this lump of tissue manufacture its own consciousness? Such bio-philosophical interpretations or hypotheses do not answer the question of what fires up the system to give it life in the first place. If this lump of tissue were fired up, so to speak, with some *life force*, only then would it be able to have consciousness. My conclusion is that the life force is what brings consciousness.

Nonetheless, when the neural signal from the sensory organs reaches the brain, it is processed there and triggers another action.

9) Where a second level of thought intercedes, which interprets what it sees or feels

Pert (1997) posits that for the brain not to be overwhelmed by the constant deluge of sensory input, some sort of filtering system must enable us to pay attention to what our "bodymind" deems the most important pieces of information, and what to largely ignore. Here is where *Level II thought* occurs. Level II thought is interpretive thought. Somehow an interpretation through thought is made, both about what is perceived and how important it is to the system. At Level II thought, we make something of or interpret what is picked up by the senses, which have been already altered by *Level I Thought*.

At least some (possibly all?) of these generated thoughts are stored in the memory centers of the brain. Perceptions, already altered by Level I thought, are stored in our memories. Some thoughts stored in our memories seem to have more importance to us than others, perhaps because of earlier thoughts that for some reason affected us in a powerful way and now cause similar new thoughts to appear to have power over us. When we perceive something—which is the same as having a thought about something, through the senses—other thoughts from our memories can come into play and affect what we think is important to us. This is all part of the interpretive process of *Level II thought*.

According to Bohm (1994), this entire system of thought works by what he calls "reflexes"; that is, thoughts trigger a reflex action that occurs throughout the system.

> When we have a thought it registers in the memory. It registers in the form of a reflex, …and conditioned reflexes can affect the feelings… I'm proposing that this whole system works by a set of reflexes—that thought is a very subtle set of reflexes which is potentially unlimited; you can add more and more and you can modify your reflexes (pp.52-53).

If the same reflex is repeated again and again, it becomes a conditioned reflex. Bohm asserts that conditioning somehow leaves a mark in the system, in the nerves, and then a reflex has been altered. A great deal of routine learning consists of establishing conditioned reflexes, such as when learning to drive a car. This conditioning seems to set up pathways in the brain that form patterns, and our thinking tends to follow along those patterns (Kotulak, 1996). This is very helpful when learning to drive a car, but sometimes these conditioned paths do not serve us well, such as when we acquire a habit of worry.

Are we simply subjected to and relegated to the conditioned reflexes we pick up? Bohm (1994) suggests we can intervene in this system. In fact, if we don't intervene, if we don't realize what is going on, we can get ourselves into difficulty:

> If we don't see how thought enters perception we may take that perception as a fact unaffected by thought, and then base our assumptions and actions and thinking on that so-called fact. Thus, we can get into a trap; for example, we may assume that people of a certain kind are no good, and then say, "I can see that they're no good" (p.117).

Bohm speculates that thought originally exists to help and protect us, but after a while it begins to run on its own. Thought also seems to include a defensive reflex that defends against any evidence that might weaken what it thinks it knows. Thus we experience one reflex after another.

10) Which stimulates other chemical changes in the brain and body;

A further problem, according to Bohm, is every thought triggers some change in the system's chemistry. A strong thought with a lot of emotion attached involves a bigger chemical change. Constant repetition of a lot of little thoughts also can build up the change. Bohm points out that researchers say experience, perception and thought establish synapse connections, and the more a pattern is repeated the stronger those connections become. After a while they get very strong and can be very hard to change. Something happens in the chemistry, in the physics, in the neurophysiological process. A reflex may connect to endorphins and produce an impulse to hold the whole pattern further.

One reflex is that Level II thought also moves the neuropeptide molecules. Pert (1997) states that thought is stored in the mind and is instantaneously transformed into physical reality. A common example is that when we have a thought of embarrassment our cheeks turn red. Pert says that's the neuropeptides at work.

305

> When a receptor is flooded with a ligand, it changes the cell membrane in a such a way that the probability of an electrical impulse traveling across the membrane where the receptor resides is facilitated or inhibited, thereafter affecting the choice of neuronal circuitry that will be used... The decisions about what becomes a thought rising to consciousness and what remains an undigestive thought pattern buried at the deeper level in the body is mediated by the receptors. I'd say that the fact that memory is encoded or stored at the receptor level means that memory and processes are emotion-driven and unconscious (but, like other receptor-mediated processes, can sometimes be made conscious) (p.143).

Thus at "step" 10 the same process occurs again that happened at "step" 7. The only difference is that it is triggered by another kind of thought—*interpretation* (Level II)—that happens through the neural circuits and the brain, which in turn stimulates more molecule movement that stimulates other chemical change.

11) Which are experienced as an emotion, mood, or other feeling

Whether from "step" 7 or 10, some reaction is then generated in the body. But this process takes time, perhaps as much as a second or two before, for example, a thought of being nervous about speaking in front of a group reaches the solar plexus and produces a queasy feeling. And, as Bohm (1994) says, "you don't realize that what you are feeling in the body has been stimulated by your thought, so you may say, 'I feel fear in the pit of my stomach...'" (p.40).

The movement of these molecules is what causes us to feel emotions (Pert, 1997). Again, this vibrational movement is triggered by thought, first at *Level I* before we perceive anything, which alters our perception in the first place, and then at *Level II* through another thought or set of thoughts that interpret and make decisions about the relative importance of what we perceive. Emotions are the result. Usually the thoughts speed by so fast that we are left only feeling the emotions and don't notice thought has anything to do with it. At that point, the emotions take over. But it is important to remember they are *after the fact* of thought.

Wilson (1998) provides an illustration of walking down the street at night and hearing footsteps. In the space of a few seconds we might have a conscious response that triggers automatic changes in our physiology. This thought causes the entire system to react or respond. If suddenly a streetlight appears and we turn around and see it's only a cat, that thought would then trigger yet another change in our physiology. We could conclude we have both primary emotions—inborn or intrinsic responses that arise from Level I Thought—and secondary emotions that arise from personalized, Level II thoughts.

Bohm (1994) points out electrical measurements have shown some electrochemical process in the brain precedes conscious intention. This may lead to the type of secondary emotion mentioned earlier. Perhaps this type of emotion is triggered by thoughts from memory within the brain. As Bohm says, "Emotion is very fast... The emotional centre is hit very quickly.... If somebody says something disturbing to you, the needle [in a polygraph] deflects about three seconds later. It takes a few seconds for the impulse to get down the spinal column..." (p.41).

From her discoveries, Pert (1997) asserts the following:

> We can no longer think of the emotions as having less validity than physical, material substance, but instead must see them as cellular signals that are involved in the process of translating information into physical reality; literally transforming mind into matter. Emotions are at the nexus between matter in mind, going back and forth between the two and influencing both (p.189).

Thus, thoughts activate the physiological response (Myss, 1996), and create emotions. Pert (1997) goes on to state that emotions and bodily sensations are intricately intertwined in a bi-directional network where they can alter one another. Sensory information goes through a filtering process as it travels across the synapses, eventually but not always reaching areas of higher processes such as the frontal lobe, where it enters our conscious awareness. According to Pert, this filtering process determines what we pay attention to at any moment. It is determined, she says, by the quantity and quality of the receptors at specific "nodal" points.

One hypothesis from Pert's data is there is reason to believe "each peptide may invoke a unique emotional tone." For example, because the intestine is lined with peptide receptors, we experience what we call "gut feelings" because "we literally feel our emotions in our gut" (Capra, 1997, p.284). Implications are, too, that this vibrational "tone" is what affects or creates what we call "moods."

In summary, Pert states that emotions and moods are constantly regulating what we experience as "reality." Our thoughts, which are somehow screened or impacted by other thoughts, are what set the system in motion to cause emotions. These biochemicals or neuropeptides, then, are "the physiological substrates of emotion, the molecular underpinnings of what we experience as feelings, sensations, thoughts, drives, perhaps even spirit or soul" (Pert, 1997, p.130).

12) These affect a third level of thought that creates an intention and decides what we are going to do about that experience

Triggered by Level II thought, these neuropeptides move and alter emotions and moods. These emotions and mood states, in turn, affect a third level of thought which, in turn, creates an intention. When Capra (1997) says that all our perceptions and thoughts are colored by emotions; he is likely referring to what I would call *Level III intentional thought*. Level II interpretive thoughts (and probably Level I protothought) create emotions and moods which, in turn, affect our intentions, which are Level III thoughts.

It is important to note that once emotions take over, we still are never ultimately "stuck" with them. Pert (1997) explains what happens:

> Fortunately…receptors are not stagnant, and can change in both sensitivity and in the arrangement they have with other proteins in the cell membrane. This means that even when we are "stuck" emotionally, fixated on a version of reality that does not serve us well, there is always a biochemical potential for change and growth. Most of our bodymind attentional shifts are subconscious. While neuropeptides are actually directing our attention by their activities, we are not consciously involved in

deciding what gets processed, remembered and learned. But we do have the possibility of bringing some of these decisions into consciousness (p.146).

Pert here is speaking of Level III *intentional* thought, because she uses the example of visualization: Visualization can actually increase blood flow into a body part, and increase oxygen and provide nutrients to carry away toxins. Visualization is intentional. Level III thought, often, is thought that we go out of our way to think, however we do that.

Physiologically, within the brain "the caudate nucleus acts as a gatekeeper that prevents unwanted thoughts from establishing self-reinforcing circuits in the brain. Like a record stuck in the same grove, unwanted thoughts keep repeating themselves and drive compulsive behavior" (Kotulak, 1998, p.24). This "wiring" can get established in the brain and, for example, can make a child fearful and hesitant. But this wiring is not fixed. It can be undone and reform into networks that make that child more outgoing and trusting (p. 62).

All this enters our consciousness. Do we have consciousness of our thoughts at all three levels, or just of Level III intentional thought? To answer this, it is very important to distinguish between consciousness and what most people think of as awareness. If our body is affected by any level of thought, our body must somehow have consciousness of it. This consciousness, however, may not register in our brains as awareness. We may not be aware a thought is affecting us, yet it still affects us. Our body, then, has a consciousness, of which our brain registers awareness only of a small part, like the tip of an iceberg. Some may call what lies below the surface the subconscious or the unconscious, but I suggest it is only different levels within the totality of our consciousness. Capra (1997) says that "to be human is to be endowed with reflective consciousness" (p.290). He seems once again to be speaking of what we are aware of.

Nonetheless, intentional thought within our consciousness often makes us want to act, even though we might not be aware of it. This sounds like a contradiction, but it is not.

13) Which leads to behavior

Any behavior begins with intentional thought. Even though we may not be aware of the specific thought, our body has consciousness of it. For example, if we take a step to walk, we are not aware that the thought "walk" precedes the moving of our legs, but that is what happens. We must have an intention to walk, or we wouldn't.

Thought, then, precedes everything. At "step" 2, Level I protothought precedes our perception. At "step" 11, Level II interpretive thought precedes our emotions. Here at "step" 13, Level III intentional thought precedes our behavior.

14) Which may affect something out in the world, which reacts or responds

Our behaviors, triggered by our thoughts and emotions, in turn often incite some action or reaction to occur "out there." Walking may not cause much of a stir out in the world (except if we happen to land on a bug or a toe), but if we were to pull out a gun and shoot someone it certainly would—and a wide variety of levels in between. Something in the outside world then reacts to or acts upon what we did—another person, in response, would go through the entire process described above, and however the process came out for that person would determine her/his behavior in return.

15) Which triggers the entire system to begin again so we can experience the result.

Then we get to experience the result of what our own thoughts, which turned into our actions, started in motion. However, we do not get a direct experience from what someone does to us. First we have a Level I thought about it, which merges with our perception of it to give us what we experience of it. By the time the signal travels the neural pathway to get to the brain and back, Level II thought has then interpreted and somehow has combined with the molecule movement started by Level I thought to affect our emotions and give us a secondary experience of it, which then sets off an intentional (Level III) thought that makes us respond or react again. Thought, at its different levels, has its fingers in the pie every step of the way. Nothing we can possibly do or experience is without thought. Any time we act or react or respond to anything, we do so through our thinking.

Further, it appears that thoughts in our consciousness, which transform into matter and affect emotions, lead us toward health or away from it. According to Kotulak (1996) brain research shows that "bad experiences affect the brain" primarily through stress hormones such as cortisol and adrenaline, and are designed to respond to psychological or physical danger, preparing the body for fight or flight. Environmental stress has been found to activate genes linked to depression and other mental problems, and stress, through its hormonal intermediaries, turns on genes that leave a memory trace of a bad feeling. While true, remember that a stressful environment and bad experiences are all brought to us by thought.

While the system is propelled by thought, stressful and other unhealthy thinking affects chemicals in our brains and bodies that, in turn, affect Level III thought that affects our behavior. For example, low seratonin levels in the brain increase impulsiveness; normal levels are associated with clear thinking and social success (Kotulak, 1996). The more our thinking affects our chemicals, the more our behavior—and our health—appears to be affected.

This entire process corresponds perfectly with what Barbara Brennan (1987) sees:

> Creation or manifestation takes place when a concept or a belief is transmitted from its source in the high levels down into the more dense levels of reality until it becomes crystallized into physical reality. We create according to our beliefs. Of course what is taking place at the lower levels also affects the higher ones (p.137).

Can We Affect This System?

If the above is how the whole system of thought-into-form works in our bodies, the next question is, does the system operate on its own, or can we somehow affect it in healthy ways? Bohm provides an answer.

Bohm (1994) suggests we have a fundamental awareness or stream of consciousness, available to us at various depths, that we can draw upon and affect the system. Unfortunately, our thinking confuses us, and this resource becomes obscured. Here is how:

Thoughts are *representations* (Bohm's term), and representations always take on a certain form. For example, a rainbow is a something formed in our minds, because a rainbow doesn't really exist in "reality"—we can't find it. It has been produced by thought, and is presented as perception. In fact, Bohm says, this is true of everything we perceive. What we are seeing is really just a lot of forms that we think are real, but thought is taking what it has represented as fact. We forget that any perception of any form has come to us through our thinking, and therefore we consider it a fact independent of thought. The more this happens, the more the brain gets "muddled up." It "goes wrong, so to speak," then this spreads and becomes a "systemic fault" that becomes some kind of "reality" that misleads us (p.133). Thus we run into a major, apparent contradiction: It looks as if thought gives us unlimited power to create whatever experience we want for ourselves, yet thought limits itself! At least we allow it to.

If thought "tricks" us so well, what can we do? Fortunately, Bohm seems to suggest that three safeguards are built into the system:

1. This system of thought-into-form is always seeking "coherence" (Bohm's term)—it wants to have everything make sense—and when it experiences incoherence it seeks to right itself.
2. Our thoughts are free to change; we are not stuck with our patterns of thinking.
3. There appears to be "insight" or "intelligence" beyond our typical reflexes of thought, something that may be outside the system, that is able to *see* whether the system is coherent or not. In other words, it is possible to have an insight from some deeper-than-usual depth that can change the system and therefore change the organism.

...the insight is probably from immense depths of subtlety—perhaps even beyond the organism for all we know. Wherever it comes from, the important point is that it works directly at the physical chemical level of the organism, along with everything else. So it really affects you through and through... [But] the reflex of thought is continually resisting and defending, because the insight may be seen as a threat to the structure which you want to hold... When we fail to see that this is happening, then we are in danger, especially if there is resistance to seeing it. And we are conditioned to resist seeing that this is happening. That's really where the self-deception arises (Bohm, 1994, pp.159-161).

This leads Bohm to distinguish between different types of thinking, although the word "types" may be inaccurate. The realm from where insight arises—wherever that is—appears different from our normal, conditioned thinking process. To Bohm, the answer lies in what he calls "clear thinking," which, he says, "implies that we are in some way awakened a little bit. Perhaps there is something beyond the reflex which is at work...but the very fact that we are sometimes able to see new things would suggest that there is the unconditioned" (Bohm, 1994, p.72). To Bohm, the system of thought is a material process. If we have an insight or a perception of truth, it will actually affect the material process, which includes all the reflexes. But, Bohm says, if we merely have intellectual knowledge of what is going on, then it does not touch this process deeply.

What can help us most, then, is "proprioception," which Bohm defines as the "self-perception of thought" (p.18). We can observe our thinking from a distance, or know we are the thinkers of our own thoughts that are giving us our experiences.

It is not simply a matter of changing negative thoughts to positive thoughts. As Bohm points out, if we engage in positive thinking to overcome negative thoughts, the negative thoughts are still there acting in us. It is still incoherence to the system, because the negative thoughts keep working and will cause trouble somewhere else. So if the answer is not positive thinking, what is it? It seems to be simply knowing that all our experience is coming from our own thinking, not from "out there," and knowing that because thinking changes we are never stuck where we are.

Bohm also points out that reassuring or pleasant thoughts can produce endorphins. We may sometimes get addicted to those thoughts. Then our thinking says, "I won't give them up, even if they're wrong; I'll believe them to be true." This is another example of how the thought process is more than simply intellectual or emotional; it is neurophysiological. It has physical and chemical elements. Bohm states that medical investigators have demonstrated this by measuring electrical waves in brain scans. Every time we think, the blood distribution shifts around, and many changes occur inside our brain and bodies. Thought can never be separated from the neurophysiological process (Bohm, 1994, p 45).

Returning to the notion of insight or intelligence, Deepak Chopra (1990) also speaks of a place of silence from which insights arise.

> [Beyond the constant activity of the mind]…lies a silent region that appears as empty as the quantum field between the stars. Yet, like that quantum field, our inner silence holds rich promise. The silence inside us is the key to the quantum mechanical body. It is not a chaotic but an organized silence. It has shape and design, purpose and processes, just like the physical body… (p.10)

Like Bohm, Chopra says our body has a silent flow of intelligence, a constant bubbling up of thoughts. Then he leaps further by saying our body *is* really that silent flow of intelligence. "The secret of life at this level is that anything in your body can be changed with the flick of an intention" (p.10)." Some may not make this leap with him. Perhaps we don't even need to; it may be enough to know that our thinking affects our health.

Carolyn Myss (1997) says that "because divine energy is inherent in our biological system, every thought that crosses our minds, every belief we nurture, every memory to which we cling translates into a positive or negative command to our bodies and spirits" (p.67). To see ourselves through this lens can be both magnificent and intimidating, for it means no part of our lives is powerless. Thought, at a deep enough level, appears to affect any part of the system. The implication is that *we may be creating our own health.*

Myss takes this notion further: "As a rule, a person's energy system transmits only the information that is essential to bring the conscious mind to an awareness of the imbalance or disease" (p.37). Once this awareness occurs, this implies we can do something about our health—perhaps even before the fact of a problem. Hunt (1997) corroborates this by saying *any physical problem begins first within a person's energy field before it even shows up in physical form.* (Keep in mind that the energy field is where Level I protothought seems to reside.) Hunt found that when a person experienced imagery of some kind, it first appeared in the field and later became evident in brain wave recordings. Turmoil in the energy field

311

signaled the experience of emotions and physiological manifestations before they happened. In laboratory tests she found that an increase in magnetic energy preceded a change in consciousness or emotion, or any dramatic change in electrical energy—as though it acted as a harbinger or facilitator.

Such incredible statements make sense if, as Bohm (1994) says, "Thought...is a more subtle form of the physical" (p.139). He uses the example of seeing someone very attractive to us, thereby affecting our chemistry, then at another time having a different thought about how that person really is, and that person doesn't attract us any more. The perception affects the chemistry. Suppose we see something from a very deep place of insight or wisdom—we now respond to that new perception "in very deep and subtle ways which may be beyond what science could even trace" (p.148). The thinking we use to guide and direct us can affect our health.

Insight from our deep intelligence, then, affects the chemistry of the system anew, or we will stay within the realm of our patterned reflexes, some of which can be destructive and lead to ill-health. This happens often in thinking related to our egos or images of self-importance, and with thinking that causes us stress.

Biochemist Iyla Prigogine discovered that at certain points of instability within the cognitive-biological system, new structures and forms of order can emerge. At these points the system metaphorically can "choose" from several possible paths or states. Which path it takes depends on factors such as the system's history and external conditions (which we now know come to us through our own thought), and the path it takes can never be predicted (in Capra, 1997, p.183). Will we move toward or away from our health at any given time? Prigogine found that a closed system will always decay or deteriorate, but he demonstrated that if energy is introduced into this system the disintegration process is altered and matter takes on a higher organization. Thus, we can have both evidence of decay, as well as the first step in the creation of the new. With new energy the system becomes rejuvenated and becomes healthier.

There is reason to believe this system of thought-into-form has vast implications for our physical health, though this is not the place to venture deeply into it. It appears, however, that we can affect this system in healthy ways by understanding the role of thought, feelings and emotions and their effects on body chemistry, and thus on our physical health and healing (Chopra, 1990; Myss, 1997; Hunt, 1996; Pert, 1997).

Pert (1997) believes that "all emotions are healthy, because emotions are what unite the mind and the body...." To repress them is to not let them flow freely, which sets up "dis-integrity in the system, causing it to act at cross-purposes rather than as a unified whole" (p. 192).

Energy is power, Myss (1996) says, and transmitting energy into the past by dwelling on painful events drains power from your body and can lead to illness.

A problem can develop at any point in this system; for example, from traumatic head injury, in a baby that acquires a chemical imbalance from her mother, during a depressive episode, etc. When this happens the entire process—the "steps" after that level—can change. Following one example, traumatic head injury may affect brain chemistry and the neural wiring in the brain, which in turn affects Level II thought, which moves the molecules, which affects the emotions, which in turn affects Level III thought, which determines how one behaves. Perhaps (depending on the extent of the physical injury) it is even conceivable, though not common, that Level I thought can intercede at a deep enough level to right the entire system.

Likewise, intervention can occur at any point within the system, once again affecting all "steps" after it. For example, acupuncture or various kinds of somatic work may get energy flowing again by removing a blockage, which may allow thoughts to flow more freely again. I am uncertain whether such practices can affect any "steps" before the intervention point, in this case above "steps" 7 or 10, which is where this type of intervention would likely occur. What does appear clear is that the higher the level (the "step") of intervention in the system, the more leverage or power it has to affect more of the whole system. This is why an intervention at Level I thought, such as through an enormous epiphany, has appeared to make miracles occur. Even a deep insight can affect the entire system below it—even at the physical level—depending on the magnitude of the insight.

Thus, this system of thought-into-form can be entered and affected at many different points. If thoughts that carry powerful emotions become converted into matter, this also lessens the mystery of cellular memory. Likewise, it answers the question of why practices such as Bioenergetics or Yoga Therapy, both of which place people in positions difficult for the body to hold, can release a flood of emotion-laden thoughts, as can other somatic work. Yet, unless people know what to do with those emotions/thoughts after the initial release, such practices may not have lasting impact. The same may be true for energy healing; an energy healer, for example, may be able to "repair" a part of one's energy field caused by faulty thinking and make the person feel better, but if that thinking has not changed it may eventually "damage" the energy field again. Conversely, it would seem important to know that *even cellular memory can change with another powerful-enough thought; it is never solid, fixed, unchangeable.*

If thoughts at a deep enough level can change the body's chemistry, and if the chemistry is altered in detrimental ways, it is not surprising that certain psychiatrically prescribed drugs would help bring the chemicals more in balance. Rather than foster dependence on such drugs to keep the chemical imbalances in check for years (if not indefinitely), it would seem wise to attempt to affect *thought* at a deep enough level to permanently alter the chemical imbalance.

Energy field science may also answer why some of newer therapies may work, such as Thought Field Therapy (The Callahan Techniques), which is an attempt to cure trauma by tapping designated spots on the body in a specific sequence in an attempt to balance the body's energy system and promote the body's own healing energy. Less clear, it may even explain EMDR (Eye Movement Desensitization and Reprocessing), which attempts to release past traumatic stress via the brain's information processing system by replicating eye movements that occur spontaneously during REM sleep (dreaming state) while simultaneously visualizing the past traumatic incident. What may be going on is with both approaches is an altering of the energy field which, as Hunt (1996), Myss (1996) and Brennan (1987) point out, has a curative effect. Again, however, *if thought is the creator, thought should also be the most basic cure.* When people understand the role that thought plays in creating their experience, they appear to have more of a handle on whatever life throws at them. A change in thinking at a deep enough level would constitute a change in the energy field and would negate the need for tapping or eye movements.

The intersection of science and spirit

The astute reader will note that the spiritual teachings cited in Chapter XIX bear uncanny resemblance to this system of thought-into-form, and both the scientific and spiritual directions appear to lend credence to the three Principles of Mind, Consciousness, and Thought uncovered by Sydney Banks (1998). Coincidence? It seems unlikely.

Pert (1997) offers a plausible explanation of the connection between the scientific and spiritual worlds.

> Where does the intelligence, the information that runs our bodymind come from? We know that information has an infinite capacity to expand and increase, and that it is beyond time and place, matter and energy. Therefore it cannot belong to the material world we apprehend with our senses, but must belong to its own realm, one that we can experience as emotion, the mind, the spirit—an inforealm! This is the term I prefer because it has a scientific ring to it, but others mean the same thing when they say the field of intelligence, innate intelligence, the wisdom of the body. Still others call it God... Reductionists will always argue that the molecules come first, are the primal forces, and that thoughts and emotions follow as a kind of epiphenomenon of the molecules. And they've got good evidence: Doesn't the flow of peptides change the physiologic response, which then create the feelings we experience? Doesn't the chemical release of endorphins cause the feeling of pain relief or the euphoria of a running high? I don't deny this, but what I'm saying is that we must recognize that there is a two way system of communication at work. Yes, the release of endorphins can cause pain relief and euphoria. But, conversely, we can bring about the release of endorphins through our state of mind...I like to think of mental phenomena as messengers bringing information and intelligence from the nonphysical world to the body, where they manifest via their physical substrate, the neuropeptides and their receptors (pp.310-311).

What are the implications? As our thinking changes, we have a different sensory experience. *If our thinking changes, we will have a different sensory experience.* Whenever we react to anything "out there" we are really reacting to what is "in here" in our own thinking. We are creating—essentially making up, often inadvertently—what we are reacting to. In other words, it is not the world out there giving me problems, it is me. My own thinking about the world out there is what is giving me problems. That means that the solution always lies "in here"—within.

In summation, it seems that interpretations from science can corroborate much of what Sydney Banks (1998) came to *see* and understand through his epiphany.

This by no means is meant to be the definitive word on this subject. I acknowledge I have only scratched the surface here. All I hope is that this suggests a direction for further inquiry. It is quite an interesting inquiry.

It seems fitting to close this chapter with a quote from Thich Nhat Hanh, a Vietnamese Buddhist teacher nominated by Martin Luther King, Jr. for the Nobel Peace Prize, from his book, *Being Peace*, first brought to my attention by Raeburn & Rootman (1998).

> Many of us worry about the situation of the world. We don't know when the bombs will explode. We feel that we are on the edge of time. As individuals we feel helpless, despairing. The situation is so dangerous, injustice is so widespread, the

danger is so close. In this kind of situation, if we panic, things will only become worse. We need to remain calm, to see clearly... I like to use the example of a small boat crossing the Gulf of Siam. In Vietnam there are many people, called boat people, who leave the country in small boats. Often the boats are caught in rough seas or storms, the people may panic and the boats can sink. But even if one person aboard can remain calm, lucid, knowing what to do and what not to do, he or she can help the boat survive. His or her expression—face, voice—communicates clarity and calmness, and people have trust in that person. They will listen to what he or she says. One such person can save the lives of many... Children understand very well that in each woman, in each man, there is a capacity of waking up, of understanding, and of loving. Many children have told me that they cannot show me anyone who does not have this capacity. Some people allow it to develop, and some do not, but everyone has it. This capacity of waking up, of being aware of what is going on in your feelings, in your body, in your perceptions, in the world, is called Buddha nature, the capacity of understanding and loving. Since the baby of that Buddha is in us, we should give him or her a chance... It is not by going out for a demonstration against nuclear missiles that we can bring about peace. It is with our capacity of smiling, breathing, and being peace that we can make peace (9-11).

XXII. BARBARA

Interview with Barbara Glaspie. *I end this book with another miracle. We see homeless crack addicts on the street and think there is no hope. But that is* only *a thought! Barbara is living proof of innate health in action. As with all the people I interviewed for this book, and so many others touched by this understanding, I feel so privileged and grateful to know her. I interviewed her at the Visitacion Valley housing project in San Francisco, California in May, 2001.*

JP: What were you like before you got this understanding?

BG: Depressed. Drama mama. Empty. I was a little empty person. I had a really, really long, dragged-out kind of past. I was addicted to crack cocaine for many years, I had been through CPS [Child Protective Services], turned in by them because I could no longer take care of my children, and I didn't have the courage to tell someone I needed help. I had been homeless. I was homeless for three or four years. I start there because in this understanding that I know now, I heard so many times that this is already in you, and the Principles are always in action, you just know it, and that kind of thing. And I just get really tickled inside because I know that it's true. It's true because for many years most of the thoughts that I hung onto were negative thoughts. Like, "I was the most terrible parent in the world," "I was a dope fiend," "I was homeless." "I was a disgrace to the population"— let alone being an African American woman, feeling like it was expected of me to fail. And I fed into that, and that all looked real to me. So for many years that's where I lived. I lived in depression, I lived in agony, I lived in pain. And that seemed like my place—that felt comfortable for me.

And I was a drama person, I liked to fight. I liked to get drunk and challenge men. I had this thing with men because they were, I felt, like, the source of what had happened to me. They took advantage of me. I was addicted to dope and I needed your money, and so you knew, in order for me to get your money you'd want to trade for sex. I had this thing with men, and I felt like I was powerful when I drank, so I would just challenge them, you know? I was challenging them, like "You're weak. You're really a weak man for taking advantage of someone when they're in such a vulnerable state." So I had all kinds of crazy stuff going on, and all in between time, I was having children. And all of this sick and insanity type of behavior that I was in—and it all just made sense to me—I thought I was in love, so if you're in love, you have a baby, or whatever.

I look at all that and I remember one time laying down in the middle of the street, Van Ness and San Francisco or something—I really wasn't familiar with my surroundings for about four years. So I laid down in the middle of the street, and I remember saying out loud, "I want to die! Just kill me!" But something inside of me really didn't want to die. And I couldn't figure out how could I think something so sane when I was feeling so insane. And that was another time when I realized the buoyancy in all of this, and how these good feelings and all this natural ability kept trying to surface. And I kept submerging it with drugs and alcohol and my behavior that I was on.

And as we talk about the Principles always being in action, and we are the Principles in action, it's true! Because I didn't know Health Realization when, for some miraculous reason, I came out of all of this stuff. I don't even really know when. I just remember I would always have thoughts of, "Oh, what if I really could be a good mother? What if there's a possibility that I am somebody?" and naturally, unfortunately, I would always not believe that part. So I'd stay in the addiction and stay in homelessness, not even make an attempt to try to find a place to live, let alone, hey, check out where are my kids. None of that ever occurred to me.

JP: When you were homeless, where were you?

BG: I was in San Francisco. I was right here.

JP: Just walking on the streets?

BG: Yeah, I just pushed a cart, like everybody else, and I'd collect the cans and whatever I could. And I stole a lot. And to me, people who steal from their family and stuff like that, I think they're sick, but I also think there's a part of them that really doesn't want to do that. Because I felt like if I stole from a family member, then that would lessen the chances of someone killing me or really causing me some bodily harm. So my family members naturally I knew loved me—didn't like what I had become but they loved me—so I would see my family here and there, and they'd be so glad to see me because I'd disappear for months at a time—any opportunity I got I'd steal something from them and sell it. Or I'd do whatever I could do—whatever made sense to me at the time to get the drug, I'd do it. So even though insane as that seems, it really makes sense to me now because I was still thinking of my safety. Even in all that behavior that I was doing in the stealing, I never stole from a store, I would never steal from other people's houses, I would always go take from my family. Because people will hurt you for taking their things, especially when you're taking things that are valuable to them, because I would get caught, and I would make up excuses to my family as to, you know, "If you just give me money I wouldn't have to steal from you," and all these things. So at some point, I really, really, really felt like I wanted to change.

JP: Do you remember what the circumstances were around that?

BG: Yeah. All my kids had been taken from me. At that time I had two children, and actually I got kicked out of a homeless hotel. I was living in a homeless hotel, and I began my drug activity there. I would sell drugs and smoke and do all that stuff. I couldn't keep appointments naturally because I was on drugs, so finally they stopped sending me my welfare check. And I would go down in an outrage to the welfare office and say, "*I need money to pay my rent!*" and all kinds of stuff, and be truly upset with the social workers because I felt like they had taken ownership of my money that they were supposed to give for me and my kids—which I never used for the kids. So people get smart to what you're up to, so they cut me off. And they kicked me out of the homeless hotel. And with me not having somewhere to stay—naturally I shouldn't have had my kids anyway because I was totally gone on drugs—they allowed me to make a decision to where I could give my kids to my mother and she would take care of them temporarily. She was really sick. That didn't matter to me at the time. I felt like anybody in the world had to be stronger than me, so even if she was sick she had to be strong enough to take care of my kids, because I couldn't do it.

So I kind of just wandered around the streets of San Francisco for the next two years, in and out of drug hotels and wherever somebody would let me lay down for the night—or in the corners of the stores, I would lay there also. And it occurred to me one day that I wanted to be—not even happy; happy was too big for me at that time—I just wanted to be content. And I wasn't even content, because I maybe wore size three and I was just fading away. I was just fading away. And when you

318

use crack cocaine a lot of people say you have illusions and all this stuff, which could be possibly true, but for me I had been up four or five days on one of my drug runs, and I went in the bathroom to my sister's house—this was when Geneva Towers was up—and I was actually staying pillar to post there, anywhere in the building that I could stay. And once I was down there and I was getting high, and I couldn't get high for some reason this day. It just wouldn't happen. I kept thinking, "Oh, I don't have enough money," and I was making all these excuses why I wasn't getting high this day, because I was always able to get high before. So I looked at myself in the mirror—and I saw something other than myself. It wasn't me! It could not have been me. I didn't recognize who the person was. And it was really scary! It was really, really scary. It scared me to death. And I couldn't tell people, because they already gave me names, like I was a dope fiend and I was crazy—all kind of things wrong with me—so people made fun of me all the time. So this was not something I was going to go run and tell people who were in the other room getting high, is that I just saw somebody else in the mirror. So I kind of sat with that and I didn't get high the rest of that day, because I was really scared. So I said, "Maybe this is a sign from God. What's going on?"

Even at night I was so tired. I had been so tired from the streets, from the drugs, from the abuse, from everything. I was tired! So it occurred to me that maybe I can get clean, maybe I can give it a try, maybe I'll try it. So what happened is, I went and tried to check myself into a residential place, and they said I had to be clean three days. To me that was impossible. I had been getting high for years every single day, every moment I was awake I was getting high. How in the heck could I stay clean for three days? But somehow I did. I don't even know how I did that. I stayed clean three days! And I went back down and I told them. And she said, "We have no space." And I just broke down. I said, "You know, if you don't take me today—if you don't see me today then I may be dead tomorrow!" And something that I said, the lady that was there felt and resonated with that. And I think that's that universal connection that we talk about, when people are not necessarily listening softly but *feeling* where somebody is coming from. And I said, "It's only by the grace of God that I have made it through your door today, and if you turn me away, I may be dead tomorrow." And she went and talked to some people, and she said, "We can get you in, but we don't have any room in our inpatient." And I'm thinking, "I'm homeless, so some of the reason for me to even try to get in here is so I could have somewhere to sleep, stay, and try to get clean. And she said, "Well, we only have outpatient." So that was scary. I was just scared. I'm thinking, "Outpatient? So that means I go home every day where there's dysfunction and people use drugs and come back here and be clean the next day?"

But, see, something was already happening inside of me at that point, because I had never made it to a drug rehabilitation place. I couldn't keep thirty-five cents to get on the bus, you know? I'd spend thirty-five cents, or put thirty-five cents with other people to make a dollar trying to get high, so what really registered for me is that it was a miracle. I got thirty-five cents, and I made it downtown to the women's alcoholism center—I made it there! And I told her how I got there. I didn't know how to keep money and I got there. And I said, "Something's going on. I can do it! I must be able to do this if I can get thirty-five cents." I'd been trying to get bus fare. This is going to sound really crazy. I had been trying to keep thirty-five cents for bus fare for over a year, saying I was going to go to the drug rehabilitation place—and I couldn't make it! I kept saying, "Tomorrow's the big day! I'll do it. This could be the first day of the rest of my life"—all these things, where my normal thinking would have been, you know, like, "Just fuck it, because I can't do it!" Somebody will have to help me up and walk me through it, or it won't get done. But I had did it myself, and that was big steps for me: Keeping the bus fare to get down there, begging for her to take me until she said, "Yes." So that's the beginning for me.

So I come back to this place, which is Geneva Towers, where drugs were in abundance all around the whole vicinity, right here where we're sitting today. This is where Geneva Towers was. So the first three days I think I was on this natural high thing. Then I started to feel myself breaking down and getting weak. But the difference this time was when I had what they call an urge—which to me now is what I understand to be the thought about using—instead of succumbing to that thinking that I could get high one time and they wouldn't know it, I didn't do it. I said, "I can't do it! If I do, then I'm doomed." So that worked. And before I knew it I was just walking through it. It had been three months and I was still going in and out of this drug-infested place, and they don't have a clue today how I was getting back and forth there, and where I was coming to when I left them every day. And before I knew it years had passed by.

JP: Years?

BG: Years! Years had passed by. But in the time when this was happening, I'm constantly moving and going forward. But I don't see it, though. I don't see myself going forward. I don't see that I'm making steps to prepare to welcome my children back into my life.

JP: Did you have a home at that point?

BG: Well, no. I was still staying with different people. My sister lived on 9, my mother lived on 12, and I had friends that lived throughout the building. I couldn't stay with them because all my friends were dope users or drug addicts.

JP: How many years are we talking about?

BG: Well, my drug abuse started in 1985. So I'm in Texas doing drugs, and I'm graduating to California. Then in 1989 I come here and actually go on a worse kind of binge thing, so 1989 was my worst, worst year of using. And 1990 was just kind of like where I was getting kind of tired, but I just kept going because I felt worthless and that was my space. My space was to be a drug addict, a dope fiend, homeless, and that just felt like what I should be doing.

JP: So what year did you enter the program?

BG: At the end of 1990.

JP: And then when you said, "It went for years—"

BG: You mean not using? Clean?

JP: Yeah. But the point where you said for years that you weren't feeling like you were getting anywhere.

BG: Right, two years, because 1992 was the last time I did drugs. In that time, I was moving forward but I still couldn't feel myself. I couldn't see that I was moving. I had already taken steps. I had made arrangements with the CPS worker so that I could have visits with my children, because I was told not to go near my children—who lived with my mother. And so I had started making arrangements to do that. I went downtown and got on the list for public housing and made arrangements. And I had put my kids on there, although I didn't have my kids. My thinking was that I would have them back someday, and so when I got my house I would have to have enough room for them.

JP: So at what point did you bump into Health Realization?

BG: Oh, man! See, let me just tell you, I was clean all those years, just think about it, from 1992. But I was still miserable—until I learned about Health Realization two years ago. So what I'm telling you is that even with me being clean and getting my kids back, I still was not complete. Because I was doing it the hard way. I was hustling and bustling and punishing myself and trying to show myself that I got to create a challenge and solve it to show people that I'm strong now, that I'm not the same dope fiend they used to know, that I'm a good mother now. And yet I didn't really know how to be a mother. I didn't know how to even nurture my children, let alone myself. So even being clean all those years, I still didn't realize where all this pain was still coming from.

JP: It still felt like you were in pain?

BG: I still felt like I was in pain. I was clean. I didn't say my life had changed; I said I had stopped using drugs! I had stopped using drugs and alcohol, but I did not know myself, and I did not know how to take care of myself still. I was in the hustle and bustle and the struggle of showing other people that I'm doing it.

JP: So bring me to that moment where you first bumped into Health Realization. What happened to you?

BG: Okay. How that occurred was, at this point in time like I said, I'm still going through the motions, I'm not really happy still, I still have a lot of pain going on even after all these years. And what I learned later was that I was still living through my past. And one day I was really actively involved, because remember I'm still trying to prove to people that even after seven years I'm clean and I'm a good parent and an active member of society—so I joined the Parent Advisory Committee at the Boys and Girls Club, which is here located in Visitacion Valley. I was the chairperson. So the guy that was over the Boys and Girls Club said one day, "Some people are coming to do a presentation." In fact, it was like a joke to people. They said it was something like "Health Revitalization" or something, and I'm thinking, "Why do you guys always want me to be the guinea pig for stuff? Why do you want me to be the one that goes?" And he's like, "Well, you have rapport with people, and we just kind of want you to sit in and bring information back to us. None of us really want to be involved, but we just want to be nice and a Dr. Mills or something is coming." And I thought, "Okay,"—because remember I'm still in this state of trying to prove myself, so I'll do this if that's what it takes.

And I went that night, and it was Roger [Mills] and Beverley [Wilson] and Barbara Bailey. I remember being there that first day and just kind of looking at them and having my own ways. Like, I thought I could only hear messages from people of color, and if they weren't of color then they didn't know my struggles, so they couldn't relate to anything that I needed. And so he came in, and "Oh God," Roger was Caucasian. And I thought, "Okay, now I'm really not going to listen because he came to brainwash us, and they want me to bring this message back to my people." And what happened during that whole time, with me sitting there doing all this thinking about these people that I had never met and never talked to—and Beverley was there, but I thought, "Okay, he has her under lock and key, too; that doesn't make any difference." So he kept talking, and he started talking about *Thought*. They started talking about Thought, and while I was sitting there listening to them I realized that the thinking I was doing was preventing me from hearing what they were saying. Because I had sat in that room at least thirty minutes and didn't hear a word they were saying. But I heard "Thought,"—that our Thought creates our experience, and that made it so real for me. Not because they said it—because I didn't believe nothing they said that day—but I was experiencing it. I was sitting in that room, thinking, "Oh, I'll be glad when they're done. What's taking so long?" and every time, the more I had all this habitual thinking about why they were there, and I didn't realize that I was almost laying down in the chair. And I thought, "How did I get here?" The more I was sitting I was thinking, and the more I thought about it, the weaker I got.

And then it occurred to me and I just leaned up in my chair, and I remember saying something to them like, "Oh, yeah, that's right, because I remember when I used drugs in the Tower, and I used to go in the garbage room and I used to think—" And it hit me, just like that! It hit me. I truly understood what they were saying about thought, and from that moment they had my attention. They had my attention and I won't say that I was all in, but I knew that there was some truth to what they had came and said. And so for the next two times, I forced myself to sit in on the training. And after that, it was like I couldn't miss one. I had to be there because something was happening to me.

JP: Now before you go there, when you said it hit you, can you describe what you felt at that—

BG: I felt a tremendous amount of energy.

JP: Really?

BG: Yeah. It hit me through my body. It went through my body. And I remember grabbing my shoulders and pushing them together because it was just feeling overwhelming. It was an overwhelming feeling like *I* was doing something. I had never, ever felt in my life that I was causing or creating *anything* that had happened to me. And I realized that I was creating some misery for myself, and I just like hugged myself, grabbed myself and squeezed really tight. And Beverley looked at me and said, "Mm, mm, mm!" And she said, "Just hold onto your seat, girl!" And I said, "No, you just don't understand what a feeling I just had." I said [emotional now], "I've been causing myself so much misery for years." Because I seen, literally, just then—even though, remember I had been clean for years—I had *seen* at that moment how much misery that I had caused my own self. *How could I do that to myself?* And then I had to go through a process of forgiving myself, and that was really hard, because I couldn't figure out what had I been instilling in my kids—if I'm making myself so miserable, what kind of message was I giving to them? But then I learned about psychological innocence. And boy, let me tell you, when I did that, I didn't even relive all those things but I recognized that they happened, and it was a beautiful thing for me to know that when I was doing those things to myself, that *I didn't know that I was.* But it was even more powerful for me to know that *I created my own experience.* I never in my life knew anything that had happened to me—from the scums of sleeping on the floor to drug abuse—that I had nothing to do with that. And it took me to a plateau I had never been to. It took me to a place like, *"Now I know!"* and all I could do was cry. I cried and I cried. I cried a lot. I cried for, like, two months. And it wasn't a painful cry. It was almost like a release, like I was releasing and forgiving. But I had released myself, and I had never in my life felt that type of freedom before. I had never felt free. Even after I got clean I had never been free. And I thought, *"Oh, my God, I can free myself! I can free myself from this!"* And that was the part that kept me crying for months, because I was truly, truly free! You know?

And then in deepening my understanding, it kept going to a different level for me. I always felt like I was stupid, and can you imagine, like three Principles—I'd hear people say, three Principles—and I said, "Oh my God, it's so much bigger than that. How do I tell my people?" Here I have to explain to them how I came to understand this understanding, so I can't do that without talking about the three Principles. You can't make up something that's not true. How do I tell my people that you are free? *You are free!*" And I hear people sometimes, getting caught up in this thing blaming people for these conditions—and that looked real to me. It was real! "If they would just do this for us." "They held us back. It took too long to learn, now some of us are really slow, and we can't understand things." And just telling people, *"Everything you need, you have."* I could never tell somebody that before. I could never have imagined how to fix my mouth to tell somebody that everything you need, you have—to be whole, to be complete, to be happy, to whatever you want.

And the thing is with this, that this is so life-altering, to me it's not even about, "You can change your life forever; let me tell you about the three Principles." It's more to me like to explain it to people that *"This is something that you were given—the gift of life!* This is something that you had when you was born."

And I remember trying to tell this lady something. I was talking to a lady over here who was still actually addicted to crack cocaine. And I remember going to her one day, and I still have moments like an overwhelming feeling of love and joy that I have—it's not the pain anymore, because I used to sit on the stairs and cry in pain. And now if I do cry, it's just like the freedom that I feel I can't explain to them. So this lady, she said, "Oh, my God, you look so well." She said, "You been clean for a long time?" I said, "Yeah, but I haven't been free." I said, "I'm free." And she was looking at me like—she knows me very well, and she also knew me when I was drama mama. And she looked at me and she said, "Please tell me how. Please tell me how!" And she's somebody that's still using that lives in this complex right now, and I went on and I started talking to her about the Principles. But I couldn't, my throat started cracking up. And that's what happens to me sometimes—and I think that's the part where I have to slow down and relax—because when I talk about this, not only do I get excited, I get emotional. Because I think of the agony and pain that I was in for so many years, and I understand that *I'm not a prisoner of that any more!* But the beautiful part to that is, sometimes I have to cry—I caused a lot of that myself and I caused it out of psychological innocence. And I couldn't even tell her anything because I just started to break down. I was telling her about the Principles and I was trying to tell her how they all work together, and you *are* the Principles, and she was just kind of looking confused. And I understood her confusion, because I remember that same confusion when they were telling me about these Principles. I couldn't see how they would ever change my life, and they have changed my life forever.

And the beautiful part to this, I always went places to give something, to be better, to do better, to be right, and I would only remember that technique for a short time, of how to do it, when to do it when you're feeling down and out, or pick up this when you're feeling like that. And now, I tell you, this understanding is just like—I can't explain it to you—I remember what a struggle I had, even when I was becoming clean. Because they said, "You do it one day at a time"—where you're talking to somebody who loved to use drugs—and a day, twenty-four hours, is a lifetime. And I can remember that whole struggle with that. And knowing now when I go to drug and rehabilitation places, I talk to the people in charge first, and I say, "Look, I'm going to say something and I don't know if it'll be okay with you or your staff, but if I can't say it, I can't talk. I have to tell these people that they can do this moment to moment. They don't have to be strong for a day." That was one of my weakest, weakest points in recovery, remembering one day at a time. And see, knowing this understanding and what I know now, I know my experiences are created moment to moment.

JP: It's like one moment at a time.

BG: One *moment* at a time! And if I'm getting through moments, then I'm going to make it. But you're talking about a day. And I'm not saying it's wrong, because I believed the Twelve Steps would work for me, and they did. So I don't have anything against that. I just can't tell people one day at a time, especially someone who is in any kind of addiction.

JP: When you said that the Twelve Steps worked—they got you off the drugs but it didn't sound like it stopped the pain.

BG: They didn't. That's what I'm saying, *it didn't stop the pain!* I was still in pain four or five years after that, still in pain. So that's where it takes me back to my thinking. When people want to be clean, that's where it comes from—the *thought* that you want it. It's not necessarily the people or the Twelve Steps, because for me the Twelve Steps were really humiliating. But I had to be strong,

323

and that was my whole thing, my whole persona. So I can do the Twelve Steps—I can go back and tell people I stole this, or "When you went out of your kitchen I took a piece of chicken, and I'm sorry for that." That was humiliating! You know what I mean? And to me there's a more loving, compassionate way to do that. And I'm not saying, "People, convert to Health Realization." It's not about a conversion. These are things we're born with. They belong to you. Use them! And I don't even know how to exercise the Principles—I think I get caught up sometimes still, but the thing is that I don't stay there long, because that's not where my happiness is, it's not where my peace is, and I used to believe that it was. And that's the sick, insane part. I can't say that because I would be hurting my neck, my back, my throat—everything inside of me would lock up because I know the pain that it is when you're going through something like that. But if I had ever, ever in my life known that my life experiences were created moment to moment, how I could relax, how I could just be myself, how I could just know that I could just *be*, and not have to try to be something that I thought people needed me to be, that I could just be Barbara—and who Barbara was was very beautiful. And I'm not an ugly person. That's what I created. And that is the beautiful thing about thought, the ability to create! And *I could create any future I wanted for myself,* Anything I wanted, I could create it, and I knew that, and the freedom, freedom, freedom, freedom, *freedom!*

And I hear the Martin Luther King speech, and people don't know the meaning that it has for me now. And I believe in heritage and all that. With my people, I'm down! I'm down with humanity now, though. Can you imagine how much bigger that is than "my people?" So my life and my possibilities and the realm I'm in is just beyond the outer limits! And it's, like, crazy for me. But that speech has something different for me now. I tell people, and I talk to teenagers sometimes, and the first thing I ask them is, "When you hear that Martin Luther King speech that he did, what do you feel?" They say, "Strong." And even though he says, "Thank God Almighty, I'm free at last!" none of them ever say that part of it. And to me that was a very intricate part of that speech. But when I used to hear it, I just used to think of a very strong, powerful Black man that had knowledge. Honestly. But when I hear that now, I hear, "Free at last! Thank whoever your creator is, almighty whoever, free at last, and I'd just like to tell you, brothers and sisters, today that *you can be free, and the choice is yours.* And I'd like to help point you to where that is!"

And my God, I'm just astounded by presentations. I don't know why they want me to do something like that, I cry too much. And my tears are always of joy and happiness, but it's just so overwhelming to me how much love and compassion that I feel for myself and other people. I was always a person who was down for myself, "What I can get, what I can do, what can you give me, what I need." Always, always, always, always, always. And I just feel so real. I feel like I'm not a fake any more. I've tried to fake to people like I was this cool person, or I was an outstanding person. I didn't believe shit of it, though, that's the cold part. But the difference today is that I know it's true, and that comes across to people when I speak to them. I don't need to be a speaker or a presenter. I don't need to be anything. I do need to be myself, because when I'm myself something shines through me that's like—Whooo, I don't know, something just shines through me, and it goes through my body and I feel it, and it's almost like other people just magnetize to it. And I think that's what they talk about, when you come in this understanding, and you are content and you are all these things, and the difference is you still have things go on in your life, you still have those same things that you had before that go on in your life, but they definitely don't hold onto you and grip you like they used to.

I used to be incapacitated, couldn't move. I'd be in the bed for five days, cause I'd be mentally sick like, "Oh my God, what am I gonna do? I don't make enough money, I have all these kids, how will I provide? What will I do? Well, how will I do it in the bed? So who was I lying through that [laughs]. I will laugh at myself sometimes and say, "Well, how would you do it in the bed?" And I'll get up, and I may not go to do anything but cut my lawn. I'll do something like that, and believe me, unbelievable, I will forget that I even had the thought of not surviving—forget all about I had that thought. It will be gone and dismissed and out of there. But yet, a few moments ago, this is the same thing that used to hold me down for weeks, just physically incapacitated cause I don't know what to do, I don't know which way to turn, I don't know to do, my life is in shambles, and the same thoughts will come back and they occur and they happen, but they never in life could ever grip me the way they did before. I know what they are: I see you passing, and I'll see you later. Because you'll be back, and I'll be here. But the difference is, it will never be the same. It can never be the same once you understand how we operate. And I think that is so important.

And I remember how to see, I see all kinds of people who really look important, and now I look at them differently. I used to look at people—I'd sit in the doctor's office and just have all this thinking about, oh, what kind of house people have, and what their life must be like, and, oh, I bet you I'm the only one in this room using low-income housing. I mean, I was at this feeling, and now it's just like so far from me now. Now it doesn't matter to me what walk or phase of life that you come through. I know that I don't need to be judgmental about that, or of anything or anybody.

JP: How did you get this Health Realization job at Visitacion Valley?

BG: Well, that's special. That is so special for me. The funny thing is, I was feeling so good about this Health Realization stuff, I had no credentials—only the fact that I had been before in the community with the people. They needed a project director and an executive assistant, where I didn't know how to type and I had minimal skills about computers. And it was amazing. I'm telling you, this understanding will blow you out of the water. I had this notion one night when I woke up—see, I wasn't going to apply for neither one of those jobs because I wasn't qualified to do either one. But somehow I had to be involved with this stuff, I couldn't let this get away from me because it had already started to change my life in a week or two. So I thought, "Oh God, I don't have these skills, I don't have anything. All I have is that I had been in this community as a homeless person, as a drug abuser, and now I'm here and I don't do anything." So I figured the only thing they can say is yes or no, we can use you or not, so I applied for the project director [laughs]. I applied for the project director, and I'm telling you, I had no thinking about it because if I'd had a thought about it there's no way I would have took my butt out there applying for a project director's job which I had no clue [laughs]. So they set up this interview. They wanted to hire people within the community, which I thought was really beautiful. So in that short period of time I told you, "Thought" was the thing that first hit me—the fact that our thoughts create our experience. So I go out there, really nervous, and I thought, "Oh, my God, I know they don't want me. They can see that I'm uneducated—they can see all these things." I didn't do any of that thinking until I got there, but seeing Elsie [Spittle] and Roger sitting there—now, remember, I'm still seeing things like I'm the ant and everybody else is a big giant. So I went in there and, God, they looked so professional. And I thought I'd dressed up that day. But I didn't feel really dressed when I got there and seeing them.

So I did the interview, and I got a call like two or three days later from Roger, and he said I didn't get the job. Well, oh my God, I couldn't even talk—and not that I even expected to get the job, but hearing it was something different. I kind of just wanted them not to call or not to say anything and let me come to my own conclusions [laughs] about not getting the job. So it was so funny. What I did was, I went earlier that morning, and I said "Beverley, can you please meet me there?" I said, "I'm really going through a lot of things. I don't really understand what this stuff is, but this stuff is really doing something to me. It's moving me in my life like nothing's ever moved me before. Can I just talk to you for a minute in confidence?" I said, "I have no credentials. I have none of this stuff. I have nothing that I think they're looking for," but see, Beverley understood about Health Realization, and she knew it was something more than what I did. But she said, "This understanding—they need you!" I could not understand her saying that for the life of me. I thought she was so full of shit, that she was saying something to make me feel good. Who would need me? I mean the way she said it was like, "They *need you*, " in a like almost made me believe it, you know? So I said, "Okay." And I went and I didn't get it, and Roger called and said, "Ann Shine got the job as project director." Well, I was going to hang up on him—not be mad at him but I needed to hang up right then because I was having a lot of feelings about that at that particular time. He said, "Oh, but we're creating a job for you." And I dropped the phone. He'll remember this very well. I dropped the phone, couldn't pick it up, all I heard was, "We're creating for you." And that's all I could keep saying in my head, and I was like, "Oh, God, this stuff is so real!" And I couldn't pick the phone up. I just looked at the phone. And after a minute I was out of shock, but no one had ever like offered something that was just for me. And then it started playing in my head what Beverley said, "Oh, they need you." I had been coming to every training, but I was coming for me, because I needed to, because whatever was happening was really, really changing my life. So I finally picked up the phone. And he said, "Hello. Are you there?" I said, "Yes. You're doing what?" "We're creating a position." I said, "Well, you know I have too many children, and I really can't take a part-time job." He said, "It is full-time." And I just started screaming, just screaming and yelling and screaming and screaming, "Oh, thank you very much, thank you very much," and I hung up on him. I guess he kind of knew my excitement and didn't worry about it, and that's how I ultimately came here.

But the beautiful part is that I was feeling like whether I got the job or not, I had to be a part of this whole thing. And I really just said, "If this thing does anything for anybody else like it does for me—see, at the time I'm still thinking of it as a concept. I haven't grasped on to what it really is yet. All I know is that it's doing something to me and now I'm recognizing my thoughts, which is saving me, because I'm having some stinkin' thinkin', don't even know about it. And it was happening so much that I didn't realize them, and I was playing them out. So that's how I got it, and it was like amazing. I could not believe it. And just like, oh God, I can't even tell you—I don't even know where I'm going, but I'm not afraid. See, I'm just not afraid.

JP: How long from the time that you first got exposed to Health Realization did the job happen?

BG: Maybe two weeks, three weeks—not a month.

JP: Oh, that blows me away. You really must have caught something.

BG: I did, I must have caught *something*! And I'm so happy for it.

JP: And when you were talking about stuff shining through you, it's been happening right here, right now!

BG: [Screams] *Ooh, God*! [laughs] Okay, good, I'm telling you! And you know what? With my kids, I said, "If I'm blessed, if I just know, I know they'll be okay." And I don't try to push it on them, but I'm the Principles in action in my house, and I can't stop doing that. And if that catches on to my kids, I'd be like, "Yes!" But it's my little kids, like seven and eight, who say stuff that would blow me out of the water. My daughter told me the other day that her quality of thinking was very mellow. And I asked her, "Well, why do you think that is?" She said, "Because I was thinking that I wish I didn't have a brother because we fight all the time, but now I'm thinking, if he wasn't here, I'd just die." I have four kids of my own, two kids are kids from drug abuse, people that I knew and went on the same path that I did, and it almost felt like my fate to take on their kids. They had no family, and I was there. So two more kids I picked up, and now they've been with me so long it's like they're my children. People say, "Are those your six kids?" The difference is the struggle is not the same. I used to feel like a housemaid. I wore different clothing. I wore different perfume. And people would walk by and say, "You smell like old women perfume or something." But unconsciously I was doing that. And I would dress different because, like, I had a certain persona that I needed to put up so that people wouldn't bother me. I can take care of my four kids and two more, but what they don't know, see, is I have a secret. It's that I live my life through the

Principles—the Principles are in me, and it just takes away a lot of the extra excess baggage that I was carrying. There's six kids in a three-bedroom house, but they feel my spirit in that house, and they know that I'm only there to love and nurture you, and I want you to be happy. I don't care what anyone else is thinking about that. Go ahead, do your thing, because I'm doing mine, and it's not worrying about what you're thinking, because I know I have no control over that.

Jack Pransky

APPENDIX A

RESULTS FROM PSYCHOLOGY OF MIND (POM) OR NEO-COGNITIVE PSYCHOTHERAPY (NCP) RESEARCH

The Minneapolis Institute of Mental Health (MIMH) showed the effects of what it called "the psychological principles introduced by Suarez and Mills" on chemically dependent adolescents, ages 12-17, at the On-Belay Group Home, a residential facility. Until 1982 this facility had been employing a disease model approach. In 1983 when it switched to "the psychological principles..." the group home reported graduating twice as many students, five times as many became reunited with their families, and the former 6-12 month average length of stay decreased by 1/3. In a one year follow-up, 13 of 23 respondents (56.5%) reported "positive changes in their addictive behavior." The MIMH concluded that the study demonstrates that the introduction of these principles at a program level could significantly impact the therapeutic progress of chemically dependent adolescents in a group home setting (Minneapolis Institute of Mental Health, 1984).

A sample of 82 outpatients who had received at least three sessions of Neo-Cognitive Psychology (NCP) as the sole treatment modality for a minimum of 3 months were randomly selected from three different clinical settings and 7 different therapists. The clients had been treated for depression, anxiety, adjustment, and chemical dependency. At follow-up, 78 of the 82 that had received NCP treatment reported either absence of symptoms or a decrease in the severity and frequency of symptoms to the level that the patient could resolve themselves. Both therapists and patients independently rated the degree of disability of diagnosed symptoms. "In all cases, there was a statistically significant difference between the pre and post therapy disability ratings for both patient and therapist" (Suarez, 1985, p.15). No significant difference in results were found for age (which ranged from 17-62), gender, education, or race.

Shuford (1987) and Ringold (1993) described three early studies assessing NCP therapeutic efficacy. One study showed that patients reported significant improvement in productivity and quality of life, higher levels of self esteem, their relationships became more enjoyable and satisfying, they spent less time worrying, had fewer conflicts and arguments, a better family life, and were more productive at home and work. At follow up, mean scores on a 7 point Likert scale (0-6) clustered around "minimally disabling" to "mildly disabling" (.60 to 2.70) compared with a previous mean of 3.65 to 5.08, "significantly disabling" to "severely disabling" (Kidoo, 1984, in Shuford, 1987, p.32). Another study showed that NCP therapy ranged from 9 to 14 visits to alleviate symptoms and averaged 16 visits for patients to consistently report high mental health, characterized by feelings of well-being, self-esteem, and psychological maturity (Miller & Sickora, 1984, in Shuford, 1987). The efficacy of neo-cognitive psychology was also shown with 25 DUI (Driving Under the Influence) court mandated clients. At a six month follow up, after weekly individual sessions for period of fifteen weeks, 13 subjects continued to abstain from alcohol use and 12 reduced their use to a nonproblemmatic level, All rated their family life, social life, and job performance improved (Stewart, C., 1987 in Ringold, 1993).

Another preliminary study in an outpatient setting showed the efficacy in an outpatient setting of a neo-cognitive (NCP) approach to psychological change. The sample consisted of 42 outpatients from the Advanced Human Studies Institute who received NCP as the sole treatment modality; they had no previous therapy. Twenty two male and 22 female patients averaging 37 years old were pre and post tested on the Profile Moods States Bi-polar Form and the Brief Symptom Inventory. The number of treatment sessions ranged from 3 to 49 with a mean of 12.7. Subjects had sought therapy for anxiety, depression, relationship concerns, child abuse, eating disorders, and alcohol abuse. Pre to post change on the BSI nine symptom factors, GSI, and on all mood states of the POMS-BI was statistically significant beyond P.<.001; the scoring on most mood states showed a near doubling in improvement. The authors stated that at termination of treatment, patients reported symptoms to be almost nonexistent and indicated that they felt "happy, relaxed confident and energetic" (Shuford & Crystal, 1988, p.21).

The first post-hoc study on the effectiveness of "Neo-cognitive psychotherapy" (NCP) using standardized testing was conducted with 85 adult patients receiving treatment for depression or anxiety, randomly selected from a pool of approximately 250 in an outpatient clinical setting at the Minneapolis Institute of Mental Health (MIMH). NCP was the sole treatment modality used by all therapists for a mean of 13 therapy sessions. Post-test follow-up ranged from 0-24 months, and data were collected over a two to three years. Pre- to post- change for both diagnostic groups on all measures was were found to be statistically significant beyond the P.= <.0001 level: Weissman Social Adjustment scale (mean: pre = 2.13; post = 1.75); SCL-90 Multidimensional Symptom Self-report Inventory (mean: pre = .935 post = .445). The same level of significance held for a 5 point Distress Scale. As with the other studies no significant differences were found for age, sex, or education. Results were suggestive of NCP treatment efficacy (Shuford, 1988).

Two case studies detailed the process and effects of Neo-cognitive/Psychology of Mind therapy. The first concerned a severely traumatized 10 year old who was repeatedly and severely sexually molested by her uncle during the previous year and a half. She had become increasingly withdrawn and symptomatic, her school work plummeted, she could no longer remain in a regular class and had to be placed in a special class for emotionally disturbed children. She went downhill for six months. The NCP therapist first helped her to calm down, gave her hope, and assured her that she was really fine, that she was "just thinking too much in her head about it." The therapist cautioned her to stay away from dwelling on the past, that it just keeps people stuck in the same unhappy, unhealthy state of mind, and that by putting the problems out of her mind, it would give her a chance to gain perspective on them; in clearing her head she would have insights. The intent of the therapy was to guide both her and her family back to their mental health. Although not dealt with directly, in the first three months the father reported not drinking as much; the mother reported no longer depending upon sleeping pills for rest. The child began almost immediately to improve in school. Her teachers reported being astonished with her friendliness and diligence. Her grades improved, and she was able enroll in regular classes (the school planning team had been shocked at this recommendation), and she did very well (Crystal, 1988).

Another case study documented effects of treatment on two patients with histories of paranoid schizophrenia, in conjunction with their regular medication regimens (Ringold, 1992). The patients received six to seven months of outpatient POM therapy. One, a 30 year old African American female had been raped at age 16 and again at 23, her father was schizophrenic, and she'd been hospitalized and in outpatient treatment continually ever since. The other, a 38 year old African American male, had begun experiencing psychological difficulties at age 23, including paranoia, sleeplessness, lack of appetite, hallucinations, a history of drug abuse, and he had been hospitalized continuously two to four times a year. Both had been unable to make any significant improvements. After six months of Psychology of Mind treatment, based on the concept "that all human beings have a core of healthy intelligence that comes alive for them and can be experienced in their own lives" (p.73), the woman reported, "I'm not hearing some strange voices and I feel better. I feel healthier" (p.27). Her family and the staff noted improvements in her behavior. Both she and the other patient no longer had to return to the hospital on a regular basis. While assessment instruments indicated a variation in degree of symptoms experienced during therapy, both patients reported that "the therapy had improved their ability to function well in their lives" (p.75). The study concluded "…POM may have some usefulness as a therapeutic approach with…paranoid schizophrenia."

In a six year post hoc follow-up study of the long-term effectiveness of Neocognitive/POM psychotherapy, 23 of 45 former patients (13 female, 10 male, White, ages 30-54) responded to the follow-up inquiry. All had been the first clients of first time NCP-trained therapists. The subjects had experienced a variety of symptoms such as depression, chemical dependency, victims of physical and sexual abuse, marital problems, phobias and other anxieties. After an average of 14.6 sessions, all respondents reported positive change. No responses fell below the median of the Quality of Life scale, and 56.7% fell into the upper quartile. On a Positive Change scale, 80-91% of respondents reported improvements in general mood, appearance, self-esteem, marriage or significant relationships. Regarding their initial presenting problems 56.5% showed a recurrence, yet only 39.1% needed to return for professional help, 5.4% relapsed; 45.9% reported great change, and 48.7% reported moderate change. For patients with major depression, 73% showed great change and 27% moderate change; for general anxiety disorder, 26% showed great change, with 72% moderate and 3% relapse; for substance abuse, 60% showed great change, 40% moderate, and 0% relapse; for adjustment disorder, 47.5% showed great change, 45% moderate, and 7.5% relapse (Bailey, Blevens, & Heath, 1988). Another study cited elsewhere examined an outpatient treatment sample of 231 outpatient clients, 31% of whom were diagnosed with some type of depressive disorder. Of those diagnosed with major depression, 94.6% experienced a significant reduction in symptoms. Of the rest, 73% experienced very significant reductions and 27% experienced moderate change (Bailey, 1989, in Ringold 1992).

The first pre-post test study of POM therapy in outpatient settings was conducted with 53 adults, using the SLC-90-R and the Weissman Social Adjustment Scales. Patients were those with depression, anxiety, and adjustment disorders. From intake to three months of therapy, six of seven scales showed significant reductions in levels of distress (P.=<.001), and from three to six months (P.=<.05). Of patients with affective disorders, of those with adjustment disorders, 79.2% showed improvement (Blevens, Bailey, Olson, & Mills, 1992).

330

Although many of these studies have design flaws and this was not stringent scientific research, the cumulative picture offers compelling evidence of the potential of three Principle-based approaches as an effective psychotherapy. More study is warranted

Jack Pransky

Appendix B(1): Bemidji Study Qnuestionnaire (compressed)

FOLLOW-UP QUESTIONNAIRE FOR HEALTH REALIZATION TRAINING
NAME (optional): _____ Code (leave blank):_____
Which Health Realization training did you attend? May, 1997: __ October, 1997: __
How would you rate this training? Excellent__ Very Good__ Good__ Fair__ Poor__
Since the training, did you seek out or otherwise participate in additional Health Realization or Psychology of Mind training or learning, including readings or tapes? Yes____ No____ If yes, please specify.
For each question below, please circle the number that best indicates your answer, and/or fill in the blanks where indicated.
1. Since your exposure to Health Realization (HR) would you say that, generally, your inner life (e.g. the feelings you generally carry with you and what drives you) has—

5	4	3	2	1
improved very much	improved	remained the same	gotten slightly worse	gotten much worse

Explain:
2. Since your exposure to HR, would you say that, generally, your feeling level at work has-

5	4	3	2	1
improved very much	improved	remained the same	gotten slightly worse	gotten much worse

Explain:
3a. On average, before the training, approximately how often would you say that you got stressed out?

10   9   8   7   6   5   4   3   2   1
very little   very often

3b. On average now, approximately how often would you say that you get stressed out?

10   9   8   7   6   5   4   3   2   1
very little   very often

4a. Since your exposure to HR, would you say that, generally, your relationship with your kids has—

5	4	3	2	1
improved very much	improved	remained the same	gotten slightly worse	gotten much worse

Explain:
4b. On average, before the training, approximately how many times per week did you get into arguments or fights with your kids? Approximately ____ times per week
4c. On average now, approximately how many times per week do you get into arguments or fights with your kids? Approximately ____ times per week
5a. Since your exposure to HR, would you say that, generally, your relationship with your spouse or partner has—

5	4	3	2	1
improved very much	improved	remained the same	gotten slightly worse	gotten much worse

Explain.
5b. On average, before the training, approximately how many times per month did you get into arguments or fights with your spouse or partner? Approximately ___ times per month
5c. On average now, approximately how many times per month do you get into arguments or fights with your spouse or partner? Approximately ____ times per month
6. Since your exposure to HR, would you say that, generally, your relationship with your friends, co-workers, and neighbors has—

5	4	3	2	1
improved very much	improved	remained the same	gotten slightly worse	gotten much worse

7. Since your exposure to HR, would you say that, generally, your relationship with your boss or supervisor has—

5	4	3	2	1
improved very much	improved	remained the same	gotten slightly worse	gotten much worse

Explain answers to questions 6 and/or 7:

8. Since your exposure to HR, would you say that, generally, your relationships with people you found difficult

has-	5	4	3	2	1
	improved very much	improved	remained the same	gotten slightly worse	gotten much worse

Explain.

9a. Describe any other changes that have occurred in your experience of life since your exposure to HR?

9b. How do you account for these changes?

10a. Briefly describe any realizations or insights that you have had as a result of your exposure to HR?

10b. What difference have these insights or realizations made for you?

10c. Is there anything specific that you recall hearing in the Health Realization training that triggered these insights, and if so, what?

11a. Circle the number that best describes what you would say was the general quality of your life or well-being prior to your exposure to HR.

very high 10   9   8   7   6   5   4   3   2   1 very low

11b. Circle the number that best describes the general quality of your life or well-being now.

very high 10   9   8   7   6   5   4   3   2   1 very low

12a. Have you tried to convey to others what you realized, heard, saw, or understood through HR?

Yes__ No____ If so, how have you done it?

13. Have you seen any differences in others as a result helping them understand HR? Yes__ No__ If so, what?

Directions: *For each question below please circle the number that best represents where you would rate yourself today. The only requirement is honesty with yourself. highest—10 9 8 7 6 5 4 3 2 1—lowest*

1. If I experience a problem that I can't seem to solve I almost always try to put it out of my mind and wait until my head is clear so a solution can pop up as if from nowhere.

highest 10   9   8   7   6   5   4   3   2   1 lowest

2. If I am bothered by something I almost always wait until my mood rises before I say anything or before I act.

highest 10   9   8   7   6   5   4   3   2   1 lowest

3. If someone yells at me or insults me or does something to me that most people would consider hurtful or disrespectful I almost never take it personally; I almost always chalk it up to the way s/he is seeing things, or to a low mood.

highest 10   9   8   7   6   5   4   3   2   1 lowest

4. I almost always realize in the moment how my usual, habitual way of seeing things is affecting my tendency to get myself in trouble or to lose my bearings.

highest 10   9   8   7   6   5   4   3   2   1 lowest

5. I am often aware that how I am seeing someone or something is affecting how I feel.

highest 10   9   8   7   6   5   4   3   2   1 lowest

6. I almost always see beyond people's appearances or actions to the health inside them, and I act as if they are the embodiment of that health

highest 10   9   8   7   6   5   4   3   2   1 lowest

7. I am usually lighthearted or see things philosophically, even when things go wrong.

highest 10   9   8   7   6   5   4   3   2   1 lowest

8. I almost always realize that at any moment I can see things differently and therefore don't take myself too seriously.

highest 10   9   8   7   6   5   4   3   2   1 lowest

9. When working with others or with a friend, child, or partner who experiences a problem, I almost always try to get them to calm down, to regain his/her bearings, and only discuss it with them once they do.

highest 10   9   8   7   6   5   4   3   2   1 lowest

10. How would I rate my general mental well-being that I live in most of the time?

highest 10   9   8   7   6   5   4   3   2   1 lowest

***Now go back through all ten questions and place a square around the number that best represents where you were before you became exposed to Health Realization training.*

Note: This is not a test! No one I know is perfect. We are all in a continual process of evolving in one direction or another.

Appendix B(2) –Bemidji Study

SUMMARY OF RESULTS OF COMPLETED FOLLOW-UP QUESTIONNAIRES
(one year after 3-day Health realization Training)
Which Health Realization training did you attend?   May, 1997: _11_ October, 1997: _12_
                                                                          n = 23 out of a possible 37 responses
How would you rate this training? Excellent_17_ Very Good_4_ Good_1_ Fair_0_ Poor_0_

Since the training, did you seek out or otherwise participate in additional Health Realization or Psychology of Mind training or learning, including readings or tapes? Yes__18__ No__5___ If yes, please specify.
For each question below, please circle the number that best indicates your answer, and/or fill in the blanks where indicated.
1. Since your exposure to Health Realization (HR) would you say that, generally, your inner life (e.g. the feelings you generally carry with you and what drives you) has—

5 - 2	4 - 19	3 - 1	2 - 1	1 - 0
improved very much	improved	remained the same	gotten slightly worse	gotten much worse

Explain:
CJ: I am more aware of my innate health, and the connection my thoughts have to my ultimate well-being. I am better able to maintain my inner health through this understanding.
WP: I love the idea that I can react in a more positive way for my health
MM: I just <u>know</u> and see the truth in the principles and how it explains all interactions - it makes so much sense, it's a relief to know I am the creator of my experience on this earth journey.
MO: Always I have the intention and general attitude of continual improvement—this training has not interfered with that intention.
EP: I try to implement what I learned so stress doesn't overtake me. I understand others better or think I do and try to realize what their agenda is. Before I just saw what I needed to get done or accomplish and assumed everyone else understood and would act accordingly. I'm still struggling with some of this
MH: There is still quite a bit of internal strife in my department. I now know that I can control my thoughts so the stress doesn't affect me near as much.
JL: more calm
MN: I still backslide and think the world would be so much easier to navigate if everyone had the same understanding! But, overall, when I'm on track, I feel more sane and much less stressed.
MW: When I take the time or am open to learning/remembering more about who and what I am, I grow. HR offers me time and insights and stretched me
GI: High stress, illness in family, work stress, got lost in my own mud.
BY: I believe I take fewer life events personally, resulting in a lower stress level and higher optimism
TA: A waxing and waning awareness of the ability to consciously choose how I react to situations
D: I now seem to be much more aware of how my moods affect how I think and what I think about.

2. Since your exposure to HR, would you say that, generally, your feeling level at work has-

5 - 3	4 - 15 (1)	3 - 2	2 - 0	1 - 0
improved very much	improved	remained the same	gotten slightly worse	gotten much worse

Explain:
SS: more calm more often
MM: Much more able to see moods in others and myself; certainly take things less personally, try to help others take things less personally, and often see us scaring ourselves
DB: There were some things happening on the job that I let REALLY get to me … it was affecting me in a very negative way—now I realize I can only control myself and how I live in my world
CJ: I take more time to see where the other person is coming from, and seem to be less critical because of this awareness of their perspective.

EP: Well for one thing I changed job environments at about that time so that helped and I work with a great bunch of people, so even though the physical plant and economics are not ideal, I continue because of the healthy attitude of those around me and those I work with.

MH: Even though there is still substantial corruption where I work, I concentrate on the good and I realize that I can only be a good role model for others if I am not only doing the right things but appear to be happy.

MN: Recognition of the role of moods has been quite significant. Some of my work with interest based collective bargaining has some interesting parallels.

MW: It has been most helpful (even fun!) to share a bond with some of the others who have experienced some of the same ways of looking at situations, selves, others

BY: Improvement is the result of residing in an immediate work community that also embraces HR concepts

TA: somewhat: It is difficult to "hang on" to these principles in work related situations

BC: on leave of absence

3a. On average, before the training, approximately how often would you say that you got stressed out?

10	9	8	7	6	5	4	3	2	1
very little							**4.2**		very often

3b. On average now, approximately how often would you say that you get stressed out?

10	9	8	7	6	5	4	3	2	1
very little			**7.0**						very often

4a. Since your exposure to HR, would you say that, generally, your relationship with your kids has-

5 - 1	4 - 12 (1)	3 - 5	2 - 0	1 - 0
improved very much	improved	remained the same	gotten slightly worse	gotten much worse

Explain:

CJ: I am more patient with with their moods, since I recognize it as such. I am less likely to react angrily, since I am less angry and more compassionate. I express my needs to them more when I'm well than when I'm in a low mood.

WP: I look at comments less personally. I recognize my moods. I let things bother me less.

MM: Much more able to see their moods and see when they lose their bearings as innocent, not purposeful

MO: Largest improvement was period before training.

EP: I definitely have improved with my eldest, but he also went off to college, so that may have helped. But when he came home I tried to remember his needs, etc. as best as possible. I remember my own youth and wanting to be independent. Also with the # 2 son. We always got along better, but when we do argue it is short lived and we start over a lot.

MW: I guess it goes back to # 1. The more my inners grow, my ability to relate to the "outside" grows too. (I especially recall the "moods" ideas with the teens:)

DB: My step sons are now adults, and that, combined with HR, has helped us accept that we are different people but share a very strong common bond (thru my husband and their dad)—recently brought to light through a family crisis revolving around my husband's health

4b. On average, before the training, approximately how many times per week did you get into arguments or fights with your kids?   Approximately __**5.6**__ times per week

4c. On average now, approximately how many times per week do you get into arguments or fights with your kids?   Approximately __**2.4**__ times per week

5a. Since your exposure to HR, would you say that, generally, your relationship with your spouse or partner has--

5 - 4	4 - 12 (1)	3 - 4	2 - 0	1 - 0
improved very much	improved	remained the same	gotten slightly worse	gotten much worse

Explain.

CJ: I listen much better during stressful times

SS: More understanding. Quicker recovery from tension and quarrels

MM: Weeks short of a divorce—prior to HR-. This is perhaps the area I've seen most change in my life. I am able to see the innocence and humility in my spouse like never before, and see his busy-mindedness in a much bigger way

MN: I'm better able to pull back and not get engaged in conflicts—or to at least recognize what's happening and stop it at an earlier point. Hard to quantify. They aren't so intense. They don't last long now, and they often end with laughter when we realize what we're doing.

DD: I do not personalize behaviors the way I use to. Listening skills have improved. Compassion for insecurity.

BY: I believe we have acquired a basis for resolution or prevention of conflict that was not present in our relationship prior to HR training.

MO: generally

EP: We have had the same problems for so long that they are part of or lives, mainly with care of our elder pernicious dad also got sick recently, so he understands more, and he has been very supportive of my mothers health and problems and time required to attend to her.

MH: Understanding about not taking things personally. Trying more to see things from her perspective

TF: Presently. spouse is working out of the country

BY: I believe we have acquired a basis for resolution or prevention of conflict that was not present in our relationship prior to HR training.

DB: I tried to control him (unconsciously of course) and his behavior, and when I finally started to let go, things came to a head, and I feel we are on a better course now, especially for him

BC: We always had a good relationship, but we are both passionate folks

5b. On average, before the training, approximately how many times per month did you get into arguments or fights with your spouse or partner? Approximately __**3.5**__ times per month

5c. On average now, approximately how many times per month do you get into arguments or fights with your spouse or partner? Approximately __**1.8**__ times per month

6. Since your exposure to HR, would you say that, generally, your relationship with your friends, co-workers, and neighbors has—

5 - 0	4 - 12 (3)	3 - 7	2 - 0	1 - 0
improved very much	improved	remained the same	gotten slightly worse	gotten much worse

7. Since your exposure to HR, would you say that, generally, your relationship with your boss or supervisor has—

5 - 0	4 - 12	3 - 6	2 - 0	1 - 0
improved very much	improved	remained the same	gotten slightly worse	gotten much worse

Explain answers to questions 6-7:

SS: I don't take comments and actions as personally as I have in the past. It has helped to realize that stress and reality are actually how we perceive them; it's something we control

GL: I am less likely to react directly to the actions; instead I am evaluating the quality of my thoughts, aware of my thinking affecting my reactions, and evaluating moods involved / trying to reach a higher plane of my mind

CJ: HR hasn't seemed to alter my relationships with these people, except perhaps the deeper conversations about HR with friends who have taken the training.

MO: self-employed

WP: Keep more positive - for my health don't let little things bother, have great friends / I don't take things so personally - it's her thinking

EP: I think I still have room for improvement and this has been a particularly trying time trying to establish a clinic and get grants and funding, basically spinning straw into gold, but it is working. If I didn't have these co-workers and co-dreamers I might have given up or abandoned the idea and dream of or clinic

MH: I don't complain as much. / I stay away from him as much as possible.

MM: was good prior to training / not a lot of interaction with supervisor

SE: I don't take comments and actions as personally as I have in the past. It has helped to realize that stress and reality are actually how we perceive them; it's something we control

MN: we've had a good working relationship all along

? I loved and respected her before, and love and respect her now. any growth = improvement
TF: working well - not taking things personally - going with the flow
GI: I made a conscious effort to use HR in this area of my life
DB: nonpersonalization of employees problems / sharing HR principles with employees
BY: My supervisor lacks something

8. Since your exposure to HR, would you say that, generally, your relationships with people you found difficult
has-   5 - 0   4 - 17   3 - 5   2 - 0   1 - 0
        improved very   improved   remained   gotten   gotten much
        much   the same   slightly worse   worse
Explain.
CJ: I see more clearly why they are the way they are, or—where they are coming from
SS: I have more patience and more humor with my own attitude
MH: Not taking things personally . Everyone has problems, not just me.
MM: Able to see the innocence in their actions and see them in their state of confusion and find myself managing more with my heart, than head—which feels so much better, as I think my decisions are much more giving the benefit of the doubt of difficult people
MN: I'm much less frustrated and more patient, with some of our most difficult employees (I'm a personnel director)
MW: I am internally reminded to accept our differences and try to listen to what they are really saying
TF: I'm more able to accept them and realize they're doing the best they can with the situation they're in
DD: Again, non personalization of others problems. Listening skills have improved.
BY: While my relationship with difficult people remains the same, HR has helped me reduce the psycho/emotional cost
MO: Partly the same as # 1 answer and they seem less important
WP: Haven't really seen either of them much
EP: I didn't find lots of people difficult but again because of my new perspective I at least try to understand where they are coming from and why they are or act that way, that I don't get along or find them "difficult"
JL: I don't find many people difficult
TA: I have not applied these principles as much as I could.
BC: I haven't had much opportunity to try this out, since I have been home alone or with people whom I enjoy.

9a. Describe any other changes that have occurred in your experience of life since your exposure to HR?

CJ: I more clearly see that my thoughts determine my reality, and I'm able to think in more positive, health-promoting ways
WP: I've helped my kids look at life through the eyes of POM/HR and I've seen good changes there. I love what my marriage has become
EP: I don't sweat the small stuff.
SS: I notice my own insights more. I have more inner calm and get involved in others' business a lot less. I volunteer more. I see more options. I trust myself more.
MH: I look for the good in situations more
JL: tends to improve my self-esteem; interrupts habitual response patterns
MM: Finding the value in deeper listening, particularly with my own children. I am amazed and delighted to listen to them explore their own ideas and find their own answers.
MN: I find it much easier to not participate in the negativity that happens at work. I recognize so much of it as "small stuff." I'm paying even more attention to the need to listen deeply—and benefiting from doing it.
GL: Moods have been better, more restful, quality of work improved
JF: The experience helped me to wake up to the experience of life and get a clearer view .
MW: I'm more aware of trying to hear what to listen to
TF: more relaxed and accepting of things
DD: I do not remain stuck in anger for days anymore. My thoughts flow better and I move on with things. I do not personalize others issues, but have more compassion for them. I understand my own insecurities better also
BC: I am more aware of low mood and not trying to "fix" things while I'm in it

9b. How do you account for these changes?

CJ: Learning about thought in the HR training enabled me to be aware of my thought. Also, learning about the range of possible ways to view a situation gave me alternatives to "taking it personally," so that I can see (think) other thoughts about a situation.
SS: Having a better understanding of mind and thought
MH: realizing that I have control over my thoughts
JL: New understanding
MM: Just tried it, found it worked, and felt so much closer to people in general.
MN: Awareness of my thinking as well as that of others
Gl: Awareness that my thinking is creating my own reality
JF: It's difficult for me to know how much HR played in the positive changes that have occurred. Just being open to what life is teaching me moment-to-moment and knowing there are many choices I have in how I perceive and think about these experiences has been helpful.
MW: I listened and heard what you said!
TF: Having the insight to put things in perspective
DD: Learning HR and POM principles — applying them as much as I can
BC: Noticing thoughts. The training.

10a. Briefly describe any realizations or insights that you have had as a result of your exposure to HR?

CJ: That low moods are very temporary, and I'll rise out of them in time
MO: via Syd Banks — understanding my experience not so anachronistic; via Ed Lemon — nothing truly important is difficult
EP: Accentuate the positive thoughts. Eliminate negative thinking.
SS: I see my moods. I have a sense of the natural wisdom in my thoughts. I don't take my car and the weather personally.
JL: I have had a hard time recognizing how strongly attached I am to my own perspective.
MM: That I'm not a very good listener, but want to be. The truth of the principles. When you share this with others, what matters most is the feeling.
GL: I can feel better about life than I was feeling before my exposure to HR
JF: That every day we have an opportunity to wake up to the moment and that is where all life and eternity is — everything else is illusion.
MW: I realize that I feel blessed and humble that I know God who I can trust and and not feel I must become a god myself
TF: You can decrease your own stress by your thinking
DD: My own moods — low and high, and when I'm in them
BY: The concept is empowering. This feels a exciting to me at times, scary at others. The scary part arises from the realization that I can't blame so much on others any more.

10b. What difference have these insights or realizations made for you?

CJ: I'm less worried about experiencing a low mood—it has less impact on my mental health, just knowing it will be temporary. I'm much less likely to get "stuck" for lengths of time
WP: I clear my mind more often, catch stress and negative thinking sooner, clear mind more easily
EP: Life is easier, in a way. Less stress, or maybe same stress level but but I don't let it sap my strength and energy. Stress is self-defeating.
SS: I can tell others where I am (mood). Peace of mind. More willing to take chances. More open to possibilities. Able to give more people benefit of the doubt.
MH: Things are now fun again.
JL: Occasionally better listening. Greater patience with low moods.
MM: Not to be so hard on myself - understanding and awareness of wanting something more - and what that is.
MN: Some aspects of my job are easier, dealing with relationships with co-workers and supervisors.
GL: Improve relations with others, especially those who are difficult.
JF: It helps me to reduce my fears by knowing that much of them are just illusions, just thoughts.

MW: In the Bible it says the kingdom is within you — to me, that means God. So then, when I remember — what a great place to retreat into! The kingdom!

TF: more at peace with myself

DD: How to handle my decision-making issues at these times [moods]. Being aware of my thoughts at those times.

TA: A richer, more connected inner life

DB: I hope I'll be slowing down now and enjoying life more

BC: greater inner peace/happiness.

10c. Is there anything specific that you recall hearing in the Health Realization training that triggered these insights, and if so, what?

CJ: Mood elevator idea of visiting different floors

MO: Syd: "the mind" free of thought, and consciousness = the base; Ed - to dip into "that stream," the source

WP: "Clear your mind" "for your own health. "It's only their thinking" talk about in when you're not in a low mood. Enjoy the moment.

EP: Just the whole mind set and way of looking at things and others in the world. The eyeball. The stress circle. The examples on the overheads. I still get the job done, but a lot more fun doing it, and Not to worry so much. Clearing the mind does work!! I can't get over it.

SS: moods. Personal/nonpersonal. Levels of understanding.

MH: Whenever I have angry thoughts, I can catch myself and I don't have to be angry or depressed.

JL: The normalcy of mood swings to the human experience

MN: I think it's really the whole package that's made the difference

GL: The identification of when my best experiences have been in my life

JF: Just taking the time to remember those people who live or have lived in health (Jesus, Mother Theresa, Gandhi, George Foreman, my grandfather, my husband) These are all people with little fear, much wisdom, courage, laughter)

TF: "don't take things personally"

BY: I think it has resulted from a synthesis of all the HR concepts I've been taught and the discovery of those concepts in the literature of other disciplines.

DB: Yes, thinking about my thinking!! That's a lot to think about.

BC: noticing

11a. Circle the number that best describes what you would say was the general quality of your life or well-being prior to your exposure to HR.

10	9	8	7	6	5	4	3	2	1
very high			**6.8**		so-so				very low

11b. Circle the number that best describes the general quality of your life or well-being now.

10	9	8	7	6	5	4	3	2	1
very high		**8.0**			so-so				very low

12a. Have you tried to convey to others what you realized, heard, saw, or understood through HR? Yes_21_ No__1__ If so, how have you done it?

13. Have you seen any differences in others as a result helping them understand HR? Yes_11_ No_7_ If so, what?

CJ: through formal presentations (HS class. Girl Scouts, Community Ed staff) and informally in conversations as input on feedback./ / I think small gains have been made with my kids in regards to their awareness of thought and their internal control of their reality through their thought.

WP: I have purchased 14 Relationships Handbooks, and given Jack's Parenting books to many (including my girls)/ Positively, it's logical. I talk about it mainly in parts./ / My brother and sister in law may even try to keep their marriage going. Also for my daughter, I see her not getting so upset about happenings:—answers come. And in working out differences - It's their thinking

SS: conversation, gave tapes, loaned books, done presentations/ /more clarity, more optimism

MH: when they are angry or overwhelmed, I can give a little advice about controlling your thoughts/interested

Jack Pransky

JL: talk, shared tapes, book/ / my husband observed his low mood one day

MM: formal presentations (attached list) and evaluations; to my children in a teachable moment/see evaluations/Y

MN: Employees I've worked with have said it's easier for them not to take things personally and to focus on their own thinking rather than blaming others (supervisors or employees) for their difficulties without assuming any personal responsibility

GL: just sharing informally with others/interested but not exactly ready to accept the whole idea—seems to simple to be real/ / some have sought out information

JF: I describe Health Realization (to my friends) as Christ Realization. Recognizing Christ in ourselves and others. Professionally, I describe it "innate health", Just by seeing it, looking for it, it is drawn out in the light of the moment./ /it has helped my husband (I think) to not take things so personally or to feel that he has to fix things when I am upset.

TF: in helping people handle their stressful situations// more content with their life

DD: some of my employees have been through trainings, Husband and children exposed to HR through my conversations. Many other community members spoken to... / an employee who is in a supervisory position - more aware of her moods and decisions, ways of handling her employee concerns with some changes.

BY: I didn't do a good job and they didn't want to hear it.

—SE: Before HR I thought (perceived) I was handling life fairly well. If you don't know there's a better way of thinking, you think you're doing OK

—

1. If I experience a problem that I can't seem to solve I almost always try to put it out of my mind and wait until my head is clear so a solution can pop up as if from nowhere.

highest 10   9   8   7   6   5   4   3   2   1 lowest

7.1- - - - - - - - - - - - - - - - - 4.4

2. If I am bothered by something I almost always wait until mood rises before I say anything or before I act.

highest 10   9   8   7   6   5   4   3   2   1 lowest

6.7- - - - - - - - - - - - - - - - 3.9

3. If someone yells at me or insults me or does something to me that most people would consider hurtful or disrespectful I almost never take it personally; I almost always chalk it up to the way s/he is seeing things, or to a low mood.

highest 10   9   8   7   6   5   4   3   2   1 lowest

7.2 - - - - - - - - - - - - - - - - - 4.2

4. I almost always realize in the moment how my usual, habitual way of seeing things is affecting my tendency to get myself in trouble or to lose my bearings.

highest 10   9   8   7   6   5   4   3   2   1 lowest

7.1 - - - - - - - - - - - - - - - - 4.1

5. I am often aware that how I am seeing someone or something is affecting how I feel.

highest 10   9   8   7   6   5   4   3   2   1 lowest

7.5 - - - - - - - - - - - - - - - 4.7

6. I almost always see beyond people's appearances or actions to the health inside them, and I act as if they are the embodiment of that health

highest 10   9   8   7   6   5   4   3   2   1 lowest

6.9 - - - - - - - - - - - - - - 4.2

7. I am usually lighthearted or see things philosophically, even when things go wrong.

highest 10   9   8   7   6   5   4   3   2   1 lowest

7.7 - - - - - - - - - - - - - 5.2

340

8. I almost always realize that at any moment I can see things differently and therefore don't take myself too seriously.

highest 10   9   8   7   6   5   4   3   2   1 lowest

6.8 - - - - - - - - - - - - - - - 4.2

9. When working with others or with a friend, child, or partner who experiences a problem, I almost always try to get them to calm down, to regain his/her bearings, and only discuss it with them once they do.

highest 10   9   8   7   6   5   4   3   2   1 lowest

7.5 - - - - - - - - - - - - - - 5.1

10. How would I rate my general mental well-being that I live in most of the time?

highest 10   9   8   7   6   5   4   3   2   1 lowest

7.7 - - - - - - - 6.2

Appendix B(3)

BEMIDJI STUDY DESIGN: A QUALITATIVE STUDY MEASURING EFFECTS OF HEALTH REALIZATION TRAINING ON PARTICPANTS

The Study: Phenomenological study question: "How do people perceive and describe their experience following Health Realization training?" Open-ended interview process.

Doctoral Study Committee "core faculty": Dr. Marvin Sussman and Dr. Donald Klein. Early assistance on study question and design provided by Dr. Clark Moustakas.

Health Realization training *participants* who also volunteered to be interviewed for this study:

DD: director of a semi-independent, private nursing service.
MM: director of Beltrami County Public Health Nursing Services
SS: a licensed mental health counselor and family therapist
CJ: a school board member, community volunteer and parent
BC: a community member from Bemidji, temporarily on leave from human services
JF: a nurse from Beltrami County Public Health Nursing Service
CA: a community development coordinator for a battered women's coalition
GL: county administrator for Beltrami County
MN: director of personnel for Beltrami County
WP: director of a kinship mentoring program
JL: a businessperson, who asked if she could attend after hearing me speak briefly at Rotary Club
MO: a psychologist and instructor for Bemidji State University
BY: director of Upward Bound, Bemidji State University

GLOSSARY OF TERMS

Study Question:
perceive — what participants see and feel and realize. Health Realization asserts it is impossible to separate "perception" from an "objective" description of experience
experience — whatever people see of their lives, or whatever people would say about their lives or the quality of their lives, or whatever they would say happens in their lives; .
Body of Study:
Consciousness – the power to experience
experience – the totality of everything that one is conscious of in the moment, including the feelings one has and the reality one perceives
field **of prevention** – individuals, groups, and institutions engaged in the study and practice of prevention
Health – the totality of one's mental, physical, and spiritual well-being
Health Realization – an inside-out approach to prevention and education based on the three Principles of Mind, Consciousness, and Thought which, together, create people's experience of life
innate health – a fundamental property of the three Principles that is an inborn, natural state of well-being or wisdom arising from pure Consciousness and accessed via a clear mind or from realizing the infinite capacity for formless creation of new experience via Thought
inside-out – beginning with what occurs inside one's being and then moves outward to affect the family, other relationships, the community, it's institutions or society
Mind – the intelligence and energy behind life; the life-force; the source of Consciousness and Thought
Neo-cognitive Therapy (NCP) – a term used in the past by Psychology of Mind practitioners to describe the psychotherapy practice of Psychology of Mind (Note: Now when Psychology of Mind is applied as psychotherapy it is most often referred to as Health Realization or principle-based psychotherapy.)
outside-in – an approach to prevention or community change that begins with what occurs in the community, it's institutions or society or other external conditions that affect people, and then moves inward to affect one's being and behavior
perceive/perception – what one has consciousness of taking in through any or all of the senses

prevention - the act of creating conditions that come before a problem so the problem cannot materialize (Pransky, 1991); the act of creating conditions that promote well-being and thereby reduce the incidence or prevalence of problem behaviors (adapted from Lofquist, 1983)

prevention practitioners – those who practice prevention out in the field or who otherwise engage in prevention efforts with people or communities

preventionists – those who engage in the study of prevention

Principle – a force in the universe or in nature that always exists, irrespective of people's awareness of it

Psychology of Mind (POM) – a name formerly used for the study and practice within the field of psychology of the three Principles of Mind, Consciousness and Thought

resiliency/resilience – the capacity to spring back, rebound, or successfully adapt in the face of adversity; that property of a material that allows it to resume its original shape after being bent, stretched, or compressed

Spirit – the realm of the intangible, formless, and nonmaterial; of, from, or pertaining to God or the soul

spiritual/spirituality – of, relating to, consisting of, or having the nature of spirit

the three Principles – The three principles underlying Psychology of Mind and Health Realization: Mind, Consciousness, and Thought

Thought – the power to create; all mental activity

thought content – an individual's specific thoughts

A Few Notes on Study Methods

I, as researcher, had no way to explore people's internal experience without their full collaboration and participation; therefore, they became "co-researchers" in the process. This is why I selected an open-ended interview process, where co-researcher responses to my questions prompted me to probe further in specific directions I would not have thought of otherwise, and in directions that they considered most important and relevant. I also chose to supplement qualitative research with a small, complementary, quantitative design to construct a more complete and inclusive understanding of issues involved, and draw upon the strengths of both approaches

A Few Notes on Data Analysis Procedure

For quantitative data: As quantitative data from questionnaire were not primary reason for research, I merely determined the mean score for each question and compared their perceptions before and after training. I did not believe further statistical analysis was necessary because its purpose was merely to show an overall picture of the percentage of training participants who experienced changes as a result of the training, and to what extent.

For the qualitative data: I followed basic procedure of analyzing qualitative data described by Creswell (1998) and adapted the phenomenological analysis for this purpose, as follows: 1) I transcribed the raw interview data; 2) I listened to each audiotape, watched each videotape and read through each interview text; 3) I read through the text again and searched for themes about co-researcher experiences, making notes of themes in the margins; 4) I re-examined the themes and clustered the meanings to find relationships between themes, placing all themes on the same page or pages; 5) I read the crossed themes and went into a state of *epoche*, clearing my mind and eliminating preconceptions; 6) from this state of *epoche* I had an insight that my initial categorical and combined themes were not of primary importance; a new classification of themes then came to mind that appeared to represent more of the crux of what the co-researchers were communicating; 7) I developed an interpretation of what appeared to take place to cause the changes in their lives, based on their statements; 8) I wrote a narrative that appeared to me to be the essence of their experience.

After I began data analysis I was influenced by Belenky, Bond & Weinstock in *A Tradition That Has No Name* (1997), where researchers sought to draw out participants' expressions of their "own voice." I found the richness of expression captured by their own words would be my preferred direction.

Study *Limitations and Concerns*

All training participants were given equal opportunity to participate in interviews for this study. All those who expressed interest in being interviewed were, with exception of a sheriff's department officer with whom I was unable to arrange a mutually convenient time for interview while I was in Bemidji. He did fill out a questionnaire.

Those who chose to be interviewed were those who perceived, at least to some extent, that the Health Realization training contributed to some level of improvement in their lives. While this was anticipated, it does

343

suggest possible limitations in the sample, as no one who felt that they got little or nothing from the training chose to be interviewed. Also, there was no control group. Both limitations are less an issue of concern for this qualitative study because I was most interested in those who perceived their lives had changed and why, but a control group would have been preferable for the quantitative portion.

Another limitation: I was both the trainer for the Health Realization trainings and the one who conducted the interviews. Ideally, the interviews should have been conducted by a more neutral party. My role might have yielded some bias in responses. To counteract this potential problem, I a member of my doctoral committee, Dr. George Brown, to write to Susan Smith, my point-person in Bemidji for the interviews, to ask her to take a sample poll of participants to determine whether they thought they would have given different responses had I not been the one conducting the interviews. This yielded a letter from Ms. Smith dated June 1, 1999 stating, "In regards to…being certain that the interview responses reflect the respondent's thoughts at the time of the interview given that Jack was both trainer and interviewer…In each case the individuals responded with a wholehearted, "Yes" and said they would have given the same answers had another person been conducting the interviews…" Further, to ensure that in my report of results I accurately portrayed what people said, Dr. Brown's letter to Ms. Smith asked her if, in her sample poll, she would share with participants a draft of the results section of this study to determine whether my specification of themes depicting their responses in fact accurately reflected those responses. Again, the letter from Ms. Smith stated, "In regards to concern # 2, all people contacted felt that their responses were contained in the categories and that all the themes accurately reflected what they said." Another way I chose to counteract potential bias was to report results largely by using direct quotes instead of using my own interpretations of what participants stated.

As do Belenky, Bond & Weinstock (1997) in their analysis of their own program, I admit my bias that prior to the interviews I hoped and anticipated that those who participated in the Health Realization training intervention would experience healthy changes in their experience of life as a result. I trust my use of their own words would dispel most of this bias.

Because perceptions of improvement in one's life is a personal matter, the following research concerns were of little or no consequence in designing this study: This inquiry was not intended to compare those who experienced improvement in their lives with those who did not. It was not intended to determine why some people attending this training had one experience and others a different experience. It was not intended to determine what about this training makes it life changing for some and not for others? All such inquiries are recommended for future study.

It is, however, a legitimate question why most participants apparently got a tremendous amount out of this training and at least a few apparently did not. Given interview responses, it is clear all participants whose lives changed had new insights about themselves and their lives, and those who experienced no change did not. Further study is warranted to answer the deeper question of why some and not others experience insights from such a training.

Co-researchers reported that the life changes they experienced were the result of the Health Realization training. Because self-reports were the primary source of data, questions may be raised about the accuracy of such reports. In my view, it does not matter whether anyone else thought participants' lives improved, because their own perceptions of their lives is what matters to them. Their own perceptions of change are what is important to them. Corroboration of their reports by others would have only added supplemental information and is recommended for further study.

Since respondents showed an increase in positive scores on all parameters, another legitimate question is whether reported changes could have occurred without this intervention, due simply to the maturation process of respondents over time, or because some other influence may have occurred in the intervening year since the training. This arises because the study design lacked a control group. However, participants did report that improvements in their lives were the direct result of understandings gained through Health Realization, either in the training itself or through their own subsequent pursuit of Health Realization due to interest sparked during that training. Previously participants reported that they did not experience anything close to this type of change.

Would similar results have occurred in any three-day preventive intervention? Without a control group this is impossible to determine. While I have been involved personally as both a trainer and a participant in numerous prevention trainings and have never seen this kind of life change after three days, this is still a legitimate question and further controlled, longitudinal studies are indicated.

While much prevention education tends to fade over time and requires booster sessions to continue to have lasting impact (Pransky, 1991), the effects of Health Realization training appear to deepen over time. Such was the case in this study, as well as in Modello and other Health Realization projects, and in my own life. People who have deep enough insights into the power of what Health Realization is pointing to appear to continue on their own to seek further understanding.

Because after the training participants decided on their own to further their understanding of Health Realization through tapes, books, other trainings or other means, does this mean the changes in their lives cannot be solely attributed to the three-day trainings? Clearly, training participants' further pursuit of Health Realization did contribute to their deepening understanding, which then further improved their lives. Nonetheless, any individual further pursuit of Health Realization was an outgrowth of the initial training. Health Realization expects that change occurs via insight, and no one can predict when an insight will occur. Sometimes this happens during the training, and sometimes after when people go back to their lives and begin to make connections. Sometimes it happens through pursuit of other Health Realization training or resources. Even so, some participants in the initial training did not participate in other training or pursue other POM-related resources, and some of their lives also improved as much as those who pursued other resources or training. Insight is unpredictable. Further study is indicated here as well.

In retrospect, it was an omission of this study that during the interviews I did not think to ask about temporal sequencing or progression of post-training experience that went on during the weeks and months following the experience. Therefore, I did not uncover whether there were ups and downs, doubts, subsequent revelations, or times when they felt they "lost it." Many of the co-researchers' stories, however, do indicate they did have ups and downs but some of their understandings appeared to deepen over time. Yet, this was one of the weakest aspects of this study.

Still another question arises concerning the population of this study. These were largely white middle class professionals, an atypical population for most prevention interventions. If this population studied were more "at risk" of developing the problems that one typically wants to prevent, would changes have been observed in problem behaviors such as substance abuse, violence, school behavior problems, teenage pregnancy and other problem behaviors? From this study, there is no way to tell. However, results from other Health Realization projects such as Modello and Coliseum Gardens, reported earlier in Section II, have found substantive reductions in such problem behaviors with these populations. While further study is advised, many of the professionals in this study were those who work with typical prevention populations. Study results suggest that in a number of cases these professionals appear to have begun to apply what they learned to their work with their clients and community or community members. Further longitudinal study is warranted here as well to determine if this indication continues over time.

Other Recommendations from the Study (besides those reported in Chapter XII)

1. compare those attending Health Realization training who experienced improvement in lives with those who didn't to determine why some attending such a training have different experiences, and specifically what about this training makes it life changing for some and not for others
2. more objectively measure behavior change among training participants other than by self-reports
3. determine whether similar results would have occurred during the same time period within a similar population in a similar setting with no intervention, or in comparison with other preventive interventions
4. measure longitudinal effects on a community over time after Health Realization training, and as compared with other prevention efforts
5. compare the relative efficacy of the new and older approaches to teaching Health Realization (teaching principles vs. teaching concepts)
6. determine efficacy in more "at risk" populations of behavior changes in which the prevention field is interested, such as substance abuse, violence, school behavior problems, teenage pregnancy, etc.
7. when professional human services providers receive training, determine whether this longitudinally leads to community change or change in problem behaviors in "at risk" populations;
8. determine what specifically it was about the Health Realization training that helped to spark the insights that made the changes occur among participants.
9. fund and conduct controlled, longitudinal studies of Health Realization efforts in accordance with above

Appendix C(1)

COMPARISON RESULTS FROM FOLLOW-UP QUESTIONNAIRES (numbers only)
FROM BEMIDJI I AND BEMIDJI II STUDIES

Which Health Realization training did you attend?
May, 1997: _11_ October, 1997: _12_ n = 23 out of a possible 37 responses = 62%
March 2000   *n= 14 out of a possible 26 responses = 54%*

How would you rate this training?
Excellent_17_ Very Good_4_ Good_1_ Fair_0_ Poor_0_
*Excellent_8_ Very Good_3_ Good_1_ Fair_2_ Poor_0_*

Since the training, did you seek out or otherwise participate in additional Health Realization or Psychology of Mind training or learning, including readings or tapes? Yes__18__ No__5___ If yes, please specify.
Yes__9__ No__5___ If yes, please specify.

For each question below, please circle the number that best indicates your answer, and/or fill in the blanks where indicated.
1. Since your exposure to Health Realization (HR) would you say that, generally, your inner life (e.g. the feelings you generally carry with you and what drives you) has--

5 - 2		4 - 19	3 - 1	2 - 1	1 - 0	
5 - 3	*(1)*	*4 - 7*	*3 - 2*	*2 - 0*	*1 - 0*	
improved very much		improved	remained the same	gotten slightly worse	gotten much worse	

2. Since your exposure to HR, would you say that, generally, your feeling level at work has-

5 - 3		4 - 15	(1)	3 - 2	2 - 0	1 - 0
5 - 3	*(1)*	*4 - 4*	*(1)*	*3 - 3*	*2 - 0*	*1 - 0*
improved very much		improved		remained the same	gotten slightly worse	gotten much worse

3a. On average, before the training, approximately how often would you say that you got stressed out?

10	9	8	7	6	5	4	3	2	1
very little						4.2			very often
very little						*3.6*			*very often*

3b. On average now, approximately how often would you say that you get stressed out?

10	9	8	7	6	5	4	3	2	1
very little			7.0						very often
very little			*6.0*						*very often*

4a. Since your exposure to HR, would you say that, generally, your relationship with your kids has-

5 - 1		4 - 12	(1)	3 - 5	2 - 0	1 - 0
5 - 2	*(1)*	*4 - 8*		*3 - 1*	*2 - 0*	*1 - 0*
improved very much		improved		remained the same	gotten slightly worse	gotten much worse

4b. On average, before the training, approximately how many times per week did you get into arguments or fights with your kids?
Approximately __5.6___ times per week
Approximately __3.75___ times per week

4c. On average now, approximately how many times per week do you get into arguments or fights with your kids?
Approximately __2.4___ times per week

346

Approximately __1.25___ times per week

5a. Since your exposure to HR, would you say that, generally, your relationship with your spouse or partner has—

5 - 4		4 - 12	(1)	3 - 4		2 - 0		1 - 0	
5 - 3	*(1)*	*4 - 3*		*3 - 3*		*2 - 0*		*1 – 0*	
						(+1 removed due to divorce)			
improved very		improved		remained		gotten		gotten much	
much				the same	slightly worse		worse		

5b. On average, before the training, approximately how many times per month did you get into arguments or fights with your spouse or partner?

Approximately __3.5__ times per month

Approximately __3.0__ times per month

5c. On average now, approximately how many times per month do you get into arguments or fights with your spouse or partner?

Approximately __1.8__ times per month

Approximately __1.15__ times per month

6. Since your exposure to HR, would you say that, generally, your relationship with your friends, co-workers, and neighbors has--

5 - 0		4 - 12	(3)	3 - 7		2 - 0		1 - 0
5 - 1	*(1)*	*4 - 7*		*3 - 3*		*2 - 0*		*1 - 0*
improved very		improved		remained		gotten		gotten much
much				the same	slightly worse		worse	

7. Since your exposure to HR, would you say that, generally, your relationship with your boss or supervisor has--

5 - 0		4 - 12		3 - 6		2 - 0		1 - 0
5 - 1		*4 - 3*		*3 - 3*		*2 - 0*		*1 - 0*
improved very		improved		remained		gotten		gotten much
much				the same	slightly worse		worse	

8. Since your exposure to HR, would you say that, generally, your relationships with people you found difficult has-

5 - 0		4 - 17		3 - 5		2 - 0		1 – 0
5 - 1	*(1)*	*4 - 8*	*(1)*	*3 - 1*		*2 - 0*		*1 - 0*
improved very		improved		remained		gotten		gotten much
much				the same	slightly worse		worse	

11a. Circle the number that best describes what you would say was the general quality of your life or well-being prior to your exposure to HR.

10	9	8	7	6	5	4	3	2	1
very high			6.8		so-so			very low	
very high			*6.1 so-so*				*very low*		

11b. Circle the number that best describes the general quality of your life or well-being now.

10	9	8	7	6	5	4	3	2	1
very high		8.0			so-so			very low	
very high	*8.6*				*so-so*			*very low*	

12a. Have you tried to convey to others what you realized, heard, saw, or understood through HR?

Yes_21_ No__1__   If so, how have you done it?

Yes_11_ No__2__

13. Have you seen any differences in others as a result helping them understand HR?   Yes_11_ No_7_

If so, what?   *Yes__7_ No_4_*

Directions: *For each question below please circle the number that best represents where you would rate yourself today. The only requirement is honesty with yourself.*

1. If I experience a problem that I can't seem to solve I almost always try to put it out of my mind and wait until my head is clear so a solution can pop up as if from nowhere.

highest 10   9   8   7   6   5   4   3   2   1 lowest

7.1- - - - - - - 4.4

6.45- - - - - -4.0

2. If I am bothered by something I almost always wait until my mood rises before I say anything or before I act.

highest 10   9   8   7   6   5   4   3   2   1 lowest

6.7- - - - - - - -3.9

6.7- - - - - - - 4.0

3. If someone yells at me or insults me or does something to me that most people would consider hurtful or disrespectful I almost never take it personally; I almost always chalk it up to the way s/he is seeing things, or to a low mood.

highest 10   9   8   7   6   5   4   3   2   1 lowest

7.2 - - - - - - - - - - - - - 4.2

6.3 - - - - - - - - - - - - - - 3.1

4. I almost always realize in the moment how my usual, habitual way of seeing things is affecting my tendency to get myself in trouble or to lose my bearings.

highest 10   9   8   7   6   5   4   3   2   1 lowest

7.1 - - - - - - - - - - - - - 4.1

7.0 - - - - - - - - - - - - - - - 3.7

5. I am often aware that how I am seeing someone or something is affecting how I feel.

highest 10   9   8   7   6   5   4   3   2   1 lowest

7.5 - - - - - - - - - - - - -4.7

7.0 - - - - - - - - - - - - 4.3

6. I almost always see beyond people's appearances or actions to the health inside them, and I act as if they are the embodiment of that health

highest 10   9   8   7   6   5   4   3   2   1 lowest

6.9 - - - - - - - - - - - 4.2

6.5 - - - - - - - - - - - - - -3.45

7. I am usually lighthearted or see things philosophically, even when things go wrong.

highest 10   9   8   7   6   5   4   3   2   1 lowest

7.7 - - - - - - - - - - -5.2

6.5 - - - - - - - - - - - - -3.8

8. I almost always realize that at any moment I can see things differently and therefore don't take myself too seriously.

highest 10   9   8   7   6   5   4   3   2   1 lowest

6.8 - - - - - - - - - - 4.2

6.9 - - - - - - - - - -4.6

9. When working with others or with a friend, child, or partner who experiences a problem, I almost always try to get them to calm down, to regain his/her bearings, and only discuss it with them once they do.

highest 10   9   8   7   6   5   4   3   2   1 lowest

7.5 - - - - - - - - - - -5.1

7.3 - - - - - - - - - - - 4.6

10. How would I rate my general mental well-being that I live in most of the time?

highest 10   9   8   7   6   5   4   3   2   1 lowest

7.7 - - - - - 6.2

7.4 - - - - - - - - - - - -4.7

Appendix C(2) – Bemidji II Study: A Supplemental Follow-Up Study

Comparison Results

The summary results questionnaire in Appendix C (1) shows comparison results between the first and second Bemidji studies. If nothing else, this second study provides some verification that the first study was not a fluke; that teaching Health Realization in either form does appear to help people live in higher levels of well-being and with reduced stress.

Issues and questions raised by these data for Health Realization practitioners

This study raises some interesting questions for Health Realization practitioners; it appears to corroborate many practitioner perceptions that teaching solely via the principles may be even more efficacious than teaching via the old Psychology of Mind Training Institute (POMTI) "concepts." While some may point to similar results such as reduction in stress and conclude it does not matter how Health Realization is conveyed, this would not appear to be an accurate conclusion, for both "quality of life" and "well-being" improvements were far lower when teaching via the concepts. This study may suggest that there is no set way to convey this understanding to have it produce results. However, these data do not suggest that Health Realization practitioners yet know the best way to convey this understanding for it to have the greatest impact on others. Every form created to convey this understanding has some flaws precisely because it is taught through a form, even when attempting to convey it with the least form possible (the principles). Concepts are made-up formulations of the mind; principles, as the term is used here, exist in the universe whether we are aware of them or not. Also, if participants can reach the same place in less time, it makes little sense to teach through the concepts.

While a lower percentage of returns came in from the third (principle-based) training, this does not suggest this training was not as well received. This 2000 survey questionnaire was sent out as a private study; I as researcher did not spend the time tracking down participants to yield a better return as I did with the first, doctoral study. Nor does the fact that a lower percentage of trainees went on to seek further training on their own mean anything, for there were a couple of very enthusiastic go-getters from the first training who went out of their way to bring other Health Realization-related trainings into Bemidji. Nor does the fact that the 2000 training was rated slightly less highly overall have anything to do with training outcomes. Results were reasonably similar, regardless of how well each training group rated it.

It may be important to note that the fact anyone changes as a result of any training is a testament to the three principles in action. In other words, no matter what the venue, if one's thinking changes, one's experience changes along with it. Another way of saying this is it is important to separate out the methodology used to convey the principles, and the fact that change happens because of the principles, no matter what methodology is used. If anyone's thinking shifts to the extent that their level of consciousness rises, that person will have a better life experience. The question is whether the change lasts. Both of these studies show at least after one year, people's new experience of life lasts.

All study limitations pertaining to the quantitative data reported in the 1999 study are true for this study also (Appendix B(3)). In addition to those, quantitative data for both studies, and in comparison with each other, needs measures of statistical significance applied. However, these data for these studies are available from Jack Pransky to anyone who wishes to do perform that task.

Recommendations

This replication study showing results of Health Realization training after one year suggests the efficacy of Health Realization training for improving lives and improving behavior, and for reducing stress, a noted precursor for alcohol and other drug abuse and a host of other problems such as violence. This would further recommend Health Realization as an effective and model approach to prevention. Of course, further rigorous, controlled, longitudinal scientific study is also recommended.

Appendix D

More detail on Health Realization history (as I understand it) [continued from Chapter VIII]

By 1987, *Sanity, Insanity and Common Sense* had been revised and coauthored with Darlene Stewart (Suarez, Mills & Stewart, 1987). The "four principles" it articulated had been honed to the following: 1) Thought as a function: The capability of each human being to formulate thoughts; 2) Separate realities: The separate reality of individual differences that every unique thought system creates; 3) Levels of consciousness: The degree to which a human being is aware that he or she is using an ability to think to formulate experience in life; 4) Feelings and emotions as indicators of levels of consciousness, or of the quality and direction of human psychological functioning.

In 1986 Jane Nelson published *Understanding*, the first self-help book based on these "four principles." It stated, "Most people act like victims of their thoughts instead of producers of their thoughts. Instead of knowing that thinking is a function or an ability, they believe that what they think is reality… As soon as we take the content of our thoughts seriously we have forgotten that we think" (p.18).

In 1989 a major leap of understanding occurred in Psychology of Mind when Banks issued a tape correcting the "neocognitive" interpretation of his experience. Three, not four, Principles, he asserted, work together to create people's psychological experience: Mind, Consciousness and Thought. The "four principles" were abandoned, and the Advanced Human Studies Institute closed.

A Psychology of Mind (POM) Training Institute formed in an attempt to provide leadership. The faculty of the Institute sought advice from a former president of the American Psychological Association (APA) in hopes this new psychology eventually would be accepted by it. His advice led to the development of a training, certification and internship program and the development of six "core concepts." These concepts, articulated by the POM core faculty around 1991-1992, were intended to present a logical conceptual framework that would help explain the three Principles. The concepts were: Innate Health; Two Modes of Thinking, Feelings and Emotions; Moods; Thought Systems; Levels of Understanding; Healthy Psychological Functioning. [Note: As these were later abandoned, I see no point amplifying them here.] "Thought Systems" was dropped as a concept when the faculty recognized it made POM sound too much like cognitive psychology, and made it appear that there was some fixed entity within the mind to content with, rather than only ever-changing thoughts.] "Core Concepts" courses were created by the faulty to officially convey this understanding. During this time, talk of spirituality within POM became taboo, largely because of the perception that the APA would not approve, and possibly because they didn't want POM to sound New-Agey and run the risk of turning people off.

In 1996, as he was writing the book, *The Renaissance of Pscyhology* (Pransky, G., 1998) (which he later took off the market when his own understanding deepened), George Pransky realized that people's understanding of the concepts was all over the map, and the concepts were not as clear as they might be even to the practitioners using them. He thus convened POM practitioners to engage in conceptual rigor. Meanwhile, the certification program did not seem to produce what the faculty intended, so it was dropped. [Note: The training I conducted in Bemidji, Minnesota and studied for my doctoral dissertation (Pransky, 1999) (Chapter XII) occurred within this stage of Psychology of Mind/Health Realization development.]

During this period a few books appeared, applying Psychology of Mind to various aspects of life, such as relationships—*Divorce is Not the Answer*, subsequently titled, *The Relationship Handbook* (Pransky, 1990), and substance abuse—*The Serenity Principle* (Bailey, 1990). After nearly a decade Mills (1995) wrote *Realizing Mental Health*, a book articulating the then-newer understanding. Richard Carlson wrote the self-help books *You Can Be Happy No Matter What* (1997) and *You Can Feel Good Again* (1993), and later hit the big time with the *New York Times* Best Seller, *Don't sweat the small stuff…:and it's all small stuff* (1997) a book loosely based on Psychology of Mind. Joe Bailey later collaborated with Carlson to write *Slowing down to the speed of life* (Carlson & Bailey, 1997). In 1997 *Parenting from the Heart* (Pransky) applied Health Realization to parenting, and in 1998 the story of *Modello* was told (Pransky).

In 1997 the international Psychology of Mind Resource Centre (now Philosophy of Living Centre) and website was created in Western Australia to promulgate this understanding.

By the end of the decade everything changed again. Sydney Banks, who normally had nothing to do with the operation of Psychology of Mind, felt he needed to step in once again. He pointed out that any "concepts" took people away from the pure understanding of the three Principles. Without realizing it and with the best of intentions Psychology of Mind had begun to go astray, becoming lost in its own formulations. The Psychology of Mind faculty disbanded, and with it its training institute.

In 1996 a Psychology of Mind Foundation had formed to proliferate Psychology of Mind, but in 1999 changed its name to the Aequinimitas Foundation and assumed leadership, returning to the articulation of this understanding solely through the purity of the three Principles. Its faculty (of which I was honored to be a member) created courses called Foundations I and Foundations II, on which the Foundation began to conduct research. The term "Psychology of Mind" began to fade from use.

The Aequanimitas Foundation then disbanded its faculty and stepped into the background, and this is where is the *West Virginia University Medical School Sydney Banks Institute for Innate Health* came into being.

A number of centers and institutes (for example, the NorthEast Health Realization Institute) and private providers have cropped up around the country and world that, independently, offer training, counseling and prevention. As of this writing no one formalized, centralized system or location is responsible for "putting out" this understanding and approach.

Lest we lose sight of this, the intent of it all is to help people realize the three Principles that at every moment create or interfere with their well-being and preclude or promote problem behaviors.

BIBLIOGRAPHY

Albee, G.W. (1996). Revolutions and counterrevolutions in prevention. *American psychologist.* 51 (11): 1130-1133.

Albee, G.W. (1983). Psychopathology, prevention, and the just society. *Journal of primary prevention.* 4, 5-40.

Albee, G.W. (1980). Social science and social change: The primary prevention of disturbance in youth. Burlington, VT: University of Vermont.

Applications: Health Realization/POM in the Community (videotape). (2000), Renton, WA: Lone Pine Media

Bailey, J. (1999). *Speed Traps.* San Francisco: Harper & Row.

Bailey, J. (1990). *The serenity principle.* San Francisco: Harper & Row.

Bailey, J. (1989). New hope for depression: A study in neo-cognitive therapy. Paper presented at the Eighth Annual Conference on Psychology of Mind, St. Petersburg, FL

Bailey, J.V., Blevens, K., & Heath, C. (1988). Early results: A six year post hoc follow-up study of the long term effectiveness of neocognitive psychotherapy. Paper presented at the Seventh Annual Conference on Psychology of Mind, Coral Gables, FL.

Bandura, A. (1989). Human agency in social cognitive theory. *American psychologist.* 44: 1175-1184.

Bandura, A. (1982). Self-efficacy mechanism in human agency. *American psychologist.* 37: 122-147

Banks, S. (2001). *The enlightened gardener.* Renton, WA: Lone Pine Publishing

Banks, S. (1998). *The missing link.* Renton, WA: Lone Pine Publishing

Banks, S. (1997). Discussing the three principles (audiotape). Bend, OR: Philosophy of Living Centre [out of print].

Banyan Foundation (1992). The Self Esteem is for Everyone Project (SEE): Program results and final report. Tampa, FL.

Bays, L. and Freeman-Longo, R. (1989). *Why did I do it again? Understanding my cycle of behaviors: Guided workbook for clients in treatment.* Orwell, VT: Safer Society Press.

Belenky, M.F., Bond, L.A. & Weinstock, J.S. (1997). A tradition that has no name: Nurturing the development of people, families, and communities. New York: Basic Books.

Belsky, J. (1980). Child maltreatment: An ecological integration. *American psychologist.* 34(4): 320-335.

Benard, B. (1996a). Musings II: Rethinking How We Do Prevention. *Western Center News.* San Francisco, CA: Far West Laboratory for Educational Research and Development (March)

Benard, B. (1996b). From research to practice: The foundations of the resiliency paradigm. *Resiliency in action.* 1(1): 7-11

Benard, B. (1996c). Roger Mills: A Community psychologist discovers Health Realization. *Resiliency in action.* (Summer).

Benard, B. (1995). Interview with Emmy Werner, 'Mother Resilience.' *Western center news.* (March) 6

Benard, B. (1994a). The Health Realization approach to resiliency. *Western center news.* San Francisco, CA: Far West Laboratory for Educational Research and Development (December).

Benard, B. (1994b). Guides for the Journey from Risk to Resiliency. *Western center news.* 7(4).

Benard, B. (1993). Resiliency paradigm validates craft knowledge. *Western center news.* (September).

Benard, B. (1991). Fostering resiliency in kids: Protective factors in the family, school, and community. Western center news. Portland, OR: Western Regional Center for Drug-Free Schools and Communities.

Benard, B. & Lorio, R. (1991). Positive approach to social ills has promise. *Western center news* (June).

Benard B. & Marshall, K. (1997). A framework for practice: Tapping innate resilience. Research practice. (Spring), 9:15. Minneapolis, MN: University of Minnesota, Center for Applied Research and Educational Imporvement.

Benard, B. et al. (1988). An overview of community-based prevention. Paper presented at the National Prevention Network's First National Conference on Prevention Research Findings, Kansas City, MO, March 26-30. Springfield, IL: Illinois Prevention Resource Center.

Bennet, C., Anderson, L., Cooper, S., Hassol, L., Klein, D., & Rosenblum, G. (1996). *Community psychology: A report of the Boston conference on the education of psychologists for community mental health.* Boston, MA: Boston University.

Benson, P.L. (1995). Uniting communities for youth: Mobilizing all sectors to create a positive future. Minneapolis, MN: Search Institute

Benson, P.L. et al. (1995). What kids need to succeed: Proven, practical ways to raise good kids. Minneapolis, MN: Search Institute.

Benson, P.L. (1992). *The troubled journey: A profile of American youth.* Minneapolis, MN: Respecteen.

Berkowitz, B. (1999). Transforming the values of preventionists. *Journal of primary prevention.* 19 (3): 251-255.

Berne, E. (1972). *What do you say after you say hello.* New York: Bantam Books.

Bittman, B., Berk, L., Lee S., Felten, D. & Westengard, J. (2001). Composite Effects of Group Drumming Music Therapy on Modulation of Neuroendocrine-Immune Parameters in Normal Subjects. *Alternative Therapies in Health & Medicine, 7(1),* 38-47.

Bjarnason, T. (1998). Parents, religion and perceived social coherence: A Durkheimian framework of adolescent anomie. *Journal for the Scientific Study of Religion, 37(4),* 742-754.

Bleick, C.R., & Abrams, A.I. (1987). The transcendental meditation program and criminal recidivism in California. *Journal of Criminal Justice, 15,* 211-230.

Blevens, K. (2001). The red road project: A Health Realization proposal for the Hualapai Health Department. La Conner, WA: Red Road Consulting

Blevens, K., Bailey, J., Olson, P., & Mills, R. (1992). Treatment effects of neo-cognitive therapy: A formative evaluation. Paper prepared for the Foundation for the Advancement of Mental health, Minneapolis, MN.

Bloom, B. L. (1986). Preventive intervention in the case of marital disruption. In National Mental Health Association Commission on the Prevention of Mental-Emotional Disabilities (eds.). *The prevention of mental-emotional disabilities: Resource papers.* Alexandria, VA: National Mental Health Association

Bloom, M. (1996) Primary prevention and resilience: Changing paradigms and changing lives. In R.L. Hampton, P. Jenkins, & T.P. Gullota, (eds.) Issues in *Children's and family's lives.* Vol. 4. Thousand Oaks, CA: Sage

Bloom, M. (1988). List of events for the historical context of primary prevention. Virginia Commonwealth University (unpublished)

Bogenschneider, K. (1996). Family related prevention programs: A ecological risk/protective theory for building prevention programs, policies, and community capacity to support youth. *Family relations.* 45. 127-138.

Bohm, D. (1994). *Thought as a system.* New York, NY: Routledge

Borg, M.B. (1997). The impact of training in the Health Realization/Community Empowerment model on affective states of psychological distress. Doctoral Dissertation. Bend, OR: Psychology of Mind Resource Center

Botvin, G.J., Baker, I., Dusenbury, L., Botvin, E.M., & Diaz, T. (1995). Long-term follow-up results of a randomized drug abuse prevention trial in a white middle-class population. *JAMA,* 273 (14): 1106-1112.

Bowman, M. (1997). *Individual differences in posttraumatic response: Problems with the adversity -distress connection.* Mahwah, NJ: Lawrence Erlbaum Assts.

Brennan, B.A. (1987). *Hands of light: A guide to healing through the human energy field.* New York, NY: Bantam Books.

Briscoe, J.E., (1990). *Guided imagery to affect depression and self-esteem in hospitalized adolescents.* Ann Arbor, Mich.: Dissertation, United States International University.

Bronfenbrenner, U. (1977). Toward an experimental ecology of human development. *American psychologist.* 32: 513-531.

Brounstein, P.J., Zweig, J.M., & Gardner, S.E. (1998). Science-based practices in substance abuse prevention: A guide. Washington, DC: Substance Abuse and Mental Health Service Administration & Center for Substance Abuse Prevention.

Burns, E.T. (1996). *From Risk to Resilience: A Journey With Heart for Our Children, Our Future.* Dallas: The Marco Polo Group.

Caplan, G. (1986). Crisis interevntion and support systems. In Kessler, M. & Goldston, S.E. (Eds.). *A decade of progress in primary prevention.* Hanover, NH: University Press of New England.

Capra, F. (1997). *The web of life: A new understanding of living systems.* New York, NY: Doubleday.

Carlson, R. (1997). *Don't sweat the small stuff...:and it's all small stuff.* New York: Hyperion.

Carlson, R. (1993). *You can feel good again.* New York, NY: Dutton

Carlson, R. (1997). *You can be happy no matter what.* Novato, CA: New World Publishers.

Carlson, R. & Bailey, J. (1997). *Slowing down to the speed of life.* San Francisco: HarperCollins.

Center for Drug Free Schools and Communities (1996). Glenwood/Lyndale program site visit. Minneapolis, MN: University of Minnesota. (February 23-24).

Center for Substance Abuse Prevention (1995). Background Report for the Development of CSAP's Prevention 2001 Curriculum. Washington, DC: CSAP, Division of Community Prevention and Training, Training and Evaluation Branch. Chapter III-12 and III-22.

Chamberlain, R.W. (1992). Preventing low birth weight, child abuse, and school failure: The need for comprehensive community-wide approaches. *Pediatrics in review.* 13(2): 64-71

Cherry, A.L. (1996). Assessment of Effectiveness using the Informed Families Outcome Evaluation Systems. Barry University School of Social Work.

Chopra, D. (1990). *Perfect Health: The complete mind/body guide.* New York, NY: Harmony Books

Churchland, P.M. (1988). *Matter and consciousness: A Contemporary introduction to the Philosophy of Mind.* Cambridge, MA: Bradford.

Cowen, E.L. (1977). Baby-steps toward primary prevention. *American journal of community psychology.* 5(1): 1-22

Cowen, E.L. et al. (1973). Long-term follow-up of early detected vulnerable children. *Journal of consulting and clinical psychology.* 41.

Creswell, J.W. (1997). Qualitative inquiry and research design: Choosing among five traditions. Thousand Oaks, CA: Sage.

Crystal, A.M. (1988). Neo-cognitive psychotherapy with the family of a severely traumatic sexually abused child: A case study. Bend, OR: Philosophy of Living Centre.

Dennett, D.C. (1991). *Consciousness explained.* Boston, MA: Little, Brown & Co.

Derezotes, D. (2000). Evaluation of yoga and meditation trainings with adolescent sex offenders. *Child and Adolescent Social Work Journal, 17(2),* 97-112.

Dillbeck, M.C., & Abrams, A.I. (1987). The application of the transcendental meditation program to corrections. *International Journal of Comparitive and Applied Criminal Justice, 11(1),* 111-132.

Donahue, M.J., & Benson, P.L. (1995). Religion and well-being of adolescents. *Journal of Social Issues, 51(2),* 145-160.

Dow, R. & Cook, S. (1996). *Turned on: Eight vital insights to energize your people, customers and profits.* New York, NY: Harper Collins.

Elliot, D.S., Huizinga, D., & Ageton, S.S. (1982). Explaining delinquency and drug use. Boulder, CO: Boulder Research Institute.

Elliot D.S. and Voss, H (1974). *Delinquency and dropout.* Lexington, MA: D.C. Heath

Epperson, C. (1996). Greater After Prison Support (GAPS). Evaluation summary. Gastonia, NC

Foreman, G. & Engel, J. (1995). *By George: The autobiography of George Foreman.* New York, NY: Villard Books

Gardner, H. (1993). *Creating minds: An anatomy of creativity seen through the lives of Freud, Einstein, Picasso, Stravinsky, Eliot, Graham and Gandhi.* New York: Basic Books

Garmezy, N. (1991). Resiliency and vulnerability to adverse developmental outcomes and associated with poverty. *American behavioral psychologist.* 34(4): 416-430

Garmezy, N. (1974). The study of competence in children at risk for severe pathology. In E. Anthony et. al. (eds.) *The child in his family. Vol. 3. Children at Psychiatric Risk.* 77-98. NY: Wiley

Gendreau, P. (1996). "The principles of effective intervention with offenders." In A.T. Harland [Ed.], Choosing correctional options that work: Defining the demand and evaluating the supply. Thousand Oaks, CA: Sage.

Gerber, R. (1988). *Vibrational medicine: New choices for healing ourselves.* Santa Fe: Bear & Co.

Glasser, W. (1985). *Control theory.* New York, NY: Harper & Row.

Glasser, W. & Powers, W.T. (1981). *Stations of the mind: New directions for Reality Therapy.* New York, NY: Harper & Row

Glenn, H.S. & Nelsen, J. (1988). *Raising self-reliant children: in a self-indulgent world.* Rocklin, CA: Prima Publishing.

Glenn, H.S. & Warner, J.W. (1983). *Developing capable young people.* Hurst, TX: Humansphere.

Grof, S. (1986). *Beyond the Brain: Birth Death and transcendence in psychotherapy.* Albany, NY: SUNY Press.

Hanh, T.N. (1987). *Being Peace.* Berkeley, CA: Parallax Press.

Hart, W. (1987). *Vipassana meditation, As Taught by S.N. Goenka: The art of living*. San Francisco, CA: Harper.

Hawkins, J.D. & Catalano, R.F. (1992). *Communities that care: Action for drug abuse prevention*. San Francisco, CA: Jossey-Bass.

Hawkins, J.D., Catalano, R.F. & Miller, J.Y. (1992). Risk and protective factors for alcohol and other drug problems in adolescence and early adulthood. *Psychological bulletin*. 112(1): 64-105.

Hawkins, J.D., Catalano, R.F., Morrison, D.M., O'Donnell, J., Abbott, R.D. & Day, L.E. (1992). The Seattle Social Development Project: Effects of the first four years on protective factors and problem behaviors. In McCord, J. & Tremblay, R. (eds.), *The prevention of antisocial behavior in children* (139-161). New York: Guilford Publications.

Hawkins, J.D. & Weiss, J.G. (1985). The Social Development Model: An integrated approach to delinquency prevention. *Journal of Primary Prevention.* 2

Heath, C.J., Emiliano, S.Y., & Usagawa, S.K. (1992). Project Mainstream Hawaii. Paper presented at the American Educational Research Association, San Francisco, CA. Bend, OR: Psychology of Mind Resource Center

Henderson, N. (1996). Resiliency in Practice: One-to-One Interactions that Foster Resiliency. *Resiliency in action*. 1(1): 15-17

Henderson, N. & Milstein, M. (1997). *Resiliency in schools: Making it happen for students and educators*. Thousand Oaks, CA: Corwin Press.

Henderson, N., Benard, B., Sharp-Light, N., Richardson, G. (1996). The philosophy of Resiliency in Action. *Resiliency in Action*. (summer).

Higgins, G.O. (1994). *Resilient adults: Overcoming a cruel past*. San Francisco: Jossey-Bass.

Hirschi, T. (1969). *Causes of delinquency*. Berkeley, CA: University of California Press.

Holder, D.W., Durant, R.H., Harris, T.L., Daniel, J.H., Obeidallah, D., & Goodman, E. (2000). The association between adolescent spirituality and voluntary sexual activity. *Journal of Adolescent Health, 26*, 295-302.

House, F.N. (1970). *The development of sociology*. Westport, CT: Greenwood Press.

Hunt, M. (1993). *The story of psychology*. New York: Doubleday.

Hunt, H.V. (1996). *Infinite mind: Science of the human vibrations of consciousness*. Malibu, CA: Malibu

Huxley, A. (1944). *The perennial philosophy*. Cleveland, OH: Meridian Books.

James, W. (1981). *The principles of psychology*. Cambridge, MA: Harvard University Press.

James, W. (2000). *Varieties of religious experience*. Westminster, MD: Modern Library Series.

Jason, L.A. (1997). *Community building: Values for a sustainable future*. Westport, CT: Praeger.

Jessor, R. (1991). Risk behavior in adolescence: A psychosocial framework for understanding and action. *Journal of adolescent health*. 12 (8): 597-605

Jessor R. & Jessor S.L. (1977). *Problem and psychological development: A longitudinal study of youth*. New York, NY: Academic Press.

Johnson, C.A., Pentz, M.A., Weber, M.D., Dwyer, J.H., Baer, N., MacKinnon, D.P., Hansen, W.B. & Flay, B.R. (1990). Relative effectiveness of comprehensive community programming for drug abuse prevention with high-risk and low-risk adolescents. *Journal of consulting and clinical psychology*. 58(4): 447-456.

Johnson, G., Bird, T., & Little, J. (1980). *Delinquency prevention: Theories and strategies*. Washington, DC: Office of Juvenile Justice and Delinquency Prevention, U.S. Department of Justice.

Jung, C.J. (1951). *Aion: Researches into the phenomenology of self.* Sir H. Read (Ed.) *Collected works of C.J. Jung.* 9 (1).

Jung, C.J. (1938). *Religion and psychology*. London, England: Oxford University Press.

Kelley, J.G. (1968). Toward an ecological conception of preventive interventions. In J.W. Carter, Jr. (Ed.). *Research contributions from psychology to community mental health*. New York, NY: Behavioral publications, Inc.

Kelley, T.M. (1996). A critique of social bonding and control theory of delinquency using the principles of Psychology of Mind. *Adolescence*. 31: 122 (321-337).

Kelley, T.M. (1996). At-risk youth and locus of control. Bend, OR: Philosophy of Living Centre

Kelley, T.M. (1993) Neo-cognitive learning theory: Implications for prevention and early intervention strategies with at-risk youth. *Adolescence*. 28 (110): 439-460.

Kelley, T.M. (1990). A neo-cognitive model of crime. *Journal of offender rehabilitation*. 16: 1-26

Kempe, R.S. & Kempe, C.H. (1978). *Child abuse*. Cambridge, MA: Harvard University Press.

Kibel, B. (1996). Evaluation using Results Mapping. *New designs for youth development*. 12(1): 9-15.

Kibel, B. (1994). Evaluation of local prevention practices: An open systems model in action. *New designs for youth development.* 11(3): 15-22.

Klein, D.C. (2001). *New vision, new reality: A Guide to Unleashing Energy, Joy, and Creativity in Your Life.* Center City, MN: Hazelden.

Klein, D.C. (1988). The power of appreciation. *American journal of community psychology.* 16(3): 305-323

Klein, D.C. (1983). A transforming view of mental health. *Journal of primary prevention.* 836, 202-206.

Klein, D.C. (1968). Community dynamics and mental health. New York: Wiley.

Klein D.C. & Goldston, S.E. (1977). *Primary prevention: An idea whose time has come.* Washington, CD: DHEW Publications No. ADM 77-477.

Kotulak, R. (1996). *Inside the brain: Revolutionary discoveries of how the mind works.* Kansas City, MO: Andrews McNeel Publishing.

Krot, S. (1983). The adolescent in the transitional family. Bend, OR: Philosophy of Living Centre

Kumpfer, K.L. (1997). What works in the prevention of drug abuse: Individual, school and family approaches. DHHS Center for Substance Abuse Prevention. Secretary's Youth Substance Abuse Prevention Initiative. Resource Paper 69-105 (March).

Kurian, M., Verdi, M.P., Caterino, L.C., & Kulhavy, R.W. (1994). Relating scales on the children's personality questionnaire to training time and belt rank in ATA taekwondo. *Perceptual and Motor Skills, 79(2),* 904-906.

Kurtz, E. & Ketcham, K. (1992). *The Spirituality of Imperfection Storytelling and the Journey to Wholeness.* New York: Bantam Books.

Layton, C., Higaonna, M., & Arneil, S. (1993). Karate for self-defense: An analysis of goju-ryu and kyokushinkai kata. *Perceptual and Motor Skills, 77(3, Pt. 1),* 829-830.

Leven, J. (1994). Religion and health: Is there an association, is it valid, and is it causal?. *Social science medicine.* 38 (11): 1475-1482.

Lederman, L. with Teresi, D. (1994). *The God Particle: If the Universe is the Answer, What is the Question?* Delta Books.

Lindsey, E.W., Kurtz, D.P., Jarvis, S., Williams, N.R., & Nackerud, L. (2000). How runaway and homeless youth navigate troubled waters: Personal strengths and resources. *Child and Adolescent Social Work Journal, 17(2),* 115-140

Lofquist, W.A. (1989). *The technology of prevention workbook.* Tucson, AZ: AYD Publications (Development Associates).

Lofquist, W. (1983). *Discovering the meaning of prevention.* Tucson, AZ: Associates for Youth Development (Development Associates).

Lohman, R. (1999). Yoga techniques applicable within drug and alcohol rehabilitation programmes. *Therapeutic Communities, 20(1)* 61-72.

Marlatt, G.A. & Gordon, J.R. (1985). *Relapse prevention.* New York: Guilford Press.

Marshall, K. (2000). Experiences implementing resilience/Health Realization in schools. Minneapolis: University of Minnesota, National Resilience Resource Center. (with update via personal communication, May 8, 2002.)

Marshall, K. (1998). Restructuring systems with resilience/Health Realization. Promising positive and behaviors in children. Fourteenth Annual Rosalynn Carter Symposium on Mental Health Policy. Atlanta, GA: The Carter Center (48-58).

Maslow, A.H. (1968). *Toward a psychology of being.* New York, NY: Van Norstrand Reinhold.

Mason, M., and Collison, B. (1995). Adolescent substance abuse treatment incorporating "rites of passage." *Alcoholism Treatment Quarterly*, 13(3), 69-79.

McCombs, B.L. (1991). Overview: Where have we been and where are we going in understanding human motivation? *Journal of experimental education.* 60(1):5-14

McCombs, B.L. (1991). Unraveling motivation: New perspectives from research and practice. *Journal of experimental education.* 60: 3-4.

McCombs, B.L. & Marzano, R.J. (1990). Putting the self in self-regulated learning: The self as agent in integrating will and skill. *Educational psychologist.* 25: 51-69

McCombs, B., Bland, C., and Shown, J. (1994). Neighbors making a difference: Community empowerment as a primary prevention strategy and foundation for collaborative partnerships. Final report to the U.S. Department of Education.

McCullough, M.E., Larson, D.B., Hoyt, W.T., Koenig, H.G., & Thoresen, C. (2000). Religious involvement and mortality: A meta-analytic review. *Health Psychology, 19(3):* in press.

357

McKinney, J.P., & McKinney, K.G. (1999). Prayer in the lives of late adolescents. *Journal of Adolescence, 22,* 279-290.

McKnight, J. (1997). *Building communities from the inside-out: A path toward finding and mobilizing a community's assets.* Acta Publications

McLeroy, K.R., Bibeau, D., Steckler, A. & Glantz, K. (1989). An ecological perspective on health promotion programs. *Health education quarterly.* 15(4): 351-377

Michello, J. (1988). Spiritual and emotional determinants of health. *Journal of religion and health.* 27(1): 62-70.

Miller, A. (1992). Comprehensive Community Revitalization Program. Bend, OR: Philosophy of Living Centre

Miller, C.E. (1991). Book Review: Prevention: The Critical Need: A User Friendly guide for 21st century parents, practitioners, and planners. *New designs for youth development.* 10(1): 28.

Miller, W.B. (1958). Lower class culture as a generating milieu of gang delinquency. *Journal of Social issues.* 3.

Mills, R.C. (1996). Psychology of Mind - Health Realization: Summary of Clinical, Prevention, and Community Empowerment Applications. Bend, OR: Psychology of Mind Resource Center

Mills, R.C. (1996). *Realizing Mental Health.* New York: Sulzberger & Graham

Mills, R.C. (1993). Individual and community empowerment: Fostering leadership and collaboration. St. Petersberg, FL: R.C. Mills & Associates.

Mills, R.C. (1991). A new understanding of self: Affect, state of mind, self-understanding, and intrinsic motivation. *Journal of experimental education.* 60: 67-81.

Mills, R.C. (1991). The Psychology of Mind applied to substance abuse, dropout, and delinquency prevention: Modello - Homestead Gardens Intervention Project. Paper presented to the Florida Alcohol and Drug Abuse Association Annual Conference, Orlando, FL.

Mills, R.C. (1990). The Modello Early Intervention Project: A model for prevention; A demonstration project based on Psychology of Mind. Presented at the Seventh Annual Conference on the Psychology of Mind. Miami, FL.

Mills, R.C. & Bailey, J. (1996). Reducing and preventing violence in at-risk communities. (unpublished)

Mills, R.C., Blevens, J.K. & Pransky, G.S. (1978). A new framework for psychology. Bend, OR: Philosophy of Living Centre

Mills, R.C., Blevens, J.K. & Pransky, G.S. (1978). The new psychology: Seeing beyond techniques, methods, and approaches. Bend, OR: Philosophy of Living Centre

Mills, R.C., Dunham, R. and Alpert, G. (1988). Working with high-risk youth in prevention and early intervention programs: Toward a comprehensive wellness model. *Adolescence.* 23(91): 643-660

Mills, R.C. & Pransky, G. (1993). Psychology of Mind: The basis for Health Realization: The founder's monograph. LaConner, WA: Psychology of Mind Training Institute.

Mills, R.C. & Kelley, J.G. (1972). Cultural adaptation and ecological analogies: analysis of three Mexican Villages. In S.E. Golann ad C. Eisdorfer (Eds.) *Handbook for community mental health.* New York: Appleton-Century-Crofts.

Mills, R.C. & Spittle, E.B. (2001). *The wisdom within.* Renton, WA: Lone Pine Publishing

Mills, R.C. & Spittle, E.B. (1998). The Health Realization primer: Empowering individuals & communities. Long Beach, CA: R.C. Mills & Associates.

Minneapolis Institute of Mental Health (1984). Preliminary report: A study of program outcome with chemically dependent adolescents. Bend, OR: Philosophy of Living Centre

Moustakas, C. (1994). *Phenomenological research methods.* Thousand Oaks, CA: Sage.

Muktananda, Swami (1992). *Mystery of the mind.* South Fallsburg, NY: SYDA Foundation.

Myss, C. (1996). *Anatomy of the Spirit. The seven stages of power and healing.* New York, NY: Three Rivers Press.

Namy Dickason, C. (1993). Spirituality of Prevention: A first conference of its kind. *New designs for youth development.* 10(3): 27-28.

Nelsen, J. (1986). *Understanding: Eliminating Stress and Dissatisfaction in life and relationships.* Fair Oaks, CA: Sunrise.

Nidich, S., Nidich, R. J., & Rainforth, M. (1986). School effectiveness: Achievement gains at the Maharishi school of the age of enlightenment. *Education, 107(1),* 49-54.

O.M.G., Inc. (1994). Final annual assessment report: Comprehensive Community Revitalization Project. Philadelphia, PA (March).

O'Connell-Higgins, G. (1994). *Resilient adults: Overcoming a cruel past.* San Francisco, CA: Jossey-Bass.

Olds, D.L. et al. (1984). Final report: The prenatal/early infancy project: A follow-up evaluation at the third year of life. Springfield, VA: U.S. Dept. of Commerce, National Technical Information Service.

Parrish, P. & Shaw, K. (1997). Positive Paths. Tucson and Tempe, AZ: Information & Referral Services and EMPACT-SPC.

Peck, N. Law, A. & Mills, R.C. (1987). Dropout prevention: What we have learned. Ann Arbor: Eric Clearinghouse.

Perry, C.L., Williams, C.L., Veblin-Mortenson, S., Toomey, T.L., Komro, K.A., Anstine, P.S., McGovern,

P.G., Finnegan, .R., Forster, J.L., Wagenaar, A.C. & Wolfson, M. (1996). Project Northland: Outcomes of a communitywide alcohol use prevention program during early adolescence. *American journal of public health.* 86(7): 956-965.

Pert, C.B. (1997). *Molecules of emotion: Why you feel the way you feel.* New York, NY: Scribner.

Pithers, W.D. (1989). Relapse prevention with sexual aggressors: A method for maintaining therapeutic gain and enhancing external supervision. In W.L. Marshall, D.R. Laws & H.E. Barabee, *Handbook of sexual assault.* New York: Plenum Press.

Polk, K. & Kobrinm, S. (1972). Delinquency prevention through youth development. Washington, DC: Department of Health, Education, & Welfare

Polsfuss, C. (1994). A new era in social work practice: Health Realization & resiliency. Paper delivered at annual Psychology of Mind Conference, July

Price, R.H. et al. (Eds.) (1988). *14 ounces of prevention: A casebook for practitioners.* Washington, DC: American Psychological Association.

Price, R.H., Ketterer, R.F., Bader, B.C., Monahan, J. (Eds.)(1980). *Prevention in mental health: Research, policy and practice.* Thousand Oaks, CA: Sage.

Pransky, G.S. (1998). *The renaissance of psychology.* New York: Sulzberger & Graham (out of print).

Pransky, G.S. (1990). *The relationship handbook* [former title, *Divorce is not the answer.* Blue Ridge Summit, PA: Tab Books]. LaConner, WA: Pransky & Assts.

Pransky, G.S. (1991). Anger: Stopping the annoyance to anger spiral. Practical psychology audio series. LaConner, WA: Pransky & Associates. (out of print)

Pransky, G.S. (1991 - 1999). Practical psychology audio and video tape series (over 60 tapes on many subjects). La Conner, WA: Pransky & Associates. (out of print)

Pransky, G.S. (1995). The Practice of Psychology of Mind Therapy. (audiotape series). LaConner, WA: Pransky & Assoc.

Pransky, G.S., Mills, R.C., Sedgeman, J.A. & Blevens, J.K. (1997). An emerging paradigm for Brief treatment and prevention. In L. Vandecreek, S. Knapp, T.J. Jackson, (eds.) *Innovations in clinical practice: A Source Book.* 15: 76-98. Sarasota, FL: Professional Resource Press.

Pransky, J. (1999). The experience of participants after Health Realization training: A one-year follow-up phenomenological study. Doctoral dissertation/Project Demonstrating Excellence prepared for The Union Institute, Cincinnati, Ohio.

Pransky, J. (1998). *Modello: A story of hope for the inner-city and beyond: An inside-out model of prevention and resiliency in action through Health Realization.* Cabot, VT: NEHRI Publications.

Pransky, J. (2001/1997). *Parenting from the Heart.* Bloomington, IN: 1stBooks Library. Cabot, VT: NEHRI Publications.

Pransky, J. (1996). Health Realization as a prevention system. Cabot, VT: NEHRI Publications.

Pransky, J. (1994). Can prevention be moved to a higher plane? *New designs for youth development.* Tucson, AZ: Development Associates. (11:2).

Pransky, J. (2001/1991). *Prevention: The critical need.* Bloomington, IN: 1stBooks Library. (Formerly, Springfield, MO: Burrell Foundation and Burlington, VT: Paradigm Press.)

Pransky, J. & Carpenos, L. (2000). *Healthy thinking/feeling/doing from the inside out: A middle school curriculum for the prevention of violence, abuse and other problem behaviors.* Brandon, VT: Safer Society Press.

Purchalski, C.M. (2000). *Role of spirituality in health and illlness.* Boston, MA: Spirituality & Healing in Medicine, Mainstreaming Spirituality: The Next Step, Harvard Medical School, Department of Continuing Education and Mind/Body Medical Institute, Caregroup, Beth Israel Deaconess Medical Center.

Raeburn, J. & Rootman, I. (1998). *People-centered health promotion.* New York, NY: John Wiley & Sons.

Reitmeyer, R. (2001). Mind over matter. *Counseling Today.* August.

Jack Pransky

Resnick, M.D., Bearman, P.S., Blum, R.Wm., Bauman, K.E., Harris, K.M., Jones, J., Tabor, J, Beuhring, T., Sieving, R.E., Shew, M., Ireland, M., Bearinger, L.H., & Udry, J.R. (1997). Protecting adolescents from harm: Findings from the national longitudinal study on adolescent health. *JAMA*, 278(10), 823-832.

Richards-Colocino, N., McKenzie, P. & Newton, R.R. (1996), Project Success: Comprehensive intervention services for middle school high-risk youth. *Journal of adolescent research.* 11(1):130-163.

Ringold, C. (1992). Changing hearts, changing minds: The usefulness of Psychology of Mind in the treatment of paranoid schizophrenia. Two case studies. Minnesota school of Professional Psychology. Unpublished doctoral dissertation.

Ritzer, G. (1988). Contemporary Sociological Theory. New York: Alfred A. Knopf

Roe, K. & Bowser, B. (1993). Health Realization Community Empowerment Project, Coliseum Gardens, Oakland, CA.: Evaluation of first year findings. Bend, OR: Philosophy of Living Centre

Rodham Clinton, H. (1996). *It takes a village: And other lessons children teach us.* New York: Touchstone Books.

Rutter, M. (1979). Protective factors in children's responses to stress and disadvantage. In M.W. Kent & J.E. Rolf (eds.) *Primary prevention of psychopathology, Vol. 3. Social competence in children* (49-74). Hanover, NH: University Press of New England.

Rutter, M. (1989). Pathways from childhood to adult life. *Journal of child psychology.* 30 (1): 23-51.

Rutter, M. (1987). Psychosocial resilience and protective mechanisms. *American Orthopsychiatric Association.* 57(3): 316-331.

Sanchez-Way, R., & Johnson, S. (2000). Cultural Practices in American Indian Prevention Programs. *Juvenile Justice, v7 n2,* 20-30. Retrieved December 24, 2001 from the World Wide Web: http://ncjrs.org/pdffilies1/172854.pdf.

Saunders, G.P. (1998). *The relationship of spirituality to adolescents' responses to loss.* Milwaukee, WI: Dissertation, The Wisconsin School of Professional Psychology.

Searle, J.R. (1994). *The rediscovery of mind.* Cambridge, MA: Bradford

Segall, R. (2000). Catch the beat. Psychology Today, July 2000 33 (4), 10.

Schorr, L.B. (1997). *Common purpose: Strengthening families and neighborhoods to rebuild America.* New York, NY: Doubleday

Schweinhart, L.J. & Weikart, D.P. (1980). *Young children grow up: The effects of the Perry Preschool program on youths through age fifteen.* Ypsilanti, MI: High/Scope Educational Research Foundation.

Search institute (1997). 40 developmental assets. Minneapolis, MN: Search Institute

Sedgeman, J. (2000). No question should go unanswered – III. Morgantown, WV: Sydney Banks Institute of Innate Health, West Virginia University School of Medicine.

Sedgeman, J. (1998). Reflections on 'Study' of the principles. Morgantown, WV: West Virginia University School of Medicine.

Sedgeman, J.A. (1997). Psychology of mind - Introduction. Psychology of Mind handbook 1997. Midland, Australia: Psychology of Mind Resource Center

Sedgeman, J.A. (2000-2003) many three principle-related articles on many subjects. www.sbiih.org.

Seligman, M.E.P. (1991). *Learned optimism.* New York: Alfred A. Knopf.

Seligman, M.E.P. (1996). *The optimistic child.* New York: Harper Perennial.

Shuford, R. (1987). Neo-cognitive psychotherapy: Initial research in a clinical setting. Paper presented at the Sixth Annual Psychology of Mind Conference, Miami, FL.

Shuford, R. & Crystal, A. (1988). The efficacy of a neo-cognitive approach to positive psychological change: A preliminary study in an outpatient setting. Paper presented at the Seventh Annual Conference on Psychology of Mind, Coral Gables, Florida.

Shumway, J & Sydney Banks Institute of Innate Health (2001). Understanding of Experience Scale. Morgantown, WV: West Virginia University School of Medicine.

Shure, M.B. & Spivak, G. (1988). Interpersonal cognitive problem solving. In Price, R.H. et al. (eds.) *14 ounces of prevention: A casebook for practitioners.* Washington, DC: American Psychological Association.

Shure, M.B. & Spivack, G. (1979). Interpersonal cognitive problem-solving and primary prevention: Programming for preschool and kindergarten children. *Journal of clinical psychology.* Summer.

Smith, J., Twemlow, S.W., & Hoover, D.W. (1999). Bullies, victims and bystanders: A method of in-school intervention and possible parental contributions. *Child Psychiatry and Human Development, 30(1),* 29-37.

Stewart, C. (1987). The efficacy of neo-cognitive psychology with DUI clients. Paper presented at the Annual Conference of Florida Alcohol and Drug Abuse Association. Miami, FL

Stewart, D.L. (1993). *Creating the teachable moment*. Blue Ridge Summit, PA: Tab Books.

Stewart, D.L. (1988). State-dependent learning: The effect of feelings and emotions on reading achievement. Bend, OR: Philosophy of Living Centre

Strecher, V.B. et al. (1986). The role of self-efficacy in achieving health behavioral change. *Health education quarterly*. 13(1): 73-79

Stokes, S. (1994). Impact on city employees of a Health Realization training. Fresno, CA: California School for Professional Psychology, Center for Psychological Services (May).

Suarez, E.M. (1985). The efficacy of a neo-cognitive approach to psychotherapy. Paper presented at the Hawaii Psychological Association Annual Conference.

Suarez, E.M., Mills, R.C., & Stewart, D. (1987). *Sanity, insanity, and common sense*. New York: Fawcett Columbine.

Suarez, E.M. & Mills, R.C. (1982). *Sanity, insanity, and common sense*. West Allis, WI: Med. Psych. Publications.

Today Show. NBC (1990, April). Videotape segment aired on the Modello/Homestead Gardens Intervention Program.

Timm, J. & Campsall, C. (1994). *Self-esteem is for everyone handbook*. Learning Advantages.

Trulson, M.E. (1986). Martial Arts Training: A novel "cure" for juvenile delinquency. *Human Relations. 39(12)*, 1131-1140.

U.S. Department of Health and Human Services (1998). Science-based substance abuse prevention. Paper prepared for National Prevention Network's conference on Joining Forces to Advance Prevention, San Antonio, Texas. Washington, DC: HHS

Walsch, N.D. (1995). *Conversations with God: Book I*. Charlottsville, VA: Hampton Roads Publishing.

Walsch, N.D. (1999). *Conversations with God: Book III*. Charlottsville, VA: Hampton Roads Publishing.

Wapnick, G. & Wapnick, K. (1995). *The most commonly asked questions about A Course in Miracles*. Roscoe, NY: Foundation for Inner Peace.

Werner, E.E. (1996). How children become resilient: Observations and Cautions. *Resiliency in action*. (Winter) 18-28

Werner, E.E. (1989). High risk children in young adulthood: A longitudinal study from birth to 32 years. *American journal of orthospychiatry*. 59: 71-81

Werner, E.E. & Smith, R. (1992). *Overcoming the odds: High-risk children from birth to adulthood*. Ithaca, NY: Cornell University Press.

Werner, E.E. & Smith, R. (1989). *Vulnerable but invincible: A longitudinal study of resilient children and youth*. New York: Adams, Bannister, and Cox

Wheatley, M. (1997). Goodbye command and control. *Leader to leader*. (Summer) 21-28.

Williams, H.S. & Webb, A.Y. (1992). *Outcome funding: A new approach to public sector grantmaking*. Rensselaerville, NY: Rensselaerville Institute.

Williams, M. and Pransky, J. (1993). Effects of the "Health Realization Model" on gang members. Paper presented at the Twelfth Annual Conference on Psychology of Mind, Burlington, VT.

Wilson, E.O. (1998). *Consilience: The unity of knowledge*. New York, NY: Knopf.

Wilson, M. (2002). Practice Unbound: A Study of Secular Spiritual and Religous Activities in Work with Adolescents. Boxboro, Mass.: New England Network for Child, Youth & Family Services

Wilson, S., Simpson, S. Pransky, J., & Johnson, S. (1996). From risk to resiliency: A training curriculum developed for the Vermont State Team for Children & Families: Waterbury, VT: Agency of Human Services

Wilber, K. (1996). *A brief history of everything*. Boston, MA: Shambhala

Wilber, K. (1997). *The eye of spirit: An internal vision for a world gone slightly mad*. Boston, MA: Shambhala

Wolf, D.B. (1999). *Effects of Hare Krsna maha mantra on stress, depression and the three gunas*.Ann Arbor, Mich.: Dissertation, Florida State University School of Social Work.

Wolin, S. and Wolin, S. (1993). The resilient self: How survivors of troubled families rise above adversity. New York: Villard Books

Zipkin, D. (1985). Relaxation techniques for handicapped children: A review of literature. *The Journal of Special Education, 19(3)*, 283-289.

Zoeller, D. (2002). The role of fath-based organization in prevention. Prevention Forum. Winter/Spring. 22:2. (6-11).

Zohar, D. and Marshall, I. (1994). *The quantum society. Mind, physics, and a new social vision.* New York: Winston Morrow & Co.

Zukav, G. (1989). *The seat of the soul.* New York: Fireside

About the Author

Jack Pransky, Ph.D. is founder/director of the *Northeast Health Realization Institute*. He authored the books, ***Prevention: The Critical Need*** (2001/1991), ***Parenting from the Heart*** (2000/1997), ***Modello: A Story of Hope for the Inner City and Beyond*** (1998), and co-authored ***Healthy Thinking/ Feeling/Doing from the Inside-Out* prevention** curriculum for middle school students (2000). Pransky has worked in the field of prevention since 1968 in a wide variety of capacities and now provides consultation and training throughout the U.S., and internationally. Jack was instrumental in creating the first state law (Vermont) requiring state agencies to plan for and conduct prevention practices, and he worked on developing national prevention policy. He is also cofounder/director of the nonprofit consulting organization, *Prevention Unlimited* which created the Spirituality of Prevention Conference. He now specializes in Health Realization and prevention from the inside-out. In 2001 his book, ***Modello*** received the Martin Luther King Storyteller's Award for the book best exemplifying King's vision of "the beloved community.

To contact Jack Pransky for trainings, workshops, seminars, speaking engagements, inside-out coaching or counseling, questions or comments, visit www.healthrealize.com or call 802-563-2730.

CPSIA information can be obtained at www.ICGtesting.com
Printed in the USA
LVOW09s2307091115

461824LV00004B/139/P